Mastering HR Management with SAP

 PRESS

SAP PRESS is issued by
Bernhard Hochlehnert, SAP AG

SAP PRESS is a joint initiative of SAP and Galileo Press. The know-how offered by SAP specialists combined with the expertise of the publishing house Galileo Press offers the reader expert books in the field. SAP PRESS features first-hand information and expert advice, and provides useful skills for professional decision-making.

SAP PRESS offers a variety of books on technical and business related topics for the SAP user. For further information, please visit our website: *www.sap-press.com*.

Krämer, Lübke, Ringling
HR Personnel Planning and Development Using SAP
How to get the most from your mySAP HR systems
2004, 552 pp., ISBN 1-59229-024-8

Brochhausen, Kielisch, Schnerring, Staeck
mySAP HR—Technical Principles and Programming
2005, 451 pp., ISBN 1-59229-055-8

Forndron, Liebermann, Thurner, Widmayer
mySAP ERP Roadmap
2006, approx. 400 pp., ISBN 1-59229-071-X

Karch, Heilig
SAP NetWeaver Roadmap
2005, 312 pp., ISBN 1-59229-041-8

Buck-Emden, Zencke
mySAP CRM
The Official Guidebook to SAP CRM 4.0
2004, 462 pp., ISBN 1-59229-029-9

Christian Krämer, Sven Ringling, Song Yang

Mastering HR Management with SAP

Galileo Press

Bonn • Boston

Contents

7 E-Recruiting 199

8   Time Management   249

9   Payroll   361

10 Benefits 431

11 Personnel Controlling 457

Invitation

Dear Reader,

You may expect a "Preface" here, but we'd rather extend an invitation.

More precisely, the authors issue three different invitations to each reader:

1. mySAP HCM is a huge topic, and every day there is something new to learn. The authors of this book are co-authoring a free e-mail newsletter about mySAP HCM, which keeps its readers up-to-date with six issues per year. To learn more about this newsletter and subscribe online, have a look at *http://www.admanus.de/english-newsletter*, or subscribe via e-mail by sending a message with "subscribe book" in the subject line to *newsletter@iprocon.com. We invite you to keep in touch!*

2. Throughout the book, you will find many process models, mostly in the form of event-driven process chains. If you are interested in getting these process models in an electronic form, we offer you a free download via *http://www.iprocon.com/book-process* (Password *innovation*). They are available in the original form as an ARIS database and as a PowerPoint file. *We invite you to download!*

3. This book shows many ways to use the potential of the system to support processes in ways other than those for which they were originally designed. The enormous flexibility of mySAP HCM provides many more opportunities than could be described in one book. So, don't stick to the straightforward solutions, but rather think out of the box! If you really understand the underlying structure and functionality of the system, you will often find an efficient way to cope with your requirements. *We invite you to innovate!*

To learn more about the authors and other people involved, have a look at Appendix E, *About the Authors*.

We recommend you read Chapter 1, *Goal of this Book*, which will help you get the best value from this book. We wish you interesting reading and many ideas that help you succeed in your project or day-to-day job with mySAP HR.

1 Goal of this Book

mySAP HR is a very extensive topic, and many people are interested in it for different reasons. But, as we all know that "the Jack of all trades is a master of none," we have to make some decisions to limit the scope of this book.

1.1 Scope of the Content

The book describes HR on the basis of the R/3 releases 4.6C and R/3 Enterprise, as well as mySAP ERP 2004. Some changes made with mySAP ERP 2005 are also taken into account, especially concerning E-Recruiting. The changes caused by the transition from R/3 Enterprise to mySAP ERP 2004 mainly affect the technological basis, which means that you can apply almost everything we say about HR within R/3 to mySAP ERP Human Capital Management (mySAP ERP HCM). As was the case with R/3 Enterprise, mySAP ERP will continuously be developed further by small updates (support packages) and larger annual supplements, while at the same time ensuring the validity of the essential statements made in this book.

SAP R/3 and mySAP ERP

Where necessary, we adapted the book to mySAP ERP 2004 (ECC 5.0). Most of the screenshots were taken from mySAP ERP 2004 (ECC 5.0) and R/3 Enterprise (4.70), while a smaller number of screenshots are from other releases. The E-Recruiting screenshots are from Version 6.0 as included in mySAP ERP 2005. Where necessary, we will notify you about substantial differences between the various releases.

As "HR" is still the term commonly used for the software now officially named "HCM", we will comply with this and use the term "HR" throughout the book on most occasions. We also use "HR" when we are talking about the business process without special reference to the SAP software. When we want to stress that we are not talking about the HR component in R/3 or in the Central Component but are looking at the broader range of the software package including systems outside R/3 or its successor (the ECC), such as E-Recruiting, portal, etc. we generally refer to it as "mySAP ERP HCM" or just "HCM".

The processes treated in this book are described in such a way that the functionalities and most important characteristics of mySAP HR become evident in the respective processes. In addition, we will describe customizing, i.e. customer-specific configuration of the system, by way of examples. In general, we have placed more emphasis on understanding the overall concept and relationships than on detailed descriptions of customizing tables.

For readers who haven't used the system in their daily work, we have provided numerous screenshots from the system. These should help illustrate the information provided in this book and thus make it more tangible.

Even using abstract description, without too many details, and avoiding a screenshot gallery that shows each and every potentially relevant screen, mySAP HR is too voluminous a topic to treat entirely in one single book. For this reason, the book focuses on the administrative processes and avoids dealing with matters related to the system basis or programming. Personnel planning and development is described in a separate book by the same authors, which was also published by SAP PRESS.[1] In that book, we draw a line of separation between the parts that SAP formerly referred to as PA and PD. Although no longer officially used, there are still reasons for making this distinction. There is a difference in the technical implementation, which is also reflected in the system configuration. Further, in the administrative processes considered, the focus is on technology and processes, while the implementation of personnel planning and development is almost entirely decided on the process-definition side.

In the country-specific sections, we mainly refer to the U.S. version. However, we always describe the general, country-independent system as well. In this way, the book can also be used by readers in other countries, while readers in the U.S. will find valuable information for international rollout projects.

Another important element of the book is the visualization of process examples. These enable a much better understanding of the processes and their IT support than would a purely textual description.

1.2   Target Group

The following target audiences will find useful information in this book:

▶ *Decision makers in HR, IT and organizational departments* will gain a critical overview of the mySAP HR functionalities. They will also develop a feeling for the basic strengths and weaknesses as well as the cost drivers.

---

1 Krämer, Lübke, Ringling: *HR Personnel Planning and Development Using SAP*, SAP PRESS 2004

- *Project managers* are provided with the most important integration aspects and success factors that are critical for the implementation.

- *Members of implementation project teams, consultants, and those responsible for customizing* will find many tips for each process. In this context, basic functionalities are described in more detail so that employees who are just assuming these roles will receive appropriate guidelines for getting started. For advanced users, the book contains many recommendations that don't go into too much detail. It is more important to understand the basic direction of each process or project.

- *Interested users* who would like to see beyond the borders of their specific activities, and key users who are also responsible for the continued development of the system, will get a good overview of the various interactions and develop a better understanding of how the system works.

- *Programmers who work close to the application in the mySAP HR environment* will find the contents of this book very helpful in facilitating communication with the user departments and the review of technical concepts.

- *Students or other interested parties* who are just learning about personnel management will develop true insight into the practice of Human Resources (HR) and its IT implementation with mySAP HR. The book's topics represent important functions of a personnel department and indicate where problems can occur. It is especially for this target group that the book provides business-related background information.

1.3   Working with this Book

You can read the individual chapters of this book in any sequence. For readers who are less familiar with mySAP HR, however, we recommend that you read Chapter 4, *Personnel Administration*, before proceeding with the other chapters.

In addition, over time, you should also get an overview of all processes, not simply the process or processes for which you are responsible or in which you work. In order to work in highly-integrated processes, a basic understanding of the additional context is absolutely beneficial.

The detailed descriptions of various customizing activities can be skipped according to your personal preferences. When working with this book for the first time, it is sufficient to read the conceptual sections first and to proceed with the descriptions of the actual implementation on a step-by-step basis. Project managers may also find it interesting to first read the critical success factors in each chapter.

2 Overview of mySAP ERP HCM

Although SAP has changed product names, transformed underlying technology, Web-enabled user interfaces, and added many new applications, most things that you knew about the central concepts of SAP R/3 HR are still true for mySAP ERP HCM. This book focuses on the basic concepts of the application rather than dealing with the latest trends in Web design or interface technology.

2.1 HR or HCM as a Part of the SAP Solutions Family

The "old" R/3 System (that is until Release 4.6C) is a business software solution that is all of one piece. Together with other modules from the areas of Logistics and Financials/Accounting, SAP R/3 HR builds the R/3 application level. All of these modules use the same technological base, the so-called "SAP Basis," which allows them to interact with each other and the rest of the world. It also provides a very good software development environment for the SAP programming languages ABAP/4 and ABAP Objects.

SAP R/3 Enterprise brought two major technological changes (see Figure 2.1):

▶ The application was split between the *Enterprise Core* and the *Enterprise Extension Sets*. The extension sets were conceived as a way to bring new functionality in well-defined portions to each module. HR has its own series of extension sets and can be updated without a major upgrade that would involve all other modules as well. Moreover, this concept keeps the number of changes in the Enterprise Core low, thus improving stability. As a rule, a new set of extension sets is issued once a year.

▶ The SAP Basis was replaced by the Web Application Server (Web AS). It brought major improvements regarding interfaces with other systems and, as its name suggests, facilitates development of Web integration.

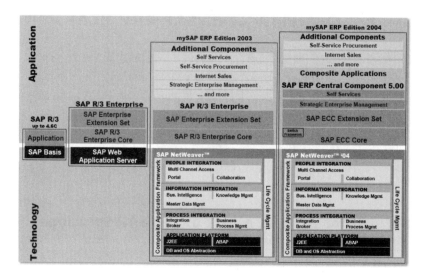

Figure 2.1 The Evolution from R/3 to mySAP ERP

New functionality was always delivered in two different ways:

▶ The enhancement of the R/3 application itself (in R/3 Enterprise, mostly via extension sets)

▶ The development of completely new products such as BW, Enterprise Portal, CRM, E-Recruiting, Learning Solution, etc. Most of these products (sometimes called New-Dimension products) are not new and date back to the 1990s. They are designed to interoperate with R/3 but also with other systems or as stand-alone applications. Under the name of "mySAP," they were bundled together with R/3 mainly for the convenience of customers who wanted to buy a whole solution family—as well as for marketing purposes.

Most of these products are now integrated in mySAP ERP 2004. In some cases, they really merged technically with the successor of R/3. In other cases, they are merely bundled—again for marketing purposes—and are connected via well-defined interfaces. Not taking into consideration that the New Dimension products already existed before, the step from R/3 Enterprise to mySAP ERP 2004 seems enormous (see Figure 2.1). In reality, although major technical improvements do occur—especially regarding integration within the mySAP product family and with third-party products—it is more of an evolution than a revolution. The integration of the different components improves step-by-step, the whole system opens more and more for third-party products, and the user interfaces get ever more Web-enabled. The version generally available in 2005 is named "edition 2004" because 2004 was the year of the ramp-up with first customers. This naming scheme is supposed to be used in the future too. So the year in the name of the version represents the year of general availability with a new version coming up each year.

As shown on the right side of Figure 2.1 mySAP ERP consists of three major parts

▶ The *ERP Central Component* (ECC) is basically the successor of R/3 Enterprise. It also uses of the concept of extension sets (named "ECC Extension Sets") in a way similar to R/3 Enterprise, as well as an underlying core ("SAP ECC Core"). The version included in mySAP ERP 2004 is the "ECC 5.0."

Major changes occurred in the technical base. *SAP NetWeaver* is much more powerful than the Web AS alone. However, many components of NetWeaver are still in their infancy, or even if technically mature lack a broad range of useful applications. As NetWeaver is central to SAP strategy, this will change very quickly. The new techniques for interfaces, process control, and Web-integration will soon have major impact on all application processes, including HCM.

▶ *Additional components* that are not technically integrated into one system.

▶ What do all these fast-paced changes mean for the readers of this book, who want to build up know-how regarding the HR component of any version of SAP products? The answer is this: Whatever the user interface looks like and whatever new interface technologies exist to leverage the collaboration with customers, suppliers, government, and employees, knowing the basic concepts of payroll, time management, and master data along with the corresponding customizing and project management will be crucial skills for the foreseeable future when you want to support your HR processes with software from SAP. In addition, the command of the technological aspects of SAP NetWeaver is important and probably will be even more so tomorrow. There are many technical books available at SAP PRESS. However, you must be aware that it is nearly impossible for one person to have detailed knowledge of mySAP HCM *and* of SAP NetWeaver. So, a team of application experts and technical experts will be needed in most cases.

To conclude this chapter, we will have a look at the so-called Solution Map for mySAP ERP 2004, as shown in Figure 2.2. Besides the line with the title "Human Capital Management," there are elements in other lines that may be interesting for your HR-department, depending on how your company is organized. These are Self Services, Workforce Analytics, Travel Management, Environment, Health & Safety, and Incentive and Commission Management. On the other hand, what SAP calls "HCM" may support processes that are not dealt with in your HR department. This might include payroll as a part of Employee Transaction Management, which often is a task of the accounting department. This shows that it is not so important in which drawer SAP decides to put a particular functionality. Customers have to look for the functions they need and use them to build their own processes on. All components of mySAP ERP are designed to interact with one another, but to different degrees. Generally, integration is better between two parts of the ECC than between an ECC-based process and an additional component. But even this need not always be true.

Self Services				
Analytics	Strategic Enterprise Management	Financial Analytics	Operations Analytics	Workforce Analytics
Financials	Financial Accounting	Management Accounting	Financial Supply Chain Management	Corporate Governance
Human Capital Management	Employee Life-Cycle Management	Employee Transaction Management	HCM Service Delivery	Workforce Deployment
Operations: Value Generation	Procurement	Inventory & Warehouse Management / Manufacturing	Transportation	Sales Order Management / Customer Service
Operations: Support	Life-Cycle Data Management	Program & Project Management	Quality Management	Enterprise Asset Management
Corporate Services	Travel Management	Environment, Health & Safety	Incentive & Commission Management	Real Estate Management

Figure 2.2 mySAP ERP 2004 Solution Map

2.2 The Elements of mySAP ERP HCM and SAP R/3 HR

By now, few people are using the terminology of HCM as shown in the solution map, given that few people actually use the term "HCM" but stick to "HR." So we will show a list of components based mainly on the elements of the SAP menu and distinguish between those that used to be a part of the R/3 system (thus now being part of the ECC) and those that didn't. Figure 2.3 shows the menu of the ECC 5.0. The payroll sub-menu shows the international approach of mySAP HCM. Actually, there are even far more country solutions than shown in the standard payroll menu. Most of them are available as enhancements from SAP or its partners.

Figure 2.3 mySAP ERP 2004 ECC 5.0: Menu

The following components are included in SAP R/3 4.6c:

▶ **Personnel Administration**
Managing personnel data and basic administrative processes

▶ **Organizational Management**
Maintenance of the organizational structure as a basis for reporting and planning purposes

▶ **Recruitment**
Managing vacancies, job advertisements, selection, and correspondence (this is not to be confused with the E-Recruiting solution, which is not part of R/3)

- ▶ **Time Management/Time Administration**
  Maintenance and evaluation of time data, managing time accounts, creating input for payroll

- ▶ **Shift Planning**
  Managing the optimal workforce deployment based on requirements and shift plans

- ▶ **Incentive Wages**
  Piece rate and premium wages for workers

- ▶ **Payroll**
  Calculation of gross and net salaries, payment, reporting to authorities, posting to the Financials module

- ▶ **Benefits**
  Pension plans, insurance, and other benefits in compliance to the specific rules of each country

- ▶ **Travel Management (this component was a part of HR initially but was moved to financials and than to corporate services)**
  Planning of trips, procurement of tickets, etc., request and approval processes, settlement and posting to financial accounting

- ▶ **Training and Event Management**
  Event catalogue, organizing events and resource planning, management of attendees, correspondence, billing and activity allocation

- ▶ **Personnel Development**
  Skill management, career and succession planning, appraisals, development plans

- ▶ **Compensation Management**
  Compensation planning for individual employees and groups, budgeting, policies, benchmarking, job pricing

- ▶ **Personnel Cost Planning**
  Planning of costs base of basic pay master data, organizational management, payroll results, and payroll simulation

- ▶ **Budget Management**
  Managing positions and budgets for the public sector

- ▶ **Environment, Health and Safety**
  Though a designated cross-application component of the corporate services field, it is included in the HR menu, because health and safety-at-work issues are the purview of the HR department in most cases.

New components in R/3 Enterprise and ECC 5.0:

▶ **Management of Global Employees**
Managing the whole process of expatriation and repatriation

▶ **Personnel Cost Planning and Simulation**
This is the successor of the old cost-planning solution. It is far more flexible and lacks many of the old solution's shortcomings.

▶ **Enterprise Compensation Management**
This is the successor of the old compensation management. There are major improvements in process integration and in benchmarking and job pricing.

▶ **Management by Objectives**
This is basically a new and more flexible appraisal component that allows the documentation and management of objectives.

Besides these new components, there are many other improvements delivered with a new version or one of the extension sets. Here are just a few examples:

▶ Context-sensitive structural authorization

▶ Long term incentive plans in compensation management

▶ Mobile solutions

▶ New calendar view in Time Manager's Workplace

▶ More flexible appraisal forms in training and event management

▶ Many country-specific improvements and new functions in payroll, benefits and personnel administration

Other components that are now part of mySAP ERP HCM but never were a part of R/3:

▶ **E-Recruiting**
This product is supposed to be the successor to the old recruitment solution, which is a part of R/3 and the ECC. It has a far better functionality because it is not merely an administrative system for applicant tracking but allows for real talent-management. It offers potential candidates a portal for registering and getting information about interesting jobs. The E-Recruiting solution can also be used as a talent-management tool for internal candidates and for succession planning. Personnel development and recruiting are beginning to merge together here.

- **Learning Solution (LSO)**
  The so called LSO basically creates a learning portal for each employee that integrates some functions of training and event management and personnel development with new functions around e-learning. It also contains an authoring environment for the development of e-learning content.

- **Knowledge Warehouse (KW)**
  The KW manages any kind of files that contain knowledge such as presentations, text documents, or videos.

- **Business Information Warehouse (BW)**
  The BW provides a wide range of analytical functions not only for HCM but for all other applications.

- **Strategic Enterprise Management (SEM)**
  The SEM provides highly aggregated information to support strategic decisions. Special features are the Balanced Scorecard (BSC) and the Business Planning and Simulation (BPS).

- **Employee Self Service (ESS)**
  Though the content of ESS may be found in an R/3 system, it always needed an additional component to work. This used to be the Internet Transaction Server, which still can be used for this purpose. For some years ESS has been integrated in the Enterprise Portal as well. Today both the stand-alone solution and the portal-based solution can be used. However, in the future the stand-alone solution is expected to be dropped.

- **Enterprise Portal**
  Besides ESS, the most important element of the Enterprise Portal from an HR point of view is the Manager's Self Service (MSS). Unlike the ESS it cannot be used without the portal.

Given the vast range of components in mySAP ERP, it is not very probable that this system would be the software of choice when looking at each individual process. However, the advantages of having a highly integrated architecture and a single user interface for all these processes can be huge. To use these advantages requires a very good knowledge of the system, especially at the points of contact between the various components.

3   mySAP HR in the Project

Project management as such certainly doesn't need to be redefined. However, a project implementing mySAP HR contains specifications in addition to the general principles of an IT project, and we will describe those specifications here.

3.1   Structure of a mySAP HR Project

3.1.1   Project Scope

Depending on the given prerequisites, there are many useful possibilities to define the scope of a first implementation. To this end, we assume that the goal is to implement the main processes described in this book:

▶ Personnel administration

▶ Recruitment

▶ Time management (depending on the industry and remuneration model including incentive wages)

▶ Payroll

▶ Benefits

▶ Personnel controlling (in so far as it is to control the processes listed above)

In addition, the following questions arise:

1. Must all these processes be implemented at the same key date?

2. Are additional supplementing processes required?

The second question can clearly be answered with "yes," based on the experience of many projects. In a company with more than 1,000 employees, organizational management should be integrated from the beginning. This makes it possible to map the actual organizational structure as a basis for reports on daily business, personnel controlling, and authorizations. Integrating organizational management later on tends to increase the costs significantly. In addition, you can regard quality assurance and authorization management as specific cross-section processes that should be taken into account from the beginning and provided with sufficient resources.

As to Question 1: With the exception of recruitment, all the processes mentioned previously are strongly dependent on each other. Therefore, if possible, they should also be implemented together. The alternative would be to build very complex interfaces to bridge the times between the individual implementations. It is better to reserve this effort for the implementation itself. Consider also that if the process is mapped continuously for most users, no navigation between the different systems is necessary. An implementation at different dates should therefore only occur if the existing capacities do not permit any other solution.

Recruitment can also be implemented in a second step (e.g., together with personnel development). However, it should be integrated in the design phase when establishing the company structure and the organizational structure (see Section 4.2.5).

We will now also comment on the processes we haven't referred to yet:

▶ Travel Management could possibly be implemented in the first step, if integration into remuneration payroll is required. However, the dependencies here are rather few, so travel management can also be implemented at a later stage. However, implementing travel management before personnel administration increases the effort considerably, as travel management requires certain personnel master data and structures of the personnel administration.

▶ If Shift Planning is required, you must check for every specific case whether this process is possible in legacy systems without any complex interface to time management in mySAP HR.

▶ Personnel Cost Planning and Compensation Management are very dependent on payroll and personnel administration. You must also check here how complex an interface from mySAP HR the old system requires. When starting the payroll on January 1st in a particular year, you should implement both of these components for the next subsequent planning round, i.e. usually in September or October.

Decentralized application ESS (Employee Self Service) and Manager's Desktop or Manager's Self Service (MSS) are applications that have a largely decentralized effect. To ensure the stability of the processes and to be able to respond to requests from decentralized users in the personnel department, an implementation is only advisable if the central processes are stable and if the users in the personnel department have constructed a secure system. This decision also depends on the already existing software. If management and employees are already used to a similar functionality, you should not revert to paper-supported processes.

For Manager's Desktop in particular it is advisable to take a closer look. In many cases, the provision of paper reports requires development work of its own. Although standard reports are suitable for online evaluation, weaknesses can emerge during printout (e.g., insufficient flexibility regarding page breaks). In this case, avoiding additional development can be reason enough to justify immediate implementation of Manager's Desktop.

In general, this is a good time to apply the basic principle that the project risk is considerably reduced if the project is divided into clear steps that also have real consequences. A planned project runtime of more than a year without a visible result is risky and often leads to deadline shifts.

In large companies, the implementation in a pilot area with subsequent rollout is recommended for this reason. In the mySAP HR processes considered here, this depends mostly on the situation and conditions of the company. If payroll itself is implemented centrally for all areas, the rollout concept is difficult to implement. This works more easily with components such as ESS, Manager's Desktop, travel management, or recruitment.

3.1.2   Project Phases

The ASAP concept (AcceleratedSAP) is used here to separate the project phases. ASAP is both a comprehensive tool to support an SAP implementation and it is a methodology. As a tool, ASAP has been replaced by SAP Solution Manager. The roadmap described here is still in use, however.

ASAP

While you can certainly check whether it makes sense to use the tool with regard to the specific requirements, the methodology is generally accepted. There are however obviously differences in the names of the phases and their content at the details level. Figure 3.1 illustrates the ASAP roadmap that delineates the project phases of an SAP project.

In the following sections we will describe the individual phases. Here we will partly deviate from the detail statements of ASAP, especially because we cannot basically assume the use of ASAP tools.

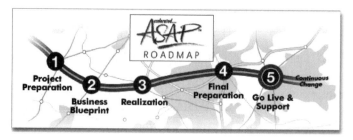

Figure 3.1 ASAP Roadmap

Project Preparation

The project preparation phase is actually self-evident and quite simple in terms of content. However, failure occurs so frequently in practice that we think it will be important to describe it in some detail. Basically the prerequisites for the actual project should be created in this phase. These include in particular:

▶ Defining the project team

▶ Training the project team and decision-makers

▶ Providing project rooms

▶ Providing the technical infrastructure

▶ Defining project standards (forms, templates, document conventions, etc.)

This all may sound simple, but in fact much time is lost in projects because these issues were not dealt with up front. These prerequisites should be clarified throughout the project, in particular for projects whose scope exceeds that of mySAP HR.

Business Blueprint

Before you start the implementation, you should know exactly what is to be implemented. In addition, the project requirements must be defined, and the project scope must be documented in a form that is understandable to all those involved. As changes during the course of the project aren't provided for by pure theory, but all the more so correspond to actual practice, an essential factor is that the documentation on requirements is always kept up-to-date as a part of the change management.

It is no longer feasible to establish requirements without any system reference once you leave the general levels and go into further detail. Responding to extensive, detailed question lists, without knowing the background to the questions, causes those involved in the project to be wary and threatens acceptance of the implemented system. In addition, there are frequent misunderstandings at this level.

Therefore, when you establish the detailed requirements you should use two means of support:

▶ Create a prototype that will be used again in the next phase for implementation

▶ Visualize the processes using modeling tools

Both means provide the project participants with alternatives and their advantages and disadvantages. The detailed requirements can thus really be established by the entire team. Both the prototype and the process models are used for further training of the project team.

An alternative to the prototype can also be a "neutral" training system such as SAP's IDES system. In this case, however, an efficient basic configuration must be carried out at the beginning of the implementation phase. No reusable project work can be carried out based on the IDES system. The IDES is pre-configured in such a way that it rules out later release changes.

> **Note** It is frequently supposed that the target processes can be defined as far as the details level without any concrete mapping of a prototype in the system "on paper" (or in some documentation tools). The hope is that afterwards only the system tables must be set according to the documentation, and that an ideally configured system exists. In practice, a process definition is not possible at the detailed level without the ability to run the processes through ever more refined development systems (prototypes). This is to be supported by a rough process definition before the start of the system configuration and a continuous refinement during the project.

Implementation

Based on the prototype, the implementation incorporates the gradual refinement of the mapped processes in system configuration and programming. Here, in particular, intensive transfer of know-how from the consultants to the internal team members takes place. In general, this transfer happens "on the job." Additional training can, however, be carried out for specific issues. This also depends on the size of the project team.

You should not lose sight of the results processed in phase two. Deviations should be agreed upon with those affected and with those responsible, and the documentation must be adapted.

Final Preparation

In this phase, the immediate preparations for taking the system live are carried out on the basis of the almost entirely configured system. Changes to the system configuration in this phase must be coordinated and approved even on the details level, as they can affect such tasks as the integration of legacy data or end-user training.

Essential elements of this phase are:

▶ Integration tests and final tuning

▶ Interface tests

▶ Role-specific end-user training

▶ GoingLive Check

Go-live and Support

The final data transfer and launch of the productive operation with the new system take place here.

A hotline must now be available for the end users. The project team gets support from the consultants' side. Especially with technical problems such as bad performance, SAP provides the relevant services.

A lot of time is frequently required to transfer legacy data. This is generally not the case for personnel master data, as its data structures are quite simple. Other data in mySAP HR, such as organizational structures, are more complex and require a higher level of effort during the interface programming, but the transfer itself is generally less time-critical than it is, for instance, in logistics, due to the difference in the quantity of data. However, an early test with real data from the legacy system is important. Such a test not only enables you to make statements on the runtime but also on the quality of the legacy data. In mySAP HR, very detailed plausibility checks usually are carried out with regard to the data entry. If this was not the case in the legacy system, the data transfer can require a large amount of subsequent work and can compromise the production start if this additional work hasn't been allowed for.

Continuous Change

In the phase of continuous improvement, the importance of phase two becomes obvious. In an implementation project carried out in a short timeframe with an unchanged team, you can frequently manage with very little documentation. However, if changes are necessary after a long period of time, new components are introduced or an upgrade is implemented, documenting the processes and system settings based on these processes is extremely helpful. Here you must ensure that the continuous change also applies to the documentation!

3.2 Tools

3.2.1 The Solution Manager

A large number of project management tools are available in the market these days. The Solution Manager, in replacing the former ASAP, provides an extensive collection of tools, specifically to accompany SAP projects. It is divided into an area for the system operation and one for project support. The latter basically contains the following components:[1]

▶ Project management helps (roadmap)

▶ Accelerators: checklists, instructions or templates for certain subjects. Links to SAP Service Marketplace

▶ Predefined scenarios (structured up to the process step level). In HR, however, there was almost no content available at the time of printing.

▶ Integration in the implementation guide (IMG) of several systems

▶ Definition of the system landscape

▶ Automatic customizing distribution

▶ Test organization

▶ Internal message management with the option to forward messages to SAP AG

To what extent the Solution Manager is specifically used in a concrete mySAP HR project depends, among other things, on the following factors:

▶ The quality and scope of the predefined HR scenarios available at the project start

---

1 You can find detailed information on ASAP on the Internet at *http://service.sap.com/asap*

- ▶ Scope of the project (additional processes in addition to HR, the number of systems involved, the number of project team members)
- ▶ Integration in the documentation and project-management tools existing in the company
- ▶ Level of experience of the project participants; in particular, use is recommended for teams with little HR and project experience

In most cases it is useful to use some of the existing checklists and forms. The same applies to the basic philosophy expressed by the roadmap, which can be used in most cases. To what extent a complete use of the Solution Manager is useful must be considered in each individual case. For rollout projects, there is special functionality available to define templates. In such projects the use of the Solution Manager is definitely worthwhile.

3.2.2   Process Modeling

Tools

A broad range of tools is available to model and optimize business processes. For the processes described in this book, *ARIS Easy Design Versions 5* and *6.1* from IDS Scheer AG was used (although the normal modeling conventions were not adhered to for reasons of space). The ARIS product family is specifically suited for use in the mySAP HR environment, because coupling with R/3 and ASAP and also HR is generally possible.

A few other products also fulfill these criteria. The following factors are particularly relevant for selection:

- ▶ Usability
- ▶ Price (huge differences!)
- ▶ Re-usability of the models (e.g., for ISO certification)
- ▶ Web-enabledness of the models
- ▶ The option of distributed modeling
- ▶ Database-based tool versus graphic tool
- ▶ Coupling with R/3
- ▶ Integration in the solution manager
- ▶ Coupling with mySAP HR
- ▶ Variety of model types offered

▶ Market share

▶ Interfaces

Whatever product you decide on, the process-oriented documentation is particularly useful in larger projects. Rollout projects rarely function without visualized and fine-tuned business processes. However, it is rarely of any use to describe extensive internal processing of the system (e.g., net payroll) in a process model. The interaction between the users and the system is much more important.

C-Business Maps of SAP AG

SAP has offered C-Business Maps for quite some time (the "C" stands for "collaborative"). These generally describe processes in which collaboration takes place across company boundaries and are therefore oriented towards e-business. In the HR environment, such scenarios are particularly relevant for recruitment, but SAP also provides other examples.[2]

A C-Business Map presents in visual form the steps of the participating business partners and the interfaces in a collaborative process. In general, each step is assigned the advantages and quantified potentials achieved by the use of cross-company e-business technologies.

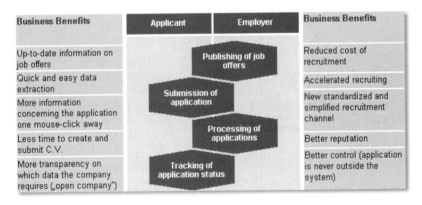

Figure 3.2 C-Business Map: Job Advertisement

Figure 3.2 shows an example of the process of a job advertisement and the application processing. This illustration is on a very general level as one step can only be ended by the change between the advertising company and the applicant. There is no quantification of the optimization

---

2 You can find examples and additional information at *http://www.sap.com/services/pdf/BWP_CBusinessMaps.pdf*

potentials in the examples available from SAP for personnel-management processes. In other areas, the specification of percentages based on project experience and customer surveys are usual. In the following sections, a particular emphasis is placed on the description of the interfaces.

Other Reference Models

In addition to the C-Business Maps, other reference models can also act as suggestions or templates, and tools for the project work. For the implementation, optimization or outsourcing of HR processes, for instance, we like to use a standardized HR services catalog. Such a catalog does not yet contain any detailed description of process flows, but rather a structured display of the services in personnel management (in general these are between 100 and 1,000 services).

This means it can be easily adapted to the specific conditions of a company and can then be used to define the project scope in a structured procedure (see Figure 3.3).[3]

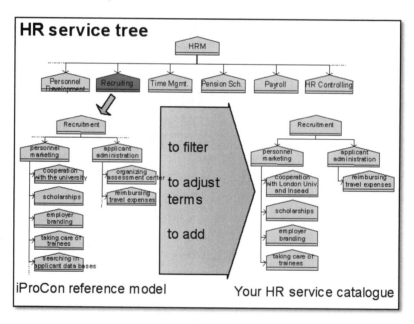

Figure 3.3 HR Services: From the Reference Model to the Project Focus

---

3 You can find further information and an example of this reference model at *http://www.iprocon.de/int/leistungen/refmods.htm*

3.2.3 Implementation Guide

You can find a brief description of the implementation guide (IMG) in Appendix A, *Cross-Process Customizing Tools*. In addition to the structured access to customizing activities, it offers functionalities for project management such as status management, degree of completion, scheduling and resource assignment, and the option to place the documentation in a useful manner.

In many cases the functionalities are insufficiently used although managing the guide is very easy to handle. In addition, it is also integrated in ASAP.

3.3 Critical Success Factors

▶ Timely definition and training of the project team

▶ Composing the project team from IT and personnel-management experts

▶ Awareness of the high complexity of customizing, in particular in payroll and time management

▶ Ensuring a stable technical infrastructure, in particular for the development and customizing systems (data backups must be carried out way before the productive operation starts)

▶ Early integration of employee representatives

▶ Clarification of the structures in mySAP HR and in particular clarification of the use of organizational management (thereby integrating the remaining processes, particularly accounting)

▶ Timely checking of the data quality in the legacy system

▶ Establishment of an extensive test environment, especially for payroll and time evaluation

▶ Modeling of the business processes at least for decentralized use

▶ Experienced project management (mySAP HR is one of the more complex processes in R/3)

▶ Creation and, in particular, maintenance of the documentation

4   Personnel Administration

Personnel administration comprises the areas of HR master data, the necessary structures, and the corresponding reporting. Administration thus forms the basis for the other areas of personnel management, while also acting as an independent essential personnel management process.

4.1   Business Principles

In addition to legal principles and structuring of work processes in personnel administration, we will stress the principles of organizational theory in this section. We will explore the significance of personnel administration as a basis for other processes of personnel management, as well as principles of personnel reporting. We also will describe the importance of a personnel database integrated across the entire enterprise. Among the remaining topics in this chapter will be approaches to decentralized personnel work.

4.1.1   Organizational Structures in the Personnel Area

Organizational theory differentiates between organizational structure and process structure (see Figure 4.1).

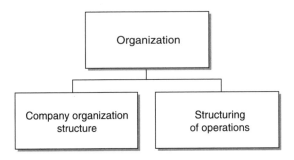

Figure 4.1 Organizational Concepts

The SAP system uses both areas of organizational theory. To structure the personnel dataset, the organizational structure discussed here is the more relevant area. The process structure will always be part of the subject matter in each chapter because of the process-oriented nature of the book, and will not be considered as part of the specific content here.

Structuring the workforce can be considered from different perspectives. First, structuring is carried out according to the "normal" organizational structure, as described in the organizational chart of a company. This structure can be seen from different viewpoints (functional, product-oriented, market-oriented, etc.), and in the case of the matrix organization two or more of these views can even be taken at the same time. There are other criteria that structure the workforce. For example, groups of employees are formed according to their status (salaried workers, industrial workers, executives), their contract type (pay-scale, non-pay-scale), or employment level (part-time, full-time). Further structures are supplied by legal rules (pay-scale law, social-insurance law) and by the location of the employee, which more and more frequently cannot be determined from the organizational chart. A further structural attribute—the project structure—is increasingly gaining in importance. In companies where work is frequently carried out on a project-basis, membership in one or more project teams is often as important a criterion as the line of command or the location.

For personnel work carried out on a daily basis, the following decisions can be derived from the structures:

▶ Validity of business regulations (payroll, time management, travel costs reimbursement, etc.)

▶ Validity of regulations according to collective agreement

▶ Validity of legal regulations

▶ Responsibility of HR administrators

▶ Responsibility of authorities

▶ Supervisors

▶ Treatment in legal statistics

▶ Treatment in statistics of the internal HR reporting

▶ Assigning personnel costs in the context of financial accounting and management accounting

This list, which is by no means complete, clearly shows the importance of the project step "clarifying the structures," regardless of the software selected. A yardstick for the quality of the structure is always the question: "Can the administrator reach all decisions mentioned and assign the appropriate statistics based on the classification of an employee in the selected structure?"

4.1.2   HR Master Data and Work Processes

The core of personnel administration is the personnel data itself. It provides the basis for reporting and the subsequent processes. To this end, completeness, quality, and timeliness are crucial.

Optimal definition of the processes for maintenance and quality assurance of the HR master data pays off in two ways:

▶ It provides an ideal information basis for the entire personnel work and therefore increases its efficiency and effectiveness. Lack of quality in this regard, however, accumulates negative impact as it moves down the process stream.

▶ Many maintenance processes run on a daily basis, so that optimal structuring provides continuous benefits.

Selecting Data

The decision as to which personnel data should be maintained is a fundamental one. The important consideration is that master data is not an end in itself. The selection of data should generally be determined by the following factors:

▶ Legal regulations (see Section 4.1.3)

▶ Requirements of evaluations and statistics (see Chapter 11, *Personnel Controlling*)

▶ Requirements of downstream processes (see Section 4.1.4 and 4.1.5)

▶ Requirements of the organization of the personnel administration itself (e.g., location of the file or responsible HR administrator)

An expansion of the database is always useless if the extra data can only be partly entered or is of a poor quality. Evaluations of the data then appear to be precise, but using the data often leads to incorrect conclusions. In this context, less is often more: Only refer to data for which you can guarantee a sufficient quality.

When selecting data, however, you should not limit yourself to data controlled in the HR department. In most companies, great potential can be yielded from the step that leads from an HR *department* information system to an overall HR information system (see Section 4.1.5).

Maintenance Processes

The quality of the data is defined insofar as it can be interpreted in a standardized and correct manner. For everyone who must maintain specific data, a standardized process must be defined. If administrator A enters the business number in the field "Phone number," but administrator B enters a private number, the data is practically worthless.

For reasons of timeliness, understanding the entire personnel management process is essential. An administrator in payroll will always ensure that the data he or she is responsible for is always up-to-date in time for the payroll run. He or she may be completely unaware that a colleague has just a week before carried out evaluations that form the basis for important decisions. These interdependencies must be realized and communicated. Along with timeliness, they are the essential criteria for organizing data maintenance.

Organization and Work Distribution

Several helpful principles can be established for personnel administration:

▶ Data entry should take place as closely as possible to when and where the information gets known

▶ Information output should meet information requirements as closely as possible

▶ Minimize the number of agents per process

▶ Minimize the number of information carriers per process (paper, e-mail, phone, IT system, etc.)

▶ Minimize the number of interruptions to a process

In the ideal situation, the employee enters all data by himself, the management and controllers evaluate all data themselves in the personnel system, and in the personnel department there is only one administrator for every employee for all areas.

The reality is often very different. The level of needed data protection and the qualifications for each role severely limit flexibility. The conflict between the required timeliness and availability of different data groups frequently blocks complete processing that is free from interruptions. However, the principles referred to should still be followed conscientiously. In cases where processing cannot be done by one person, teams can be formed.

The advantages of modern data-processing (DP) systems can only be fully exploited if decentralized concepts are used and a clearly defined work distribution is implemented in a seamless manner.

4.1.3 Legal Principles

Personnel administration is regulated through a variety of legal requirements, which differ from country to country and from state to state. The most important areas these regulations deal with are:

- ▶ Data protection
- ▶ Employment law (especially the equal-employment-opportunity regulations, which are very important in North America but become more and more important in Europe as well)
- ▶ Tax regulations
- ▶ Collective agreements (especially in the more unionized European countries)
- ▶ Social Security

In general, these and other laws provide no detailed rules to implement HR processes in a DP system. Legal limits generally provide little scope within which to exploit ideal processes.

These restrictions apply to the U.S. as well as to most other countries, although to very different extents. Make sure that you know about the specific regulation when doing a rollout project to another country. There may even be differences between different states.

4.1.4 A Basis for Other Personnel Management Processes

The quality of other personnel processes—above all personnel controlling—depends on the quality of the personnel administration. This dependency is particularly clear if you are working with an integrated DP system, which should always be the essential goal. Lack of timeliness and poor quality of data maintenance have an immediate impact on the results of the other management areas. This problem is, however, basically independent of the system. Even if work is being carried out in isolated systems or exclusively on paper, specific information is indispensable as a basis for the processes that are described in more detail in the following sections.

Time Management

When you do time recording via time recording terminals, time management depends most heavily on the timeliness of data. The employees generally expect their time accounts to be updated daily at the time-recording terminal. If a lack of quality in the basic data leads to errors, this leads to more time and effort on the part of staff, due to enquiries, and a basic mistrust of employees towards the system. Where access-control systems are linked, errors can even completely "lock out" employees.

Essential master data for time management includes:

▶ Organizational data that determines the assignment of employees to certain business regulations

▶ Assignment of the employee to a relevant time administrator

▶ Time model/shift plan

▶ Leave entitlement

▶ Assignment of the employee to the respective time-recording terminal

Payroll

The payroll processes a particularly large quantity of personnel data. This data does not need to be updated on a daily basis but rather on a monthly basis, and it must be up-to-date at the day of payroll. Erroneous results are problematic in their own way because, in contrast to time management, corrections cannot be made daily but only in the subsequent month, as otherwise it would require much effort. The transfer of results to public institutions such as tax agencies underlines the importance of a high data quality.

A basic problem is the need to remunerate employees before the end of the month for which payment is to be made. Because it is inevitable that not all data pertaining to the month can be known, the salary calculated is more or less an estimated value. When setting the due date for payment, the increased process costs of an earlier point in time should also be taken into consideration. Payroll systems available on the market can indeed process subsequent changes, but the effort involved in inputting these changes rises, and at the same time the employee's understanding of the remuneration payroll suffers. In the case of assumed fixed monthly salaries, it is surprising how many unexpected changes arise in the second half of the month due to overtime, unpaid absence, changes to the tax data, etc.

The following essential basic data is relevant to remuneration by the date of payroll:

▶ Organizational data that determines the classification by company, pay scale, and legal regulations

▶ Gross remuneration, including one-off payments

▶ Tax and social-insurance data

▶ Other services such as direct insurance, company car, etc.

▶ Address data to dispatch remuneration statements

▶ Data for the company pension plan

▶ Bank details

Personnel Planning and Development

Personnel planning and development processes also depend on data which must be updated on a daily basis. However, this dependency is all too often forgotten due to frequent structural separation of the processes of administration, time management and payroll. In extreme cases, personnel development managers have to face the fact that only at the time of the remuneration payment can they safely rely on the basic administration data.

Even if the organization places great value on the importance of personnel planning and development, the processes of data retrieval and recording frequently focus only the goal of transferring the correct amount to the correct account on payday.

Therefore care must be taken to ensure that the planning departments are provided with administrative information for their daily work. For example, this information can include:

▶ Pay scale grouping

▶ Agreed gross salary

▶ Organizational assignment with history

▶ Residency permit

▶ Native language

▶ Working time

▶ Scheduled absence times

It often happens that an employee has not even been entered in the system when the personnel development wants to maintain a training schedule for this employee.

4.1.5 Companywide Integration of HR Data

In practice, many HR information systems are in fact HR *department* information systems. Beyond the HR department, data from the central system is used most frequently in the form of paper lists provided by the HR department. On the other hand, various types HR data are maintained on a companywide basis. For example:

▶ Absence lists (whether on the basis of Microsoft Excel or a large chart) in all departments

▶ Birthday lists and anniversary lists in all departments

▶ Lists with salaries, paid bonuses, and objectives which the management uses for budgeting and annual appraisals

▶ Remaining leave lists, which often show numbers different from those maintained by the HR department (in the worst case, the paper lists of the department office are more up-to-date than the central HR information system)

▶ Lists of assets such as laptops and company cars, for which, in the context of asset accounting, the employee who uses the items is also entered

▶ Data from the loan department of a bank concerning employee loans

▶ Service phone numbers maintained by the technical service, as well as room numbers, and their publication in an internal phone book

▶ Assignment of keys and access cards for employees maintained by the security service in a file

▶ Organizational charts created by the organizational department that go down to employee levels in separate "org-chart" software

▶ List in Microsoft Excel format maintained by the security manager in order to check the timeliness of first-aid courses and hazardous-material training

Such structures have often grown historically and may have been useful at the time of their implementation. However, the availability of a modern system with a central database and potential for decentralized access provides much more useful options. The decentralized use of a companywide HR information system provides many advantages:

- Lower costs through elimination of duplicate entries
- Savings on system costs in the decentralized area and a decrease in the proportion of the TCO (Total Costs of Ownership) allocated to the HR department in the personnel system
- Improved data quality due to an improved communication between decentralized users and the HR department
- Elimination of contradictory datasets
- Increased data security through integration of previously decentralized data in the central security concept
- Improved transparency of existing datasets
- The possibility of aggregating previously separate datasets (e.g., on the department level)
- Having all the data in one system makes it possible to provide people with necessary information about changes, e.g., new hires, or transfers. This can be managed by an interface with the company's e-mail system (e.g., MS Outlook) so that messages are generated automatically whenever a predefined event occurs.
- Considerably improved data protection due to access control for the central system, as well as transparency

In this context, the last item is definitely one of the most important. However, it can also become a problem, as the transparency which is suddenly available uncovers past failures. The existence of decentralized HR data is not always agreed upon by the data-protection officers. Often, the potential we have described above is not fully used, in order to avoid such problems. At this point, the only solution is an open dialogue and the awareness of the opportunity to solve a widespread problem.

Other obstacles which must be overcome on the way to companywide, integrated HR information systems can be:

Other obstacles

- A blockade by decentralized users who regard the integration of "their" datasets into the entire system as an encroachment upon their "sovereign territory"
- The difficulty of identifying decentralized datasets, especially if they were not recorded in digital format
- The problem of converting decentralized datasets, which are mostly maintained without conventions or with very different conventions

▶ Complicated assignment-to-data of the central system because only names have been maintained instead of personnel numbers

▶ A lack of acceptance of standards by the decentralized users

▶ A shift of costs that increase the workload in certain places despite the reduction of the overall cost structure

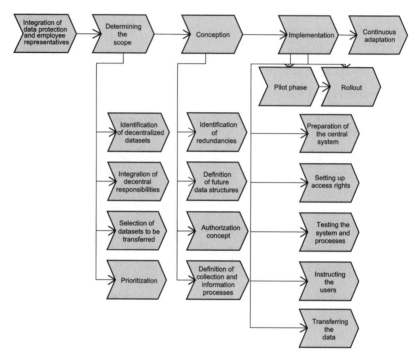

Figure 4.2 Process for Companywide Integration of HR Data

The procedure to establish a companywide integrated HR information system is illustrated in Figure 4.2. The detailed image suggests that the planning appears more complex than it actually is. In less extensive actions of this type, the project phases are not always as detailed as illustrated in the diagram. However, all the steps shown in this process are essential for the successful integration.

4.2 The mySAP HR Concept

HR inevitably follows the aforementioned principles. In doing so, it effectively fulfills business requirements in the area of personnel administration, although it must be admitted that there are both strengths and weaknesses. In the following sections we will discuss in particular the weak points and how they are handled. In addition, we will describe the basic concepts, the essential application components, and the fundamental as well as critical customizing activities. We will specifically focus on those aspects of implementation or optimization projects where important decisions are made—for example in the company and employee structures. The data maintenance of infotypes and the data-maintenance processes are other essential aspects treated here. National specifics, in particular in the area of infotypes, are only touched on in examples.

As an introduction to the system-relevant subjects, this chapter is more detailed than the sections on the other processes. Experienced users will skim over some sections, but will still find many interesting tips.

4.2.1 Personnel Numbers

The Importance of Personnel Numbers

The personnel number is the system's central classification criterion for all personnel data. Each individual data record is assigned to the correct employee using the personnel number. This is true for master data organized in infotypes (see Section 4.2.2) as well as for the results of payroll, time management, company pension plans, and travel expense reports. It will be clear that it is practically impossible to make a subsequent change in a personnel number without creating inconsistencies in the database or losing the entire history of an employee.

In HR, the personnel number can be a maximum of eight characters and is composed only of digits.

The Assignment of Numbers

Assigning "meaningful" personnel numbers (e.g., "personnel numbers of managers start with a '9' ") is absolutely not recommended. Because the smallest amounts of information occasionally read from the personnel numbers are absolutely static, meaningful personnel numbers always lead to unsolvable problems if the "coded" information is changed. Examples of this are the change of cost center, change of position, or ending the apprenticeship.

No meaningful numbers

However, it is not generally necessary to hide additional information in the personnel numbers in R/3. All employee characteristics are documented through the structuring and data-entry options that we will describe in the following sections. Essential information that the administrator always wants to have access to when processing the data for an employee can be displayed in a suitable form. For example, it can be shown in the remuneration statement or as header information in all screens of HR data processing. Figure 4.3 shows an example for header details. Essentially, the content of the headers can be flexibly adjusted.

Personnel No.	100244	
Name	John Kent	Corporate - United States
	Active	Philadelphia
	Salaried staff	SSN 700-07-7024

Figure 4.3 Header Entries in the HR Data Maintenance

There are two different options for personnel number assignment:

▶ In external number assignment the administrator manually enters a personnel number for each new employee. The assignment can then be carried out in any sequence.

▶ For internal number assignments the system automatically determines the next free number. In this case the administrator cannot make any changes.

Number ranges   In both cases, the available numbers can be limited by using the number range. Number ranges can for example be assigned separately for each subsidiary. However, you must remember that the information gained gets lost or becomes incorrect when an employee moves to another subsidiary.

Setting the number range and assigning it to parts of the enterprise structure is done through the IMG menu path **Personnel Management · Personnel Administration · Basic Settings · Maintain number range intervals for personnel numbers & Determine defaults for number ranges**.

The current number in particular can be read or changed there (only upwards!), and decisions can be made as to whether internal or external assignments will be done. In the example in Figure 4.4 the numbers of the intervals 01 and 02 are to be assigned internally, while for interval 03 the personnel numbers must be assigned by the user. Which of the three intervals is relevant for a specific hiring action is determined in the IMG item **Determine defaults for number ranges**.

It is generally advisable to have an internal number assignment. Having a single number range for the entire company simplifies changes between the individual subsidiaries.

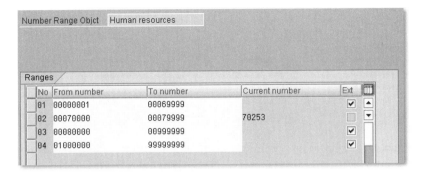

Figure 4.4 Number Ranges for Personnel Numbers

The Concept of the Reference Personnel Number

One of the weaknesses in the HR data structure lies at the personnel-number level. The personnel number is the ultimate key criterion for all data; it is not possible to enter several employment contracts for one person. The solution is to create a new HR master record for each employment relationship. This, however, leads to a redundant entry of a large part of the personnel data as the address or name of the employee, for instance, don't change through the additional employment contract.

The problem is partly solved through the concept of the reference personnel number. As the second employment contract is entered, it is connected to the first one by the **Reference personnel number** field. Certain data is then copied from the original personnel number and during the course of time additional changes such as a new address of one of the two personnel numbers always affects the other one as well. In contrast, other data points, such as the salaries for each contract, remain independent from one another.

Reference personnel number

The data (i.e., infotypes) that is or is not mirrored here is defined via the IMG: **Personnel management · Personnel administration · Customizing Procedures · Infotypes · Infotypes · Infotype ·** Selection box **"copy infotype".** There, for example, Infotype 0002 ("Personal Data") is keyed to be mirrored. The corresponding field of the customizing screen (**Copy infotype)** is selected in Figure 4.5.

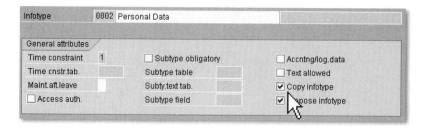

Figure 4.5 Setting the Relevance of the Infotype for Reference Personnel Numbers

Examples of the use of reference personnel numbers include the following:

▶ There are several contracts each with a low working time, as is often the case at universities offering several jobs to students.

▶ The work time for an employee is divided between two connected companies (e.g., a caretaker is employed by two affiliated companies located in the same building). However, if possible this should be stipulated in one contract, and the costs should be split between the two companies.

The Concept of Concurrent Employment

Since Release R/3 Enterprise, the concept of concurrent employment is available. This concept maps the case of concurrent employment relationships for one person better than the concept of the reference personnel number. Concurrent employment can also be adequately covered in other areas, such as payroll or time management.

Note that this concept is only implemented for the U.S. and Canada. OSS Note 517071 provides precise information on the release of the functionality.

In order to be able to use concurrent employment, it must first be released in Customizing. This can be done via IMG path **Personnel management · Personnel administration · Basic settings · Basic settings for concurrent employment · Activate concurrent employment**.

After this, the "old" personnel number only stands for an employment contract. The person is identified through the "(external) person ID" or "personal identification number," which is stored in Infotype 0709. The personal ID consists of 18 characters and can be structured alphanumerically. This infotype must be maintained before activating the concurrent employment for all employment contracts. This can be carried out through report HR_CE_GENERATE_PERSONID_EXT. Infotype 0712 identifies the main employment contract.

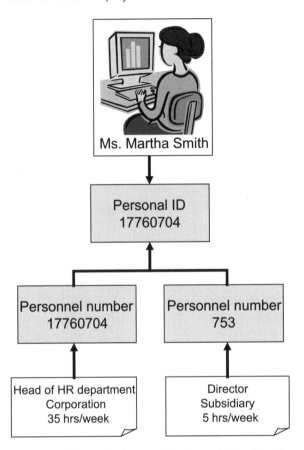

Figure 4.6 Relationship Between the Personal ID and the Personnel Number

Thus, an employee who has several employment contracts has a clear ID and several "personnel numbers" which now stand for contract numbers (see Figure 4.6). In the application (e.g., in the master-data maintenance), the user can therefore select a person by his or her ID and determine which employment contract is currently to be processed. Through the user parameter HR_CCURE_ PIDSL you can deactivate the person ID also for each individual user. This is particularly useful in environments where a personnel administrator does not possess access rights for more than one employment contract (for example, if the contracts are basically located in different companies, which also have different personnel administrators).

Searching for Employees

Even if the personnel number is the essential criterion for the DP system, it is unacceptable to mandate that a user always know the personnel number in order to maintain an HR master record. HR offers extensive options for selecting the personnel numbers to be processed according to various criteria. These should be sufficiently dealt with in the user training, since daily work becomes considerably more efficient by their use. Person selection is described in detail in the sections "Selecting the Personnel Number" and "The Object Manager" (see Section 4.2.3).

4.2.2 The Infotype Concept

Entering master data in HR is carried out via information types (infotypes). In order to facilitate the data maintenance, the infotypes can be combined into infogroups for the implementation of personnel actions or into infotype menus for individual maintenance.

Infotypes

An Infotype is the combination of professional data which belongs together, e.g., addresses, bank details, additional payment, etc. For the user, it is displayed as a screen for data entry. An infotype can contain plausibility controls, obligatory fields, can be divided into subtypes, and always has a period of validity.

In addition to its name an infotype can be identified by a four-digit number. Here the number ranges are defined as follows:

- 0000–0999 personnel administration (or recruitment)
- 1000–1999 personnel planning and development
- 2000–2999 time management
- 3000–3999 logistics integration
- 4000–4999 exclusively recruitment
- 9000–9999 customer-specific infotypes

Note to programmers

For those interested in programming: In the database in administration and time management, the data for Infotype "nnnn" is always stored in the database table "PAnnnn" (Recruitment: "PBnnnn"), with the exception of Infotype 2011, which represents Table TEVEN.

The interface of the infotype screen can vary according to the status of the Customizing settings, depending on the data currently entered or other data of the same employee. For example, in Infotype 0016 ("Contract elements") for temporary employment relationships there is a field for the limit date.

Customizing the interfaces of the infotypes can also be carried out independently of the data of the processed employees via Customizing (see section "Customizing infotypes"). For this reason, the examples shown here will deviate partially from the interfaces of your systems.

Subtypes

Subtypes partition an infotype into screens of similar content. An example of this is Infotype 0009 ("Bank Details") with the subtypes "Main bank", "Other bank" and "Travel expenses" (see Figure 4.7).

The interfaces of an infotype can differ in appearance according to the subtype or can carry out other plausibility checks. For example, Infotype "Family" has different screens for spouses and children.

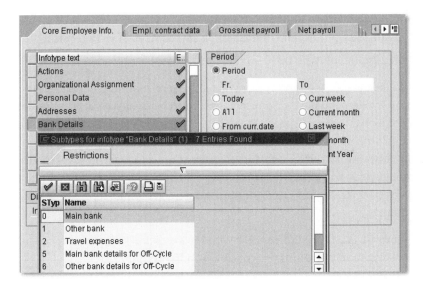

Figure 4.7 Subtypes in the Example of the Bank Details

Time Constraint

Time constraint is one of the essential attributes of the infotype concept in R/3. It allows HR administration to build a history of data that changes with time. Time constraint describes to what extent an infotype or subtype can exist on a multiple basis and can contain gaps. It can be defined for a complete infotype or per subtype.

Personnel administration primarily uses the following four time constraint types:

▶ **Time constraint 0**
Exactly one record must exist during the entire period of validity of the person and it must always be the same one.

(Example: Infotype 0003—"Payroll Status"

▶ **Time constraint 1**
For one point in time, there must be exactly one valid record and overlaps are not possible.

(Example: Infotype 0002—"Personal Data," in particular the name of the employee)

▶ **Time constraint 2**
For each point in time, there can be a maximum of one valid record. Gaps are allowed, overlaps are not possible.

(Example: Infotype 0004—"Disability")

▶ **Time constraint 3**
For each point in time, there can be any number of valid records.

(Example: Infotype 0030—"Powers of Attorney")

The meaning of the time constraint can be seen in Infotype 0021 ("Family"). While subtype 1 ("Spouse"), has time constraint 2—at least in the European culture group—subtype 2 ("Child") allows several entries at the same time, and therefore has time constraint 3. For subtype 1, time constraint 3 would correspond to polygamy. Time constraint 1 for a spouse would mean an enforced marriage, even if not always necessarily with the same partner. A lifelong partnership would correspond to the time constraint 0.

Figure 4.8 illustrates this concept with the exception of the special case of time constraint 0, which only occurs with Infotype 0003.

Note You should prepare your users for time constraints, because many errors and problems in the HR application arise due to incorrect execution when making changes, copying, and inserting infotypes. It is similarly essential to understand different time constraints in order to successfully create and interpret evaluations for standard reports as well as to create specific queries or reports.

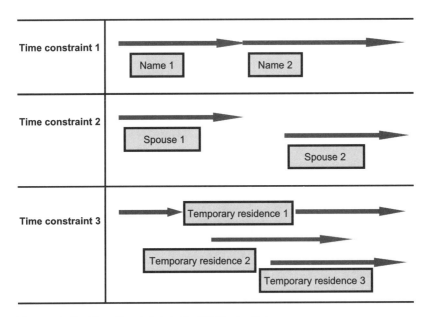

Figure 4.8 The Time Constraints in the HR Master Data

4.2.3 Data Maintenance in Infotypes

HR data is maintained completely by using infotypes. This section describes the work with personnel administration infotypes and in particular the "most popular" stumbling blocks. In doing so, we will limit ourselves first of all to maintaining individual infotypes, as this is the best way of clearly showing the underlying concept.

Specific interfaces sometimes combine several infotypes or segments from several infotypes to a screen. This is a trend that in the course of further development of mySAP HR will definitely be promoted in order to offer users tailored interfaces for specific situations (especially when Adobe forms will be used as user interface technology as it is planned for the future). Although this undoubtedly means an improvement for the end users, it makes customizing and programming more difficult. When working in the system configuration, it is often important to know the individual infotypes and their numbering.

Master-data maintenance—Initial Screen

Maintaining HR master data is carried out through the menu path **Human Resources · Personnel management · Administration · HR master data**

- **Maintain**. The basic screen for master-data maintenance (see Figure 4.9) is divided into the object manager (left) and the actual maintenance screen (right).

Figure 4.9 Master-data Maintenance—Initial Screen

Because this screen represents a large part of the daily work of an administrator, like the maintenance screens for frequently used infotypes, much emphasis must be placed on optimal system configuration and user training. In comparison to payroll or time management, master-data maintenance can at first seem to be relatively simple. It is exactly this misperception that leads to frequent failures.

It is indeed quite possible to implement a functioning master-data maintenance with very little difficulty—and it can be used without much training—but in most cases neglecting this area leads to inefficiency and poor data quality. The current release of mySAP HR now provides options to increase efficiency and the quality of the processes in this seemingly simple component. These are discussed as the chapter progresses, since their thorough use is recommended. Master-data maintenance is sometimes perfectly suitable for system and process optimization six months after the start of production. Then, the first experiences of the users can be integrated in the optimization process. Due to the absence of deadline pressure and the knowledge that already had been gathered internally, optimization can be implemented with very little external support.

Using the basic screen for infotype maintenance is intuitive. Basically, you must fill out the selection fields for personnel numbers, information types and subtype ("type"), as well as for the period. Then you can use the menu or the pushbutton bar to select the required action.

Selecting the Infotype

There are several ways to select the required infotype:

▶ You can enter the infotype number

▶ You can enter the infotype name

▶ You can select the infotype field via the input help (F4 help)

▶ You can select a tab

The tab selection is particularly user-friendly and can be used to structure a task-specific interface (see Section "The Infotype Menu"). pg 66

Selecting the Personnel Number

The selection of the personnel number is supported in various ways. The users should also be aware of this support, as otherwise much time can be lost. When calling the input help, several search helps are provided by matchcodes and through free search (see Figure 4.10).

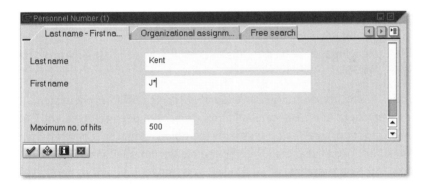

Figure 4.10 Search Help for Personnel Numbers

Most frequently, a name search is carried out here. This can also be used without F4 Help by entering "=n.Surname.Forename" or only the beginning of the name in the personnel number field. In particular for large organizations, searching through organizational assignment is very helpful. For example, this allows you to combine the search for surnames and personnel sub-areas. The free search provides even more options, but a free search is more laborious due to the numerous possible search criteria. Search criteria grouped according to infotypes and freely selectable are used in the same way as they are in the ad-hoc query (see Chapter 11, *Personnel Controlling*).

"Other search help" Users who are provided with free search as a first input help are often confused and cannot find their way back to the desired search help. In this case, you can use the **Other search help** button displayed in Figure 4.11.

Figure 4.11 Changing the Search Help

The search helps are generally usable in all screens that permit the entry of personnel numbers, and also in the selection screens for reports. Customer-specific search helps can be set up via the IMG (**Personnel management · Personnel administration · Basic settings · Maintain search helps**).

The Object Manager

The object manager permits the users to select personnel numbers and to maintain them in a personal to-do list. Selection is done through the matchcode options already referred to (here under "collective search help") as well as the free search and through the search term. An infotype can be maintained for the personnel numbers selected in the to-do list without having to return each time to the initial screen of the master-data maintenance.

The to-do list remains available even after logging off from the system. If it is very large (for instance, if all employees have been selected without any restrictions), calling screens with the object manager can take a long time. The to-do list should then be reduced or emptied via a new selection. If the object manager is not used or is impeded due to its configuration (screen size, PC capacity), it can be switched off at any time using the path **Settings · Hide object manager**.

Customer-specific adjustments to the object manager are possible in the IMG. If necessary, use the path **Personnel management · Global settings in Personnel management · Settings for Object manager**. The settings to be implemented there are not limited to the object manager in the HR master-data maintenance. Further variants are also used in other HR transactions.

Basic Functions for Working with Infotypes

The actual work with infotypes involves the following activities:

▶ **Creation**
Creating a new record with beginning and end date. Other records are deleted or limited according to the time constraint. Examples:

  ▶ The birth of a child necessitates the creation of a corresponding record of Infotype 0021.

  ▶ After relocation, a new record is created in Infotype 0006 from 03/04/2002. In addition, the old address is limited with the end date of 03/03/2002.

▶ **Change**
An existing record of an infotype is changed for its entire period of validity. An example of this would be error corrections (e.g., an incorrectly written family name).

▶ **Copying**
Similar to creation, with the difference that an old record is used as a template. Example: Changing the family name as of 03/10/2002 because of marriage. Note: Changing instead of copying frequently causes errors and destroys the history!

▶ **Delimiting**
Upon entering a delimitation date, all records valid for this date are provided. After selecting the required records and clicking the **Delimit** button, the respective selected end date is set to the day before the delimitation date. Delimiting as such is only permitted for infotypes with time constraints 2 and 3. For infotypes with time constraints 1 and 2, creating and copying records can possibly automatically trigger delimitation, as no parallel records are permitted. The system notifies you about this by issuing a warning.

▶ **Displaying**
In the display mode the user can see data but cannot change them. In many cases displaying something is the only function a user is authorized to use. But even if you have change authorization you should always use the display mode if you do not intend to maintain data. This protects against accidental changes and, in addition, other users cannot process HR master data as long as you are in the maintenance mode for this HR master data (locking mechanism).

► **List entry**

List entry is only permitted for certain infotypes: those for which an entry in a row is possible. These are, notably, the infotypes for time management.

► **Locking/unlocking**

Locked records of an infotype are overlooked in further processing, in particular for payroll. Thus, this functionality is helpful if you are not sure of a specific data entry and there is still need for clarification, or if the effect of a deletion should be tested up front. In particular the locked data entry and subsequent unlocking by another user is done in order to implement the dual-control principle. This is also supported by the authorization concept of R/3.

► **Deletion**

Infotypes with time constraint 1 must be continuously available. Thus it is not possible to delete all data records of such an infotype. When deleting a data record, the system extends the predecessor to such an extent that in turn there are no gaps. This is signaled by a warning message.

► **Overview**

An overview shows all entries of an infotype in the selection period in form of a list. Some of the functions for individual records described here can be executed directly from the list (see Figure 4.12).

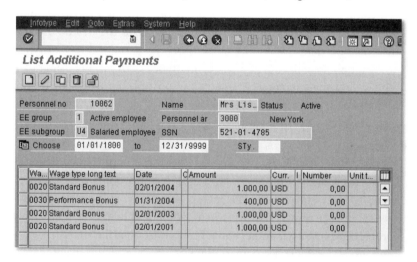

Figure 4.12 Overview of the Records of an Infotype

General Information on Maintenance in the Infotype Screens

Maintenance of the data fields in the screens occurs individually per info-type. This is described for selected infotypes in the following sections. Let's first make some general remarks concerning the maintenance of infotypes.

Fixed entry options exist for many data fields. These options are generally controlled by Customizing tables through which the selection then can be defined according to the specific company. However, you should be aware that some of these tables are not or are only partially supposed to be changed via Customizing. This is described in further detail in the IMG documentation and is signaled by a warning when an entry is changed that should only be changed by SAP itself. You can also change those tables. An upgrade to a new release, however, might set back the changes. In addition, you must check whether legal requirements pro-hibit the change.

To improve user-friendliness, the interfaces in HR are becoming more and more "key-free": The user works solely with the "complete texts" (e.g., "Angola") instead of the system-internal key (e.g., "AO"). For the system configuration or evaluation, it is still often helpful to know the system-internal key or to know how to reach the Customizing table that deter-mines the selection.

By using the **Customizing of Local Layout** button or pressing **Alt + F12** and then choosing **Options**, you can reach the options menu of the SAP GUI.

In the **Expert** tab you can tick the **Show keys in all dropdown lists** option to see the keys in the respective fields. Figure 4.13 shows the **Language** and **Nationality** keys in Infotype 0002 without keys and with keys.

Figure 4.13 Input Help Without and With Key

If key-free help is always to be deactivated, you can adjust this via the GUI settings according to the respective PC installations (see Figure 4.14).

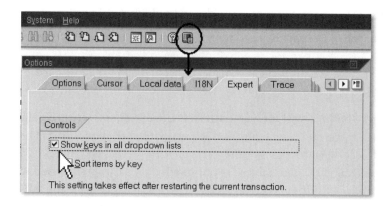

Figure 4.14 Deactivating Key-Free Input Helps

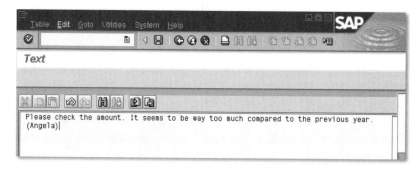

Figure 4.15 Maintaining an Additional Text for the Infotype

Background text For many infotypes, it is possible to enter additional texts. Additional text generally does not appear directly on the screen of the infotype but rather in a background editor, which you can reach through the menu path **Edit · Maintain text** (see Figure 4.15).

It is a useful convention to always maintain such texts when an infotype record is locked due to an existing clarification requirement.

You can recognize the existing background text and the lock identifier in the screen by the two symbols displayed in Figure 4.16.

Be aware that the background texts are difficult to evaluate. Even SAP Query doesn't provide these texts for evaluation, as they are not stored in transparent database tables. Therefore, a somewhat more complex additional programming is necessary for evaluation purposes. In general, data that is required in evaluations should not be entered in this way. Even entering data in the wrong row can lead to incorrect lists, even in the case of self-programmed evaluations. Instead, the infotype should be enhanced with customer-specific fields. These fields can then be evaluated via SAP Query and can be very easily implemented (see Section "Enhancing Infotypes").

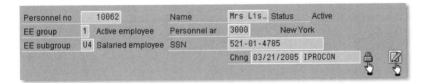

Personnel no	10062		Name		Mrs Lis…	Status	Active
EE group	1	Active employee	Personnel ar		3000	New York	
EE subgroup	U4	Salaried employee	SSN		521-01-4785		
					Chng	03/21/2005 IPROCON	

Figure 4.16 Symbols for Locks and Background Text

Some infotypes show a part of the background text in the basic screen. However, the same limitations also exist there with regard to their scope for evaluation. Figure 4.17 illustrates this in the example of Infotype 0030 ("Powers of Attorney"). The comments field in this infotype is an extract of the background text and is thus hardly suitable for evaluations.

Other special functions which you can access through the menu for all or some infotypes include the following:

▶ Assigning and displaying documents of an optical archive via menu path **Extras · Display all facsimiles**

▶ Navigation to the overview of all records of the infotype

▶ Display and maintenance of data for costs assignments via menu path **Edit · Maintain cost assignment** …

Another essential piece of information is the display of the date and the user name for the last change of the entry. You can find this information in the bottom line of the header data (see Figure 4.38 for an example). However, it is not logged here when the change to the validity ending occurs, because of a delimitation that was initiated by creation of a new record. This situation can sometimes lead to confusion. Clearly, deletions aren't entered either, because the modified record then wouldn't exist. In order to get a complete change history for reasons of revision or to understand errors, you should log the infotype changes using the standard tool provided for this.

Logging infotype changes can be implemented via the following IMG path: **Personnel management · Personnel administration · Tools · Revision · Set up change document**. There you can define which changes are to be logged on both the infotype and field levels.

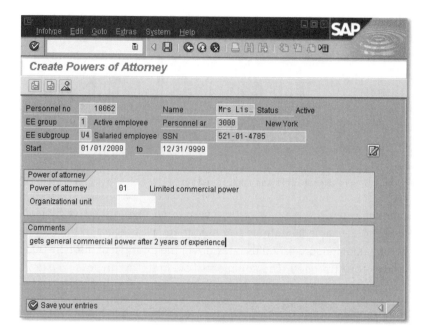

Figure 4.17 Background Text Partially Displayed

Within the application, the evaluation of the change documents occurs via menu path **Human Resources · Personnel management · Administration · Info system · Documents · Infotype change**.

4.2.4 System Adjustments in Master-Data Maintenance

The Infotype Menu

You can enter the master-data maintenance by selecting different tabs. The structure of the individual tabs as well as the selection of available tabs can be defined as user-dependent via Customizing.

The settings can be done via IMG path **Personnel management · Personnel administration · Customizing Procedures · Infotype menus**. The connection between the individual IMG activities is described here in more detail for three reasons:

▶ The documentation is quite unclear and old fashioned at this point. The user parameter PMN, which is referred to in the documentation, is no longer supported.

▶ In addition to the HR master-data maintenance, other menus are also controlled at this point. Furthermore, very similar user group-dependent customizing once again takes place regarding personnel actions (see Section 4.4.1).

▶ This is the first extensive Customizing activity to be described in this book.

SAP uses the Infotype menu concept here for an individual tab, while the concept Infotype menu selection is used for the summary of the described tabs.

Customizing is carried out in five steps:

Customizing

1. In order to be able to control user-dependent customizing—which is desirable in the context of the role-based application—the user parameter UGR (user group) must be maintained in all user master records. User parameters are maintained in the user administration or—provided they have the necessary authorization—by the user themselves via menu path **System · User profiles · Own data ·** tab **Parameters** (see Figure 4.18).

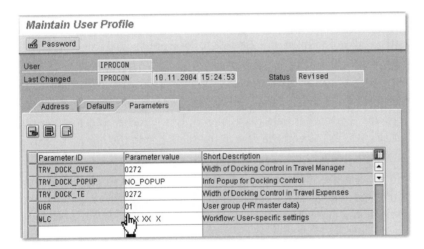

Figure 4.18 Maintaining the User Parameter UGR

2. First the individual tabs are defined in the IMG activity **Infotype menu · User group dependency on menus and info groups** (see Figure 4.19). This step can be left out if infotypes are only to be inserted or deleted in an existing tab. In this Customizing view, you can define whether the display is to be user-dependent, which default value (reference user group) should be set for the parameter UGR, or whether a warning or an error is to be raised if the parameter UGR is not maintained.

The mySAP HR Concept **67**

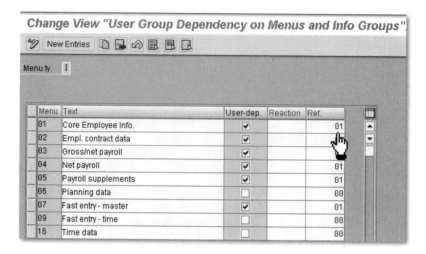

Figure 4.19 Defining an Infotype Menu with Reference User Group

3. Finally, the IMG activity **Infotype menu · Infotype menu** defines the infotypes that appear on the tab, depending on the Parameter UGR (see Figure 4.20). If a reference user group was entered in the previous step, this group must at least exist for one entry.

4. After the individual tabs (infotype menus) have been defined, you must define the infotype menu selection via IMG activity **Determine choice of infotype menus · User group dependency on menus and info groups**. For master-data maintenance, this is carried out through the Menu 01 key. As was the case in the second step the question of user group dependency is also handled here (see Figure 4.21).

5. In the last step (IMG activity **Determine choice of infotype menus · infotype menus**), you define which tabs are displayed. In the pre-selection you must again select Menu 01. Then you define which tabs are displayed in connection with the individual user groups (i.e., the characteristics of the parameter UGR, see Figure 4.22). As the structure of the tabs has already been set in steps 2 and 3, the appearance of the master-data maintenance screen has now been completely defined.

Note   In contrast to what is specified in the documentation, you can only integrate ten tabs into a menu. You should keep this in mind from the very beginning of your concept!

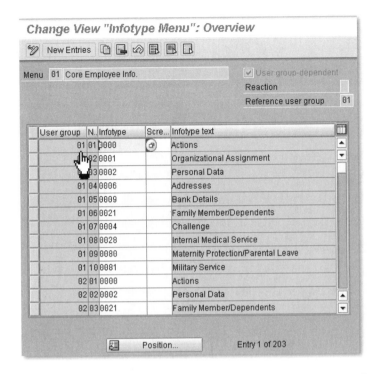

Figure 4.20 Assigning Infotypes to an Infotype Menu (User Group-Dependent)

Change View "User Group Dependency on Menus and Info Groups"

New Entries 📇 🔒 🖉 📑 🖩 📑

Menu ty.   S

Menu	Text	User-dep.	Reaction	Ref.	
01	HR master data	☑		01	
32	Payroll Information	☑			
BP	Benefits profile	☑			
EP	Employee profile	☑		94	
HP	HR manager profile	☑		95	
LP	Line manager profile	☑		96	
PP	Payroll profile	☑		91	
SP	Security profile	☑		92	
TC	Trainer profile	☑		90	
TP	Travel planning	☐		00	
TD	Travel expenses	☐		00	

Figure 4.21 Maintaining the Menu Selection with Reference User Group

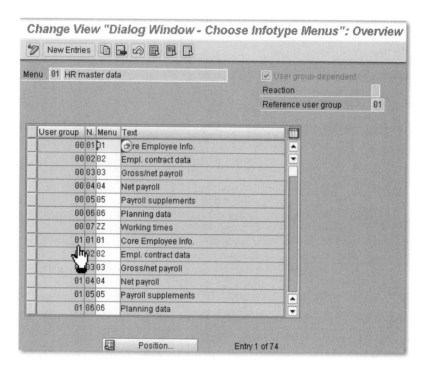

Figure 4.22 Defining the Infotype Menu to be Displayed (User Group-Dependent)

Excessive detailing of the user-dependent setting of this and other interfaces frequently leads to increased maintenance work. In this case, even slight task shifts or the substitution of an employee can then require a modification of the Customizing settings.

Adjusting Infotypes

For many infotypes, there are individual options to customize screens, default values, input helps, and plausibility checks. These options are distributed in several subgroups in IMG path **Personnel management · Personnel administration** (see Figure 4.23) and some of them are dealt with in connection with the respective infotypes in the following sections of this chapter. First, we will describe the adjustment options generally provided for all infotypes.

The adjustment options essentially amount to three processes whose IMG paths are as follows:

▶ Screen control: **Personnel management · Personnel administration · Customizing User Interfaces · Change Screen Modifications**

▶ General infotype properties: **Personnel management** · **Personnel administration** · **Customizing Procedures** · **Infotypes** · **Defining fields relevant for retroactive accounting**

▶ Dynpro header: **Personnel management** · **Personnel administration** · **Customizing User Interfaces** · **Change Screen header**

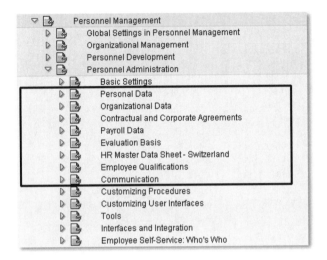

Figure 4.23 Infotype-Specific Settings in Personnel Administration

Screen control permits you to hide individual fields of an infotype, or to declare them as output-only or as a mandatory field.

Screen control

In order to use the table in the IMG, you must first know exactly which dynpro (screen) you actually want to adjust. To do so you must call the system status from the entry screen of the infotype (menu path **System · Status**). The two fields, **Program (screen)** and **Screen number** (see Figure 4.24) indicate the entry to be processed for adjustment (see Figure 4.25).

In general, the name of the module pool is MP<infotype number>00, while 2000 is the dynpro number for the full screen. For country-dependent screens, the dynpro number for the U.S. is generally 2010. For other countries other dynpro numbers are relevant, the last two digits of which generally correspond to the country grouping.[1] However, there are exceptions to this: for Canada, for example, the number 2010 is often used instead of 2007.

---

1 Selected country groupings are: 07: Canada; 08: UK; 10: USA; 11: Ireland; 13: Australia; 16: South Africa; 40: India; 43: New Zealand

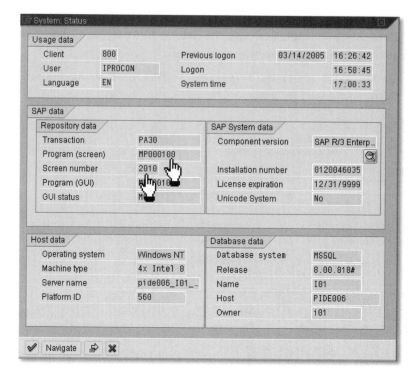

Figure 4.24 Determining the Current Dynpro from the System Status

Mod. pool	Screen	Feature	Variable key	Alt. screen
MP000100	2000	P0001		2000
MP000100	2000		10	2010

Figure 4.25 Screen control: Basic Entry and Entry for U.S. Dynpro

As the maintenance interfaces must differ according to various criteria, there are usually a few additional entries for each basic entry. For this reason, there is a so called feature stored with the basic entry, which supplies a variable key as a result. The maintenance of features is described in Appendix C. Criteria considered by each of the features are in general organizational attributes but also can be infotype-specific attributes such as the subtype. Very often, the variable key provided by the feature depends on the respective country.

The actual relevant entry is identified depending on the value in the screen controls table. Thus, for example, the standard setting for Infotype 0001 for Sweden goes to a separate row with variable Key 23, and from there calls Dynpro 2023 instead of Dynpro 2000. Even though for Japan variable Key 22 calls Dynpro number 2000, the individual entry enables you to show additional fields or to declare them as mandatory fields. As the infotypes for recruitment are also controlled by this table, a differentiation by transaction classes is predominantly carried out (A = Administration, B = Recruitment). In the example of Infotype 0001, variable key B leads to Dynpro 2100 for recruitment.

Further details are sufficiently explained in the documentation. It is worthwhile to comprehend the example of Infotype 0001 with the feature P0001 in order to understand the concept.

A few important tips on this subject:

Tips

▶ Converting mandatory fields to optional fields should be performed with caution. In general, the fields keyed as mandatory by default are actually required for a clean processing.

▶ You can also control custom dynpros using this table (good knowledge of dynpro programming is a prerequisite). For full screens, it is important that you use the area between 2000 and 2999, whereas for list screens you should use the area between 3000 and 3999. As this is not a customer namespace, it technically represents a modification. If possible you should therefore not work with custom dynpros but rather with enhanced standard dynpros.

▶ You should refer to the documentation for the **Subsequent dynpro** field if this field is not set to zero.

▶ Some fields can only be shown or hidden together as a group. This is because they have a joint grouping (see Figure 4.26). Developers who enhance infotypes or who define their own infotypes should be aware that this grouping is the third grouping in the attributes of the dynpro field. If there is no grouping entered there, the field cannot be controlled by the screen control.

Screen Control									
Grp	Field Name	Field text	Std	RF	Opt.	Outp	Hide	Init	
001	P0001-BUKRS	Company Code	◉	○	○	○	○	○	
	P0001-WERKS	Personnel Area	◉	○	○	○	○	○	
	P0001-KOSTL	Cost Center	○	○	◉	○	○	○	
004	P0001-PERSG	Employee Group	◉	○	○	○	○	○	

Figure 4.26 Grouping in the Screen Control

It can also be very helpful to adjust the general infotype properties. The individual settings are sufficiently documented, so we only want to describe the most essential options of these customizing activities here:

▶ Defining whether the subtype must be entered before calling the infotype (this should be the case if dynpro modifications or different checks and default values are controlled with regard to the subtype.)

▶ Choosing whether to enter the assignments to objects of cost accounting and logistics (e.g., non-recurring payments)

▶ Behavior of the infotype in connection with the reference personnel numbers

▶ Choosing whether to maintain a background text

▶ Taking action for entering employees who have left

▶ Time dependency of authorization checks

▶ Interpreting beginning and end dates when making selections through master-data maintenance

▶ Taking action regarding retroactive calculations in time management and payroll (This is one of the most important properties and will be dealt with especially in the respective chapters.)

▶ Dynpro numbers (before any modifications are carried out via screen control)

▶ The number of the dynpro-header

▶ The text of the infotype

▶ Possible reasons for changes (The reasons specified here can be entered for information purposes when changing an infotype. For some infotypes the field must first be shown by using the screen control. For other infotypes it is not available at all.)

The last general customization option refers to the dynpro-header. The header contains certain pieces of information on an employee which should always be displayed when working with master data (e.g., name and cost center). The data displayed in each case can be defined according to the specific infotype here. The settings are country-dependent.

We will now describe the individual steps to be performed (see Figure 4.27): Via the infotype properties, each infotype is assigned a dynpro header number. Each dynpro header number, in turn, is then assigned a header modification in the form of a two-digit key. In the next step, all fields that are to be displayed in the header are assigned to the dynpro modification. The most important action is to carry out a generation afterwards using the button beneath the control table. If necessary, this generation must also be performed after a completely new installation of a standard system. As the field names automatically taken from the data dictionary can sometimes be confusing, you can replace them with your own texts. It is also possible to display a photo. To do this, however, the photos must first be stored in the system.

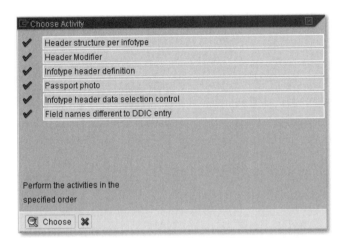

Figure 4.27 Steps for Customizing the Infotype-Header

Discussions often arise concerning the displayed data, as each user assumes a different key date. As a rule, you can display the data as valid on the current date or the start date of the current infotype. Either method can be useful. The most important thing is that the users are aware of this.

Enhancing Infotypes

Enhancing infotypes is actually a part of user interface programming and we will therefore only deal with it in brief. It is important to know that enhancement of an infotype by additional fields is rather simple and can be done without any modifications. If no special processing or check logic is required for the new fields, then enhancement can essentially be done without programming knowledge. However, a basic understanding of the data dictionary and the table structure in the system is required.

The enhancement is carried out via Transaction PM01 using the **Enhance Infotype** and **Enhance List Screen** tabs. The online documentation describes the process very well and in detail. We recommend you use the

Create All button, which should guide you through the entire process. There is, however, one restriction: The additional fields appear at the bottom edge of the screen.

> **Tip** Programmers who want to deal with the subject in more detail should know that if additional fields are to be displayed in the dynpro without additional fields being required in the database, automatic generation does not function at first. You need to make an entry in the customer include of the database structure. However, in order to still be able to work with the enhancement that is convenient and does not require modification, it is advisable to integrate a dummy field in the customer include of the structure, which is then removed again from the user interface. If the customer include of the dynpro is then available after the automatic generation, existing fields or fields to be calculated then can be integrated there. A frequently used example is the display of additional communication numbers that are known from the U.S. version of Infotype 0006 and also on the dynpros of other countries. Infotype 0006 provides these fields for phone, fax, pagers, mobile phones, etc. In some country-specific versions such as the German one, these fields are not available in the dynpro and also cannot be displayed via screen control. As the use of the dynpro for another country would turn off the specific entry checks, it is a good idea to enhance the specified country dynpro.

Creating New Infotypes

Basically, the creation of new infotypes is as simple as enhancing the existing ones. You are also supported by Transaction PM01 whose online documentation is very helpful.

You can implement infotypes with simple interfaces very easily without calculations and checks. Typical applications are infotypes that are only used to store historical data from legacy systems and will no longer require maintenance in the future. You can, however, implement much more complex applications that result in a correspondingly high level of effort in programming.

In general, you should store in new infotypes all personnel data for which there are no entry options in the standard version. This enables you to make complete use of cross-infotype standard processing. Custom infotypes are completely integrated in normal master-data maintenance, cross-infotype customizing and the evaluation via queries.

tomer namespace between 9000 and 9999. In addition, you must be able
to manage the data dictionary and the table structure and have basic
knowledge of the screen painter.

Plausibility Checks and Default Values

For each infotype, you can store default values or plausibility checks that
go beyond the customizing options. You can do this through programming in two function exits in SAP enhancement PBAS0001:

▶ EXIT_SAPFP50M_001 is called when an infotype is created or copied.
Here you can program suggested values in particular.

▶ EXIT_SAPFP50M_002 is called after each data release (**Enter** or **Save**).
You can store entry checks here and also change field content depending on entries made.

To do this, you need to have programming knowledge and project-management knowledge concerning SAP enhancements. As the documentation contains examples in the system, implementation is then quite simple. The function exits do not represent a modification.

For the project manager or key user, it is of prime importance just to
know that this option exists. The actual implementation is then easy for a
programmer if he or she knows the data structures of HR and observes
the documentation of the function exits.

From Release 4.6C on, there is an even more powerful option available in
order to access the infotype processing, for instance through additional
checks or suggested values. BADI (Business Add-In) HRPAD00INFTY
enables you to store customer-specific programming codes in three different places (processing times):

▶ PBO (Process Before Output)
Here you can interfere immediately before the data is output on the
screen.

▶ PAI (Process After Input)
This point in time is particularly suitable for entry checks.

▶ IN_UPDATE
At this point you can call processing at the time of saving.

A prerequisite for using this method is also the knowledge of HR data
structures and the technical infotype concept. In addition, the programmer must be familiar with ABAP Objects and BADI technology.

4.2.5 Structures in Personnel Administration

As described in Section 4.1.1, clearly defined structures are an essential factor in structuring a DP-supported personnel administration system. We will now present the different views of the structure in HR. We will specifically explore the controlling effect of the individual structuring attributes and the evaluation aspect. Both aspects are crucial for defining the structure at the beginning of a project. Even if these definitions are changed as the project progresses, a precise description is necessary at the beginning as Customizing also relies on these results to a large extent.

The Enterprise Structure

The structural outline in HR is primarily carried out through the concepts of the personnel area and the personnel sub-area. They represent the "company" and "location" views but can be resettled for evaluation and tax reasons on a lower level of the hierarchy.

The two concepts are integrated in the accounting structures. Here you must ensure that a company code (independent accounting unit) is on a higher (or equal) hierarchy level than the personnel area. Hence, a personnel area is assigned to exactly one company code. The cost center and the business area can also divide the head count as further structural elements of accounting. They are not integrated into the hierarchy of the personnel area and the sub-area; that is, employees of different personnel areas can theoretically be assigned to the same cost center. The meaning of this and other structural concepts will be more closely considered in the context of Infotype 0001 ("Organizational assignment") in Section 4.3.2.

As a result, the integration concept looks like the one illustrated in the simplified graphic in Figure 4.28. There, abstractions are made from special cases and the connections between the HR enterprise structure, HR organizational management, and accounting are illustrated. Organizational management is described in further detail in Chapter 5, *Organizational Management in mySAP HR*.

The client is the major organization criterion above all other components in the system. It represents a self-enclosed world of its own, (we will ignore at this point the coupling of different systems via ALE as a special case which creates an artificially enlarged client).

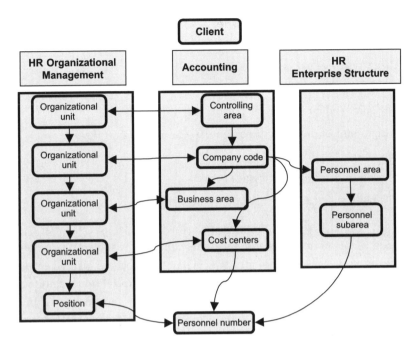

Figure 4.28 Integration Context of the HR Structures

The essential decision criteria for forming personnel areas are:

▶ Company code
▶ Country version for payroll

For the personnel sub-area, the main criteria are:

▶ Location
▶ Public holiday calendar

The personnel area/sub-area combination mainly controls the following functionalities:

▶ Public holiday calendar
▶ Bonus calculation
▶ Eligibility of wage types
▶ Eligibility and quota deduction of leave types
▶ Eligibility and quota deduction of time quotas
▶ Eligibility and design of work schedules
▶ Eligibility, counting, and validation of absence and attendance types

- ▶ Time evaluation and error messages in time evaluation
- ▶ Wage-type generation
- ▶ Wage-type evaluation
- ▶ Plausibility checks in infotypes
- ▶ Eligibility and evaluation of substitutes
- ▶ Assignment of pay-scale type and pay-scale area
- ▶ Assignment to a legal entity
- ▶ Exception handling in statistics
- ▶ Eligibility check and calculation in travel expenses

This list, which is still incomplete, makes it immediately clear that the division of personnel areas and personnel sub-areas is subject to numerous external factors. In addition, two hierarchy levels are insufficient in order to structure a medium-sized or larger organization. Additional structuring through company code and cost center can be helpful but also are subject to constraints on the accounting side that may counteract the requirements of personnel management. The additional structuring options for Infotype 0001, organizational unit, and organizational key do not permit any sufficient and manageable hierarchy. Therefore we recommend that you implement organizational management to map the organizational structure (see Chapter 5, Organizational Management in mySAP HR) and to regard the enterprise structure described here as a control element for the administrative processes.

Copy function You can maintain personnel areas and sub-areas via the following IMG path: **Enterprise structure · Definition · Human Resources Management**. We strongly recommend here that you create new elements by using the copy function only. When copying from the personnel sub-areas, you will have to get used to the copy tool asking from which area you want to copy a specific sub-area. But if you always stick closely to the documentation and user guide, you won't get confused. As a matter of fact, the copy function works quite well! The assignment of personnel areas to company codes and of personnel sub-areas to personnel areas is done via the path **Enterprise structure · Assignment · Human Resources Management**.

The Employee Structure

Irrespective of their organizational assignment, employees can be divided into employee groups and subgroups. The employee group is the more general criterion (e.g., active, pensioner, external). The employee subgroup, on the other hand, is the more precise criterion (e.g., hourly paid workers, salaried staff, senior staff, and temporary staff) and is subordinate to the group. An employee subgroup can be permissible in all groups or can be limited to just one group. In addition, a specific employee structure can be defined for each country.

The employee structure controls the following aspects:

▶ Pay scale structure

▶ Eligibility of wage types

▶ Processing in payroll

▶ Processing in time management

▶ Default values and plausibility checks in the infotype maintenance

▶ Eligibility and removal of time quotas

▶ Eligibility and evaluation of time models

▶ Eligibility of incentive wages

▶ Treatment in internal and external statistics

Like the enterprise structure, the employee structure is also responsible for numerous control tasks. For personnel planning and development and for HR controlling you generally require a different grouping which is less geared towards formal criteria (such as salaried or industrial workers), but more towards content criteria (engineer or loan officer). For this purpose the position concept is available in organizational management (see Chapter 5, *Organizational Management in mySAP HR*).

The Payroll Structure

The payroll structure is based on the payroll area. It contains a lot less control functions than the two other structures which have been described up to now. The employees are merely summarized from the perspective of the payroll organization. All employees which are to be accounted for on the same day in the same payroll run are assigned to the same payroll area.

In addition to the payroll date this assignment also controls the following aspects:

▶ The broadest possible retro active calculation (which however can be further limited on the levels of individual employees)

▶ The release of payroll-relevant data for maintenance

Assignment to a payroll area is done via a field in Infotype 0001. Default values can be generated for this through various indicators, such as employee subunit, personnel area, etc., so that basically, when you hire a new employee the payroll area doesn't need to be entered manually.

As the payroll area exclusively controls the payroll organization it will be described in more detail in Chapter 9, *Payroll*.

Further Structures

You can also structure the staff according to many different points of view and, as a matter of fact, you should do so. Most of these structuring options only affect individual aspects (e.g., an individual infotype and some evaluations).

Examples of additional structures (with the relevant infotype indicated):

▶ Pay scale structure (Infotype 0008)

▶ Assignment to administrator (Infotype 0001)

▶ Assignment to a supervisor (Infotype 0001)

▶ Nationalities structure (Infotype 0002)

▶ Gender structure (Infotype 0002)

▶ Temporary/permanent (Infotype 0016)

▶ Assignment to travel cost regulations (Infotype 0017)

▶ Education structure (Infotype 0022)

Like the main structures described above, the structures in this list also always have two functions:

▶ Control of the system behavior, although most of the times in narrowly defined areas

▶ Selection within evaluations

The latter is to some degree severely limited in the standard evaluations, as not all of the criteria referred to here can be used for selection. For this, however, the system provides a solution through an enhanced selection as well as a selection via ad hoc queries (see Chapter 11, *Personnel Controlling*).

Many of these structures can be derived from the main structures. For instance, the travel-cost regulation for the employee subgroup "sales representative" regarding the use of private cars may be different from the regulation that is valid for the rest of the staff. Therefore, by default, the main structures can be combined under different viewpoints to "new" structures.

Combining Structural Elements

In HR, deriving a new structure from existing main structures and further criteria is generally referred to as *grouping*. The term *modifier*, which comes from the days of Release 2.2, is also still used. Suitable definition of the basic structures and subsequent grouping is the most important customizing activity in the area of personnel administration. This should be carried out in collaboration with an experienced consultant, but should not be put completely in the hands of people outside the enterprise, because an understanding of the structures created is a prerequisite for subsequent maintenance of the system.

A simple example involves the grouping of employee groups and subgroups from the point of view of eligibility of primary wage types (wage types entered in infotypes). This enables in-depth control of eligibility and, consequently, of plausibility checks in data entry, without having to enter the wage types that are eligible for each individual employee subgroup.

In Customizing, grouping is basically performed in three ways:

Customizing grouping

1. Maintenance views for customizing tables map the given structure in a specified manner to the structure to be defined (e.g., the assignment of a public holiday calendar to a personnel sub-area). In the IMG, these groupings are generally assigned to the relevant aspects at a suitable point. You can access the example of the public holiday calendar via IMG path **Time Management · Work Schedules · Work Schedule Rules and Work Schedules · Define Groupings for the Public Holiday Calendar**, and this is illustrated in Figure 4.29. For the most important groupings, maintenance views V_001P_ALL ("Personnel areas and subareas") and V_503_ALL ("Employee groups and subgroups")—which you can reach via Transaction SM31—provide a very good overview. This type of combination is very easy to maintain, but is not all that flexible. Copying personnel areas, personnel sub-areas, employee groups and subgroups using the IMG copy tool also copies these groupings.

Personnel area	Personnel Area Text	Personnel subar...	Pers. subarea text	Holi...
300	Corporate - United States	0001	Philadelphia	US
300	Corporate - United States	0002	Chesterbrook	US
300	Corporate - United States	0003	Los Angeles	US
3000	New York	0001	Manhattan	US
3100	Chicago	0001	Chicago	US
3100	Chicago	0002	St. Louis	US
3100	Chicago	0003	Ohio district	US
3100	Chicago	0004	Minneapolis	US
3200	Atlanta	0001	Atlanta	US
3300	Los Angeles	0001	Foster City	US
3400	Boston	0001	Boston	US
3500	Philadelphia	0001	Philadelphia	US
3600	Corporate - SAPCOE II	0001	Corporate	US
3600	Corporate - SAPCOE II	0002	Electric	US
3600	Corporate - SAPCOE II	0003	Gas	US
S300	Atlanta (Services USA)	0001	Atlanta	US

Figure 4.29 Grouping for the Public Holiday Calendar

2. Features integrate an employee through a decision tree into the new structure. The maintenance of features is described in further detail in Appendix A, *Cross-Prozess Customizing Tools*. For example, let's take a look at feature CONTR, which sets default valus for some fields of Infotype 0016 and thus performs a structuring with regard to the form of contracts (duration of sick pay, probationary period, notice period). Figure 4.30 shows a simple form of the CONTR feature. Here all contract elements are set for Australia, Italy, Portugal, and Norway. For Hong Kong and Argentina, only some fields are set. Figure 4.31, for example shows how a certain employee (employee of a German personnel area) is assigned to a group of contract elements. As in this example, the return values of a feature often only provide default values for specific infotype fields.

	Variable key	F	C	Operations
000010			D	TCLAS
000020	A		D	MOLGA
000030	A 13		D	PERSG " AUSTRALIA
000040	A 13 *		D	PERSK " AUSTRALIA
000050	A 13 * **			&CONTR=42/010-6/012-3/012-04-04-01, " AUSTRALIA
000060	A 15			&CONTR=03/010-1/012-3/012-13-13-01, " ITALY
000070	A 19			&CONTR=3/010-0/012-6/012-04-04-01, " PORTUGAL
000080	A 20		D	PERSG " NORWAY
000090	A 20 *		D	PERSK " NORWAY
000100	A 20 * **			&CONTR=16/010-12/012-6/012-13-13-01, " NORWAY
000110	A 27			&CONTR= / - / -3/012- -10-01, " HONG KONG
000120	A 29		D	PERSG " ARGENTINA
000130	A 29 *		D	PERSK " ARGENTINA
000140	A 29 * **			&CONTR= / -/ -3/012-04-04-21, " ARGENTINA

Status   X

Figure 4.30 Example of the CONTR Feature

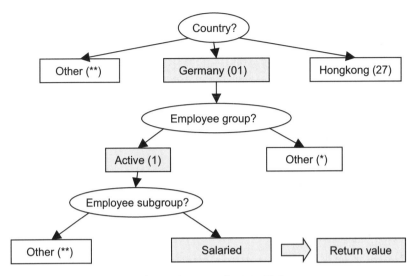

Figure 4.31 Grouping a Specific Employee via the CONTR Feature

3. The detail flow of payroll and time evaluation is controlled by calculation rules (see Chapter 8, *Time Management*, and Chapter 9, *Payroll*). These rules contain similar decision trees in the same way features do, and they can control processing in particular through the main structures.

When copying structural elements, the features and calculation rules are not automatically supplemented. Although the copy tool does provide a list of all potentially affected features, this list contains many standard examples provided by SAP that are not relevant for your specific installation. We therefore recommend that you document in a simple form the use of personnel areas, personnel sub-areas, employee groups, and subgroups in calculation rules and features. By doing so, you can establish quickly which additions are necessary when creating new structural elements.

In order to simplify the maintenance of calculation rules in the case of structural changes, it is advisable to use the "Employee subgroup grouping for personnel calculation rule" (see view V_503_ALL). In addition, the decisions derived from the structures should as much as possible be based with the initializing calculation rules MODT and TMOD (and their customer-specific copies).

4.2.6 Organizational Management

Organizational management is the most varied and flexible option to structure the enterprise from an HR perspective. This is described in more detail in Chapter 5, *Organizational Management in mySAP HR*.

4.3 Selected Infotypes for Personnel Administration

4.3.1 Actions (0000)

The action concept is described in further detail in Section 4.4.1.

4.3.2 Organizational Assignment (0001)

The Infotype "Organizational assignment" is one of the most important infotypes and must exist for each employee from the time he or she is first entered in the system. It is retained even after the employee has left. Most other infotypes can only be entered in the validity period of the Infotype 0001. Only infotypes that solely contain personal information and bear no relation to the relationship between the person and the company can start before the beginning of the first organizational assignment. Examples for this are the Infotypes "Personal Data" (0002) and "Education" (0022).

Customizing of the Infotype 0001 can be reached via IMG path **Personnel management · Personnel administration · Organizational data · Organizational assignment**.

Infotype 0001 basically fulfills four functions:

▶ Classification of the employee in the enterprise structure
▶ Classification of the employee in the personnel structure
▶ Classification of the employee in the organizational structure
▶ Assignment of the employee to support the process structure

Classification in the enterprise structure

First of all in Infotype 0001, assignment of an employee to a *personnel area* and a *personnel sub-area* is entered. As designated through assignment to a legal entity and a company code (and indirectly a controlling area) is derived as per Customizing. The cost center is also maintained here for the most part. However, if the integration into the organizational management is active, the cost center is derived from this and is no longer changeable in Infotype 0001. This situation is also illustrated in Figure 4.32.

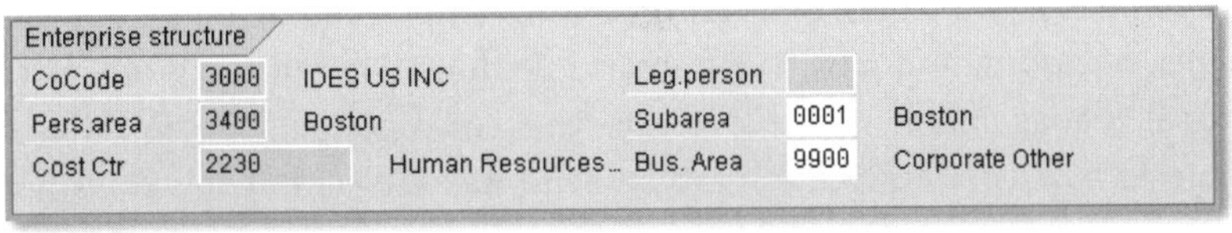

Figure 4.32 Enterprise Structure in Infotype 0001

Also, the personnel area cannot be changed through simple maintenance in the infotype. To make this change, you must carry out an action (e.g., "organizational change"), which enables you to change the personnel area (see Section 4.4.1). The reason for this is the importance of control within the personnel area. Making a change without an action and without including other data (e.g., the basic amounts to change the pay scale area) can lead to data inconsistencies. As this danger also exists for other data of Infotype 0001, the company-specific conditions should be checked. From this check, conventions can be derived for which an action is needed via Infotypes 0000/0302 for organizational changes, for reasons of data quality or evaluation.

The business area is freely maintained. Its use must comply with accounting, as it will also be transferred into accounting through the posting interface of the payroll.

With regard to direct maintenance for employee group and subgroup, the same applies as for the personnel area. The payroll area can basically be freely accessed. In general, though, it is derived from other fields of the Infotype 0001. Therefore, you can use the feature ABKRS to implement the suggestion of a default value, e.g., depending on the employee group. In the example in Figure 4.33 the payroll area U.S. is suggested based on the employee subgroup.

Classification in the personnel structure

In this case, the work contract is only maintained in exceptional circumstances. It is used in Germany for different statistics based on legal limits and can normally be derived through the employee subgroup. For other countries, this field should be used for individual analyses, if necessary. You can store the possible adjustments in Customizing for the Infotype 0001.

Figure 4.33 Personnel Structure in Infotype 0001

Infotype 0001 enables the assignment of employees to organizational units, positions, and jobs. This can also be done without using organizational management. You can create the corresponding organizational objects by customizing the infotype in simple tables, but this does not allow you to map any real structure. For this reason, and because of the additional functionalities, the use of organizational management is strongly advisable for enterprises of 1,000 employees and more. This is also often useful for smaller companies. You should, however, ensure that the maintenance is not an end in itself but is rather carried out based on simple, pragmatic principles.

Integration of organizational management is effected in two steps:

1. In IMG path **Personnel management · Organizational management · Integration · Integration with personnel administration · Set up integration with personnel administration** the entry PLOGI-ORGA in the Basic settings must be set to "X" (see Figure 4.34). There are more control options in the same table, and these are well-documented. You cannot access the documentation intuitively: Rather, position the cursor on the entry in the column **sm. Code** (semantic code)—and click on the **Documentation** button (see Figure 4.34). Do not become confused by the seemingly technical appearance of the table. It is only a collection of individual control indicators that are each individually documented. It appears very frequently in a similar form in customizing the personnel planning and development.

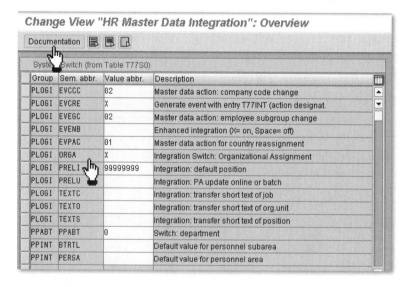

Figure 4.34 Control Options for the Integration into Organizational Management

2. Now that the integration is basically activated, you must establish in the second step which employees participate in the integration. In some companies these are all employees; in others pensioners or part-time employees are excluded. This control can be carried out through the feature PLOGI, which you can reach through the same IMG path. In the simple example in Figure 4.35 the integration is activated for all employees.

For active integration you only have to maintain the position in Infotype 0001. Job and organizational unit (and cost center) are then automatically derived from this. The organization of this structure is described in more detail in Chapter 5, *Organizational Management in mySAP HR*.

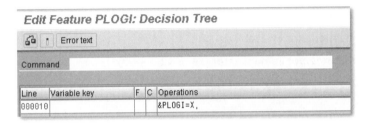

Figure 4.35 Integration Through the Feature PLOGI is Generally Active

The organizational key is in many cases a very helpful field. It can be populated manually or according to fixed rules from further fields of Infotype 0001 (also through non-displayed fields such as the employee name). It is also possible to provide a table with permitted entry values. In the example in Figure 4.36, the organizational key includes the personnel area and cost center (with leading zeros). How it is composed and whether the value determined can be manually overwritten are defined by Customizing for Infotype 0001 ("Set up organizational key").

The organizational key is not only available as a selection criterion for most of the reports but is also available in the authorization check. Thus, you can use it to carry out an authorization check indirectly through cost centers (which is not possible directly) or through combining the personnel area and beginning letters of the surnames (if your processing is organized in this manner).

The following information is important for programming and also for creating queries: The data derived from the organizational management (cost center, organizational unit, and job) and the company code derived from customizing are redundantly saved in the database in the relevant infotype record. They are not dynamically derived when the infotype is called. This simplifies programming.

Assigning an employee to Administrators as the last function of the Infotype 0001 (see Figure 4.37) can be regarded as an aspect of organizational structure. However, this assignment mainly serves to control the process structure within the personnel department. In the system, the assignment particularly affects:

▶ Dynamically generated e-mails that are directed to the responsible administrator (see, e.g., Section 4.4.2)

▶ Authorization for the HR master record maintenance

▶ Employee information regarding his responsible administrator (e.g., on the remuneration statement)

▶ Selection criteria for evaluations

▶ Task monitoring per administrator (see Section 4.3.6)

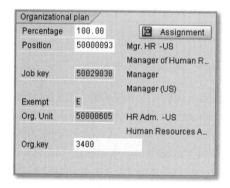

Figure 4.36 Organizational Structure in Infotype 0001

mySAP HR provides three administrator fields. The supervisor field can be used as a further assignment, though that does not deliver the same functionality.

Figure 4.37 Infotype 0001 Also Supports the Process Structure

Employees are assigned three different administrators in Infotype 0001 (see Figure 4.37, left). In most country versions (although not for the U.S. and Canada) these can then be subdivided in administrator groups (see Figure 4.37, right).

The administrators must be defined in the Customizing for Infotype 0001. During this process, they are divided by administrator group but not by "administrator type," i.e., all transactional users can be assigned to the relevant group respectively as time, payroll, or HR administrators. In order to structure this cleanly, it is advisable that you create number conventions. Names, phone numbers, and in particular SAP user names are maintained per administrator. The user names are particularly required in order to guarantee the functionality of dynamic e-mail.

Assigning an employee to the administrator group is done through the feature PINCH (similarly in Customizing for Infotype 0001).

4.3.3 Personal Data (0002)

Infotype 0002 is as important as Infotype 0001 because it defines the existence of the employee as a person by storing the name and date of birth (see Figure 4.38). Other infotypes generally cannot exist before the beginning date of Infotype 0002.

Change Personal Data

Personnel no	10062		Name	Mrs Lis… Status	Active
EE group	1	Active employee	Personnel ar	3000	New York
EE subgroup	U4	Salaried employee	SSN	521-01-4785	
Start	05/15/1960	To	12/31/9999	Chng 10/19/2000 BONIN	

Name

Form of addr	Mrs	Name format	
Last name	Johnson	Birth name	
First name	Lisa	Second name	
Mid. name		Initials	
Designation		Known as	
Suffix			
Name	Mrs Lisa Johnson		

HR data

SSN	521-01-4785	Gender	
Birth date	05/15/1960	● Female ○ Male ○ TBD	
Comm.lang.	English		
Nationality	American		
Mar.status			

Figure 4.38 Infotype 0002 — Personal Data

The data to be saved in Infotype 0002 is also strongly dependent on the country. In the U.S., for example, a Social Security number is saved. In other countries, there are frequently other fields and plausibility checks, and the selection option **TBD** (to be declared) is missing for the **Gender** field.

Insofar as other countries are not supported by the system as delivered, an enhancement of the infotype is required. This is not critical, however.

One of the most important fields is **Comm.lang.** (Communication Language). This does not only serve as additional information but is also used at certain points of the system if documents or e-mails are output for the employee.

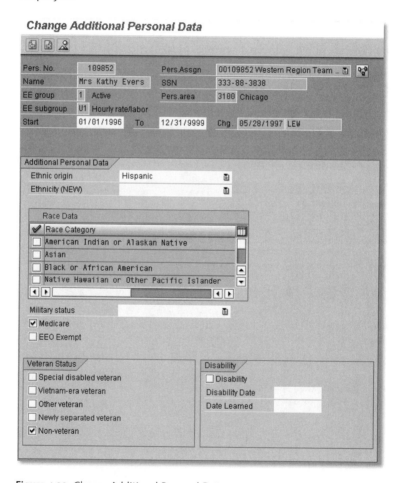

Figure 4.39 Change Additional Personal Data

For instance, when outputting the time statement you can determine that it is to be created in the employee language. In this case, the language of communication of Infotype 0002 is relevant. Therefore, if you create the documents for the employees in a selection of languages (e.g., English, German, Spanish, and French), but not necessarily in the mother tongue of the employee (e.g., Croatian), this field should be populated with the chosen language of communication. The mother tongue can then be maintained for information purposes in another place (e.g., in a customer-specific field).

Customizing for Infotype 0002 can be found via IMG path **Personnel management · Personnel administration · Personal data · Personal data**.

For the U.S., there is also the Infotype "Additional personal data" (0077), in which data on military status, veteran status, and disability are maintained (see Figure 4.39).

4.3.4 Address (0006)

Addresses are probably the most country-specific information besides the data on net payroll (tax, social insurance, etc.). One of the most obvious reasons is the difference in postal code formats. Figure 4.40 shows the standard delivery screen for the U.S.

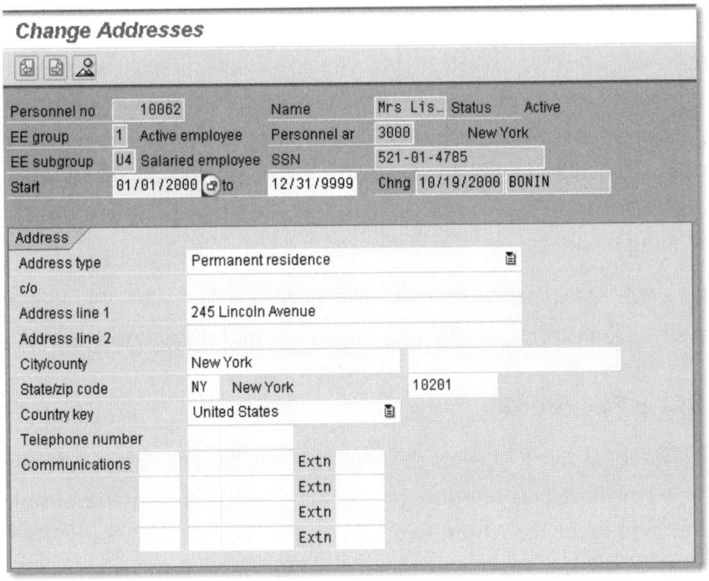

Figure 4.40 U.S. Address Data

Beside the address format, there can also be further specifications for other countries. In the German payroll version, the field **distance in kilometers** (between place of residence and workplace) calculates the imputed income of company cars (together with Infotype 0032).

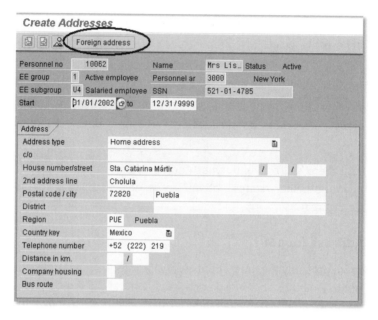

Figure 4.41 Foreign Address Mexico

When creating a new address record you can use the **Foreign address** button to select another country. This allows you to enter an address in Mexican format, for example (see Figure 4.41.) In addition, Infotype 0006 offers several subtypes. Here you can enter temporary residences, for example. The subtype "permanent residence" is generally used when outputting correspondence. In some cases this can be controlled instead by customizing or directly by the application.

Customizing for Infotype 0006 can be found via IMG path **Personnel management · Personnel administration · Personal data · Addresses**.

4.3.5 Basic Pay (0008)

Customizing for Infotype 0008 is the most extensive. This is because the complete pay scale structure is integrated. Figure 4.42 shows an example of a salaried employee for whom two wage types are indirectly evaluated. Indirect evaluation is treated in detail in Chapter 9, *Payroll*. This basically means that the amount of the wage type is not manually but indirectly maintained (e.g., through a pay scale table or derived from other wage types). This is indicated by the "I" next to the currency column. In order to decrease the maintenance effort and to increase the data quality, indirect evaluation should be used as frequently as possible.

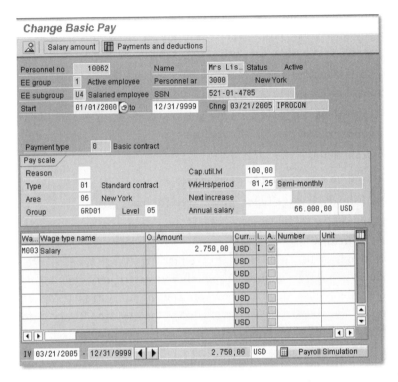

Figure 4.42 Basic Pay with Indirect Evaluation Through Pay Scale

In one record of the Infotype 0008, you can enter 40 wage types (up to Release 4.6C "only" 20). This is usually not required, though, if you really limit yourself to the basic pay and in addition use the Infotypes 0014 ("Recurring payments and deductions") and 0015 ("additional payments and deductions").

Note A frequent application error is that a wage type to be indirectly evaluated is changed manually because, for example, the pay-scale table has not yet been updated. From this time onwards, however, the wage type of this employee is directly evaluated (the "I" is omitted), and the next update of the pay scale table does not have any impact. Where possible, indirectly evaluated wage types should be customized so that the amounts cannot be manually overwritten.

Customizing of the Infotype 0008 can be performed via IMG path **Personnel management · Personnel administration · Payroll data · Basic pay**. There, you must essentially make the following settings that are documented in detail in the IMG:

▶ **Group employee subgroups from the pay scale point of view**
Do not differentiate more than is necessary, as this grouping is the key in very heavy-maintenance customizing tables!

▶ **Pay scale structure**
Combine pay scale areas, if the same rules apply.

▶ **Default values for pay scale type and pay scale area, depending on the company and personnel structure**

▶ **Pay-scale tables**

▶ **Working time according to pay scale**

▶ **Establish which wage types are allowed for basic pay**

▶ **Default values for wage types, depending on personnel and enterprise structure**
This item is particularly helpful. In the first step (**Wage types · Enterprise structure for wage type model**) you determine codes for the wage-type models, depending on your specific structures, via the feature LGMST. These codes are populated in the next step (**Wage types · Revise default wage types**). This eventually determines which wage types are actually suggested and also whether they can be manually changed. The time that you invest here pays off in the form of more efficient processes and a higher accounting quality.

▶ **Display a button through which you can reference the simulation of the employee's payroll**
This functionality is new with Release 4.6c and usually highly appreciated by administrators.

4.3.6 Monitoring of Tasks (0019)

Infotype 0019 enables you to create tracking deadlines for different subjects (date types). These, however, do not trigger pop-ups to appear when you log onto a system, in the way that you know all to well from many e-mail systems. That would also not be appropriate, due to the number of deadlines an HR administrator generally has to observe. For instance, there can be a flood of deadlines at the end of the quarter (end of the probationary period, phasing out of part-time agreements, etc.). In general, it is more useful for the administrator to determine his own work rhythm and check the deadlines at a suitable time, for example when probationary periods are due to expire during the coming four weeks. A convenient evaluation is provided via menu path **Human Resources · Personnel management · Administration · Infosystem · Reports · Employee · Date monitoring**.

You enter the tasks to be monitored in Infotype 0019 (see Figure 4.43). In most cases (e.g., the end of the probationary period, or the end of a temporary work contract etc.) you can create default settings for task monitoring via a dynamic action so the administrator only has to save it. At this point it is worthwhile to exploit the benefits of dynamic processes (see Section 4.4.2). **Dynamic action**

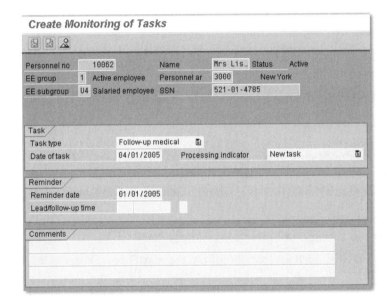

Figure 4.43 Task Monitoring in the "Follow-up Medical" Example

Customizing of task monitoring can be performed through IMG path **Personnel management · Personnel administration · Evaluation basis · monitoring of tasks**. There, you only have to create the different task types and characterize them particularly with regard to the lead time. Please note while doing this that often the administrator who monitors the deadlines, as well as the employees or management to be involved, require some lead time. Always create a task type "other deadlines" which can be further characterized via user-defined text depending on the situation.

4.3.7 Cost Distribution (0027)

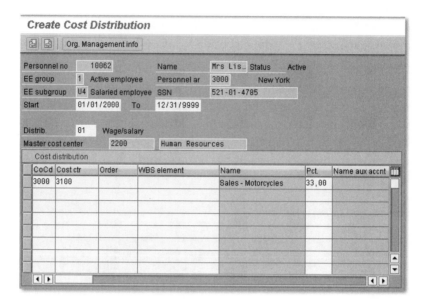

Figure 4.44 Cost Distribution to the Cost Center

In many cases, the employee costs are distributed across several cost centers over longer periods of time This can be very easily done via Infotype 0027 (see Figure 4.44). However, you should note the following:

▶ For evaluations in mySAP HR the employee is always selected under his or her master cost center from Infotype 0001.

▶ Enter only the portions that differ from the master cost center in Infotype 0027; the rest will automatically be posted to the master cost center. If you enter the master cost center redundantly (e.g., with 75%) and the rest at 25% to a different cost center, the new master cost center will be completely ignored in case of an organizational change and the old cost center will still be debited at 75%. In certain circumstances, it is useful to integrate Infotype 0027 in the action "organizational change".

▶ Even if a different company code is entered here—if, for example 25% of the expense is posted through the posting interface on this company code—the company code that makes the payment is always 100% of the master company code from Infotype 0001. The percentage rate apportioned to the different company code accumulates to the document split account and must be balanced via a company code clearing. Alternatively, you can automatically post to company-code-clearing accounts. This must be reconciled with financial accounting.

▶ There are different subtypes for wage/salary and travel expenses. Thus it is possible to indicate that an employee only performs 10% of his working time but 50% of his journeys for a different cost center. Since Release 4.6B, a distribution from the wage/salary subtype is completely ignored by the travel expense module. In previous releases or old patch levels, the distribution of wage/salary is considered for travel expenses as well, if there no travel expenses subtype is maintained.

▶ Besides cost centers, you can distribute the costs to orders or projects (WBS elements). In the public sector there are also funds available.

4.3.8 External Transfers (0011)

The infotype "External transfers" can trigger any number of employee-related transfers to a third party, which are generally retained from the net amount paid to the employee. Examples include are rent payments or loan repayments, which in some countries (e.g., Slovenia) are frequently directly transferred by the employer.

The infotype can also be used to make up for missing country-specific requirements such as garnishments in country versions which do not support specific garnishment processes. In these cases, the specific checks and calculations are not supported but at least the process can be reflected in an integrated manner.

In addition to the transfer to predefined recipients, which are created in Customizing for the Infotype 0011, recipient data can also be entered directly.

Attention The field "First payment period" always leads to confusion and errors (just like in Infotype 0014—recurring payments). Most administrators interpret this as the very first payment in the first year of the validity of the infotype. In fact, this field is reconsidered every year. If "11" is entered as the first payment period, and "1" is selected as the interval, the payment in the first year (provided that there is a monthly payroll) is made in November and December, and then not for the next 10 months (see Figure 4.45). The payment will only resume in November and December of the second year. If there should be a monthly payment in the future from November of the first year, you should leave the field **First payment period** empty. You can guarantee the November start through the begin date of the record that must then be located in November. This example should also provide an incentive to use the **F1** help button as often as possible at the beginning.

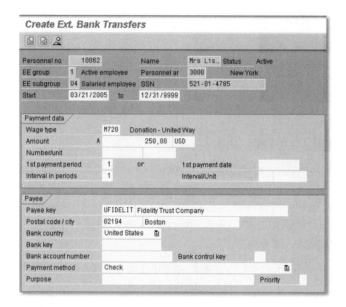

Figure 4.45 Rent Payment Through External Bank Transfers

4.3.9 Education

In Infotype 0022, the education of an employee is documented. This can include school and high school attendance but also individual training courses. The latter can be documented in Infotype 0022 if the training and event management is not implemented. Figure 4.46 shows the documentation of a Ph.D.

For each phase of school and professional training (Elementary School, Junior High School, High School, College, University, ...) an individual record for the infotype is created. The central concept in Infotype 0022 is the educational establishment type (high school, business school, etc.) It defines the following:

▶ Which certificates are available for the entry?

▶ Which branches of study are permissible?

▶ Is it a course? (There are additional fields ready for input for a course, see Figure 4.47).

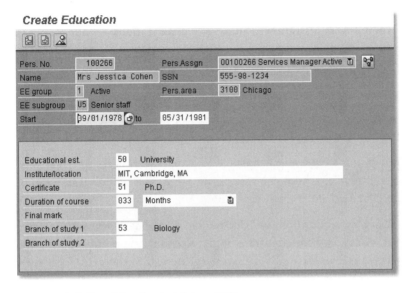

Create Education

Pers. No.	100266	Pers.Assgn	00100266 Services Manager Active
Name	Mrs Jessica Cohen	SSN	555-98-1234
EE group	1 Active	Pers.area	3100 Chicago
EE subgroup	U5 Senior staff		
Start	09/01/1978 to	05/31/1981	

Educational est.	50	University
Institute/location	MIT, Cambridge, MA	
Certificate	51	Ph.D.
Duration of course	033	Months
Final mark		
Branch of study 1	53	Biology
Branch of study 2		

Figure 4.46 College Education in Infotype 0022

Tip If the validity period of such a record corresponds to the validity of the repayment obligation and if the infotype is included in the leaving action, the transactional user will be notified automatically of the due repayment at the time the employee leaves the company.

Personnel no	10062	Name	Mrs Lis... Status Active
EE group	1 Active employee	Personnel ar	3000 New York
EE subgroup	U4 Salaried employee	SSN	521-01-4785
Start	03/21/2005 to	03/22/2005	Chng 03/21/2005 IPROCON

Educational est.	AD	External course/sem.
Institute/location	SAP	
Certificate	A0	No final certificate
Duration of course	002	Days
Final mark		
Branch of study 1	72	Human Resource Management
Branch of study 2		
Course appraisal	Personnel Administration R/3	
Course fees	1.000,00 USD	☑ Repayment obligation

Figure 4.47 Course in Infotype 0022

Customizing is here carried out via IMG path **Personnel management ·** **Personnel administration · Employee qualifications · Education and** **Training**. Here you must carry out the following steps:

▶ Create the permissible school types and flag as "course," if necessary

▶ Create the permissible certificates and branches of study

▶ Assign the certificates and branches of study to the corresponding school types

Through this structure it is possible to assign a certificate or a branch of study to several school types. For example, a high school degree can be earned at a public or a private school.

The field "education/training" (hidden in SAP standard delivery and in figure 4.46) is completely separate from the school type in customizing. This means that every school type can be combined in the entry with every type of education/training. In general, the field is used in order to enter a professional training or a study goal. Permissible educations are similarly defined through the afore-mentioned IMG path and combined into categories (e.g., "degrees in business" or "degrees in language"). The education and training category can then also be used for evaluation purposes.

The education data of employees is indeed frequently required, but in many companies it is not entered in the system. Evaluations are abstained from instead, and in individual cases the personnel file is consulted. This is because the data entry is quite complex. A solution for this problem is to delegate the entry through ESS to the employee himself.

4.3.10 Additional Personal Data (Infotype 0077)

Apart from standard personal data stored in Infotype 0002, other personal data is stored in Infotype 0077. Information in this infotype is used mainly for statistical and reporting purpose.

For some employers in the U.S. Public Sector, it is a legal requirement to submit reports containing the following information periodically:

▶ **Ethnic origin**
This is the only required field for this infotype. The standard values are delivered by SAP. You can define your own values via IMG path **Personnel Administration · Personal Data · Additional Personal Data ·** **Enter Ethnic Origin**.

▶ **Race Data**
Check the race applicable to the employee.

- ▶ **Military status**

  Stores the military information of the employee. The possible values can be maintained via IMG path **Personnel Administration · Personal Data · Additional Personal Data · Enter Military status**.

- ▶ **Veteran status**

- ▶ **Disability**

  If this infotype is to be used, we recommend that you have this information record included in the New Hire Action. Authorizations to access this infotype should be strictly controlled because it contains confidential personal information.

4.3.11 Residence Status (Infotype 0094)

According to U.S. law *Immigration Reform and Control Act (IRCA)*, the employer must verify whether the employee is legally allowed to work in the U.S. The employee needs to provide proper identification and other legal documents. Infotype 0094 can be used to store residency status and other information collected during the verification process and later used for statistics and reporting. The information is divided into two parts:

Personal identification

- ▶ Residency status indicates the legal status of the employee. Standard settings include:

  - ▶ A   Non-resident alien

  - ▶ C   Citizen

  - ▶ N   Non-Citizen resident

- ▶ ID types, ID number and ID expiration date are used to record the ID used for the employee's identification.

Employment Verification

Work permit type, number, and expiry of work permit are used to store information of work permit issued by authorities. Those fields are only for non-U.S. citizens.

If the **Expiry of Work Perm** field is filled and the residence status is set to A (Non-resident alien) in the Personal Identification section, upon saving, the system will prompt to create an Infotype 0019 Monitoring of Tasks, subtype 71 (work permit expires).

You can change the customizing by IMG path: **Personnel Administration · Personal Data · Residence Status · Residence Status**. By selecting different options in the **Choose Activity** window, you can define residence status, ID types and work permit types.

4.3.12 Infotypes for U.S. Employee Tax Information

There are several infotypes used to store tax information for U.S. payroll. Those infotypes serve the legal requirements and are therefore of great importance. The data accuracy must be ensured.

Infotype Residence Tax Area (0207) is the U.S. specific infotype that stores the residence tax area of the employee. An employee's taxation largely depends on the residence tax area. The net payroll calculation reads this infotype for taxation purpose. The U.S. tax calculation is partly done by a third-party tool, *BSI TaxFactory*, which will be described in Chapter 9, *Payroll*.

Employee's Work Tax Area (0208) is needed when the employee works in more than one locality within one tax year and is required to pay tax to a work location other than the resident tax area. The tax-area information in Infotype 0208 overrides information in Infotype 0207 to a certain percentage. Thus the tax can be distributed to different work areas and residence areas proportionally. The IMG for setting up a tax area under USA would be: **Payroll · Tax · Tax Data Maintenance · Tax areas**.

Infotype Unemployment State (0209) is another infotype related to U.S. tax. It is used to assign an unemployment state for employee's payment of unemployment insurance.

Most of the customizing for those infotypes is delivered by SAP as standard setting for U.S. taxation. Although the user can make changes to the settings in IMG, it is recommended that you update the tax area only through the HR Hot Packages (formerly known as LCP).

4.4 Procedures in Personnel Administration

In order to support procedures in personnel administration, three concepts are available that vary in their implementation with regard to their flexibility and complexity. Figure 4.48 shows a brief overview of the options.

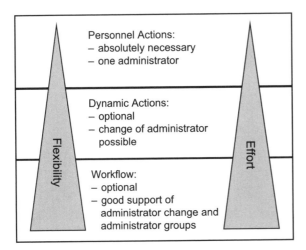

Figure 4.48 Options to Support Workflows

4.4.1 Personnel Actions

An action essentially fulfills two tasks:

Concept of
personnel actions

▶ First, it allows you to maintain a previously defined sequence of info-types, without each infotype having to be called individually. This saves time and also ensures quality as it supports the observance of standard procedure. It represents a sort of "mini-workflow" in which the trans-actional user doesn't change.

▶ Second, it documents essential events in the history of an employee. In particular, the change of different attributes of an employee can only be effected via an action (e.g., employee group and subgroup, person-nel area, and employment status). This further enables quality assur-ance: The attributes referred to have an extensive control function in the master data area. For instance, if the employee subgroup is changed without checking the infotypes controlled by it, there will more than likely be inconsistencies. An example would be changing the employee subgroups to non-pay scale employees while there is still pay scale pay stored in the basic pay infotype. When making a change via an action, all the critical infotypes can be integrated in the process so that no essential adjustment is overlooked.

Examples of personnel actions are:

▶ Hire

▶ Leave

▶ Retirement

▶ Organizational change

▶ Promotion

▶ Increase of basic pay

▶ Beginning of semiretirement

▶ Beginning of a part-time employment during parental leave

Personnel actions are basically saved in Infotype 0000 ("Actions"). The list screen of this infotype gives an overview of the history of the employee (see Figure 4.49).

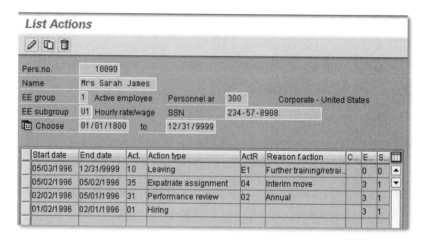

List Actions

Pers.no.	10090						
Name	Mrs Sarah James						
EE group	1 Active employee	Personnel ar	300		Corporate - United States		
EE subgroup	U1 Hourly rate/wage	SSN	234-57-8908				
Choose	01/01/1800 to	12/31/9999					

Start date	End date	Act.	Action type	ActR	Reason f.action	C...	E...	S...
05/03/1996	12/31/9999	10	Leaving	E1	Further training/retrai...	0	0	
05/02/1996	05/02/1996	35	Expatriate assignment	04	Interim move	3	1	
02/02/1996	05/01/1996	31	Performance review	02	Annual	3	1	
01/02/1996	02/01/1996	01	Hiring			3	1	

Figure 4.49 List Screen of the Actions

Infotype 0000 saves the type and reason for the processes, and also the status of the employee regarding employment and special payments, as well as a customer-specific status. In general, every status is available in the evaluations as a selection criterion. The type of action controls the infotype sequence to be maintained, and, like the action reason, also serves information purposes.

In addition, action type and reason have different country- and industry-specific control functionalities, for example:

▶ Germany: Reasons for notification (public social security)

▶ Austria: "Damaging actions/action reasons" to determine tax days

▶ Switzerland: Exceptional actions concerning reduced working hours

▶ Spain: Seniority calculation

The Employment Status

The employment status is quite significant. It determines whether an employee is still active. Non-active HR masters are divided into departed employees, pensioners, or employees with inactive work relationships.

The employment status is considered in evaluations such as payroll, time management, travel management, company pension plans, training and event management, compensation management, and organizational management. After they leave, employees cannot be posted to training sessions and receive no basic pay.

Additional Actions

Infotype 0000 must by its nature have time constraint 1. After all, an employee cannot have two different employment statuses at the same time. This leads to problems if two actions are to be entered on the same day (e.g., organizational change and promotion).

The solution has been provided by Infotype 0302 since Release 4.0 ("Additional actions"). It has time constraint 3 and can basically save all actions.

Determining which actions are to be saved in Infotype 0000—in particular if there are several actions on one day—is accomplished by a prioritization in Customizing. Here, you must ensure that actions that change the status must always save a record in Infotype 0000 and therefore must not conflict with one another.

As Infotype 0000 is generally incomplete due to the actions carried out on the same day, Infotype 0302 should always be evaluated for self-created queries or reports. Customizing should always be controlled so that all processes are stored in IT 0302—even those which are already saved in Infotype 0000. This leads to the following division for evaluations through query and custom developments:

▶ Evaluation via actions and action reasons (related to key dates): Infotype 0302
▶ Evaluations via the status of an employee (related to the period): Infotype 0000

Infotype 0000 is suitable for display in the master data. The additional actions that occur in the period of the record displayed are shown in the display (see Figure 4.50). A direct maintenance or display of Infotype 0302 in the HR master data is not possible.

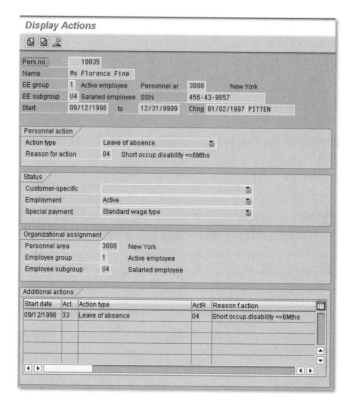

Figure 4.50 Single Screen "Actions" with Integrated View of the Actions to be Added

Data Maintenance in Actions

Actions are called through the action menu via the menu path **Human Resources · Personnel management · Administration · HR master data · Personnel actions**.

After selecting a personnel number, a start date, and the desired action, the action is launched via the **Execute** button. Please note the following special characteristics:

▶ No personnel number is entered for a setting as long as no external personnel number allocation is activated.

▶ When an employee leaves, the start date is entered as the last day that the employee belonged to the company. However, Infotype 0000 is then saved with the start date of the following day. Thus, while the entry corresponds to common language use ("Left on 12/31/2001"), the data is correctly stored for evaluation purposes (the employee still counts as a member of staff on 12/31/2001).

▶ Some actions enable a change to the personnel area, employee group, and subgroup. In such cases, you can and should maintain this data immediately in the action menu (first screen). This ensures that the possible control mechanisms that depend on this data are already correctly supported at the start of the action (e.g., "relevance for the organizational management").

After calling an action, the maintenance screen for Infotype 0000 is displayed. Position, personnel area, employee group, and subgroup are already maintained here (provided the type of action actually permits maintenance), although they actually display the data of Infotype 0000.

At this point you can insert additional infotypes for the action using the **Change info group** function. However, in a later change or display of the action the change to the infogroup is no longer visible, which means this procedure is in general not very advantageous. The concept of the infogroup is explained in more detail in the next section.

Saving the action infotype then triggers additional infotypes of the action. During this process, infotypes for creation, copying, changing, or display can be suggested. The latter is scarcely used but is definitely quite useful if certain subjects are to be checked in connection with an action. For instance in a change of department, displaying the objects on loan can be helpful in order to reclaim an item such as a key.

Subsequent correction of actions is often quite complicated. Through the maintenance of Infotype 0000, all infotypes of the action can be maintained in sequence via the **Execute info group** function. Changing the date is problematic. For this purpose, the date entries of the individual infotypes must be changed and Infotype 0000 must then be deleted and recreated. Only for changing entry and leaving dates is there a special function provided through the menu path **Human Resources · Personnel management · Administration · HR master data · Maintain · Utilities · Change entry/leaving date**. Before you use this, you should refer to the detailed notes in the online documentation.

Changing to a different country presents a unique problem if the country assignment for payroll is changed at the same time. In this case, you must assign a new personnel number, which is supported by the system if the action used is customized correspondingly. This is not necessary if it is a temporary assignment and the employee will continue to be accounted for according to the law of the previous country, or if payroll for this employee is not activated.

Organizational change

The process of organizational change is shown in an example in Figure 4.51 and in Figure 4.52. The infotypes thus included in the actions represent a useful selection but can vary according to enterprise-specific requirements.

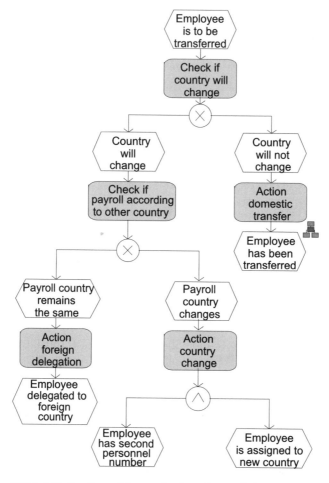

Figure 4.51 The General Process for Organizational Change

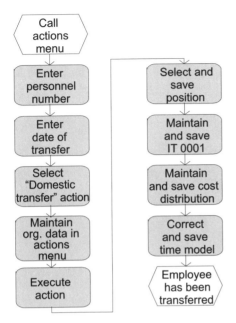

Figure 4.52 "Domestic Transfer" as a Subprocess of the Organizational Change

Fast Entry for Actions

For some actions, maintaining only a few fields in several different info-types is inefficient. It is then clearer and faster to maintain all of these fields on one screen. Fast entry can be used for this, as only selected fields of the infotypes are shown. The organizational change or the mini-master entry of external employees for settlement of travel expenses is often a useful application of this method.

You can reach fast entry via menu path **Human Resources · Personnel management · Administration · HR master data · Fast entry: actions**. Then the previous data of the HR master data will be applied. Figure 4.54 shows an example of this.

If additional fields are also to be maintained for individual infotypes, the fast-entry screen offers the option of selecting these infotypes. Maintenance for these infotypes is then provided once the fast-entry screen is saved. The example in Figure 4.53 shows this selection for Infotype "Basic pay".

Pers.No.	100299
Start	10/02/2005

Org. Assignment

Personnel area	3400	Boston
Personnel subarea	0001	
Employee group	1	
Employee subgroup	U4	

Cost Center		Position	
Organizational unit	0	Job key	0	☐ Org.assignment

Working time

Work schedule rule	☑		☐ Working time

Basic pay

Pay scale type	
Pay Scale Area	
Pay Scale Group	/	☑ Basic pay

Figure 4.53 Fast Entry for the Action "Organizational Change"

The screens for fast entry for actions also can be configured enterprise-specific field by field. IMG path **Personnel management · Personnel administration · Customizing user interfaces · Fast entry for actions** provides the customizing tool for the fast entry for actions (see Figure 4.54).

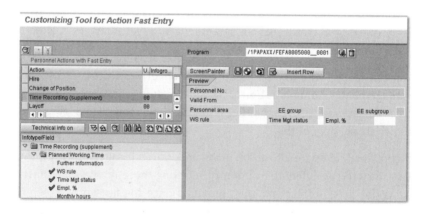

Figure 4.54 Customizing Tool for Action Fast Entry

The following steps are required here in order to define a new user interface for fast entry for actions:

1. Select the action type
2. Select the fields in the field selection (bottom left)
3. Define an infotype basis by selecting the infotype in the field selection
4. Select "Further information" in the field selection, if you want to be able during the action fast entry to call the full screen for the corresponding infotype via a checkbox
5. Call the Screen Painter if the layout of the user interface still has to be designed. (For this you need basic knowledge in the use of the Screen Painter. In-depth knowledge of interface programming is generally not required.)
6. Generate the interface
7. Maintain a short description for the user interface
8. Activate the user interface thus defined so that it is called instead of the standard interface when calling the fast entry

In this process, you must ensure that it is not possible to maintain inconsistent datasets (you must take particular care of mandatory fields). Plausibility checks and default values can be individually programmed through BAdi HR_FAST_ACTION_CHECK.

Customizing Actions

Enterprise-specific adjustments in customizing essentially define:

▶ Available personnel actions in the action menu
▶ Infotypes called in an action (summarized in an infogroup)
▶ Miscellaneous additional properties of the actions themselves

P9-60

Similar to the infotype menus (see Section 4.2.4), the first two items can be controlled, dependent on the user group. Figure 4.55 provides an overview of the context.

Customizing for personnel actions can be found via IMG path **Personnel management · Personnel administration · Customizing procedures · Actions**.

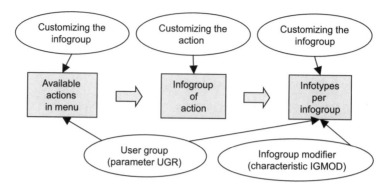

Figure 4.55 Context of the Customizing of Actions

Here, as is so often the case, the IMG items are arranged in the sequence in which they are to be processed (an infogroup must first be created before it can be assigned to the action). To understand the design, however, you must proceed the other way around; that is you first must consider which actions you require before you determine which infotypes have to be assigned to them via infogroups.

Customizing steps   The process consists of the following steps (please refer to the standard documentation):

1. Create the required action types through the item **Set up personnel actions**. If possible, copy these from default templates and do not concern yourself with further properties and priorities in the first step.

2. Define the action menu (depending on the user group).

3. Check which actions should depend on the user group or on organizational attributes of the employees (Example: For employee subgroup "Temporary personnel," Infotype 0022 "Education" should not appear in the hiring action.)

4. For default variants of the respective actions, maintain the infogroups (depending on the user group). Use the standard templates from SAP as examples, in particular with regard to leaving operations. If possible, never use the operation MOD ("Change").

5. In the feature IGMOD (**Define infogroups · Infogroup modifier**), create a decision tree which differentiates employees to be treated differently in actions (e.g., according to country grouping and employee subgroup). The return value of the feature (Infogroup modifier) is then the key in the infogroup definition. Leave the return value empty for the standard variant already created. Here you should not make too detailed a differentiation. It is better to accept an non-required

infotype in an action than to put up with a system which has become unmanageable due to excessive customizing. Note that the number of user groups and infogroup modifiers multiplies if you implement the infogroups in the next step.

6. For each combination of user group and infogroup modifiers, define which infotypes should be contained in the action.

7. Assign the correct infogroups to the actions through **Set up personnel actions · Personnel action types**.

8. Then, define further properties for the actions and, if necessary, the prioritization regarding infotypes 0000 and 0302. In the maintenance view **Set up personnel actions · Personnel action types**, refer to the field help (**F1**) of the respective fields and follow the default examples.

9. For each action type create at least one reason. This can be empty— and indeed should be, if the action concerned has only one reason— in order to reduce maintenance effort. You also can create further reasons for evaluation and information purposes. Depending on the country, certain actions (especially leaving the company) require differentiation according to different reasons (e.g., termination by employee, termination by employer, death).

10. Observe as necessary other country-specific customizing of actions and reasons. Otherwise creating new action reasons or actions can lead to errors in payroll or its post-processing.

After this, you can execute the actions. The infotypes to be maintained and the available actions and reasons are defined.

Item 8 defines the following essential properties of the actions:

▶ Is it an initial hiring or an hiring action through the recruitment module (see Chapter 6, *Recruitment*, and Chapter 7, *E-Recruiting*)?

▶ Which status is set, and how? Note that not all actions can change the status!

▶ Which specific check routines are run for the sequence of actions (e.g., re-entry only after previous leave)? These checks are also based on the employment status.

▶ Which organizational attributes are maintained in the action?

▶ Does the action record start at the action date entered (e.g., entry) or on the following day (e.g., termination)?

▶ Is a record saved in Infotype 0000 and/or in Infotype 0302?

▶ Is it a change of country regarding payroll?

This shows that an action is far more than the progression of certain info-types. Dealing incorrectly with actions or avoiding them through direct maintenance of infotypes usually leads to errors in further processes built on administration.

The special case of country change will not be further discussed. The only important thing to remember here is that using a workflow is necessary for an extensively automated treatment (see Section 4.4.3).

Customer-specific status | Customer-specific status is an important last point. You can use this to obtain additional selection options in evaluations or control options in time management and payroll. You can maintain your own entry options through **Create customer-specific status**. For instance, if you have three fundamentally different business regulations due to mergers or takeovers, but the employees involved are thoroughly mixed at an organizational level, this attribute can be used as a means of differentiation.

4.4.2 Dynamic Actions

The Concept of Dynamic Actions

Dynamic actions can be started automatically from the processing of personnel administration infotypes (including time management) or from applicant data administration. When specific events occur, you can execute pre-defined actions.

You can consider the following triggering events:

▶ Creating an infotype record

▶ Changing an infotype record

▶ Deleting an infotype record

These three events can trigger the following actions:

▶ Checking additional conditions before the actual action is triggered (e.g., checking if the field **Social security number** is maintained). You cannot carry out any plausibility checks on the data maintenance with this action. The check only controls if the actions of the dynamic action defined in the following section are executed.

▶ Calling another infotype and setting specific values (e.g., end of probation period, depending on how the corresponding field is maintained in Infotype 0016).

▶ Sending an e-mail to a defined recipient (or distribution list) or to a transactional user responsible for the employee (according to Infotype

0001, "Organizational assignment"). This makes it possible to integrate other agents or to inform third parties in a workflow. If you completely exploit the options of SAP Office for this (substitution, forwarding, distribution lists), you can often avoid the much more complicated use of SAP Business Workflow.

▶ Calling a custom program routine. This variant provides considerable flexibility. Any form can be called in an ABAP/4 program that is to be named. Restrictions arise only because of the limited option of value transfer between the program that performs the call and the infotype to be called.

The standard release already works in some places with dynamic actions. In personnel administration, these are mostly useful but not always necessary examples. In recruitment the entire process cannot function without the supplied dynamic actions.

Figure 4.56 shows the process of a dynamic action as it is supplied by default: Depending on the time-management status for the employee to be processed, after maintaining Infotype 0007 ("Planned working time") Infotype 0050 ("Time recording information") is called. This happens because maintenance of a time-recording ID is required only in the case of a positive entry for the time-management status.

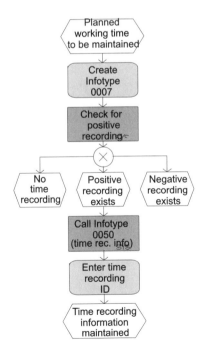

Figure 4.56 Process for a Dynamic Call of Time-Recording Information

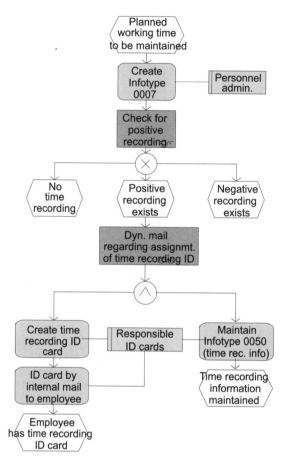

Figure 4.57 Dynamically Calling the Time Recording Information with a Change of the Agent

In Figure 4.57, the same example is slightly modified. Depending on the organization of the work, it can be useful to have the time-recording ID maintained in a different department. In this example, the department responsible for IDs automatically receives information that a new ID is required. In order to avoid further dividing the process, the number of the newly created ID is also entered in the HR master data by this department.

Customizing Dynamic Actions

You can set dynamic actions via IMG path **Personnel management · Personnel administration · Customizing procedures · Dynamic actions**. Dynamic e-mails that represent a special form of dynamic actions are described in a separate section (see the following section).

Dynamic E-mail

Dynamic e-mails are set via IMG path **Personnel management · Personnel administration · Customizing procedures · Setting up mail connection for infotype changes**.

The customizing corresponds to the other dynamic actions and is carried out through the same customizing view. This also means that a dynamic e-mail can be triggered along with other actions and that the same additional checks (action "P") can be integrated up front. Triggering an e-mail is carried out via action "M." In the variable function part, a feature is then addressed which determines the properties of the e-mail.

In the feature, the following settings are done:

▶ Text of the e-mail (Here in particular, variables from the addressed HR master data can be included. If the e-mail is generated because of a change to the infotype record, you must know whether you want to integrate the content with the status before or after the change.)

▶ Recipient

▶ Send attributes (storage in the sent items folder, etc.)

▶ Processing of infotypes from the e-mail (Example: By clicking within the e-mail Infotype 0050 is called to be maintained for the affected employee.)

The feature M0001 delivered in the standard package provides a suitable copy template. Both the documentation of this feature and that available in the IMG provide a very good description of customizing at the details level. Figure 4.58 gives you an overview of the control of dynamic e-mails: The processed infotype, the type of processing and optional additional checks on the content of infotype fields determine whether an e-mail is triggered and which feature is processed. The feature then determines the e-mail more precisely. If the feature determines one or more of the transactional users assigned in Infotype 0001 as a recipient, then this infotype is also essential for sending the e-mail. The title of a standard text determined in the feature must also be filled with content via the standard text maintenance.

If dynamic e-mails are used to a large extent or the decision trees in the feature are deep, it is advisable to distribute the logic across several features. It is, for example, useful to use one feature per infotype. This means you can also avoid the infotype number as a criterion at the root of the feature.

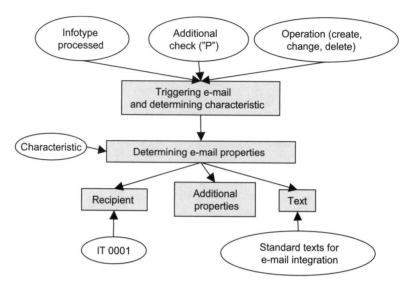

Figure 4.58 Customizing Dynamic E-mails: An Overview

It is also advisable from the beginning to use the transactional class as a decision criterion ("A" for personnel administration and "B" for applicant data), even if the recruitment module is not used at the start. Otherwise there must be a complete revision of the dynamic actions during a later implementation of recruitment as in most cases their behavior should not be the same for applicants and employees.

Dynamic e-mails are extremely suitable for informing different people about new employees, transfers, etc. Their potential is rarely fully utilized. This is often because the use of the concept is limited to e-mails within R/3 (SAP Office). External mail systems such as MS Exchange can generally be integrated with R/3 with little effort. This means that even employees who do not generally work with R/3 (e.g., those responsible for access control or the distribution of mobile phones and laptop computers) can be informed.

If you are building an extensive communication concept on the basis of the dynamic e-mails in HR, two recommendations must definitely be considered:

▶ Always use distribution lists as recipients, and never use individual e-mail addresses. This makes maintenance considerably easier even if the distribution lists sometimes only consist of one address.

▶ Document the different mails clearly in table form according to the triggering events, recipients and texts.

4.4.3 Business Workflow in HR

In contrast to dynamic actions, workflow is still somewhat more complex and therefore provides various possibilities for use. In this section we should only deal in brief with the essential differences between workflow and dynamic actions, as there are entire books available that deal with the subject of workflow[2].

By using Business Workflow, you can map entire business processes in the system and can control their flow. Tasks can be sent, their fulfillment can be monitored, and their transactional users can be prompted to react. Workflow- management systems control processes according to a pre-defined model. The objective of such a system is to provide a comprehensive support of business processes. The area of workflow use is far more extensive than that of the dynamic actions.

Dynamic E-mail vs. Work items

One area in which Workflow is used is the improvement of the information flow. If dynamic e-mails are sent to several responsible agents (distribution lists), for instance due to infotype changes, then there is no guarantee that the tasks are actually completed or that parallel work on the same task is avoided.

In contrast to dynamic actions, Workflow does not send any e-mails but rather work items. These work items can be sent to several transactional users. The vital thing about Workflow is that a work item disappears from the inbox of the other recipients as soon as the transactional user of this work item has accepted it for processing. This ensures that two or more users cannot attempt to process the same case.

By processing the work item, you can make sure that the Workflow can, for instance, send a message to the sender of the work item if the work item was not accepted within a defined period. In addition, dialog work items can be sent which require addressees to make a certain decision and to document this in the dialog with the work item.

Dynamic Actions vs. Controlling Complex Approval Procedures

A workflow system can also be used to control complex processes such as approval procedures. A classic example of this is the leave request, which a transactional user fills out in electronic format by starting a workflow

**Example:
Leave request**

---

2 For example, Rickayzen, Dart, Brennecke, Schneider: *Practical Workflow for SAP*, SAP PRESS 2002

that begins with a form. The user enters the request data into this form. The work item "leave request" is sent to the superior. The superior decides on the fate of this request by clicking the mouse button. If the leave request is not approved in its current form, a workflow system can ensure in contrast to the dynamic actions that the request is returned to the original sender for revision. The process then continues until a final denial or approval of the request is reached. While the work item "leave request" is still in circulation, the workflow system can remind either the transactional user of the work item or the sender of the outstanding processing request at predefined intervals. Figure 4.59 shows a classic leave request workflow.

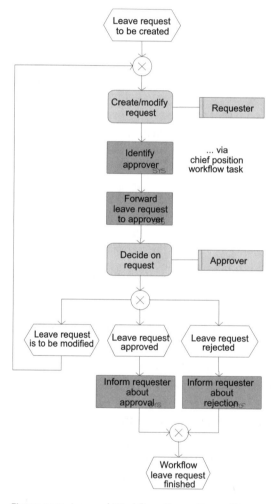

Figure 4.59 Approval Workflow, "Leave Request"

As previously described, addressees of the dynamic e-mails can be the administrators from Infotype 0001, "Organizational assignment," explicitly specified system users, or distribution lists. However, for the example of the leave request this would not be sufficient as in general the superior of an employee must be informed. In this case the workflow system uses the organizational management structure. For example, in order to determine the superior of an employee, workflow can recognize the superior through the assigned organizational unit and identify the director of this or a superior organizational unit (chief position). For a further understanding of how this works, see Chapter 5, *Organizational Management in mySAP HR*, and Figure 4.60. The important lesson is that the workflow system is very flexible; as soon as the manager of a department changes, the new manager automatically receives the leave requests as he then occupies the chief position.

By assigning workflow tasks, the system can be enabled to identify potential recipients for tasks which occur in a system. Workflow tasks are assigned to positions, a fact which ensures that the actual holder of the position is identified as the recipient.

Workflow tasks

Using organizational management for workflow requires at least a basic organizational structure. This structure must contain at least organizational units and positions. You will find more detailed information on the subject of organizational management in Chapter 5, *Organizational Management in mySAP HR*.

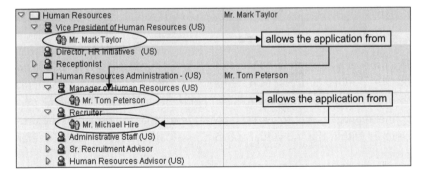

Figure 4.60 Identifying the Superiors (Chief Positions)

Dynamic Actions vs. Controlling Individual Processes

Unlike dynamic actions, a workflow system can control a process if you must react to an error within a process.

Using Workflow Templates

SAP provides more than 100 workflow templates which you should check for usability, and adjust if necessary. For personnel management alone, there now are about 46 template processes. At this point we'd like to refer you to the online documentation (**SAP NetWeaver · SAP Web Application Server · Business Management · SAP Business Workflow · Reference documentation · Workflow Scenarios in the applications · PA Personnel management: Workflow Scenarios**). Before a workflow is implemented in the company, you must document the business processes (actual), analyze and if necessary size them down (planned/SAP planned). Then you should check the workflow templates for their usability.

Workflow Information System

You cannot monitor the runtime of dynamic actions. That's why it is difficult to draw a conclusion as to how the implementation of dynamic actions has actually affected the runtimes of processes. The evaluation options of workflow systems, for instance, can be used to determine the lead times of individual processes.

4.5 Process Examples

The examples partly integrate organizational management, the conception of which in mySAP HR is described in Chapter 5, *Organizational Management in mySAP HR*.

4.5.1 Hiring an Employee

The process is illustrated in Figures 4.61 and 4.62 and shows an overview of the outline process from emergence of workforce requirements through hiring the employee to his or her integration with the overall personnel management processes. It is important that the design of the procedures within the individual sub-processes always supports the overall process.

Figure 4.62 shows the importance of organizational management for the first process steps. Recruitment is based on vacant positions. In order to hire an employee, the position for maintaining the organizational assignment must be known.

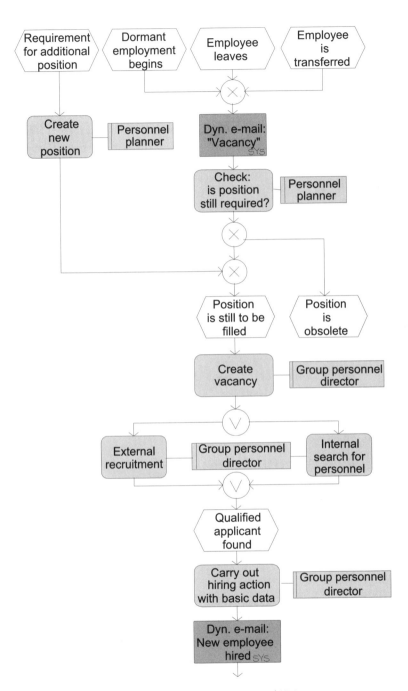

Figure 4.61 Workforce Requirements, Recruitment, and Hiring

In order to be able to include the employee as quickly as possible in personnel administration after a successful search for staff, it is advisable to add the applicant data to the basic data already known. Even if some information is still missing, such as tax data, social insurance number, etc., which are required for payroll, the entry of basic data as early as possible is nevertheless useful. Here is why:

▶ You can use dynamic e-mails to inform other company areas about the new employee so that the numerous processes involved in hiring can be triggered (providing a phone, PC work place, network user, canteen card, etc.).

▶ Statistics for personnel controlling can then take the new employee already into account.

▶ The HR department can immediately book the employee for training in event management systems.

▶ The employee can already participate in ESS on the first workday and if necessary maintain some of his or her own data.

Once the complete documents are available you can enter them using a second action (see Figure 4.62).

For customizing this means that in general when hiring a new employee through the recruitment component three different hiring actions are required:

▶ An action for the ideal case that, in concluding the contract, all the required data exists

▶ An action to enter the essential basic data (Infotypes 0000, 0001, 0002 and, if necessary, further data known from recruitment such as address, bank details, etc.)

▶ An additional action to complement the basic data with data that will be available at a later stage, in particular a great deal of payroll-relevant data

The first two actions are identified as transferring applicant data and are saved in Infotype 0000. The last one is merely an additional action and is therefore only stored in Infotype 0302.

> **Note** Such a process or a similar outline process should be posted prominently in every HR department in order to remind the employees that the quality of the entire process depends on their participation. This is particularly helpful if the team composition is not customer-oriented but function-oriented.

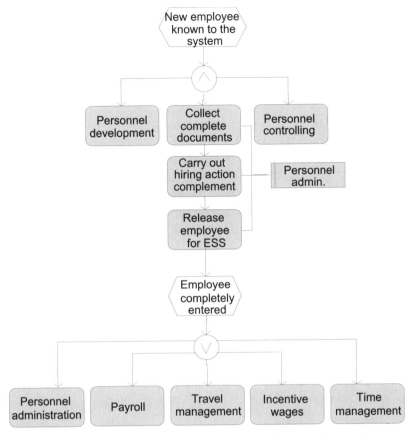

Figure 4.62 Integrating the Newly Hired Employee from the System Perspective

4.5.2 Decentralized Use of Personnel Data

As already described in Section 4.1.5, mySAP HR should not be implemented only for the HR department. Only by expanding implementation beyond HR can you fully use the very high potential of the system. This expansion is often blocked due to fears that data protection could be violated. However, the authorization concept in mySAP HR provides for detailed limitations, and the simple processes described in the following section can be simply and securely implemented with regard to authorizations.

It is often the seemingly "unimportant" infotypes, those not particularly relevant for time management and payroll, that are most useful if they are implemented in a decentralized manner. One common feature in all the following process examples is that integration in the HR master data in mySAP HR reduces the effort involved in entering specialized additional data and improves the evaluation options, in contrast to isolated solutions such as those based on office products. Finally, name and organizational assignment are always maintained, and the entirety of the data generates greatly improved combination options in reporting.

The Loans Department

In many areas of a company, it is necessary to know the power-of-attorney and competencies formally granted to employees. In the loans business of a bank, the loan-allocation competence is an important piece of information. This is usually stored in the user master records of the corresponding IT systems of the loans department. However, a separate summary is often required which is partly supplemented with further personnel data.

Infotype 0030 | Basically Infotype 0030 ("Powers of attorney") is suitable for this. This infotype enables you to enter the following data (see Figure 4.63):

▶ The type of power of attorney (credit allocation competence, general commercial power of attorney, etc.), which represents the subtype of Infotype 0030

▶ The area of validity of the power of attorney in the form of an organizational unit (e.g., "Commercial real estate department")

▶ A free commentary, although this cannot be evaluated easily

As loan-allocation competencies in particular often vary strongly with regard to the amounts that can be allocated, it is not always useful to create an individual subtype for every loan limit that is conceivable. Therefore it is a good idea to enhance the infotype by a customer-specific amount field, and it makes even more sense to supplement it with a currency field.

In addition, the integration into the process of personnel administration must be ensured. In the case of displacement, leaving, or the beginning of dormant employment, the person responsible for the powers of attorney maintenance should preferably be automatically informed. For this reason you should use the concept of dynamic actions (see Section 4.4.2).

Customizing the types of power of attorney is carried out via IMG path **Personnel management · Personnel administration · Contractual and corporate agreements · Powers of attorney.**

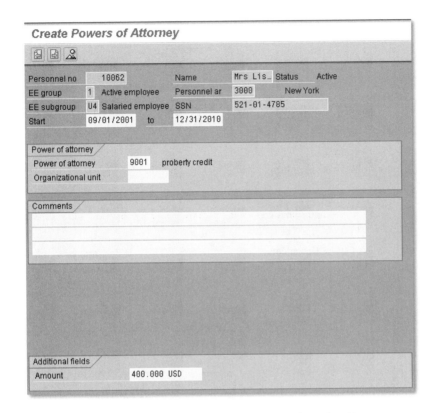

Figure 4.63 Infotype 0030 ("Powers of Attorney") with Additional Field

As access authorization can also be limited on the subtype level, it can be ensured that loan allocation competences, for instance, can be maintained in the loan department, whereas general commercial powers of attorney are maintained in the HR department.

You can ideally round off this process if you connect an optical archive to mySAP HR. It is even possible to assign scanned signatures to Infotype 0030. Figure 4.64 shows an overview of a sample process.

Optical archive

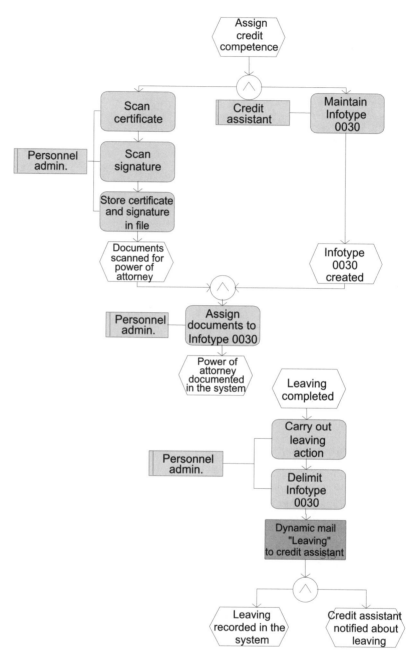

Figure 4.64 Decentralized Use of Infotype 0030 ("Powers of Attorney")

Administering Objects on Loan

Lists are drawn up at many places in an organization in order to establish which employees are provided by the company with which working materials. These range from keys and access cards through books and mobile phones to laptops; often there are many different lists in many different formats at different places. If an employee then leaves the company or is transferred to a different location, it is often uncertain whether the objects on loan are reclaimed. On the other hand, if the items are reclaimed, a process card is then used which the employee must work through step by step on the last day or days of work. The entire process is more reminiscent of retirement day from the army in the 19th Century than representative of management in a modern company.

Infotype 0040 ("Objects on Loan") can be used here. The various types of objects on loan in turn represent the subtypes. In addition, a free text field is available (see Figure 4.65). For actions for organizational change or leaving, the objects on loan can be integrated and messages for the responsible departments can be generated. Decentralized maintenance at various points is once again non-problematic, as access can be limited to the subtype levels by the authorization concept.

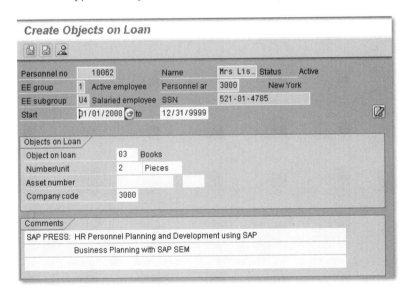

Figure 4.65 Objects on Loan in the Infotype 0040

The **Asset number** field enables integration into asset accounting. This way, you can immediately send a notification message including the asset number to asset accounting in the case of a loss or damage.

Customizing for the objects on loan can be reached via IMG path **Personnel management · Personnel administration · Contractual and corporate agreements · Objects on loan**. There you also can activate the integration into asset accounting in addition to defining the possible subtypes.

Verifying Instructions

It is often necessary to verify and document various different instructions and briefings that must be repeated on a regular basis. For example, the security officer must check regularly if certain employees are regularly instructed in the use of hazardous materials or fire prevention. Banks must provide evidence of compliance instructions for certain groups of employees.

In mySAP HR all this is mapped through Infotype 0035 ("Company Instructions"). For instructions that are periodically repeated it is advisable to set the end of the validity period correspondingly (see Figure 4.66) and also to remind employees of repeat instructions by implementing task monitoring. Task monitoring can be created through a dynamic action when saving Infotype 0035; but it depends on the infotype's subtype.

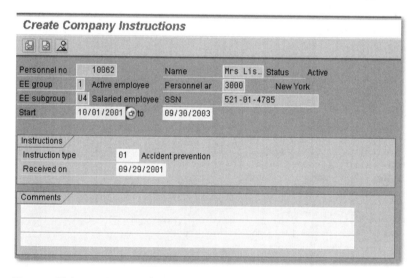

Figure 4.66 Instructions in Infotype 0035

Customizing instructions can be reached via IMG path **Personnel management · Personnel administration · Contractual and corporate agreements · Company instructions**. There you can only define the instruction types.

More than a Phone Directory: Who's Who in ESS

In many companies, a Web-based telephone directory is created with great effort. In most cases there are even several telephone directories that indicate the room, the organizational assignment, and the function of an employee. Some of these directories still contain employees who left the company a long time ago.

But particularly scary is the fact that such a phone directory is the most reliable organizational manual in many companies. The data there is more up-to-date than that contained in each org chart or personnel capacity planning document. The reason for this is clear: The first thing that every employee needs is a telephone. For this reason, the relevant department is best informed about new employees, their phone numbers and work places.

You should make use of this situation and have the corresponding service department directly maintain the phone number in mySAP HR. Depending on the relevant convention, this can be done in Infotypes 0032 ("Internal Data") or 0105 ("Communication").

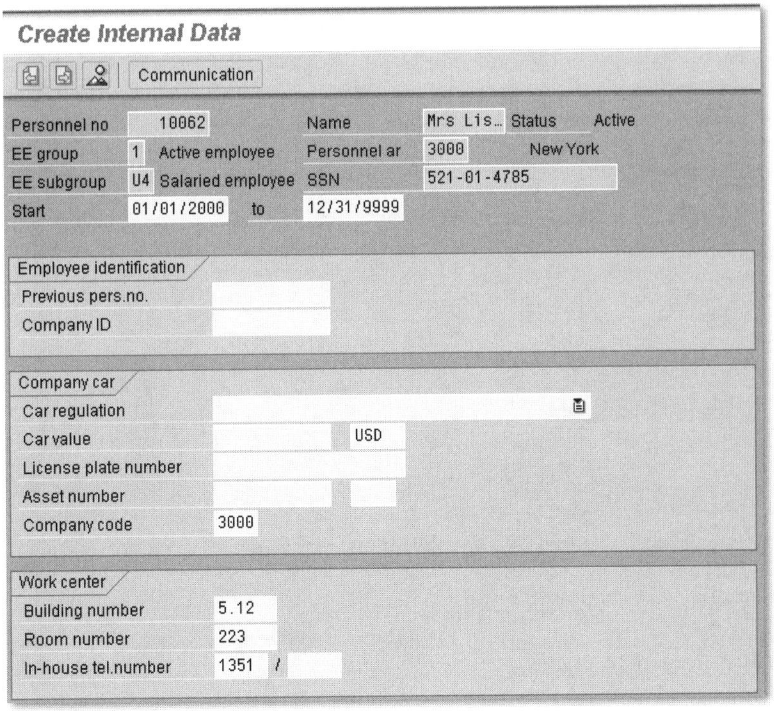

Figure 4.67 In Addition to Phone Numbers Infotype 0032 Contains Other Data.

Infotype 0105 uses an individual subtype for each number (phone, fax, company credit card, SAP user name, etc.). This allows for a fine structuring of the access authorization. Customizing for the different types of communication can be reached via IMG path **Personnel management · Personnel administration · Communication · Create communication types**.

The third variant would be the maintenance of the objects **Work place** or **Position** in organizational management which will not be considered in more detail here.

The "Who's Who" of mySAP HR Employee Self Service is based on information from HR administration and enables each employee to access an employee directory, locating the relevant phone numbers and department names and even photos of the individual employees through their Web browser.

Figure 4.68 Customizing the ESS Employee Directory

Customizing for the Who's Who (previous installation and setting up of ESS is assumed) is done via IMG path **Personnel management · Personnel administration · Employee Self Service · Employee Self Service (ITS-Version) · Office**. There the following items can be defined:

▶ The document type in which the photos of the employees are stored

▶ Limitations of the employees integrated in the directory

▶ Country-specific structure of the employee directory concerning selection fields and the data to be displayed. You can do this similarly to the infoset query (see Figure 4.68). In addition, the settings to be carried out also depend on the selected ESS service for the employee directory.

4.5.3 Managing Expatriates

The "Management of global employees" component with extension 1.10 of R/3 Enterprise represents a comprehensive tool to map international employee assignments. The component is based on the concurrent employment technology (see Section 4.2.1). Here, too, every employee is given a clear personal ID while the "old" personnel numbers identify the individual employment contracts. However, these work relationships must exist in different countries, i.e., they must be assigned to different groupings for wage and salary payroll (MOLGA).

As a component of an extension, this function must also be activated in order for you to use it. The activation must not be undone, as is the case with other components of the extension. At present the "Management of global employees" function is provided for pilot customers only. Therefore, a modification will be necessary if you want to activate the function. You can perform this modification in the CHECK_ RELEASED method of the CL_HRCE_MASTERSWITCHES class. There you must activate the line "ce_is_released = true."; that is, you must remove the asterisk at the beginning of the line. Only after doing this can you maintain the CCURE switch in Table T77S0. Please also refer to the most up-to-date version of OSS Note 540451 for the activation process.

In general, if the component is activated it can be separately controlled for each individual user. The user parameter HR_CCURE_PIDSL with the value "-" is used to hide the personal ID in the master data display and maintenance screens (see Figure 4.69), so that the selection can once again be carried out with the personnel number.

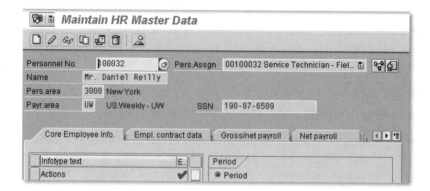

Figure 4.69 Selection with Personnel Number

The entire process from planning via assignment to return (or alternatively to changing to another global assignment) is supported by the system (see Figure 4.70). There are some additional infotypes, actions and Customizing tables involved in this process. We will not go into detail on customizing here, as it is quite extensive and probably only affects a few readers. The important aspect for the majority of users and decision-makers is the basic scope of functionality.

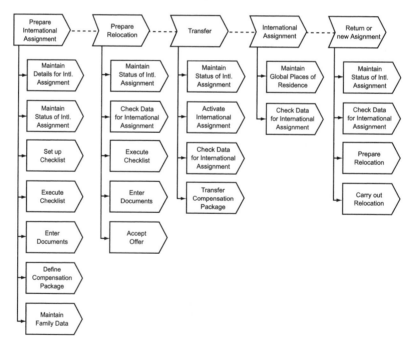

Figure 4.70 The Basic Process to Manage Global Employees

The individual phases (see Figure 4.70) are initiated through actions. In the following sections we will discuss these actions briefly.

The preparation of the international assignment is triggered with the action "Planning Global Assignment." For the time being the employee (along with his or her new contract) has the employment status "left company" in order to indicate that the international assignment is planned. The general conditions for the international assignment are documented in the infotypes described below:

Preparing an international assignment

▶ **Details on global assignment (0710)**

You must first maintain this infotype. It determines the essential attributes of the assignment: The duration and family accompaniment affect the compensation package in Infotype 0706. Furthermore, it is indicated whether the employee will be promoted due to the assignment and who is the responsible manager in the home country. Figure 4.71 provides an overview of the additional information provided by Infotype 0710.

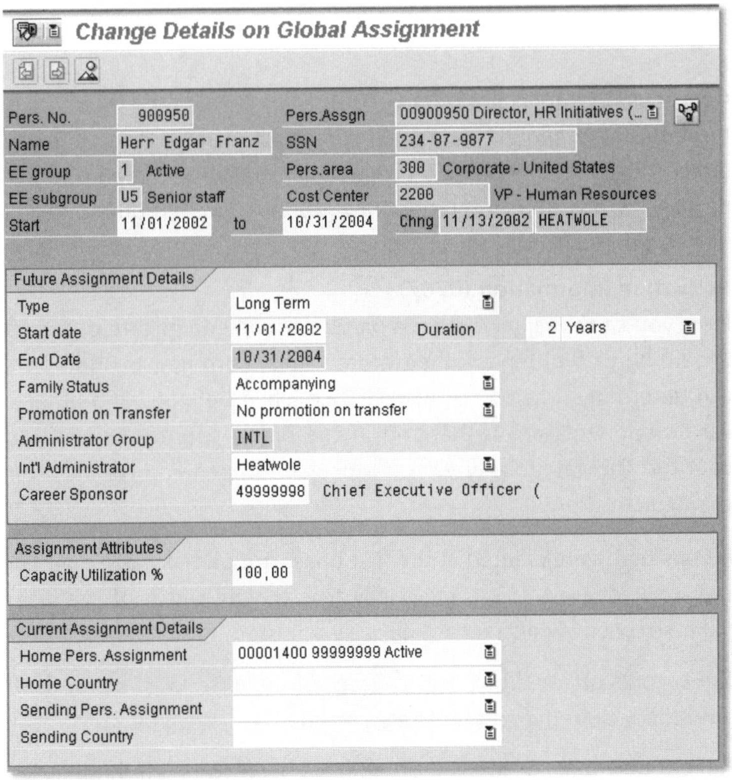

Figure 4.71 Infotype 710 with the Main Characteristics of a Global Assignment

▶ **Status of global assignment (0715)**
This infotype is to be maintained next. This sequence is also defined in the default actions. It documents the status of the assignment from planning to end. The "Refused by management" or "Refused by employee" statuses are both possible here. "In process" means the employee is currently on an international assignment.

▶ **Documents (0702 and 0703)**
The most important information for the necessary documents (passport, visas, etc.) is maintained in Infotype 0702. Infotype 0703 fulfills the same functions for the family members.

▶ **Information on dependants (0704)**
The relevant information for the family members is stored here (Who accompanies the employee? Which schools are required?)

▶ **Information on check list (0705)**
A check list is structured using this infotype. It enables you to control many tasks of the assignment process. There is a responsible person and a status stored for each check list item. In addition, you can define which items must necessarily be completed before a transfer can take place.

▶ **Compensation package offer (0706)**
In addition to general data such as exchange rate and cost-of-living index this infotype contains the different items of the compensation package. A possible integration into payroll and the required flexibility due to the many relevant countries makes customizing very extensive.

▶ **Activation information (0707)**
Here you can specify whether a particular percentage rate of the salary should be paid out in another (more stable) currency. In addition, you can determine if taxes, social insurance, child benefits, and other similar components are to be paid in the home country or in the host country. The category types are processed depending on the country during activation.

Infotypes that were created in the first phase are partially also maintained in the other phases. This is especially true for the status of the international assignment which is continuously adjusted.

Preparing the relocation   In the second phase the checklist from Infotype 0705 is mainly worked off and the required documents are provided.

Transfer   If the required steps of the first phase have been completed (in particular the mandatory items in the check list) and the employee has accepted the offer, the new employment contract can be activated. To do this, report RPMGE_ACTI VATION is activated, which simultaneously launches the activation in the host country. A requirement for the activation is that Infotype 0715, subtype HOST, has the status "Must be activated." Upon activation, the employee receives the employment status "active" while the activation date is entered in Infotype 0707. Infotypes 0008, 0014 and 0015 that are used to define the salary are derived from the compensation package offer. The personal data remains the same. Then the report is used to carry out the activation in the home country. The actual employee contract receives the employment status dormant.

During the international assignment, the "normal" processes of personnel administration and payroll continue as before. If necessary, the absence times during the assignment are documented in Infotype 0708 ("Details of global commuting"). This infotype is used to monitor tax regulations (e.g., the 183 day rule that applies in Germany). However, it is not taken into consideration by the time management, remuneration payroll, or travel-cost management components.

International assignment

Upon return the relocation process starts again. As an alternative to moving back into the home country another assignment can follow immediately.

Return

4.6 Critical Success Factors

Organizational management is integrated here in so far as it is required as the basis for the processes described in this book.

▶ Free yourself from the terminology. In mySAP HR many terms are used in an unusual manner or in another sense than you are used to in your daily business. This cannot be avoided when working with a standard software package. Try to apprehend expressions such as "employee subgroup", "job," and "position" in the system environment as what they represent in mySAP HR. There are more important things to discuss than names.

▶ Clarify the HR structures by considering the structures of other processes as well.

▶ At an early stage, clarify the processes for data maintenance, in particular the work distribution and decentralized entry. This process definition should be supported by employees or consultants with a high degree of experience in mySAP HR. This is the only way of fully utilizing the options of the system.

▶ Do not limit the use of mySAP HR to the HR department.

▶ In Customizing, personnel administration appears to be very simple in contrast to time management or payroll. However, it provides an enormous number of options that optimally support your daily tasks. The amount of resources invested here depends on the frequency of the processes supported and in particular on the number of employees. In any case, for larger companies with more than 5000 employees, an optimal configuration of the data entry process is definitely worthwhile.

▶ Consider right from the beginning not only the requirements of payroll and time management but also the central and decentralized evaluation requirements.

▶ Do not enter any data that you do not actually require, just because there happens to be a suitable infotype for it.

▶ The authorization concept for data entry and reporting is of great importance. It should be considered in connection with the role concept[3] (see Chapter 13, *Role-Based Portal Solution*). Involve the data-protection officer as early as possible.

▶ Avoid processes where the work is divided between too many persons. The days of the separation between salary accountants and personnel attendants on the one hand and workers responsible for data entry on the other are definitely over. The processes are only slowed down and made more expensive by this separation.

---

3 You can find more detailed information on the HR role and authorization concept in the following books: Brochhausen, Kielisch, Schnerring, Staeck: *mySAP HR— Technical Principles and Programming*, SAP PRESS 2005; Krämer, Lübke, Ringling: *HR Personnel Planning and Development Using SAP*, SAP PRESS 2004, Chapter 3

5 Organizational Management in mySAP HR

Organizational management is a very powerful and flexible component. It not only describes the basis for the personnel planning and development processes, but is also required for optimal implementation of personnel administration, and in particular for personnel controlling. In addition, it offers extensive options for defining and evaluating structures.

5.1 Classification in the Overall System and in HR

5.1.1 Importance for Personnel Administration

Organizational management is actually assigned to the planning components of HR, which are not part of the subject-matter of this book. However, because it represents a utility for structuring even without the use of personnel planning and development, it should be mentioned here. Use of organizational management when using personnel administration is definitely advisable as a basis for structuring and evaluation. In addition, the component serves as an essential basis for evaluations in all other processes and is of particular importance for recruitment. In this context, the complete functional scope is not required. It will suffice to discuss a pragmatic implementation using the following objects, which will be described in more detail in the course of the book.

▶ Organizational units and their integration in the organizational structure

▶ Positions, their integration in the organizational structure and the assignment of owners

▶ Jobs as a means to describe and classify positions

Organizational management is of particular importance in the mySAP HR authorization check. By activating the structural authorization check, it is possible to assign authorizations based on the organizational structure. We will only introduce organizational management in general terms in this chapter. You will find a detailed description in the book "HR Personnel Planning and Development Using SAP" from the same team of authors, also published by SAP PRESS.

5.1.2 Importance for Personnel Planning and Development

The object types mentioned above are an indispensable basis for the personnel planning and development processes. Only event management would be able to function without organizational management, but even it would be extremely limited in terms of carrying out evaluations.

For the remaining processes of personnel planning and development, the basic objects of positions, jobs, and—frequently—organizational units are further characterized with regard to the following attributes:

▶ Requirement profiles
▶ Career paths
▶ Development plans
▶ Employee goals
▶ Appraisal models
▶ Planned costs
▶ Requirements
▶ Budgets
▶ Compensation

5.1.3 Importance for the Decentralized Use of HR

Specific interfaces for decentralized use also require the clean maintenance of the organizational structure in many cases:

▶ The MDT (Manager's Desktop) or the MSS (Manager's Self Service) cannot be used without organizational management.
▶ In TMW (Time Manager's Workplace), organizational management can also be used for selecting the employees to be processed. There are other ways of doing this, however.

5.1.4 Importance for R/3 in General

Organizational management is a basis for the following cross-process functionalities:

▶ SAP Business Workflow
▶ Assigning roles to users
▶ Cross-module company organization along with controlling

5.2 Structure of Organizational Management

The Concept of the Plan Version

A plan version describes a specific world from the personnel planning and development view. Different plan versions are specifically used in order to run through alternative planning scenarios. Therefore it is possible to copy plan versions.

The active plan version or integration plan version has a special status. It is only set once during the initial implementation (mostly to 01) and must not be changed after that. The integration plan version is the only plan version whose changes impact the active integration of personnel administration.

Integration plan version

In order to change the plan version currently displayed or processed, you can use the menu path **Personnel · Organizational management · Settings · Set plan version** (see Figure 5.1).

Figure 5.1 Selecting the Plan Version

Objects, Relationships, Infotypes

While in personnel administration the "person" represents merely a type of information object, in organizational management different object types are processed. These are, for instance:

▶ Organizational unit

▶ Position

▶ Job

▶ Task

In addition external object types are also addressed. These represent objects that do not belong to organizational management and are not saved in its object structure, but that are quite important for organizational management. These are, in particular:

▶ Person from personnel administration

▶ Applicants from recruiting

▶ Cost center from cost accounting

In order to create relationships between these objects, relationship types are used. Each relationship possesses specific semantics such as:

▶ "Belongs to/Incorporates" (between organizational unit and position)

▶ "Holder" (between position and person)

▶ "Manages/is managed by" (between position and organizational unit)

This means different structures can be based on objects and relationships.

Infotypes are used in order to further describe objects beyond their structure relationship in the same way as in personnel administration. The infotype concept is very similar to that used in administration, even though the technical implementation deviates in some respects. In particular, not all infotypes are permitted for all object types here. Thus, for instance the Infotype "Vacancy" exists for a position, but not for an organizational unit.

The concept of objects, relationships and infotypes described here also applies to the other processes of personnel planning and development. Here, in particular, object types of different processes (e.g., organizational units and events) can be related to each other. The same infotype can also be used for objects of different processes. The number range for infotypes in personnel planning and development ranges between 1000 and 1999.

Customizing for objects, infotypes, and relationships is carried out via IMG path **Personnel management · Organizational management · Basic settings Enhancement · Data modeling**. For our present purpose, i.e., to use organizational management in a simple form as a basis for personnel administration and personnel controlling, no settings are required there.

Selected Object Types

Organizational unit — Basically, an organizational unit is an object of the organizational structure that has not been further specified. It can represent a business area, a team, an authority, a plant, or a department, among other things. This very general definition enables you to map as far into the depth of an organizational hierarchy as you want by using superordinate and subordinate organizational units.

Position — In simple terms, a position is a place that a specific employee can occupy. A position can also be vacant, which means for recruitment that personnel are required and an employee should be searched for. Positions are assigned to an organizational unit by the relationship type "belongs to."

The chief position has specific characteristics. The owner of this position manages the corresponding organizational unit. From a technical point of view, a chief position emerges when a link of the type "manages" is created between a position and an organizational unit. The chief position is important in many areas. For example, it can be used in order to assign specific tasks in Workflow, to identify the manager for the Manager's Desktop (see Section 13.3), or to grant access rights to subordinate employees via the structural authorization check.

A job can be regarded as a prototype or template for a position. While for instance, "loan officers" usually describes a job, "loan officer no. 3 in the commercial real estate department" is a position. In general, jobs and positions are named in the same way. In the example, the position would therefore also be called "loan officer." However, you can ascertain which position is meant from the hierarchical classification in the organizational structure. Jobs and positions are linked via the relationship types "describes" or "is described by." Thus the job concept provides a structure for the positions which can also be used for evaluation purposes.

Job

Selected Infotypes

In many maintenance interfaces, the individual infotypes rarely appear. They are rather integrated in cross-application interfaces in order to align the process of the daily maintenance work with the tasks of a user role. You can reach the maintenance for individual infotypes through the menu path **Personnel · Organizational management · Expert mode**. Maintenance screens are provided there for organizational units, jobs, and positions for infotypes (see Figure 5.2). Under the menu item **General**, you can maintain infotypes for any objects.

The Infotype "Object" represents the object itself. It contains a name and an abbreviation, which may change over time. An object can be clearly identified using an eight-digit object ID. Infotype 1000 is thus comparable to Infotype 0002 in personnel administration. The name and abbreviation correspond to the name of an employee and the object ID of the personnel number. Figure 5.3 shows Infoype 1000.

Object (Infotype 1000)

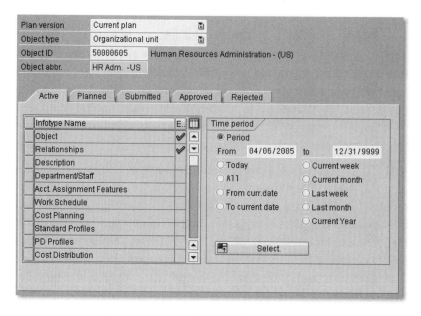

Figure 5.2 Expert Mode Independent of Object Types

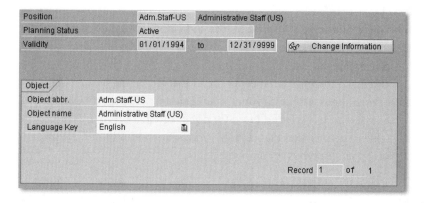

Figure 5.3 Infotype 1000 (Object)

Relationship
(Infotype 1001)

Relationships are also stored in an infotype where the relationship type represents the subtype. Direct maintenance of Infotype 1001, however, is an exception. The integrated maintenance interfaces enable reassignments, relationships, and simultaneous regeneration with relationships, without the direct maintenance of Infotype 1001. The infotype contains the relationship type and the related object (see Figure 5.4).

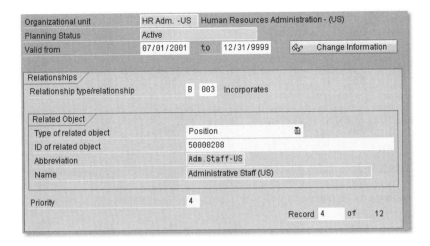

Organizational unit	HR Adm. -US	Human Resources Administration - (US)
Planning Status	Active	
Valid from	07/01/2001	to 12/31/9999 ό Change Information

Relationships

| Relationship type/relationship | B | 003 | Incorporates |

Related Object

Type of related object	Position	
ID of related object	50000208	
Abbreviation	Adm.Staff-US	
Name	Administrative Staff (US)	

| Priority | 4 | |
| | | Record 4 of 12 |

Figure 5.4 Relating the Organizational Unit to the Position

When a relationship is created, the corresponding relationship is also automatically created in the opposite direction. Thus, if the relationship "Position belongs to organizational unit" is created, the system automatically also creates "Organizational unit comprises position." Figure 5.5 shows the inverse relationship that corresponds to Figure 5.4.

Position	Adm.Staff-US	Administrative Staff (US)
Planning Status	Active	
Valid from	07/01/2001	to 12/31/9999 ό Change Information

Relationships

| Relationship type/relationship | A | 003 | Belongs to |

Related Object

Type of related object	Organizational unit	
ID of related object	50000605	
Abbreviation	HR Adm. -US	
Name	Human Resources Administration - (US)	

| Priority | 4 | |
| | | Record 1 of 3 |

Figure 5.5 Relating the Position to the Organizational Unit

Infotype "Department/staff" enables you to identify an organizational unit as a staff unit. This can be evaluated and displayed in a graphic. In addition, these department IDs can also be used to distinguish real departments from groups. This affects both evaluations and the integra-

Department/staff (Infotype 1003)

tion with personnel administration (see Section 5.2.2). Figure 5.6 illustrates an example of Infotype 1003.

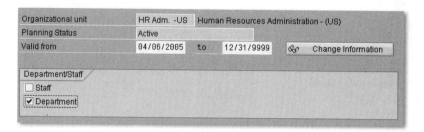

Figure 5.6 Department Identifier and Staff Identifier in Infotype 1003

Vacancy (Infotype 1007) Information on the vacancy is an essential element of manpower-requirement planning and recruitment. In order to be able to really support requirement planning, the vacancy should be created as soon as the departure or transfer of an employee becomes known. This generally occurs automatically in the action "Organizational change" or "Leaving."

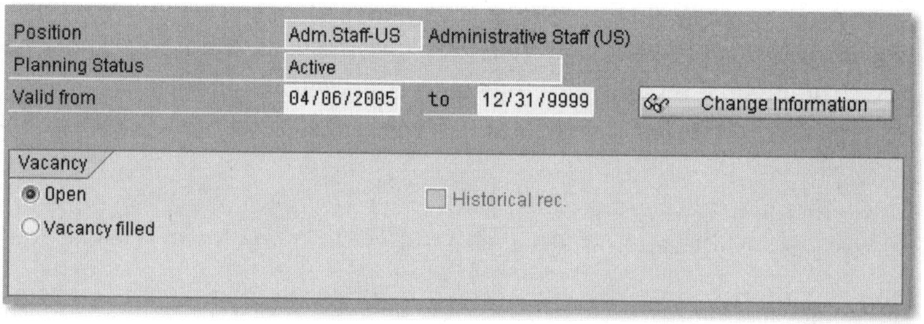

Figure 5.7 Infotype 1007 (Vacancy)

The infotype itself contains a status indication for the vacancy (see Figure 5.7). **Open** means that the search for personnel can begin immediately, while **Vacancy filled** doesn't require any immediate action.

5.2.1 Designing the Organizational Structure

The organizational structure is initially created via the menu path **Personnel · Organizational management · Organizational structure · Organization and staff assignment · Create**, in order to publish the root of the structure. You then can carry out further maintenance through the path **Personnel · Organizational management · Organizational structure · Organization and staff assignment · Change**.

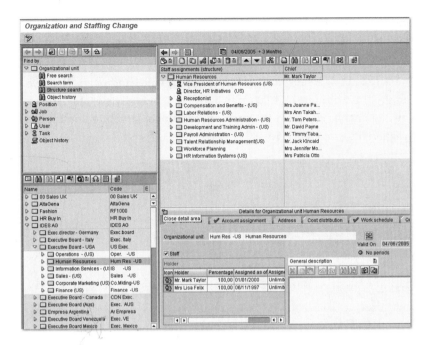

Figure 5.8 Maintenance Interface Divided into Four Parts

To a large extent, the integrated maintenance interface abstracts from the infotypes, and is divided into four areas (see Figure 5.8). Due to the split-screen technology, the four areas can be enlarged or reduced using the mouse, as is required for the current activity.

The upper left-hand pane is used to select objects and works like the Object Manager in personnel administration (see Figure 5.9).

Figure 5.9 Selecting Objects

The lower left-hand pane manages the pool of objects already selected (see Figure 5.10). These can be selected as root objects for the work area or can be assigned to objects of the work area by Drag&Drop.

The actual work area is located in the upper right-hand pane. There you can use the **Goto** button to change between different views. In particular you can change between the pure organizational structure and the staff assignments (see Figure 5.11).

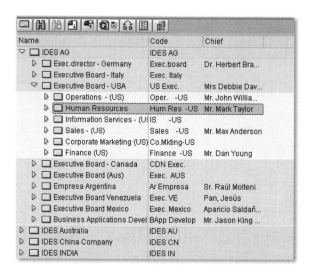

Figure 5.10 Object Pool

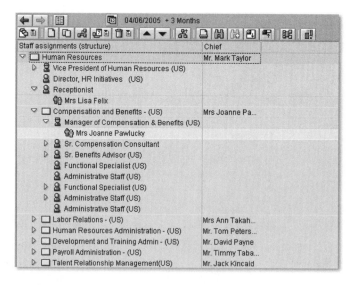

Figure 5.11 Staff Assignments in the Work Area

The following functionalities are available here:

▶ Creating, reassigning, delimiting, and deleting organizational units

▶ Creating, reassigning, delimiting, and deleting positions

▶ Changing the display sequence

▶ Assigning cost centers

▶ Assigning management functions

▶ Selecting objects for the details area

If you selected an object for the details area by double-clicking on it, different maintenance functions are available in several tabs (see Figure 5.12). Which tabs are available depends on the object type and the customizing settings.

This configuration of the entire maintenance screen occurs via the IMG path **Personnel management · Organizational management · Hierarchy framework**.

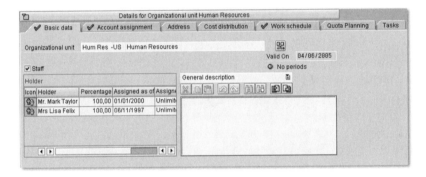

Figure 5.12 Maintenance via Tabs

5.2.2 Integration with Personnel Administration

The functionalities described so far are sufficient for supporting personnel administration and personnel controlling. The functionality of the integration is described in more detail in Chapter 4, *Personnel Administration*, in correlation with Infotype 0001. Nevertheless here are some important remarks on integration:

▶ The teams which maintain the organizational management and personnel administration in the system must be completely aware of the integration aspects, as well as their effects on the work of their colleagues.

► Note that retroactive organizational changes trigger recalculations in remuneration payroll that may lead to extensive adjustments in cost accounting.

► You should also pay particular attention to the integration with recruitment and manpower requirement planning. These are based on the following prerequisites:

  ► Vacancies must be maintained in a timely and correct manner.

  ► Vacant positions must be delimited if they are definitely no longer required.

  ► Positions for new employees must be created and correspondingly named.

► For a simple implementation of organizational management, as we seek to enable in this book, no customizing settings are required at first except for the definition of the integration itself via the characteristic PLOGI and the entries in the system table T77S0 for the group PLOGI.

6 Recruitment

This chapter deals with the characteristics of recruitment, starting with the different recruitment methods and continuing through selecting applicants to hiring an employee. The individual steps in mySAP HR are also described in the same way.

6.1 Business Principles

Business principles provide the starting points for implementing the requirements in a personnel-management system. In addition to legal requirements, especially as regards data protection, the different recruitment paths are of great importance when it comes to recruiting specialists and executives who are particularly scarce in the labor market. However, recruitment of junior employees and trainees in large numbers is a central issue for applicant selection. The descriptions in this section are also relevant for Chapter 7, *E-Recruiting*.

6.1.1 Goals of the Recruitment Process

For recruitment, human resources should be made available through searches and provision so the workforce requirements can be met from quantitative and qualitative viewpoints. The goal of any recruitment process is therefore to achieve the following targets in addition to providing qualified personnel:

▶ Quantity target
Human resources should be recruited in sufficient quantities (number of jobs) and for a sufficient duration (hours of work for each job).

▶ Time target
Human resources should be employed promptly at the time scheduled for filling the job. In addition, the employee should be recruited for the desired staff assignment (fixed term or unlimited).

6.1.2 Recruitment Media

Before selecting the recruitment media, specific decisions need to be made. First you must decide if human resources are to be recruited internally or externally.

A preference for either internal or external recruitment will often be derived from the corporate HR strategy. In a strongly unionized environment, you often will be forced to focus on internal recruitment whenever possible.

Media for Internal Advertising

▶ "Blackboard"
In practice, for internal job advertisements, standardized forms are frequently used which provide a job description, important requirements, the time of the staff assignment, and the pay-scale category of the job to be filled. In addition to the classic "blackboard," which can be found in most cafeteria or canteen areas, internal advertisements are being advertised more frequently on the intranet or by circulating an e-mail, thanks to increased use of intranets.

▶ Direct selection and address
While jobs are being advertising on the blackboard, in practice there is generally also a direct addressing and targeted selection of a candidate for certain jobs to be filled. A prerequisite for such a process is functioning succession and personnel-development planning.

▶ Advertising on the intranet/career platform
Companies are increasingly advertising certain jobs on the intranet as well as on the blackboard. Individuals in the commercial area are mainly approached here. Occasionally there are also mailings to all employees stating that applications from employees' acquaintances are also welcome.

Media for External Advertising

AIDA principle ▶ Job advertisements
Advertisements are still the most important instrument for external recruitment. The decision as to which newspaper should be selected strongly depends on whom the advertisement is to address. In designing the advertisement, the proven AIDA principle should be observed (**A**ttention **I**nterest **D**esire **A**ction). First of all, the applicant's attention should be drawn to the advertisement (Attention). For well-known companies, the company logo can already achieve this effect. The required attention can also be raised by directly addressing the reader. Interest in the advertised job (Interest) can be generated by highlighting a few task areas or by mentioning the characteristics of the company culture. The desire to apply for the job (Desire) can be generated by emphasizing particular employee benefits of the company or the

career opportunities related to the advertised job. Last but not least, there should be a request for action to the applicant to apply. A contact address or contact person should be provided.

▶ **Job agencies (public or private)**
Job agencies are often a possibility to find new staff at relatively low cost. This applies especially to public agencies. However, in some countries and regions these agencies do not have a good reputation among the most-wanted groups of candidates. Moreover, public agencies tend to focus on candidates that are already unemployed. As a result, employers will not be able to reach potential employees who currently have jobs but are looking for new opportunities.

▶ **Headhunting**
Researchers seek out target groups or persons who currently hold positions corresponding to those the company desires to fill, and they ascertain those individuals' willingness to move. Due to high costs, headhunters are thus generally only used for recruiting executives and specialists who are rarely found in the labor market. The advantage of these recruitment methods is that applicants who are currently not looking for a position are also addressed. In addition, the competition can possibly be weakened by this, while at the same time the personnel department in your own company can be relieved of work.

▶ **Personnel leasing**
This method of recruitment is used to cover short-term requirements. In general, this doesn't involve any application process; instead, a few temp agencies are addressed directly. Many countries have legal restrictions regarding the duration for which temporary staff are allowed to be employed for.

▶ **Internet**
For certain target groups, in particular in the area of IT, it has become normal in recent years to publish advertisements on the Internet. Other occupational groups are also increasingly being addressed by Internet recruiting. Due to the multiple methods of recruitment through the Internet and the possible connections to existing ERP software, this subject is dealt with separately in Section 6.1.6.

▶ **Career platform**
An open career platform represents a specific form of recruitment over the Internet. Future candidates who are not currently willing to move can become interested in the company in this way. Chapter 7 describes this concept in further detail.

► **Personal recommendation**

A lot of hiring is based on personal recommendation. Employees, customers or suppliers can make such recommendations. The advantage of this method lies in the fact that a relationship of trust is already created between the candidates and the potential employer.

► **Other (university contacts, allocation of degree dissertations, workshops, etc.)**

These recruitment methods are generally used to recruit junior staff directly from universities and colleges.

Decision Criteria for External Recruitment Media

If external recruitment is decided on, you must consider what external recruitment medium is to be used or who carries out recruitment. There are several criteria here which should be taken into account when trying to get a decision (see Figure 6.1).

Decision criteria for external recruitment

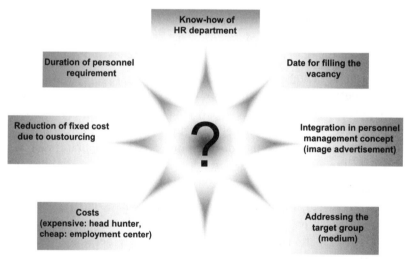

Figure 6.1 Decision Criteria for External Recruitment

6.1.3 Managing the Application Process

By managing the application process we mean all actions, from receipt of the application to the creation and delivery of the employment contract to the new employee.

In today's labor market situation, especially with regard to specialists and executives, and particularly in the IT sector it is increasingly important for a company to appear as an attractive employer. This can be achieved up front by the design and contents of the recruitment media; however, it should not stop there. Again and again, companies that looked attractive from the outside made serious mistakes when managing the application process.

However, managing other applicants such as junior staff and trainees, places great demands on the respective administrators and thus also on the software used. Because applications for trainee positions are received in many ways, mastering the huge number of such applications is always a challenge for the HR department An initial pre-selection takes place when the application files are reviewed and applications that are obviously incomplete are filtered out.

Requirements for the Application Process from the Applicants' Point of View

▶ If you placed yourself in the position of an applicant, you would find out quickly what is important in managing the application process. You would want to know, for example:

▶ **Fast feedback upon receipt of the application**
If a company has succeeded in attracting applicants, it is extremely important to respond as quickly as possible to interesting applicants. This begins with informing the applicant as soon as possible that their application has arrived and is already being processed. In the context of quality assurance, many companies have determined specific response times, which should not exceed a maximum of two weeks in this area. When supporting such a goal, it is important to use the correct instrument. This instrument should enable you to enter and evaluate applicant data in as efficient and uncomplicated a manner as possible, and also to enable fast correspondence.

▶ **Fast availability of the status of the application**
It should be possible immediately to provide a statement on the status of an application upon an applicant's request. A status statement might include such information as the person currently in charge, departmental flow, or correspondence. Moreover, this point is also of great importance internally, as all those with access rights constantly have information on the whereabouts of applicant files and the status of the application.

Requirements for the Application Process from the Point of View of the User Departments

▶ **Simple entry of applicant data**

Entering the applicant data—especially when dealing with large quantities—must be manageable in an uncomplicated and simple way.

▶ **Identification of duplicate applications**

You must be able to detect duplicate applications automatically. Here you must make a distinction between identifying multiple applicants and previous employees.

▶ **Ensuring comparability**

The data basis for the selection process should be as equal as possible, i.e., the same information content should be available for all applicants. In addition, it is generally necessary to enter additional data for an applicant in a later step. For instance, the bank details must be entered if there is to be an interview or assessment center in order to settle the travel espenses of an applicant.

▶ **Maintaining and monitoring the status of the application**

In order to manage the selection process, it is necessary to enter all the planned and completed activities for an applicant within a selection process (e.g., sending confirmation of receipt, transferring applicant files, interview). In addition, the status of an application must be available quickly and across different departments so that information can be received on it at any time. This information requirement is internal from the user department point of view and also external from an applicant point of view.

Equal Employment Opportunities (EEO)

EEO delivers some very important criteria for a proper recruitment process. There are several laws in the U.S. to enforce EEO. These include:

▶ Title VII of the *Civil Rights Act of 1964*, which prohibits employment discrimination based on race, color, religion, sex, or national origin.

▶ Age Discrimination in *Employment Act of 1967*, which protects individuals who are 40 years of age or older.

▶ Title I and Title V of the *Americans with Disabilities Act of 1990*, which prohibit employment discrimination against qualified individuals with disabilities.

Different regulations may apply in other countries. Thus, you have to check the legal requirements in every country in which you want to

implement a recruitment process. The HR system should be able to provide the necessary information to answer inquiries from the U.S. EEO
Commission and do the mandatory reporting.

6.1.4 Applicant Selection

In this section, we will first give you a brief overview of the process of
pre-selection of applicants and then describe the actual selection process
and the different selection procedures in further detail.

Pre-selection

In the applicant pre-selection, the incoming applications are divided into
three categories:

▶ **A applicants**
These applicants seem to be suitable based on the documents provided. You want to consider the applicant in more detail in an interview. The A criteria can be derived from

  ▶ Request for personnel from the user department

  ▶ Requirements profile

  ▶ Job description

  ▶ Company principles (e.g., to employ university graduates only)

  ▶ Application principles

  A criteria typically include: "A" applicant
                                                                   criteria
  ▶ Completeness of the application documents

  ▶ Age

  ▶ Industry experience

  ▶ Years of work experience

  ▶ Final qualification

▶ **B applicants**
Interesting applicants who are not assigned to group A due to smaller
irregularities in their CV or for similar reasons. These applicants provide
a reserve in case some applicants from group A have turned out not to
be suitable or have canceled their application.

▶ **C applicants**
Applicants who, based on their qualifications, do not suit the advertised job or whose application documents are incomplete. These applicants are generally refused immediately.

Selection Process

The applicant selection can be carried out in different ways. This depends on several factors:

▶ **Applicant group**
If this involves, for instance, trainees, then proficiency tests, group exercises, and subsequent interviews or preliminary interviews are often carried out. The selection of specialists, on the other hand, is generally done through first and, if necessary, second interviews.

▶ **Type of job to be occupied**
If specialists and executives must be selected, assessment centers are generally carried out in which the applicants go through different test scenarios for at least one day.

6.1.5 Recruitment Controlling

Recruiting incurs costs for the external/internal recruitment media and above all ties up human resources. The task of recruitment controlling is to find out the level of success related to the resources used. The efficiency of recruitment actions is to be determined in order to make decisions for or against specific actions. Recruitment controlling controls personnel-management work and must be considered as operational controlling.

A prerequisite for an effective recruitment controlling is high transparency of the costs related to HR processes. In order to determine these costs, the following question must be answered (example: recruiting new employees):

▶ Which parts of the company can be involved?

  ▷ Personnel marketing: Publish information on the Internet, recruiting days, participate in applicant forums, etc.

  ▷ Psychological service: Creating a selection process and its constant revision (e.g., AC, tests, interview guidelines)

  ▷ Recruitment: Implementing the selection process, concluding the contract, etc.

▶ How can you identify the costs?

  ▷ Defining a cost unit "Specialist recruitment"

  ▷ Post individual cost-unit costs (personnel costs, media costs, etc.) directly to the cost unit

- Post overhead cost-unit costs to the cost unit (first option: apportionment of current costs; from the costs of the psychological service X% is assigned to the creation of an AC for specialists; second option: working with a planned allocation rate)

The second block of information is the use, for instance of recruitment media. This can then be quantitatively determined if the incoming applications are assigned to a recruitment medium. This means evaluations can be made throughout the recruitment flow, which enables a statement on how many applications related to a specific medium. Qualitative success can be determined on the basis of the number of applications that refer to a specific medium and have led to the conclusion of a contract.

What is still problematic in this context is the monetary evaluation of this success. For sales employees, for instance, it is rather easy to evaluate the success of their activities in monetary terms (number and volume of contracts concluded), whereas for HR administrators this is much more difficult. The dilemma is that while the costs can be identified on a quantitative basis, success can only be expressed in terms of quality. There are different examples of how you can work around or solve this problem. One option is to define the desired benefit. With regard to executives, this might translate to low fluctuation in the respective department. This benefit can then be evaluated on a monetary basis, if you take into account the costs saved by avoiding the recruitment of new employees.

Monetary success evaluation

6.1.6 Internet Recruiting

The latest figures show a rapid increase in the number of online users. Up until a few years ago on the Internet, you could practically only find university graduates in IT-related occupational groups. Today, however, you can find the whole range of the labor market.

There are several ways for companies to recruit personnel on the Internet:

- **Recruitment through their own website**
  The option of creating online applications directly for job advertisements and transferring the data directly to an existing ERP system relieves the HR department considerably from administrative tasks such as entering applicant master data. In order to "lure" applicants to a specific website, there are traffic generators such as entering the website into search machines (Altavista, Fireball, Google, Lycos) and directories such as Web.de or Yahoo. Entries in meta job exchanges in which only career-relevant websites are entered (e.g., *www.mon-*

ster.com, *www.careerbuilder.com*, *http://hotjobs.yahoo.com*) are possible.

▶ **Using commercial job exchanges**
There is now a large offering in this area, ranging from the job exchange that provides the entire range of jobs, through specific job exchanges for specialists and executives, to regional job exchanges. The range of activities of these exchanges generally includes the following:

  ▶ Entering the company profile

  ▶ Entering the job offers

  ▶ Online applications

  ▶ Job-search database

  ▶ Link to the company website

▶ **Job-search databases**
The active search of companies for new employees is the focus here. In job-search databases, you must beware of non-active individuals who have been listed there for a long time. It is crucial that the data be up-to-date.

The integration of online applications with HR management systems means that many steps can be automated:

▶ Automatic delivery of applications to the correct administrator

▶ Informing applicants by mouse-click on receipt of the application

▶ Making information on the status of the application available online in the recruitment process

▶ Applicant correspondence by e-mail

Media mix Relying 100% on the Internet for personnel searches is only of use in a few cases. Instead you should use a combination of different media. A job advertisement in the newspaper can for instance contain a reference to the website and additional information about the company.

6.2 The mySAP HR Concept

6.2.1 Integration in the Organizational Structure

Recruitment uses the mySAP organizational structure to the extent that it uses vacant positions from organizational management. The vacancies are created using the infotype "Vacancy" at a position of the organizational management (**Personnel · Personnel management · Recruitment · Advertising · Vacancy · Maintain**). The positions to be filled are made accessible to application management by assigning this infotype (see Figure 6.2).

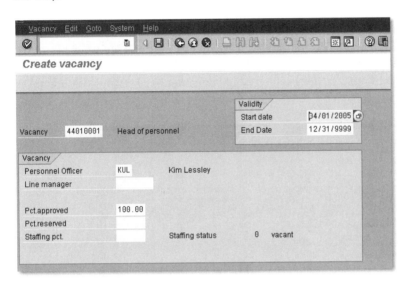

Figure 6.2 Setting Position as Vacant

Another way to use organizational management in recruiting is the creation of requirement profiles for the position. Together with their counterpart, the qualifications profile of the applicant, these enable a profile comparison to support the applicant selection. We will only deal in brief here with the options of organizational management for creating a requirement profile, as this subject is part of personnel development, which will not specifically be dealt with here.

Requirements and qualifications profile

The prerequisite for both requirement and for qualifications profiles is the creation of a qualifications catalog. Our discussion has less to do with maintaining this catalog in mySAP HR and more to do with the design activity in creating such a catalog. Determining the qualifications that already exist in a company and the selection of those qualifications to be implemented in the system represents quite a challenge. The easiest way of doing this is to compile qualifications if there is a clear policy in a company regarding the requirements for a position. This is particularly the case in public services, as there are straightforward job descriptions compiled from different activities which in turn result in the grouping to a specific pay scale. The counterpart to this, the qualifications profile and an example of a profile comparison, are described in Section 6.2.3.

The final use of organizational management for applicant management is implemented by creating a job advertisement. In this step, the vacancies previously created are assigned to the job advertisements (see Figure 6.3). It is problematic if the job advertisement involves trainee positions, as this generally involves several positions of the same type. The problem here is the necessity of having to create several similar vacancies in order to be able to document how many trainee positions are to be occupied. This occurs because there is no option in R/3 to—for instance—relate a quantity to a vacancy, which would document how many positions are to be occupied.

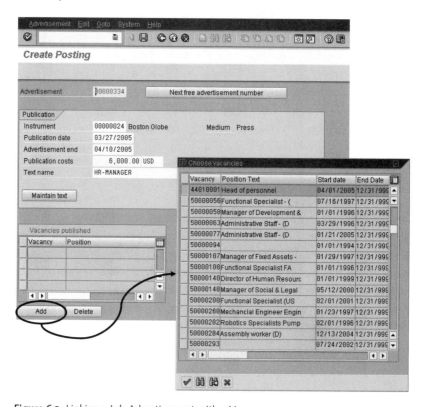

Figure 6.3 Linking a Job Advertisement with a Vacancy

6.2.2 Media and Instruments

It is first necessary to draw a distinction between the concepts of media and instruments.

Media A few examples, such as press or Internet/intranet, make it clear what is meant by the term media. This involves classifications and groupings that enable you to combine several instruments. In addition, you can assign a medium to unsolicited applicants through which they have contacted the company.

Media are created in the recruitment customizing via the IMG path **Personnel management · Recruitment · Workforce requirements and Advertisements · Create media**. A characteristic of the medium is the applicant class assigned to it, which specifies if a medium is used to advertise internal or external applicants (see Figure 6.4).

Change View "Medium": Overview

New Entries

Medium	Name of medium	Applicant class	Applicant class text
01	Press	AP	External applicant
02	Employment office	AP	External applicant
03	Exec.search agency	AP	External applicant
04	Internal Job Posting	P	Internal applicant
05	Mail	P	Internal applicant
06	Internal press	P	Internal applicant
10	University	AP	External applicant
11	Trade fairs	AP	External applicant
12	Headhunter	AP	External applicant
13	Employee Referral	AP	External applicant
14	Walk In	AP	External applicant
15	Internet	AP	External applicant

Figure 6.4 Creating Media

In the recruitment instruments the type and methods of recruitment are mapped, for instance the placing of advertisements in the print media, personal contacts through headhunting or referral by an employment center or recruitment agencies.

Instruments

Recruitment instruments are further classified according to the medium used (e.g., press, Internet, recruitment agency).

Recruitment instruments are created in the customizing (IMG) for recruitment via **Personnel management · Recruitment · Workforce requirements and Advertising · Create recruitment instruments** (see Figure 6.5). A prerequisite for this is the creation of a recruitment medium, given that recruitment instruments are divided according to the medium used. For each recruitment instrument, you can store a contact person and an address key. You maintain the address of the contact person for the respective recruitment instrument through the work step "Create addresses for recruitment instruments" (**Personnel management · Recruitment · Workforce requirements and Advertising**) (see Figure 6.5).

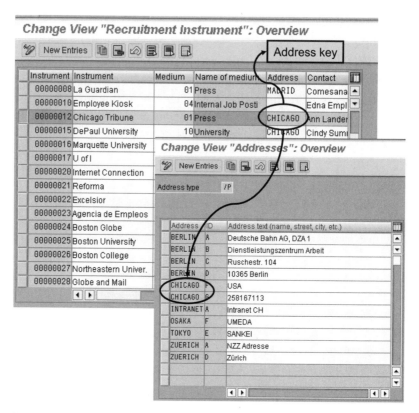

Figure 6.5 Creating Recruitment Instruments

Advertisements The recruitment media and instruments are used when creating an advertisement (see Figure 6.6). In addition to the applicant, the central object in applicant management in mySAP HR is the advertisement.

The purpose of assigning recruitment instruments to advertisements lies in recruitment controlling, in which we evaluate how successful a specific advertisement instrument was in comparison to the others. You can measure this, for example, by contrasting the number of applications and their quality (e.g., measurable by the number of people hired based on an advertisement) with the recruitment instrument. If several instruments are used for an advertisement, a separate advertisement must be created for each of these instruments. This could well seem cumbersome, but it enables you to evaluate the effectiveness of instruments, as the incoming applications are assigned to the advertisement to which they refer (e.g., advertisement in *The Economist*).

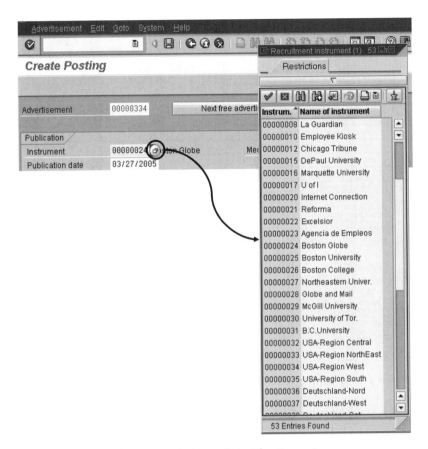

Figure 6.6 Assigning Recruitment Instruments to Advertisements

6.2.3 Applicant Master Data

The collection of applicant master data often represents a big challenge for the HR department, in that a large quantity of applicant documents must be viewed in some fashion, and the interesting applications must be entered into a system. It is important to have an instrument at hand that enables you to enter the data as quickly and in as structured a way as possible. Figure 6.7 shows an example of an entry screen for the applicant master data. You can see the individual areas can be individually customized.

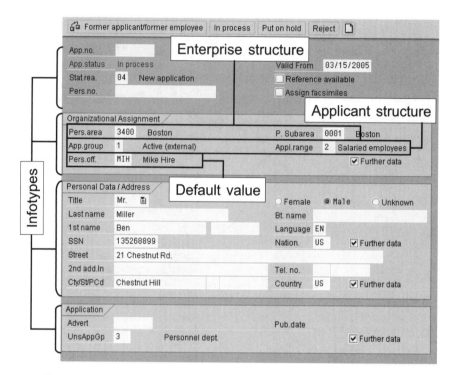

Figure 6.7 Entry Screen for Applicant Master Data

Applicant Structure

In comparison to the structure in the personnel administration (see Section 4.2.5), structures used in the application management are also necessary for control and evaluation functions.

Even if the definition of the applicant structure is subject to changes throughout the course of the project, clarification should be as precise as possible from the beginning of the project, because customizing of applicant management is to some extent based on these early results. As well as assigning applicants to the company structure displayed by the organizational structure of HR, the applicants are assigned to applicant groups and applicant subgroups (details on the definition and functions of the company structure with the personnel areas and sub-areas can also be found in Section 4.2.5).

Applicant groups
Like the employee groups in personnel administration, the applicant groups are the result of a basic division of employees (e.g., employees with unlimited/fixed term employment contracts, trainees, temps). Here, the decisive criterion is the type of employment relationship to be entered into. The applicant class is a property of the applicant group that

states whether an applicant group comprises internal or external applicants (indicator P = internal applicant, indicator AP = external applicant, see Figure 6.8). Applicant groups are maintained in the IMG via the path **Personnel management · Recruitment · Manage applicants · Applicant structure · Create applicant groups**.

Applicant group	Applicant group text	Applicant class	Applicant class text
1	Active (external)	AP	External applicant
2	Active (internal)	P	Internal applicant
3	Student employee	AP	External applicant
4	Temporary worker	AP	External applicant
5	Retiree	P	Internal applicant

Figure 6.8 Creating Applicant Groups

Contrary to the applicant group, the applicant ranges represent a more refined breakdown of the applicant structure. The applicant range is a freely selectable structuring criterion by which applicants are generally structured according to hierarchical criteria (e.g., executives, senior managers, employees) or according to functional criteria (e.g., corporate management, sales, and production).

Applicant subgroups

For applications that are not directly related to an advertisement and thus to a vacancy, unsolicited applicant groups can be set up. The unsolicited applicant group is a freely selectable criterion to structure unsolicited applicants. For instance it is possible to summarize unsolicited applicants according to their desired position in the company (e.g., sales employee, personnel department employee). Each unsolicited applicant group must be assigned a group personnel director. This director acts as a suggested value in entering the master data when an applicant is assigned the corresponding unsolicited applicant group. A prerequisite for assigning a group personnel director is that these group personnel directors working in the company have been created in the system (IMG: **Personnel management · Recruitment · Manage applicants · Create group personnel directors**).

Unsolicited applicant groups

In order to facilitate the decision of which applicant groups and subgroups are created, you must clarify what requirements the applicant structure should fulfill with regard to the following points:

▶ Different processing of different applicants with regard to

　▷ Applicant processes (see Section 6.2.4)

　▷ Applicant correspondence (see Section 6.2.5)

▷ Applicant responsibility (Who processes whom?)

▶ Selection for the evaluation

▶ Authorization check

The more differentiated the controls are to be in this area, the more refined the applicant structure must be.

When the applicant data is initially entered, the system checks whether the application is a duplicate application. Here, the last name in combination with the first name and the date of birth are used as a basis for comparison. When there is a hit, the system shows the result of the comparison. From here, you can navigate to the data of the person found (see Figure 6.9) in order to find out if it is the same person and what advertisement the application refers to. If you have recognized the person, you can confirm this in the system, and the applicant is set to the status "renewed application." In addition, the master data already entered is transferred (see Figure 6.10).

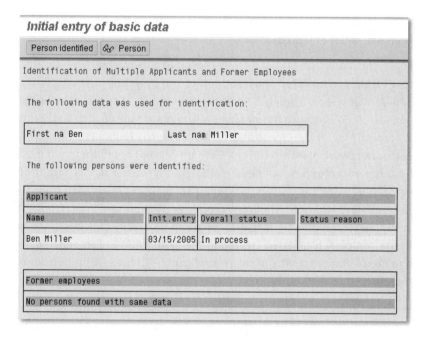

Figure 6.9 Recognizing Applicants

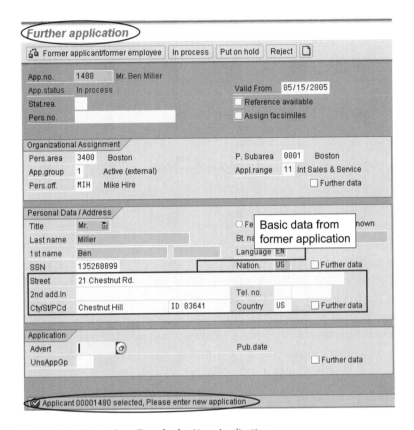

Figure 6.10 Master Data Transfer for New Application

Short Profile

By defining one or several short profiles of the applicants, evaluations can be defined individually by the customer. An example is the report to evaluate the applications received (more detail in Section 6.2.4), for which a short profile can be called in each case for individual applicants. It is useful to create different short profiles which meet the different requirements in the company. For instance, the short profile provided for a transactional user should meet certain administrative criteria. These might include displaying the applicant processes or the current status of the applicant in the application process. Line-manager applicants, on the other hand, would instead need short profiles that contain CVs and qualifications.

SAP provides two templates to create the short profile. These can be reached through the IMG path **Personnel management · Recruitment · Manage applicants · Short profile**. These templates can be copied and customized. For these documents the following information is available as text variables from the applicant master data (extract):

▶ Fields of the organizational assignment of the applicant: Personnel (sub-)area, applicant group/subgroup, etc.

▶ Fields of the personal data of an applicant: First name, last name, gender, etc.

▶ Address fields: Address

▶ Qualification fields: Education, certificates, etc.

▶ Qualification fields: Qualifications and their characteristics

▶ Overall status of the applicant

▶ Completed/planned processes

The data to be included in a short profile and the data of the applicant should be included at all depends strongly on the information the data is supposed to provide. For a pure administration of the applicants without system support when selecting the suitable applicants, master data are sufficient, such as address, personal data and the vacancy and advertisement assignment. However, if a company also needs support when selecting a suitable applicant, either for certain occupational groups or in general, further data is required. This is because both the requirements of the vacancy and the qualifications of the applicants are necessary if, for instance, profile comparisons are to be carried out.

Qualifications Profiles and Profile Comparisons

The use of profiles and profile comparisons is part of the personnel development components in mySAP HR and can support the decision-making processes regarding the selection of suitable applicants or successors respectively. As personnel development is not part of this book, we will only briefly describe the subject of profiles and profile comparisons here.

The requirements profile was already discussed briefly in Section 6.2.1. Creating a qualifications profile is the logical counterpart here if profile comparisons are to be referred to in selecting applicants. A predetermined qualifications catalog is required here too, which is used as a basis for both the requirements and the qualifications profiles. A qualifications profile consists of several components (see Figure 6.11):

- **Qualifications**
  The existing qualifications and their characteristics are entered here.
- **Potentials**
  You can enter whether a person has potential to occupy a specific position/job.
- **Preferences**
  If an employee is interested in a specific task or position, this can be entered here.
- **Dislikes**
  In order to avoid offering someone a specific position or task, this can be entered here as an exclusion criterion.
- **Appraisals received as appraisee**
  For an applicant these can be appraisals from an assessment center, and in the case of an employee, these can be appraisals by a superior.

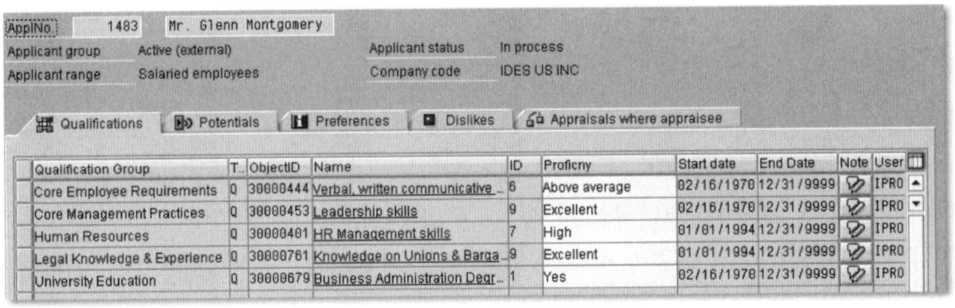

Qualification Group	T..	ObjectID	Name	ID	Proficny	Start date	End Date	Note	User
Core Employee Requirements	Q	30000444	Verbal, written communicative ...	6	Above average	02/16/1970	12/31/9999		IPRO
Core Management Practices	Q	30000453	Leadership skills	9	Excellent	02/16/1970	12/31/9999		IPRO
Human Resources	Q	30000401	HR Management skills	7	High	01/01/1994	12/31/9999		IPRO
Legal Knowledge & Experience	Q	30000761	Knowledge on Unions & Barga...	9	Excellent	01/01/1994	12/31/9999		IPRO
University Education	Q	30000679	Business Administration Degr...	1	Yes	02/16/1970	12/31/9999		IPRO

Figure 6.11 Qualifications Profile

In order to support the applicant selection, there is the option to contrast the qualifications profiles of the applicants with the requirements profiles of positions or jobs. A result of this comparison is shown in Figure 6.12.

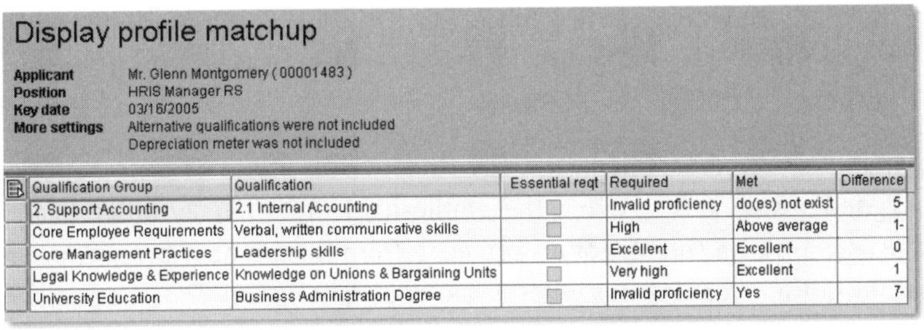

Qualification Group	Qualification	Essential reqt	Required	Met	Difference
2. Support Accounting	2.1 Internal Accounting		Invalid proficiency	do(es) not exist	5-
Core Employee Requirements	Verbal, written communicative skills		High	Above average	1-
Core Management Practices	Leadership skills		Excellent	Excellent	0
Legal Knowledge & Experience	Knowledge on Unions & Bargaining Units		Very high	Excellent	1
University Education	Business Administration Degree		Invalid proficiency	Yes	7-

Figure 6.12 Profile Comparison Between Applicants and Positions

6.2.4 Status, Actions, Processes

In order to be able to systematically log the process of an applicant from the first entry of his data in the applicant master data through the various selection processes to hiring or refusal, processes and actions are carried out in mySAP HR that document the respective status of the applicant.

You will find that mySAP HR basically differentiates between two types of selection processes in recruitment:

▶ **Global selection process**
Each applicant entered takes part in the global selection process of a company. This process decides if an applicant is of interest for the company. If an applicant is not refused, he or she can participate in one or several selection processes for a vacancy.

▶ **Selection process for each vacancy**
Here, the applicant is assigned to the relevant vacancies.

Status

Both in the global selection process and in the selection processes for a vacancy, you can decide at any time whether the interest in an applicant persists. The respective status of an applicant in a selection process is mapped in the applicant status. There are two types of applicant status with regard to the selection processes:

▶ **Overall status**
This status specifies the current status (e.g., in process, on hold, interview required) an applicant has in the global selection process of the company.

▶ **Status of the vacancy assignment**
This defines which current status (e.g., in process, on hold, interview required) an applicant has in the selection process for a specific vacancy.

Depending on the system settings, the overall status is automatically assigned via an action when the applicant data is initially entered and must always be available for an applicant from this point in time. You can see from the overall status whether an applicant currently participates in at least one selection process (e.g., overall status "in process," "on hold," "interview required"), or if all selection processes have already been completed for him (overall status "refused" or "employ").

An applicant receives a status-of-the-vacancy assignment as soon as he or she has been assigned to a vacancy. If an applicant has several vacancy assignments, a status of the vacancy assignment is available for all of these assignments. A selection process is completed if all applicants who are participating in the selection process have the status "rejected" or the status "to be employed."

The applicant statuses provided by SAP should be regarded as a default and not be supplemented. The following different status categories for applicants are provided by SAP:

▶ "In process"

▶ "To be employed"

▶ "On hold"

▶ "Rejected"

▶ "Contract offered"

▶ "Offer refused"

▶ "Invite"

For some of the status categories, it can be necessary to specify reasons. **Status reason** For example, it can be possible to connect the information on why someone has the status 4, "rejected," with a reason for the refusal. In this case, reasons such as "insufficient qualifications," "rejected after conclusion of the selection process," and the like would be conceivable. The status reason can be purely informational, but it can also be used for instance to establish which text templates are assigned to the relevant applicant process during automatic creation, and thus which letter the applicant will receive. The status reasons can be assigned to individual statuses (see Figure 6.13).

Change View "Admissible Combination of Status and Reason": Overview

New Entries

Status	Text for applicant status	Status reason	Text for status reason
1	In process	04	New application
3	On hold	03	Overqualified
3	On hold	05	No requirement
4	Rejected	01	Insufficient qualifications
4	Rejected	02	Formal error
4	Rejected	03	Overqualified
4	Rejected	05	No requirement
4	Rejected	06	

Figure 6.13 Admissibility of Status Reasons

In recruitment customizing, you establish which combinations between the overall status and the status of the vacancy assignment are admissible. It may not be permitted in a company, for example, to assign an invitation for interview to applicants who have the overall status "Contract offered" for another vacancy. This is controlled by assigning the admissible statuses of the vacancy assignment to the individual overall status. You can see an overview of the possible combinations in Figure 6.14.

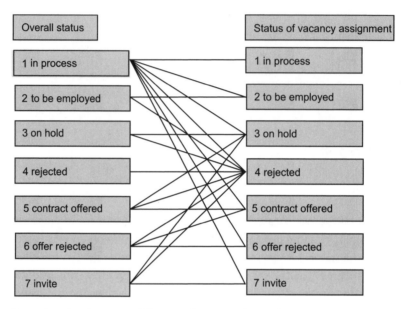

Figure 6.14 Combinations of the Overall Status with the Status of the Vacancy Assignment

The overall status of an applicant is set via the applicant actions in recruitment (e.g., the applicant action "**Initial core data**" sets the overall status: "**In process**").

Actions

In mySAP HR, actions refer to a sequencing of infotypes, for instance "organizational assignment" and "address," carried out in personnel management for an applicant or employee for a particular reason such as initial entry of applicant data, hiring, change of cost center, leaving, etc. (see Figure 6.15). The infotype concept is described in more detail in Section 4.2.2.

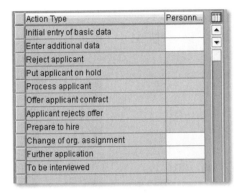

Action Type	Personn...	
Initial entry of basic data		
Enter additional data		
Reject applicant		
Put applicant on hold		
Process applicant		
Offer applicant contract		
Applicant rejects offer		
Prepare to hire		
Change of org. assignment		
Further application		
To be interviewed		

Figure 6.15 Applicant Actions

The type and sequence of infotypes to be processed in recruitment by using actions is defined in the recruitment customizing. Here, as in personnel administration, you can create info groups (sequences of infotypes, see Figure 6.16). SAP provides a range of applicant actions (see Figure 6.15). Customizing applicant actions is easy.

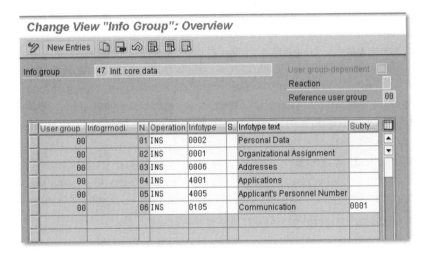

Change View "Info Group": Overview

New Entries

Info group   47 Init. core data   User group-dependent

Reaction

Reference user group   00

User group	Infogrmodi.	N.	Operation	Infotype	S.	Infotype text	Subty...
00		01	INS	0002		Personal Data	
00		02	INS	0001		Organizational Assignment	
00		03	INS	0006		Addresses	
00		04	INS	4001		Applications	
00		05	INS	4005		Applicant's Personnel Number	
00		06	INS	0105		Communication	0001

Figure 6.16 Info Groups of the Action "Initial Core Data"

You can navigate to the applicant actions via the IMG path **Personnel management · Recruitment · Selecting applicants · Change infogroups/applicant actions.** In recruitment, the following administration infotypes are available:

▶ Organizational assignment (0001)

▶ Personal data (0002)

- Addresses (0006)
- Education (0022)
- Other/previous employers (0023)
- Qualifications (over 0024)
- Bank details (0009)
- Contract elements (0016)
- Basic Pay (0008)
- Recurring payments and deductions (0014)
- Additional payments (0015)
- Planned working time (0007)

If required, other recruitment infotypes can be made available. In addition to the personnel administration infotypes mentioned above, there are specific infotypes for applicants. These are as follows:

- **Applicant actions (4000)**
  Here, all actions are stored that have been carried out for an applicant. These can be processes for data entry (e.g., initial entry of applicant data, entry of additional data), but they can also be processes that change the overall status of the applicant (e.g., reject applicant, put applicant on hold). In addition to the action type carried out for an applicant, you can enter in the "applicant actions" infotype wheter an applicant can produce a reference. If this is the case you can select the personnel number of the reference from the administration HR master data in a separate field.

- **Application (4001)**
  In this infotype you can enter if an application refers to an advertisement (vacancy) or arrived unsolicitedly (unsolicited applicant group).

- **Vacancy assignment (4002)**
  Here you enter which vacancies an applicant is assigned to.

- **Applicant activities (4003)**
  The entry, logging and planning of activities for an applicant within the selection process is carried out via the applicant activities. Thus, applicant activities are administrative steps that an applicant runs through in the course of his or her application. In addition, the applicant correspondence is carried out through the applicant activities (more detailed information on the applicant activities is contained in Section 6.2.4).

- ▶ **Applicant's personnel number (4005)**

  The system automatically fills the infotype for all internal applicants. This means every internal applicant has a data record of this infotype.

- ▶ **Aplicant activity status (4004)**

  There is exactly one data record of this infotype in the system for each applicant. The system automatically creates and updates this data record. The infotype displays the status of the processes carried out and supports the search for applicant data efficiently.

- ▶ **Employee's applicant number (0139)**

  This infotype is used in personnel administration in the following cases:

  - ▶ The external applicant joins the company as an employee

  - ▶ The internal applicant and thus an existing employee in the company occupies the vacant job

  You store the applicant number and the employee personnel number in this infotype. This means the infotype identifies the applicant with the employee.

When combining info groups and thus actions, you must note that the infotype "organizational assignment" (0001) must always be created as one of the first infotypes as it is used for authorization checks, screen layout, and plausibility checks within other infotypes.

Apart from the sequence of infotypes, you can also define which fields are to be shown during the initial entry of applicant data. In addition, the two-level process for the initial entry of data is defined here, establishing which data belongs to the core data and which belongs to the additional data.

This two-level process is especially useful for the initial entry of applicant data. First you enter the core applicant data, and then, in a second step, you can enter additional data. The basic data must be entered for each applicant, as it includes basic information for statistical purposes, such as the assignment of applicants to personnel (sub-)areas, applicant groups/ranges, names, and for sending out letters, e.g., the address. Additional data is only entered for those applicants who are of further interest for the company. Using the applicant action "Enter additional data," you can for instance assign an applicant to one or several vacancies. In addition, you can use this applicant action to enter applicant data on education, qualifications and previous employers.

As it is necessary in the administration of a selection process to enter all planned and completed activities for an applicant (e.g., sending a confirmation of receipt, transferring applicant documents, interview) in the scope of a selection process, the logging and planning of activities for an applicant is carried out through applicant activities.

Activities

Applicant activities are administrative steps which an applicant runs through in the course of his or her application. Applicant activities are created and processed for each action carried out with an applicant. The system creates some of the applicant activities automatically. For instance, the applicant activity "Confirmation of receipt" is automatically created after the action "Initial entry of applicant data." The applicant activities are partly created explicitly (e.g., transfer of applicant data to the user department). In deciding when and which applicant activities are to be created automatically, you are free to set the selection process yourself using your own customized actions and the automatic activities to be created.

The activities of an application have the following properties:

▶ **Activity type**
You can use the activity type to determine the specific activity that is to be carried out for an applicant (e.g., sending out the confirmation of receipt, invitation for an interview, date of the interview).

▶ **Activity status**
For each applicant activity, it is determined if the activity for an applicant is still to be carried out (activity status "planned") or if it has already been completed (activity status "completed").

▶ **Execution date**
Regarding planned activities, the execution date specifies up to what day or on what day the activity should take place, and for completed activities it specifies when the activity took place.

▶ **Activity administrator**
The administrator is responsible for ensuring that the relevant activity takes place on the specified date, or he or she assumes responsibility for carrying out the activity in the correct manner.

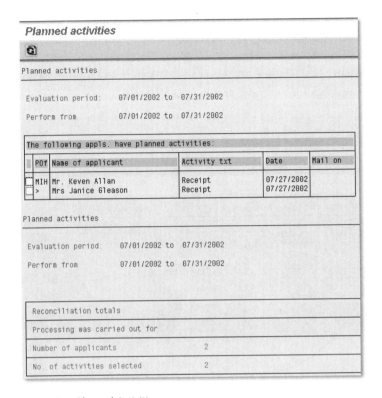

Figure 6.17 Planned Activities

The properties of the applicant processes enables you to carry out a control via the individual selection processes. The most important control instruments for the selection process are:

Control instruments

▶ **Planned activities**
This evaluation monitors the planned activities according to the group personnel director. Thus, the recruiter can get an overview of the planned activities for each applicant (see Figure 6.17).

▶ **Applications**
This report outputs a list of all applications (see Figure 6.18). The list contains the following information:

▷ Applicant's name

▷ Date of receipt of the application

▷ Advertisement or unsolicited applicant group the application refers to

By entering selection criteria, the output quantity can be reduced. For instance, in the receipt of application you can determine that only the applicants are selected who applied within the relevant time interval. From the evaluation result, you can navigate to a short profile for individual applicants that can be adjusted according to your individual requirements (see Figure 6.18). You can find a short description of the possible settings for the short profile in Section 6.2.3.

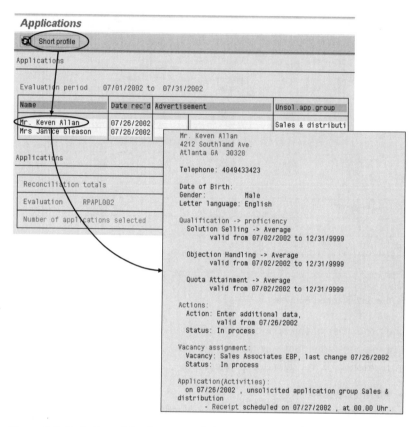

Figure 6.18 Evaluation of Applications and Short Profile

6.2.5 Controlling the Work Flow and Correspondence

The work flows in the applicant administration are basically controlled via the personnel actions and the activities which arise from this. Here, dynamic actions (see Section 4.4.2) play a decisive role, as they control the triggering of actions during the maintenance of a recruitment info-type record. The standard settings provided by SAP can be described as follows:

1. If the infotype "Applicant activities" (4000) is changed through one of the following actions, activities are automatically created in connection with the PACTV feature. The corresponding actions are: "Reapplication," "Initial core data," "Put applicant on hold," "Reject applicant," "Offer applicant contract," "Applicant rejects offer," "Prepare for hiring."

2. If the overall status of an applicant is changed through one of the following actions in infotype "Applicant activities" (4000), a report is launched in which you can maintain the applicant's vacancy assignments. The corresponding actions are: "Set applicant to 'in process'," "Offer applicant contract," "Applicant rejects offer," "Prepare for hiring."

3. If the overall status of an applicant is changed through one of the following actions in infotype "Applicant activities" (4000), the status of the vacancy assignments for the applicant is automatically set to the value of its overall status. The corresponding actions are: "Put applicant on hold," "Reject applicant."

4. If the overall status of the applicant is set to either the value "to be employed," "Contract offered" or "Offer rejected," in the infotype "Applicant activities" (4000), a report is launched which you can use to change the status of those applicants that are also assigned to this vacancy.

5. If the status of the applicant is set to one of the values "To be employed," "Contract offered" or "Offer rejected" in the infotype "Vacancy assignment" (4002), a screen is provided to maintain the staffing/reservation percentage.

As mentioned in item Number 1 of the previous list, you control the automatic creation of activities through the feature PACTV (IMG path **Personnel management · Recruitment · Applicant selection · Applicant activities · Applicant activity types · Change automatic creation of applicant activities**). The following settings can be made for the activity to be created:

▶ **Process activity in online or in background**
"Online" means the activity is created in a dialog with the user, i.e. the user must enter data for the activity. "In background" means that the activity is created completely in the background and is provided with all the necessary data. The activity "Receipt confirmation" is processed in the background, as it merely establishes that the applicant should receive a receipt confirmation.

▶ **Execution date**

If an activity is processed in the background, it must be provided with an execution date and, if necessary, with an execution time.

▶ **"Recurring work" flag**

If this flag is defined for an activity, "Recurring work" is automatically checked when the activity is created, and the activity can then be carried out through mass processing and set to the "completed" status.

▶ **"Send mail" flag**

This flag specifies if an e-mail is sent when the activity is created (reference to the MAIL feature).

▶ **Name of the text template**

If an activity for the applicant correspondence is involved, the activity can be provided with the name of the text template.

Figure 6.19 shows an activity that was automatically created by the system on the basis of the initial entry of applicant data. The group personnel director can then create the correspondence for the applicant on the basis of this process. You can see an example of a confirmation of receipt in Figure 6.19.

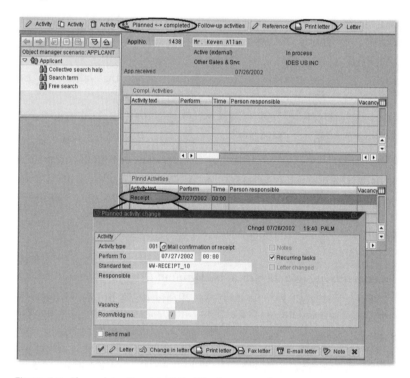

Figure 6.19 Planned Applicant Activity "Confirmation of Receipt"

In particular the activities implemented for almost every applicant, such as the printing of the confirmation of receipt, are generally not called individually through the individual applicants and set to the status "Completed" but are rather carried out via "Recurring work." In the mySAP menu call **Personnel management · Recruitment · Applicant activity · Print letters** (to create correspondence for several applicants at the same time) and **Complete activities** (to change the status of the processes for several applicants at the same time).

The connection between applicant actions and the activities and letters that arise from this is once again clarified by an activity taken from practice (see Section 6.3.3).

For the applicant correspondence there are two possible word-processing systems available: SAPscript and Microsoft Word. When using Microsoft Word as a word processing system in recruitment you must note the following points:

Applicant correspondence via word processing

▶ Since HR Support Packages 58–62, it is absolutely necessary to use one of the following SAP GUIs, as otherwise the Word interface will no longer function correctly:

  ▶ SAP GUI 46D with at least patch level 505 or higher

  ▶ SAP GUI 610 with at least patch level 12 or higher

  ▶ SAP GUI 620 with at least patch level 1 or higher

▶ In the presentation system you must install a 32-bit operating system (at least Windows 95 or Windows NT).

▶ In the operating system of the presentation server you must maintain the environment variable Path_to_codepage (this generally occurs automatically during installation).

▶ You must fill the feature WPROC:

  ▶ By setting the return value RTF (see Figure 6.20) you can determine that Word is to be used for word processing.

  ▶ You must also specify which Word versions you are using in the company. You can transfer this through a structured return, and the system then checks the registry of the corresponding work station computer as to which version is being used and then automatically uses this version (example for Word 8.0 and 9.0, see Figure 6.20).

  ▶ A structured return is possible for versions from Word 8.0.

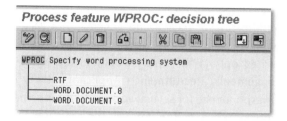

Figure 6.20 Feature WPROC

Due to the high degree of convenience, outputting letters through the Microsoft Word interface is highly recommended.

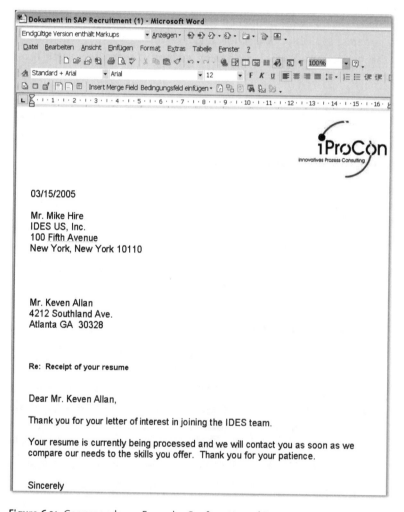

Figure 6.21 Correspondence Example: Confirmation of Receipt

Applicant correspondence by mail

In order to be able to send mails to the applicants from an activity, it is necessary to connect e-mail software such as MS Outlook or Lotus Notes to the R/3 system. A technical prerequisite is the installation of the SAP Exchange Connector. By using the **E-mail letter** button you can determine from an activity that the correspondence with this applicant should be carried out by e-mail (see Figure 6.22).

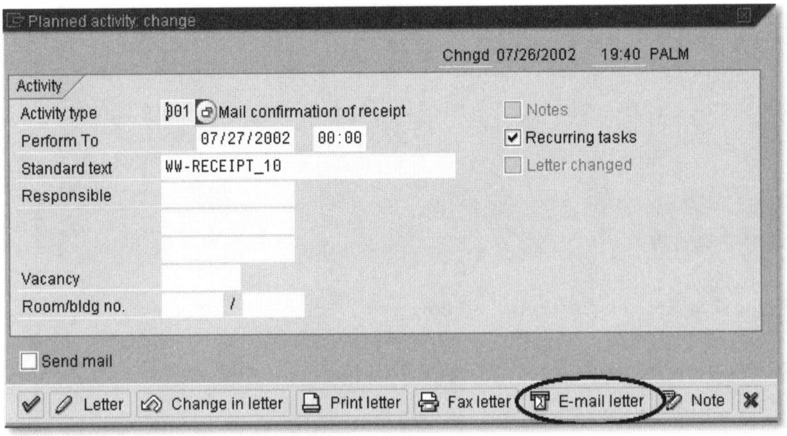

Figure 6.22 Sending an Activity Letter as an E-Mail

By default the document is then sent as a PDF attachment to the mail. The feature WPROC enables you to control that the user is given the option to decide via selection buttons whether the correspondence occurs by letter, e-mail or fax (see Figure 6.23). A prerequisite is that a blank character " " instead of RTF is returned (i.e., SAPscript instead of Word), in the feature WPROC. Then Transaction PBAT (Print letters) calls a program for SAPscript print.

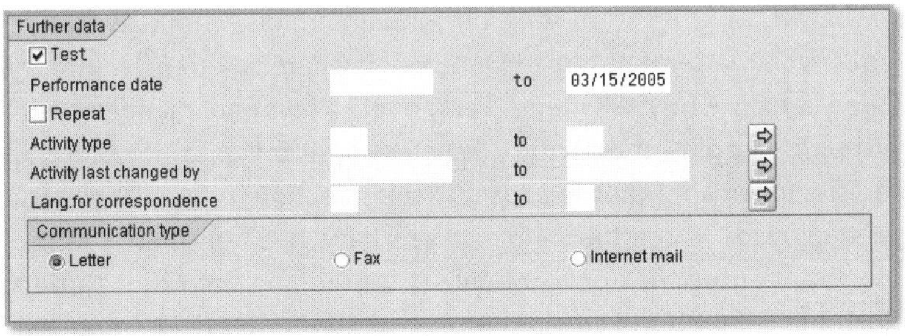

Figure 6.23 Selecting the Sending Type for a Letter

When sending the letter by mail and fax the data is retrieved from the following infotypes.

▶ Mail address from Infotype 0105/subtype 0010

    ▶ A list with mail addresses is displayed in order to select the required mail address from several mail addresses (see Figure 6.24).

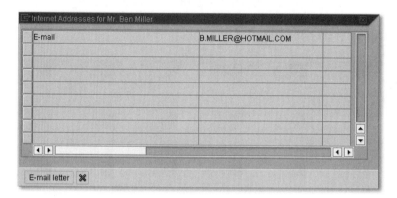

Figure 6.24 Selecting the E-Mail Address

▶ Fax number from Infotype 0006 "Address" or Infotype 0105 "Communication"/subtype 0005

    ▶ For an individual printout, all numbers are provided for selection

    ▶ For a mass printout all fax numbers from Infotype 0006 "Address" are used

The decision for SAPscript as a word processor is a basic decision, as no option exists in the default to switch between Word for letters and SAPscript for mail. It is also not possible to manipulate the subject line and mail text when sending mails.

Hiring An employee is hired at the end of a successful recruitment process. Due to integration with personnel administration mySAP HR provides the option, based on integration with personnel administration, to transfer the application master data already entered through data transfer into the employee database (mySAP menu: **Personnel · Personnel management · Recruitment · Applicant activity · Transfer applicant data · Execute**). A prerequisite for an applicant to appear in this selection is the overall status "to be employed." Once the hiring actions have been entered, the program for transferring the applicant data is started and then runs through the individual infotypes of the info group, similar to hiring without using recruitment. The applicant receives a personnel number and his or her master data from the applicant administration will be complemented, if necessary. At the end of the action the administrator receives a statistic with information on the progression of the transfer (see Figure 6.25).

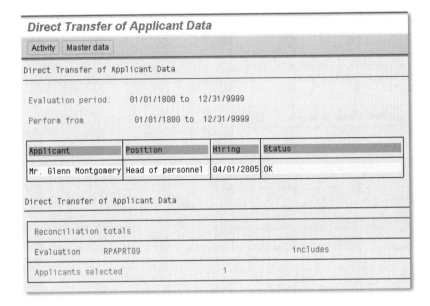

Direct Transfer of Applicant Data

Activity	Master data

Direct Transfer of Applicant Data

Evaluation period: 01/01/1800 to 12/31/9999

Perform from   01/01/1800 to 12/31/9999

Applicant	Position	Hiring	Status
Mr. Glenn Montgomery	Head of personnel	04/01/2005	OK

Direct Transfer of Applicant Data

Reconciliation totals		
Evaluation RPAPRT09		includes
Applicants selected	1	

Figure 6.25 Result of the Data Transfer

6.2.6 Controlling

The aim of controlling in recruitment is to contrast the costs which have arisen from the recruitment process with the benefits. mySAP HR supports this by providing an option to enter the costs, e.g., of an advertisement and also by providing the option to evaluate the recruitment instruments and media based on the following criteria:

▶ Costs of the recruitment instrument (see Figure 6.26)

▶ Status of the applicants (see Figure 6.27)

▶ The number of applicants per advertisement instrument (see Figure 6.28)

Evaluate Recruitment Instruments

𝒦 Instrument	Evaluate advert	Applicant statistics	Applicant list

Evaluate Recruitment Instruments

Instrument	Number of adverts	Number of applications	Total cost	Cost per application
New York Times	3	102	2,253.50 USD	22.09 USD
Boston Globe	1	1	500.00 USD	500.00 USD

Figure 6.26 Costs of the Recruitment Instrument

Applicant status (overall)	Number
In process	115
On hold	7
Rejected	9
To be hired	17
Contract offered	4
Offer rejected	0
Invite	2
Total	154

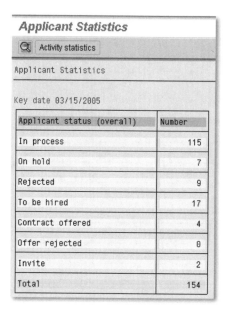

Figure 6.27 Applicant Statistics of the Recruitment Instrument

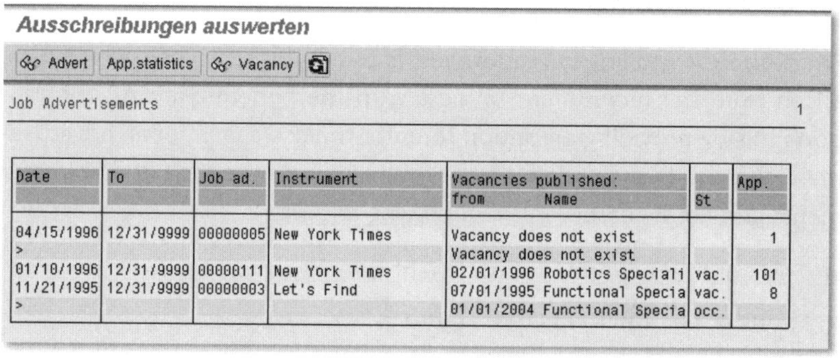

Date	To	Job ad.	Instrument	Vacancies published: from Name	St	App.
04/15/1996	12/31/9999	00000005	New York Times	Vacancy does not exist		1
>				Vacancy does not exist		
01/10/1996	12/31/9999	00000111	New York Times	02/01/1996 Robotics Speciali	vac.	101
11/21/1995	12/31/9999	00000003	Let's Find	07/01/1995 Functional Specia	vac.	8
>				01/01/2004 Functional Specia	occ.	

Figure 6.28 Number of Applicants per Advertisement

6.2.7 Integration with the Internet

In the course of the increased use of the Internet for recruitment (see Section 6.1.6) there is also the option to integrate recruitment in mySAP HR with the Internet. In addition, integrating intranet scenarios with mySAP HR recruitment is useful for internal recruitment.

The following scenarios are currently supported in mySAP HR recruitment:

▶ **Job offers**

The Internet application component "Job offers" supports companies in providing the following options for external applicants:

- ▶ Display of company job advertisements
- ▶ Applying to positions advertised in the company
- ▶ Unsolicited application with the company (unsolicited applications)
- ▶ Electronic transfer of application documents to the company

▶ **Application status**

The Internet application component "application status" currently provides the option to support a cost-effective and efficient recruitment process that enables external applicants to inquire about the status of their applications themselves over the Internet. This Internet application component saves the personnel department administrative work which emerges due to answering applicant queries.

Chapter 7, *E-Recruiting*, provides an outlook on a more comprehensive and far-reaching solution then mySAP HR recruitment, with a focus on intranet and Internet scenarios.

6.3 Process Examples

The outline process of applicant administration is displayed in Figure 6.29. This contains on a basic level all steps which are implemented, from advertising to contract creation in the system. This process is already described in a similar form for personnel administration in Section 4.5.1. It has merely been supplemented with a few components for the applicant administration. The process represents an ideal situation, considering that creating a requirements profile for a job or position and a qualifications profile as well as carrying out a profile comparison requires the use of the personnel-development component.

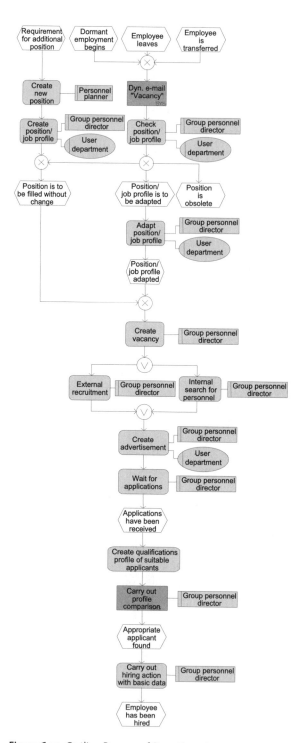

Figure 6.29 Outline Process of Recruitment

6.3.1 Advertisement

In order to understand the process description for job advertisements in Figure 6.30, knowledge of organizational management is required (see Chapter 5, *Organizational Management in mySAP HR*). You should at least be aware of the concepts of job and position.

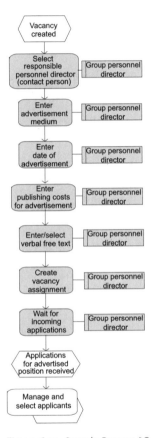

Figure 6.30 Sample Process "Create Advertisement"

As you can see in Figure 6.30, the advertisement requires the existence of a vacancy. If this vacancy is created, you can begin entering the advertisement.

6.3.2 Receipt of Application

Based on the process of the job advertisement, you can navigate to the process of receipt of application, once applications have been received for advertised jobs (see Figure 6.31). The process of the receipt of applications once again shows clearly when the system carries out checks (duplicate application) and when it automatically creates an application process. The next step is the selection process.

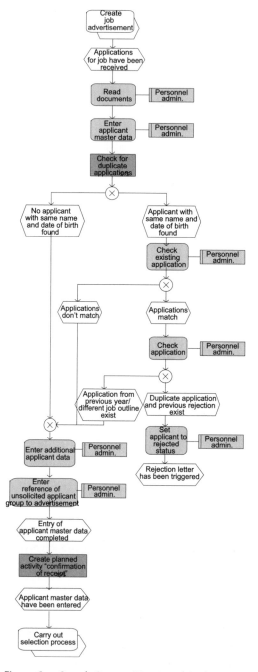

Figure 6.31 Sample Process "Receipt of Application"

6.3.3 Single-Level Selection Process

This process once again clarifies in detail the relationship between actions and activities in the applicant administration to control the application process. The first part of the process is concluded with the applicant rejecting the invitation for an interview and therefore receives a specific rejection letter.

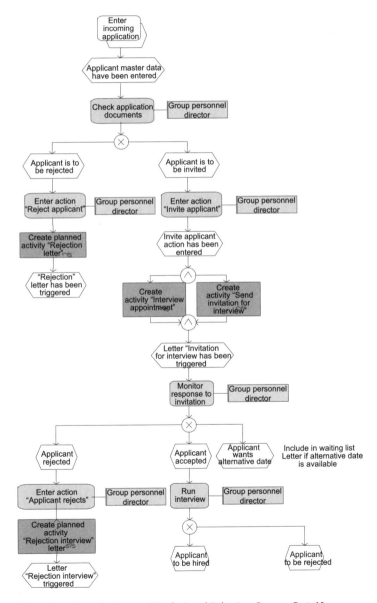

Figure 6.32 Sample Process "Single-Level Selection Process Part 1"

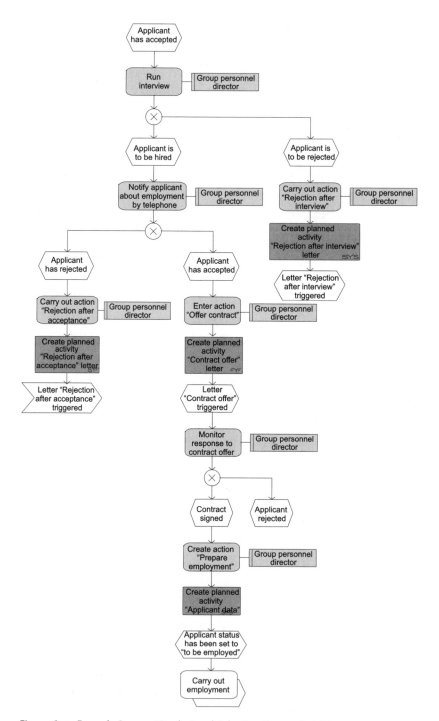

Figure 6.33 Example Process "Single-Level Selection Process Part 2"

An alternative conclusion to the process is also described: The applicant accepts the appointment for the interview and is to be hired after the interview (see Figure 6.32). Figure 6.33 displays the actions that are necessary for hiring. It also illustrates how the process continues if the applicant is to be rejected after the interview.

6.3.4 Contract Creation

A lot of information on the applicant is necessary for contract creation. This ranges from the address through the planned working time to salary and leave entitlement. This data on the applicant can be entered by using the option to integrate the infotypes from personnel administration into recruitment, and it can be used when creating the contract. Figure 6.34 shows which infotypes provide useful data for the contract creation.

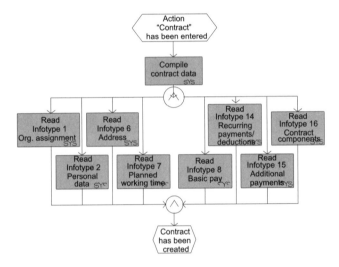

Figure 6.34 Sample Process "Contract Creation"

6.4 Critical Success Factors

This section will point out and summarize factors that should be particularly taken into account when implementing recruitment.

▶ **Applicant structure**
   As part of the conceptual considerations for structuring the applicants, you should ensure that the structure is adapted to the requirements regarding details of evaluations, controlling authorizations, and different processing of different applicants, with regard to applicant activities, applicant correspondence, and the responsability for the appli-

cants. In addition, the selection options in evaluation are characterized by the selected applicant structure.

▶ **Processes**
Based on the options for structuring the recruitment processes, the processes to be mapped must be known and documented as early as possible. This must be carried out before the beginning of the implementation, because basic changes to the processes shortly before production startup can lead to complex customizing effort.

▶ **Correspondence**
Due to electronic means of correspondence and the functions for automatically creating applicant correspondence, it is necessary to define standard letters. The conception of such standard letters entails a certain degree of effort which requires a huge amount of adaptation in most companies. This means you should deal with the creation of company-specific standard letters at an early stage.

▶ **Microsoft Word interface**
Due to the integration of Microsoft Word with mySAP HR recruitment, it is necessary to check at an early stage which versions of Word are installed at the relevant work centers. A standardized version structure is almost inevitable. In addition, extensive tests of the Word interface must be carried out both in the test environment and on the client computers.

▶ **E-Recruiting solution as an alternative**
Before investing time and money in implementing or enhancing (e.g., web-enabling) this solution, you should always investigate whether this is really the better alternative compared to the E-Recruiting solution described in Chapter 7, *E-Recruiting*. Consider not only the current functional requirements and possibilities, but also future developments. Last but not least, ask your account manager at SAP about the maintenance of the recruitment module described in this chapter.

7   E-Recruiting

The E-Recruiting solution within mySAP ERP HCM is com-
pletely new and doesn't have much in common with the
recruitment solution described in the previous chapter. The
new design built on a new technological basis takes into
account the new labor market where it takes a proactive
approach to capture the best talents.

7.1   Business Principles

Most of what is said in Section 6.1 is also true for E-Recruiting, as we are
talking primarily about a different technical approach. However, the new
technology allows some major changes to the business processes, which
have to be discussed here.

7.1.1   War for Talent

Even in countries with high unemployment it is more and more difficult
for companies to attract specialized or high-potential candidates, as you
can see in several European countries these days. Most organizations
expect this problem to grow, given the aging population in many parts of
the industrialized world and ever-increasing skill requirements for the top
technical and managerial positions.

On the other hand, most organizations see a sharp increase of applications from candidates with only average or low skills. The challenge to the
HR department will be to manage this workload efficiently while still finding the best candidates to ensure their companies' competitiveness.

7.1.2   Sourcing and Retention

Considering that the highly talented tend to behave as self-confident
business partners in the labor market today, the traditional recruitment
process is just not enough. What you need is a comprehensive talent-
relationship management.

Research shows that the majority of employees are neither 100% loyal to
their employers nor actively looking for a new job. More than 50% are
generally interested in a good opportunity but may not even read the
help-wanted section of the newspaper. A company that attracts talent
and builds relationships with talented people even before they are

urgently looking for a new job has a considerable advantage. That's the idea behind the concept of the talent pool. Employees who are screening the job market without an immediate wish to change their employers are invited to an uncommitted registration. They can look around and get acquainted with the company. When a promising opening arises, they are available without the need for much advertising. Moreover, the talent pool allows for a reasonable segmentation of candidates so that you can concentrate on your target groups.

Thus, you can apply well-known principals of customer-relationship management to your recruiting processes. It is more efficient and more effective to build and maintain long-term relationships than to search for short-term contacts every time you need them and then lose them again.

What is true for external candidates is also true for internal talent. After all, your best employees are potential candidates for your competitors, and it would be naïve to assume that they do not watch the job market. So, since they are watching anyway, why not make sure that the internal job market of your company is at the top of their list? Allow your employees what you allow external candidates. When change is due, it is better they choose a new job in your company than leave for the competition.

7.1.3   Controlling Recruitment Processes

Measurement of the recruitment performance is becoming more and more important. There are well known key figures such as

▶ **Cost per hire**
All internal (e.g., time spent by recruiters) and external (e.g., cost of a job advert) costs that are spent to fill a position

▶ **Time to fill**
Time that passes from the opening of a position to the hiring of a new employee

▶ **Cost of staff turnover**
All costs caused by the leaving of an employee (including hiring and training costs as well as the costs caused by the vacancy, to name but the most important components)

With E-Recruiting, it is often more difficult to assign the costs to a specific hiring, because the costs for the talent pool must be shared by all hiring activities in some way. Moreover, there are often requirements for more detailed information. One way of dividing the time to fill a vacancy is as follows:

- The time from the moment the vacancy is known to the moment when a job advertisement is published (online or in print)
- The time between the publishing of the advertisement and the invitations to first interviews
- The time between the interviews and the hiring decision
- Other

With a specialized e-recruitment system, the expectations in this area are particularly high.

7.1.4   Processes and Organization

This new world of recruitment can be quite a challenge for the HR department. It differs from the traditional process in a number of ways.

- The candidates can contact the company in many different ways, and they want to decide how to go about it.
- Working with a talent pool requires completely new processes, because, after the initial registration, the initiative often must come from the employer.
- Besides the processes surrounding applications and job openings, something must be done for the retention of talent in the pool.
- Line managers expect to be involved more actively in the selection process and get quicker results so they can respond to changing market requirements
- "Cost per hire" is an important key figure, and budgets for HR are often limited.
- Recruitment, staff retention, succession planning, and career development are interacting strongly. They even can be seen as parts of the same complex process.

All this requires significant changes to the old organization and processes.

7.1.5   Recruitment Service Providing

In recent years, more and more companies have outsourced parts of their recruitment processes or built corporate service centers to act as service providers. The pressure to reduce costs, together with the increasing complexity of the processes, may be major reasons for this.

However, with this step, the processes often get even more complex because of increased coordination requirements. So, it is even more important to have well defined and sensible processes and a clear organization with an appropriate IT-support.

7.1.6 Technology

Most organizations seriously working with E-Recruiting have to face technological challenges. These include the following.

▶ Candidates send in information in many different forms. Not only must paper-based applications be processed but also electronic documents in a variety of formats such as Microsoft Word, PDF, TIF, and JPG. One possibility is to have all applicants fill in an online form with the most important information.

▶ Data security is always an issue, and it has two sides:

  ▶ Candidates who register and enter confidential data want to be sure that no unauthorized access of this data is possible.

  ▶ It makes sense that the recruiting system interacts with the operative HR system. Because this interaction opens up a connection between the HR system and the outside world via the Internet, technology must guarantee that data of the operative HR system cannot be accessed from outside the organization.

▶ International recruitment is often a reason for changing from traditional recruitment processes to E-Recruiting. However, this means that the system has to

  ▶ Comply with legislation of different countries regarding data security, accessibility, etc.

  ▶ Be multilingual

  ▶ Deal with different formats for addresses, names, etc.

  ▶ Take into account the different education systems and grading systems

7.2   The Process in mySAP ERP HCM

7.2.1   Overview

Figure 7.1 shows the main functional areas of the solution. In the center of the whole process stands the **Talent pool**, where candidates can maintain their data. How much data they enter can be decided by the candidates within the restrictions that the employer sets in the Customizing.

Registration is the first step. At this point, it is generally not required that the candidate enters all the data. We can expect, rather, that many candidates will enter more and more data with time and only offer the full set of data when they find an attractive vacancy.

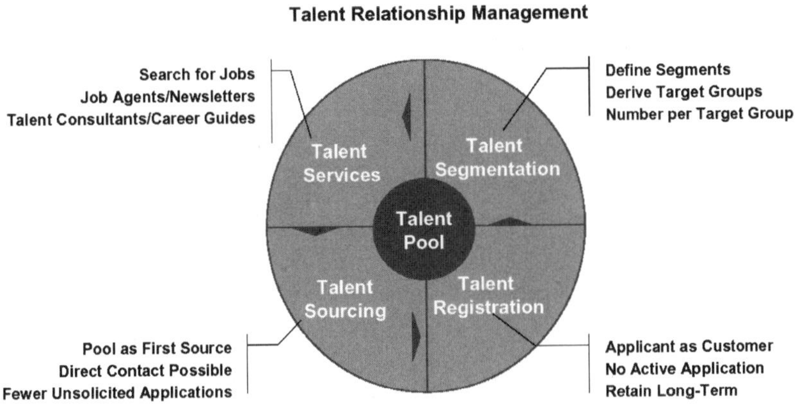

Talent Relationship Management

Search for Jobs
Job Agents/Newsletters
Talent Consultants/Career Guides

Define Segments
Derive Target Groups
Number per Target Group

Talent Services
Talent Segmentation
Talent Pool
Talent Sourcing
Talent Registration

Pool as First Source
Direct Contact Possible
Fewer Unsolicited Applications

Applicant as Customer
No Active Application
Retain Long-Term

Figure 7.1 Functional Overview of mySAP E-Recruiting

The data maintained in the talent pool usually includes:

▶ Personal data

▶ Communication data (address, e-mail, phone, etc.)

▶ Employment preferences (such as functional area and salary expectations)

▶ Work experience

▶ Education

▶ Skills profile (qualifications)

▶ A range of attachments such as certificates and reference letters

▶ A cover letter

Although it is possible at this stage to see active applications for a particular vacancy, and although in most cases this is encouraged, the employer's main aim in registration is developing a long-term relationship.

How much effort is invested in this relationship and whether a candidate receives invitations to apply for specific jobs can be decided in the talent **segmentation** process. It allows the employer to assign candidates to a talent group (see Section 7.2.6) and to assess candidates in a detailed appraisal form (questionnaire) (see Section 7.2.5) that can be fully customized.

To retain candidates in the pool, several services can be offered to them (as shown in Figure 7.1). Whatever the value-added services may be, the most important points for the candidate are:

▶ Searching for interesting job postings

▶ Getting qualified job offers or invitations to apply from a recruiter, based on the candidate profile.

From the employer's point of view, the three functional areas described so far build the basis for the real purpose of the system: **talent sourcing**. With a broad pool of talent and substantial information about candidates at hand, many vacancies can be filled from this pool. So, the pool is the first place to look for new employees before any other expensive and time-consuming measures such as placing job advertisements or hiring head-hunters are necessary. To fulfill this purpose, requisition management (see Section 7.2.3) is a very important feature of the solution. Recruiters define the requisitions and related job postings that are requested by the managers who are looking for new employees. These requisitions hold the data about the job requirements that will be matched with the candidates' data.

Note that the whole system works for internal candidates as well as for external ones. With Version 6.0, succession planning is included as an explicit component represented by its own role, the Succession Planner. This shows an important development within mySAP HCM: Recruiting and personnel development get more and more integrated in the **Talent Management** solution. With this development, the software is ahead of many HR departments, where these two functions are still much too separated from each other. As a matter of fact, recruitment and personnel development are often alternative or even hybrid solutions to the same problem. So, they should be dealt with together as mySAP HCM suggests.

7.2.2 Process and Roles

The application is based on several roles, which are described in detail in Section 7.3. A role is not merely a set of authorizations, as it is sometimes understood. In the context of E-Recruiting, a role represents a set of functions together with the corresponding user interface tailored to the requirements of the role. The most important roles and their interactions are represented in Figure 7.2. This figure shows the main process, starting with a candidate's interest in the company and the creation of a vacancy, up to the application. Of course, this process as shown is rather simplified as it does not take into account the various outcomes each step could have. It merely concentrates on "the most interesting" outcomes that keep the process going.

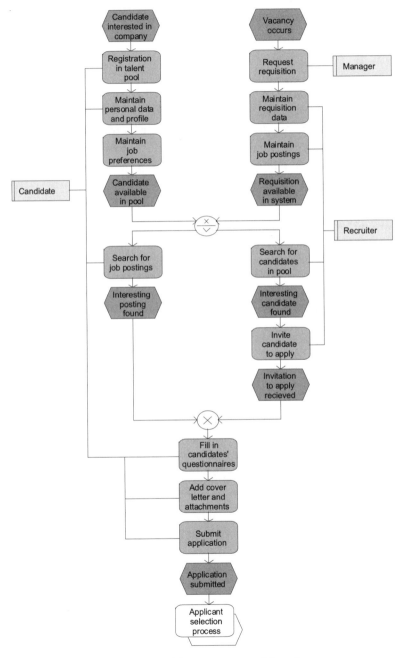

Figure 7.2 Process Overview: Candidate, Manager, and Recruiter

The first part of the process shows two independent branches:

▶ The candidate registers in the talent pool and maintains some data.

▶ A manager needs a new employee and requests a requisition, which is created by the recruiter along with one or more postings.

The second part of the process shows, how the candidate and the requisition—or rather a job posting contained in the requisition—can get together. There are two ways for this to happen:

▶ The candidate searches for interesting positions and finds a match.

▶ The recruiter searches for candidates matching his requisition and finds one. In this case, he would invite the candidate to apply for the position in question and provide all necessary data.

In both cases, the candidate will complete his or her data. Usually he or she will upload a cover letter and other attachments and may have to fill in one or several questionnaires. This done, he or she can submit the application.

Of course the process doesn't stop there, but will go the usual course of a selection process with correspondence, interviews, etc., and further roles are likely to be involved. The process flow is controlled by so called process templates (see Section 7.2.4) together with SAP Workflow.

In the following sections, we will discuss the most important concepts of the solution and then look at the different roles.

7.2.3 Requisitions

Together with the candidates themselves, requisitions are the central objects of the whole solution. Requisitions provide the means to get vacancies communicated to the users of the talent warehouse as well as to all other persons involved.

Each requisition contains one or more job postings that are dealt with together and have similar requirements. Each job posting can be published via one or more publications (see Figure 7.3).

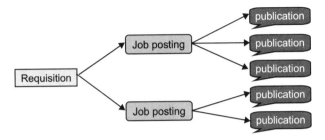

Figure 7.3 Structure of a Requisition

A requisition is maintained in nine steps, which do not all have to occur in every organization.

1. Maintain general job information, which contains administrative data about the requisition process and the basic job details such as description, function, and salary (see Figure 7.4).

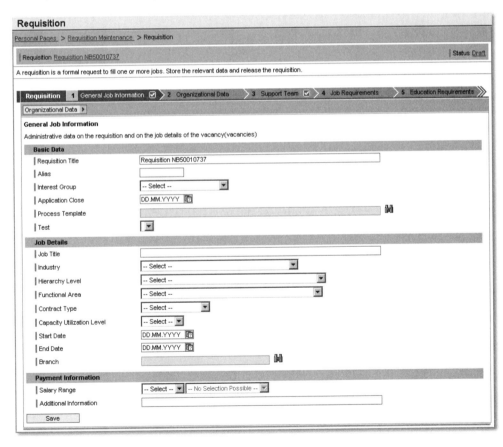

Figure 7.4 Creating a Requisition

2. Maintain organizational data.

3. Define the support team: This is the team working with the requisition in several roles (see Figure 7.5). You needn't define all possible roles for a requisition. The extent to which you define them depends on your process. Generally a recruiter and a requesting manager are involved at least. Other roles that could be involved include a decision maker to approve the postings, an administrator, or a data-entry assistant.

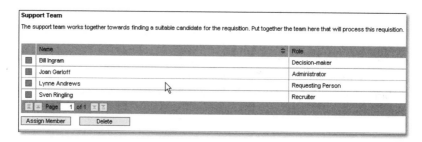

Figure 7.5 Defining the Support Team

4. Maintain job requirements relating to the employment experience of the future position holder.

5. Maintain education requirements.

6. Add attachments (such as a detailed job description in the form of a PDF file).

7. Set the status of the requisition; only if the requisition is released can the included postings can be published for the talent pool.

8. The data overview shows the recruiter, what data has been maintained so that he can easily identify any missing data.

9. In the last step, the job postings are included in the requisition.

Figure 7.4 shows the design of a step-by-step procedure typical for the E-Recruiting solution. A step that is often included in such procedures is the data overview, though this is not shown in the figure. Step nine leads to another step-by-step procedure as shown in Figure 7.6. While the requisition is an object for merely internal use (though the data assigned, such as salary and requirements, has important external effects), the job posting is meant for the outside world. This is clear particularly when you note the multilingual descriptions that can be seen on the lower tabs in Figure 7.6. After all, it is not the requisition but the job (posting), a candidate is looking for.

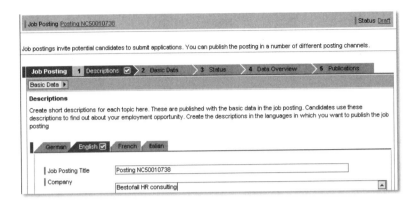

Figure 7.6 Creating a Job Posting

Most of the data a job posting needs is already maintained on the level of the requisition, so there are only five steps involved in creating the posting:

1. The general description

2. Some basic data of administrative character

3. The status, which has a similar meaning as the status of the requisition

4. The data overview mentioned above

5. The publications of the posting (see Figure 7.7).

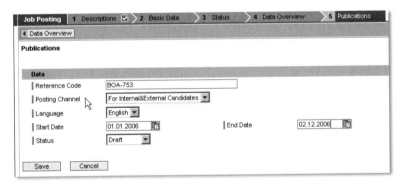

Figure 7.7 Maintaining a Publication

Readers who are familiar with the traditional solution described in Chapter 6, *Recruitment*, will be pleased to see that it is not necessary to create a new posting for each publication. Instead, it is possible to assign several publications to one posting. In this regard, the data structure of the E-Recruiting solution does represent the real world much better than the traditional solution. The publication gets most of its data from the posting and the requisition, so that most important information is the posting channel and the time period through which the publication is continued. As with requisitions and postings, the publication has a status. The status shown in Figure 7.7 is "draft," which means, that it cannot be seen by candidates. A publication can only be "released," when both the posting and the requisition are released.

7.2.4 Process Templates

The tracking process of an application for a particular posting is defined by a so-called process template. It consists of an ordered set of process steps and activities and is assigned to a requisition. Through the template, the recruiter is guided through the process, but he is not forced to perform all steps or to perform them in a predefined order.

Although the process template does more or less take the role of actions, activities and the feature PACTV of the traditional recruitment solution, there are some significant differences.

▶ A process template is defined by the end-user (e.g., the recruiter) in the normal application, while the feature PACTV must be maintained in customizing.

▶ The concept of the process template is more flexible. It is much easier to establish different processes for different target groups.

▶ To achieve the same level of guidance, workflow must be included.

The concept of the process template has four levels:

1. The process template itself (e.g., "High potentials North America")

2. A set of process steps or sub-processes (e.g., "Application-Entry" or "Prescreening") is assigned to the template. They are called just "process" in the system.

3. A set of activities (e.g., "first interview" or "rejection after interview") is assigned to each process. Note, that the types of activities as well as the processes available are defined in customizing (see Section 7.4.5 for this and for the categories of activities). Only the assignment can be done by the recruiter.

4. Special content such as letters or questionnaires (see Section 7.2.5) can be assigned to each activity.

The recruiter can create a new process template via the path **Process Templates · Create Process Template**. At first, some header data as shown in Figure 7.8 must be entered. The most important data is the status. The template can only be assigned to a requisition when it has the status "released." You should only release it, when it is definitely ready, as later changes can be difficult, when the template is already included in a requisition.

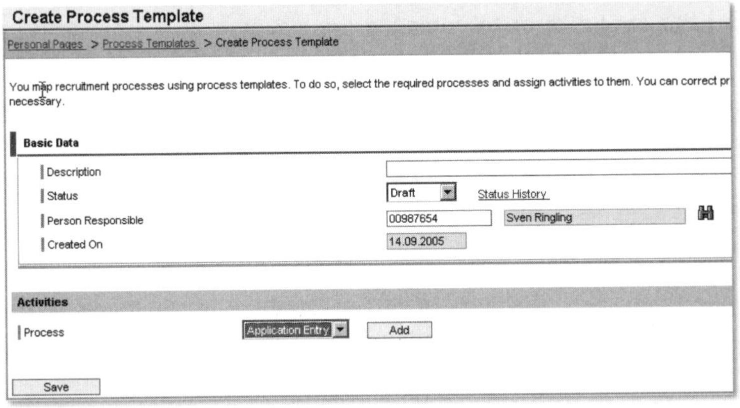

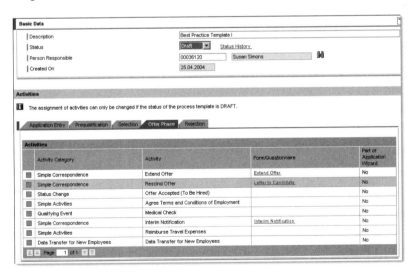

Figure 7.8 Header Data of a Process Template

Figure 7.9 shows a complete process template in which the processes "Application Entry," "Prequalification," "Selection," "Offer Phase" and "Rejection" are represented by the five tabs. Eight activities are assigned to the process "Offer Phase," and three of them have a letter form assigned.

Figure 7.9 Process Template with Five Processes

7.2.5 Questionnaires

Questionnaires are a very flexible tool that allows to get almost every information from or about a candidate in a well structured way. There are two types of questionnaires:

▶ General questionnaires, that can be used to get additional information from the candidate or to enter the impression that the manager or decision-maker got from the candidate in an interview.

▶ EEO questionnaires are designed for the specific purpose of obtaining data necessary to comply with the U.S. EEO (Equal Employment Opportunities) regulations. EEO questionnaires are based on the same concept as general questionnaires but contain a special type of questions.

Each questionnaire is composed of a set of questions from a pool of available questions. Both questions and questionnaires can be maintained by the end-user, usually the recruiter or an administrator. Each question can be assigned to several questionnaires.

As with process templates, the status field is important fro questionnaires and questions. Both can only be used, when the status is "released." Keep the status set on "draft" as long as the question or questionnaire is not completed.

The questions for general questionnaires can be of five different types.

▶ Single selection: a field where an answer from a given choice of predefined answers can be selected.

▶ Input field: a field where a short text can be maintained freely.

▶ Multiple selections: more than one answer can be selected from a given choice of answers.

▶ Predefined scale: the answer can be chosen from a scale defined in customizing.

▶ Input area: an area to maintain a text; similar to the input field, but with more space.

Figure 7.10 shows one example for each of these types and Figure 7.11 shows them included in a questionnaire in the preview mode. This is exactly how a questionnaire would look to the candidate or anybody else asked to fill it in online.

▣	Have you ever bought a product from our company?	Single Selection
▣	Describe your experience in intercultural management	Input Field
▣	Which of these countries have you ever worked in?	Multiple Selection
▣	How would you rate your coffee brewing skills?	Predefined Scale
▣	Describe you prblem solving approach!	Input Area

Figure 7.10 Questions of Five Different Types

Have you ever bought a product from our company?
- ⦿ | Not Specified
- ○ | Yes
- ○ | No
- ○ | Not sure

Describe your experience in intercultural management

Which of these countries have you ever worked in?
- ☐ | Canada
- ☐ | USA
- ☐ | Bolivia
- ☐ | United Kingdom
- ☐ | Germany
- ☐ | Sweden
- ☐ | Namibia
- ☐ | India

How would you rate your coffee brewing skills?
- ⦿ | Not Specified
- ○ | Very limited
- ○ | Limited
- ○ | Elementary
- ○ | Adequate
- ○ | Average
- ○ | Above average
- ○ | High
- ○ | Very High
- ○ | Excellent

Describe you prblem solving approach!

Figure 7.11 The Five Question Types in Preview

The maintenance of questions can be accessed by the recruiter via the activity **Question Maintenance** in the box **Administration**. Then he receives an overview, as shown in Figure 7.12, where he can display, change or create new questions. The questions are assigned to one of four tabs for structuring purposes:

▶ Other

▶ Candidate related

▶ Decision-maker related

▶ Job related

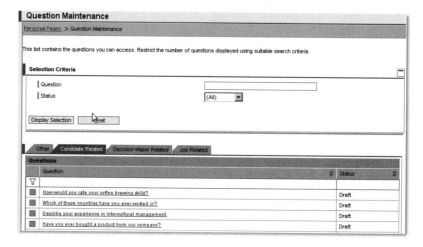

Figure 7.12 Question Maintenance—Overview

Figure 7.13 shows, how an input field question is created. Just maintain the text of the question as it shall presented on the questionnaire and choose **Input field** as the response type. When the question is ready for use in questionnaires, change the status to "released." As there are no predefined answers, the lower part of the screen containing the responses is empty.

In Figure 7.14, a question with a multiple selection is maintained. Here, you have to assign all the possible responses. These are taken from a catalogue of responses that can be maintained by the recruiter. Make sure that responses are re-used whenever possible. Especially common answers like "Yes" or "No," will occur very often in the catalogue, when you do not check whether a response you need is already available before you create a new one.

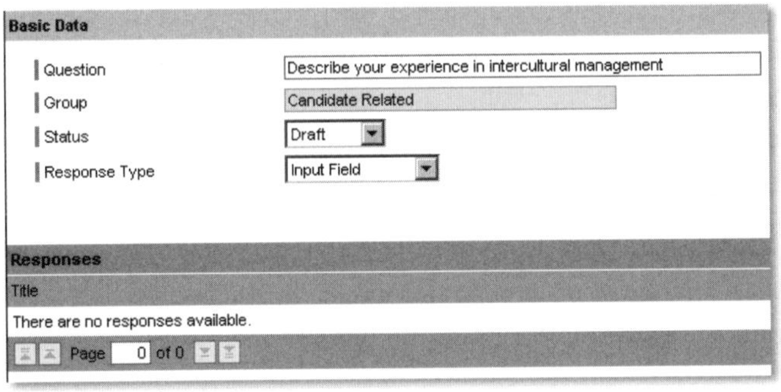

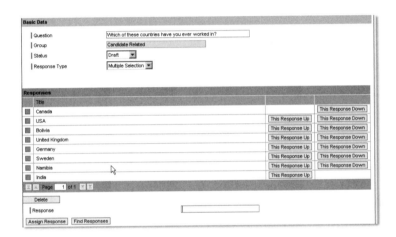

Figure 7.13 Maintain a Question with an Input Field

Figure 7.14 Maintain a Question with Multiple Selection

EEO questions are very similar to other questions. However, there are the additional fields **Reporting Area** and **Field** to make sure the data complies with the requirements of EEO reporting (see Figure 7.15). The options for these fields are maintained in customizing and come with a default setting from SAP.

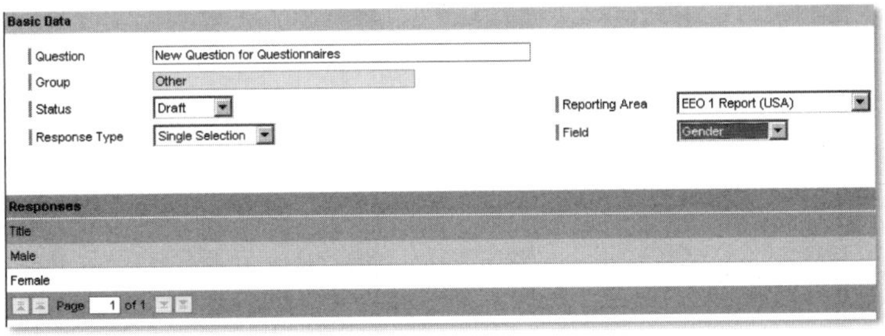

Figure 7.15 Maintain EEO Question

Once the necessary questions are available, the recruiter can start building questionnaires using the item **Questionnaire Maintenance** in the box **Administration**. Because it is possible to create new questions right out of the questionnaire-maintenance screen, you can proceed to this step right away. However, if there are several questions to be maintained, it is more convenient to stick to the sequence described here.

The first screen of the questionnaire maintenance looks exactly as for the question maintenance (see Figure 7.16) and has the same purpose.

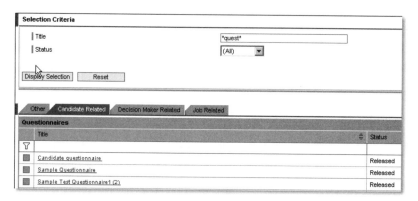

Figure 7.16 Questionnaire Maintenance—Overview

The maintenance of questionnaires involves three steps:

▶ Maintain a title

▶ Assign questions and define their sequence (see Figure 7.17)

▶ Rate responses. Besides the rating of the responses (that is giving marks to each possible answer), some responses can also be declared to be the "expected response." A candidate who does not select an expected response is deemed unsuitable. For example, when a specific job requires that the candidate has worked in Sweden before, then your questionnaire could include the question "In which of these countries have you worked before?" with the answer "Sweden" an expected response within the multiple selection. Note, that the rating of the responses does not happen in question maintenance but always in the context of the questionnaire.

While maintaining the questionnaire, you can get a preview with the "attributes," showing the whole questionnaire with the rating of each answer and the expected-response flags (see Figure 7.18).

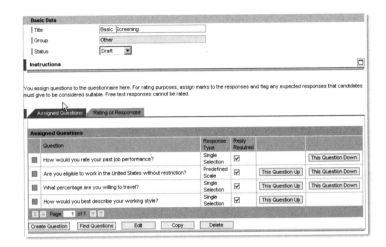

Figure 7.17 Assign Questions to a Questionnaire

Attributes of Questionnaire

This page displays the technical attributes of the questionnaire. The questions are displayed with the response rating. You can also see whether a response is an expected response.

Basic Screening (Maximum Score : 151)

Please complete the following questions below.

	Marks	Expected Response
How would you rate your past job performance? *		
⊙ Not Specified	0	
○ Unsatisfactory	0	
○ Poor	0	
○ Average	10	
○ Above average	40	
○ Excellent	50	
Are you eligible to work in the United States without restriction? *		
⊙ Not Specified	0	
○ No	0	
○ Yes	1	⚑
What percentage are you willing to travel? *		
⊙ Not Specified	0	
○ 0-25%	0	
○ 26-50%	25	
○ 51-75%	50	
○ Up to 100%	50	
How would you best describe your working style? *		
⊙ Not Specified	0	
○ Very independent	25	
○ Independent, but like to work in a team	50	
○ Prefer to work in a team	0	

Questionnaire Preview

Figure 7.18 Preview of Questionnaire with Attributes

When the questionnaires are ready, they can be included in the process via the process template. An applicant can be asked to fill in a questionnaire, either as one step of the application wizard when applying for a job or via an e-mail sent by the recruiter. This e-mail contains a link to the questionnaire within the E-Recruiting platform and requires the candidate to log in before answering the questions online.

7.2.6 Further Important Terms

Talent Pool

The talent pool comprises all candidates registered in the platform, including internal candidates.

Talent Groups

Via the respective item in the **Talent Relationship Management** box, the recruiter can assign candidates to talent groups as a measure of talent segmentation.

Object types

There are five types of objects used in the e-recruitment solution:

▶ Candidates (NA)

▶ Requisition (NB)

▶ Posting (NC)

▶ Application (ND)

▶ Candidacy (NE) — a candidacy occurs only when a candidate is assigned to a job posting. When this has not (yet) happened, it is an application.

Technically, these objects are used much like object types of organizational management, and the data is stored in infotypes 5100 to 5199. However, this structure is hidden from the end-user. In Customizing, it is important to know the object types, as they are sometimes used to assign any items such as activities.

Statuses and Status Reasons

As in the traditional recruitment solution, statuses are used in E-Recruiting as well. However, different statuses are available per object type. The statuses for an application or a candidacy are:

- ▶ Draft
- ▶ In process
- ▶ Withdrawn
- ▶ Rejected
- ▶ To be hired

The statuses for a posting are:

- ▶ Draft
- ▶ Released
- ▶ Closed (meaning "do not use anymore")
- ▶ To be deleted (but it can only be deleted when it is no longer used in active processes)

The same statuses can apply to requisitions, but for those there is a fifth status called "on hold."

A candidate can have only two statuses:

- ▶ Locked (meaning that this user is not considered for vacancies)
- ▶ Released (meaning that this candidate can work on the platform and can be found by the recruiter for openings)

This is an important difference to the traditional recruitment solution: The status of a candidate does not correspond to the status of his of her application. This difference results from the completely different concept of E-Recruiting. The candidate is considered to be interesting not simply because one or more applications are pending. The long-term relationship E-Recruiting is aiming at can begin long before the first application and can go on afterwards.

Status reasons can be maintained in Customizing and assigned when the status of an object is changed through an activity.

7.3 Looking at the Different Roles in E-Recruiting

As noted earlier, the E-Recruiting solution is completely role-based. Each role is characterized by a set of functions. These are displayed on the start page, the so called **Personal Pages**, in several boxes representing a kind of functional areas (see Figure 7.21).

All roles have a box called **Personal Settings** with one item as shown in Figure 7.19. These settings do not affect the process flow in any way but are merely used to adapt the user interface according to the user's preferences.

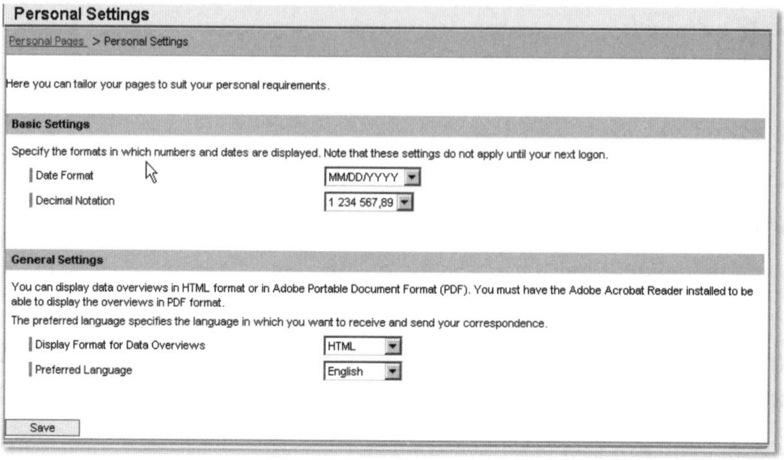

Figure 7.19 Personal Settings for All Users

7.3.1 The External Candidate

The external candidate is probably the most important role, because he is the one you want to attract to your company and who is most likely to be put off when the application is not well designed. As the visual appearance is more important for this role than for any other, we support this section of the book with plenty of screenshots for the reader to get an impression of the solution from the candidate's point of view. Note that most of the fields available for maintenance and the dropdown lists are subject to custom configuration and that the layout is usually adapted to the corporate design of the organization. These points apply not only for the candidate but for all roles.

The first step for an external candidate is the registration (see Figure 7.20). This is a process very similar to other registration processes known elsewhere on the Web, be it for an online shopping portal or a communication platform. An important issue here is the data privacy statement. According to the laws of many countries, you must make sure that the candidate accepts such a statement, and you may need different statements when working in different countries.

Registration

Do you want to find out more about your career options in our company?

We are constantly looking for talented and motivated new employees who can contribute to the success of our company. Take a look at our Job&Career pages and you will find valuable information about our company and current employment opportunities. If you are interested in a job, you can apply for it online directly. If you do not find any suitable vacancies but would still like to work for our company, you can register with us. We will contact you as soon as an employment opportunity arises that may interest you.

Name

| First Name * | Steven |
| Last Name * | Tether |

User Data

User Name *	steven
Password *	••••••••
Repeat Password *	••••••••
E-Mail *	steven.tether@hotmail.com

Data Privacy Statement

We endeavour to ensure that the data you submit to us remains confidential and is used only for the purposes stated in the data privacy statement. Please confirm acceptance of our data privacy statement. Data Privacy Statement

☑ Yes, I have read the data privacy statement and I accept it

Register

Figure 7.20 Registration with Acceptance of Privacy Statement

After registration and with each further logging in, the candidate gets his or her personal pages as shown in Figure 7.21. Besides the maintenance of personal data and communication data and the personal settings seen on the right side of the screen, there are two major functional areas in this role:

▶ The maintenance of the candidate profile

▶ The employment opportunities where the candidate can search for jobs and submit applications

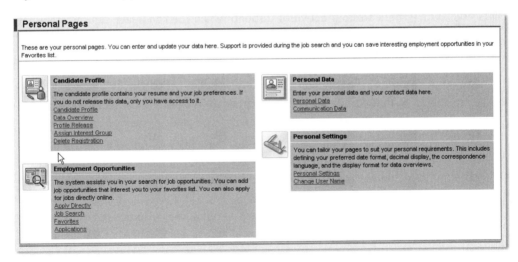

Personal Pages

These are your personal pages. You can enter and update your data here. Support is provided during the job search and you can save interesting employment opportunities in your Favorites list.

Candidate Profile

The candidate profile contains your resume and your job preferences. If you do not release this data, only you have access to it.
Candidate Profile
Data Overview
Profile Release
Assign Interest Group
Delete Registration

Personal Data

Enter your personal data and your contact data here.
Personal Data
Communication Data

Personal Settings

You can tailor your pages to suit your personal requirements. This includes defining your preferred date format, decimal display, the correspondence language, and the display format for data overviews.
Personal Settings
Change User Name

Employment Opportunities

The system assists you in your search for job opportunities. You can add job opportunities that interest you to your favorites list. You can also apply for jobs directly online.
Apply Directly
Job Search
Favorites
Applications

Figure 7.21 Personal Pages for an External Candidate

As one of the strong points of E-Recruiting is its global availability, a multilingual user interface can be very important. Figure 7.22 shows what a Spanish-speaking candidate would see on her personal pages. For the benefit of the reader of this book, however, we will stick to English in the remaining part of this chapter.

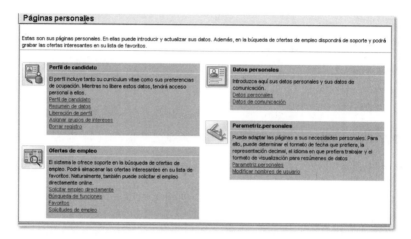

Figure 7.22 Personal Pages in Spanish: a Multilingual Platform

After registration, the candidate is not obliged to maintain any further data. It is his or her choice whether he maintains a comprehensive profile right at the beginning or just looks around a bit for interesting jobs. However, the employer may define some mandatory fields.

There are four activities through which the candidate can maintain data about himself:

▶ The first step would probably be to maintain some **Personal Data** such as gender and date of birth in the box **Personal Data**.

▶ In the same box via **Communication Data** the contact data such as e-mail address, phone numbers, and postal address are maintained.

▶ In the box **Candidate Profile** via the activity **Assign Interest Group** he can choose a group to be assigned to. This can include groups such as executives, lower management, technical staff, internships, etc. It is up to the employer whether to offer this option and how to use it. Considering that the profile data is extensive and not always maintained completely, the interest group can be handy for a first segmentation of the talent pool.

▶ The most important activity is the maintenance of the Candidate Profile, which can also be found in the box **Candidate Profile**. This is what we want to focus on in the following paragraphs.

The candidate profile is maintained in eight steps, and the user is guided through these with the navigation bar shown in Figure 7.23. It is not necessary to complete each step before going to the next one. It is up to the candidate how much information he wants to reveal at which point of time. Although it is tempting to demand a huge amount of data from the candidates before considering them for any postings, it may be wise to allow candidates to concentrate on the essentials. With more and more online recruiting sites available working in a similar way, candidates may not want to be bothered with maintaining too much data again and again. After all, the data is available in the resume and other attachments, so that from a candidate's point of view it is redundant work to enter the data online again for each employer. While demanding extensive profile data makes the process more efficient and reporting more interesting for the employer, some candidates might be put off.

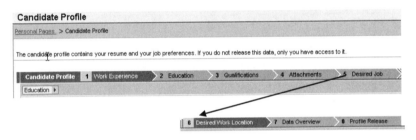

Figure 7.23 Candidate Profile: Eight Steps

Here are the eight steps of the profile maintenance as shown in Figure 7.23:

1. In the work-experience step, data for all former jobs can be maintained. Figure 7.24 shows an example with data maintained for one position held by the candidate in the past. The data refers to the employer and to the position itself. While some fields can be freely filled with any text, others have predefined options in dropdown boxes. These options (here and for the following steps as well) are mostly defined via Customizing in a straightforward way.

   As there can be more than one former employers, the work experience view consists of a list with all former positions (see Figure 7.25), and each entry can be maintained in the detailed view as described above. This combination of overview list and detailed view is also used for other steps.

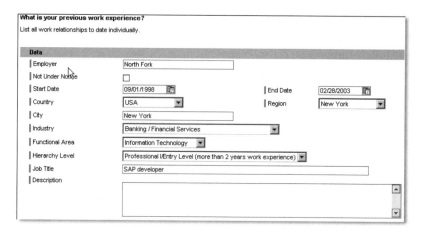

Figure 7.24 Work Experience: One Former Employer in Detail

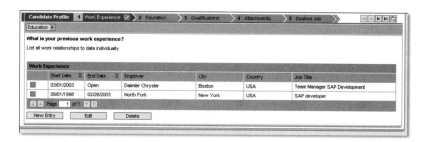

Figure 7.25 Work Experience Overview

2. The education view is designed in exactly the same way. A list of educational institutes attended by the candidate is built via a detailed view, where data concerning the institute (e.g., school or university) and the type, content, and grades of the education (e.g., Ph.D in information science/cryptology rated "summa cum laude").

3. Under **Qualifications**, the candidate describes his skills profile. The skills the employer is particularly interested in are available in several qualification groups and the candidate can select the skills he has and rate them in a self-assessment (see Figure 7.26). The catalogue behind these qualifications is based on the same technical framework as the qualifications catalogue used in the personnel-development component of mySAP HCM. For information on its maintenance, refer to the SAP PRESS book HR Personnel Planning and Development using SAP. However the same catalogue is rarely used for E-Recruiting and for personnel development for several reasons:

- The internal skills catalogue is probably much too large to bother the candidates with.

- The internal catalogue may include skills descriptions that cannot be understood by an external person.

- Not all skills that are interesting from a development point of view are necessarily interesting for the recruiter and the other way round.

- You may not want the outside world to see your full skills catalogue. This might not only allow insides into your HR processes but also betray your business strategy to your competitor (assuming that your personnel development is aligned to the overall strategy of your organization).

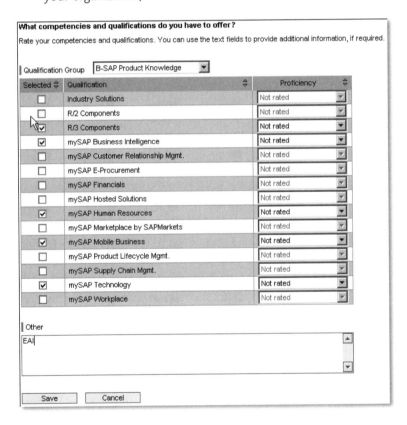

Figure 7.26 Qualifications per Group

4. Attachments can be all kinds of documents such as Microsoft Word, PDF, or TIF. However, you should restrict the options for the candidate to those document types you can process easily with your IT infrastructure. We recommend accepting PDF files as this is a widely accept for-

mat. As most candidates will have access to an office product creating DOC files but not necessarily to a PDF converter, it will be difficult to exclude the DOC format. Figure 7.27 shows how an attachment is uploaded and included into the profile. The attachment type describes for the content. The types allowed are maintained in customizing and can include reference letters, resumes, certificates, etc. Cover letters are also uploaded as attachments, but in most cases this will only happen, when an application is submitted but not when the profile is maintained initially.

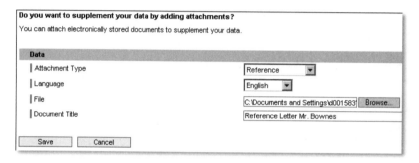

Figure 7.27 Upload Attachments

5. For the recruiter, it is not only important to get data about the candidate, her experience and her skills, but also to learn about her expectations regarding her future job. Moreover, it is important to show the candidate that the employer is not only interested in what he can get from the candidate but that he also listens to the candidate's expectations. Figure 7.28 shows how employment references concerning the industry, functional area, and hierarchy level are maintained as well as expectations towards the contract such as salary and working time.

6. The maintenance of the desired work location is very similar to the step describes before. This is particularly important for organizations with various locations.

7. Step seven gives the candidate an overview of the data maintained, so that he or she can perform corrections or add missing data before releasing the profile.

8. The profile release (see Figure 7.29) is the final step. With the release, the profile is available for the recruiter so that he can find the candidate and offer her appropriate jobs. As long as the data is not yet maintained as the candidate wants it to be or for as long as she does not yet want to be contacted for job offers, she leaves the profile status "locked." Note

that in this step the candidate is reminded of the data privacy statement she accepted upon registration. This acceptance cannot be withdrawn, because if it were, the candidate would have to leave the talent pool.

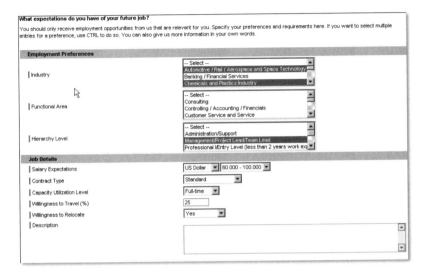

Figure 7.28 Expectations of the Desired Job

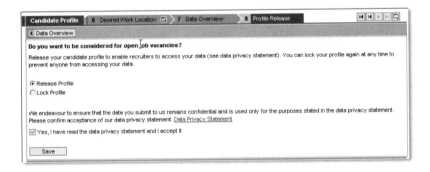

Figure 7.29 Release Candidates Profile

Now, that the profile is released, the candidate can wait for the employer to contact her. However, she also can actively search for jobs and apply. To search for jobs, she can use the activity **Job Search** in the **Employment Opportunities** box. As Figure 7.30 indicates, there are two options for searching, which can also be combined:

▶ Full-text search

▶ Search using the predefined criteria as they are maintained as information in the requisition data

Each search can be saved as a search query and thus be re-used later.

Note that the match percentage is calculated a bit awkwardly. The calculation scheme used by the search engine is not really transparent and does as a rule not deliver exactly 100% when all search criteria are perfectly matched. However, the percentage is nevertheless a good indicator for the matching. Just be sure you understand it not as a true percentage but as an open ranking, and—even if you are looking for perfect matches only—do not set the minimum matching percentage to 100%.

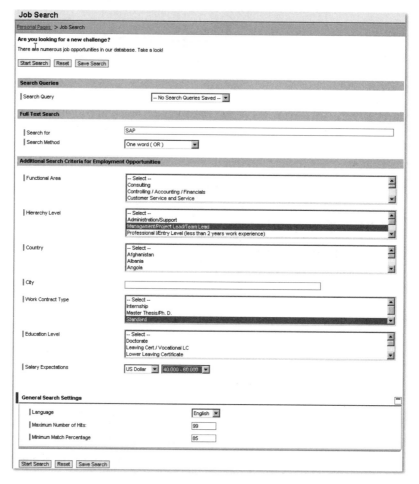

Figure 7.30 Searching for Job Postings

The candidate then gets a result list with jobs matching her search (see Figure 7.31) and has the following options for each posting:

- ▶ Display the data overview (see Figure 7.33)
- ▶ Add to the favorites list
- ▶ Apply

When the jobs are already on the favorites list or an application has already been submitted, there are even more options as described in the following paragraph.

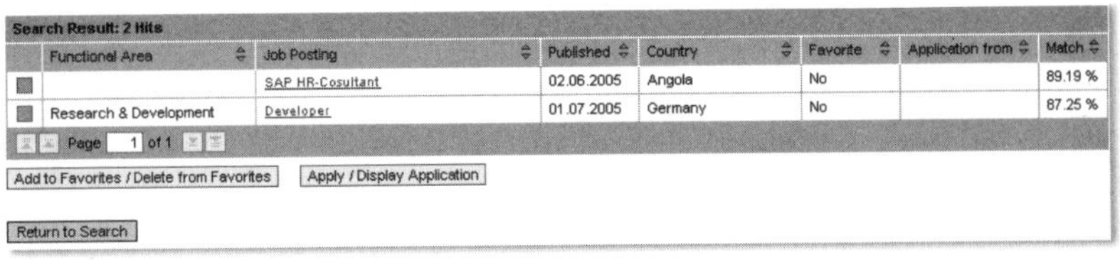

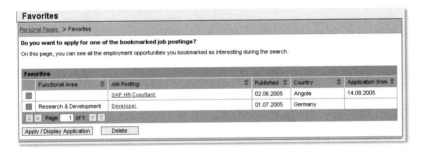

Figure 7.31 Results: Interesting Job Postings

Once a job has been added to the favorite list, it can be accessed through the activity Favorites in the **Employment Opportunities** box. Apart from displaying the data overview (see Figure 7.33) and applying for the job, the posting can also be removed from the favorites list (see Figure 7.32), and existing applications can be displayed.

Figure 7.32 Favorite Job Postings with Applications

The data overview for the job posting (see Figure 7.33) can be displayed in PDF or HTML format, according to the personal settings (see Figure 7.19). In our example, PDF format has been chosen. In this case, the data overview is not used to check data for completeness and correctness but to get information about the posting. The data overviews referred to on other occasions (e.g., requisition or candidate profile) look similar.

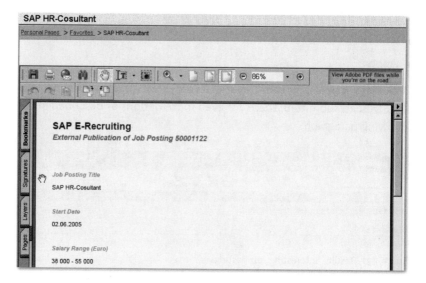

Figure 7.33 Overview of a Job Posting as a PDF File

The candidate has three ways to apply for a job:

▶ Applying for a job found on a search result list.

▶ Applying for a job on the favorites list.

▶ Applying directly for a job using the activity **Apply Directly** in the **Employment Opportunities** box. To do this, the candidate must know the reference code of the job posting (e.g., from a job advertisement in a newspaper).

In each of these three cases, the application wizard is started. As indicated in Figure 7.34 and Figure 7.35, this wizard guides the candidate through ten steps. However, steps one to seven contain activities already done when maintaining the candidate profile. So, if the candidate thinks that her profile is complete, she might as well start with the data overview in step eight to check the data and than proceed to the two final steps. Other steps could be included, however (especially questionnaires), depending on the custom configuration.

These final steps (see Figure 7.35) include:

▶ Uploading a cover letter (similar to uploading other attachments)

▶ Sending the application

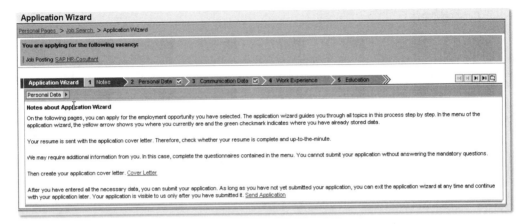

Figure 7.34 Application Wizard: Apply and Complete Profile Information

Figure 7.35 Application Wizard: Send Application with Cover Letter

All applications can be accessed via the activity Applications in the box **Employment Opportunities**.

After the application is submitted, the process will not be completed. On the contrary: If the candidate is well suited for the job, there will be many more steps including correspondence, questionnaires, interviews, etc., where other roles are involved as well (especially the recruiter). These steps depend very much on custom configuration and on the process template assigned to the requisition. How this can be designed has already been discussed in Section 7.2.

7.3.2 The Internal Candidate

The role of the internal candidate is very similar to that of the external one, as can be seen from its personal pages in Figure 7.36.

The main differences arise from the fact that the employee is already represented in mySAP HR with his master data, while some activities of the external candidate are not available here.

An employee could register and apply like any external candidate. However, this would not make much sense because he would have to reveal his identity when he applies.

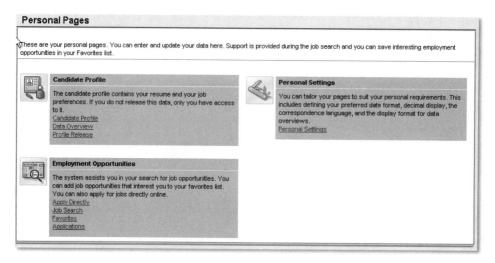

Figure 7.36 Personal Pages for Internal Candidate

7.3.3 The Manager

The requesting manager plays a very important role in the whole process. Besides the candidate, he is one of the persons who initiate the process as shown in Figure 7.2.

As the personal pages in Figure 7.37 indicate, the manager can he involved in defining the requisition and in the selection process. It is strongly recommended that each manager performs these activities himself on the system, as it is the most efficient process. This is especially true for the selection activities. However it will often happen that the communication between the e-recruitment system and the manager is paper-based and involves an administrative assistant or the recruiter in actually maintaining the data. It is a major task in any e-recruitment project to convince the managers of the added value they get from working directly with the system and using the possibilities of interactivity.

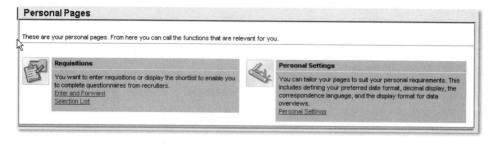

Figure 7.37 Personal Pages for Manager

If the managers do not feel able or claim not to have enough time to maintain the data of the requisition request online, you may have to make a concession to them by having this done by the recruiter. As this is quite a lot of data to maintain (see Figure 7.38) and does not happen too often, you can get an efficient process in spite of this delegation. However, you should stick to a design where the manager is actively involved in the selection process online.

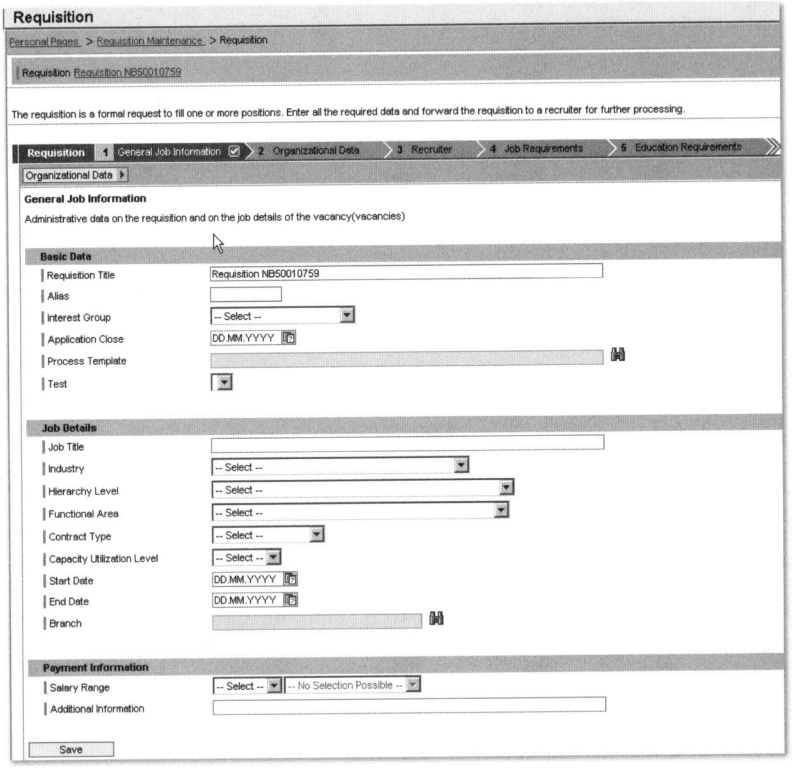

Figure 7.38 Requesting a Requisition

7.3.4 The Recruiter

As can be seen from its personal pages in Figure 7.39, the role of the recruiter has the broadest range of functions. We have already dealt with the content of the box Administration in Section 7.2.4 and Section 7.2.5 and with personal setting in at the beginning of Section 7.3. We will not go into detail regarding reporting. This can be freely defined via SAP Query based on three standard infosets or custom infosets (see Chapter 11, *Personnel Controlling*) or the Business Information Warehouse (BW).

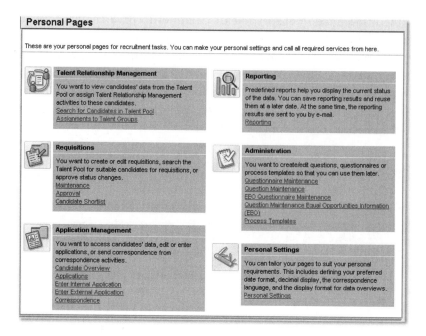

Personal Pages

These are your personal pages for recruitment tasks. You can make your personal settings and call all required services from here.

Talent Relationship Management

You want to view candidates' data from the Talent Pool or assign Talent Relationship Management activities to these candidates.
Search for Candidates in Talent Pool
Assignments to Talent Groups

Reporting

Predefined reports help you display the current status of the data. You can save reporting results and reuse them at a later date. At the same time, the reporting results are sent to you by e-mail.
Reporting

Requisitions

You want to create or edit requisitions, search the Talent Pool for suitable candidates for requisitions, or approve status changes.
Maintenance
Approval
Candidate Shortlist

Administration

You want to create/edit questions, questionnaires or process templates so that you can use them later.
Questionnaire Maintenance
Question Maintenance
EEO Questionnaire Maintenance
Question Maintenance Equal Opportunities Information (EEO)
Process Templates

Application Management

You want to access candidates' data, edit or enter applications, or send correspondence from correspondence activities.
Candidate Overview
Applications
Enter Internal Application
Enter External Application
Correspondence

Personal Settings

You can tailor your pages to suit your personal requirements. This includes defining your preferred date format, decimal display, the correspondence language, and the display format for data overviews.
Personal Settings

Figure 7.39 Personal Pages for the Recruiter

The three boxes on the left side remain for us to discuss here. Assignments to Talent Groups is the simpler activity in the box Talent Relationship Management. It is a straightforward method of talent segmentation where each candidate can be assigned to a group from a predefined list.

The more unusual activity is the **Search for Candidates in the Pool**. The search functionality (see Figure 7.40) is designed similarly to the search for jobs in the role of the external candidate, and everything explained there can be applied here as well.

However, there are two major differences:

▶ The search criteria can be weighted.

▶ Besides the normal search template elements, qualifications and questionnaires can be used for the search. The search templates are defined in Customizing.

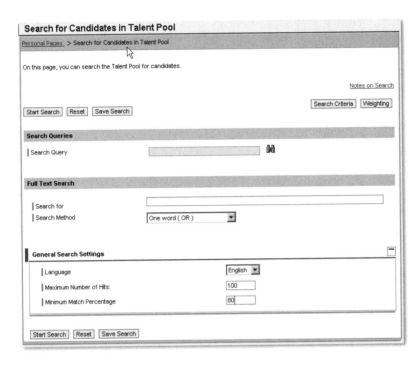

Figure 7.40 Recruiter Looks for Candidates in the Talent Pool

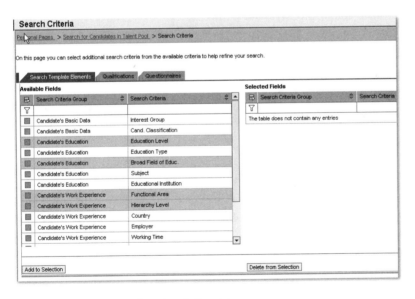

Figure 7.41 Search Criteria from Search Template

It may seem awkward to have the recruiter maintain all the search criteria. After all, the requirements for the job are maintained with the requi-

sition data and in theory could be used as search criteria. It can be argued, though, that these criteria are often too restrictive or that other criteria usually must be added. Although this may be true in many cases, it is one of the weak points of the system that at this point in the process no reference can be made to the data already maintained earlier. This is to some extent compensated by the feature that any search once conducted can be saved as a search query.

Figure 7.42 shows the precise search criteria and groups selected in Figure 7.41.

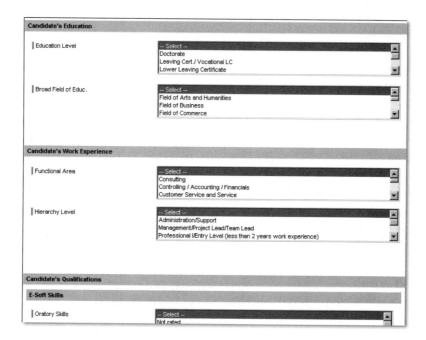

Figure 7.42 Filling in the Search Criteria

The maintenance and approval of requisitions have already been discussed. The remaining activity in the Requisitions box is the **Candidate Shortlist**. The recruiter can assign candidates to a short list for a posting and based on this short list he can organize the management of the requisitions and candidacies. Figure 7.43 shows the selection of assigned candidates ordered by process (the processes are represented by tabs). You can also see that the candidates can be ranked by criteria entered via the tab Ranking Criteria. For each candidate, the profile, the data overview, and the activities assigned can be displayed.

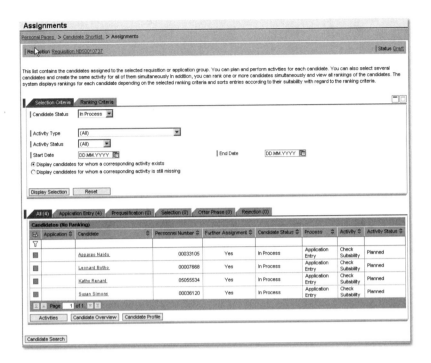

Figure 7.43 Working with Assigned Candidates

Most of the functions in the box Application Management are controlled via the process templates discussed in Section 7.2.4. As we did with the role of the external candidate, we won't take a detailed look at the process of application management here. However, we want to mention that the recruiter has the option to maintain an internal or external application with all the necessary data via the activities Enter Internal Application and Enter External Application. This is necessary if an application has not been submitted via the E-Recruiting system. Figure 7.44 shows how such a data entry screen could look.

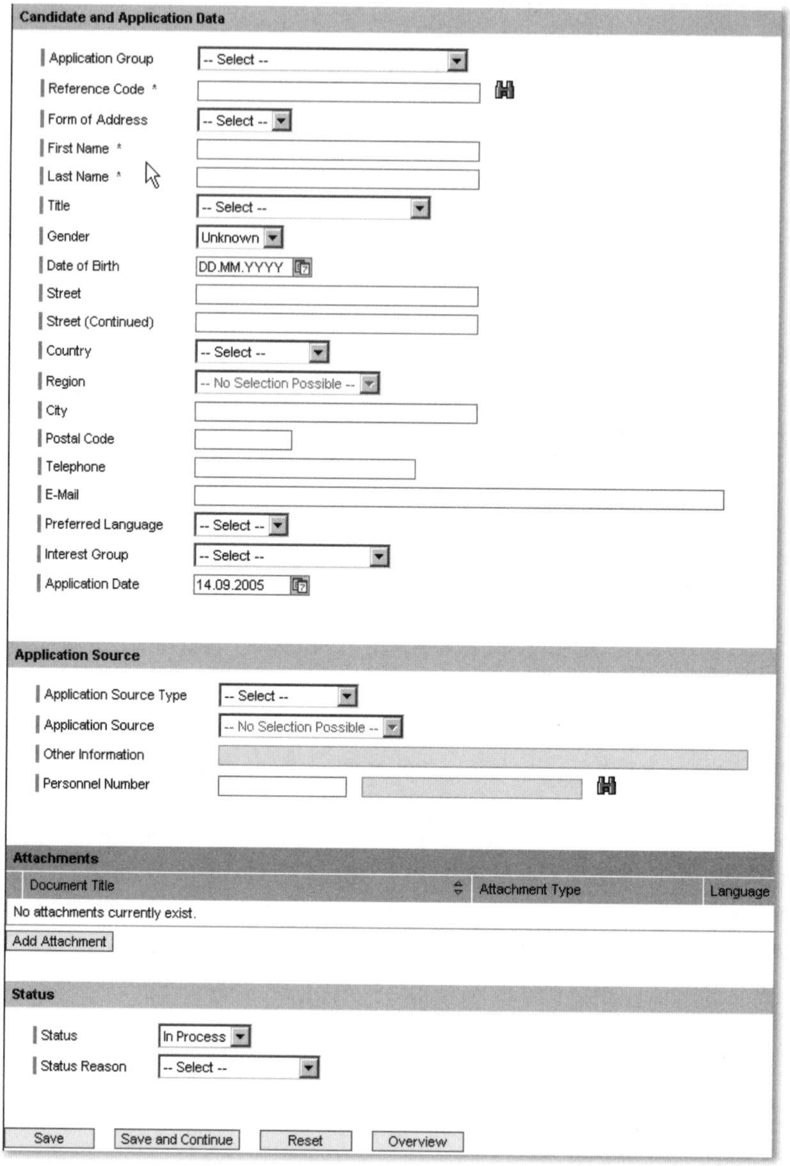

Candidate and Application Data

Application Group	-- Select --
Reference Code *	
Form of Address	-- Select --
First Name *	
Last Name *	
Title	-- Select --
Gender	Unknown
Date of Birth	DD.MM.YYYY
Street	
Street (Continued)	
Country	-- Select --
Region	-- No Selection Possible --
City	
Postal Code	
Telephone	
E-Mail	
Preferred Language	-- Select --
Interest Group	-- Select --
Application Date	14.09.2005

Application Source

Application Source Type	-- Select --
Application Source	-- No Selection Possible --
Other Information	
Personnel Number	

Attachments

Document Title	Attachment Type	Language
No attachments currently exist.		

Add Attachment

Status

Status	In Process
Status Reason	-- Select --

Save   Save and Continue   Reset   Overview

Figure 7.44 Entering an Application Manually

7.3.5 The Administrator

The administrator is responsible to provide the prerequisites for the management of candidates and requisitions:

▶ Maintain the internal users

▶ Delete the registration for external candidates and the external candidates. Because the users for external candidates are created automatically with registration, no user maintenance is required. However, it may be necessary to de-register inactive users.

▶ Maintain other current settings such as branches and talent groups.

All these functions are accessed via the administrator pages (see Figure 7.45.

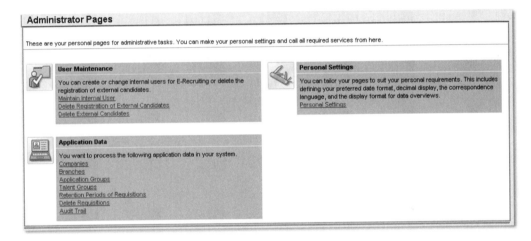

Figure 7.45 Administrator Pages

The administrator often is a key user or the person responsible for the customizing as well. His functions within the recruiting process itself are very limited.

7.3.6 Succession Planner

The succession planner is a new role with mySAP ERP 2005. We will not discuss it further, because succession planning is not the subject of this book. You can see from the start screen of the succession planner in Figure 7.46 that this role is similar to the role of the recruiter but is missing some of those functions. In particular, there is no application management included, as succession planning doesn't require applications.

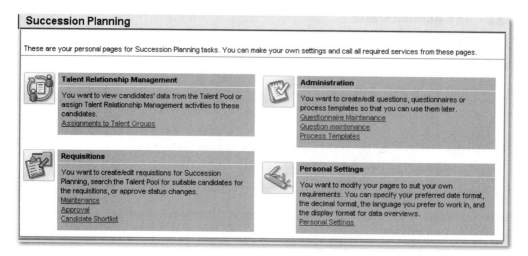

Succession Planning

These are your personal pages for Succession Planning tasks. You can make your own settings and call all required services from these pages.

Talent Relationship Management

You want to view candidates' data from the Talent Pool or assign Talent Relationship Management activities to these candidates.
Assignments to Talent Groups

Administration

You want to create/edit questions, questionnaires or process templates so that you can use them later.
Questionnaire Maintenance
Question maintenance
Process Templates

Requisitions

You want to create/edit requisitions for Succession Planning, search the Talent Pool for suitable candidates for the requisitions, or approve status changes.
Maintenance
Approval
Candidate Shortlist

Personal Settings

You want to modify your pages to suit your own requirements. You can specify your preferred date format, the decimal format, the language you prefer to work in, and the display format for data overviews.
Personal Settings

Figure 7.46 Personal Pages for Succession Planner

7.4 Customizing and Technology

The Customizing for E-Recruiting can be found in the IMG under **SAP E-Recruiting** and is divided into five major parts:

▶ Technical settings

▶ Basic settings

▶ Recruitment

▶ Succession planning

▶ Tools

It is neither possible nor necessary to describe all Customizing activities step by step. This is already done in the available documentation from SAP. We will discuss the first three points here and go into detail for several examples.

7.4.1 Technical Settings

Besides a variety of technical prerequisites, which should not be overlooked, and the configuration for reporting, we want to look at two points:

Start Pages

Via the IMG path **Technical Settings · User Interfaces · Start pages** you can decide how the start pages (personal pages) look like. This is done in three steps.

1. Define the links representing the activities. SAP delivers about 40 pre-defined functions.

2. Combine these links to form the groups representing the boxes on the start page.

3. Assign the groups to the start pages.

Field Configuration

Via the IMG path **Technical Settings · User Interfaces · Flexibilization · Fields · Modify Fields** in Interfaces, you can decide whether a field shall be displayed of hidden, input or output-only, optional or required.

Via the IMG path **Technical Settings · User Interfaces · Flexibilization · Fields · Define Additional** Fields you find a description how to create new fields via BAdIs. This is not possible for every single screen but for most of the screens where it could make sense.

7.4.2 Basic Settings

Besides the languages available, there are three aspects that can all be maintained in a straightforward way:

▶ Enterprise structure: companies are defined in a simple table and branches are assigned to them. Note that the branches come from the SAP business partner data.

▶ Attachment types: You define attachment types in a simple table and you can implement the BAdI **HRRCF00_DOC_UPLOAD** to perform specific checks on the attachments such as:

  ▶ File type

  ▶ Size of the file

  ▶ Number of files

  ▶ Virus check

You can even perform a conversion from one type to another via this BAdI, but you need suitable third-party software to do this.

7.4.3 Talent Warehouse

The Customizing for the talent warehouse is pretty straightforward, once you know what exactly is needed. Most of the Customizing items here define the options for fields with dropdown boxes such as:

- ▶ Industries (for work experience and desired employment)
- ▶ Education types
- ▶ Interest groups

As one example Figure 7.47 shows the maintenance of salary ranges reached via the IMG path **Talent Warehouse · Candidate · Work Experience/Desired Employment · Salary ranges · Define Salary Ranges**. Note that this table and some others are not only used in the candidate profile but in the requisition too.

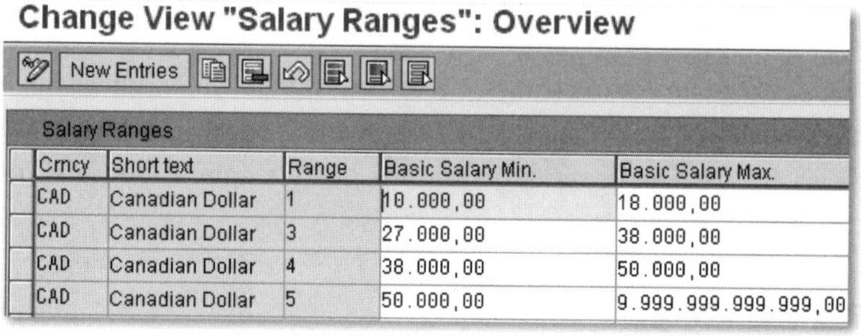

Change View "Salary Ranges": Overview

Crncy	Short text	Range	Basic Salary Min.	Basic Salary Max.
CAD	Canadian Dollar	1	10.000,00	18.000,00
CAD	Canadian Dollar	3	27.000,00	38.000,00
CAD	Canadian Dollar	4	38.000,00	50.000,00
CAD	Canadian Dollar	5	50.000,00	9.999.999.999.999,00

Figure 7.47 Maintain Salary Ranges

Another very important point here is the Customizing for the search functions. The definition of Search Profiles and Search Templates requires a considerable effort, especially when done for the first time. However it is worth the effort, as searching is a very important feature for candidates as well as for recruiters and it makes sense to adapt it as good as possible to your requirements. Each step is described in the SAP documentation within the IMG.

7.4.4 Applicant Tracking

This is probably the most intensive activity in Customizing, as the framework for process templates must be defined here.

We should examine the definition of scales for ranking and reporting. These scales are so called quality scales, which means that they contain clearly defined countable (discrete) proficiencies. Via the path **Applicant Tracking · Define Scales for Ranking and Reporting** you get the table shown in Figure 7.48, where each scale is defined by a text. Then, the proficiencies are assigned (see Figure 7.49).

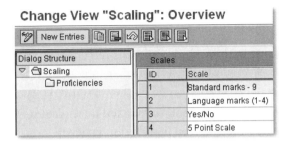

Figure 7.48 Maintain Scales

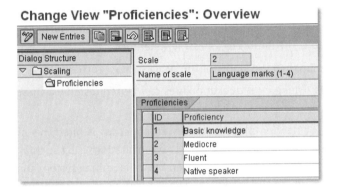

Figure 7.49 Define Proficiencies for a Scale

Each scale can be assigned to one or more scale types via the path **Applicant Tracking · Assign Scales to Scale Types**. This determines where the scale can be used. There are three scale types available:

▶ Candidate ranking

▶ Ranking of candidates' assignments to requisitions

▶ Weighting of criteria for Search&Match.

7.4.5 Activities

Although the Customizing for activities only provides the basis for the definition of process templates (outside Customizing) but does not control the process flow directly, you should know how your processes will look before doing this Customizing.

The first step would be to define the processes via the IMG path **Applicant Tracking · Activities · Define Processes**. The group must always be recruiting as we are not dealing with succession planning here.

The second step requires some effort. You have to define the activity types and assign them to one of the seven categories.

▶ Simple activities: They just serve as a task list for the recruiter but have no specific behavior (call requesting manager after interview). They contain the data field's status, due date, and employee responsible.

▶ Qualifying events: They refer to an event, so that additional data such as time and address must be maintained (e.g., first interview)

▶ Simple correspondence: Here a letter form is assigned (e.g., interim notification)

▶ Invitation: Activities of this category have a letter form assigned and refer to a qualifying event. This letter can include data of this qualifying event as well (e.g., invitation to assessment center).

▶ Status change: Change the status of the process (e.g., rejection).

▶ Questionnaires: Filling in of questionnaires can be requested via these activities.

▶ Data transfer for new employees: When an applicant is hired, his or her data can be transferred to personnel administration using such an activity. To do so, the connection between the E-Recruiting system and the ECC system where the employee data is maintained must be configured accordingly.

When created, the activity types are assigned to the processes they occur in and to the objects they can be used for. Figure 7.50 shows some activities that can be used for candidacies and some that can be used for applications.

Change View "Assignment of Activity Type to Object Types": Overview

Type	Name	O.	Object type text	
0010	Check Suitability	NE	Candidacy	
0050	Reimburse Travel Expenses	NE	Candidacy	
0070	Find Suitable Requisitions	ND	Application	
0100	Agree Terms and Conditions of Employment	ND	Application	
0100	Agree Terms and Conditions of Employment	NE	Candidacy	

Figure 7.50 Assign Activity Types to Object Types

The further items in this part of the IMG deal with settings for activity types of specific categories and with the workflow that can be started after an activity has been created.

Activities with correspondence must have assigned a form containing the letter via the IMG path **Applicant Tracking · Activities · Correspondence · Assign Forms to Activity types**. These forms must have been defined as smart forms (see Figure 7.51) before using the IMG path **Applicant Tracking · Activities · Correspondence · Create Form** (or Transaction SMART-FORMS). For further information on Smart forms, refer to the SAP PRESS book *SAP Smart Forms by Werner Hertleif and Christoph Wachter*.

Figure 7.51 Maintain Forms for Letters with SAP Smart Forms

7.4.6 Questionnaires

The questionnaires are defined by the recruiter in the application as described in Section 7.2.5. There is not much Customizing to be done except for the scales, which are the same as shown in Figure 7.48. There are two questionnaire categories (job-related information and EEO), and they are created automatically in the customizing via the path **Applicant Tracking · Questionnaires · Update categories**. When assigning these categories to activity types, you also decide whether the questionnaires are integrated into the application wizard. If not, a link to the question-naire must be sent via e-mail.

Some special customizing settings deal with EEO questionnaires (path **Applicant Tracking · Questionnaires · Equal Employment Opportunity**).

7.4.7 Requisition Management

Besides the approval workflows for requisitions and job postings, the Customizing for the requisition management is very similar to that of the talent warehouse:

▶ The options for the dropdown-boxes in various fields of the requisition data and the job posting data are maintained (e.g., work contract types or industries).

▶ Search profiles and search templates can be defined.

7.4.8 Further Technical Issues

Here is some additional information concerning the technical basis:

▶ The Web-based user interfaces are implemented using Business Server Pages (BSPs). To learn more about BSPs, refer to the SAP PRESS books *Advanced BSP Programming* by Brian McKellar and Thomas Jung and *BSP Extensions: How to Master Web Reporting with HTMLB* by Frédéric Heinemann.

▶ Correspondence is realized with the Smart Forms technology. An inter-face to Microsoft Word is not available but could be designed through a custom development.

▶ Many issues arise when you require a connection to the ECC system where the HR is running (for example organizational management or transfer of candidate to the employee master data). When SAP E-Recruiting, Release 300 or higher, and SAP ECC 5.0, Human Resources Extension (EA-HR 500) or higher are used, both E-Recruiting and the ECC can be run on the same instance. However, this is usually avoided for security reasons. To connect both systems, you need to configure ALE as described via the IMG path **Technical settings · SAP ERP Central Component (ECC) Integration · Software runs on different instances**.

▶ The search functionality is provided by the search engine *Text Retrieval and Information Extraction (TREX)*. It works much like the search engines you know from the Web. This search engine is also used in the

SAP Enterprise Portal. However, for E-Recruiting purposes it must be installed in the configuration designed for a non-portal environment. You will find the installation guide *Installing Retrieval and Classification (TREX) in a Non-Portal Environment* on the SAP Service Marketplace (*service.sap.com*).

7.5   Critical Success Factors

Most of what is said in Chapter 6, *Recruitment,* applies here as well. However there are some particular issues to observe:

▶ When transitioning from a traditional recruitment solution, you mustn't consider the implementation of E-Recruiting as a mere change of the technical basis, where the processes aren't changed much except that e-mail is used more extensively for communication. As discussed in Section 7.1 and Section 7.2, the concept is completely different from the old solution and allows and requires completely different processes.

▶ Make sure you have the necessary skill set available for your project. It should include:

  ▷ One person (probably a consultant) who has a very good knowledge of mySAP HCM as a whole (especially the data structure of personnel planning and development), Customizing and processes in the SAP e-recruitment solution (knowledge of the traditional recruitment solution will also help to some extend), and recruitment processes in general.

  ▷ Design and programming of BSPs. It depends on your requirements whether any changes to BSPs are necessary.

  ▷ Design and programming of smart forms

  ▷ Workflow: It depends on your requirements how much workflow will be used.

  ▷ Web Application Server / NetWeaver: It is necessary for the integration with the ECC system and the TREX search engine.

  ▷ Architecture and security of Web-based applications

  ▷ SAP Query

  ▷ Possibly BW

  ▷ Possibly ABAP Objects

▶ Make sure that the managers are involved online in the whole process, especially in the selection. As they may be on high hierarchy levels, it can be difficult for an E-Recruiting project manager to succeed in this without the help of a powerful project sponsor from the top-management.

▶ When coming from the traditional recruitment solution, make sure that you have a solution for printed correspondence that complies with your requirements, as the new solution lacks some of the flexibility you have when using Microsoft Word in the traditional solution.

8   Time Management

We describe time management, first, as the recording and processing of times of the normal working day, especially for purposes of managing time accounts and the monetary evaluation of time. Time management also concerns the recording and processing of times for a company's activity output, in particular for the purposes of incentive wage calculation.

8.1   Business Principles

8.1.1   Objectives of Time Management

Time management documents the behavior of employees in regard to working time in general. This includes:

► Duration and position of attendance times

► Duration and position of break times

► Working times outside the company (e.g., business trips)

► Special absences (sickness, vacation, etc.)

► Types of activity during the times entered (productive hours, overtime, etc.)

In the area of incentive wages, this information is also combined with production data, such as:

► Number of pieces completed

► Standard times

► Scrap

Further information is then derived from this primary data. In addition, company regulations such as work schedules, flextime regulations, and rules for bonus calculation are applied. This time evaluation then supplies the following sorts of results.

► Status of the leave account

► Status of the flextime account and/or long-term account

► Overtime hours to be paid

► Bonuses for overtime, nightwork, work on Sundays and public holidays.

- ▶ Bonuses to be paid for special activities
- ▶ Action required when the working-time law or the company's core-time regulations have been violated

In the incentive wage environment, piecework or premium regulations of the incentive wage components are used to calculate the remuneration.

Entering working times in order to calculate compensation in the form of money and/or time is not comprehensive enough as a primary goal of time management. This activity is, rather, a way to manage the "working-time" resource, and therefore is the basis for the output and performance of the employee.

Working time is the time that the company would like to implement most efficiently in the pursuit of its objectives. On the other hand, an employee who is working loses time that he or she otherwise could spend achieving personal goals. An interesting tension field emerges where those involved pursue contradictory goals, such as

- ▶ Provision of working times corresponding to the requirements for the activity output of the company
- ▶ Availability of free time corresponding to the private requirements of the employee
- ▶ Capability to plan free time for the employee
- ▶ Flexible availability of working time for the company

The primary goal of modern working-time management is to harmonize these goals as far as possible for the following reasons:

- ▶ Fulfilling company requirements, due to the pressure of the market, requires increasing flexibility of working time.
- ▶ Taking into account the requirements of the employees helps to bind them to the company and to use available working time optimally through the ability and willingness to perform at a high level.

Further goals are defined through legal or collective agreements, for which compliance must be monitored and documented, and also through personnel controlling.

To achieve the primary goals, the following are some of the approaches pursued in company regulations or collective agreements.

- Payment of bonuses for work performed during weekends or nights (In some countries the payment of such bonuses are taxed at a lower tax rate.)
- Flexible working-time models that are beneficial for both the private interests of the employee and the company
- Implementation of long-term time accounts which can be used for a sabbatical.
- Delegation of responsibility for planning working times to the employees themselves (time-autonomous work groups)
- Possibility to donate leave entitlement to colleagues in special situations (such as severe illness of a child, spouse, or other relative)

Such and similar regulations are described in the following sections with regard to their implementation in mySAP HR.

We can assume that in the area of time management great value is placed on correct maintenance of time data. Less emphasis, however, is placed on what is really done during this time. The question "How long was the employee present in this month?" is often answered as far as the fourth decimal place. But the question "What has the employee achieved in this month?" is often neglected. Time management as a method for efficient use of an important and expensive resource is actually a management task that all too often is delegated to a time-recording system.

Quantity and quality

This state of affairs is certainly due in part to the fact that it is far easier to measure time accurately than it is to measure performance. Thus, this chapter also mainly deals with the recording and formal evaluation of attendance times. However, you should always be aware of the danger that this simplification involves. The emergence of a "seconds-counting culture" should definitely be avoided. Whether avoiding the recording of all work times represents the best solution, is questionable as well, however. For most employees, being able to prove their working times is reassuring, and should at least remain as an early- warning system for employees being overburdened or under-challenged (regardless of whether this is quantitative or qualitative).

Emerging developments in this area are certainly interesting, but in the medium term are not likely to completely replace the familiar forms of time recording and evaluation. Modern forms of work such as teleworking speak against classic time recording. Developments such as life-working-time accounts further promote it.

8.1.2 Forms of Time Recording

You can basically differentiate between positive time recording and negative time recording (see Figure 8.1).

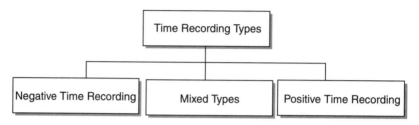

Figure 8.1 Forms of Time Recording

Negative time recording Negative time recording is based on a defined working time model, i.e., daily working time, weekly work schedule, etc. Only deviations to this are entered. This generally leads to consideration of overtime or shortfall of more than, say, 15 minutes as well as all-day absences or significant absences lasting less than one day, while smaller deviations are not considered. Only working duration is entered; the circumstances of working time are generally not relevant as long as these have no effects on payment (e.g., through night-work bonuses). The recording is mainly carried out manually by the employee and is then entered and processed at central points, supported by the system. PC-supported recording (e.g., via Web-based interfaces) is still rare but useful, as this clearly reduces administrative effort at central points.

Positive time recording Positive time recording is based on a working time model as well. However, it is not only larger deviations that are recorded here but also all clock-in and clock-out times. In conjunction with additional data such as absences, the deviations from the work schedule can be calculated and evaluated automatically. Time- recording terminals are used for positive time recording in general (and partly also Web-supported recording or even recording via WAP-capable mobile phones). Manual recording is also possible, but is rarely done.

Mixed form In a mixed form both kinds of time recording are combined. This could mean that in the management area negative time recording is implemented, while in the production area positive recording is implemented. In practice, positive time recording is almost never implemented on a companywide basis, because many jobs are not compatible with this.

The basis of this book is essentially positive time recording, because it is more extensive and because the system design for negative time recording can be derived easily from this.

8.1.3 Legal Principles

A variety of regulations address working time. Some of them originate from legislation, others from collective agreements with trade unions or company- specific regulations. Most of them differ from country to country, and some even depend on the industry sector or the individual employee (e.g., restrictions for minors or pregnant women).

A very important issue is regulation of safety at work, which often requires clearly defined breaks, restrictions on the total working time of a person per day, or the time of exposure to certain conditions (e.g., to radiation).

In case of accidents or potential job-related illnesses, the employer should be able to prove with records from the IT system that all regulations were observed. To allow managers to be proactive, it is a good idea to provide them with the necessary current data.

8.1.4 Concepts of Flexible Working Hours Policy

The scope of a policy for flexible working hours is to a great extent characterized by the form that activity output takes for the company in question. Factors which influence this are primarily:

▶ Adhering to fixed service times for the customers

▶ Adhering to specific reaction times to customer requests

▶ Attachment to fixed locations to guarantee these service times (call centers offer much more options than retail stores)

▶ Exchangeability of employees (coupling/decoupling of the person and function)

▶ The option of producing in the warehouse

▶ Necessity of replacement capacities for peak times and emergencies

▶ Ability to plan contracts

▶ Working in groups and on assembly lines, which makes it necessary for all those involved to carry out their work at the same time

Essentially, maneuverability is greater the further you diverge from working time as a measure of all things related to work results (with the familiar problems of measurability).

Despite the inherent necessities linking time to performance, concepts for decoupling working time from service and production times have already been implemented for several decades. Less-fixed methods are being used to provide the necessary capacity, while efforts are under way to better adapt the number of staff to the requirements. It is in the area of services that personnel bottlenecks can be cleared by the use of part-time staff.

The following concepts are being implemented in order to achieve the goals described in Section 8.1.1.

▶ **"Classic" flextime**
The employee achieves his daily target time within a specified time-frame. If this is exceeded or fallen short of, the deviation is managed within a flextime account that generally shows an upper limit of 15 to 50 hours. Within a specified core time, the employee must be present.

▶ **Flextime without core time**
Core times are generally stored in EDP systems, and the core time deviations run to time administrators or the personnel department. There, they are either ignored or discussed with management to determine that this did not affect the regular operations. From experience, we see that core times only cause hassle. The scheduling of working time within the scope of flextime should be the responsibility of management.

▶ **Flextime with staffing guarantees**
The staffing guarantee is the team-related further development of core time that is geared towards internal or external customers. Within a team, certain staff numbers are defined for certain time periods. Scheduling is the responsibility of management.

▶ **Time-autonomous work groups**
The responsibility for staff numbers lies within the team itself (see Section 8.6.4).

▶ **Flextime or choice of working time**
Within an adequate notification period (e.g., six months) an employee can freely select his or her weekly working time within a defined corridor (e.g., 16–42 hours). This means long-term variations of the business workload can be reacted to, wherein special incentives are set for increasing or reducing working time.

► **Sabbaticals**

They primarily serve the interests of the employee and are therefore an instrument of employee retention. By supporting sabbaticals in times of slow business, however, the objectives of the company can also be addressed.

In some countries special effects on taxes and social security have to be observed.

► **Annual working time**

The classic flextime account is not adequate when capacity requirements depend on the season and are subject to fluctuations. There are different methods of distributing working time sensibly throughout the year. The introduction of such a system is best scheduled for the beginning of a period of a high workload, as you can avoid the psychological problem of negative flextime balances.

► **Life working time**

As the times in a life-working-time account are to a large extent outside the scope of scheduling, the account merely serves as a means of employee retention and long-term increases of capacity.

However, this concept requires a strong controlling of the working time invested by the managers. It is all to easy for employees to earn a huge leave entitlement by lingering in the company although no work is being done.

► **Home work/telework**

While home work was earlier the domain of manufacturing, where work was carried out for piecerate wages at home, telework now offers more options. Modern time-recording systems even enable "stamping" via the Internet. The extent to which this is useful is questionable. Telework demands mutual trust anyway and should be used to consider work results instead of working time. However, it frequently makes sense for the employee to perform PC-supported daily entries, even for reasons of self-control.

8.2 Design in the SAP System

In this section, we will describe the basic design in the system. The particularities which emerge due to specific interfaces for data entry (TMW, mobile applications, ESS, MSS) are dealt with following this chapter and in Chapter 13, *Role-based Portal Solution*.

8.2.1 Structures in Time Management

The structures of time management are based on the structures described in Chapter 4, *Personnel Administration*. Essentially, the combinations of employee subgroup and group and of the personnel area and sub-area are grouped under different aspects of time management. The requirements of time management definitely have to be considered when defining these structures. The grouping for the public holiday calendar is often an essential criterion for the definition of the structures. The country grouping (MOLGA) may also be relevant.

The following essential groupings of the personnel area and the personnel sub-area (customizing view V_001P_ALL) exists.

▶ Grouping for working schedule

▶ Grouping for time recording (used in many customizing steps, such as time types and time evaluation messages)

▶ Grouping for additional time data such as absences and attendances, absence/attendance counting, leave types, time quota types, substitution and stand-by-duty

▶ Assignment to a public holiday calendar

The essential groupings of employee groups and subgroups (Customizing view V_503_ALL) are:

▶ Grouping for personnel calculation rules for control in the time-evaluation schema (is also used in payroll calculation)

▶ Grouping for time quota types

▶ Grouping for working schedule

▶ Indicator for participation in the incentive wage

Other structures which are important for time management are entered directly in the personnel master:

▶ Time administrator in Infotype 0001

▶ Separation of part-time and full-time staff via part-time indicator in Infotype 0007

▶ Grouping to control the subsystem connection in Infotype 0050 (for time events, subsystems, employee expenses, access control)

▶ The grouping for the time evaluation rule in Infotype 0050. This is not used by the standard time evaluation, but can be used in a custom evaluation scheme for structuring and as a decision criterion.

The multitudes of groupings that directly affect time management appear very confusing at first. They are however very helpful, both in mapping different rules and in forming useful combinations, to keep the number of entries in the customizing tables as low as possible. It is therefore advisable to make distinctions only if it is really necessary. Otherwise, all employees should be controlled on the same grouping.

8.2.2 Public-Holiday Calendar

In the public-holiday calendar you can define which days are public holidays. When defining the public holidays, you determine the rule under which the public holiday is created and which holiday class is assigned to it. The holiday class is used as a control criterion in time evaluation and the assignment of daily work schedules. The following holiday classes are possible: normal public holidays; half public holidays (e.g., New Year's Eve); and company-specific holidays, for which no bonuses are paid for working hours.

The R/3 public-holiday calendar also maps guaranteed holidays, which are made up for when they fall on a day that is off anyway. This is, for instance, practiced in Luxembourg and the UK.

Note Ensure that the public holiday calendar is cross-client and is used in R/3 by several modules (e.g., production planning, IS banking). You should only implement changes with the agreement of the system administration. You can also use your own calendars for HR, though this causes redundant maintenance and disadvantages regarding integration.

You must check while setting up time management whether it is necessary to use several public holiday calendars. This is generally the case if the company is located in several states or regions. Do not use more public holiday calendars than necessary, as the number of calendars also determines the number of the work schedule rules.

Customizing in mySAP ERP is carried out via IMG path **SAP NetWeaver · General Settings · Maintain Calendar** (in earlier versions you find it under "cross-application components"). Note that the automatic transport connection is not active here—transport must be called manually.

In addition to time management, event management and payroll also use the public-holiday calendar.

8.2.3 Concepts Explanations for Time Management

For a better understanding of the following sections, some of the HR concepts will first be explained.

Time Types

The concept of time type is similar to that of the wage type in payroll. The calculation for a time evaluation is implemented in the time evaluation and is partly also saved and evaluated there. Time types can represent time balances or accounts (e.g., flextime balance), serve certain evaluation purposes (e.g., to the total of the work times over ten hours a day), or can be simply required for internal calculation of time evaluation (e.g., overtime). Time types are created using IMG path **Time Management · Time Evaluation · Time Evaluation Settings · Define Time Types**. There, you can set whether the values of the time type should be saved as per day or per month, whether they are reset to zero at the end of a month or year, and whether they represent a time account.

In addition to each time type saved as a balance, a time type can be entered to store the balance of the previous month or previous year. These time types can, for instance, be used in order to print out previous monthly balances on the time statement of the current month. Figure 8.2 shows the definition of a time type.

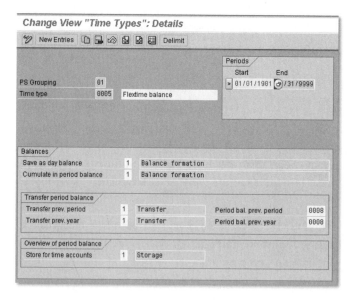

Figure 8.2 Time Type Settings for the Example of the Flextime Balance According to the Standard Supply

Time Balance

This is a special case of the time type. Time balances are saved on a monthly or daily basis. Other time types are only used for internal calculations, are not saved, and can therefore not be evaluated. In general, however, you key all time types in such a way that they can at least be saved on a daily basis.

Time Account

A time account is also a special case of the time type. Time accounts are generally managed progressively (Example: flextime balance). In other words, a time account is not generally set to zero at the beginning of the month (however this does not rule out a capping, e.g., at 25 hours). Time accounts receive a particular tab in the time types table and are therefore prepared to display in the time recording terminal.

Time Quota

This generally means an absence quota. These are entered in Infotype 2006 (see Section 4.1.5). This concept represents an alternative to the time type for the mapping of time accounts and balances. In this case, there is little or no manual maintenance. The quota status in Infotype 2006 is automatically supplied from the time evaluation. The advantage of the absence quota is that the quota status, in contrast to a time type, can be read directly without a special report by displaying Infotype 2006. In addition, when entering absences that reduce the account, you can define in Customizing the online checking for the quota available. The concept of the time type, in contrast, allows for more flexible handling in the definition of the time-evaluation schema. For releases lower than 4.5A, it is generally advisable to use the time type for the management of time accounts. As the effort involved in conversion tends to be very high, you would be likely to use this variant for later upgrades.

Time-wage types

Wage types populated with information in figures (hours, pieces, etc.) and transferred to payroll for monetary evaluation and, if necessary, to payment, are time-wage types. Time-wage types are the basis of the automatic interface between time management and payroll.

Time Evaluation, Time Accounting

Time evaluation is a program that runs at least daily or even more frequently and which calculates the essential results of time management (balance statuses, info time types, time-wage types, quotas) from the recorded employee data (including time stamps). You can call it via the following menu path: **Human Resources · Time Management · Administration · Time Evaluation · Time Evaluation**. It can however also be called from the to-do list of the time administrator. In general it also runs as a regular job. The time-evaluation flow is controlled by the customer-specific adapted schema (see Section 8.2.7).

Time Statement

The time statement is the form (online or as a printout), on which the essential results of time evaluation for the employee are displayed. Calling the time statement does not trigger a new calculation but rather merely displays the saved results of time evaluation. It is either called through the menu path **Human Resources · Time Management · Administration · Time Evaluation · Time Statement** or from the to-do list of the time administrator. It makes sense and is usual to ensure this is available in Employee Self-Service (ESS).

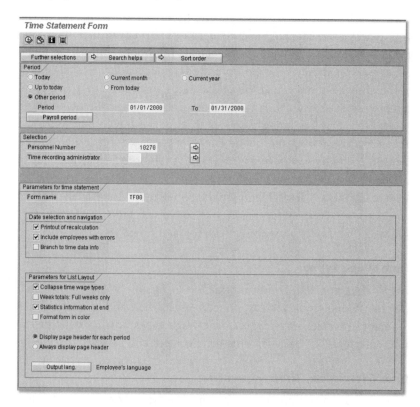

Figure 8.3 Example of a Time Statement Form

Figure 8.4 shows an example of a time statement and Figure 8.3 shows its selection screen (note the output language!). The form used here is of particular importance. You can call the form via IMG path **Time Management · Time Evaluation · Evaluations and the Time Management Pool · Time Statement Form · Set Up Time Statement Using Form Editor**. The Form Editor for Release 4.6C (as is the case with R/3 Enterprise and mySAP ERP) is simple to handle and is sufficiently documented. The most important thing is that the time types to be displayed are saved with the balances required in each case (daily balance or monthly balance).

```
IDES US INC               Time Statement List          Page :   1
                          ====================

Philadelphia
Pers No.    :   00010270  Name: Mr. Henry Miller       EE Group: 1
Personnel area:  300      Cost ctr:   3200             EE subgrouU4

Payroll Period  :  200001 From 01/01/2000 - 01/31/2000   WS Rule:  FLEX

                          Individual Results
                          ==================
Day Text        In   Out  From  To    Rec.  Skeleton Flex   CViol OT    DWS

03                        07:50 17:05  9,25   8,09  0,09   0,00  0,00   FLEX

04                        07:40 17:07  9,45   8,12  0,12   0,00  0,00   FLEX

05                        07:55 17:13  9,31   8,23  0,23   0,00  0,00   FLEX

06                        07:57 17:05  9,13   8,09  0,09   0,00  0,00   FLEX

07                        07:53 17:02  9,16   9,04  1,04   0,00  0,00   FLEX

10                        07:43 17:17  9,56   9,29  1,29   0,00  0,00   FLEX

11                        07:55 17:05  9,16   9,09  1,09   0,00  0,00   FLEX

12                        07:51 17:11  9,33   9,19  1,19   0,00  0,00   FLEX

13                        07:42 17:12  9,50   9,21  1,21   0,00  0,00   FLEX

14                        07:43 17:17  9,57   9,29  1,29   0,00  0,00   FLEX

17  M.L.K. Day            07:56 17:13  9,28   8,00  0,00   0,00  0,00   FLEX
     from

27                        07:51 17:01  9,17   9,03  1,03   0,00  0,00   FLEX

28                        07:47 17:08  9,35   9,14  1,14   0,00  0,00   FLEX

31                        07:40 17:12  9,53   9,21  1,21   0,00  0,00   FLEX


                          Totals Overview
                          ===============
Type                      Working Time        Overtime

Previous month's             15,00              0,00
Planned time                168,00
Working time                187,36
Revision                      0,00              0,00
Balance                      15,00              0,00
Excess/insuffici             19,36
Remaining leave               0,00
```

Figure 8.4 Calling the Time Statement Form

If forms were first processed through the maintenance for individual views, and are now to be maintained through the Form Editor after an upgrade, there can be problems. Frequently checking and resaving all form settings in the Form Editor is sufficient.

Time Events

Time events are actions related to points in time that supply the essential information for the calculation in the time evaluation. Examples are: "Clock-in," "Clock-out," "Time ticket start," etc.

Time Pair

A time pair is the time span between two time-points, which may be formed through time events, attendance or absence entered, and corner times of the time model. The time pairs are the most important objects for processing the time-evaluation schema. In addition to the pure time span, they are identified through numerous attributes (e.g., overtime pair, break, origin, etc.). These attributes can then in turn determine the processing run in the schema.

Time Evaluation Messages

Time evaluation provides error or information messages for certain statuses that the time administrator can edit during error-handling of the to-do list. Errors can be keyed so that the time evaluation remains at the day where the error occurred, until the error is removed or further calculated. In the case of error messages, the employee receives out-of-date information about this day (through the terminal or the ESS); in the case of information messages, he can receive incorrect information in certain circumstances. The error messages are triggered in the time-evaluation schema and implemented via IMG path **Time Management · Time Evaluation · Time Evaluation with Clock Times · Message Output · Create Message Descriptions**. As in the definition of the time types, take care that the personnel sub-area grouping is used for time recording. You can also set whether the employee is shown a message at the terminal. For retroactive calculations, messages are always recreated if necessary. You can generally assume that the administrator or the employee took the hint and acted on the message. By using the "Create once" tab, you can avoid multiple creation of the same message for the same reason.

8.2.4 Work Schedules

The concept of the work schedule enables you to determine the scheduled working time for the individual employee for each day in terms of position and duration. Moreover, additional information such as core times, flextime limits, general overtime approvals, etc. are assigned. The SAP concept appears to be confusing at first glance. On closer inspection, however, you recognize that the multi-level concept makes it possible to extensively reuse parts that have been defined. This means the solution enables a swift mapping of rotating shift schedules. It appears to be quite cumbersome, on the other hand, for companies that have no rotating shifts. This means working schedules based on the public- holiday calendar are the basis for the complete time evaluation and also for time recording.

Customizing the working schedules is done via IMG path **Time Management · Work Schedules** with several subdirectories.

The Daily Work Schedule

The concept daily work schedule does not really refer to the content that it maps. Not only can you define working time within a calendar day, but also across several days, for instance in the case of a night shift. The single limitation is the scope of 24 hours. Each daily work schedule is thus assigned to the day on which it begins.

The daily work schedule generally also contains a work break schedule (see Figure 8.5). This is required before creating the daily work schedule.

Work break schedule

Grpg	Break	N.	Start	End	P	Unpaid	Paid	After	RefTim	Type 1	Type 2
90	3SCH	01	01:00	01:15	☑	0,25					
90	3SCH	02	04:00	04:45	☑	0,75					
90	3SCH	03	09:00	09:15	☐	0,25					
90	3SCH	04	12:00	12:45	☐	0,75					
90	3SCH	05	17:00	17:15	☐	0,25					
90	3SCH	06	20:00	20:45	☐	0,75					

Figure 8.5 Work Break Schedule

You execute the following settings in the work break schedule:

▶ Situation of breaks with fixed time or in the context of a break

▶ The situation of breaks relative to the work start and planned working-time start.

▶ Assigning the break to the previous day for cross-day models

▶ Identification as a paid or unpaid break.

Paid breaks frequently are not documented in the system. That can have the following disadvantages:

▶ The break time cannot be evaluated.

▶ Regulations that automatically assume and deduct a defined break time for the employee cannot take the paid breaks into consideration.

▶ Adhering to regulations such as the working-time law in Germany and other countries cannot be monitored with the support of the system.

The work-break schedule has the same groupings as the daily work schedule.

Daily work schedule The daily working time of the employee is stored in the daily work schedule itself. The system provides different options for mapping these.

▶ You define the working time as a fixed working time. In this case, enter a planned working time. The system calculates the planned working times from this by considering the work-break schedule. All times that fall outside the planned working time are not favorably taken into consideration for the employee. However, if this is required, an adjustment in the schema or the entry of an attendance quota is required.

▶ You define the working time as flextime. In this case, you specify a working time frame, and within this frame establish the normal working time. The planned working hours are calculated from the normal working time. All times that lie within the planned working time are favorably taken into consideration for the employee. In the standard version, the portion in excess of the planned working time is posted to the flextime account. Another form of processing is possible by adjustment of the schema.

In addition, the following information is stored in the daily work schedule:

▶ **Core times**
In the standard version, violating the core time triggers a warning message for the time administrator.

▶ **Tolerances**
Clock-in or clock-out entries are always set to the fixed time within the range of tolerance. Example: The normal work start is 8 a.m., and the begin tolerance is 7.45 to 8 a.m. In this case, each stamp that occurs in

the period between 7.45 and 8.00 is automatically set to 8.00. The tolerance regulations can be mapped more flexibly in the schema (e.g., rounding all postings to the nearest five minutes).

▶ **Minimal, maximal working time and compensation time**
You can enter these as fixed values and process them in the time evaluation. However, this information is not considered in the standard supply of the schema.

▶ **Daily work schedule class**
This is an essential element of time evaluation and wage-types generation and acts as a control criterion. Thus, you can classify between, for example, night-shift models and other models and prevent a bonus being paid in the wage types generation, if an employee arrives for the early shift before 6 a.m. In the time-evaluation schema , you can use this criterion for decisions in processing. The importance of each individual daily work-schedule class depends individually on its settings in wage-types generation and time evaluation. Therefore, significant documentation is extremely important. The daily work schedule class 0 is reserved for "off work." Models of other classes can also have a planned working time of zero hours. You must set the corresponding tab here.

The daily work schedule (see Figure 8.6) provides a description of an individual working day with regard to the working time. In addition, it defines which daily work schedule is assigned to a certain day for a certain employee.

Variants of the Daily Work Schedule

Frequently, an otherwise regular working time deviates from the normal value (e.g., on Fridays, before public holidays, and on half days). This means several variants can be defined for each daily work schedule.

The assignment of a variants to a certain day occurs through the daily work schedule selection rule. This is defined in Customizing and is assigned to each individual daily work schedule. Depending on the public holiday class for the current day, the subsequent day and the weekday a variants is selected. In the example shown in Figure 8.7, in rule 90, the variant B is assigned to all public holidays of public-holiday class 2 (in the standard variants, half public holidays) and apart from that on every Friday (weekday number 5).

Daily work schedule selection rule

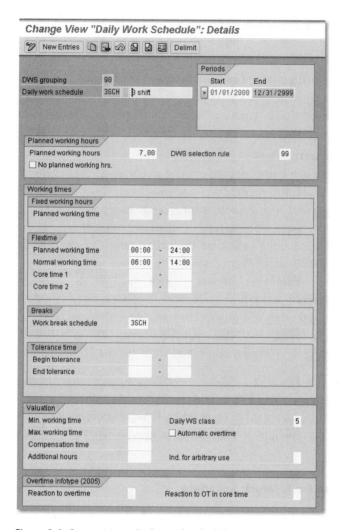

Figure 8.6 Customizing a Daily Work Schedule

Rule	No	Holiday class	Hol.cl.next day	Weekday	Variant
		b123456789	b123456789	1234567	
☐ 90	01	..X......	XXXXXXXXXX	XXXXXXX	B
☐ 90	02	XX.XXXXXX	XXXXXXXXXX	....X..	B

Figure 8.7 Daily Work Schedule Selection Rule

In addition, you can also select variants depending on an absence (on days for which there is a half day's leave, for instance, a variant without a core time and without a break is selected). However, this occurs in the customizing of absence types.

The Period Work Schedule

The period work schedule determines the sequence of the daily work schedules. It is the basis for the work schedule and sets the work rhythm. It can comprise one week and several weeks. It also can define periods that cannot be divided by seven. In this case you must conclude your period with "*". The example in Figure 8.8 shows a three-week schedule in which the free days change each week. However, the model 3SCH is always assigned for the work days.

Grpg	PWS	Period WS text	Wee	01	02	03	04	05	06	07
90	3SCH	3 shift	001	3SCH	3SCH	3SCH	3SCH	3SCH	FREE	FREE
90	3SCH	3 shift	002	3SCH	3SCH	3SCH	FREE	FREE	FREE	3SCH
90	3SCH	3 shift	003	3SCH	3SCH	FREE	FREE	3SCH	3SCH	3SCH

Figure 8.8 Period Work Schedule

The period work schedule has the same groupings as the daily work schedule. Period work schedules are also classified. This both supports the counting of absences and enables evaluation within the time evaluation and wage-type generation. Therefore, analyze precisely the content that is connected to a period work schedule, such as overtime, shift bonus, etc. It's important to implement this concept early on, to avoid a conceptual redesign during implementation and time evaluation. It is generally useful to classify shift-rotation schedules and also classic part-time schedules separately, as these frequently must be handled with special care in bonus generation.

The Work Schedule Rule

The work schedule rule establishes the time frame in which the employee works: daily, weekly, monthly, and annually. Further, it establishes the connection of the period work schedule to the real calendar. The reference date, for instance 01/07/2002 and the starting point, for example 001, determine that the period work schedule starts on Monday 01/07/2002 and executes its rolling rhythm from then on. It is useful to select a Monday as a starting point, as the period work schedules also begin on Mondays and the assignment is then easier. It is not necessary to have assigned a particular employee to this work schedule at the starting point date. It is purely the abstract beginning of the rhythm of the period work schedule.

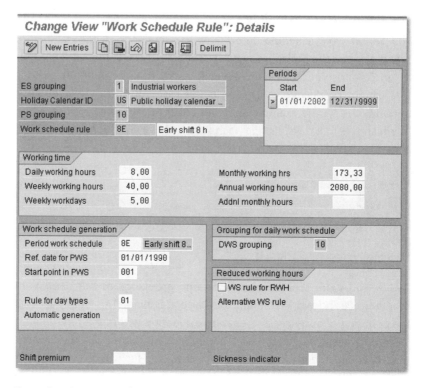

Figure 8.9 Customizing the Work Schedule Rule

For reduced working hours, you can store an alternative work schedule and a percentage record for a shift bonus, which is not evaluated in the standard schema. In addition, a rule is assigned to determine the day type (e.g., this means weekend bonuses can be defined differently or completely disabled). Customizing the work-schedule rule is displayed in Figure 8.9.

The Work Schedule

The work schedule contains the essential information for each individual work day. It is not manually maintained, but rather is generated on the basis of work schedule rules, period schedules, and public-holiday calendars. A work schedule is stored for each combination of work-schedule rules, groupings of the employee subgroups for work schedules, public-holiday calendars, and groupings for the personnel sub-areas for work schedules and daily work schedules. The resulting work schedule is then assigned to an employee based on the respective employee subgroup and personnel sub-area. This plan can then be changed for the individual employee, but only after entering other time data (e.g., substitutions).

The user does not directly assign the generated work schedule. The assignment rather takes place in Infotype 0007 (Planned Working Time) via the work schedule rule. This therefore can take into consideration a change of the public-holiday calendar that is due to an employee transfer, without having to maintain Infotype 0007.

Generating work schedules should occur approximately up to three years in advance, in order to enable the recording of longer absences (e.g., parental leave). Although the time evaluation functions correctly if no generation has occurred, it does generate temporary work schedules and therefore does not perform as well. The behavior of time management for non-generated work schedules is set in the customizing of work schedule rules (see Figure 8.10). It is advisable to transfer the standard supply, so the time evaluation does run free of errors, but a warning message regarding missing generation is created.

Work schedule generation

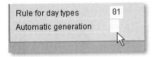

Figure 8.10 Tab to Generate the Work Schedule Rule

Figure 8.11 shows a work schedule for the month of January 2000. It contains the information as to which calendar day, which day's work schedule, and which version is to be worked on. In addition, it also contains the public-holiday class from the holiday calendar.

The work schedule is assigned to the employee in Infotype 0007 for the employee. You can assign standard values in this infotype via different features, which facilitate master data entry.

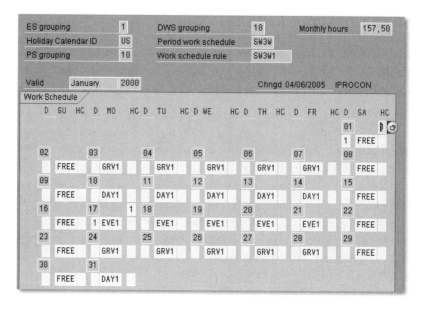

Figure 8.11 Generated Work Schedule

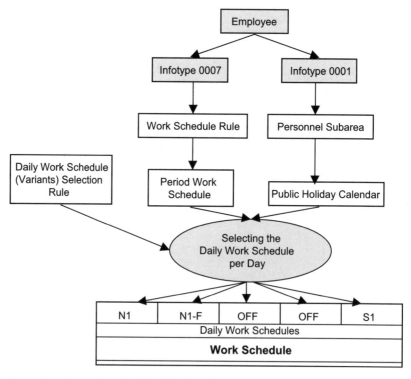

Figure 8.12 Customizing the Time Model and Connection to the Employee

Figure 8.12 shows an overview of the context in which you customize the work schedule. The work schedule sets the basis for time recording and time evaluation. In the following section, the entry of time data on the application side is dealt with, along with the corresponding customizing.

8.2.5 Time Data Entry

Entering the time data is also done in infotypes. This practice basically corresponds to the infotype concept in personnel administration. The number area for time infotypes ranges from 2000 to 2999.

Maintaining these infotypes is carried out via the following menu path: **Human Resources · Time Management · Administration · Time Data · Maintain**.

In this section, we will not only describe the pure entry of time data but also the way it displays its effect in the time evaluation and the relevant customizing.

Collision Check in Time Data Maintenance

A peculiarity of time infotypes can be found in the collision check. For the infotypes described up to this point, only records of the same infotypes collide with one another, depending on the time constraint, and these records can delimit themselves from each other. In time management, this is also possible for records of different infotypes.

The time-constraint class that is determined in the Customizing for the individual infotypes controls the reactions between the individual infotypes. Customizing the reactions for collisions can be carried out via the following IMG path: **Time Management · Time Data Recording and Administration · Specify System Reaction to Overlapping Time Infotypes**. For each combination of infotype and the relevant time-constraint class, a reaction is defined for the collision with any additional combination of infotype and relevant time-constraint class.

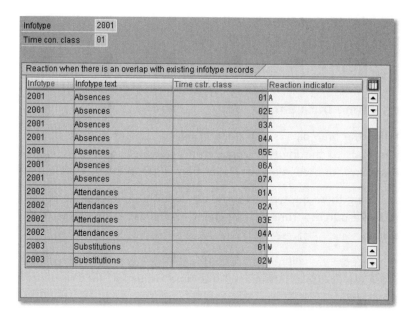

| Infotype | 2001 |
| Time con. class | 01 |

Reaction when there is an overlap with existing infotype records

Infotype	Infotype text	Time cstr. class	Reaction indicator
2001	Absences	01	A
2001	Absences	02	E
2001	Absences	03	A
2001	Absences	04	A
2001	Absences	05	E
2001	Absences	06	A
2001	Absences	07	A
2002	Attendances	01	A
2002	Attendances	02	A
2002	Attendances	03	E
2002	Attendances	04	A
2003	Substitutions	01	W
2003	Substitutions	02	W

Figure 8.13 Time Constraint Reaction for Time Management Infotypes

The example in Figure 8.13 is based on Infotype 2001 with time-constraint class 01 and shows the reactions of the infotypes depending on their time-constraint class. The reactions tab can have the following characteristics:

▶ A—the old record is delimited, collisions are displayed

▶ E—the new record cannot be inserted, collisions are displayed

▶ W—the new record can be added, collisions are displayed

▶ N—like W, collisions are not displayed

If a corresponding collision occurs during the data maintenance, a warning message or error message occurs, and if necessary an existing record is delimited.

A realistic example is the collision of sickness and vacation (both are subtypes of Infotype 2001 with different time-constraint classes), as predefined in the standard version. If a sickness record is entered in an existing leave record, the former is delimited after a system warning. In the reverse case, the system does not allow the entry.

Substitutions (Infotype 2003)

As substitutions in Infotype 2003 immediately change the work schedule of an employee, they are dealt with directly in the connection to Section 8.2.4. For a period or an individual day the employee can be assigned a deviating planned working time (see Figure 8.14). This means that the use of this infotype far exceeds the classic understanding of the concept substitution.

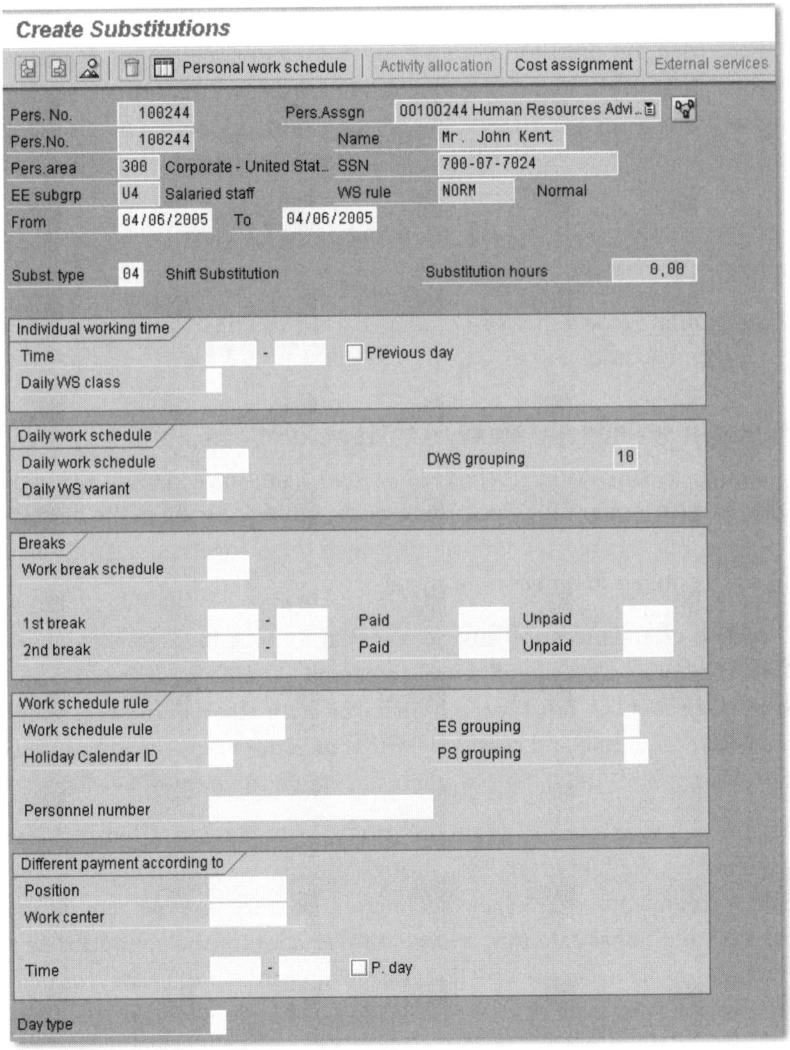

Figure 8.14 Infotype 2003: Substitutions

The deviating planned working time should occur if possible by assignment of a daily work schedule or a work schedule rule. The direct entry of times (also break times) or the assignment of a day type are also possible. If a real substitution exists, the deviating work schedule rule can be determined via the substituted personnel number.

It also can directly affect the payment: If the employee accepts a high-value activity, this is entered by assigning a position or a work place. A deviating payment can be determined from this.

Customizing the substitutions is carried out via IMG path **Time Management · Time Data Recording and Administration · Substitutions**. The substitution types are mainly defined there and are identified according to their relevance for shift-time compensation (payroll then ensures that the employee is not at a financial disadvantage due to the substitutions) and reduced working hours. The time-constraint class is also assigned according to substitution type here.

A suggestion value can also be defined for the **Substitution type** field through the feature VTART.

Attendances and Absences (Infotypes 2001 and 2002)

Attendances and absences are dealt with in a similar manner in Customizing and are also grouped according to the same grouping in the personnel area. For this reason, we will deal with them together, even though they are entered in different infotypes.

Originally attendances and absences are part of time management. However, they have a strong influence on payroll. Absences can be paid and unpaid. Account information can be linked with attendance/absence for financial accounting and cost accounting. In addition, paid absences also can affect the payroll if the payment is made on the basis of averages.

Absences Absences are entered in Infotype 2001. The individual absence types (mapped via the subtypes) differ strongly in some ways with regard to the data to be maintained. Sicknesses in many country versions require the entry of additional data that impacts the duration of the continued pay. Examples of absences are vacation, sickness, health cure, flexday, or military service.

Figure 8.15 shows the entry screen for vacation, which basically only contains the start and end dates (for records lasting less than one day, and also start and end times) and also the absence counts. Here you can differentiate in particular between absence days and calendar days, as days that are off from work anyway are not counted as absent days. In addition, the field **Quota used** shows how many days are deducted from the leave entitlement. The entry screen for vacation generally corresponds to most other absence types.

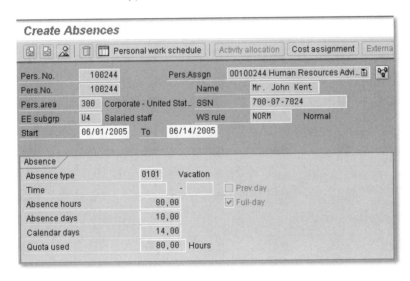

Figure 8.15 Absence: Vacation

Figure 8.16 shows additional data used only for the substyle "sickness." This, along with other data, is used to calculate sick pay.

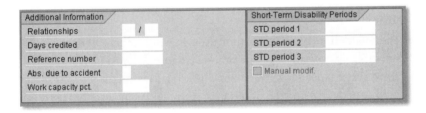

Figure 8.16 Limited Absence with Continued Pay

Attendances are maintained in Infotype 2002. Their entry is more standardized than that of absences. Examples of attendances are business trips (see Figure 8.17), seminar visits, training school, etc. There is frequent confusion regarding the concept behind selection of attendances, as such events are casually referred to also as absences. In HR terminology, they are constantly referred to as attendances if they are part of the working time.

Attendances

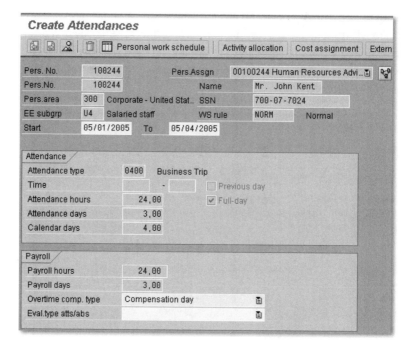

Figure 8.17 Attendance: Business Trip

In addition to information on the period and counting, similar to absences, attendances provide two additional entry options:

▶ The field **Overtime compensation type** specifies how overtime that occurs due to attendance is to be handled. In our example, it is remunerated.

▶ The **Evaluation type** field is not used in the standard version. It can however be used through the time-evaluation schema in order to generate wage types for specific activities (e.g., instructor activities). For correspondingly created interfaces, this field can also be used for absences. However, this is generally not a good idea.

In general, the attendance times for an employee are derived from the time stamps at the terminal and are only entered in exceptional cases (such as occasions when the employee cannot stamp because he or she is working outside the plant or office) via Infotype 2002. However, there are different recording scenarios, where all work times of the employees are recorded as attendances, and, if necessary, are supplemented with additional information (e.g., the assignment of times to cost centers, projects or financial funds).

Customizing for Attendance and Absences

The settings can be carried out via the following IMG paths: **Time Management · Time Data Recording and Administration · Absences · Absence catalogue** and **Time Management · Time Data Recording and Administration · Attendances**. Many settings are maintained for attendances and absences in the same way. All customizing activities mentioned in this paragraph are to be found via these two paths.

First the activities "Define Attendance and Absence Types" and "Determine Entry Screens and Time Constraint Classes " are to be carried out. Here, you mainly specify how the attendance or absence can be recorded, how it behaves during the recording, and which values are enabled. The settings are easy to understand and are well documented. You should however edit them in a detailed manner as the plausibility checks help to improve the data quality. The field **Screen number** is worthy of special mention (see Figure 8.18). Without reading the help screen, you would never realize that this field determines whether the absence type deducts a quota (e.g., the leave quota). The documentation for this field must be closely considered in other respects.

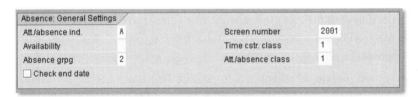

Absence: General Settings			
Att./absence ind.	A	Screen number	2001
Availability		Time cstr. class	1
Absence grpg	2	Att./absence class	1
☐ Check end date			

Figure 8.18 Customizing Item "Entry Screens and Time Constraint Classes"

Even the activity "Define Indicators for the Personal Calendar" is easy to understand. Consider exactly what you see in the calendar view and would like to enter.

Counting (Absences or attendances) is much more complex. You must define here how many hours and/or days of a certain attendance or absence are calculated, if it involves the deduction of quotas or payment. A detailed description would be beyond the scope of this book and would essentially repeat the already extensive documentation of the IMG. Therefore, at this point we will just make a few points:

▶ First, consider the complete documentation on these customizing sections and the concepts of the attendance quotas and absence quotas.

- If required, use the option of controlling the counting via the counting class of the period work schedule. This saves you having to create different absence types for the same content.

- In any case you should use the new variant of the rules for absence counting. Note that in specific customizing views old and new control parameters are mixed. The old ones are then identified.

- Note the new field **Deduction over interval end** in the view **Assign Counting Rules to Absence Types**. This means you can map the widely used regulation that the remaining leave from the previous year expires at a certain date, but that a vacation that has begun before the end of the deduction period is valid and can be taken beyond the expiration date of the remaining leave.

- Depending on absences, you can also define which variant of the daily work schedule has to be used. This can be necessary if you are processing working times. Suppose, for example, that you have an average daily working time of eight hours for a five-day week. However, from Monday to Thursday you work eight-and-a-half hours, and only six hours on Friday. Absences are generally deemed to be eight hours. In this case, you can assign a corresponding daily work schedule in connection with the rules for variants, using the above field. Note that the work-schedule selection rule must be assigned in the daily work schedule.

- You can define whether a quota can also be negative. From a business viewpoint it is useful if a vacation is taken in times of lower workload, even if the leave quota is depleted. This is especially true when at the end of the year there is usually little work, and management would be pleased if fewer leave days were taken in the following summer when there is a higher workload expected.

- The core of the process is the "Define Counting Rules" activity. In the counting rules, you use a variety of criteria to specify how days and hours are to be counted. The sheer number of criteria at first glance seems overwhelming, but usually only a few are required. It rarely makes sense, for example, to count leave days on Mondays at 20%, Tuesdays at 40%, and other days at 77%. However, take note in each case that the daily schedule class 0 stands for days off and thus is generally not taken into consideration in absence counting. That saves you having to carry out the control via weekdays, which doesn't work in many shift models anyway. In the deduction rules, you can define the sequence in which quotas are to be deducted (Example: The number of leave days taken is to use up the quota "special leave" first, and only then the "annual leave entitlement"). In the last category, rounding rules are defined which can be used in the counting rules.

The setting of attendance and absence types is generally concluded with the customizing of counting. All that is missing now are the activities for special absence data (maternity protection, parental leave, military service), which are pretty self-explanatory. It is some comfort that this complex customizing provides many options for company-specific adjustment—and that the settings for the other infotypes are much simpler.

Availability (Infotype 2004)

Dealing with availability is generally a very company-specific process. Many default settings of the system above all refer to the German public sector, but can also be adjusted for other industries.

Using Infotype 2004 with automatic generation of free-time compensation or payment is very complex in customizing, and is also complicated to some extent for data entry (according to the usage type). For lower volumes it is therefore worth thinking about the options that Infotype 2004 is either not maintained at all or only for information purposes, and the payment or free-time compensation can only be entered directly via the Infotypes 2010 and 2012/2006.

There are two basic options for entering the infotypes: the direct entry of times or determination of the availability times using specific working time models (daily work schedules or work schedule rules). The former, because it is easier to customize, is more immediately flexible for unscheduled requirements. However, interpreting a start and end time through a longer period is problematic. According to the parameterization of the P2004 function in the schema, the complete period between the start time on the first day and the end time on the last day is calculated as availability time, and the same is true for each individual day the period between the start and end times (see example in Figure 8.19).

Figure 8.20 structures the options for availability recording, and gives a basic description of the decision process regarding the mapping of availabilities in the system. In addition to the number of availability scenarios, there are other company-specific requirements that function as decision criteria. For reasons of simplicity, all are not all detailed here.

Entry

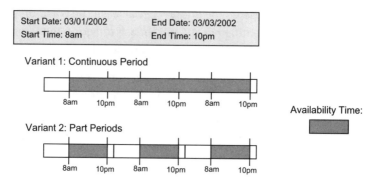

Variant 1: Continuous Period

Variant 2: Part Periods

Figure 8.19 Interpretation of Availability Times

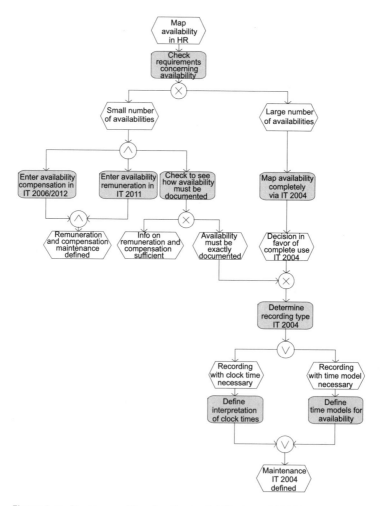

Figure 8.20 Decision on Mapping the Availability in mySAP HR

If you are using the functionality of availabilities in Infotype 2004 to its full extent, you must adjust the customizing in the IMG and in the schema of the time evaluation correspondingly. You create the prerequisite that availabilities are to be taken into consideration by the time evaluation, mainly by using function P2004, which is available in the standard version but not yet integrated in the schema. We will go into more detail on maintaining the schema in Section 8.2.7. You can navigate to further customizing via IMG path **Time Management · Time Data Recording and Administration · Availability**.

Essential properties are linked to the availability types that affect the time data "Maintenance," "Time evaluation" and "Capacity planning." However, the most decisive factor is how the availability process actually takes place: When is an availability recorded, how is it credited, what happens if an employee has an off-site assignment, etc?

Overtime (Infotype 2005)

Overtime should be maintained for the most part in time management. If you enter the payroll amounts directly, information on when exactly the remuneration originated is lost. This means some options of the system—esp. in reporting but also in some country-specific tax schemes—are not being used optimally.

Infotype 2005 should only be used for negative time recording, as overtime here is maintained in a fixed manner. In positive time recording, the attendance times for the employee are known already because of the stamps. Here it makes much more sense to maintain overtime through attendance quotas in Infotype 2007, or rather to authorize them.

In Infotype 2005, overtime is entered precisely to the second with break times, or as a pure hourly figure. Using the second option means losing the information about when exactly the overtime occurred.

Maintaining and customizing Infotype 2005 is quite easy. It is only processing the overtime in the time evaluation schema that can be difficult. This is largely controlled by the overtime compensation type, which besides Infotype 2005 can also be used in Infotypes 2010, 2007 and 2002. It specifies which parts of the overtime are remunerated, or compensated for with free time. By default, the following overtime compensation types are provided, which can also be processed in the schema by default:

- ▶ Remuneration (basic pay and if applicable, bonus)
- ▶ Free time for basic pay (and bonus remuneration)
- ▶ Free time compensation (basic pay and, if applicable, bonus)

You can create additional compensation types via IMG path **Time Management · Time Data Recording and Administration · Overtime · Define Types of Overtime Compensation**. However, you must then populate this with data in the time evaluation schema.

From release status 4.6 A, the relevant data fields are also available in Infotype 2002, which also means that this can be used to maintain overtime data. That is particularly useful if the overtime times are covered by entering attendance times. In the future, you will not have to deal with Infotype 2005, and this makes good sense for especially if you are just starting your implementation of SAP time management.

Absence Quotas (Infotype 2006)

Basic   Absence quotas can map different subjects, which allow for employees to have paid or unpaid absences. An essential characteristic is quota deduction. The combination of absences and absence quotas enables you to follow how often an employee is entitled to a certain absence.

Possible types of absence quotas are:

- ▶ Annual leave entitlement
- ▶ Winter vacation
- ▶ Educational leave
- ▶ Free time due to overtime
- ▶ Weekend compensation

Entry   Leave quotas in older release statuses were exclusively managed via Infotype 0005 ("Leave Entitlement"). Although this can still be used in the R/3 enterprise, it is not further maintained by SAP. A new implementation of time management should therefore use the Infotype 2006 in each case. In existing systems, if a good opportunity presents itself (fiscal year change), you should replace the Infotype 0005 by infotype 2006. SAP provides corresponding migration tools.

Absence quotas (i.e., requirements) can be structured in the following ways:

▶ **Manual Entry in Infotype 2006**

An essential piece of information besides the quota amount is the deduction period. This enables you to implement, for instance, the company regulation that leave days must be used up by March 31st of the following year (see Figure 8.21).

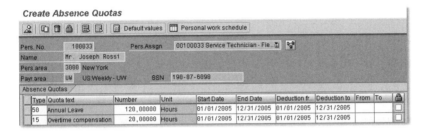

Figure 8.21 Entering Leave Entitlement as an Absence Quota

▶ **Entering a quota correction in Infotype 2013**

This is used if the quota is not manually entered, but rather is automatically constructed in the time evaluation (see Figure 8.22).

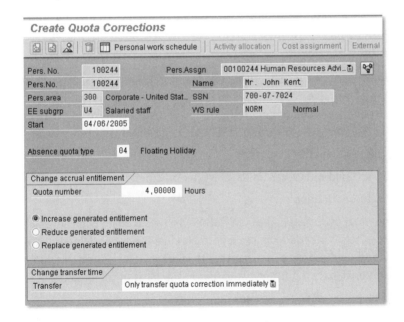

Figure 8.22 Increasing a Quota by Four Hours via Infotype 2013

▶ **Automatic Creation in Time Evaluation**

Quotas thus structured cannot be changed manually in Infotype 2006 but rather at most via Infotype 2013. (For instance, for each night shift, the quota "night shift bonus" is increased by an hour. Or: at month's end, the flextime is capped at 20 hours and the figure in excess of this is transferred to the "Annual working time account").

► **Mass generation**
Absence quotas are generated via Report RPTQTA00.

They can be deducted as follows:

► Manual maintenance in Infotypes 2006 or 2013

► Automatic deduction in the time evaluation based on company-specific facts (Example: If the flextime account is negative at months end it is canceled out by the quota "Annual working time account.")

► Entering absences that are keyed for the respective quota with regard to the deduction

► Compensation via Infotype 0416 (this also replaces Infotype 0083 in the case of vacation, if Infotype 0005 is replaced by Infotype 2006)

Customizing — Customizing for the counting of absences and partly also for deducting quotas has already been described. Through the IMG path **Time Management · Time Data Recording and Administration · Managing Time Accounts Using Attendance/Absence Quotas** the following settings can be performed:

► Definition of the attendance and absence quota types used with essential characteristics such as the type of deduction, rounding, time constraint class, deduction permission in excess of the existing entitlement, and restrictions regarding start and end times (see Figure 8.23)

► Calculating the entitlements

► Rules to build up quotas (initializing, periodic or current)

► Rules to deduct quotas

► Evaluating deducted quotas in the payroll (Example: If an absence record "Vacation" deducts the quota "Annual leave entitlement," it is valuated on the basis of a three-month average. If it deducts the quota "Additional leave," it is only valuated on the basis of the basic pay)

► Rules and valuation for payment

► Layout and content of the quota overview (you can reach this via the menu path **Human Resources · Time Management · Administration · Time Data · Quota Overview**)

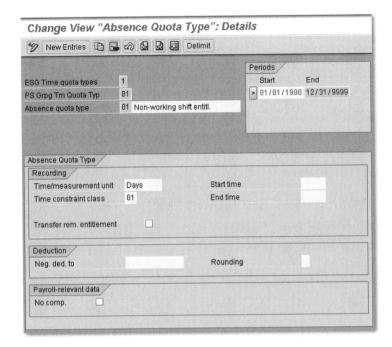

Figure 8.23 Customizing Absence Quota Types

Absence Quotas vs. Time Accounts in Time Types

Previously, time accounts such as annual account, free time due to over-time etc. were mostly executed in the time evaluation as time types. The extensive functionality of Infotype 2006 and its integration in evaluations and maintenance interfaces makes it advisable to map time-off entitlement through it as far as possible. For a new implementation of time management you can use the following rules of thumb:

▶ Manage the flextime account via the time type 0005 (using standard functionality).

▶ Manage other time accounts via Infotype 2006 and—if possible—automatically control its creation through the time management schema.

Attendance Quotas (Infotype 2007)

Attendance quotas strongly correspond with absence quotas. We will not go into further detail on the corresponding customizing. Their treatment in the time evaluation schema follows in Section 8.2.7.

The important thing is to recognize the basic importance of attendance quotas. They have the following functions:

▶ Authorization of the attendance of employees at unusual times (days off, times outside working hours), which otherwise would not be considered in favour of the employee.

▶ Valuation of attendance times (if possible also within working hours) regarding compensation or remuneration (for this purpose the overtime compensation type is also entered in an attendance quota in addition to the times)

The deduction of attendance quotas generally occurs as follows:

▶ Attendances from Infotype 2002

▶ Attendances which result from employee time stamps (Infotype 2011)

They are generally created by direct maintenance of Infotype 2007 (see Figure 8.24).

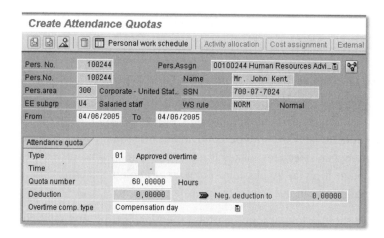

Figure 8.24 Authorization of 60 Overtime Hours for Which Payment is to be Made

The advantage of using an attendance quota for overtime authorization, in contrast to a fixed entry of overtime (Infotype 2005), lies in the fact that the exact times don't need to be known yet at the time of entry. For example, it is possible to assign a quota of 10 hours for a specific period or to allow overtime between 8 p.m. and 10 p.m. every day. The actual overtime is then determined automatically by the time evaluation, based on employee time stamps in the scope of the quota. This means it is sufficient to enter the overtime authorization (generally in advance). Every further step up to payment is done automatically, is documented and can be evaluated. The part of the quota which has already been used (if for example 60 hours of overtime were authorized due to a software project for the period 12/01/2001 to 01/31/2002) can be directly read in Infotype 2007 (see Figure 8.24).

Employee Remuneration Info (Infotype 2010)

Even if employee remuneration information is stored in a time-management infotype, they are processed by the payroll. Data that emerges from specific working times of the employee and frequently accumulates in the area of the time administrator or the incentive wage administrator is maintained here.

All facts not automatically determined by time evaluation or the incentive wage, are maintained via Infotype 2010, such as dirty-work bonuses for certain periods or piecework rates for parts finished at home. Basically, this infotype allows you to enter hours, pieces and/or amounts that are then transferred into payroll and valuated, if necessary. In addition, the valuation of hours or pieces entered by entering a deviating valuation basis can be influenced in different ways (see Figure 8.25).

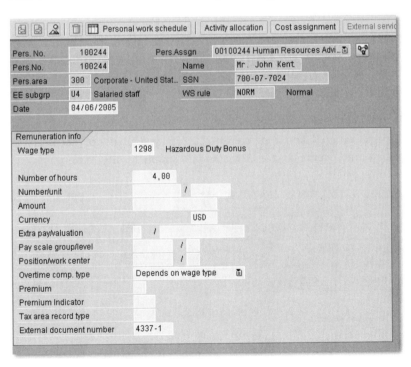

Figure 8.25 Dirty Work Bonus as Employee Remuneration Info with Reference to the Document Number of a Paper Document

Time Transfer Specifications (Infotype 2012)

Time transfers are used in order to modify the values of time balances, time-wage types and/or absence quotas. Here, the pure increase or decrease of an individual value is possible, as well as a transfer (e.g., transfer of x hours from the flextime balance to the annual working time account or posting the flextime balance into the time wage type "basic wage overtime," which corresponds to a disbursement of the balance).

The enhanced functionality of Infotype 2006, together with Infotype 0416 ("Time Quota compensation") only partially replaces the functionality of Infotype 2012. A tool to directly change the values of certain time types is mostly also required. Maintaining the infotype is quite simple (see Figure 8.26). The corresponding customizing is carried out via IMG path **Time Management · Time Evaluation · Time Evaluation with Clock Times · Processing Balances · Time Transfer**. There are two essential steps to be carried out there:

▶ The time transfer type must be created with an abbreviation and long text (sometimes with additional checks).

▶ The transfers must be defined with the following questions: From which time types, time-wage types or absence quotas is the value entered in the infotype drawn or added to? Here you can also work with percentage rates (e.g., 23%, in order to generate a flexiday from four days of availability time saved up). For real transfers, at least two such rules are necessary.

The actual transfer is performed by time evaluation, which analyzes the infotype entered and the relevant customizing. It is not necessary to change the schema vis-à-vis the standard supply for this reason.

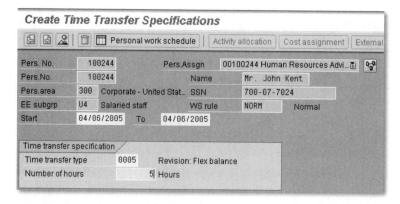

Figure 8.26 Correction to the Flextime Account (as a Time Type) via Infotype 2012

Quota Corrections (Infotype 2013)

Infotype 2013 changes absence quotas, in particular those which were generated by time evaluation and are thus not directly manually maintained.

The hourly figure entered can increase, decrease or completely overwrite the entitlement in Infotype 2006. You must also ensure here that maintenance in Infotype 2013 is not executed directly, but rather via time evaluation in Infotype 2006. As this is not necessarily updated daily, only at the month's end of the time evaluation can you accelerate this via the **Transfer** field in the quota correction.

Time Events (Infotype 2011)

Time events are generally entered via time recording or PDC terminals (see Section 8.2.6). It is also possible to enter them manually and to change them via Infotype 2011 (see Figure 8.27). If you are familiar with the functionality of this infotype, the integration of a terminal only represents another technical path for maintenance.

Entry

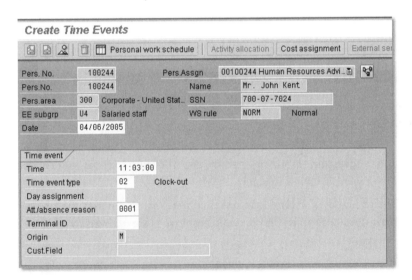

Figure 8.27 Clock-Out Entry with Absence Reason Entered Manually

For reasons of revision, it is relevant that all time events be identified according to their origin (manual entry or terminal posting), and that the originals still exist in the database table TEVEN even after a manual change or deletion.

The essential information for a time event is the date, time and type (clock-in, clock-out, etc.). In addition, the attendance and absence reason enables the triggering of the automatic generation of records of Infotype 2001 or 2002. A clock-out entry with the reason "flexday following day" then avoids the manual message and entry of a flexday via Infotype 2001. In standard Customizing, however, the time administrator then receives a message on such automatically generated absences and must release it.

In addition, extensive additional information can be entered that is not supported by all terminal manufacturers.

Time recording information
The recording of time events—whether this is done manually or through a terminal—requires the correct maintenance of Infotype 0050 ("Time Recording Info"). It contains in particular the following information:

▶ The **Time Recording ID Number** enables the assignment of a time-recording ID card, and thus the postings at the time recording terminal for the employee. Even if time events are exclusively maintained manually, this must always be maintained in the standard version and must be unique. Otherwise you cannot save the infotype. This is even the case if the field is hidden via Customizing.

> **Tip** In such cases, pre-allocate the field with the personnel number which is unequivocal as well (see Section 4.2).

▶ The **time event type group** determines the permitted time events.

▶ The **subsystem** grouping determines the terminals at which the employee is allowed to stamp.

▶ The grouping of **attendance/absence reasons** determines the reasons permitted (Example: Only specific employees are allowed to post "off-site work").

▶ The grouping **employee expenses** determines which wage types can be posted through the subsystem (e.g., parking fees).

▶ The **access control group** is then relevant, provided that the same subsystem is used for access control and determines when and how the employee has access.

Customizing
Customizing for time events and Infotype 0050 are closely connected with each other and can be reached via IMG path **Time Management · Personnel Time Events** (for the PDC connection also **Time Management**

• **Plant Data Collection**). In particular, the properties and effects of the grouping maintained in Infotype 0050 are set.

The customizing itself is easily executed by means of documentation. The important thing is to consider the groupings precisely in advance, and to leave scope for expansions of the three-digit abbreviations in naming conventions.

With regard to the time events enabled (by assigning the personnel time event type groups), we advise that you mainly use Time event type 03 "Clock-in/-out." It enables the HR system to decide which posting should exist now (based on the previous posting and the time model), and considerably decreases the complexity involved in manual correction of missing postings. For the most part, only the time-event types set by default are usable.

Additional Information on Time Data

Additional data can be maintained according to the Customizing for most of the time data which can be entered. These comprise the following areas:

▶ **Cost assignment**
Costs which are assigned to the data record via payroll, can be assigned a different cost unit as primary costs (see Figure 8.28). This assignment occurs through the normal posting interface in payroll.

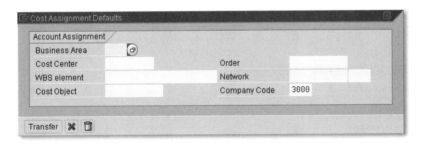

Figure 8.28 Entering a Different Primary Cost Assignment

▶ **Cost allocation**
Using the information provided by Report RPTPDOC0 (Menu path **Human Resources · Time Management · Administration · Environment · Activity Allocation**), a secondary costs allocation can be carried out between the sender and the recipient. For this reason, the entry of a performance type for cost accounting is of particular importance. An

example is the compensation of a business trip that takes place to support another department or because of a project (see Figure 8.29). In addition, the costs can be assigned to the sender as primary costs via payroll. However, the sender is normally the master cost center for the employee.

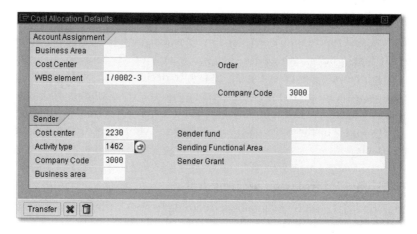

Figure 8.29 Debiting a Project (WBS Element) and Crediting the Master Cost Center (2230)

▶ **External services**
Integration to the R/3 component MM SRV is supported here. If the times of external service providers are entered in HR, or also through the schema TM02, additional information can be stored here. These are provided to purchasing as purchasing documents, positions, and activity numbers for checking and settlement (see Figure 8.30).

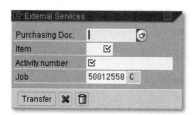

Figure 8.30 Entering Information on External Services

▶ **Different payment**
This additional data enables you to assign a special payment to certain times. In the simplest case, this would be an hourly rate entered manually as a valuation basis (see Figure 8.31). Examples would be bonuses for instructor activities (entered as attendance in Infotype 2002) or

noise bonuses for times which are spent in a particularly loud environment (entered through the time recording terminal or directly in Infotype 2011).

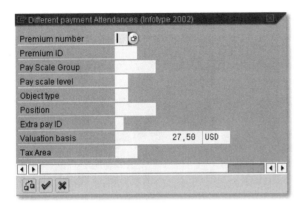

Figure 8.31 Valuation of an Attendance at a Fixed Hourly Rate

Weekly, Monthly and Annual Entry

Previously, only the entry of individual facts was shown, and was supplemented by simple list entry screens as necessary. However, there now are
further options for weekly, monthly and annual entries, and for general
list entry with additional data. These maintenance screens are primarily
used for cost allocation, cost distribution and external services, and can
be found via the following menu path: **Human Resources · Time Management · Administration · Time Data · Maintain Additional Data**.

The weekly entry (see Figure 8.32) is mainly used to maintain attendance
records and their handling in cost allocation and cost distribution. Typical
examples of the use of the weekly entry are project-time recording or
compensation for times of service employees who maintain machines
from different cost centers. In a similar way, the list entry records external
services.

Weekly entry/ list entry

Monthly entry maintains data for an individual employee from the overview of a calendar month. They should only rarely be used to support the
optimal processes, because the form of the maintenance does not correspond to the usual data access. However, this can be frequently used if
obsolete processes are mapped, in which for instance monthly time
recording cards are manually maintained in settlements and entered in
the central personnel department. However, this can only be merely an
interim solution until the implementation of decentralized entry concepts
(e.g., via ESS).

Monthly entry

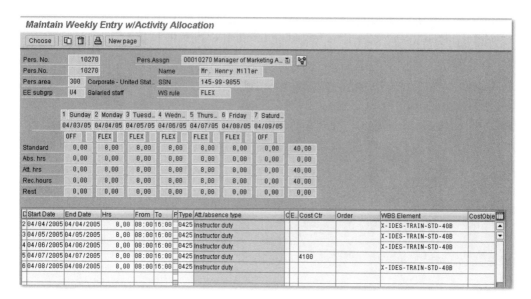

Figure 8.32 Project Time Recording via Weekly Entry

Annual calendar The annual calendar provides a good overview of any 12-month period for an employee (see Figure 8.33). Depending on Customizing, it can show all attendances and absences. It is less suitable for maintenance, although there are exceptions to this. As a display tool, it is very suitable. You should ensure that records lasting one day are displayed in lowercase letters.

Via IMG path **Time Management · Time Data Recording and Administration · Absences · Absence Catalog · Define Indicators for the Personal Calendar** you can define which absences are represented by which letters (proceed in the same way for attendances).

As is the case for the monthly entry, and to a limited extent for the weekly entry, the annual calendar becomes obsolete in many areas due to the Time Manager's Workplace (TMW), in particular the calendar view, as described in Section 8.4.

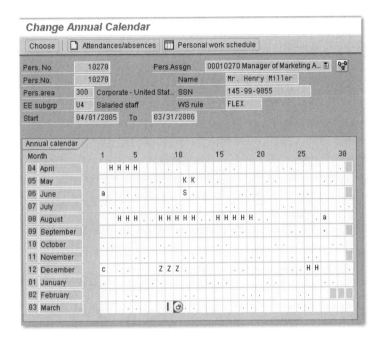

Figure 8.33 Annual Calendar with Attendances and Absences

Time Management Pool

The time management pool summarizes the essential tasks of the time administrator. This is not to be confused with the TMW (see Sections 8.3 and 8.4) that is implemented user-specifically and is strongly recommended for decentralized processing by the time administrator. You can replace the time management pool almost completely with the TMW or use it in parallel for central processing. The time management pool is, however, sufficient for pure central processing or for use by smaller companies. It can be used with a lot less configuration difficulty than can the TMW.

You can reach the time management pool via the following menu path: **Human Resources · Time Management · Administration · Time Evaluation · Time Management Pool**. There are extensive options for selecting the employees to be considered. Selection through the time administrator enables each administrator to select his or her area of responsibility. You can reach the individual components of the to-do-list directly by using the same path.

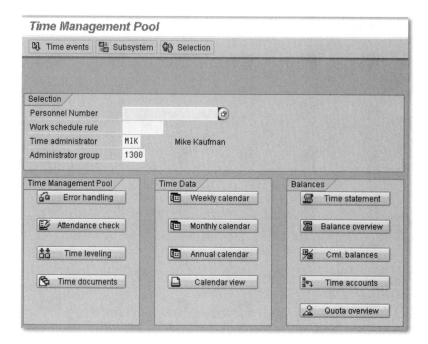

Figure 8.34 Time Management Pool

The following are the most important components of the time management pool that also display the daily business of the time administrator in HR (see also Figure 8.34):

▶ **Error handling**
All information and error messages for the selected employees can be overseen and processed here. Figure 8.35 shows the time management pool with several information messages and error messages.

▶ **Time leveling**
In the incentive wage area for instance, you can identify which attendances for the employee are not covered by time tickets.

▶ **The calendar views** that already have been described (weekly, monthly, and annual view)

▶ The cross-person entry

▶ Calling the time statement

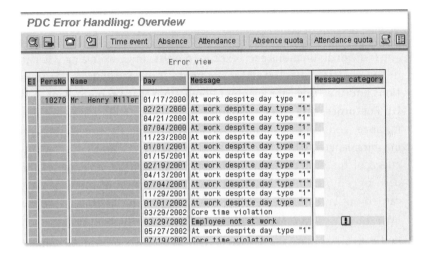

Figure 8.35 Error-Handling/Time Evaluation Messages

▶ **Balance overview**

It provides an overview of the essential time balances for the employee (see Figure 8.36). The reason for a balance overview is the need for a form that can be implemented in the same Form Editor in Customizing, as can the time statement.

Pers No.	Name	CCtr	WrkTime	FlexTime	Ref. Date
00100036	Mr. David Johnson	4120	187,00	*51,00-	01/31/2002
00100036	Mr. David Johnson	4120	160,00	*51,00-	02/28/2002
00100036	Mr. David Johnson	4120	160,00	*59,00-	03/31/2002
00010270	Mr. Henry Miller	3200	187,49	15,00	01/31/2002
00010270	Mr. Henry Miller	3200	162,95	15,00	02/28/2002
00010270	Mr. Henry Miller	3200	163,47	10,47	03/28/2002

Figure 8.36 Balance Overview

▶ The report RPTBAL00 can be created using the **Cumulated balances** button. This is an excellent way of evaluating time types on a daily and monthly basis as well as time-wage types. It is also an instrument of quality control for the system settings and to control the resource work time. Its functionality is only limited insofar as the time evaluation provides the required info time types. For this reason the settings for time evaluation should in particular be derived from the evaluation requirements.

▶ Further displays provide an overview of the time accounts and quotas.

▶ Last but not least, communication with the subsystem which normally takes place via background jobs can be controlled.

The time management pool can be adapted in Customizing in two ways to fit the specifics of your company:

1. The individual functions each execute reports. In Customizing you can define via IMG path **Time Management · Time Evaluation · Evaluations and the Time Management Pool · Time Management Pool · Set Up Postprocessing**, which variant is to be executed in each case. For instance, you can determine which form the time statement uses and in which language it should be called (while it is useful to use the language of the employee for a monthly print out, the language of the user logged on should be used here). The selection of the variants is carried out in feature LLREP, which is integrated in the IMG. Note the IMG documentation and the documentation for the feature.

2. In the error handling the time data is always shown in the environment of the error or the message. You can limit the display for specific groups of employees in a company-specific manner via the following IMG path: **Time Management · Time Evaluation · Evaluations and the Time Management Pool · Time Management Pool · Limit display to general data only** or **of data to errors only**. This generally occurs via the feature REPTA. Depending on the time-recording tab (Infotype 0007), this goes immediately to the sub-features REPT1 (no time recording and negative time recording) and REPT2 (positive time recording of different forms). In an error-dependent case, you must simply maintain one table per message.

8.2.6 Connecting Time Clocks

Time recording as displayed here comprises several areas. The categorization in Figure 8.37, for the sake of completeness, also contains the manual entry. Entry via the Employee Self Service (ESS) is a good alternative, which can be used through the normal Web browser. For smaller branches in particular, for whom attaching terminals is not worthwhile, ESS entry is more useful than sending times by paper forms or by e-mail to a central entry point. In this section the entry via terminals is described.

The person-time recording refers to pure people-related time events, e.g., clock-in, clock-out, start of break, etc. It is possible since Release 4.5, to carry out person-time recording in two ways: Through the transceiver solution, and through a Business Application Programming Interface (BAPI) with extensive options to transfer additional data.

Working-time recording refers to time events that originate from the employee's activities, e.g., setting up, tearing down, changing tools, etc.

In each case you must note the work distribution between the subsystem and HR. It is sufficient if the subsystem delivers the pure time events, or with extra information added. No further processing or interpretation is required; in fact, processing or interpretation would even be disruptive. The interpretation of time events in conjunction with other time data is incumbent on mySAP HR time management—beginning with the pair formation and ending with the transfer to payroll.

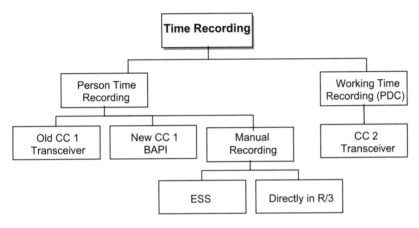

Figure 8.37 Variants for Time Recording

Some manufacturers of subsystems provide functionality similar to HR time evaluation. This is only useful if payroll occurs in another system than mySAP HR that provides insufficient functionality in time management. The direct connection of a complete external time management system to HR payroll is possible, but should be an exceptional activity (for instance, if very special functionalities are required that HR cannot map or can only do so with great difficulty). Unfortunately, many system providers are always trying to sell additional functionalities that are much better handled in HR. This not only boosts license and maintenance costs, but also makes the processes unnecessarily complicated.

The following questions will now be dealt with:

▶ How do personnel-time and working-time recording interact with each other?

▶ How do the old and new communication channel 1 (CC1) function?

▶ What should you consider during analysis and conception?

Person-Time Recording

Time recording system

SAP AG provides a certified process for the providers of time-recording systems. As the certification does not encompass the entire process of subsystem connection, it is possible that a provider is only partly certified. This would mean they are not in the position to provide all functionalities that the connection basically provides. Therefore, check closely to what extent the interface of your potential time recording system provider is certified by SAP AG.

In the following section, both interface processes are described. If you still use the old process from an older release status, a conversion is only needed if you require new functionality. The old process will basically continue to function in a stable manner.

Older CC1 transceiver

The old CC1 establishes the communication between R/3 and the time recording system (subsystem) via transceivers. The time-recording system provides a data record at the operation system level. Transceivers accept this data record and make it available to the R/3. It is provided and posted there via Application Link Enabling (ALE) and Intermediate Documents (IDOCs) for time management in HR.

Apart from the technical integration, you must maintain the functionality of the entire connection. Define in such a way as to answer the following:

▶ Are the participants to be classified in the time recording, i.e., grouped for the subsystem?

▶ Should attendance/absence reasons be entered in the terminal?

▶ Should information be displayed at the terminals?

▶ Should additional data such as canteen data be entered?

Infotype 0050 maps the connection between the personnel master data and the subsystem.

New CC1 BAPI

The new CC1 is also based like the old CC1 on IDOCs. However, for communication it uses a BAPI. In addition, it provides extended functionality. It is then possible to enter, for instance, a differing payment and cost assignment at the terminal. In addition, freely definable fields are available. Additional time event types such as change or info postings are supported. For the design of the new CC1, the same limits apply as for the old CC1, supplemented with the additional functionality.

Working Time recording (PDC)

Working time recording, also referred to as plant data collection (PDC), is based on communication channel 2 (CC2). The following modules can be tied to this interface:

▶ Production planning and control (PP)

▶ Production planning and control/Process industry (PP/PI)

▶ Maintenance or service management (PP/SM)

▶ Project system (PS)

Two processes are possible here:

▶ Confirmation occurs in relation to a certain point in time, i.e., work time events (e.g., start of setup time) are transferred. Time tickets are generated in the time evaluation.

▶ Confirmation depends on the processing duration, i.e., the number of hours transferred. Data can be directly posted as time tickets without time evaluation.

Time-spot-related confirmation generally means less difficulty in making entries in production, but also more complex and finicky solutions in R/3 as well as in the subsystem.

In order to reach a basic decision between both of these processes, an exact definition of the target process is necessary while considering technical determining factors. Here, the following areas are to be integrated in the conception:

▶ Data emergence in logistics

▶ Incentive wage

▶ Time management

▶ Payroll in general

▶ Cost accounting

Define the cross-area process at an early stage. This not only affects the customizing settings, but also on the conception of the subsequent processes, the selection of hardware and software, and even on the cabling and the elements which form the design in production.

For CC2, also check the certification of your time recording system provider and in particular all specific requirements which derive from your process, e.g., support for the operation use of multiple machines or machine cards.

Interaction of CC1 and CC2 in the Incentive Wage

As each communication channels fulfills different tasks that span the entire working time for one employee, it is necessary for these to work in tandem. We will not name the exact tables involved here.

The starting point for the collaboration could be a clock-in entry for the employee at 6 a.m. In the database you can only see one record with this information (see Table 8.1).

Time	Pair type	Time event info
06:00	At work	Person time event

Table 8.1 Database After Clock-In Entry

The employee reports at 6.15 a.m. "setup start time," at 6.30 a.m. "end of setup time," at 2 p.m. "end of series of operations" and at 2.30 p.m. "clock-out." You can now find the relevant information in the database (see Table 8.2).

Time	Communication channel 1	Time event info
06:00	CC1	Clock-in
06:15	CC2	Beginning of setup time
06:30	CC2	End of setup time
14:00	CC2	End of series of operations
14:30	CC1	Clock-out

Table 8.2 Database with Postings After One Day

In the course of the time evaluation the time pairs displayed in Table 8.3 are mapped.

Current. No.	from to	Time pair info	Time ticket info
1	06:00–06:15	Personnel time	No time ticket
2	06:15–06:30	Setup time	Time ticket setup
3	06:30–09:00	Order time	Time ticket order
4	09:00–09:15	Break	

Table 8.3 Time Pairs After Pair Formation

Current. No.	from to	Time pair info	Time ticket info
5	09:15–12:00	Order time	Time ticket order
6	12:00–12:45	Break	
7	12:45–14:00	Order time	Time ticket order
8	14:00–14:30	Personnel time	No time ticket

Table 8.3 Time Pairs After Pair Formation (cont.)

As you can see, not only the time events from the CC1 have been linked with the work time events of the CC2, but also the entire process has been validated against the daily work timetable.

The time tickets generated are now provided for the incentive wages through integration. The settings necessary for this are available in the standard SAP version and can be adapted to the specific company requirements without modifications.

> **Note** Note that the executions for the CC2 are only relevant for HR, provided that time tickets must be generated in the time management from logistic time events. If they are generated from time-confirmation tickets in logistics (i.e., logistics supplies time-related information to HR, with no time-spots), the CC2 has no impact in HR.

8.2.7 Time Evaluation

Time evaluation occurs via Report RPTIME00. In order to maintain optimal flexibility with regard to company-specific adaptations, the behavior of RPTIME00 is not only controlled via customizing tables, but also via a schema. The schema consists of functions, sub-schemas, and calculation rules. The latter are similar in their structure to the characteristics and consist of operations. Figure 8.38 shows the time-evaluation customizing context. The entire schema is also a component of Customizing and must in general be more or less radically adapted. Unfortunately, the processing is quite complex and the syntax of the available commands is not very intuitive. It is very similar to assembler programming. The schema should not be changed without experienced support.

Basic

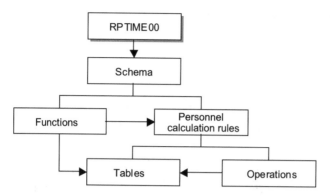

Figure 8.38 Overview: Customizing for Time Evaluation

The direction of development, however, shows that the importance of customizing in the schema is decreasing and in parts replaced by customizing tables. To this end, a customizing table was provided for Release 4.6 to support the complex processing of time balance limits (capping, warning, updating, etc).

The customizing in the schema is also supported via the IMG. Via IMG path **Time Management · Time Evaluation · Time Evaluation With Clock Times** (for negative recording: **Time Evaluation Without Clock Times**) the normal activities needed to adapt the behavior of the time evaluation are carried out. Normal customizing tables belong to this category, as do points in the schema and certain calculation rules, for which sufficient instructions can be found in the documentation. Always work as close as possible to this guide.

In the following sections you should get a feel for the complexity and the options of customizing. In addition, you will receive basic tips on the process and will get to know the basics about the contexts and selected details also.

It is not possible to handle the subject of schemas and calculation rules sufficiently within the scope of this book. The documentation provided by SAP is however very extensive and helpful in many places. At the beginning, an experienced coach should always be available.

The Schema

SAP provides different schemas in the standard version:

▶ TM00—Personnel time events (positive recording)

▶ TM01—Work schedule deviations (negative time recording)

- ▶ TM02 — External services management

- ▶ TM04 — Without clock times

In the following explanation, we will refer to the Schema TM00.

A schema consists of functions that on the one hand process fixed parameters stored in tables, and on the other hand call part schemas or personnel calculation rules. Calling a personnel-calculation rule can also be linked with parameters.

You can call the schema maintenance via Transaction PE01 or via menu path **Human Resources · Time Management · Administration · Tools · Tools Selection · Maintain Schemas**. Transaction PE02 for the maintenance of calculation rules is adjacent in the menu.

Figure 8.39 shows an extract from the standard schema TM00 and gives an overview in the schema editor. You can see which functions, rules, and part schemas it contains. By double-clicking on the corresponding part schema, you can navigate to this schema.

000180	BLOCK	BEG			
000190	IF		NOT	SIMF	
000200	PERT	TD20			
000210	P2011				
000220	ACTIO	TD10			
000230	A2003				
000240	ACTIO	TD60	AB		
000250	P2001				
000260	P2002				
000270	PTIP	TD80	GEN		
000280	ACTIO	TD90			
000290	P2005			*	
000300	PTIP	TD40	GEN	*	
000310	ACTIO	TD30			
000320	DYNWS			*	

Figure 8.39 Extract from Schema TM00

The source code of the schema is listed. By clicking in the function fields **Par1** to **Par4** and calling the **F1** help, you can go to the documentation for the corresponding function.

The basic structure of the schema corresponds to the sections of the IMG for **Time Evaluation with Clock Times**:

Structure of the schema

▶ **Initial Steps**

In addition to specific checks, different groupings are set for the employees.

▶ **Providing Time Data**

Time events, other time data such as absences and work schedules are read in and mixed, so the time pairs are available at the end. These are provided in Table TIP and are processed throughout the run of the schema.

▶ **Time Data Processing**

On the basis of time pairs in Table TIP and different Customizing settings, the following processings are executed:

- ▶ Processing beginning and end tolerances

- ▶ Error checking and outputting messages such as "Employee at work despite vacation"

- ▶ Characterizing time pairs via time types (attendance time, absence time, etc.)

- ▶ Determining break times

- ▶ Determining planned times

- ▶ Processing absences (e.g., decreasing flextime balances in the case of absence "flexday")

▶ **Time Wage Type Selection**

Attendance quotas in particular are processed here and time-wage types for overtime and other times (e.g., nightwork) are generated.

▶ **Overtime Compensation**

The wage types generated in the previous step are then further processed, in connection with the selected compensation. Here it is to be decided which parts are compensated by free time and which are transferred to payroll for payment. A monetary valuation does not occur here! The wage types are transferred with the number of hors, along with additional information if needed. Valuation with an hourly rate occurs in payroll.

▶ **Processing Balances and Message Output**

The time accounts and time balances are processed according to company regulations (e.g., capping, or transferring to another account when exceeding an upper limit). Time transfers (infotype 2012) are considered here. In addition to time types, attendance quotas are also generated. In addition, messages can be generated, depending on the status of the balances.

▶ **Month's-End Processing**

Here, in turn, balance-processing is implemented on a monthly level. In addition, info time types can be mapped and messages can be output.

▶ **Storing Evaluation Results**

This also belongs to month's-end processing and provides the results for evaluations and subsequent processes.

Calculation Rules

Calculation rules are essential components of the schema. They are called as parameters of some functions and control the processing in a detailed manner. The calculation rules provide the option of constructing a decision tree, and of using a large template of operations that shows the essential element of flexibility of time evaluation.

You can maintain the rules via Transaction PE02 (menu path **Human Resources · Time Management · Administration · Tools · Tools Selection · Maintain Personnel Calculation Rules**). In general, the standard rules should not be changed, but rather copied to custom rules and then adapted. We will not go into further detail on maintaining rules, as we would have to dedicate a whole book to this area. Remember that calculation rules provide high flexibility, but the often high once-off and maintenance complexity should not be underestimated. Figure 8.40 shows Calculation rule TC40 as an example of overtime compensation which also calls Rule TC41 as a sub-rule.

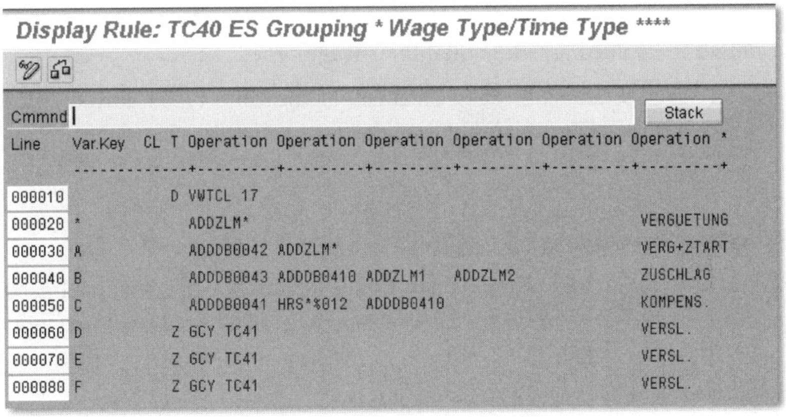

```
Display Rule: TC40 ES Grouping * Wage Type/Time Type ****

Cmmnd |                                                          Stack

Line   Var.Key  CL T Operation Operation Operation Operation Operation Operation *
       ---------+---------+---------+---------+---------+---------+---------+
000010           D VWTCL 17
000020  *          ADDZLM*                                        VERGUETUNG
000030  A          ADDDB0042 ADDZLM*                              VERG+ZTART
000040  B          ADDDB0043 ADDDB0410 ADDZLM1   ADDZLM2          ZUSCHLAG
000050  C          ADDDB0041 HRS*%012  ADDDB0410                  KOMPENS.
000060  D        Z GCY TC41                                       VERSL.
000070  E        Z GCY TC41                                       VERSL.
000080  F        Z GCY TC41                                       VERSL.
```

Figure 8.40 Example of a Calculation Rule

Basic Processing Logic

Even though we will not go into all the details, we will summarize the logic in time evaluation. If you are familiar with the basic tables, you can build on this by doing some study yourself (if possible with the support of a coach).

Time evaluation works in daily processing primarily with six internal tables (there are still some others that from the point of view of logic are not essential):

▶ Table TIP contains all time pairs and is created every day in the first part of the processing. The time pairs are provided with numerous tabs in this table, which are essential for the creation of completely new processing steps. The documentation of these tabs as well as additional tables can be found in the SAP library via the following path: **Personnel Time Management · Time Evaluation · Appendix · Internal Tables in Time Evaluation**. This is an essential section of the documentation for those who are more involved with customzing the time evaluation.

▶ Daily balances of the time types are collected in Table TES. At the end of the day processing it contains for instance the positive flextime balance for the day in time type 0005. The TES is generally populated when calculation rules process the table TIP and, if applicable, additional data, and thus derive the values for individual time types.

▶ In tables ZML (overtime) and DZL, the time-wage types , in particular with the number of hours, and, if necessary, with start and end times are collected on a daily basis. The tables are generally populated when calculation rules process Table TIP and possibly other data, and thus derive the values for individual time-wage types.

▶ In the end processing, daily balances of the time types and also the time wage types are accumulated in monthly tables. This occurs in the Tables SALDO and ZL.

Selected Processing

The settings for some of the relevant time evaluation aspects were already described in the previous sections. Here, two additional essential processing types are described in more detail: the time wage types generation, and the processing of balance limits.

Time-wage types generation
A main aim of time management lies in preparing payroll-relevant facts in time management for subsequent processing in payroll. The wage type generation which generates wage types for payroll is the interface for this.

The functions DAYMO and GWT, along with the tables for the time wage types generation rules, provide you with powerful tools to carry out these tasks. The settings are carried out via the following IMG path: **Time Management · Time Evaluation · Time Evaluation With Clock Times · Time Wage Type Selection and Overtime Compensation · Define Generation Rules**. Time wage type selection rules are primarily entered here, which describe the conditions for the emergence of a wage type (see Figure 8.41). On first glance, this table appears confusing. If you have clarified the conditions for the creation of wage types on a technical level, however, the maintenance of the table is not critical. Note that you do not necessarily require all the criteria offered.

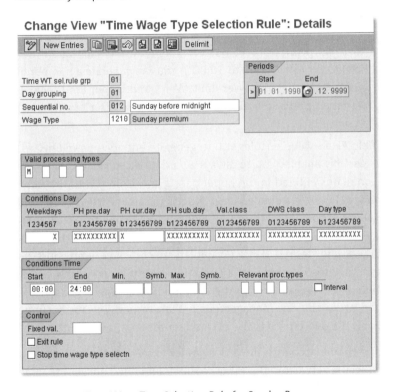

Figure 8.41 A Time Wage Type Selection Rule for Sunday Bonuses

The following criteria are available:

▶ The time wage types selection rule group and the day grouping are set in the calling schema via the function DAYMO and the calculation rule MODT.

▶ The valid processing type is assigned a time pair in the time evaluation in Table TIP (e.g., "M" for overtime, "S" for planned working time).

▶ The generation rule gets the conditions for the current day from the personal shift plan (PSP) for the employee. In the example shown, there are only limitations regarding the day of the week (Sunday) and the public holiday class (not a public holiday). The wage type in the example is formed independently of the public-holiday class of the previous day and the subsequent day, of the period-work-schedule evaluation class, of the daily work schedule class, and of the day type. All these criteria could also be used in order to further break down the generation rules (e.g., in the case of daily working-time schedules for the night shift, if a rotating shift is worked on Sundays that follow a public holiday, a wage type must then be generated).

▶ The generation rule then gets the time conditions from Table TIP. The restrictions to the times is of particular relevance for the night bonuses (note that nightwork from 10 p.m. to 6 a.m. on the subsequent day must be entered with "22:00 to 30:00"). You can generate a number of hours via the parameters **Lower limit (Min.)** and **Upper limit (Max.)**, e.g., overtime up to two hours with a 25% bonus, aftter two hours at a 50% bonus.

▶ The field **Fixed value** enables you to generate entrance premiums, for instance. This enables you to always award an attendance that meets the conditions entered in the upper part of the screen, with the same number of hours of a defined wage type. This can in particular be used for special actions such as an SAP going-live preparation over Christmas. For this reason the rule is to be limited to the precise period of validity at the desired dates (Example: An employee who must be present at Christmas receives an additional eight hours on his or her flextime account regardless of the duration of attendance.) Such rules can be easily abused. Management is then responsible for ensuring that only the overtime actually required for the company is authorized.

Balance limits The limits of time accounts, the processes for exceeding these limits, and the interaction between different accounts frequently conceal the large company-specific adjustment requirement. While older releases imposed considerable complexity on creating new calculation rules, the standard Customizing to some extent now provides extensive control tables. In the schema, the processing according to the Customizing settings is simply called via the LIMIT function which is also contained in the standard schema.

You can reach the settings via the following IMG path: **Time Management · Time Evaluation · Time Evaluation With Clock Times · Processing Balances · Balance Formation · Balance Limits**.

Basically the following options of limit processing are available respectively for monthly balances and daily balances:

▶ First, always determine which threshold value (constant or variable from the time evaluation) is drawn on, and whether this is an upper or lower threshold. The time type (accumulated, or as minimum/maximum) is then entered and must be compared with the threshold value.

▶ The checks can be daily or monthly (the latter for monthly balances on a monthly basis). However, you can define the times for the checks yourself, for example weekly.

▶ Then you enter how the system will react to a violation to the threshold value. The following options are available here:

  ▶ Creating a time-evaluation message

  ▶ Capping the balance

  ▶ Switching excess to another time type

  ▶ Transferring excess in a wage type

  ▶ Transferring the old value of the processed balance in another time type so that it is still available for evaluation purposes

▶ It is even possible to output a message in order to provide a warning shortly before reaching the threshold value. To do this, you must specify a tolerance that enters at what interval for the threshold value the message is to be generated.

▶ By limiting the limit rule regarding the age of the employee, you can, for instance, generate a message if a violation of the youth labor law occurs.

8.2.8 Incentive Wage

The Data Sources

The rules in the incentive wage are company-specific. As a result, the remuneration also has to account for particular circumstances in production. This means there frequently are different incentive wage models within a company and even within a plant. In the following section, we will describe the standard solution as well as strengths and weaknesses.

HR requires basic data on the incentive wage in time tickets. These entry screens are similar to paper time tickets still used today for the initial entry of data that is relevant to wages. The time ticket data can be transferred to HR via three different paths:

▶ Manual entry via the following menu path: **Human Resources · Time Management · Incentive Wages · Time Tickets**

▶ Time evaluation that generates time tickets from work time events in logistics

▶ Transfer of time tickets from logistics via the following menu path: **Human Resources · Time Management · Incentive Wages · Environment · Subsystem connection · Logistics Integration · Time Tickets · Create session**

The last two variants are preferable because of data quality and entry effort. They must meet the following prerequisites:

▶ Logistics must be operational in the same system as HR, or an ALE connection to the logistics system must be set up.

▶ The confirmations must be assigned to personnel numbers in logistics.

▶ Run schedule headers are not used (the notification of goods receipt for run-schedule headers does not allow the entry of personnel numbers—an useful integration demands the modification of the system at several points):

▶ Only individual incentive wages; no group incentive wage are calculated. (Group numbers for HR cannot be supplied in logistics. By assembling user exits, you can implement an integration with suitable conventions for group incentive wages without carrying out modifications.)

The Systematics of Result Calculation

The further processing now occurs in the incentive-wage components. Figure 8.42 shows an overview of the process. The dates of the time tickets are processed for groups and/or employee levels according to the rules of a premium formula,, and they then supply the result (e.g., performance efficiency rate).

The time-ticket values are first accumulated (actual times, standard times, time credits, etc.) via accumulation rules in collectors (result types). The result is finally calculated from these values, and additional parameters (e.g., a quality factor determined monthly) or a step function (can even lead to capping) can be integrated.

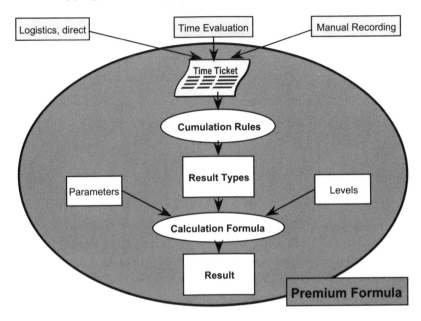

Figure 8.42 Results Calculation According to a Premium Formula

In general, at least one premium formula is required for each remuneration scenario in the incentive wage. The result determined via the premium formula on the time-ticket level or on the period level ultimately becomes the basis for the monetary valuation in the payroll.

There is a high flexibility in the calculation rule in particular. It even enables the integration of customer-specific ABAP coding, so that almost every calculation rule can be implemented.

You can reach the Customizing settings for the premium formula via the following IMG path: **Time Management · Incentive Wages · Premium Formulas**. A prerequisite is that the systematics displayed in Figure 8.42 were made specific from a company-specific viewpoint. Formulate the required formulas for the calculation rules, and clarify how the individual components of the formulas are to be determined (for instance, what counts as "secondary processing times," if these are required in the calculation). The differentiation between different types of actual times mainly occurs through the time-ticket types in which the times are entered.

Time Ticket Types

Time tickets contain the information which is required to calculate the results. These are mainly current and target values for working time, setup time, tear down time and machine time as well as quantities and scrap.

SAP HR uses the following time ticket types in the standard version:

▶ **Premium time tickets**
They contain times and quantities for individual employees (see Figure 8.43). A result can be formed here according to the time ticket (e.g., performance efficiency rate) and not only according to the period. The data for the premium time ticket is used exclusively to calculate individual premiums.

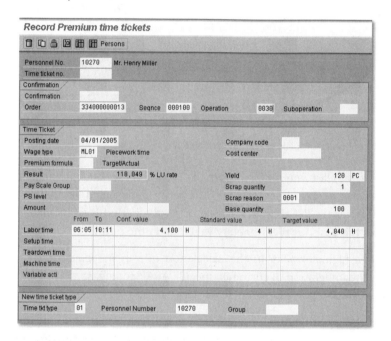

Figure 8.43 Example of a Premium Time Ticket (Individual Premium)

▶ **Quantity time tickets**
They contain quantities for a work group. As the times are not to be directly assigned here, a group result can only be calculated on the period level. The data for the quantity time ticket is used exclusively to calculate group premiums.

▶ **Person time tickets**
These contain the attendance times for an employee in a group. In this case, an employee can to all intents and purposes be active in different

groups on the same day in rotation. The data for the person time ticket is used exclusively to calculate group premiums.

▶ **Time-related time tickets**

These contain the times for an employee that are generally not evaluated in the premium pay, but rather in the normal time wage. If necessary, however, the time is also valuated with a piece-work average (e.g., the current month). In addition, the times of the time tickets can also influence the incentive wage results, for instance if they are input as malfunction periods or as secondary processing times in the calculation rule. There are several types of time tickets in one company, whose times are to be treated differently with regard to payment or evaluation.

▶ **Foreman time tickets**

They are a mixture of premium time ticket, quantity time ticket, and person time tickets. They are used if a certain member of an incentive wage group (e.g., the foreman) not only contributes to the group result but also gathers an individual premium.

The customizing of time tickets can be carried out via the following IMG path: **Time Management · Incentive Wages · Time Ticket Types**. To create your own time ticket types, you should copy the standard time tickets. Note during conception that the time ticket type can be used as a control criterion for accumulation in result types. The options to adapt time tickets, in particular showing of free customer fields, have been described in sufficient detail. Interfaces can be adjusted more extensively, simply by copying and changing a Dynpro using the Screen Painter. However, as this falls into the area of interface programming, we will not go into the topic in more detail.

Additional Settings

Additional Customizing settings are basically quite simple. However, a few settings are merely provided to activate user exits and business add-ins, which then find their use if the corresponding programming is executed. You should therefore try to manage with as few user exits as possible. Although in theory user exits are "release durable," the user exits in the incentive wage have often required adjustments when changes have been made to standard structures.

Under the IMG path **Time Management · Incentive Wages · Default Settings**, the following settings are of particular importance:

- Definition of the employee subgroups that participate in the incentive wage model

- Settings for maximal retroactive calculation for the incentive wage

  Keeping the open period for retroactive calculations (and retroactive entries) as short as possible, in order to avoid incorrect entries (e.g., incorrect annual figure).

- Using different parameters on the system, transaction and user levels. The essential parameters are:

  - Flag indicating whether or not the breaks from the daily work schedule of the employees for should be considered calculating the actual time in the time ticket (do not set, if the breaks are not precisely adhered to)

  - Tabs, whether accumulations are to be formed not only on monthly levels but also on daily levels

  - Activating messages when creating, maintaining, and displaying time tickets; if required they can be overridden on the user level.

  - Initialization of fields when creating, maintaining, and displaying time tickets; if required this can be overridden on the user level.

  - Activation of user exits

Groups must not be created in advance in Customizing. Under the IMG path **Time Management · Incentive Wages · Groups** only permissible group numbers are defined.

The integration to logistics is primarily a question of the subsystem settings (for the variants through PDC work time events) and the process definition in alignment with logistics. Via IMG path **Time Management · Incentive Wages · Integration with Logistics**, the subsequent changeability of time tickets from logistics is determined. In addition you can set small integration here. This means that in manual entry of the time tickets, certain data is read from logistics (e.g., standard values) and set in the time ticket, based on the confirmation number that is entered or the order and sequence numbers.

Strengths and Weaknesses of the HR Incentive Wage

In order to decide if the incentive wage processing is to be set in HR, you must consider the following points. Alternatives include use of an external system or manual written entry where the completed remuneration data is provided manually or by machine via Infotype 2010 for the payroll.

The following are the strengths of incentive wage processing:

Strengths

▶ The options for entering are quite comprehensive in the standard version.

▶ You can implement the confidentiality principle.

▶ The calculation process for the performance efficiency rate or additional results is extremely flexible.

▶ There is a high degree of flexibility in evaluating the payroll.

▶ An integration in the companywide data pool with personnel, logistics, and cost-accounting data is possible.

▶ The integrated process from logistics to HR, minimizes the complexity in making entries and maximises the data quality.

▶ Time-leveling enables the checking of covered times for production employees.

On the other hand, you can identify the following weaknesses:

Weaknesses

▶ You can only produce flexibility with a very high degree of complexity in Customizing and programming.

▶ Only a few reporting options are offered by default.

▶ The authorization concept and the locking concept for groups with frequent group changes are disruptive and in certain cases very disruptive.

▶ The ergonomics in the time ticket entry are far from ideal.

▶ The integration from logistics for serial orders and group premiums is problematic.

▶ The mapping of time tickets kept in reserve to improve the piece-rate during slack periods is quite unsatisfactory.

8.2.9 Reporting in Time Management

For the systematics of reporting and the use of queries, you can apply the same information that is detailed in Chapter 11 for *Personnel Controlling*.

The evaluations for time management are primarily based on the following points:

▶ Time types assigned as daily or period balances from time evaluation

▶ Time wage types that must be formed in the time evaluation (if the monetary valuation is to be integrated in the evaluation, the evaluation must occur in payroll)

▶ Infotypes of time management

▶ Time ticket data, results and accumulation of the incentive wage

The following section describes a few especially helpful reports by means of example. You can reach all these evaluations via the following menu path: **Human Resources · Time Management · Administration · Information System · Report Selection**

▶ **Attendance and absence overview graphic**
This evaluation should replace the Microsoft Excel-supported leave lists in the individual departments. It is an exceptional online tool that enables you to navigate from the overview screen to the details data. Figure 8.44 shows this overview by means of an example. It is possible to provide this evaluation to management decentrally via the MDT (see Section 13.3). However, for their vacation planning managers also need the leave requests of their employees that usually are not yet entered in the system as absence records. At this point it is possible to introduce a new "absence type" that could be called "Leave request." The employee can then enable the maintenance via the ESS (see Chapter 13, *Role-based Portal Solution*). After completing the vacation planning the wishes can be transformed into real leave records.

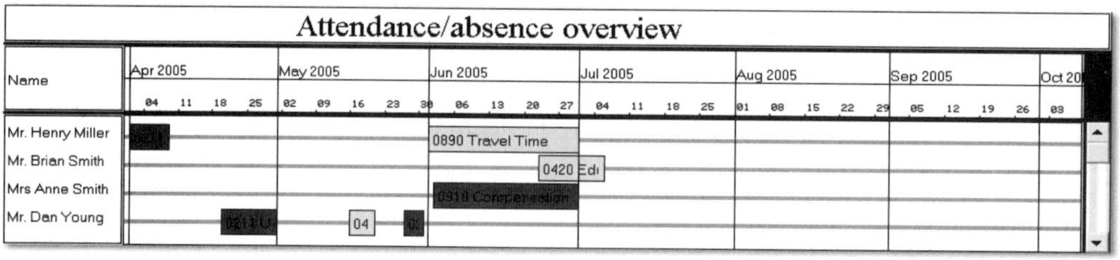

Figure 8.44 Attendances and Absences Overview Graphic

▶ **Evaluation attendance/absence data overview**
It enables creation of different forms of absence statistics. For instance, the overview aggregates the absence times in general or those restricted to certain types, and connects them to the planned time. This also enables comparable statuses for employee sickness for individual departments.

▶ **Evaluation of cumulated time evaluation results**
It enables almost any kind of meaningful evaluation which is based on daily balances, monthly balances or time-wage types. Different summation levels are also possible here. The only limitation: It is not possible

to display several time types in columns near each other. If several time types are being evaluated this only makes sense if they are to be added.

▶ **Time balances overview**
It provides an overview of several time types, but is however less flexible in the output. The time-balance overview must first be set using the Form Editor of the time statement in Customizing. It is very useful in providing management with evaluations that can always be compared and which give an overview of the balance statuses of employees.

▶ **Quota overview**
It provides a similar functionality for quotas from Infotype 2006 (display absence quota information).

8.2.10 Integration Aspects

The integration of time management in R/3 also contains module-internal components within HR and module-external components in relation to accounting and logistics (see Figure 8.45).

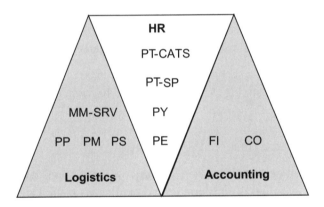

Figure 8.45 Integration Aspects of Time Management

Module-Internal Integration

Module-internal integration spans the collaboration with the part components CATS Cross-Application Time Sheet, PT SP Shift Planning, PE Training and Event Management, and PY Payroll.

The cross-application timesheet enables you to enter time data across modules and to transfer data to other modules. Plausibility controls are available within the entry. This means, for example, that it is possible to check order numbers or cost centers. The transition is carried out via a defined interface.

You can plan the assignment of employees quantitatively and qualitatively and in relation to the present or the future with resource planning. As this functionality is a component of time management, you can access the current status at any time, create a target plan on this basis, and if necessary transfer this as a new current status in time management.

Seminar participations or assignments as instructors in training and event management can automatically generate attendance records in Infotype 2002, in cases where the corresponding integration is activated in Customizing in event management.

Payroll accesses data records created in time management (time-wage types, absences, personal work schedules) and processes these in the payroll run.

Module-External Integration

Module-external integration concerns the processes of logistics and accounting. This is particularly relevant in logistics MM SRV—External Services, PP—Product Planning, PM—Maintenance and P—Project System. In accounting, controlling (CO) and also financial accounting (FI) are affected. For the public sector, you also must consider funds management.

For the logistics module, data such as attendances/absences is provided and entered for capacity planning. An example would be working times for external employees by Cross-Application Time Sheet (CATS). Further, logistics data is provided for time management, for example through confirmations for order-related times or incentive wages.

Integration in accounting can be carried out in two ways. Time data expressed in monetary values is transferred to accounting via payroll and financial accounting. Pure time information, i.e. hours, is transferred to controlling and is evaluated there according to activity types and used in cost allocation.

8.3 Time Manager's Workplace

8.3.1 Application and Functionalities

Introduction

In most companies, time administration is carried out in a decentralized manner. Checking and error removal for postings via time clocks, the recording of attendance times (if no terminals are being used) and absences are being shifted more and more to decentralized units. This is supposed to facilitate the processes by recording the information where it occurs and making it easier to process queries. Administrative assistants or other employees take on the role of decentralized time administrators. For these employees time recording is only a "sideline job" that they accept along with their main job. This makes an easy-to-manage and easy-to-use interface especially important. Users who previously worked in decentralized island solutions, which weren't integrated with central evaluation systems and payroll, find the requirements of an integrated environment very complex anyway. Acceptance should therefore not be threatened further by unnecessarily complicated data entry, where the user has to navigate through many different screens.

Time Manager's Workplace (TMW) was specifically created by SAP AG for decentralized time administrators in departments, production islands, branches, or affiliates. The essential advantage here is that all administrative activities of time management are basically possible without a change of transaction. The TMW compiles all information of the different infotypes of time management into one interface that is attached to the existing data structures. It enables considerably easier maintenance than is possible through the individual infotypes of time management. The information entered through TMW is stored in the familiar infotypes of time management (e.g., absences in Infotype 2001).

Introduction in the TMW

When you first use the TMW, you must enter the profile and definition area for IDs. The profile determines the complete layout and the adjustable functionalities of the TMW. Instead of attendance or absence types and quota types, the TMW works with IDs that are compiled in the definition quantity and, if necessary, existing subsets of this definition area.

Figure 8.46 shows the initial screen for calling the TMW (Transaction PTMW, Easy Access menu: **Human Resources · Time Management · Administration · Time Manager's Workplace**).

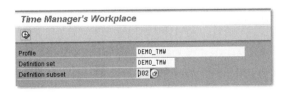

Figure 8.46 Initial Screen for the Initial Call of the TMW

The data is then stored in the user defaults as parameters PT_TMW_PRO-FILE (for the profile) and PT_TMW_TDLANGU (for the definition area and subset). If you want to avoid the initial screen, you can maintain this data upfront via the following menu: **System · User Profile · Own Data**. In the **Parameters** tab, you can enter the corresponding values. Here the subset of the definition area is to be connected to the definitions area, separated by a slash (e.g., definitions area DEMO_TMW and subset 001, entry: TMW_DEMO/001). However, the simplest variant for the user is to specify the user parameter centrally through the user administration.

The Basic Structure

The TMW is divided into different screen areas. Figure 8.47 gives an initial overview of the graphical screen areas within the TMW. In the standard version, the **Dialog messages** area is located below the **Processing of time data in detail** area. However, for reasons of clarity we recommend you place the dialog messages above the info area.

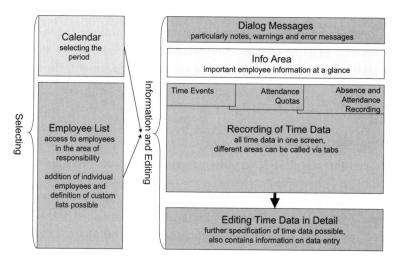

Figure 8.47 Layout and Screen Areas in TMW

The adjustment is executed via the system table T77SO. Figure 8.48 shows the required settings.

Figure 8.48 Entry in the System Table (T77SO) to Position the Message Line in the Upper Screen Area

The TMW provides the following views in the data-entry section that refer to the period and the employees:

▶ **One-day view**

Places an employee into the data-entry section for maintenance on a specific selected day.

▶ **Multi-day view**

Enables you to maintain a period for an employee that is previously selected through the calendar.

▶ **Multi-Person view**

Permits the maintenance of time data for several employees at the same time for a selected day. You can transfer several employees into the data entry section by selecting the employees (hold down the **Shift** or **Ctrl** key and select) and then clicking the button to transfer the selected records. In the multi-person view, you can for inszance maintain a one-day vacation absence for a team in one step.

Figure 8.49 shows the use of the TMW.

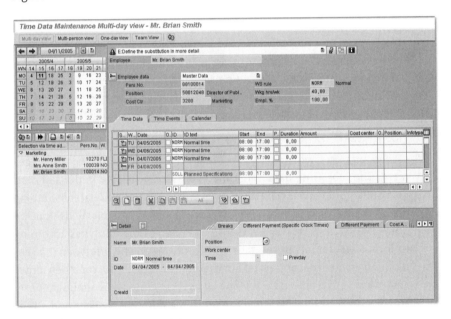

Figure 8.49 Time Manager's Workplace in Use

The views can be called via the corresponding buttons in the upper part of the calendar. Via Customizing, you can define the available views, the tabs that are visible in each view, and the data to be displayed and maintained.

Working in the TMW

The period selection is very simple in the calendar. By clicking on the day, the week, the month, or by selecting a period, the days of the selected period are provided in the multi-day view in the data entry section for making entries.

The employees assigned to the time administrators appear in the employee list. You can structure the selection of employees for the employee list very flexibly in Customizing. In this way, you can make a selection for instance via the time administrators from Infotype 0001 or via a pre-defined selection path. This also gives you the option to create your own employee lists in the application. This can be done by using the button **Employee List · Maintain your own employee list** in a selection screen similar to the ad-hoc query. The temporary addition of individual employees in the employee list is possible through this button. The employee list can also be adjusted in the layout without a problem. The adjustment is carried out similarly to the layout formation in SAP list viewer.

The employee information is not immediately visible upon calling the TMW, rather you must click on the **Detail** button or select an entry from the selection list for it to be displayed. The employee information is defined in Customizing and can be selected from a variety of master and time data. The implementation of new fields (e.g., from customer-specific infotypes) is possible through Customizing.

The data-entry section consists of tabs in which the data maintenance is carried out, and which actually contain the infotypes of time management. The tabs **Time data** and **Time events** are available in the standard version; a company-specific adjustment (showing additional tabs, hiding previous tabs or renaming them, tabs to expand or limit fields) can be done in Customizing. It makes sense to integrate the infotypes according to logical viewpoints in the tabs and to only map the infotypes that are required by the decentralized time administrators. You can then enter and manage the time data for one or several employees simultaneously and flexibly by using IDs. The IDs refer to the different absence and attendance types, quotas, substitutions, availabilities, time events, etc. of the time-management types. The assignment takes place in Customizing. If you consider the data-entry section in more detail, you will notice that the entry of events for several days in the entry section no longer seems possible, as only one day can be edited at a time. It helps to open the details area, in which the data for events of several days can also be entered.

You can call the details area by selecting the tab and activating the **Detail** button under the period display in the data entry section, or by double-clicking on the **ID** field. In this details area, you can carry out more detailed specifications to the time data entered in the data-entry section. You can see and store even more information in the details area, such as the information which must be added to an attendance quota (How many hours does it comprise, are the hours entered to be paid for or transferred to a time account, etc?) or additional information that can be entered as plain text.

Establishing which information is displayed and maintained here is carried out in Customizing. You can make a selection here from a variety of data which is already available as standard. It is also possible to adjust both the tab itself and the tab content.

However, the TMW has a grave weakness when making entries: Field properties which were changed in Table T588M (see Section 4.2.4, e.g., Figure 4.25 and 4.26) are ignored when making entries in the TMW. This leads to constant problems if certain field content is required for a smooth flow of time management including time evaluation. The definition of a compulsory field in Table T588M is sufficient for direct entry in time management infotypes. When using TMWs, it is nevertheless possible to forget the maintenance of fields. It is advisable here to integrate programmed plausibility checks.

In the **Dialog messages** area, the user receives notes, warnings, and error messages as confirmations of their entries. In this area, you also can process error notifications (previously **Time management pool,** Transaction PT40). You can call the message processing in the menu via **Goto · Process Messages**. The user can click on the line of the employee to be processed, after which the data for this employee appears in the entry section and, if necessary, in the details area. The error removal is then carried out there.

8.3.2 Customizing for the TMW

Customizing the TMW is characterized less by complexity and more by a considerable scope. Nearly all screen areas can be flexibly adjusted to the company requirements. Customizing is carried out in the IMG via **Time Management · Time Manager's Workplace**.

The Profile in TMW

The central concept in customizing the TMW is the profile that is created for different user groups with the same requirements and activities. Therefore, depending on the specifics of the company, it makes sense to define several profiles. It would be conceivable here to have a profile for the administrative assistants who handle the employees in time management and a profile for those who are responsible for maintaining industrial workers. The TMW is called through the profile. This compiles nearly all settings, and in this way looks after the layout, the information displayed, the data which can be maintained, and the available functionalities. The TMW establishes the following:

▶ Use of the initial period (the period selected in the calendar)

▶ Tasks that the users are allowed to execute (only managing time data or also message processing)

▶ Permissable menu functions (navigating from the TMW to the display or also the maintenance of master data, starting the time evaluation, and displaying the time statement)

▶ Available employee information for the users

▶ Available views (one-day, multi-day and multi-person view) for the users

▶ Messages in the scope of message processing

▶ Available processing instructions (checkboxes that can be used to generate customer-specific records for Infotype 2012, which the time administrators no longer have to generate manually)

▶ Display of the names of the employees in the employee list and in the multi- person view

▶ Selection options for the users in the employee list and available fields in the list layout

▶ Appearance of the lines in the time recording area when called

It is merely the IDs and the message-processing control that are not assigned to the profile.

Basic Systematics of TMW Customizing

The basic systematics for customizing appear quite simple. The difficulty—as is often the case—lies in the detail. Only an optimal well-thought-out customizing of the details level guarantees that the TMW actually reaches its aim: the efficient support of time administrators in their daily business. Figure 8.50 will clarify the basic process.

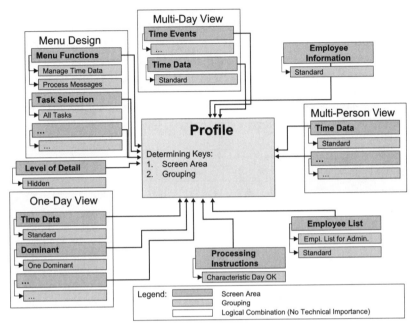

Figure 8.50 Systematics of TMW Customizing

For Figure 8.50 it is noteworthy that all the screen areas display summarized information, data, and functionalities in TMW under a rubric (the screen area). No new screen areas can be defined.

Customizing is carried out—besides the exceptions mentioned before— in a three-step process:

1. A "Grouping" is defined. The grouping, however, will not be named as such. Concepts such as field selection, selection ID, or layout ID will be used.

2. You establish which information, data or functionalities the groupings span.

3. The grouping is assigned to the profile. You specifically establish here which information and data defined in the second step are visible to the user or can be maintained, and also that functionalities can be called.

The Task Selection

Customizing will be introduced in detail on the basis of the example of task selection. In the IMG the two items **Time Management · Time Manager's Workplace · Menu Design · Define Task Selection · Create profiles and assign field selections** are processed. The task selection is a screen area (abbreviation TSK) and it controls which tasks can be selected in the menu of the TMW under **Goto**.

The first step is now to set the grouping that in this case is called **Field selection**. Figure 8.51 shows a new entry in the customizing table.

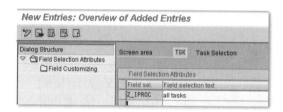

Figure 8.51 Forming a Grouping for the Task Selection

The second step is to establish the tasks which the grouping Z_IPROC spans (see Figure 8.52).

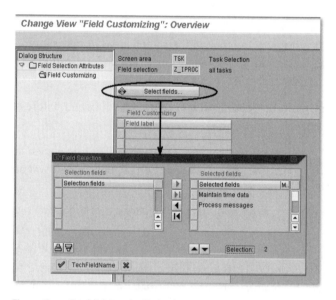

Figure 8.52 Establishing the Tasks that Can Be Executed

The last step is then to assign the field selection to the profile (see Figure 8.53).

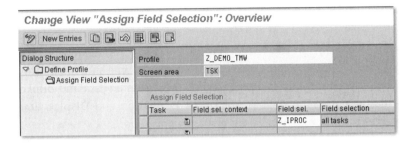

Figure 8.53 Assigning the Field Selection to the Profile

Figure 8.54 then shows the results of the Customizing settings in the application.

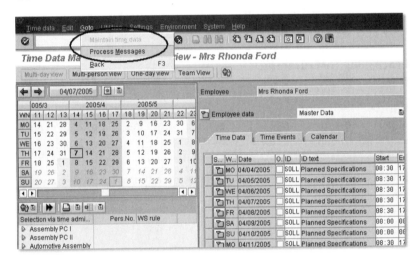

Figure 8.54 Results for the Customizing in the Task Selection

Additional Customizing settings for the TMW will now only be explained briefly as the process basically flows according to the template introduced. Nonetheless, we will name the special features.

Assigning Views

For both tasks (managing time data and processing messages) you can define which views are available (one-day, multi-day, and multi-person view) by calling the respective task. For example it is possible to avoid the multi-person view in message processing. Customizing for these views can be carried out in the IMG via **Time Management · Time Manager's Workplace · Menu Design · Define Views for Tasks · Create profiles and assign field selections**.

Menu Functions

Menu functions represent the option to go directly from the TMW to other transactions. In the TMW, you can call these transactions via the menu items **Utilities** (start time evaluation, display time statement form, call employee) and **Environment** (maintain HR master data and display HR master data). The utilities **Start time evaluation** and **Display time statement form** represent time-management reports. If these menu functions are used, you must create the variants of the report and store them in the feature LLREP. The structure used for the feature allows for a very fine control up to the user level or a transaction. You will find more information on working with features in Appendix 1. You can define the settings in the IMG via **Time Management · Time Manager's Workplace · Menu Design · Define Menu Functions/Create Profiles and Assign Field Selections**.

Processing Instructions

In the TMW, processing instructions are represented by checkboxes from which a data record of the infotype "Time transfer specifications" (2012) is generated. This spares the time administrators the task of data maintenance for frequently recurring cases. An example of this would be the regular authorization of overtime hours. In order to implement this functionality, it is necessary to define previous time types, to create new personnel calculation rules in time management, and to adjust the schema of time management correspondingly. The settings will therefore not be dealt with in more detail here.

Employee List and Employee Info

The fields displayed in the **Employee list** are also implemented in Customizing according to the process introduced here (IMG: **Time Management · Time Manager's Workplace · Screen Areas · Employee List · Define Employee List Display / Assign Field Selections to Profiles**). In addition, you have the option of displaying the employee list with a one- or two-level hierarchy.

The **Employee information** area involves the INF screen area. Here, the standard version contains predefined field selections that can be assigned to the profile. The definition of new field selections with fields is then only required if the standard is insufficient. For this reason, you must define the master data or time data upfront in the IMG via **Time Management · Time Manager's Workplace · Basic Settings · Select HR Master**

Data and Time Data in order to define master data or time data, and to integrate it subsequently in a layout for employee information. The layouts are then accepted in the INF screen area and assigned to a profile.

Configuring the Data Entry

Customizing the data entry section is somewhat more difficult as the groupings are not immediately recognizable here and the definition of the column configurations occurs at an unexpected point.

The data-entry section can be set up separately for the one-day, multiday, and multi-person views (IMG: **Time Management · Time Manager's Workplace · Screen Areas · Time Data Maintenance**). The **Time Data** and **Time Events** tabs are available in the standard version. Both of these tabs can be set flexibly in terms of column configurations (i.e., which fields are displayed and which of those are prepared for entries for data maintenance). It is also possible to define additional tabs and to incorporate different views.

Additional tabs can be defined by copying existing sample entries provided by SAP. In each case a sample entry similar to the tabs **Time Data** and **Time Events** is available. You must copy sample entries because technical settings are attached to the sample entries that are urgently required for the new tabs. You can integrate a new tabstrip in the data entry section in field-customizing of the IMG activity **Add Tabs in Time Data Maintenance Screen Area** and not—as you might possibly have expected—when defining the field selection for the profile.

The column configuration for a new tab is carried out in the table of the tabs that the copy is based on. If a new tab was created on the basis of the tab **Time Data**, the column configuration is carried out in the IMG activity **Define Table for Time Data**. Here you must create a new field selection with the corresponding field-customizing (Answering the question: "Which information should the columns displayed contain?"). Finally, the assignment of the field selection to the profile for the screen area **Time Events** or **Time Data** is carried out (one-day, multi-day, or multi-person view), not in the (one-day, multi-day, or multi-person view) **Tabs**. Figure 8.55 clarifies the contexts.

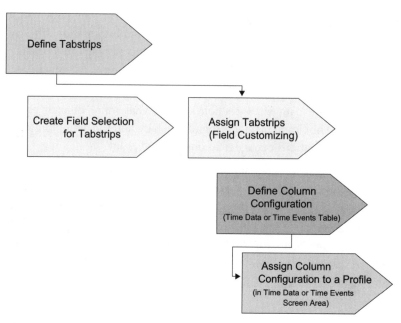

Figure 8.55 Customizing Context of Tabs

You can only populate fields in the time-data table via user exits according to your rules, but not in the time-events table.

In the time-data entry area, you can also control whether certain lines in the TMW should be shown or hidden at start-up. If the decision is made in favor for hidden lines when entering the TMW, you can display these lines by clicking on the **Detail** button.

For the time data, you can define additional detail information according to infotype in the corresponding screen section. It is displayed as in the time recording area in tabs, **A fixed**, defined quantity of tabs is available per infotype and for the individual work schedule. The existing tabs can be hidden according to the company-specific requirements. The names of the tabs can also be adjusted.

Employee Selection

The selection of the employees assigned to the time administrators can be defined in the IMG via the area **Time Management · Time Manager's Workplace · Employee Selection**. The definition of selection IDs specifies the actual selection of employees. The following options are available to establish the selection:

- Selection via a freely definable evaluation path
- Selection via the characteristics of different fields (e.g., via time administrators)
- Selection via a function module
- Selection by combining alternatives already mentioned

The selections defined can be assigned to the time administrators via profile assignment in the TMW and are then available by default in the application. It also is possible to allow the user in the TMW to define his or her own selection interactively. The selection is carried out similarly to an ad-hoc query. This view is based on an infoset, which is defined in customizing via IMG activity **Create InfoSets for HR**. The selection IDs defined are assigned to a group in the next step and then are finally assigned to a profile. This makes it possible to eliminate interactive employee selection, as the profile is not assigned any selection ID for the interactive search.

> **Tip** Align the time administrators' authorizations to the employee selection (e.g., by using the same evaluation path). This ensures against unpleasant surprises if the authorisations permitted are more extensive than the set selection, and the employee is permitted to make an interactive selection based on an infoset.

Entire View of the Profile

The profile as central key for the TMW, on which nearly all settings depend, can be totally adjusted in the IMG activity **Check and Complete Profiles**. Here you can find all the settings that were previously only partially available, in the form of a navigation tree. This is always helpful if the customizing knowledge is so good that the concepts used can be directly assigned to an area in the application. This means the changes can be carried out quickly and easily, provided the assignments of previous settings have already been completed.

Parameter Transactions

The implementation of parameter transactions is also relevant. Their use is also recommended if several profiles are being used. A parameter transaction calls the TMW with the assigned profile and the definition set and, if necessary, the IDs and definition subset, as this transaction is assigned via the authorization of a specific role. The user can only call the TMW with parameters assigned to it in the role

The Message Processing

Finally we will describe the areas without direct profile assignment. Message processing belongs to these areas including the description of the messages. Messages can be summarized according to criteria such as the same processing procedures or similar message type (e.g., all types of violation against working time laws or flextime regulation). The functional area is the superordinate term for the messages that were summarized. In Customizing the definition of the functional areas is carried out first and then the assignment of the messages to the functional areas. All messages that are assigned to a functional area are displayed in the message view under the nodes of a message functional area. The time administrators then can call the entire message functional area here.

A further help for the time administrators is the processing methods for messages. Processing methods should support the time administrators in processing messages, by showing them a specific note text and defined contextual information. Customizing occurs in the IMG via **Time Management · Time Manager's Workplace · Basic Settings · Set Up Message Processing · Define Processing Method** and the additional IMG activities underneath **Define Processing Method**. However, processing methods do not necessarily have to be used.

IDs for Time Data

IDs is another area without direct profile assignment. The IDs support a simplified data maintenance by the time administrators. The events lie behind the IDs (absences, attendances, substitutions, etc.) of time management. Their importance should not be underestimated

> **Tip** We recommend that you assign single-digit IDs for the time-management events that are most used (e.g., S for sickness with medical certificate or A for annual leave entitlement). In addition, you should select the ID so that in alphanumeric sorting facts which belong together (e.g., all types of vacation) are executed immediately after one another. This represents a great relief to the time administrators responsible for data maintenance.

Customizing of the IDs is carried out in the IMG via **Time Management · Time Manager's Workplace · IDs for Time Data**. Several events such as absences can be stored per ID; one of them, however, must be specified as priority. The event defined as a priority is then created as standard under the ID, but can be overwritten by one of the other events defined under this ID. However, we advise against assigning an ID to several events as this regularly leads to misunderstandings and problems in the application.

In mySAP HR, the concepts of the definition area and the definition subset are used to limit the IDs. The definition quantity is nothing other than the grouping of IDs. As the definition area is stored in the user parameters of the user, it means that the users do not have to reach a selection from the IDs that are available throughout the whole company. The subset represents another option for grouping within the definition area and can therefore further limit the selection of IDs. The use of the definitions area, and if necessary the definition subset, is always advisable if different employee groups are to be processed separately by different time administrators. You could, for example, determine a definitions area for administrative assistants and supervisors here. Administrative assistants provide the employees with rolling working time. Supervisors are responsible for industrial workers with shift service.

8.3.3   Amended Delivery in R/3 Enterprise

TMW is not provided with the core in R/3 Enterprise, but is available with Extension 1.1. This does not mean any initial changes to the functionality, but it does mean that after a release change to R/3 Enterprise you must activate the extension for HR, as long as the TMW is being used. The calendar views of the TMW represent the major change to the R/3 Enterprise, and these will be described in the following section.

8.4   Calendar View in the TMW

The graphical calendar views provide quick processing and a quick overview of the employee time data. Information referring to less than one day is also in the foreground for the daily and weekly calendar. In the monthly and annual calendar, there is a quick overview of all-day information.

The calendar views are based on the "normal" TMW as it has already been described in the previous section. In this section we will describe the specific characteristics in the calendar views.

8.4.1 Calendar Types

Four views for the calendar maintenance are available in **Time Manager's Workplace**:

▶ **Annual calendar**

The annual calendar provides a complete overview of the situation and frequency of all-day and multi-day time-data referring, such as shifts and absences of employees for a calendar year or an individually selected period.

▶ **Monthly calendar**

The monthly calendar enables a quick classification of employee multi-day and all-day time information and information referring to less than one day that refers to a day of the week, through the period of a calendar month and an individually selected period of several weeks.

▶ **Weekly calendar**

The weekly calendar, shown in Figure 8.56, provides a very good overview of the time situation of all-day time information and time information relating to less than one day, for the period of a week.

▶ **One-day calendar**

The one-day calendar shows an overview of an employee's time data related to a time spot for one day.

8.4.2 Functional Span

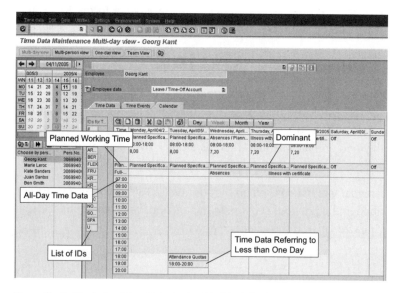

Figure 8.56 Displaying Time Data in the Weekly Calendar

The information for the day is processed in both of the following categories:

Dominant

The most important information for the day in each case is displayed in the dominant. A dominant always represents a full-day piece of information. You can display information from the following infotypes in the dominants line:

▶ Infotype "Planned Working Time" (0007)

▶ Infotype "Absences" (2001)

▶ Infotype "Attendances" (2002)

▶ Infotype "Substitutions" (2003)

The dominant is always at the foreground in all views. It the time data for a day is hidden in the multi-day view and the multi-person view, only the dominant information is available.

Planned Working Time

This displays the personal work schedule for the employee. If there is no existing current change to the planned working time for the employee, the regular work schedule is displayed for the employee.

Time Data for the Day

Here we avoid all-day time data or time data referring to less than one day, such as attendances and absences or remuneration documents for the day.

8.4.3 Processing Time Data

▶ The IDs identified in color are executed in a legend column beside the calendar view. You can accept the IDs with Drag&Drop and insert them in the calendar. You must select the ID. By re-clicking on it, you can drag this by holding down the mouse to the desired position in the calendar view.

▶ The dominant is overwritten, depending on the time recording, or an all-day record is generated by dragging the ID to the dominant's line.

▶ As an alternative to this process, you can select a day in the calendar and transfer this to an ID by double-clicking on it.

- By double-clicking on any line of any day—excluding the date line—you can enter multi-day information, all-day information or information referring to less than one day. The details view is automatically opened for this, in which you can specify time data, in a way similar to making entries in other views.

- In order to change time data that has already been entered, or the planned specification, the details view will be highlighted as in other views.

- If time data was entered for the wrong day by mistake, you can remove this. For this reason the relevant time data can simply be dragged to the desired new position by Drag&Drop. The same is also true for multi-day time data.

- All functions for the deletion, creation etc. of time data are available in the list-oriented views. In the annual and monthly calendar in particular, for example, more frequently emerging time data can be quickly entered. You can also copy and delete multi-day time data in the calendar views.

- By selecting a period in the **Calendar** screen, the system automatically selects the relevant view. If you click on an individual day in the calendar, you can call the daily schedule.

- You can switch between the different calendar views as follows:

  - By clicking on the **Day**, **Week**, **Month**, and **Year** buttons in any calendar view

  - By double-clicking on the **Current date**, **Calendar week**, or **Month** in the view, which is further detailed by one degree in each case (depending on the calendar view in which you are currently located, you can reach the corresponding view)

8.4.4 Customizing

The calendar views are mainly provided in R/3 Enterprise and mySAP ERP. However, it is possible to request SAP AG to pre-install this in Release 4.6C. In this case, customizing activities are not integrated in the IMG. For this reason we will describe the customizing using the maintenance view. This can be used in all releases.

Including the Calendar in the Time Data Entry Screen Area

In order to include the tab for the calendar in the multi-day view, you must carry out the following steps:

1. In the implementation guide you must carry out the activity **Time Management · Time Manager's Workplace · Screen Areas · Time Data Maintenance · Multi-Day View · Add Tabs in Time Data Maintenance Screen Area**

2. Edit the action in the screen area **Add Tabs in Time Data Maintenance Screen Area**.

3. Select the field selection which is to be added to the calendar.

4. In the dialog structure, select the customizing field by double-clicking on it.

5. Click on Select fields.

6. Complement the selection with the field Calendar.

Defining Data Sources of the Time Data

Here you define the data sources from which the information is displayed in the calendars.

1. Call Transaction SM34.

2. Enter VC_PT_FIELD_SELECTION_INF in the view cluster and select **Maintain**.

3. In order to process the time data, select the **CAI** screen area.

4. Select the field selection to be processed.

5. Finally select the **Field Customizing** by double-clicking on it.

6. Select **Select fields**.

7. You must select a maximum of two desired data sources and transfer them to the **Selected fields** area.

8. Then you must include the calendar type in the implementation guide for time management: **Time Management · Time Manager's Workplace · Profiles · Check and Complete Profiles**.

9. Select the profile in which this new field selection is to appear.

10. Select the selection **Assign multi-day view** in the dialog structure by double-clicking on it.

11. Enter this in the screen area **CAI** and select **Enter**.

12. Enter the individual calendar types for the data sources required in each case.

Defining Information to be Displayed

In this activity you can determine the visual appearance of the calendar:

1. Select Transaction SM34.
2. Enter VC_PT_FIELD_SELECTION_INF in the view cluster and select the screen area **CAL.**
3. Select the field selection to be processed, and select **Field Customizing** by double-clicking on it.
4. Select **Select fields**.
5. Here you can select the information blocks to be displayed in the respective calendars. If required, you can enter a separating line between the individual blocks and change the sequence of the individual blocks.
6. Then you must include the calendar type in the implementation guide in **Time Management · Time Manager's Workplace · Profile · Check and Complete Profiles**.
7. Select the profile in which this new field selection is to appear.
8. Assign the selection **Assign multi-day view** in the dialog structure by double-clicking on it.
9. Enter the screen area **CAL** and select **Enter**.
10. Here you can process the optical appearance by entering the individual calendar types for the desired field selection.

Defining the Layout of the Dominant Lines

In this activity you can define which information is to be output in the dominant lines of the daily schedule, weekly calendar and monthly calendar.

In general, you can output fields from the following infotypes in the dominants line:

▶ Infotype "Planned Working Time" (0007)
▶ Infotype "Absences" (2001)
▶ Infotype "Attendances" (2002)
▶ Infotype "Substitutions" (2003)

Customer-specific fields can also be output in the dominant lines. There are three text fields and three hourly fields which can be populated with SAP expansion PTIMTMW.

In the annual calendar it generally makes sense to output dominants as the information displayed there is output once again either during the planned time or as time data. In the annual calendar it is advisable not to output any dominants.

The dominant for a day as it also appears in the list-oriented views, is always displayed. Depending on the width of the column, the ID of the dominant or the text of the dominant is output.

The following steps are necessary in order to maintain the dominant lines:

1. Select Transaction SM34.

2. Enter VC_PT_FIELD_SELECTION_INF in the view cluster and select the screen area **CAL**.

3. Select **New Entries**.

4. Create a field selection for the daily schedule, weekly calendar and monthly calendar and specify a relevant name.

5. Select **Enter** and select a field selection.

6. Finally select the **Field Customizing** by double-clicking on it.

7. Select **Select fields**.

8. Now you can select the fields which are to be output and determine the sequence.

9. Select **Next**.

10. If necessary, you can specify in the **Display type** field if the value or the text of a time recording is to be displayed. If nothing is entered here the system automatically transfers the value.

11. Save the entries and carry out the following IMG activity: **Time Management · Time Manager's Workplace · Profile · Check and Complete Profiles**.

12. Select the profile which the list should read out when not using that set as default.

13. Select **Assign multi-day view** the dialog structure by double-clicking on it.

14. Enter the screen area **CAD** and select **Enter**.

15. For the individual calendar types you must enter the desired field selection to display the dominant line in each case.

Defining Input Help for the IDs

With this activity you can form the list of the IDs for the type of the time recording at the left margin. These settings are also valid for the calendar types and the IDs.

There are the following options:

► For experienced users it is possible to only output the IDs (field selection **HIDE**).

► For less experienced users you should output these with the texts of the IDs (field selection **TEXT**).

► The list can be completely hidden so that the users can enter new time data only via the details screen (field selection **TDTYPE**).

Implement the following steps in the IMG:

1. Select the activity **Time Management · Time Manager's Workplace**.

2. Check the path **Profile · Check and complete Profiles** and complete it in the implementation guide.

3. Select the profile which the list should read out when not using that set as default.

4. Select **Assign multi-day view** in the dialog structure by double-clicking on it.

5. Enter the screen area **TDT** and select **Enter**.

6. Select **New Entries** and maintain the desired field selection.

8.5   The Mobile Solutions of Time Management

SAP AG's Mobile Solutions is based on the premise of making useful applications accessible for mobile devices also such as laptops, mobiles and handheld devices. Here the increase in personal productivity on the part of the user and the provision of information for employees round the clock, for instance in order to reach decisions, is in the foreground of mobile business.

SAP Mobile Solutions are an enhancement to company-relevant applications for all users, independent of time, place and availability of network connections via mobile devices such as cell phones or palmtop devices. However, no complete applications are transferred to these tiny computer devices, and the need for desktop devices is eliminated.

In this section, we will consider time management Mobile Solutions. This refers to the option of entering time-management data such as confirmations for activities which can be invoiced and that were carried out on-location by customers or by entering absences. Further, it involves the provision of time management information such as employee time accounts.

With SAP NetWeaver and SAP Exchange Infrastructure (XI), a better integration of mobile services can be expected for future releases.

8.5.1 Types of Web Applications and Mobile Applications

Basically, you must differentiate between different scenarios and applications. There are applications that can run offline on laptops and whose contents are transferred during the earliest contact with the company network. Then there are "real" mobile solutions that enable you to transfer data to the company network and call data from there using mobiles and palms. In the time-management area there are three different types of Web and mobile applications: iViews, WAP applications, and Internet application components.

By iViews we mean small applications that run in the company portal (e.g., mySAP Enterprise Portal) and individual services, such as displaying the working time accounts or which cover the simple entry of working times. Internet-application components can also be integrated in company portals and cover more complex services such as absence notifications or complex entries of working times. Data can be exchanged between WAP-capable devices such as mobiles or palmtops and the R/3 using WAP applications. First we will briefly the "offline application" CATS notebook.

8.5.2 CATS Notebook

CATS (Cross Application Time Sheet) is a cross-application solution for entering times and their assignment to cost centers, projects, orders, employees, absence reasons, evaluation records etc.

The application CATS Notebook enables field staff to enter their confirmations—such as time per customer project—offline on laptops and to synchronize the data to a specific time spot with R/3. Especially for field staff who travel a lot and are active on behalf of several customers, it is of great importance to enter working times as precisely as possible. As the data entered must undergo a range of follow-up business processes such as invoice creation or processing for payroll, it must be available as quickly as possible in SAP R/3. An offline solution is optimal, in that it brings the advantages of the online application to the laptop that is not constantly connected to SAP R/3.

The Business Process "CATS Notebook"

The CATS Notebook business process practically runs on two systems. On the one hand, there are work steps which occur directly in SAP R/3, such as creating accounting objects and confirmation positions and authorizing times and triggering the subsequent processes such as invoices and payroll. On the other hand, there is the actual mobile application for offline entry and for releasing the times by the employee on the laptop. The release and authorization of times is an optional function there (see Figure 8.57).

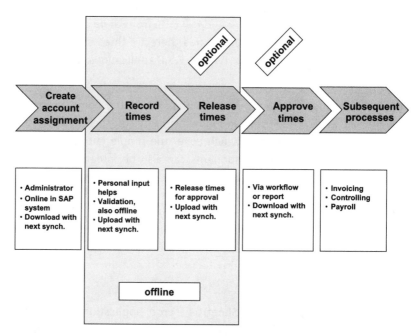

Figure 8.57 CATS Notebook Business Process

The Application "CATS Notebook"

In the application, CATS Notebook provides the following: The employees report their times for a certain period on their laptops by entering the project and the number of hours. In addition, the employees can confirm absences such as vacation or sicknesses through this application. Incorrect hours or hours which have not been released can be highlighted in color, if necessary. If an employee has a network connection, he or she transfer the confirmation data directly to the R/3 where further processes are triggered (see Figure 8.58).

⚡	Ab.Type	WBS Element	Sum	MO	TU	WE	TH	FR	SA	SU
⏱			36,00	8,00	8,00	8,00	8,00	4,00	0,00	0,00
📊			36,00	8,00	8,00	8,00	8,00	4,00	0,00	0,00
☐		PV-12	4,00	4,00						
☐		EF-2	11,00	4,00	2,00		5,00			
☐		EF-32	17,00		6,00	8,00	3,00			
☐	0100		4,00					4,00		
☐			0,00							
☐			0,00							

Figure 8.58 CATS Notebook: Confirmation of the Hours Performed

The CATS notebook is a Web-based application which can also be integrated into the company portal as self-service. The following technical prerequisites must be fulfilled for the operation:

▶ SAP R/3 4.6C or higher

▶ Plug-In 2002 or higher

▶ Notebook with Internet Explorer 5.5

▶ ITS (Internet Transaction Server) including additional services for synchronisation/SAP NetWeaver

▶ Mobile Engine 1.0

As already mentioned in addition to "offline applications" such as CATS Notebook, there are also applications for mobiles and PDAs that enable direct entries in fields of the R/3.

8.5.3 WAP Applications of Time Management

SAP provides mobile access to mySAP HR Time Management—currently still in the prototype phase– for field staff who cannot carry out a constant adjustment with the R/3 by using a laptop and the application CATS Notebook. WAP-capable mobiles enable employees to enter their working times directly and keep themselves up-to-date on their time accounts. In addition to the advantages for the employees, the companies also have the advantage of always having current data on the employees.

Example for WAP Applications "Absence Notification"

The employee makes entries concerning absences via an attendance/absence type that enables him to enter the fact that he was ill. In addition, the employee could request a vacation by entering the absence type "vacation" together with the desired period. For absences lasting less than one day the times can be entered with the time or hours.

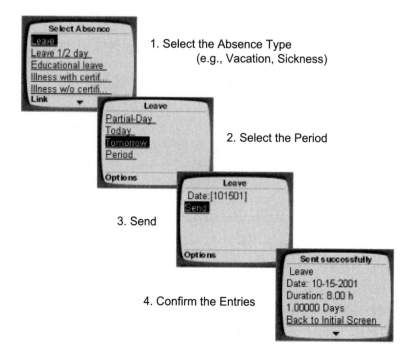

Figure 8.59 WAP Application "Absence Notification"

The data transferred via the absence notification is created in R/3 in Infotype 2001 ("Absences") with the relevant absence type. As the absence types for the WAP application are not provided with keys, a situation familiar from Infotype 2001, but rather are assigned meaningful names, entry by the employees is facilitated. The assignment of the self-defined absence key for the WAP application is transferred from the customizing of the absence notification of the ESS. You can reach this customizing via IMG **Time Management · Web applications · Leave Request (New)**. From the ESS application "Leave request" you can also use the services "Cancellation leave request." This also gives you an overview of the status of requested absences.

Many time recording systems give the user the option to see their time accounts. There is also a WAP service for these requests i.e. the WAP application "time accounts."

Further examples of WAP applications are:

- Working time recording
- Clock-in/clock-out
- Time accounts

8.5.4 Conclusion

If many employees work as field staff, the mobile solutions provided can be useful. There was a conscious effort made not to transfer complex applications to small devices, but rather to provide only the most necessary and useful input options. In the future there will definitely be more application options in time management.

8.6 Process Examples

8.6.1 Flextime Model with Traffic Lights

Flextime accounts in most companies have a fixed upper limit. When this limit is exceeded, the balance is often capped. The aim of not allowing flextime accounts to turn into self-service shops is definitely the right idea. However, the automatic capping shifts a management problem to the IT system. Balance statuses that are too high are caused by employees using their time irresponsibly or by a workload that is actually too high. The latter is more often than not a case of a lack of planning on the part of management.

Capping often serves to demotivate the employees. The traffic light model which is often used is more useful. Once the yellow phase is reached, a conversation is triggered between the employee and the supervisor. As a result, the supervisor plans the working time of the employee restrictively and must therefore send him or her home if he or she is not absolutely needed. Once the red phase is reached, another conversation takes place, in which the personnel department and if necessary the employee representatives participate. Measures to improve the workload are then discussed with superiors. The planning of working time can be directly manipulated by the HR department.

The model could appear to be unrealistic. In practice, however, this often quickly leads to a responsible treatment of working time as a resource. This also provides as much, if not more, room for maneuver for lower threshold values as for upper threshold values. This lets the employee know that a positive balance status is not seen in a positive light.

Mapping in HR Mapping in HR is quite simple. In the standard version, the creation of a flextime balance is done via time type 0005. The threshold values must now be stored in the system. This can be done via the table of constants T511k (see Figure 8.60). You can freely select the codes for the constants within the customer namespace.

ZZMRE	🛈	Flextime negative red	01/01/2000	12/31/9999	60,00
ZZMYE	🛈	Flextime negative yellow	01/01/2000	12/31/9999	40,00
ZZPRE	🛈	Flextime positive red	01/01/2000	12/31/9999	50,00
ZZPYE	🛈	Flextime positive yellow	01/01/2000	12/31/9999	30,00

Figure 8.60 Traffic Light Values in the Table of Constants

In the second step, you generate the messages to be created in case the values are exceeded (see Figure 8.61). You can reach the settings via IMG path **Time Management · Time Evaluation · Time Evaluation With Clock Times · Processing Balances · Balance Formation · Balance Limits**.

Change View "Time Evaluation Messages": Overview

New Entries 🗋 🗐 🖉 🖺 🖺 🖺

| PSGpg | Ty. | MessTy | Message long text | Mail | List ID | Balance | 🔲 |
| 02 | 1 | Z1 | Flextime traffic light red:maximum | 1 | 0 | | ▲ |

Figure 8.61 Time Evaluation Message for a Red Traffic Light

You can define the reaction when the threshold value is exceeded via the same path. You only need a part of the extensive customizing screens: definition of the comparison (time type 0005 with the table of payroll parameters T511k) and the message output. Figure 8.62 shows entries made for a red traffic light when the upper limits are exceeded.

Thus, the red and yellow traffic light stages are provided as notes in error-handling. In addition, an e-mail flag is transferred to the time recording terminal that can be provided with a corresponding text there.

If the management is to monitor the traffic light status outside error handling, you can also use the evaluation RPTBAL00 (**cumulated time evaluation results**) that should ideally be integrated in the manager's desktop for this reason.

In order to identify when threshold values are exceeded in this evaluation, you can maintain the attributes LIMIE, LIMIS and LIMIZ via the following IMG path: **Time Management · Time Evaluation · Evaluations and the Time Management Pool · Set Value Limits for Cumulated Evaluation Results**. Figure 8.63 shows an overview of the process.

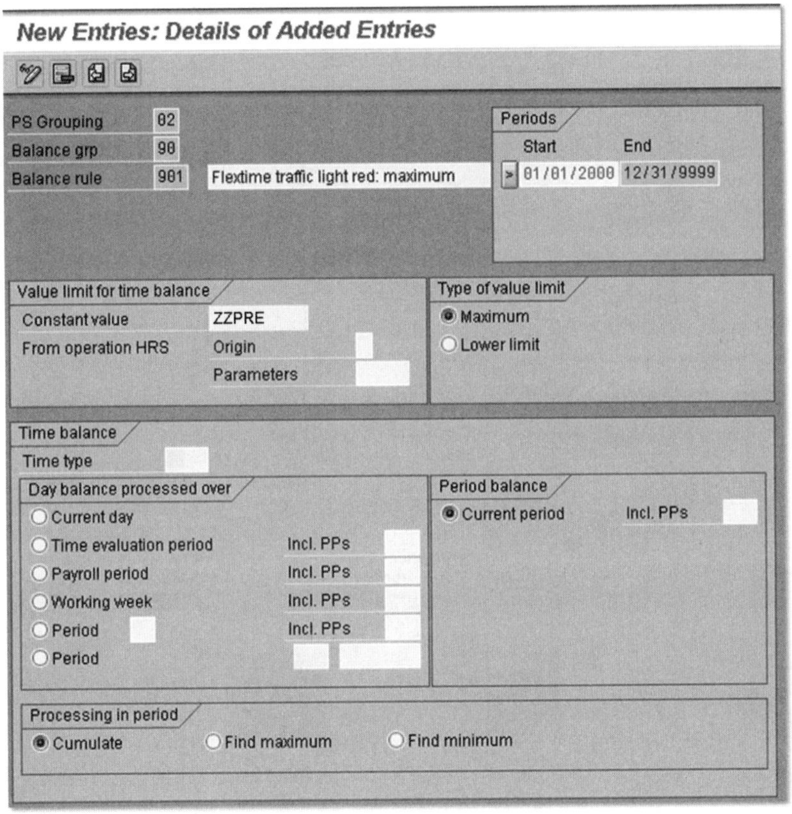

New Entries: Details of Added Entries

PS Grouping	02
Balance grp	90
Balance rule	901	Flextime traffic light red: maximum

Periods

| | Start | End |
| > | 01/01/2000 | 12/31/9999 |

Value limit for time balance

Constant value	ZZPRE
From operation HRS	Origin
	Parameters

Type of value limit

- ◉ Maximum
- ○ Lower limit

Time balance

Time type

Day balance processed over

- ○ Current day
- ○ Time evaluation period — Incl. PPs
- ○ Payroll period — Incl. PPs
- ○ Working week — Incl. PPs
- ○ Period — Incl. PPs
- ○ Period

Period balance

- ◉ Current period — Incl. PPs

Processing in period

- ◉ Cumulate ○ Find maximum ○ Find minimum

Figure 8.62 Activating a Message for a Red Traffic Light (Customizing)

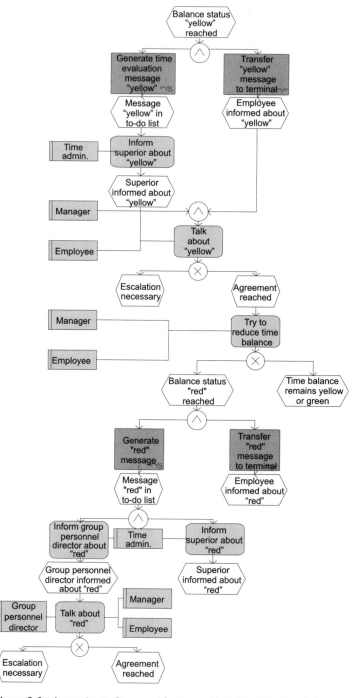

Figure 8.63 Approximate Process—Flextime with Traffic Light Regulation

8.6.2 Part-Time Model

Part-time models are widely available in some sectors today and are based on very different individual working time agreements. If there are 1,000 part-time staff in a company, there are often more than 500 different work schedule rules. This means the working time is ideally tailored towards the requirements of the employees on the one hand and the company on the other hand. An advantage of part-time staff is mostly higher flexibility. Even if, for instance, eight hours are agreed on Mondays and Wednesdays, short-term changes upon agreement, can however often be allowed for in the general rules (e.g., rush order in the department or a child's birthday).

However, it is not necessary that working time agreements should be precisely mapped to a time model in the HR system. It is completely sufficient for flextime calculation to know the weekly working time and to distribute it equally, for instance to five days. An exact distribution of working time can be done within these conditions by written or oral agreement between the employees and management.

For this reason, for a five-day week, you only need one time model in the system for constant flextime conditions. This is assigned to the employees via Infotype 0007 and supplemented there with the desired hourly figure or the part-time percentage rate (see Figure 8.64). Everything else is dynamically calculated by the system.

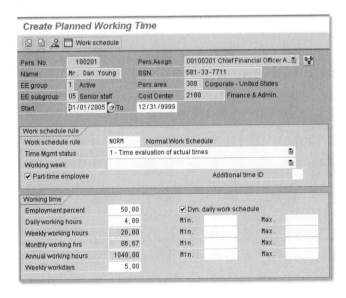

Figure 8.64 Part-time with 50%

In this case, no additional maintenance activities are necessary as long as the weekly working time for the employee has not changed. The system accepts the same working time each day, and as long as the employee plans the attendance within the scope of flextime, no further interference is necessary.

Maintenance complexity In contrast to this, the detailed mapping of all time models in the system leads to considerable maintenance complexity, as the process in Figure 8.65 also shows:

▶ From the beginning of part-time work, a model must frequently be created. As creation occurs in Customizing, this cannot be carried out by decentralized time administrators. This merely then assigns the newly created model.

▶ If the distribution of working time is changed over a longer period, the same complexity is necessary as at the beginning.

▶ Short-term changes to planning without information from the time administrators lead to error messages in time evaluation (e.g., "Employee present on a day off"). A telephone call is then usually made, and the change is then mapped by entering a substitution in Infotype 2003.

▶ The time administrator who is responsible for customizing the time model and the time administrator must always involved, which is not the case for a flexible part-time model. The time administrator must merely be involved there, when changes are made to the weekly working time.

You should reckon with a large number of part-time staff. Therefore you must by all means avoid the detailed entry of working-time distribution in time models.

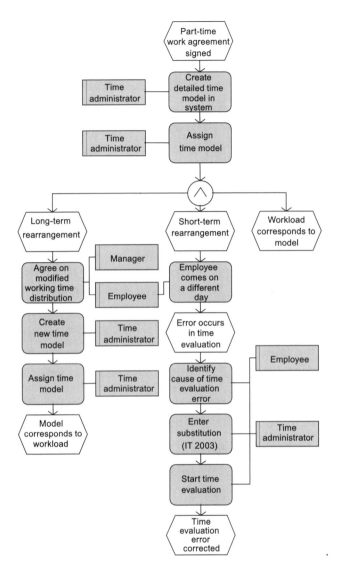

Figure 8.65 The Process with Detail Models is Generally Inefficient

8.6.3 Time-Autonomous Work Groups

Flat hierarchies often lead to situations where management insufficiently controls the working-time planning for their employees. In most cases however, this control is not even necessary. The employees for a team who have to process a joint task are generally capable of doing so. The idea of time-autonomous working groups is based on this reality. You find developments with fixed group spokesmen, rolling spokesmen, or without spokesmen.

Management, does not rob itself of responsibility, but rather coaches the group in time planning and transfers the following tasks to the group:

▶ Covering the required service time or fulfilling the distributed project/production goals by reconciling the individual working times of the group members

▶ Reconciling the break times, if required

▶ Planning vacation times and other plannable absences

▶ Autonomous reaction to unforeseen events (high workloads, sickness, etc.)

▶ Increase of capacity, for instance due to temporary workers, in the defined scope if necessary and without the authorization of management

▶ Early notification to management if the tasks are not to be fulfilled within the scope of planning, or if additional tasks are required to relieve the existing capacity

How can the group be supported by mySAP HR in these tasks? First of all, the employees of the group can also be integrated in a positive or negative time recording like the employees outside the group. The planning options within the group can only be decisively improved when a group member assumes responsibility for the tasks of a time administrator, and is thus supported by the functionalities of the TMW.

For management, key figures that can be gained via standard evaluations can be used to identify erroneous trends at an early stage. These include in particular:

▶ Balance statuses for the group (see Section 8.6.1)

▶ Violation to the working-time law

▶ Remaining leave

▶ Times carried out by temporary personnel

A very extensive support for working-time planning is also provided by workforce planning, but that topic is outside the scope of this book. However, you can also create useful evaluations with the more simple tools of time management. Regular group discussions are also common, in which both future planning and past planning are checked. In this context, you can find out if it corresponded to actual requirements, and how future planning can be improved, if necessary.

It has proven useful here to make an evaluation available to the group that has calculated the distribution of staff numbers in the past and provide this in a spreadsheet. The time spans to be observed in each case depend on the specific tasks of the group (for call centers or branches with consumer communication, it is necessary to consider week days as well as times). The task of the group is then to estimate in each case if the staffing was sufficient to carry out the tasks.

	Staff	Assessment	Staff	Assessment	Staff	Assessment	Staff	Assessment	Staff	Assessment
	Mon		Tue		Wed		Thu		Fri	
7:30 - 8:00	2	O	1	O	1	O	1	O	1	O
8:00-10:00	3	O	3	+	3	+	3	+	3	O
10:00-12:00	4	O	5	O	5	O	5	O	5	O
12:00-13:00	3	-	3	O	3	O	3	O	3	-
13:00-14:00	3	O	3	-	2	-	3	O	3	- -
14:00-17:00	5	O	3	- -	5	O	5	O	6	-
17:00-19:00	5	+	5	O	5	+	5	O	7	O
19:00-20:00	3	O	3	O	3	+	4	+	3	-
20:00-20:30	1	O	1	O	1	O	1	O	2	-

Assessment		
	- -	extremely understaffed
	-	understaffed
	O	just right
	+	overstaffed
	++	extremely overstaffed

Figure 8.66 Control Sheet—Time Autonomous Group

Figure 8.66 shows such a utility in the example of a service branch that is open to the public from Monday until Friday between 8 a.m. and 8 p.m. While the capacity figures are provided by HR time management, the group itself provides the valuation of the respective staffing and correspondingly adjusts the future planning.

8.6.4 Life-Working-Time Accounts

Life-working-time accounts are a popular means of employee retention and can be used to optimally control working time as a resource. The following section will illustrate a possible implementation in mySAP HR. However, we will not go into detail here, as these are often very specific to the company and also depend strongly on legal regulations in the respective country.

The normal flextime account forms the basis of the model described that should move within the predefined limits. At month's end, a section of the flextime account is then transferred to the annual account. In addition, overtime that is subject to bonuses, beyond flextime, is set up in the annual account, as long as it is not immediately paid out. It is only at year's end that you must decide which part of the accumulated times in the annual account is paid out, and which part is transferred to the life-working-time account.

Flextime account and annual accounts are managed in time management in hours. The times which are included in the life-working-time account should in contrast be evaluated on a monetary basis so that this account can be managed in dollars or in another currency.

Advantages of managing in dollars Managing life-working-time accounts in dollars instead of in hours has the following advantages:

▶ During change in the company (and also on a intra-company basis) it is easily transferable. Even in the case of a cost-center change, the old cost center manager would probably not want to take over any legacy with more than 1,000 hours of time-off entitlement. For this reason it is easier to transfer a valuated account.

▶ A clearly defined interest calculation is possible.

▶ If the account is for instance to be paid out after 30 years, its value strongly depends on the carrier development of the employees. If the time saved as a sales assistant is paid out as a director of an international subsidiary, this is an interest return that cannot be justified by anything.

▶ The value of the credit is constantly known so that the corresponding provisions can be built up and an insolvency insurance can be put in place.

At first glance, the annual account can appear to be an unnecessary intermediate step. However, it is very useful to clearly separate the planning ranges. In particular, it should prevent short or long-term planning being executed using the life-working-time account. In addition, payment from the life-working-time account is an exception. The annual account gives the employee the option to have the money paid out to them at year's end. The flextime account on the other hand, provides short-term scope for planning for the employee. It can extract any number of times from it, as long as it does not contradict the company requirements. For this reason, the values that can accumulate on an annual account are considerably too high.

The annual account adjusts itself to specific company requirements in exactly the same way as the transfer occurs between flextime accounts and working-time accounts, with regard to limits and authorization processes. This is also the case for the transfer into life-working-time accounts, where legal regulations come increasingly into play. The following methods are advisable to carry out mappings in time management:

▶ Run the flextime account as in the standard version via the time type 0005.

▶ Manage the annual account via a time type or an absence quota. The transfer into an annual account can be mapped via the following IMG path: **Time Management · Time Evaluation · Time Evaluation With Clock Times · Processing Balances · Balance Formation · Balance Limits**.

▶ The life-working-time account can be built up by transferring the times of the annual account through a balance transfer or quota correction into a time-wage type called "life-working-time account." This is then provided to payroll for monetary valuation. Interest calculation should also be processed in payroll. As payroll is always aware of an employee's hourly rate, it can constantly display the value of the account in terms of hours or days (e.g., in the remuneration statement). The withdrawal in terms of time can then occur via a custom absence type called "withdrawal of life working time" which is also transferred via the same time wage type to payroll. The withdrawal in terms of money is first of all even easier by entering a specific wage type in Infotype 0015.

▶ If it's possible for the employee to shorten his or her life working time by about four years after 30 years by working one hour overtime every day, it is the management's duty to treat the working time responsibly. This includes monitoring the development of balance statuses. If these statuses increase due to a high workload and don't decrease again at lower workloads, controlled intervention may be necessary. The provision of corresponding evaluation options is technically well supported by mySAP HR. The aim should be to provide the relevant reports as online evaluations through the Manager's Desktop.

The general process to build up a life-working-time account is illustrated in Figure 8.67.

▶ The model can also be supplemented by giving employees the option to extend their long-term account by waiving a part of their remuneration.

▶ In any case it makes sense (and is not too complicated), to notify the employees regularly not just of their status but also on the development of their long-term accounts. The simplest way of doing this is to use a (customer-specific) ESS scenario.

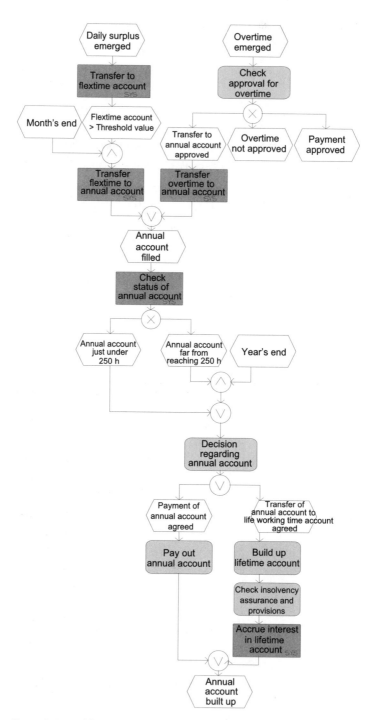

Figure 8.67 Building Up a Life Working Time Account

8.7 Critical Success Factors in Time Management

▶ Exact knowledge of the actual processes (in particular in branch offices/branches). Knowledge of the collective agreements and official company regulations alone does not suffice.

▶ A clear definition of overtime processes. The approval processes should be sufficient and not require any exceptions. Following this principle, you must eliminate exceptions (you must avoid requirements such as, for overtime on Sundays, to pay half the bonus and to transfer the other half to the life account and place the basic salary in the flextime account).

▶ An end to reporting on paper. Information on working time must be current. That is only possible online.

▶ Use the environments provided for decentralized information and processing: ESS, MSS, Time Manager's Workplace and Manager's Desktop

▶ No detailed description of time models in the system

▶ Early clarification of the extensive processes of logistics and accounting

▶ Early clarification of data entry processes, in particular for master data which is relevant for time management and for time data which is relevant for payroll. Work distribution with other processes is important for efficient flows. The change of processors must therefore be kept to a minimum.

▶ Well-trained time administrators with extensive competencies so that work is carried out mainly on a decentralized basis. The central personnel department assumes the task of advisor and controller.

▶ Optimally structured user interfaces for time administrators (and those responsible for time ticket entries such as office supervisor writers). In most cases, the TMW is the optimal solution. Simple and efficient interface creation is especially important if the time administrators only spend a very small amount of their working time with data maintenance in the R/3.

▶ Use of only the most necessary mobile solutions. Complicated entry processes on a mobile display or long maintenance times due to limited bandwidth, both limit user acceptance.

▶ No delegation of management responsibility to the time-management system

▶ Early integration test with the sub systems

▶ Quality-assurance environment with a sufficient number of documented test cases. Changes in the customizing of the schema frequently have unexpected side effects, which are not picked up without a suitable quality-assurance environment.

▶ Abolition of regulations that were justified in older systems or in manual time management, but that just increase the workload in mySAP HR. This mainly includes all types of rounding.

9 Payroll

Payroll is based on the results of personnel administration, time management and—in some cases—on the results of travel management and incentive wage. It is divided into the sub-processes gross payroll, net payroll, and subsequent processing. The subsequent processing comprises legal and company-specific components.

9.1 Business Principles

This chapter will convey the basic concepts and background of payroll. This is not a complete guide to setting up payroll, as this would be outside the scope of this book due to the complexity of the application.

We will try to avoid country and sector specifics, as legal restrictions do not leave much room for flexibility. These specifics also are frequently subject to legal amendments and are presumably only of interest to a small number of readers.

9.1.1 Basic Forms of Remuneration

The following section will provide a description of the basic forms of remuneration. There are numerous possible hybrid forms based on the basic forms. These are supplemented by additional remuneration components (see Section 9.1.3).

Incentive Wage

In the case of incentive wages, the employee is remunerated based on work results and not the time worked. It is generally assumed that this approach increases an employee's motivation.

The individual piecework is the value of the individual employee's piece performance. For each completed piece, he is credited a standard time that is measured against the actual time required. This relationship between standard and required time is referred to as the performance efficiency rate.

Performance efficiency rate [%] = Standard time x piece number / required time

If an employee exceeds a 100% performance efficiency rate, he or she can thus increase the hourly wage. A performance efficiency rate of less than 100% on the other hand leads to a reduction, which is however limited in many pay scales. More complex, team-oriented production flows frequently do not allow any individual incentive wages. By introducing group incentive wages, an attempt is made to remunerate a team, such as a manufacturing center. Here the performance efficiency rate is calculated similarly to the individual piecework, with the difference that times and number of pieces of the entire group are included. The group performance efficiency rate is then applied to the individual hourly rate for the employees. While the piecework only remunerates target quantities, the premium wage incorporates other target figures, such as quality.

Hourly Wage

In the case of hourly wages, the employee is paid for merely being present. He or she is remunerated a constant amount per hour. The hourly wage is particularly useful if the assignment of work results is difficult.

Monthly or Weekly Wage

In spite of constant weekly hours of work, an employee paid an hourly wage each month receives a different transfer amount, given that the months have different numbers of workdays. The monthly wage is an attempt to stabilize the basic wage of the employee by making sure that he or she receives a constant monthly amount. A semimonthly or two-week calculation of the remuneration is also possible.

In some remuneration models, absences of the employee (e.g., due to public holidays, vacation leave, sickness) are paid at the basic hourly wage plus an average value earned in the previous months. A performance variable is incorporated in this average (e.g., piecework) as well as a time variable (see Section 9.1.2).

9.1.2 Influencing Variables of Gross Payroll

In addition to basic remuneration forms, other circumstances also affect the remuneration.

Overtime and Bonuses

If the work in question cannot be covered with the existing employee capacity, overtime is often implemented. This overtime is to be paid for separately from regular salaries. In general, overtime bonuses accrue in addition to the basic hourly wage. However, employers frequently try to cushion short-term overtime through flexi-time regulation, as this means overtime bonuses can be saved. Overtime that accrues in one month is credited to a time account and can later be retrieved by the employee if there is less work to be done.

Times Subject to Bonuses

If the working time occurs during the night, during the weekend, or on a public holiday, additional bonuses can accrue. This makes working time more expensive.

Expenses

When the employee is working for the employer, additional costs occur (e.g., work clothes or telephone). These can be reimbursed by the employer. In many countries, these expenses are completely or partially exempt from tax and social insurance.

Non-Recurring Payments

Non-recurring payments such as bonuses or vacation bonus are not part of the monthly remuneration. Due to their lack of regularity, in many countries they are subject to special regulations with regard to taxation and social contributions.

Absences

In terms of absences, there must be a basic differentiation between paid and unpaid absences. Unpaid absences reduce the basic remuneration.

Performance-Dependent Remuneration Components

With the exception of incentive wages, basic forms of pay do not take employee results into account. For reasons of motivation and fair remuneration, these basic forms are supplemented by a performance-dependent component which should preferably be oriented towards company goals.

Modern companies derive the employee targets which are relevant for remuneration from a companywide balanced scorecard. This ensures alignment with company targets.

9.1.3 Net Payroll

In net payroll, national legal regulations are taken into account, i.e., the taxes to be deducted and the social insurance amounts are calculated.

However, U.S.-payroll in SAP HR does not include the full tax calculation scheme. You need an interface to an external BSI TaxFactory database. This sets the U.S. version apart from most other country-specific payroll solutions within SAP HR.

Special Processes

Within net payroll, a range of special processes is supported according to national laws. They considerably reduce the necessary process cycle times and therefore also the effort involved. In general, they are carried out through country-specific infotypes.

In the U.S., the following special processes are among those supported:

▶ Loans

▶ Garnishments

▶ Benefits (see Chapter 10, *Benefits*)

▶ FLSA

▶ Off-cycle payments

▶ Tip processing

9.2 Payroll Conception in mySAP HR

Basically flexibility can only be bought through complexity. This is particularly the case with payroll in mySAP HR. By normal Customizing, extensive adjustments can already be carried out. The payroll can be accessed through schemes and rules in almost any existing run and even complex regulations from collective agreements and company agreements can be implemented. If the limits are also reached here, the advantages of an open source system come into play. Standard processing can be accessed via numerous customer exits and Business Add-Ins (BAdIs). There are even tools available to modify the coding in SAP, which considerably simplifies maintenance and thereby makes modification as a more alternative option.

9.2.1 Structures for Remuneration Calculation

For the calculation, the selected settings of Infotype 0001, Organizational Assignment, are of great importance.

The enterprise structure is mapped through the personnel area and the personnel sub-area. While the personnel area is linked with the company code (which is generally a legally independent accounting unit) and therefore determines where wages and salaries are posted and where they are paid from, the personnel sub-area represents the location of the enterprise. Pay-scale information and a variety of other settings and national indicators (e.g., region and district, employer ID and industry code, tax company[1] and EEO data) are derived from this.

Enterprise structure

The personnel structure consisting of employee groups and employee subgroup also determines the essential aspects of the payroll. On this basis it is decided whether an employee is a salaried employee or a worker and if he is paid monthly or on an hourly basis. Similar to the concept of adjusting infotypes, in the payroll most settings are to be implemented according to the personnel structure and the enterprise structure.

Personnel structure

All employees of an enterprise who are to be included in payroll at a specific key date are combined in a payroll area. This area also controls the locking concept for the payroll, i.e., if the employees of a payroll area are processed; the master data of these employees is locked for maintenance (excluding data which is relevant to the future). In addition, the payroll area is a component of the logical databases PNP and PNPCE and is therefore available as a selection criterion in almost all evaluations.

Payroll area

In this context a payroll area can easily combine employees of different companies (personnel areas), as long as they are included in payroll at the same key date.

The cost center specifies the target account assignment for the personnel costs to be posted in Controlling. The cost center is also used for the travel- costs component for assigning travel costs as long as nothing else is specified there. If the organization management component is not active with active integration in personnel administration, the cost center is maintained for every employee in Infotype 0001. Otherwise this infor-

Cost center

---

1 The legal entity for tax reporting purposes. In SAP U.S. HR it should have a one-to-one relationship with the *Employer Identification Number (EIN)*.

mation is automatically forwarded from the organization chart to the employee master data.

Once these structures are in use, it is difficult to adjust them later on—especially since many essential elements in Customizing are not provided with start and end dates, and therefore cannot be easily limited if they are no longer required. For this reason, it is advisable to check the organizational structures to be used precisely in terms of their suitability from all viewpoints (master data, authorization concept, time management, payroll, reporting).

9.2.2 Payroll Principles

The Wage Type Concept

Wage types are the central processing instruments of the payroll. Entries are made using wage types in the provided payroll-relevant infotypes, e.g., as basic salary or overtime. The entire additional processing is carried out using wage types as well. Specific wage types are mapped in the net payroll for instance for the tax and social insurance to be paid. The result of the payroll—the payroll account—contains the wage types used and calculated in the employee's payroll.

The wage types thus form the basis of the payroll. They are dependent on the country, i.e., one and the same wage type can have a different meaning in a German payroll than in a payroll in the U.S. They also have a validity period within which they can be used. This also means that one wage type can exist at different times with different properties. This becomes necessary if the characteristics of a wage type change at a particular time, an example being an anniversary bonus which is subject to tax from January 1st.

A wage type is identified by a four-digit key composed of figures, letters and special characters. The related text is language-dependent:

▶ Different texts can be displayed for the same wage type for a German and for an English transactional user who each log on in their native language.

▶ A German-speaking employee can have German texts printed on the remuneration statement, and an English-speaking employee can have them printed in English.

The following conventions exist when creating four-digit wage type keys in mySAP HR:

▶ Wage types which begin with a slash (/) are called technical wage types. Most of the processing work is carried out using these technical wage types. They represent the rules for the payroll. For U.S. payroll there are about 900 of these types.[2]

▶ Wage types that begin with a number from 0 to 9 are freely available to the customer. This area is always empty in a newly supplied system.

▶ Wage types that begin with an M are SAP model wage types. So as not to have to re-invent the wheel each time, these can be used as templates for each wage type.

If the rules for payroll are controlled by wage types, it is useful to keep these up-to-date with SAP. This is the reason for the aforementioned customer namespace for wage types. All other wage types can be and are overwritten by SAP when importing updates (support packages) and in this way are constantly adjusted to the newest conditions. This is also the case with model wage types. For this reason, they should also not be used productively. A payroll with model wage types would be unstable, especially if these were customized.

The wage types used by customers always begin with a digit and are generally created by copying them from a model wage type.

Customizing Wage Types

The wage type copier was especially developed by SAP for this purpose (Transaction PU30). It copies and deletes all properties of a wage type, independent of whether it is a model wage type or another already existing wage type that is to be copied (see Figure 9.1).

In order to be able to process wage types more simply, they are summarized into wage-type groups. For example, for each infotype that contains wage types there is a specific wage-type group. This ensures that the maintenance interface for wage types remains manageable. Wage types can also be contained in several wage-type groups.

---

2 The number of technical wage types can be a first indicator for the complexity of a payroll solution within SAP. German payroll has about twice as many technical wage types as U.S. payroll, while the UK solution has only about 500. A low number of technical wage types can indicate either that payroll in the respective country is really easy or that the SAP-based solution does not cover the whole range of legal requirements.

The characteristics of wage types are determined by an amount field, a quantity field, and an amount-per-unit field. This means wage types are capable of saving any values. Whether and how a wage type is processed depends on Customizing.

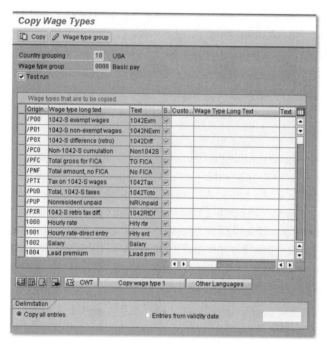

Figure 9.1 The Wage Types Copier (PU30)

Each wage type contains the following control information:

▶ **Valuation**

If an amount is not directly provided along with a wage type, payroll must carry out this task and determine the relevant amount itself. However, the amount can only be determined if the wage type contains a quantity. For instance, for overtime accrued, overtime wage types are recorded in terms of hours. These wage types must then contain the information that their evaluation basis is the personal hourly wage of the employee (if necessary in connection with a percentage rate that reflects an overtime bonus).

▶ **Cumulation**

Pools are formed using accumulation. These pools represent the interface for the net payroll, i.e., the accumulation must be completed at the end of the gross payroll. By accumulating a wage type in certain pools, specific characteristics are defined in the wage type. For instance a wage type which is subject to tax is accumulated in the "gross tax amount" pool. These pools are integrated in mySAP HR as technical wage types. They begin with "/1".

▶ **Processing classes**
Processing classes group wage types according to their characteristics. The characteristics of the processing classes of a wage type, rather than the wage type itself, are read from the payroll, and then the necessary processing steps are carried out. Abstracting a wage type itself offers more flexibility. The payroll does not have to have knowledge of every existing wage type. The characteristics of wage types can be changed simply. Processing Class 10, for instance, controls whether and how a wage type is reduced in connection with unpaid absences (see Section 9.2.5). The accumulation of a wage type can be controlled by various additional processing classes. There, the time in the payroll at which the wage type is calculated determines the processing class to be used for accumulation. In order to avoid burdening the payroll with unnecessary wage types, a wage type should be accumulated and shut down, i.e. transferred to the payroll account, as soon as a calculation is completed.

▶ **Evaluation classes**
Characteristics of the wage types are determined in the evaluation classes for printing in the remuneration statement or in other statements.

▶ **Account assignment**
Each wage type contains information on whether the wage type is to be posted to accounts and which accounts they are to be posted to.

You can analyze which wage types should have which characteristics using the report RPDLGA20. Here you can see for instance that the wage type 1212 is evaluated using the pay scale group from the pay scale table (see Figure 9.2).

We will now use an example to describe the valuation of wage types: Assuming an employee has done three hours overtime, which are to be paid out. Regulations provide that he also receives an overtime bonus in the amount of 25%.

Valuating wage types

Wage type MM10 is entered manually or transferred from time management and its number field is filled with three hours. In the field valuation basis of the wage type MM10 "01" is to be entered. All technical wage types that begin with "/0" are evaluation bases in mySAP HR. This means that the relevant hourly wage can be found in wage type /001 ("/0" + "01"). The wage type /001 in mySAP HR standard delivery always contains the currently valid hourly wage for the employee.

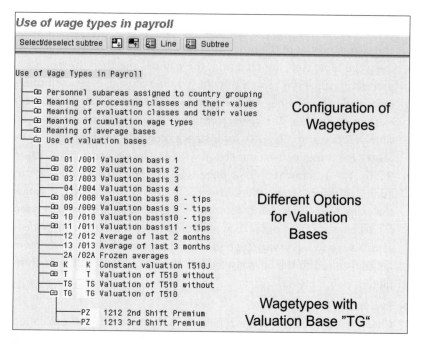

Figure 9.2 Distribution of Wage Types (RPDLGA20)

So much for the valuation basis: Now we must calculate the overtime bonus, which is 25% of the whole amount only. In order to have a better basis for later evaluations, you should use two wage types here: one for the normal hourly wage (100%) and one for the overtime bonus (25%). Here we require derived wage types. The basic pay is mapped by wage type MM10. This wage type is supplemented by the percentage rate 100. A new wage type is entered for the overtime bonus, which is similarly valuated with the hourly wage of the employee (i.e. 01). However, you must change the percentage rate to 25%, as only a 25% overtime bonus is to be paid.

Through the derivation process, a wage type can generate up to two other wage types. However, this only works once; a derived wage type cannot create other derived wage types (see Figure 9.3).

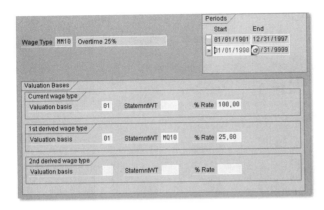

Figure 9.3 Evaluating a Wage Type (T512W)

Other fixed evaluation principles can be used in addition to the technical wage types /0**. For instance, you can establish that an employee receives an hourly bonus for hazardous or unpleasant work of $1 U.S. As shown in the previous example, the constant amount can be found on a cross-employee basis or in connection with pay scale information in Infotype 0008 ("Basic Pay") for the employee. Table 9.1 provides an overview of possible valuation base of wage types.

Valuation base	The amount-per-unit field is transferred from:
nn	The amount-per-unit field of the wage type /0nn
K	Table T510J (constant value), employee-independent
TS	The pay-scale table T510, which uses keys to search for pay-scale type, pay-scale area, pay-scale group, pay-scale level and wage type (all from Infotype 0008 "Basic Pay," except for the wage type)
TG	The pay scale table T510 is similarly accessed as with TS, however with the difference being that: pay scale level = not filled
T	The pay scale table T510 is similarly accessed as with TG, however with the difference being that: pay scale group = not filled

Table 9.1 Possible Valuation bases of a Wage Type

If a wage type is to be recorded in an infotype, it is referred to as a dialog wage type. For these types, additional information must be maintained (see Figure 9.4):

Dialog wage wage types

▶ Entries are permitted based on the enterprise and personnel structures

▶ Minimum and maximum values for the number and amount fields

▶ Several entries are permitted per month (time constraint)

▶ Indirect evaluation conducted by pay-scale tables

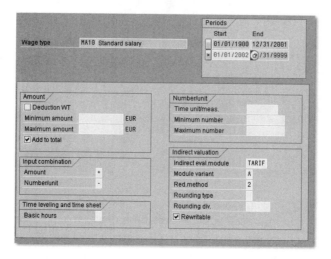

Figure 9.4 Dialog Characteristics of a Wage Type (T511)

Indirect Valuation

There is one basic issue to be dealt with in dialog wage types, i.e., whether or not these are to be valuated by entering a value manually, or if the valuation should occur indirectly by using a pay-scale table.

If a dialog wage type is indirectly valuated, this needs to be set in the dialog properties (see Figure 9.4). Here you work with modules and module variants. The combination describes the process according to which the relevant amount is transferred. Most processes work with the pay-scale table (see Figure 9.5). This is, however, not absolutely necessary.

If the amount of a wage type is automatically transferred from mySAP HR by an indirect valuation, other settings are required in order to make this powerful instrument suitable for actual practice. You must deal with the issue of what will happen if the employee works less or more than 100%.

How should this impact an employee's remuneration? A range of reduction methods is available, including rounding rules. The most useful reduction method provides the reduction by using the employment level from Infotype 0008, Basic Pay.

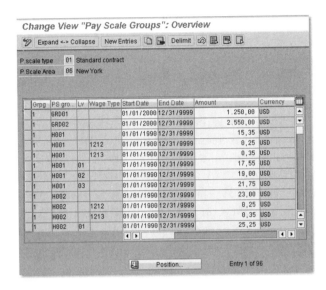

Change View "Pay Scale Groups": Overview

Expand <-> Collapse   New Entries   Delimit

P.scale type   01 Standard contract
P.Scale Area   06 New York

Grpg	PS gro...	Lv	Wage Type	Start Date	End Date	Amount	Currency
1	GRD01			01/01/2000	12/31/9999	1.250,00	USD
1	GRD02			01/01/2000	12/31/9999	2.550,00	USD
1	H001			01/01/1990	12/31/9999	15,35	USD
1	H001		1212	01/01/1900	12/31/9999	0,25	USD
1	H001		1213	01/01/1900	12/31/9999	0,35	USD
1	H001	01		01/01/1990	12/31/9999	17,55	USD
1	H001	02		01/01/1990	12/31/9999	19,00	USD
1	H001	03		01/01/1990	12/31/9999	21,75	USD
1	H002			01/01/1990	12/31/9999	23,00	USD
1	H002		1212	01/01/1900	12/31/9999	0,25	USD
1	H002		1213	01/01/1900	12/31/9999	0,35	USD
1	H002	01		01/01/1990	12/31/9999	25,25	USD

Position...   Entry 1 of 96

Figure 9.5 Pay-Scale Table (T510)

For indirectly valuated wage types no amount is saved in the database. This value is usually re-calculated by accessing infotypes, by payroll or reports. The disadvantage of the relatively complicated access to the concrete values is compensated for through simplifications during compilation and pay-scale increases. At the time of a pay-scale increase only the pay-scale table must be adjusted. The master data of all affected employees is automatically updated, as they have saved no values, but rather have calculated these during runtime from the amended pay-scale table.

As of Release 4.6C, custom modules can be implemented as business add-ins. This opens an entire range of new options. You can now make allowance for the fact that wage types can already be valuated by indirect valuation at the time of entry and not only through payroll. This not only ensures a better quality assurance when recording data but makes it possible to directly evaluate wage types from the infotypes with standard reporting (or SAP query), without having to refer to the payroll account and without the influence of the reduction of the payroll.

Unfortunately, the concept of the custom modules for indirect valuation cannot build upon an existing module of mySAP HR and attach a small add-on. This frequently covers all requirements. More often it is expected in this case that the entire existing functionality will be reprogrammed in the template.

Split Indicators

If Infotype 0008, Basic Pay, or the tax data and social-insurance data for that matter, change during a payroll period, several partial periods are created, and these must be separately taken into consideration during payroll.

Let's assume an employee has a basic salary of $3,000 U.S. On 01/20/2004 he receives a salary increase so that the new salary is $3,500. Now there are two partial periods: one from 01/01/2004 to 01/19/2004 and the other from 01/20/2004 to 01/31/2004. The basic salary is mapped through wage type M003. The payroll creates two wage types M003, one for each partial period. In order to clearly assign the wage types to the corresponding partial periods, a split indicator is used. Payroll creates a table WPBP (Work Place Basic Pay) with the work center data according to Table 9.2.

WPBP split	From	To	Calendar days	Further identifiers
01	01/01/2004	01/19/2004	20	
02	01/20/2004	01/31/2004	10	

Table 9.2 WPBP After a Salary Increase on 01/20/2004

The wage types are created from Infotype 0008 (Basic Pay) according to Table 9.3.

Wage type	WPBP split	Amount
M003	01	$3,000
M003	02	$3,500

Table 9.3 WPBP Available Loan Types After a Salary Increase on 01/20/2004

Tables 9.2 and 9.3 are linked with each other via the split identifier. If the relevant calendar days are requested in the M003 wage type, they can be transferred using the WPBP split identifier from Table WPBP (see Figure 9.6). In order to ensure that the employee does not receive $6,500, the amounts are reduced in the payroll at a later time so that in the precise calculations approximately $3,193 emerges as a weighted average value throughout the entire month (see Section 9.2.5).

Split identifiers are a technical utility to "attach" additional information to wage types.

Table WPBP

No	From	To	Action	ActionTxt	Cust.	Empl.
01	01/01/2004	01/19/2004	01	Hire		3
02	01/20/2004	01/31/2004	01	Hire		3

Table IT

A Wage type	APC1C2C3ABKoReBTAwvTvn One amount/one number	Amount
2 M003 Pay Period 01		3.000,00
2 M003 Pay Period 02		3.500,00

Figure 9.6 Wage Types with Split Identifiers

Retroactive Calculations

Retroactive calculations are always necessary if facts become known after the payroll process, which necessitate a change to the payroll data. The payroll must therefore be repeated as it is no longer correct. What is problematic about this situation, however, is that the employee has already received the remuneration statement as well as the transfer, the personnel costs for financial accounting and controlling have been transferred, and the taxes and the social insurance amounts have already been paid. A correction is therefore no longer possible. The error can be corrected at the earliest during the subsequent payroll.

How can you deal with this relatively frequent situation? This is an instance where mySAP HR displays one of its greatest strengths. It has a complete retroactive calculation function. You must only correct the incorrect entry in the respective infotype. The rest happens automatically.

The system recognizes that data has been changed in a period for which the payroll has already run. It marks these periods for correction. In the next payroll run, the payroll will be repeated for this period. A retroactive calculation takes place. The resulting difference is transferred to the current period, as the relevant period is in the past and therefore nothing more can be changed.

If the system is capable of repeating payrolls for previous periods, this means that the entire Customizing of the payroll must be time-dependent. Each adjustment to the payroll because of legal, pay scale or business reasons must be integrated in a way so that it is becomes valid at a specific date. This is the only way of ensuring that in case of a retroactive calculation the payroll logic did not change in the interim period and lead to misleading results. This is one of the reasons why the payroll is so enormously complex.

For reasons of revision the old result cannot just be changed. The retroactive calculation then creates an additional result for this period. In order not to lose the overview, we will work with the "for-period" and "in-period" concepts: In the case of an employee for whom retroactive calculation has been used, there are two payroll results for the same period, each of which has a different "in" period.

In order to better understand this complicated concept, we must carry out another example: After a successful payroll for 01/2002, we find out that we forgot to pay an employee an allowance for special services of $100 for 01/2002. This is corrected, say in infotype 0015, and after the payroll run for 02/2002 the results can be found in the database (see Table 9.4, each row of the table represents a payroll result).

For period	In period	Description
01/2002	01/2002	Original payroll 01/2002 including the error, i.e. without the allowance for special services
01/2002	02/2002	Correction to the payroll for 01/2002 during the payroll run 02/2002 (with allowance for special services)
02/2002	02/2002	Original payroll 02/2002

Table 9.4 Payroll Results After Payroll 02/2002 with Retroactive Calculation for 01/2002

From a technical point of view, retroactive calculations can be carried out as frequently as necessary. It is a very powerful instrument for avoiding inconsistencies between the payroll and the parts of mySAP HR that provide the necessary data for this.

Payroll-Relevant Master Data

In order to ensure that master data changes trigger retroactive calculations for periods when a payroll already exists, a special check logic must be active. In Infotype 0003, Payroll Status, the payroll saves the last date the employee has been accounted for (**Accounted to** field). In addition, it saves the latest date since the last payroll run on which a master data change to the payroll-relevant master data has be carried out (**Earliest MD change** field). Using this field, the payroll determines the earliest period for which a retroactive calculation will be necessary. This field is always deleted by the productive payroll (see Figure 9.7).

The logic to fill the **Earliest MD change** field is integrated in the processing logic of the infotypes. In the infotype characteristics, you only have to specify if the infotype is relevant for the payroll and must therefore trigger retroactive payroll calculation. In this context, either the entire infotype can be identified as completely relevant for payroll or merely individual fields (see Figure 9.8). For instance, the phone number of an employee is not payroll-relevant although his bank details would definitely be.

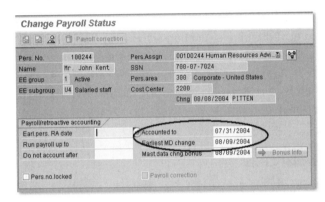

Figure 9.7 Infotype 0003 — Payroll Status

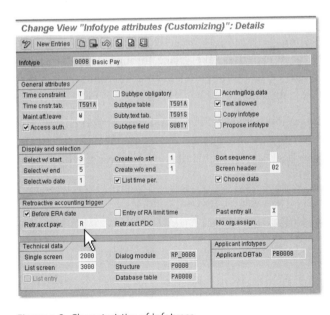

Figure 9.8 Characteristics of Infotypes

Results of Time Management

The results of the time evaluation (cluster B2) of the respective periods are read by payroll in order to receive the following data:

▶ The personal work schedule for the employee, including all attendances and absences. It contains, for instance, the planned working time as well as paid and unpaid absences of the employee.

▶ A table with wage types, which generally contain time and shift bonuses, overtime, and time accounts paid out (possibly also deductions due to negative time accounts). The task of the payroll is to valuate these wage types that are provided in terms of hours.

▶ Because the results of the time evaluation are read by the payroll, the time evaluation directly influences the payroll, in the same way as an entry in a payroll-relevant infotype. For this reason, retroactive calculation is triggered by the time evaluation for payroll if changes are implemented in the periods for which payroll has already been carried out.

Results of the Travel Costs

Similar to time management, the payroll also reads the results of travel costs (cluster TE/TX), which were created in the respective periods of the payroll. The travel costs settlement transfers a table of wage types to the payroll.

This integration has not necessarily to be active. You only need it if the reimbursement of travel expenses takes place through payroll accounting[3] or if payroll needs certain information such as reimbursements that are considered taxable income.

To activate the integration between travel management and payroll, the sub-schema UREI (for the U.S.) has to be active in your payroll schema. Additionally, feature TRVPA must be maintained (observe the documentation of the feature):

▶ Entry "L+G" must have a value between 1 and 4

▶ Entry "PA3" should have the value 1

---

3 Alternatively, it can take place through accounts payable in financial accounting, by a special DME (Data medium exchange) or by check.

9.2.3 Payroll Process

The Payroll Control Record

Each payroll area has a payroll control record (Transaction PA03) with the task of performing lock administration. This lock administration should ensure that all the master data entries are considered in the payroll. To this end you must work with the statuses "Released for Payroll," "Released for Correction," "Exit Payroll" and "Check Payroll Results." Apart from the status, a period counter is required to make clear which period is being referred to. When you change the status from "Exit Payroll" to "Released for Payroll" (beginning of a new payroll run) the period counter is automatically counted up one period. Apart from that, the period counter cannot be influenced.

The individual statuses affect the employees of the corresponding payroll area, as shown in Table 9.5.

Status	Effect of master data	Effect on the payroll
"released"	The master data is lokked for the current period and the past. Maintenance for the future is still possible.	Payroll is possible with the released period.
"correction"	A complete maintenance is possible. Payroll-relevant changes set the matchcode "W". for the employee (payroll correction)	No productive payroll is possible.
"check"	The master data is lokked for the current period and the past. Maintenance for the future is still possible.	No productive payroll is possible.
"ended"	A complete maintenance is possible.	No productive payroll is possible.

Table 9.5 Status of the Payroll Control Record

If according to the payroll control record the status in the payroll run is "ended," it is completely finished and cannot be changed. All corrections are then carried out by retroactive calculation.

In addition, the earliest retroactive accounting period is saved in the payroll control record. This establishes to what an extent a correction of master data is possible in the past and to what extent retroactive calculation can be carried out. This can only be changed directly in Transaction PA03 if the status of the payroll control record has just been set to "Exit Payroll" (see Figure 9.9).

At the same time, the earliest retroactive calculation determines the earliest retroactive accounting period for which retroactive calculation can be carried out. For this reason it can only be changed if no retroactive accounting has been set for any employees. The only instance that guarantees this is the moment, the "Exit" status is set.

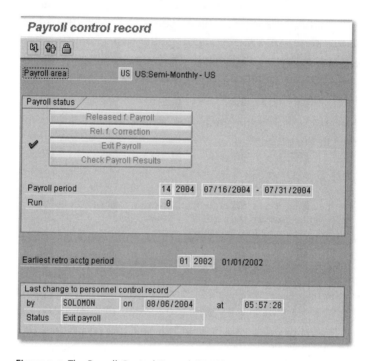

Figure 9.9 The Payroll Control Record (PA03)

The upper left corner of the payroll control record displays a range of icons, which can simplify the execution of the payroll run (see Figure 9.10). The user has the following options—restricted to the assigned payroll area:

Figure 9.10 Additional Icons of the Payroll Control Period

▶ Display matchcode "W" (employees whose payroll needs a correction before control record can be set to "Exit")

- View the list of assigned employees

- Display the employees currently locked for processing via infotype 0003

The payroll control record logs the history of the changes, so that you can see at a later stage which user carried out which status change (see Figure 9.11).

Chngd on	Time	User Name	PP	PayY	Control record status...	SpRn
10/03/2003	21:35:14	PITTEN	14	2003	Exit payroll	
10/03/2003	21:04:58	PITTEN	14	2003	Released for payroll	
10/03/2003	18:46:17	PITTEN	13	2003	Exit payroll	
10/03/2003	15:39:19	PITTEN	13	2003	Released for payroll	
06/19/2003	18:12:52	HEATWOLE	12	2003	Exit payroll	
06/19/2003	18:12:46	HEATWOLE	12	2003	Released for payroll	
06/19/2003	18:12:40	HEATWOLE	11	2003	Created new	
06/19/2003	18:12:32	HEATWOLE	12	2003	Deleted	

Figure 9.11 Log of the Payroll Control Record

Payroll Run

The payroll run is started for a payroll control record (representing a payroll area) which establishes the period for which the payroll is to be performed. The assigned payroll area determines the employees for whom payroll is to be carried out. For each individual employee, it is then determined if retroactive calculation is necessary and if so for which period. This information is extracted from Infotype 0003, Payroll Status. Payroll for an employee is chronologically implemented from the oldest to the newest period. Figure 9.12 shows the principle of the payroll program. The "basic version" RPCALCX0 displays an international template. The same principle is also used in the U.S. version RPCALCU0 and the other country versions. Some of these country versions (e.g., for the East European countries) are not delivered with the standard system but rather as add-ons.

Payroll Driver RPCALCX0

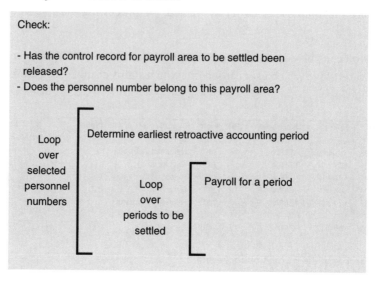

Check:

- Has the control record for payroll area to be settled been released?
- Does the personnel number belong to this payroll area?

Loop over selected personnel numbers

Determine earliest retroactive accounting period

Loop over periods to be settled

Payroll for a period

Figure 9.12 Payroll Structure

Payroll Cluster

The payroll calculates the gross components for all employees of a payroll area, while in the net payroll it calculates the relevant amounts to be paid out. These are saved in clusters. In order to avoid redundant data records and possible inconsistencies, all programs that require these results access them directly. In this context, the payroll results are stored according to the procedure described in the "Retroactive Calculation" section (see Section 9.2.2) and can be displayed using Report RPCLSTRU (U.S. version) (see Figure 9.13).

The payroll cluster then saves a multitude of data. In addition to a range of master data and data from time management the calculated wage types are also saved (see Figure 9.14).

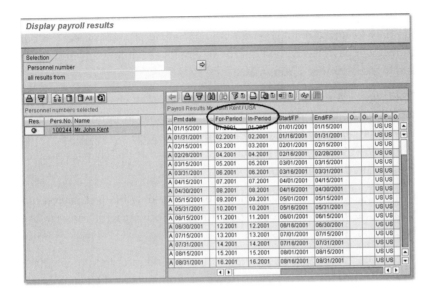

Figure 9.13 Payroll Results for an Employee

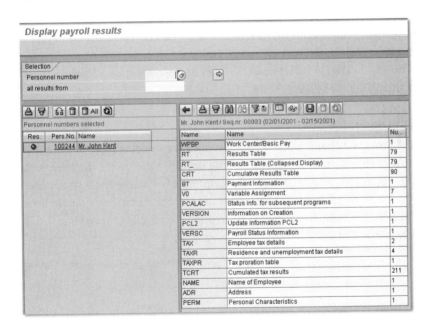

Figure 9.14 Payroll Result for a Period

Matchcode "W"

If, during the payroll run, the payroll for an individual employee is canceled (e.g., due to errors in the basic remuneration), these employees are transferred to matchcode "W." This makes it possible to repeat the payroll run only for those employees for whom the payroll was not carried out correctly. If payroll is carried out for an employee without any errors, the employee is removed from matchcode "W."

Employees are also transferred to matchcode "W" if changes to the payroll-relevant master data have been implemented in periods for which payroll has already been carried out. This is the case, for instance, in the "correction" status of the payroll control record if the changes are not implemented for the future.

Thus matchcode "W" ensures that in each case only the first payroll run for a period for all employees is performed. All other payroll runs can use matchcode "W." This saves time.

Matchcode "W" is visible as **Payroll correction** indicator in Infotype 0003 (Payroll Status) for an employee. However, from Release 4.6x on only the information from Table T52MCW is displayed. It can be changed, however, via the maintenance screen of Infotype 0003 (which can be reached through the menu path **Utilities · Change payroll status** from the master data maintenance) through the menu items **Extras · Set correction run** or **Extras · Delete Correction run**. Employees of a payroll control record who are located in matchcode "W" can be seen most clearly using Transaction PA03 (see Figure 9.10).

Subsequent Activities

Payment The term "subsequent activities" describes the necessary process steps to be carried out upon completion of the payroll, for instance the transfer of the net wages and salaries or the printing of remuneration statements. From a technical point of view, you can carry this out at any point in time. There is however the following basic principle for all components of subsequent activities:

> *All necessary data for the subsequent activities is saved in the payroll result or can be retrieved from there.*

As soon as the control record has the status "exit," the master data can be changed again. This also applies to master data that relates to a period for which the payroll has just been completed. The components of the subsequent activities must, however, provide identical results no matter when they are carried out. If they were to revert back to the master data, the result would be dependent on the changes already carried out.

With the bank transfer, all the transfer amounts established during the payroll process are transferred to the respective bank accounts. These are generally the net wages and salaries as well as diverse national transfers (in Germany for instance the company pension and the garnishment). For this, not only the wage types but also the relevant bank details are saved in the payroll system.

The bank transfer itself is carried out in three steps:

1. In the first step, you create an extract of the transfer data through the so-called preliminary program. The extract is identified by the date and time of the program run where the last digit of the seconds is replaced with a "P." The preliminary program selects all the transfers contained in the extract by supplementing the respective transfers in the payroll results with the program-run identification of the extract. This avoids transfers being carried out several times. In addition—for instance by using the selection field "wage type,"—you can access the preliminary program so that the garnishments are transferred at a different time. You can then exclude the wage type for garnishment transfers so they can be written to another extract.

2. Finally you must create the DME. The DME represents the nationally valid format of a data to communicate with banks. For this reason, the program used for this comes from financial accounting. It requires the program identification of the extract from the preliminary program. The "P" at the end of the program-run identification ensures that the individual transactions contained in the DME in financial accounting cannot be seen.

3. In the last step, the DME created can be copied to a diskette and sent.

A separate payment run independent of the payroll can be implemented by using Report RPCDTBU0. It reads data from Infotypes 0011, 0014 and 0015 and—as is the case with the normal preliminary program—provides these in an extract. The records thus created are locked against changes until the next payroll run and are integrated in the payroll results. A prerequisite for correct processing in the payroll is the relevant Customizing of the wage types used. By using this process, down payments between two payroll runs can be implemented.

Payroll posting runs in two steps. In the first step, all employees are checked to see if *debit = credit* is valid for the posting to be created. Only when this condition has been fulfilled are the posting dates of the employee transferred to the complete posting. **Posting**

The posting program recognizes three types of posting runs:

▶ In the test run "T" it is only checked, if the condition *debit = credit* is fulfilled for the employees.

▶ The simulation run "S" creates a simulation document for posting. Here all warnings and errors emerge as they would at a later production run (e.g., locked cost centers or unavailable accounts).

▶ Production run "P" creates the same data as in the simulation run. The posting run however has the "productive" status and can therefore be released and posted (this is the second step). In addition, all employees for whom the necessary prerequisite *debit = credit* was fulfilled are provided with an indicator, so that multiple postings can be avoided. The production run can be repeated until no more employees exist with *debit = credit*. The frequent reason for such an inconsistency is that wage types were not accounted for.

The simulation and production runs can be seen using Transaction PCP0 (see Figure 9.15).

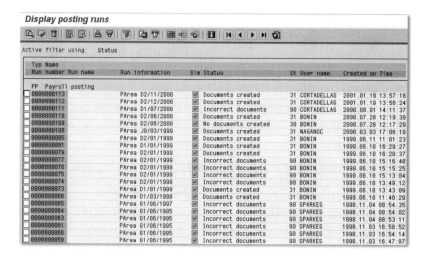

Figure 9.15 Posting Runs (Transaction PCP0)

In the run history you can trace who carried out which steps (see Figure 9.16).

The run attributes display whether all employees have been transferred to financial accounting (see Figure 9.17).

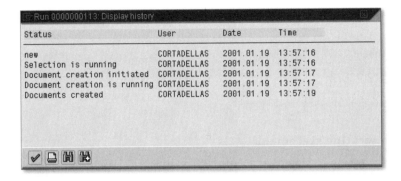

Figure 9.16 Run History

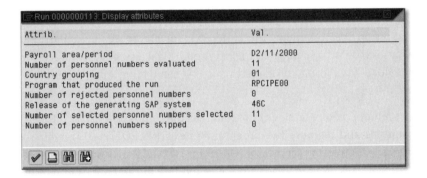

Figure 9.17 Run Attributes

Production runs must be released and posted for transfer into financial accounting. It is not important at this point whether HR and FI are located in two different systems. The payroll posting is ALE-capable, i.e., the existing system landscape is not visible in the posting process.

If a production run is deleted, all the flags set for the effected employees will be deleted again in the background so that a repetition of the production run is possible.

> **Warning** Deleting the flag takes place asynchronously to the dialog, i.e., it takes a few minutes until this process is completed by the system according to the amount of personnel numbers. Production runs which have already been booked can also be directly cancelled from here.

There are a range of evaluations which can read the payroll cluster and can display it in different processed forms (see Table 9.6).

Evaluations

Report	Technical Name	Period	Main focus
Payroll accounts	RPCKTOX0 (no U.S.-version)	For-Period	Employee
Payroll journal	RPCLJNU0	In-Period	Employee
Wage type reporter	H99CWTR0	Both	Wage type

Table 9.6 Evaluating the Payroll Results

Remuneration statement

The remuneration statement is also called the pay slip. Although the remuneration statement is not the only method of communication between the payroll department and employees, it certainly is the most important one. A well-designed remuneration statement clearly explains the details for the employee's pay and deductions. The clearer the information on the statement, the easier it is for employees to understand what exactly is happening to their payroll. It will also greatly reduce the workload for the payroll department, by eliminating many queries on such issues.

Program to create remuneration statements

The remuneration statement program has different versions for different countries and regions. The program name is RPCEDT<x>0, in which x stands for the country indicator (U for U.S., K for Canada, and X for international). This program reads employee master data and the payroll result cluster and prints that information in a predefined layout. The modifications to the remuneration statement do not have consequences for the generated payroll data. Sometimes it is necessary for the payroll data to be presented in a different way than the payroll result. For example, the amounts of some deduction wage types need to be grouped together and printed in one line item as a total. The layout of the remuneration statements is defined through forms. Figure 9.18 shows the selection screen of the remuneration statement program RPCEDTU0.

The parameters on the selection screen can control how the program runs. Following are some of the most important parameters:

The parameters in the field **Print retroactive runs** control whether retroactive runs are printed. There are three possible options:

▶ " " (space): Retroactive runs are never printed.

▶ "X": Retroactive runs are always printed.

▶ "L": Retroactive runs are only printed if a difference occurs with respect to the next to last payroll run for a wage type marked appropriately in table T512E in the field DIFAR.

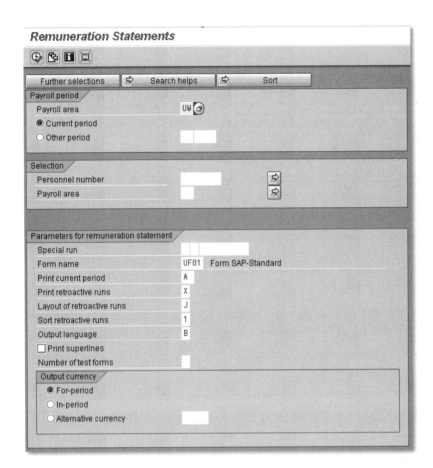

Remuneration Statements

Further selections ⇨ Search helps ⇨ Sort

Payroll period

Payroll area   UW ⊕
- ● Current period
- ○ Other period

Selection

Personnel number   ⇨
Payroll area   ⇨

Parameters for remuneration statement

Special run	
Form name	UF01 Form SAP-Standard
Print current period	A
Print retroactive runs	X
Layout of retroactive runs	J
Sort retroactive runs	1
Output language	B
☐ Print superlines	
Number of test forms	

Output currency
- ● For-period
- ○ In-period
- ○ Alternative currency

Figure 9.18 Run RPCEDTU0

As shown in Figure 9.19, in table T512E, the first three shown wage types are marked with **R** in column **Dif**, which is different from the last one. The changes can also be made within the Form Editor, through **window · groups · DifRel** field.

During the program run, all wage types with this indicator are checked to see if there are changes to the **period's second to last payroll run**. If a difference is found in at least one wage type, the form for retroactive accounting is printed. Those flags should be set only to the wage types for which changes are important (for example, insurance deductions). Changes to the rest of the wage types are ignored. Therefore, no retroactive statement will be printed out. This not only saves paper, it also decreases confusion among employees.

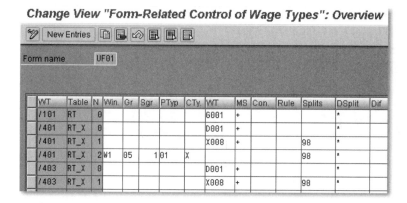

New Entries

Form name   UF01

WT	Table	N	Win.	Gr	Sgr	PTyp	CTy.	WT	MS	Con.	Rule	Splits	DSplit	Dif
/101	RT	0						6001	+				*	
/401	RT_X	0						D001	+				*	
/401	RT_X	1						X008	+			98	*	
/401	RT_X	2	W1	05		1	01	X				98	*	
/403	RT_X	0						D001	+				*	
/403	RT_X	1						X008	+			98	*	

Figure 9.19 Print Control of Retroactive Run

The parameter **Layout of retroactive runs** determines how retroactive runs are printed:

▶ "A": Retroactive accounting differences are printed on the same form as the values for the payroll period

▶ "D": Retroactive accounting differences are printed on a separate form for each period

▶ "J": Retroactive runs are printed on a separate form for each period

▶ "S": Retroactive accounting differences are cumulated on a wage-type-by-wage-type basis and then printed on the form for the payroll period

The field **Sort retroactive runs** determines how wage types are sorted for retroactive accounting printouts. The detailed information for each program parameter can be displayed by pressing the key **F1** while the cursor is put in the field. The control of retroactive payroll printouts significantly increased the complexity of the printing process of the remuneration statement, because it required special form-editing tools other than the standard SAPscript. The most commonly used tool is the Form Editor.

Form Editor

The Form Editor is a tool to modify forms used in HR. It can be accessed via or transaction code PE51 or the IMG path: **Payroll: USA · Forms · Remuneration Statement · Setup Remuneration Statement**.

Because the forms are processed by country-specific programs such as remuneration statement printing program, a country grouping must be specified for each form. For each form, the following sub-objects need to be maintained in the Form Editor.

- **Attributes**

  Attributes include the basic information of the form. The responsible person and maximum size can be maintained here.

- **Background**

  The background defines the information on the statement background.

- **Single fields**

  The single field refers to a field with value. The value can be a language-independent fixed text string, a language-dependent text module or a variable value from a table field.

- **Window**

  A window is an area defined in the form. Fields can be located in any position within a window. For example, wage types to be printed on the remuneration statement can be printed in windows.

- **Line layout**

  A line layout defines how texts in one line are arranged for printing.

- **Cumulation IDs**

  Cumulation IDs are used to group together the same kinds of wage types, time quota or absence types so that their values can be summed up together. For example, a Cumulation ID can be created on the remuneration statement to show the total deduction of an employee, which may include wage types for benefit deduction, tax deduction, and all other deductions.

- **Text modules**

  Text modules contain texts for different languages. By using text modules, a text object can be defined to be printed at a specified position despite of the text language.

- **Rules**

  Rules in HR Form Editor refer to the logic that determines whether a field should be printed out or not based on certain criteria.

- **Documentation**

  As with many other SAP objects, it is possible to store the documentation of the form together with the form itself.

Figure 9.20 shows the relationships between the form elements. Fields and groups in windows contain information to be printed on remuneration statements. The modularized structure makes it easier to change the layout. Only the position of each element needs to be adjusted; the definition of contents can remain the same.

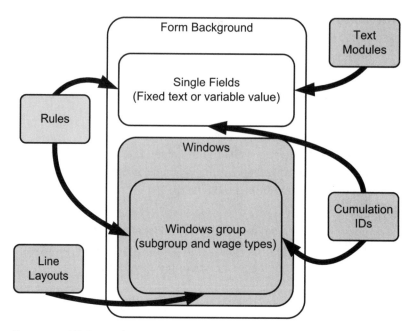

Figure 9.20 HR Form Editor

The adjustments to a single field, windows, and groups are described in detail in following paragraphs. When you double-click on a field, a pop-up window appears with all attributes to be maintained for this field. Figure 9.21 shows the properties for the employee name field, whose value comes from employee master data table P0001. In the position information, you can also specify if this element is to be printed on every page or only on the first page or last page.

The print data section describes the source of the data for this field. The field value can be fixed as a constant, or a text module that can be different for each language. It can also be a value from a table that can be determined only at run time. The pop-up window in Figure 9.21 shows some of the possible tables that can be used.

Table RT, CRT and SCRT are commonly used for wage-type-related information. If cumulation identifications are used, the table begins with Z, and contains the cumulation information. For example, ZRT contains information for cumulation wage types. You can get a full list of usable tables with possible entries (**F4**) function.

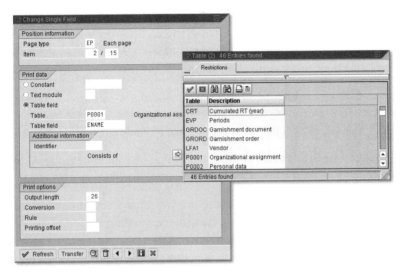

Figure 9.21 HR Form Single Field

There are two types of controls for the printing of wage types in the remuneration statement:

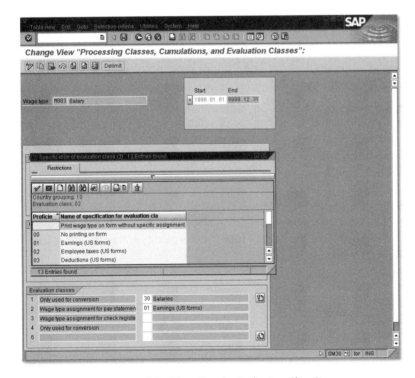

Figure 9.22 Printing Control for Wage Type by Evaluation Class 2

You can print out a wage type on the remuneration statement by maintaining evaluation class 02 in the table V_512W_D for the wage type. The IMG path for this is: **Payroll · Forms · Bases · Maintain evaluation classes and their processing class values**.

The value 01 to 03 determines in which group in the windows the wage type is printed on forms. For example, if a wage type for state tax to be printed, the value 02 is to be set for this wage type's evaluation class 2.

If the wage type is not to be printed, then value 00 should be assigned to the evaluation class for the wage type.

In the second type of control, you can use groups and subgroups of windows to directly include a wage type or cumulation identifier to be printed on the remuneration statement. The group and subgroup can be used to determine the sequence in which the wage types or cumulation identifier are printed. Giving group numbers to each wage type means that the wage types are printed in the ascending order of group numbers given. For wage types in same group, the subgroup number is used. Wage types with same group and sub-group are printed by the ascending order of wage-type names (see Figure 9.22).

Double-clicking on the window area of the form, triggers a pop-up window that shows all the group definition within the windows. Double-clicking on the group item again brings up another pop-up window for maintaining the detail of a group. Here you can maintain the wage types you want to print by referring to the wage-type table and the wage type directly. Subgroup (**Sgr**) is a mandatory field. You can also maintain other columns of the wage type as required, such as the condition rule for printing this element. For detailed meaning for each column, use **F1** to get help information.

Because the elements within the group can only be displayed after double- clicking on the group entry, it is difficult later to find out the group with the wage type you want. Putting some quality summary information in the group text is a good way to help the search.

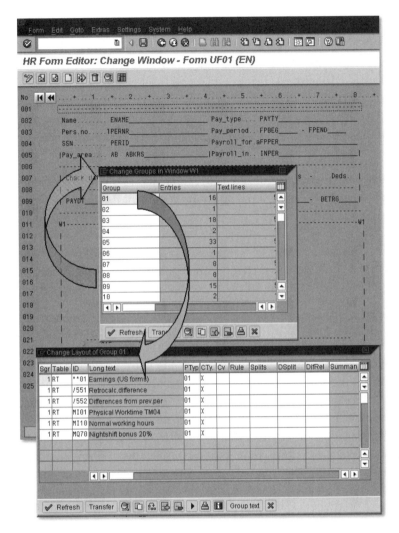

Figure 9.23 Form Window

In Figure 9.23, all the wage types have **Ptyp 01** and **Cty X**. Those items are to be printed in the corresponding line layout shown in Figure 9.24.

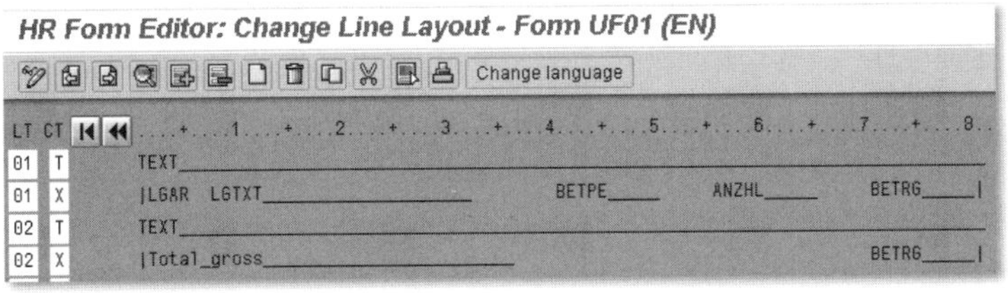

Figure 9.24 Line Layout in Form Editor

The settings for line layout are the same as those for single fields.

Although HR Form Editor already offers great flexibility, there still could be some requirement that cannot be met, such as information that has to be calculated from several fields. In that case, user exit RPCEDS29 can be used for enhancement. In this program, you can design your customized tables and fields, together with the logic to process them. However, before those tables and fields can be used in Form Editor, they must be first registered in table T514K and T514N.

All the development effort devoted to remuneration statement should be well documented. Usually, a remuneration statement has to be modified to meet legal and business requirements. At the same time, the documentation is crucial to understanding what was done before making new changes. We suggest that at least a text version of the documents be saved in the Form Editor with the documentation option. Thus, as long as the remuneration statement is there, the document can be easily found together with it.

HR Form Workplace

The remuneration statements printed from the Form Editor can only be text–based: the Form Editor neither supports the change of fonts nor any graphics. SAPscript can provide the rich format and graphics, but is not flexible enough for a complex remuneration-statement run logic. The HR Form Workplace is a newly developed tool from SAP to flexibly create and run various HR reports with advanced visual effects From Enterprise HR Extension 2.00, the U.S. version of remuneration statement is supported (Form name SAP_PAYSLIP_US). HR Form Workplace (transaction code HRFORMS) is used both to define and execute the HR Smart Forms, including remuneration statement.

As shown in Figure 9.25, a remuneration statement in HR Form Workbench can have embedded graphics, different fonts, and shaded boxes. For more information about Smart Forms, please refer to the book SAP Smart Forms from SAP PRESS.

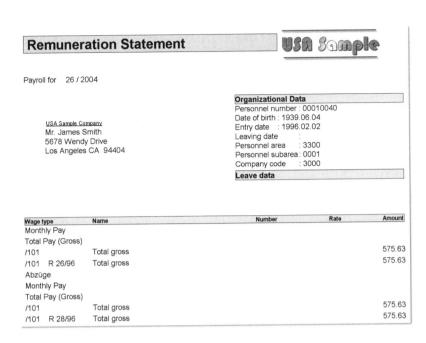

Remuneration Statement

USA Sample

Payroll for   26 / 2004

USA Sample Company
Mr. James Smith
5678 Wendy Drive
Los Angeles CA 94404

Organizational Data
Personnel number : 00010040
Date of birth : 1939.06.04
Entry date   : 1996.02.02
Leaving date   :
Personnel area   : 3300
Personnel subarea : 0001
Company code   : 3000

Leave data

Wage type	Name	Number	Rate	Amount
Monthly Pay				
Total Pay (Gross)				
/101	Total gross			575.63
/101 R 26/96	Total gross			575.63
Abzüge				
Monthly Pay				
Total Pay (Gross)				
/101	Total gross			575.63
/101 R 28/96	Total gross			575.63

Figure 9.25 HR Form Workbench—Remuneration Statement

Tax Reporter

In the U.S., as a legal requirement, a company has to produce payroll tax reports to government authorities periodically. This could involve a lot of work if done manually. SAP provides a tool for this called **Tax Reporter** that is closely integrated with payroll. The integration of the tax reporter with the payroll ensures the accuracy of the data on tax forms. You can use Tax Reporter to generate following forms:

▶ Form 940—Employer's Annual Federal Unemployment Tax Return

▶ Form 941—Employer's Quarterly Federal Tax Return

▶ Form 941C—Supporting Statement To Correct Information

▶ Form W-2—Wage and Tax Statement

▶ Form W-2C—Corrected Wage and Tax Statement

▶ 1099-R

▶ 1099-RC

▶ Multiple Worksite Report (Combined format for Bureau of Labor Statistics)

▶ Unemployment Insurance reports for all states

W-4 Withholding Allowance Report

| | | | | Tax Jurisdiction : CA |
| | | | | Allowance Threshold: 00 |

Per. no.	Employee name	Employee SSN	Effective date	Claimed Status	Claimed Allow	Mandated Status	Mandated Allow.
00010807	Natascha Pelster	777889999	1996.01.01	01	01	00	00
00010811	Milene Fisk	444332222	1996.01.01	01	01	00	00
00010812	Caroline Douglas	666443333	1996.01.01	01	01	00	00
00010813	Chris Zweber	666554444	1996.01.01	01	01	00	00
00010050	Matthew Stephens	777881234	1996.01.12	01	01	00	00
00010806	Bette Kay	666778888	1996.01.01	01	01	00	00
00010602	Carl Raymond	555221234	1995.05.18	01	01	00	00
00010603	Mary Ferguson	555998765	1996.01.01	01	01	00	00
00010604	Carl Jackson	555443333	1996.02.01	01	01	00	00
00010800	Frank Costello	556784567	1996.02.01	01	01	00	00
00010805	Butch Masters	555667777	1996.01.01	01	01	00	00
00010814	David Taylor	777665555	1996.01.01	01	01	00	00
00010009	Mike Eckert	555199991	1996.02.01	01	02	00	00
00010021	Anthony Benett	472998888	1996.01.04	01	05	00	00
00010817	Jane Simon	444335555	1996.01.01	01	01	00	00

Figure 9.26 Tax Reporter

When the tax reporting runs, it reads the payroll result from the payroll cluster tables and third party remittance and generates the tax forms. The forms can be printed out or saved to disks, according to the setup of the output options.

Tax reporter cluster After generating the Tax Reporter forms, all the results for each employee as well as for the entire tax company are stored in the cluster PCL4 at field level. The advantage of storing the tax data in a cluster is obvious. This will allow the users to reproduce the forms already generated easily without repeating the calculation. When the retroactive payroll run is performed, you need to rerun the tax report to get the latest tax report result. The new result will be updated in PCL4 automatically when you rerun the Tax Reporter.

The menu path for running Tax Reporter is: **US Payroll · Subsequent activities · Period-independent · Payroll supplement · Tax Reporter**. Figure 9.26 shows the output screen for Tax Reporter.

The tax reports are generated based on the payroll results of the entire tax company, which is linked to the employee indirectly by personnel area and personnel sub-area. You can define the tax company via IMG path **Payroll · Payroll USA · Tax · Tax companies · Assign tax company to personal area**.

When running the tax reports for a tax company, especially when many employees are involved, we suggest running this report in the background to avoid timeout errors. Splitting the employee into batches by defining program variants for different selection ranges can also help to shorten the runtime.

Please note that legal requirements for the tax forms, including formula and layout may change occasionally. SAP delivers the corresponding changes through HR support packages. Please make sure you have the correct packages installed before using the Tax Reporter.

Garnishment

Garnishment is a legal process to withdraw an employee's income directly from the employer to pay debts owned by the employee. SAP U.S. Payroll fully supports this functionality.

Garnishment can be processed only after a court order is issued requesting garnishment. The garnishment request information is stored in infotypes for later processing.

Several infotypes are used to support garnishment. A garnishment document (Infotype 0194) needs to be created for a garnishment request. Subsequently, a garnishment order (Infotype 0195) also needs to be created to store further detailed garnishment information, such as creditor information (as a vendor in the FI module) and process information. These are the mandatory infotypes for the garnishment process. If an adjustment is required such as a new balance or refund, the infotype 0216 garnishment adjustment is created to reflect the change.

Figure 9.27 shows the garnishment process originated from a court order.

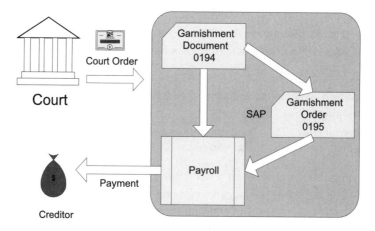

Figure 9.27 Garnishment Process

During the net-payroll processing, the garnishment infotypes are read and garnishment deductions are made to employee's pay according to the Customizing.

To implement the garnishment functionality, the following settings are essential:

▶ Wage types have to be set up to represent the garnishments. Processing class 60 has to be set up for each wage type relevant to garnishment.

▶ Garnishment order types define the required fields and field rules for the garnishment document. They also define the priority for deduction when more than one garnishment deductions is needed.

▶ In SAP U.S. Payroll, schema UGRN is used to process garnishment. The concept of schema and payroll driver will be described in following section in this chapter.

9.2.4 HR Process Workbench

The payroll run happens periodically and repeatedly for any organization. To finish one complete cycle, the payroll administrator has to run the payroll, and all necessary subsequent activities such as posting and check printing. If an error occurs during any step, the administrator has to fix the problem and probably restart the whole process. That's not all. If different groups of employees need to run payroll separately, a similar process has to be run again and again. Even for the most experienced payroll administrator, to execute all these manually is a challenging job.

It is a good idea to schedule parallel jobs for a payroll run to save some time. The report RPCSC000 can be used for parallel job-scheduling. By defining deferent program variants with separate groups of employees, it is possible to run all the jobs simultaneously.

But for the payroll run, subsequent steps and all dependencies also need to be considered. Some of these steps use the results from the previous steps. In the event of an error with some employees, the whole process must be able to either stop, or move forward with rest of the group. Those requirements are beyond the capacity of a simple job scheduler.

HR Process Workbench is an advanced tool to define, schedule, run and monitor payroll run processes. Like program RPCSC000, it can schedule jobs in parallel to greatly speed up the payroll calculation. From Release 4.7, it also supports the job scheduling on separate servers to further enhance the performance.

To get benefits from the process workbench, process models must be defined. A process models is a sequence of elements that include programs that can be run one after another or in parallel.

Depending on the purpose of the process models, they must be given assignments, which can be regular payroll run, off-cycle payroll run, or interface toolbox. The system comes with predefined process models that are suitable for different assignments as templates. We recommend that you copy the predefined template process model to your own process models and apply your own changes.

The tool to define the process model is process model editor. The transaction code call process model editor is PEST. **Human Resources · Payroll USA · Tools · Customizing Tools · Maintain Process Model**.

There are three major areas on the process model editor's screen: Display Area, Navigation Area and Insertable Object Area. As shown in Figure 9.28, the process model is displayed in the Display Area; the Navigation Area is used to control which part of the process model is displayed in the Display Area, and the Insertable Object Area provides the template of objects that can be used in the process model as steps.

Programs are the key elements for a process model. The programs used in the process model are exactly the same programs used for a manual run. In order to feed input such as selection criteria into the program while running in background, program variants are used.

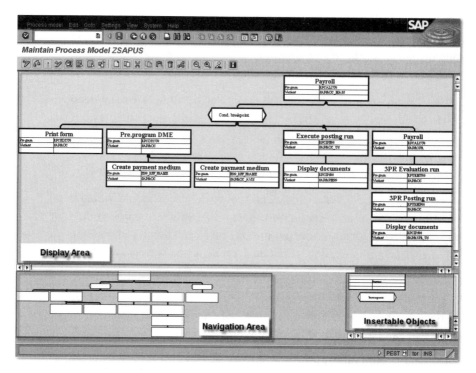

Figure 9.28 HR Process Workbench

Please note that it is very important that the correct variant is predefined and selected for a program element. This is especially true when a template process model is copied and modified. For example, if you copy a process model for production payroll run into a test-run model, you have to make sure the variant in the new process model includes the **test** flag checked.

Apart from the programs, a process model has to include a selection program that determines which employee numbers will be included in this process. The selection program defines the scope of the process run, so it must be defined at the creation of the process model. Please note that the selection program is not a step of the process, but an attached attribute of the whole process model.

A process workbench may also include breakpoints or wait points. A breakpoint is set where you want the process to stop with or without condition. Once the process is stopped, you can restart the process for the conditional breakpoint or continue to run the process from the steps after the unconditional breakpoint.

Wait points are always conditional. When a wait point is triggered, the process will go to "wait" status until a specified event occurs due to other HR activities in the system. The event can be a system event, workflow event or simply the end of other steps within the process model. Once the specified event comes out (for example, an operation mode switch which indicates the time window for background processing begins), the standby process will continue automatically. You cannot rerun the same process while it is at wait status.

The process models defined in the process workbench are also used on off-cycle workbench to perform post-payroll run activities, such as posting and check printing.

The transaction PUST is used to run a process model. Each run of the process module is a process. SAP online help has detailed instruction on how to run a payroll process.

9.2.5 The Payroll Calculation

Payroll is a matter of getting correct numbers for employees' payments and deductions. All the data and customizing are designed and maintained to support the calculation itself. A payroll calculation program is the core component of payroll.

For conversional software programs, any change in the logic requires a program change. SAP system is designed as a standard system, which means it is designed to have common functionalities for all clients and, at the same time, the flexibility to be customized based on individual customer's needs. It is impossible to do this in a conversional way because programmers can not foresee all the possibilities. To make the calculation logic easily customized without changing the calculation programs all the time, SAP developed the concept of schemas and rules.

Concept

Unlike a conversional program that has all logic including sub-modules in one program, SAP takes some of the logic controls out of its payroll program and makes those controls customizable. The core payroll calculation program is called payroll driver in SAP. The payroll driver contains only the commonly used program modules or sub-routines for calculation. Schemas and rules are used to flexibly control the how the payroll driver behaves in various circumstances.

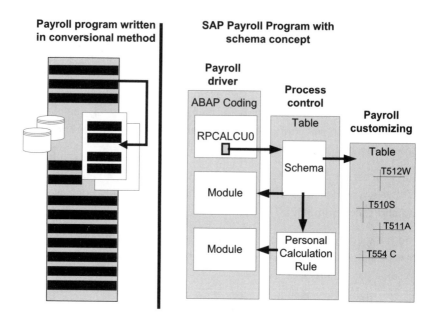

Figure 9.29 Schema Concept

The schema has a similar concept to that of a macro. It contains entries representing various pieces of code (sub-modules) within the payroll driver program. Reorganizing the entries in the schema has the same effect as rewriting the main program in a conversional program to include selected sub-modules in a specific order. After the payroll driver is triggered during the payroll run, the payroll driver refers to the schema and rules to decide which sub-routines are called, in what sequence and under what conditions.

By offering customizable schemas and rules, it is possible to change the payroll calculation process without having programming knowledge.

Figure 9.29 shows how the SAP payroll works differently from a conversional program.

Because legal requirements and business practices vary from country to country, SAP developed different standard versions of payroll calculation programs to reflect the various needs of different countries and regions. The payroll driver program name is RPCALC_0. The '_' represents a country indicator, e.g., U for U.S., K for Canada, and X for international payroll driver. The international payroll driver is used in regions that do not have a country-specific driver available, and it calculates only gross payroll. For U.S. payroll, the payroll driver program is RPCALCU0.

Schema

A personnel calculation schema consists of a number of functions in sequence. The term "function" in payroll means something different than it does in ABAP programming. A function in payroll schema is linked to a piece of ABAP code that will be called by the payroll driver when using the schema.

A function may use a rule. Functions usually provide data and rules process them (see Figure 9.30). For example, function P0015 reads the Infotype 0015 from employee master data. The rule follow the function decides what's next.

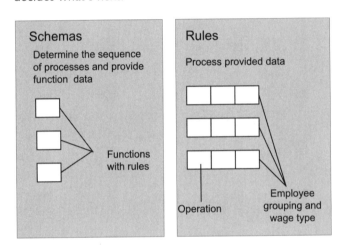

Figure 9.30 Schemas and Rules

Schema editor PE01 can be used to edit and display a schema. Figure 9.31 shows the system default U.S. payroll schema, U000. Usually the main payroll schema to be executed by the payroll driver contains only sub-schemas.

As shown in the Figure, each line of a schema includes following columns:

▶ Line number to indicate the sequence of current line within the schema.

▶ One Function column followed by up to four parameter columns where you can put a function name and parameters used by the function.

- Column D is used to indicate if current line is active or not. If the value in this column is * , it means the whole line is not active. When the driver program reads this line, it will simply be ignored.

- At the end of each line, a text can be maintained. This can be a note, comment or anything you want to put.

	Func.	Par1	Par2	Par3	Par4	D	Text
000010	COPY	UIN0					US Payroll: Initialization of payroll
000020	COPY	UODP				*	On-demand regular (no need after 4.5A)
000030	COPY	UBD0					Basic data processing
000040	COPY	UPR0					Read previous result of current period
000050	COPY	ULR0					Import previous payroll results
000060	COPY	UMO0					Determine payroll modifiers
000070	COPY	UT00					Gross compensation and time evaluation
000080	COPY	UREI				*	Travel expense
000090	BLOCK	BEG					Gross cumulation and tax processing
000100	IF		NAMC				if non-authorized manual check (*)
000110	COPY	UMC0					Process Non authorized check (*)
000120	ELSE						else if non authorized manual check (*)
000130	COPY	UAP0					Process add. payments and deductions
000140	COPY	UAL0					Proration and cumulation gross
000150	COPY	UTBS					Save tables for iteration
000160	LPBEG						Begin of iteration
000170	COPY	UTBL					Load saved tables
000180	COPY	UDD0					Process deductions, Benefits
000190	COPY	UTX0					Calculate taxes
000200	COPY	UGRN					Calculate garnishments
000210	COPY	UNA0					Calculate net
000220	COPY	UDNT					Deductions not taken during loop ?
000230	LPEND						End of iteration
000240	ENDIF						to: if non authorized manual check (*)
000250	BLOCK	END					
000260	COPY	UGRR					Garnishment Retroactive
000270	COPY	URR0					Retroactive accounting
000280	COPY	UNN0					Net processing
000290	COPY	UAC0					Month end accruals
000300	COPY	UEND					Final processing

Figure 9.31 Schema U000

Writing a schema is very much like writing a program. Schemas can be modularized for easy maintenance and reusability. There are several functions are used for structuring the schemas.

Functions for structural control in schema

Function COPY is used to include a sub-schema. This is just like an INCLUDE statement in ABAP programming. Whenever the payroll driver reads function COPY, it jumps into the included schema and continues from there.

COM creates a comment line in the schema text. It can be put in any place in a schema. Payroll driver always ignore these lines. However, they are not useless. It is very important to keep short be meaningful comment lines to briefly explain what the schema does.

BLOCK is another function used for structure control. The BLOCK BEGIN and BLOCK END always come in pair. They indicate the parts between those two lines as a block. In releases since 4.0, the schema logs are organized in a tree-like structure. With the block defined, the log information for a block will be displayed under one node. Blocks can be nested.

Function IF/ELSE/ENDIF provides a conditional route control for schema. There are two ways to set a condition: symbolic names or rules. Predefined symbolic names are populated automatically at certain points of the payroll run. A customer rule can also be used as condition, in which the operation SCOND is used to set the condition value. If the value to be set to **True**, **SCOND=T IF** should be included in the rule, **SCOND=F IF** is used to set the value to **False**. Nesting is also supported.

Loop functionality is implemented with LPBEG and LPEND. The LPBEG indicates the beginning of the loop and LPEND indicates the end. When the loop does not have a parameter, operation SCOND can be used in a rule within the loop to allow one more loop. To avoid a dead loop, the loop will stop by default.

Apart from above structural control functions, there are other three types of commonly used functions used in schema:

▶ Functions that read data from infotypes

▶ Functions that process data according to the Customizing

▶ Functions that update the wage types

Some of those functions will be explained later within the context of a schema. However, it's not possible to cover the use of all those functions in this book. Details for a function can be displayed in schema editor PE01 by pressing key **F1** while placing cursor on the function.

If the system-delivered schema cannot meet the requirements, you can make changes to it. We strongly suggest you do so in a customer client. Once you make changes to a standard schema in customer client, a copy of standard schema with your changes will form a new customer schema

Make changes based on standard schema

with the same name. The standard schema remains unchanged in client 000. Please note that the standard schemas may change during system upgrade or applying patches. Those SAP-delivered changes will not apply automatically to the customer schemas. It is important to manually compare the standard schema and customer schema after a system upgrade. If those changes reflect latest legal requirements, you have to make corresponding changes manually to your customer schemas.

Due to the complexity and importance of the schema, only experts should be allowed to make changes.

Rules

Personnel calculation rules are used to process data made available by functions. A rule contains one or more operations. The operations define the value calculation statements in payroll run and also the sequence of the statements.

Unlike the standard schemas and customer schemas, all rules can be modified the same way. You also can create your own rules in a suggested customer naming range. If a rule is to be modified, it is recommended to do the following:

1. Copy the rule into a new one with customer naming range (begins with Z or Y)
2. Only make changes to the new copy
3. Duplicate the line in the schema that calls the rule
4. Make the original line in the schema as comment (put a * in D column)
5. Change the new line to refer to the new rule name that copied

The structure of rule is a decision tree. In the tool to edit rules (transaction code PE02), a rule can be displayed either in a text table or in tree-like structural graphic.

Display a combined view of sub-schemas and rules   RPDASC00 is used to display a combined view of sub-schemas and rules within a main schema. It can expand and include all schema lines and rules detail into one continues text while maintaining the sequence in which they are called by payroll driver. Figure 9.32 shows an expanded view of schema U000 in report RPDASC00.

For those special requirements in payroll calculation that have to be implemented with new operations in ABAP coding, SAP allows an enhancement to do it. New operations can be implemented in the reports and later used in the personnel-calculation rules. Report RPCBURZO is used for international customer operations, and RPCBURZ_O is for country specific customer operations ("_" is the country indicator). After the enhancement for customer operations are done, the newly created operations need to be declared using transaction PE04. You can also use this transaction to display ABAP codes related to existing functions and operations.

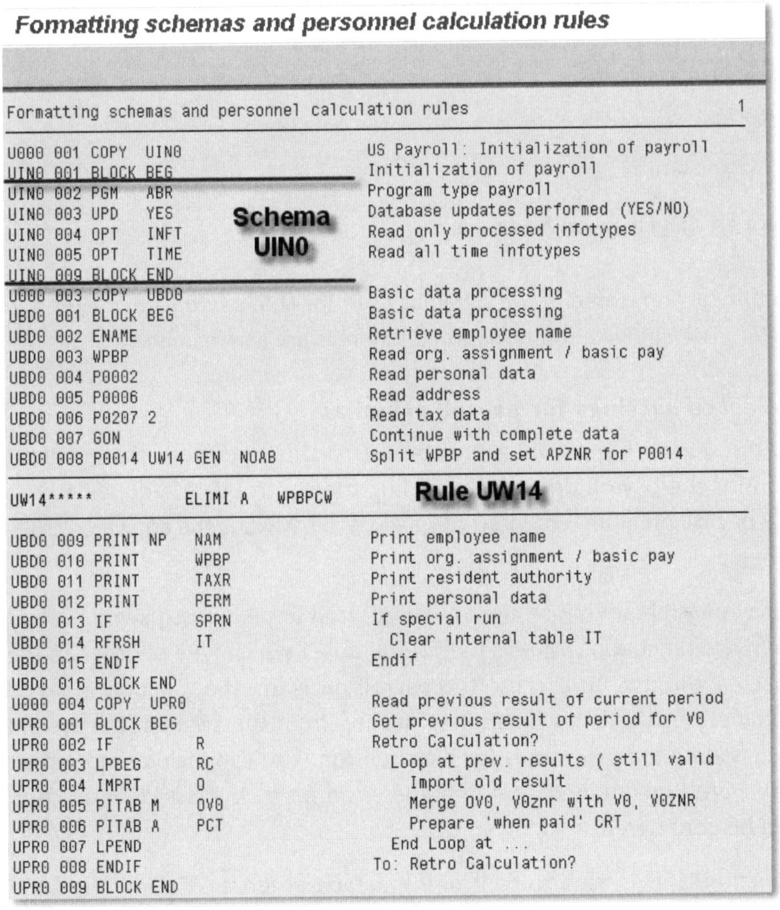

Formatting schemas and personnel calculation rules

```
Formatting schemas and personnel calculation rules                          1

U000 001 COPY  UIN0                    US Payroll: Initialization of payroll
UIN0 001 BLOCK BEG                     Initialization of payroll
UIN0 002 PGM   ABR                     Program type payroll
UIN0 003 UPD   YES    Schema           Database updates performed (YES/NO)
UIN0 004 OPT   INFT                    Read only processed infotypes
UIN0 005 OPT   TIME   UIN0             Read all time infotypes
UIN0 009 BLOCK END
U000 003 COPY  UBD0                    Basic data processing
UBD0 001 BLOCK BEG                     Basic data processing
UBD0 002 ENAME                         Retrieve employee name
UBD0 003 WPBP                          Read org. assignment / basic pay
UBD0 004 P0002                         Read personal data
UBD0 005 P0006                         Read address
UBD0 006 P0207 2                       Read tax data
UBD0 007 GON                           Continue with complete data
UBD0 008 P0014 UW14 GEN  NOAB          Split WPBP and set APZNR for P0014

UW14*****          ELIMI A   WPBPCW    Rule UW14

UBD0 009 PRINT NP    NAM               Print employee name
UBD0 010 PRINT       WPBP              Print org. assignment / basic pay
UBD0 011 PRINT       TAXR              Print resident authority
UBD0 012 PRINT       PERM              Print personal data
UBD0 013 IF          SPRN              If special run
UBD0 014 RFRSH       IT                  Clear internal table IT
UBD0 015 ENDIF                         Endif
UBD0 016 BLOCK END
U000 004 COPY  UPR0                    Read previous result of current period
UPR0 001 BLOCK BEG                     Get previous result of period for V0
UPR0 002 IF          R                 Retro Calculation?
UPR0 003 LPBEG       RC                  Loop at prev. results ( still valid
UPR0 004 IMPRT       O                    Import old result
UPR0 005 PITAB M     OV0                  Merge OV0, V0znr with V0, V0ZNR
UPR0 006 PITAB A     PCT                  Prepare 'when paid' CRT
UPR0 007 LPEND                            End Loop at ...
UPR0 008 ENDIF                         To: Retro Calculation?
UPR0 009 BLOCK END
```

Figure 9.32 Schemas and Rules (RPDASC00)

The SAP technical wage types, schemas, and rules are delivered to reflect the country-specific rules. Even small changes to those may cause recurring maintenance and also potential problems with future upgrading to new SAP releases. Therefore, adjustments to the net payroll should be made only in urgent cases.

Enhancements to operations of rules

The functionalities in payroll can be divided into gross payroll and net payroll. This applies both to payroll driver and to schema. Table 9.7 shows the contents for both gross payroll and net payroll.

Gross Payroll (USA)	Net Payroll (USA)
Read Basic data	Deductions
Read previous result of current period	Benefits
Import previous payroll results	Taxes
Gross compensation	Garnishment
Read time data and time evaluation	Net cumulation
Gross cumulation	

Table 9.7 Steps in Payroll Processing

In this section, some of the schemas used for U.S. payroll are analyzed in detail. The equivalent international schemas are also named.

Selected settings for payroll schemas

At the start of the payroll run, sub-schema UIN0 performs the initialization for the payroll driver by providing the control data required to run the payroll program. For international payroll, XIN0 is the equivalent sub-schema.

A payroll program can be used to run payroll or do a post-payroll evaluation. The function PGM tells the payroll driver which type of program the schema will use. To execute the payroll program, the function is set to parameter ABR. If this function is missing from the schema, the system will assume the program is for a payroll run. You can include more than one PGM function here, but only the value set by the last PGM function will be considered.

Function UPD is used to control the database update. Calling this function with parameter YES or NO controls whether the payroll results are updated into a database or only available during runtime. This applies only to a real payroll run. If the payroll run has been set to test run, function UPD will not update the database even when the parameter for UPD is set to **YES**.

Function OPT stands for optimize. This function is designed to enhance performance by reducing the infotypes to read during the payroll run. To import only the infotypes required in the functions within the schema, set the parameter to INFT. If the parameter TIME is set, all time infotypes are imported.

As shown in Figure 9.33, **CHECK ABR** is a function used to check the status of the employee's payroll area. When the function is used, only if the employees in payroll area with "released for payroll" status can be run. In a production client (for which client role T000-CCCATEGORY is set to "P"), this function is mandatory in order to keep the data consistency. For schemas used for test purposes, the status check for payroll control record is not necessary. To disable this check, this line should be changed to comment text.

Activate payroll area status check

```
        Func.  Par1 Par2 Par3 Par4 D  Text
000010  BLOCK  BEG                     Initialization of payroll
000020  PGM    ABR                     Program type payroll
000030  UPD    YES                     Database updates performed (YES/NO)
000040  OPT    INFT                    Read only processed infotypes
000050  OPT    TIME                    Read all time infotypes
000060  OPT    DEC                 *   Hourly rates with more than 2 decimals
000070  CHECK       ABR            *   Check over PA03
000080  OPT    BSI                 *   Set switch BSI
000090  BLOCK  END
```

Figure 9.33 Initializing Payroll Schema UIN0

> **Note** CHECK ABR is deactivated by default (see Figure 9.33). Make sure it is activated before finalizing the payroll Customizing. If a test flag is marked for a payroll run, this check is disabled automatically. There is no need to keep a different version of a schema which has CHECK ABR deactivated in a production system.

Read basic data

Schema UBD0

Schema UBD0 is a subschema used to read the basic data for payroll. The basic data includes: employee name, event, scheduled work time, basic pay, address, and relevant tax area data. The international equivalent schema is XBD0.

The function WPBP (work center basic pay) fills the employee master data, work center data, and basic pay data valid for the payroll period into the internal table WPBP. Function WPBP also fills internal table IT with the basic pay wage types.

A function with name PXXXX where XXXX represents an infotype number is used to read and process infotype information. For example, P0002 reads personal data infotype 0002, and P0014 reads and processes data from infotype 0014. For some functions, rules can be used to further restrict the process of the infotype.

Time schema **Time matters in payroll**

When the time-management module is implemented, if the time evaluation for the payroll period has not been run, the payroll program can do the evaluation from payroll perspective. In U.S. payroll schema U000, sub- schema UT00 is used to process time data including the time evaluation. Within the subschema UT00, function DAYPR calls the time evaluation schema for payroll TC00. The payroll schema for all regions shares the same time evaluation schemas XT00.

Both schema TC00 and TC04 can be used for time evaluation in payroll. TC00 deals with time data recorded in clock time format and full day records. TC04 only processes time data in hourly format.

In the schema UT00, if the PDC (Plant Data Collection) is active for the payroll period being processed, the time wage types should already exist in table ZL of cluster B2. Then the system imports the cluster and processes only the days that have not been processed yet for the payroll period. The wage types that still have to be generated are formed according to the work schedule, which triggers retroactive accounting in the subsequent payroll period.

Time wage types are stored in internal table IT after the time data and employee remuneration information has been processed. Further process to the internal-table IT is done using function PIT (process input table). Function PIT is widely used throughout the whole payroll schema. It reads personnel calculation rules in order to read Customizing table and process the internal table accordingly.

Valuation base and rule X015 Like other wage types, time wage types are valuated using valuation bases. Based on the settings in view V_512W_B for each wage type, the valuation base can be one of the following:

▶ Valuation bases entered in a table as a constant

▶ Valuation bases calculated according to basic pay

▶ Valuation bases calculated as an average of several previous periods

Rule X015 checks whether each line in a wage-type internal table already has an amount. If this has not yet happened, then this rule tries to read table T512W to get the valuation base for the wage type. If the valuation base is set to K or TS, the constant from table T510 or T510J is used. If the valuation based set to a number nn, the secondary wage type /0nn is used for the calculation. If no valuation base is found, X016 is called to evaluate the time wage type according to the principle of averages. X016 requires processing class 15.

The wage type that represents an element of the remuneration can follow different rules for different groups of employee. Modifier is used to separate the different table entries in the Customizing tables. Function MOD is used to determine modifiers by calling a personnel calculation rule. The rule uses operation MODIF that sets the modifier for table access. Table 9.8 shows the tables that a modifier can be set and the corresponding MODIF operations used.

Table	Function of the table	Operation
T510S	Wage type generation	MODIF 1=**
T510J	Constant valuations	MODIF 2=**
T510L	Levels table	MODIF 5=**
T599Y	Convert External Wage Types	MODIF 6=**
T599Z	Time Wage Types to External Systems	MODIF 7=**
T554C	Absence valuation rule	MODIF A=**
T51D1	Limits for deductions	MODIF B=**

Function MOD

Table 9.8 Table of Modifier Assignment by MODIF

In schema UT00, the function ZLIT is used to valuate the absences. There are two basic principles for processing absences.

The first option is to valuate using an average or fixed amount. The other option is to valuate the absence "as if" the employee had worked. The function PAB processed the absences according to the settings for each absence wage type in V_T554C.

Factoring

The process of getting pro rata calculation of remuneration for a partial payroll period is called factoring. The process happens when the employee does not work for a complete payroll period, or during a period when the remuneration base for the work has changed, such as when salary has increased or scheduled working hours have been reduced.

When master data changes in the middle of a payroll period for an employee, the change may affect the gross payroll in such a way that the master data set before the change and after the change is used to calculate only remuneration for part of the payroll period. In this case, the calculation is done separately for each set of data and the prorated result is used to form the result for the whole pay period.

The payroll program checks the following infotypes to determine if factoring is needed:

▶ Personnel Actions (0000)

▶ Organizational Assignment (0001)

▶ Planned Working Time (0007)

▶ Basic Pay (0008)

▶ Recurring Payments/Deductions (0014)

▶ Additional Payments (0015)

▶ Absences (2001)

Formulas for factoring A factor with a value between 0 and 1 is required to calculate partial period amounts. The factor is determined based on the times obtained from employee's personal work schedule or absence data.

The formula used to calculate the factor has to be carefully selected according to the needs. Because not all pay periods have the same length, it is possible that under certain circumstances a formula creates unwanted results. The commonly used formulas are:

Deduction method—this method assumes the employee works for the whole period with the exception of the absences.

Factor = 1 – absence/general period work time

You need an average working time for all periods as a calculation base. For example, 22 working days is used for general period of work time for monthly payroll. This naturally causes problem when the pay period has different work time than the general period work time and the absence time is relatively big. An extreme example would involve absence for a whole period. If the period has 23 actual working days, then the factor becomes negative, while in a shorter period with only 20 working days, the factor is not zero and the employee gets paid even if he didn't work at all.

Payment method—This method first assumes an employee does not work, and then gives payment to the employee according to the actual hours worked for the period.

Factor = (planned working time – absence) / general period working time

Like the deduction method, this one does not suit all scenarios. For example, if an employee has one-day absence in a 23-day period, the factor is one, giving the employee a "free absence." On the other hand, if the same scenario happens in a short period with 20 actual working days, although the employee works 95% of the time, he gets paid only 83% of the monthly salary. This is obviously unfair.

Personal Work Schedule method—this method uses the ratio of actual work time to "should work" time.

Factor = 1 – absence / planned period working time

This seems fair, but there is a problem if the two periods have different scheduled working times. In that case, the same absence (for example one day) leads to different deductions from payment.

No method seems perfect. During the implementation, the different scenarios need to be closely examined so that different methods are used for different circumstances.

In payroll calculation, factors are stored in RTE fields of wage types from /801 to /816. The factor /801 to /809 can be freely used during the Customizing. while /810 to /816 has special meanings in the system. These wage types are generated by function GEN/8. The value is multiplied by 10,000 (KGENAU) to increase the accuracy of calculation.

In schema UAL0 (U.S. version of XAL0), function PIT calls rule XPPF, XPP0 and XPP1 to calculate the factors. The actual formulas are maintained here. For example, in rule XPP1, the default rule reads:

RTE=TSSOLLRTE-TSAU** RTE*KGENAURTE/TSDIVIADDWT *

Here TSSOLL stands for partial planned working hours, TSAU** stands for sum of all unpaid absence, and TSDIVI stands for the total working hours according to the employee's working schedule. So the formula means:

▶ Rate (the value of the factor) = Planned working hours

▶ Rate = Rate—Total of unpaid absences

▶ Rate = Rate * 10,000 (for accuracy)

- Rate = Rate / Total working hours according to the schedule
- Add the wage type for factor to wage type table.

This is the personal work schedule method mentioned above. In default settings, it is used for factor wage type /801.

> **Note** Because a division operation is involved, make checks when writing formulas to make sure the divisor has a non-zero value, in order to avoid an illegal operation.

Cumulation

During the payroll run, many wage types need to be cumulated, for example, the absence time, and 410k contributions. The cumulation happens in different stages of the payroll run, depending on the wage types' attributes. Following shows the cumulation in U.S. payroll schema.

Rule X020 Personnel calculation rule X020 is used at the end of UT00 to cumulate the time wage types based on the processing class 03. All time wage types already have been valuated. Processing class 3 for each time wage type defines in which cumulation wage types it should be included, and how it is stored in the result table. The amounts of time wage types are cumulated to gross cumulation wage types /1nn and average base /2nn. Overtime hours can be cumulated into wage type /852.

In subschema UAL0, the rule X023 is called to cumulate gross wage types. Processing class 20 is used to determine the cumulation wage type in which the basic pay wage type should be included and how the wage types is stored in the result table. The wage types are cumulated to wage types /1nn.

At the end of payroll run, in sub schema UEND, function ADDCU adds the wage types into annual result table CRT. Processing class 30 is used here to determine how the wage type is cumulated in annual table.

Symbolic account ### Interface to accounting

Different wage types and the amounts for each wage type represent the results for payroll. All the dollars calculated by the payroll program have to have a source and destination in the accounting system. When SAP HR module is integrated with FI CO modules, the expense and costs that occur during the payroll run can be posted to FI and CO. Symbolic account is the central concept for this posting process.

In payroll, a symbolic account is attached to the wage types whose amount needs to be posted, The account assignment type of the corresponding symbolic account determines the type of posting (for example, posting to expense accounts, debit posting, credit posting) and the process that the system uses in table T030 (Standard Account Table) to search for the assigned financial account. It also determines the source table for the item to be posted within the payroll. Figure 9.34 shows a list of account assignment types.

AA type	Name
C	Posting to expense account
CN	Posting to expense account(w/o quantity)
D	Posting to personal customer accounts
DF	Posting to fixed customers
F	Posting to balance sheet account
FL	Posting to check RA balance
FO	Posting to bal.sheet acc. in 0-per.only
K	Post to personal vendor accounts
KF	Posting to fixed vendor accounts
L	Posting to customer per loan
Q	Posting to bal.sheet acc. with pers.no.
R	Posting to expense account (for R/2)

Figure 9.34 Account Assignment Types for Symbolic Accounts

Each of the symbolic accounts is linked to an actual G/L account. Thus the posting program can post the amount placed on a symbolic account by payroll directly to the financial account.

A wage type can be assigned to more than one symbolic account if the wage types should be posted as both expenses and payables (for example, wage types for the employer's contribution for benefit plans). If the account in Financial Accounting is an expense account, it is usually assigned a cost element in Controlling (SAP CO). This is used for posting personnel costs.

Figure 9.35 illustrates the process of posting to FI via symbolic account. Several symbolic accounts can be assigned to the same account in FI. The amounts that are posted via one symbolic account to FI can also be redirected to different financial accounts, based on the employee grouping for account determination (feature PPMOD).

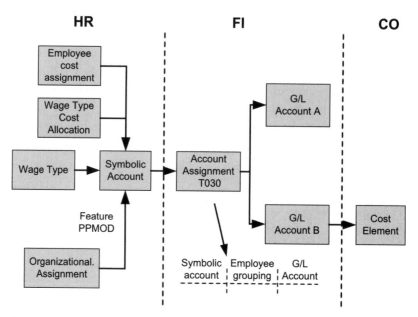

Figure 9.35 Symbolic Accounts

TaxFactory for U.S.

Unlike the net payroll programs for many countries, net payroll for the U.S. uses third-party software to calculate tax. The software product is TaxFactory, provided by a company named BSI (Business Software Inc.). The software needs to be installed separately and support SAP payroll as a server. As a client, SAP connects to the BSI TaxFactory via RFC (Remote Function Call) link. Though TaxFactory does the actual tax calculation, SAP still performs all the steps before and after calling the remote function. The payroll driver determines which taxes will be applied for each payment or deduction wage type. These steps depend largely on the configuration of wage types, tax types, tax authorities, and taxability models in IMG.

For each wage type, the payroll driver reads its tax class (value of processing class 71). For example, the value of processing class 71 for wage type M003 (Salary) is 1 (Regular wages).

Based on the applicable tax area and tax authority read from the employee master data, the payroll driver selects a taxability model for this combination of tax class, tax area, and tax authority. Then the payroll driver determines which tax types must be applied to the wage type amount based on the model.

Wage type amount and the relevant tax types are then sent to BSI via remote function call. The TaxFactory server decides which calculation formula to use based on the tax types passed and return the result of tax calculation including tax amounts for each wage type and tax type. The tax wage types determined in this process are stored in the payroll results cluster for the employee.

To use TaxFactory for tax calculation, the U.S.-specific schema for tax calculation must be correctly configured with TaxFactory information. UPAR1 BSI is used to indicate the correct version number for the TaxFactory (see Table 9.9). For example, if TaxFactory version 7.0 is to be used for tax calculation, the following entry has to be maintained in UTX0.

TaxFactory installation check

Func.	Par1	Par2	Par3	Par4	D	Text
UPAR1	BSI	70				BSI Version Flag

Table 9.9 TaxFactory Version Check

Besides Customizing in payroll calculation, technical settings also need to be done, such as installation of BSI server and registration of an RFC link for TaxFactory in SAP. Report RPUBTCU0 can be used to check whether all the technical settings have been done correctly.

9.3 Process Examples

9.3.1 Off-Cycle Workbench

Apart from the regular payroll, there is the need to run payroll and other subsequent activities for individual employees. For example, if an employee is newly hired and the employee's personal information required for payroll cannot yet be updated in the system, a separate off-cycle payroll run is needed for this employee. Other examples include issuance of a replacement check after the original check is lost or damaged, running a payroll for a special bonus, or making corrections to previous payroll results.

All those off-cycle payroll activities can be performed in a dedicated tool in SAP payroll, **Off-Cycle Workbench**. The Easy SAP menu path to start this tool is: **Human Resources · Payroll · <Country> · Off-cycle · Off-Cycle Workbench**. The corresponding transaction code is PUOC_<nn> where <nn> represents the country grouping; for example, for U.S., the transaction code is PUOC_10.

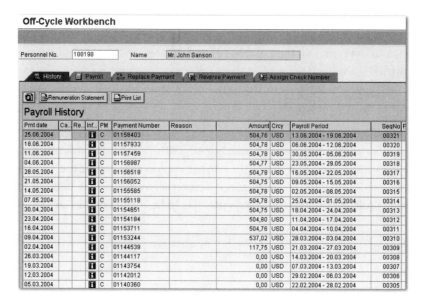

Off-Cycle Workbench

| Personnel No. | 100190 | | Name | Mr. John Sanson |

Pmt date	Ca..	Re..	Inf..	PM	Payment Number	Reason	Amount	Crcy	Payroll Period	SeqNo	F
25.06.2004			ⓘ	C	01158403		504,76	USD	13.06.2004 - 19.06.2004	00321	
18.06.2004			ⓘ	C	01157933		504,78	USD	06.06.2004 - 12.06.2004	00320	
11.06.2004			ⓘ	C	01157459		504,78	USD	30.05.2004 - 05.06.2004	00319	
04.06.2004			ⓘ	C	01156987		504,77	USD	23.05.2004 - 29.05.2004	00318	
28.05.2004			ⓘ	C	01156519		504,78	USD	16.05.2004 - 22.05.2004	00317	
21.05.2004			ⓘ	C	01156052		504,75	USD	09.05.2004 - 15.05.2004	00316	
14.05.2004			ⓘ	C	01155585		504,78	USD	02.05.2004 - 08.05.2004	00315	
07.05.2004			ⓘ	C	01155118		504,78	USD	25.04.2004 - 01.05.2004	00314	
30.04.2004			ⓘ	C	01154651		504,75	USD	18.04.2004 - 24.04.2004	00313	
23.04.2004			ⓘ	C	01154184		504,80	USD	11.04.2004 - 17.04.2004	00312	
16.04.2004			ⓘ	C	01153711		504,76	USD	04.04.2004 - 10.04.2004	00311	
09.04.2004			ⓘ	C	01153244		537,02	USD	28.03.2004 - 03.04.2004	00310	
02.04.2004			ⓘ	C	01144539		117,75	USD	21.03.2004 - 27.03.2004	00309	
26.03.2004			ⓘ	C	01144117		0,00	USD	14.03.2004 - 20.03.2004	00308	
19.03.2004			ⓘ	C	01143754		0,00	USD	07.03.2004 - 13.03.2004	00307	
12.03.2004			ⓘ	C	01142012		0,00	USD	29.02.2004 - 06.03.2004	00306	
05.03.2004			ⓘ	C	01140360		0,00	USD	22.02.2004 - 28.02.2004	00305	

Figure 9.36 Payroll History Displayed in Off-Cycle Workbench

After the **Off-Cycle Workbench** is started, enter the personnel number for which the off-cycle activity will be performed. The search help is available for this field.

After filling in the employee number and hitting key enter, the employee's name is displayed and, all past payroll runs for this employee are listed in the history tab. The information listed includes payment date, payment method, payment number, and amount currency (see Figure 9.36).

To make a special payment to an employee, select the corresponding reason and the payment date for this special payment. The payment method also needs to be specified. In this example, a manual check will be issued (see Figure 9.37). After all information needed is in place, press button **Start Payroll**.

An additional section called **Payroll Result** is displayed on the screen with a list of wage types and corresponding amount for each wage type (see Figure 9.38).

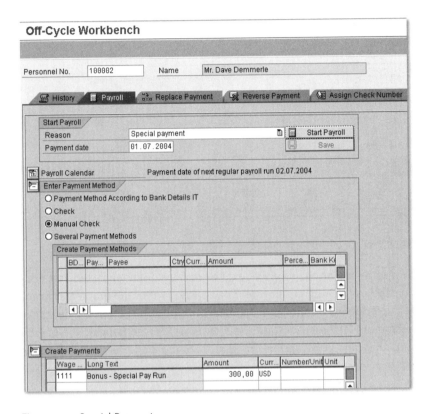

Figure 9.37 Special Payment

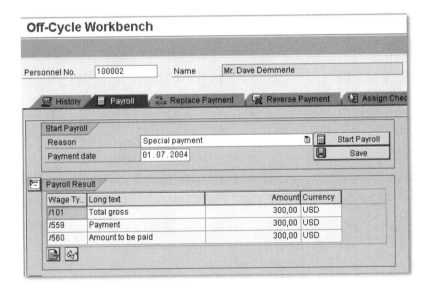

Figure 9.38 Off-Cycle Payroll Result

You can review the result here and determine whether it is OK save the result.

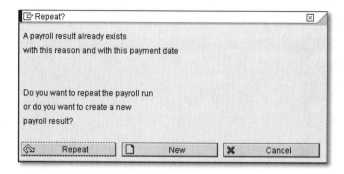

Figure 9.39 Confirmation to Repeat an Offline Payroll

If for some reason the displayed payroll result is not as expected, it is possible to rerun the special payment payroll again after the problem is fixed. At the time the rerun starts, a dialogue pops up asking if this is a new payroll run or just a repeat of last run. For rerun, choose **Repeat**. The payroll continues and runs again. The rerun can be done as many times as wanted.

The button in the payroll result area under the wage type is used to display the remuneration statement created for this special payment run (see Figure 9.40).

Remuneration Statement

```
Philadelphia                      Check #   : <Not assigned>
123 Market Street                 Check Date: 01.07.2004
Philadelphia          19111       Pay Period: 01.07.2004  -

Mr. Dave Demmerle     Tax Status       Add W/H  Gross          300,00
SSN.   445-55-5555                              Taxes            0,00
Employee#.  100002                              Deductions       0,00
Base Pay:                                       Net Retro        0,00
Cost Center:  4205                                         _____
 Work scheduling                                Net Pay        300,00

EARNINGS    HOURS      RATE      CURRENT            YTD

Bon-sp       0,00      0,00      300,00           300,00
Reg time     8,00      0,00        0,00        12.402,80
Holiday                                            614,00
                    _____
Total        8,00      0,00      300,00        13.316,80
```

Figure 9.40 Remuneration Statement

After the work is done in the Off-Cycle Workbench, subsequent processes are needed to finish the run. Depending on the requirements of different business scenarios for the off-cycle payroll, different subsequent activities may be required. For example, for a bonus payroll with check payment, the printing of check, printing of remuneration statement, and posting to FI are all needed. In contrast, a check is issued to replace a lost paycheck may need no other steps but the check printing. All those different scenarios need to be defined as process models in advance with HR Process Workbench.

The Easy SAP menu path to start this tool is: **Human Resources · Payroll · <Country> · Off-cycle · OC Batch: Follow-up for payroll**. The transaction for this is PUOCBA (see Figure 9.41).

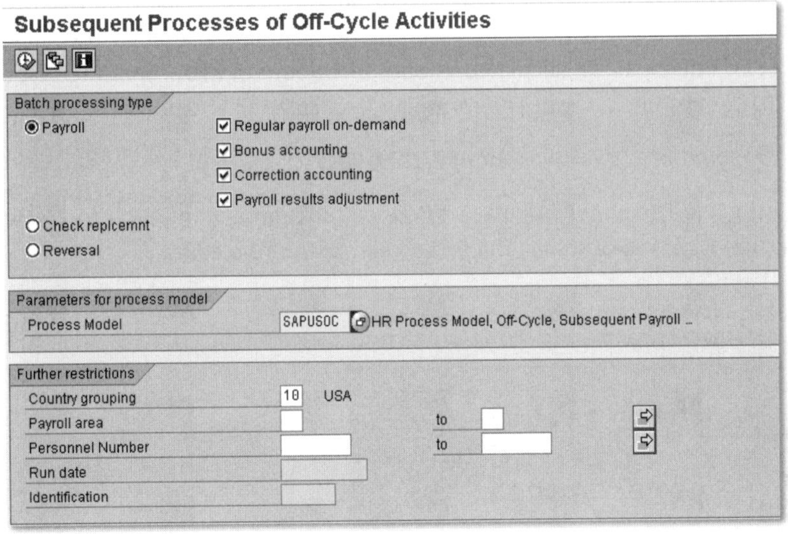

Figure 9.41 Post Process for Off-Cycle Payment

This program then triggers the whole set of programs defined in process model to finish the rest of the tasks for a complete off-cycle payroll run.

Please note that the variant used in the process model steps has to be correctly defined to include the parameters needed to complete the tasks.

9.3.2   Samples for Personnel Calculation Rules

Process Wage Type in Internal Tables

Personnel calculation rules play very important roles in processing the wage types. The wage types are stored in various internal tables during the payroll run. When the rules that process the wage types are called, the internal table loops and put each single line into a working area. Then the payroll driver checks if the rule applies to the wage type for this line. If it does, the processing steps defined in the rule are performed. When the processing is done, this line can be put back to the internal table from the working area.

We will use a sample rule to show how to create a rule to process the wage type. What this rule does is very simple: It uses wage type ZT01 to calculate wage type ZT02 and store the result to internal table. The value of ZT02 needs to be calculated as 85% of amount of ZT02. The wage type ZT01 keeps unchanged. The formula for calculation is as following:

*Amount of ZT02 = Amount of ZT01 * 0.85*

First go to Personnel Calculation Rule editor (transaction PE02) to create a rule. Figure 9.42 shows the first screen of the rule editor.

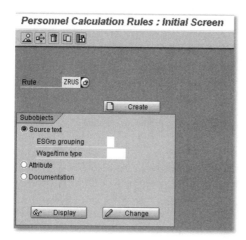

Figure 9.42 Post Process for Off-Cycle Payment

After input the rule name, press button **Create**, the attribute screen for the rule shows up (see Figure 9.43).

The program class (rule for payroll or for time evaluation) and country grouping are mandatory. C means this rule will be used for payroll; 10 is the country grouping for U.S. If the checkbox "changes only by person responsible" is checked, the system prevents another user from changing the rule, even if the other user has the authorization to edit a rule. This helps keep the rule from being changed unexpectedly.

After inputting all the information on the screen, save the attribute as shown in Figure 9.43 and go back to the first screen. Now the rule is created with empty source text.

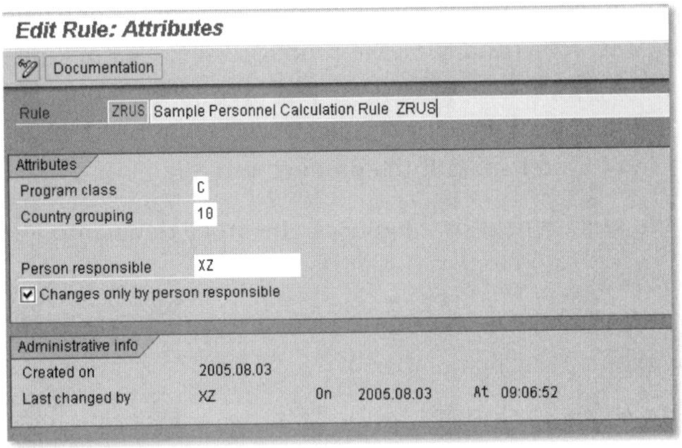

Edit Rule: Attributes

📝 Documentation	

Rule	ZRUS	Sample Personnel Calculation Rule ZRUS

Attributes
Program class	C
Country grouping	10

Person responsible	XZ
☑ Changes only by person responsible	

Administrative info
Created on	2005.08.03			
Last changed by	XZ	On	2005.08.03	At 09:06:52

Figure 9.43 Edit Rule—Attributes

To make the rule process wage type ZT01 without affecting other wage types, the wage type has to be specified for the rule. To edit the rule logic for wage type ZT01, input the wage type and click on button **Change** (see Figure 9.44).

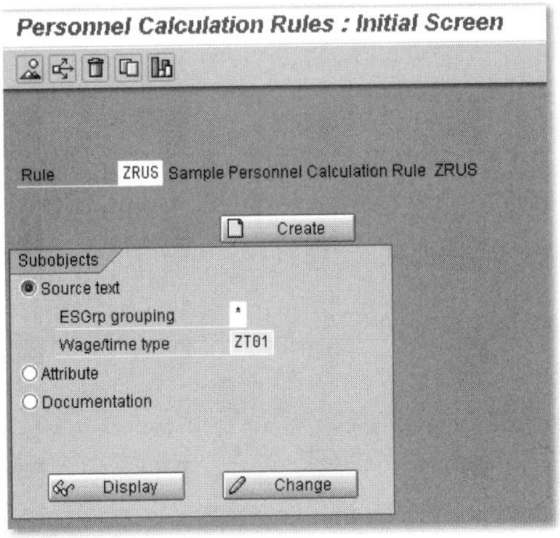

Personnel Calculation Rules : Initial Screen

Rule	ZRUS	Sample Personnel Calculation Rule ZRUS

	📄 Create

Subobjects
- ● Source text
    - ESGrp grouping | * |
    - Wage/time type | ZT01 |
- ○ Attribute
- ○ Documentation

👓 Display	✏ Change

Figure 9.44 Specifying Wage Type for Rule

In the source text of rules, for each wage type, AMT, NUM and RTE are used to represent the fields for amount, number and rate. The calculation result is written back to those fields before the internal table is updated.

Operation ADDWT reads the wage type in the working area and appends it to an internal table. If a different wage type is specified after the ADDWT, the working area will be added as a new wage type entry in the internal table.

Operation MULTI is used to multiply values in any two fields (or one field with itself) of the AMT, NUM and RTE. The product is then put into one of the three. The initial character of each field is used to represent this field when used in the operation. For example, MULTI NRA means: Multiply N (number) and R (rate) and put the product into A (amount).

In this example, the requirement of the rule can be broke down into following:

1. Keep the wage type ZT01, which means move the wage type ZT01 into output table without changing number.
2. Use a temporary variant to store the factor 0.85. The NUM field can be used as the temporary variant.
3. Then multiply the amount of ZT02 with 0.85 and put result back to the amount field.
4. Store the result as wage type ZT02.

So the above can be translated to:

1. ADDWT *
2. NUM=0.85
3. MULTI ANA
4. ADDWT ZT02

In the rule editor, the operations can be written in one line as shown in Figure 9.45.

Edit Rule: ZRUS ES Grouping * Wage Type/Time Type ZT01

Line	Var.Key	CL	T	Operation	Operation	Operation	Operation	Operation	Operation
000010				ADDWT *	NUM=0.85	MULTI ANA	ADDWTZT02		
000020									
000030									

Figure 9.45 Sample Rule

Note: that the first character of each operation must be aligned with the plus sign shown as ruler. Unlike the schema, the rule does not need to be generated to get active. Once saved, it affects the payroll immediately.

The above rule can also be written in several lines, as shown in Figure 9.46. An indicator must be placed to tell there is a following line. The following lines also need to be numbered in sequence.

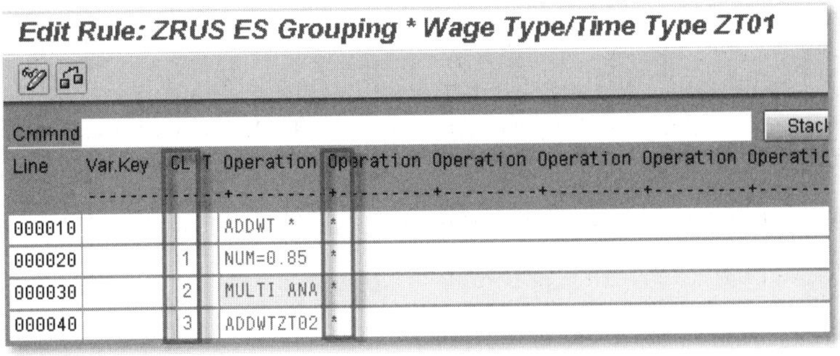

Edit Rule: ZRUS ES Grouping * Wage Type/Time Type ZT01

Line	Var.Key	CL	T	Operation	Operation	Operation	Operation	Operation	Operation	Operatic
000010				ADDWT *	*					
000020		1		NUM=0.85	*					
000030		2		MULTI ANA	*					
000040		3		ADDWTZT02	*					

Figure 9.46 Rule with Multiple Lines

By running the payroll simulation with the schema that includes the rule, the contents of the internal table before and after the process of the rule can be displayed in the log. Figure 9.47 shows the time type ZT01 in the internal table before the rule is called.

A	Wage type	APC1C2C3ABKoReBTAwvTvn	One amount/one number	Amount
2	ZT01	01		1.750,00

Table IT

Figure 9.47 Internal Table Before the Rule Process

After the rule process, as shown in Figure 9.48, the ZT01 stays in the table unchanged; a new entry for wage type ZT02 is added. The number field is assigned with value 0.85 and the result is the product of amount ZT01 and 0.85.

A	Wage type	APC1C2C3ABKoReBTAwvTvn	One amount/one number	Amount
2	ZT01	01		1.750,00
2	ZT02	01	0,85	1.487,50

Table IT

Figure 9.48 Internal Table After the Rule Process

Sample of using payroll constant

Although above rule works, we strongly suggested you not hard-code any factor number into the personnel calculation rule. The reason is easier maintenance. If you do so, then each time the factor changes, someone has to go and make changes to the rule. If the same factor is used in many different rules, it is difficult to make sure it is corrected in each and every place.

The correct approach is to create a constant in table V_511K. This table stores all constants that are used in payroll calculation. The constants defined in this table can be read by the payroll driver and be made available for rules to access.

To define a constant, call transaction SM30 and edit the view V_T511K (see Figure 9.49).

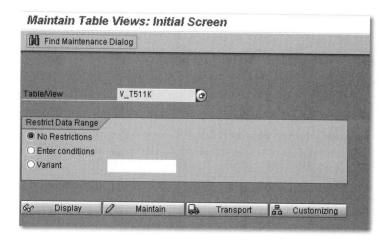

Figure 9.49 Maintenance of Constant Table

The constants are country-grouping specific, which means the same constant name may mean differently. Figure 9.50 shows the change screen for view V_T511W. Press the button **New Entries** to create new entries.

Give a name to the constant first. We suggest using a name beginning with Y or Z to avoid it being overwritten by later SAP upgrades. The constant also has a validation period, and we suggest that—unless there is a good reason—you use 99991231 as the end date. Last and the most important, value has to be maintained.

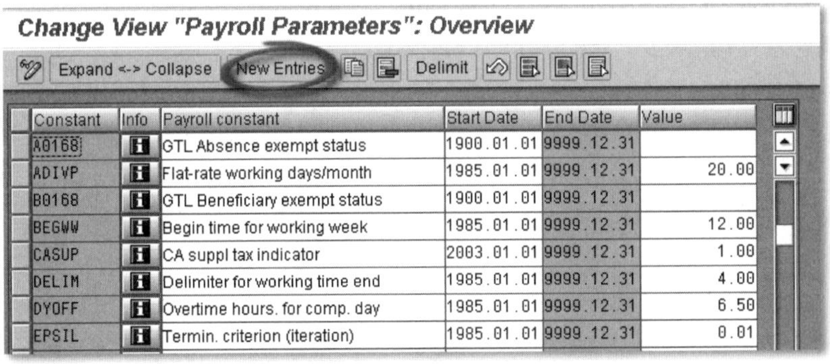

Change View "Payroll Parameters": Overview

Expand <-> Collapse | New Entries | Delimit

Constant	Info	Payroll constant	Start Date	End Date	Value
A0168	i	GTL Absence exempt status	1900.01.01	9999.12.31	
ADIVP	i	Flat-rate working days/month	1985.01.01	9999.12.31	20.00
B0168	i	GTL Beneficiary exempt status	1900.01.01	9999.12.31	
BEGWW	i	Begin time for working week	1985.01.01	9999.12.31	12.00
CASUP	i	CA suppl tax indicator	2003.01.01	9999.12.31	1.00
DELIM	i	Delimiter for working time end	1985.01.01	9999.12.31	4.00
DYOFF	i	Overtime hours. for comp. day	1985.01.01	9999.12.31	6.50
EPSIL	i	Termin. criterion (iteration)	1985.01.01	9999.12.31	0.01

Figure 9.50 View V_T511W

For the same example above, a new constant ZCLYR is created to replace the value 0.85 (see Figure 9.51).

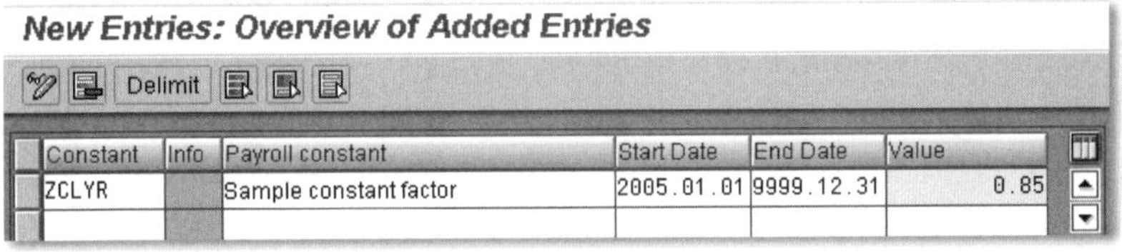

New Entries: Overview of Added Entries

Delimit

Constant	Info	Payroll constant	Start Date	End Date	Value
ZCLYR		Sample constant factor	2005.01.01	9999.12.31	0.85

Figure 9.51 Edit Constant Value

Once the constant is defined, the rule in above sample can be rewritten as shown in Figure 9.52. A letter K is added in front of the constant to indicate that the name following means a constant name in table T511W.

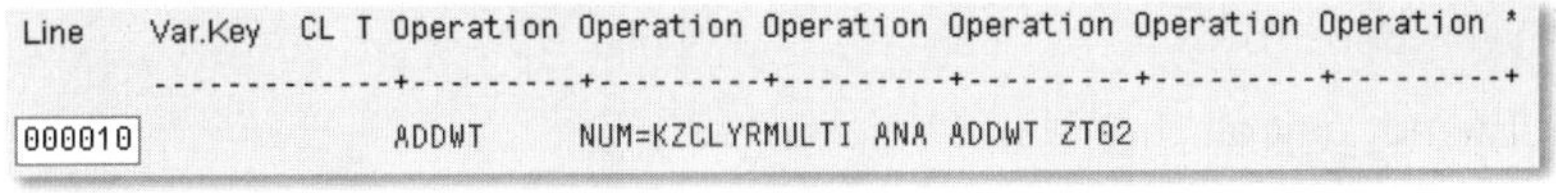

```
Line    Var.Key  CL T Operation Operation Operation Operation Operation Operation *
         -------------+---------+---------+---------+---------+---------+---------+
000010            ADDWT     NUM=KZCLYRMULTI ANA ADDWT ZT02
```

Figure 9.52 Rule Using Constant

This rule does the same job as the one with a hard-coded factor, but it is much easier to change the factor's value. Simply change the value in the view V_T511W and the calculation will use the new value. Furthermore, by splitting the constant into different validation periods, the constant value can vary in different time periods. Thus makes it possible to have only one formula in the calculation rule, based on different constant values. For example, if the factor in the above example changes annually, the new values can be maintained in separate validation period (see Figure 9.53). When the rule is called for calculation for year 2006, the new value

0.88 will be used. If a retroactive payroll run occurs for a period in 2005, it is possible to use the value for 2005.

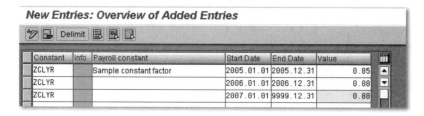

Figure 9.53 Split Constant by Validation Period

9.4   Critical Success Factors

▶ The organizational structures must be clearly structured and verified. They must all conform to the relevant requirements in terms of master data, payroll, authorization concept, and personnel reporting. A subsequent restructuring is very difficult.

▶ The wage-type catalog must be cleaned up before mapping it in mySAP HR. There the concepts must consider technical wage types, evaluation, and accounting for wage types.

▶ Regarding the allocation of wage types, an early adjustment with accounting and controlling is necessary.

▶ A clean, permanent quality assurance is absolutely necessary. This is the only way of ensuring that requirements already realized deliver the expected results even after the mapping of additional requirements. Any automation tool which is available should be used here (e.g., Test Workbench).

▶ The net payroll should not be changed.

▶ Special cases frequently require extensive maintenance-intensive adjustments. In this case, you must check if they are actually to be mapped in this form.

▶ As the system permanently continues to develop even after a successful production start, the maintenance process must be clearly described.

10   Benefits

This chapter will describe how information in the SAP Bene-fits Administration module is organized, how to perform the user setup, and how to run the module. SAP manages employee benefits based on plans. Employees' benefit-related information is stored in various infotypes. Benefits adminis-tration programs perform different activities according to employees' master data and corresponding plan settings. Most of the chapter applies to all geographic regions. At the end of this chapter, some U.S.-specific functionalities such as COBRA and FSA will be briefly introduced.

10.1   Business Principles

This section will introduce the basic business concept behind SAP Bene-fits Administration. From here on, all IMG paths described in the chapter will be found under **Personnel Management · Benefits**.

The HR system is mainly used to manage information for employees. For SAP Benefits Administration, the focus is on management of the proper-ties and process rules for benefit packages as well as maintenance of rela-tionships between employees and the packages.

Benefit packages are usually introduced to employees as plans, such as health plans, insurance plans, savings plans, or stock-purchase plans. To accurately describe a plan, many attributes of the plan have to be clearly defined. The following are very important attributes for benefit-plan administration and therefore need to be set up and managed in any ben-efit-management system.

Benefit plans

▶ Availability
  Is the plan still available, yet to come, or obsolete?

▶ Eligibility
  Which employees can join the plan? The rules can be based on the years of service, position level, location, and personal status, among other considerations.

▶ Participation status
  Who is in the plan, and who is not? During what period of time is the employee in the plan?

- ▶ **Beneficiaries and dependents**

  Who will get the benefit from this plan? Who is covered under the plan?

- ▶ **Cost**

  How much does the plan cost the employee and/or the employer?

- ▶ **Communication**

  What kind of communication is needed whenever an action is taken?

All this information for each plan and each plan participant needs to be captured and organized by the benefit administrator. Apart from that, all communications such as letters to employees, statistic reports for management teams, payment deduction to payroll departments, and information exchanges between employer and benefit providers also need to be managed.

In later sections of this chapter, we will explain the SAP solution for all the issues listed above. At the end, a sample plan will be used to illustrate key settings as well as some commonly used operations.

Benefits administration is not a stand-alone activity. It is closely connected with other HR processes, like hiring, termination, and payroll-processing. Information needs to be exchanged between different business functional divisions as well as between the employer and the employee, and the employer and benefit-service providers.

In the next section of this chapter, we will explain how the SAP Benefits Administration module integrates with other modules, how benefit data is transferred to service providers, and how benefit information is directed to employees via paper form or online.

10.2 Implementation in SAP HR

10.2.1 Basic Conceptions

Benefit Area

The benefit area is the highest organizational structure in SAP Benefits Administration. It is used to administer use of different benefit options. For example, if a nationwide U.S. company offers one set of benefit plans for East Coast employees and a different set of plans for employees on the West Coast, a separate benefit area is created for each group of employees to enable different options.

Please note that only one currency can be used within one benefit area. In the above example, if this company opens another new office in Vancouver, Canada, even if all the benefit packages offered are exactly the same for the rest of the employees living on the West Coast of the U.S., a separate benefit area has to be created simply because Canadian dollar will be used for those plans.

The IMG path for defining a benefit area is **Basic Settings · Define Benefit Area**.

Plan Categories

SAP uses the following different plan categories:

▶ Health Plans

▶ Insurance Plans

▶ Savings Plans

▶ Stock Purchase Plans

▶ Flexible Spending Accounts

▶ Credit Plans

Another category, Miscellaneous Plans, can be used for all plans not easily categorized into the above groups, such as employee-assistance programs, company car programs, or club memberships.

SAP products for handling benefits programs deal with different categories of plans in different ways. For example, if the plan in question is a health plan, the system will manage dependents and coverage. For an insurance plan, it will manage beneficiaries.

Since the processing logic for plan categories is built in standard SAP code, you cannot define new plan categories without changing the programs to make them recognizable by the system.

Plan Types

Unlike plan categories, plan types are left to the user to define, thus further reflecting the client's specific requirements. Please note that each plan type permits only one enrollment per employee. So if an employee must be enrolled simultaneously in multiple plans, those plans must belong to different plan types.

The IMG path for plan type definition is **Basic Settings · Plan Attributes · Define Plan Types**.

The plan type value is assigned to an individual plan when maintaining the general plan values. For example, to assign the plan type for a saving plan, the IMG path is **Plans · Saving Plans · Define Saving Plan General Data**.

Group and Grouping

Both group and grouping are widely used in the SAP HR system. Both are used to organize objects with similar attributes into several circles for easier handling. Confusion results from the use of similar names ("Aren't they the same thing?", "Why are two different words used?").

Generally speaking, group is used in most cases to combine objects with the same value or the same range of values in a certain field. Grouping is used to combine different objects that must be handled in the same way, no matter what attribute values they have. Grouping provides a more flexible way for the user to differentiate various business scenarios, while group is just a simple partition. Simply put: Group is by value, and grouping is by action.

For example, an employee age group contains all employees whose ages are in the same range. A cost grouping, by contrast, indicates employees who will use the same cost rule, regardless of their ages, salaries or other attributes.

In some cases, features are used to check a combination of values, in order to determine a new value for a group of objects that share the same logic.

Feature

A feature is a decision-tree object used by SAP programs. It can be used to determine certain values based on other field values already known within the HR data structure.

For example, after the cost groupings are defined, feature CSTV1 can be used to determine which cost grouping an employee belongs to (see Figure 10.1). If the CSTV1 definition shows that an employee belongs to EE group 1, EE subgroup U4, and his benefit area is U.S., then the value for his cost grouping is set to SLRY.

A feature can be edited by using transaction code PE03 and selecting the corresponding feature name.

> **Note** If a feature is changed after it has been used, the old value determined by the previous feature rule will not be updated automatically based on new rules. When changing the features, please remember that data inconsistency may exist.

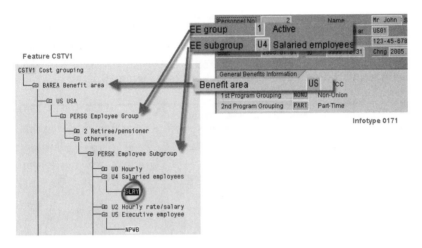

Figure 10.1 Use of Feature CSTV1

10.2.2 Benefit Plans

For plans in different plan categories, different settings have to be considered. Some settings are shared by more than one plan category. For example, both an insurance plan and a saving plan have beneficiary settings. Such settings exist under different IMG paths for different plan categories, but since they are the same, we will explain using them with only one IMG path as a detailed example.

Plan Status

By assigning the plan a plan status, you decide whether the plan should have active participants. You also define whether the plan can accept new enrollment.

The IMG path for plan status setting is **Basic Settings · Plan Attributes · Define Benefit Plan Status**.

Default Plans and Automatic Plans

There can be a gap between the time an event happens to an employee and the time an employee decides to participate in preferred plans. For

Default plans

example, a new hire needs several days to complete his benefit paperwork, due to communication within the organization. A default plan can be used as a temporary plan to provide minimal coverage to the employee. Usually such a plan has very little flexibility regarding terms.

Automatic plans Some benefit plans are offered "as is," and do not need employees to make election. Those plans can be defined as automatic plans and can be enrolled in by employees at any time.

Whether a plan is a default plan or an automatic plan is defined in **Flexible Administration · Standard Selections** (see Figure 10.2).

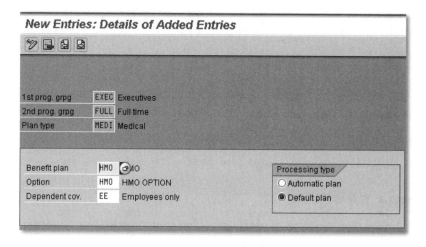

Figure 10.2 Standard Selection

Prerequisite Plans and Co-requisite Plans

Both prerequisite plans and co-requisite plans can be used to define dependencies between plans. However, there are differences between them.

If plan A is a prerequisite plan of plan B, the employee must have been enrolled into plan A on the date of enrolling to plan B; if plan A is co-requisite with plan B, then plan A has to be enrolled in together with plan B.

The IMG path to set up the prerequisite plans and co-requisite plans is **Flexible Administration · Prerequisites and Corequisites**.

Costs, Contributions and Credits

Costs variants and cost-rule settings are used to determine the costs for a benefit plan. They work together to make the cost settings flexible and efficient. When costs are to be calculated, the cost variant that a user specifies will read an employee's master data to get all information needed to look up the pre-defined costs in a cost-rule table. Then, if such an entry is found, the costs details in this entry will be used as employee's plan costs.

For example, Figure 10.3 shows that if the cost variant EE is selected for plan HMO by the employee, the costs are determined through cost variant and cost rules. First, according to the variant, the data to determine the costs comes from the employee master data. Then, because the cost grouping is flagged, the cost grouping value for the employee is set by feature CSTV1. (See Figure 10.1 for details on how the feature works.) When all these steps are done, the system looks up the cost-rule table for the cost variant of the plan. The highlighted entry is the result, and the cost factors stored in this entry are used.

Variants and rules

The IMG path for health plan cost variant and cost rule is **Plans · Health plans · Maintain Cost Variant Maintain Cost Rules**.

Similar IMG paths can be found under other plan categories' settings.

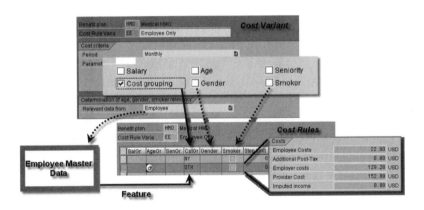

Figure 10.3 Usage of Cost Variant and Cost Rules

Contribution is used in most plan categories. It usually includes employee contribution and employer contribution. The way to set up a link between an employee and a certain contribution calculation rule is the same grouping-variant-rule mechanism. The IMG path for defining contribution groupings is under **Basic Settings · Define Employee Groupings**.

Contributions

During the enrollment, contribution limits are copied to an employee's plan master data. If the limit rules change after the enrollment, the limit may no longer be valid. Report RPLBEN18 should be used to check those conflicts after each modification to the contribution rules.

Credits   The credits designation applies to credit plans and to some miscellaneous plans. The concept for credit can be seen as "negative cost." The setting is very much the same as that of a cost plan.

The IMG path for defining cost groupings is under **Basic Settings · Define Employee Groupings**.

Evidence of Insurability (EOI)

For some health-plan and insurance-plan options, evidence of insurability needs to be presented before the coverage becomes effective.

Dependents and Beneficiaries

Dependent settings apply to health plans, and beneficiary settings apply to other plans.

All dependents to be used in plans must first be maintained in an employee's family/related person infotype (0021). In the dependents eligibility rule settings, the person who can participate in certain plans can be further restricted using a subtype of Infotype 0021, and even further using family member groupings.

Change View "Benefit Dependent Coverage": Overview

Dependent Coverage	Description	Min.No.Dependents	Max.No.of Dependents
E+DP	E+DP	1	3
EE	Employee Only		
WAIV	Waived Coverage		

Figure 10.4 Define Dependent Coverage Options

All the characteristics ascribed to dependents also apply to beneficiaries with two exceptions: when the beneficiary is the employee himself, or when the beneficiary is an organization.

In the beneficiary-eligibility variant, you can set an indicator to allow the employee to be the beneficiary. For example, if it is necessary to have an employee as beneficiary for disability insurance.

When any eligibility rule is assigned to a plan, organizations are automatically eligible. No extra settings are needed. However, as with the use of Infotype 0021, external organizations need to be maintained in Infotype 0219 in order to be assigned as beneficiaries.

Via IMG path **Benefit Settings · Dependent and Beneficiaries**, you can define which data stored in the related person infotypes can be displayed in the selection list of dependents and beneficiaries. In each of the plan settings the eligibility for dependents and beneficiaries can be further restricted. For example, in IMG **Plans · Health Plans · Define Dependent Coverage Options**, the minimum and maximum number of the dependents for each coverage option is defined (see Figure 10.4).

Coverage

Coverage applies to insurance plans and may also apply to some miscellaneous plans, depending on the plan settings.

Controlling coverage settings is similar to controlling cost. Here we also use the variant and rule combination to direct the coverage that an employee should get for a particular plan.

Coverage grouping settings can be found under IMG path **Basic Settings · Define Employee Groupings**.

The IMG paths for coverage settings are under each plan category, for example, for insurance plan, the IMG path is **Plans · Insurance Plans · Define Coverage Rules and Define Coverage Variants**.

10.2.3 Master Data

All employees' benefit-related information is stored in certain infotypes. The system will use such information to determine how to process a benefit of an employee.

General Benefits Information (Infotype 0171)

Infotype 0171 is the most important infotype for Benefits Administration. An employee has to have this infotype created before enrolling in any benefit plan. Figure 10.5 shows the **General Benefits Information** display.

This infotype stores the **Benefit area**, **1st program grouping**, and **2nd program grouping** assignments of the employee.

The **Benefit Area** default value can be determined automatically using feature BAREA with reference to information in other basic infotypes like 0001, 0002.

In Benefits Administration, **1st program grouping** and **2nd program grouping** are used to distinguish different employees using different sets of benefit programs.

Features BENGR and BSTAT are used to set default values for an employee's **1st program grouping** and **2nd program grouping**.

> **Note** The features only create default values. It is possible to override the default value manually by inputting a new value as an exception. However, if such "exceptions" happens too often you would do better to modify the feature and include the new rule.

Report RPLBEN13 can be used to display a report of all Infotype 0171 in which values maintained do not comply with the latest corresponding features.

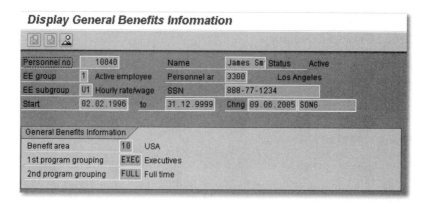

Figure 10.5 General Benefits Information (Infotype 0171)

Plan Infotypes

After enrollment in a benefit plan, a plan infotype record is created automatically to store employee-specific information for this plan. For each benefit plan in which the employee participates, a separate record is used. The plan category determines which infotype to use for each plan. The plan type is the subtype of the infotype.

Following are the infotypes used to store plan data:

- Health Plans (Infotype 0167); see Figure 10.6

- Insurance Plans (Infotype 0168)

- Savings Plans (Infotype 0169)

- Credit Plans (Infotype 0236)

- Stock Purchase Plans (Infotype 0379)

- Miscellaneous Plans (Infotype 0377)

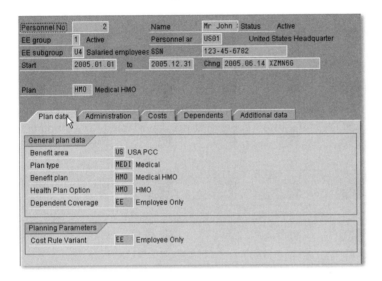

Figure 10.6 Health Plan (Infotype 0167)

Depending the setting of the benefit plan, some of the following information is stored in the infotype:

- Plan data such as plan type, plan option, etc.

- Administration data

- Coverage

- Costs

- Credits

- Contributions

- Dependents

- Beneficiaries

- Vesting

- Investments

- Additional information

Although it is possible to create and maintain a plan infotype directly using PA30, we do not suggest doing so. Using only the benefit administration transactions such as enrollment (HRBEN0001) can ensure that all plan rules, such as eligibility and cost-rule checks, are being carried out while processing the plans.

10.2.4 Enrollment

Enrollment is used to create a new benefit plan or to make changes to an existing plan for an employee. For example, if an employee gets married, then he or she needs to join a family medical insurance plan to have his or her family covered.

Benefit Offer During the enrollment, the system will automatically check the master data against the pre-defined eligibility rules in customizing; if the conditions are met, then the offers containing plans available to the employee will be displayed (see Figure 10.7).

Offer selection					
⬦	Get offer	🗋	Print form	⚠	Error list
Possible offers			**Enrollment period**		
Open offer			1998.10.01 - 2005.11.30		
Anytime changes			1800.01.01 - 9999.12.31		
Automatic offer					
Default offer					

Figure 10.7 Enrollment Offer

Four types of offers are available:

▶ **Open offer**
Offer contains all eligible plans that are currently in an open enrollment period.

▶ **Adjustment offer (Anytime changes)**
Offer contains only plans for which an employee has a corresponding adjustment reason.

▶ **Automatic offer**
Offer contains all plans flagged as automatic plans during customizing of the standard selection.

▶ **Default offer**
Offer contains all plans flagged as default plans during customizing of the standard selection.

Adjustment offers displayed on the offer list appear under the corresponding adjustment reason names. The adjustment reason defines an event, such as a birth or a divorce, which may require an employee's benefit plans to change.

In the adjustment reason definition, the time period that the adjustment to the benefit plan has to take place has to be set. The adjustment reason can be defined as change at anytime, which means there is no time limit for the change. If not, an infotype record that stores such an adjustment reason (0378) must be created before the offer can be taken.

During the enrollment process, the system checks whether the grouping the adjustment reason belongs to is permitted to make changes to certain plans.

The adjustment reasons can be defined via IMG path **Flexible Administration · Benefits Adjustment Reasons · Define Benefit Adjustment Reasons and Define Benefit Adjustment Reason Groupings**. The options under **Define Adjustment Permissions** are used to set the permitted adjustment reasons for each plan.

To enroll an employee in a benefit plan, from **Easy Access menu**, select **Human Resources · Personnel Management · Benefits · Enrollment**.

▶ First, in the employee selection area, double-click on the employee in the selection list.

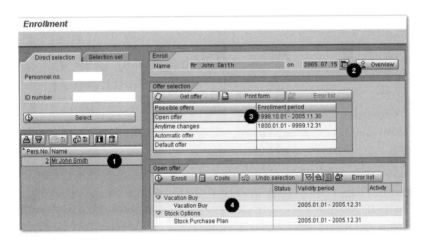

Figure 10.8 Enrollment

▶ Then, set the date for the enrollment.

▶ Next, select an offer that you want and click on the button **Get offer**. Select the plan you would like to enroll this employee in, and a dialog window with detailed plan data will pop up (see Figure 10.8 and Figure 10.9).

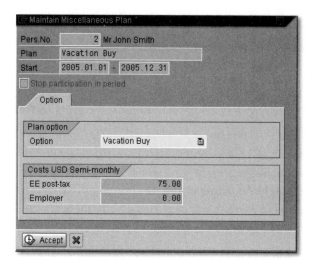

Figure 10.9 Enrollment—Plan Detail

▶ Go through the plan details. You can make changes to the default values. Click the button **Accept** to accept it. The accepted plan will have a green check next to it (see Figure 10.10).

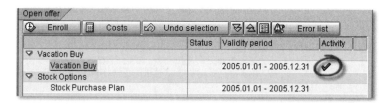

Figure 10.10 Enrollment—Plan Accepted

▶ After finishing the selection of all plans in the offer, click on the button **Enroll**. Another dialogue box will show up asking for the user's confirmation. It lists all the actions to be taken. Here, you click on **Enroll** again and the actual enrollment will take place (see Figure 10.11).

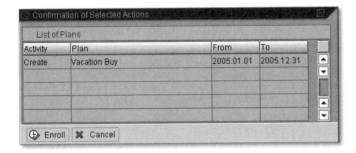

Figure 10.11 Confirmation of Selected Actions

▶ After the system finished the enrollment, a message box shows up with a success message (see Figure 10.12).

Figure 10.12 Enrollment Confirmation

▶ If you select the button **Confirmation**, a confirmation letter will be printed. The button **Continue** brings you back to the main enrollment screen. The enrollment is done.

Upon the completion of enrollment, the enrollment program creates an infotype for the corresponding benefit plan automatically. In this example, a miscellaneous plan Infotype 0337 is created. Now, go to PA20 to display the Infotype 0337 for this employee, where a corresponding entry has been created (see Figure 10.13). The subtype of the infotype is the same as the plan name.

Personnel No	2		Name	Mr John..	Status	Active
EE group	1 Active		Personnel ar	US01	United States Headquarter	
EE subgroup	U4 Salaried employe..		SSN	123-45-6782		
Choose	1800.01.01	to 9999.12.31		STy.		

	Start Date	End Date	Type	Text	Plan	Text
	2005.01.01	2005.12.31	VACB	Vacation Buy	VACB	Vacation Buy

Figure 10.13 Enrollment—Infotype Created

The plan information accepted during the enrollment is stored in the infotype. Figure 10.14 shows the cost data for the plan, the same as shown in Figure 10.9.

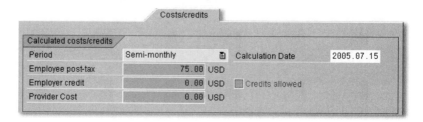

Figure 10.14 Plan Cost Information

10.2.5 Miscellaneous

Benefit Forms

Upon enrollment or changes to the plan, benefit forms usually are sent to employees for legal and information purposes. SAP can generate enrollment and confirmation forms using pre-defined form templates (see Figure 10.15).

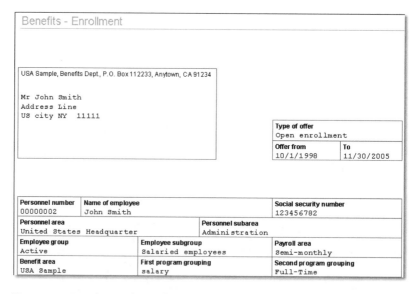

Figure 10.15 Sample Benefit Enrollment Form (SAPscript)

You can set up the form template to be either a SAPscript form or a Word document template. Based on the setting, the system either triggers the SAPscript printing or brings up a Word document for users to print. The

IMG path to determine which form print method to use is **Flexible Administration · Form Setup** (see Figure 10.16).

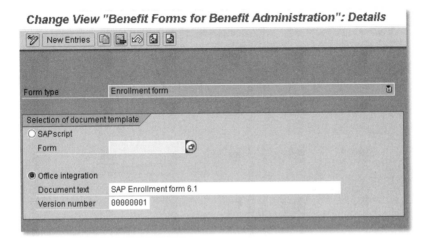

Figure 10.16 Form Setup

Please note that using Word template forms requires the printing user to log on with a transactional session, and the front-end machine has to have the Microsoft Word application installed. Although there are other applications that can recognize Microsoft Word files, you must have the Microsoft Word application to run the macros defined in the templates. If you need to have forms printed in a background job, please choose the SAPscript method.

For enrollment and confirmation forms, Microsoft Word templates are both provided by SAP as standard. You can copy them and make changes according to your needs. You need SAPscript knowledge to modify a SAP-script form.

> **Note** In the Word templates provided by SAP, there are macros embedded that will get the data feed from Benefits Administration and put data into correct fields in the Word file. When making changes to the Word template, always copy the SAP template and be careful not to damage the field definitions in the template file.

The transaction to copy and edit the Word templates for benefit forms is HRBEN0050. Figure 10.17 shows an embedded Word template for enrollment.

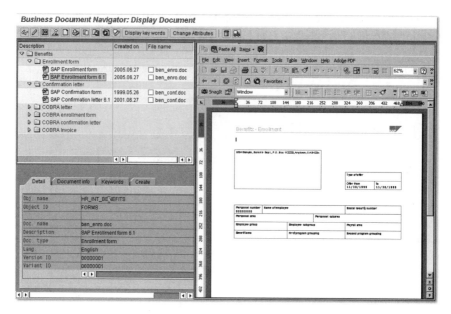

Figure 10.17 Enrollment letter—Microsoft Word Template

Benefit Employee Self Service

To input plan data for many employees is a major effort. Employee Self Service (ESS) allows individual employees to be responsible for the benefit-data input. It gives employees the flexibility to update and monitor their own benefit plans.

The following ESS services are available with the Benefits Administration component, as shown in Table 10.1.

Service	Description
PZ14	Enrollment
PZ07	Participation Overview
PZ43	Retirement Benefits
PZ40	Spending Account Claims (USA only)

Table 10.1 ESS Services for Benefits Administration

Standard Benefit Reports

The SAP Benefits Administration module provides many standard reports for various functions, as shown in Table 10.2. The reports can be run via SA38 or corresponding transaction codes.

You can also define your own reports using standard reporting tools.

Report Category	Description	Report Name	Transaction Code
Participation analysis	Eligible Employees	RPLBEN01	HRBEN0071
	Benefit Plan Participation	RPLBEN02	HRBEN0072
	Changes in Benefit Elections	RPLBEN07	HRBEN0077
	Changes in Eligibility	RPLBEN09	HRBEN0079
	Changes in Default Values for General Benefits Information	RPLBEN13	HRBEN0083
Cost and contribution analysis	Health Plan Costs	RPLBEN03	HRBEN0073
	Insurance Plan Costs	RPLBEN04	HRBEN0074
	Savings Plan Costs	RPLBEN05	RPLBEN05
	Flexible Spending Account Contributions	RPLBEN08	HRBEN0078
	Stock Purchase Plan Contributions	RPLBEN16	HRBEN0083
	Costs/Contributions for Miscellaneous Plans	RPLBEN15	HRBEN0085
	Vesting Percentages	RPLBEN06	HRBEN0076
	Contribution Limit Check	RPLBEN18	HRBEN0088
Statistical analysis	Employee Demographics	RPLBEN11	HRBEN0081
	Benefits Election Analysis	RPLBEN17	HRBEN0087
	Enrollment Statistics	RPLBEN19	HRBEN0089
Customizing analysis	Plan Overview	RPUBEN09	HRBEN0009
	Benefit Customizing Consistency Check	RPUBEN42	HRBEN0042
	Plan Cost Summary	RPUBEN46	HRBEN0046

Table 10.2 Standard Benefit Reports

Integration

SAP Benefits Administration is closely integrated with other HR sub-modules. For example, data from Personnel Management is used in the eligibility check and calculation. Deductions and taxable benefits can also be directly taken into consideration during payroll calculation, and the result can be reflected directly in an employee's pay slip. Employee time-management data such as total hours worked during a given period of time also can be used to decide if the employee is eligible for certain plan options.

Among all those, the payroll integration is the most important and will be discussed in more detail in the following section.

Payroll integration

Benefits are closely integrated with the payroll. Plans with associated costs, deductions or contributions need to be taken into account when the payroll is processed. By assigning wage types to each benefit plan, the deduction amount can be brought to the payroll for calculation. Follow IMG path **Payroll · US Payroll · Benefit Integration** to make the payroll settings.

> **Please note** If the costs or contributions are calculated during payroll runs, it is possible that the actual deduction for a pay period is different from the figure shown in master data infotype for the plan, for which the costs or contributions are calculated upon enrollment.

After the U.S. payroll run, all accumulated benefit costs are stored in the following infotypes for reporting purposes (see Table 10.3).

Infotype	Description
0496	Benefits contributions/deductions: per payroll period
0497	Benefits contributions/deductions: monthly cumulations
0498	Benefits contributions/deductions: quarterly cumulations
0499	Benefits contributions/deductions: annual cumulations
0500	Benefits contributions/deductions: per payroll period from the arrears table
0501	Benefits contributions/deductions: per payroll period from the deductions not taken table:

Table 10.3 Infotypes for Benefits Contribution and Deductions Cumulation

Benefit plan settings that are payroll-related have to be set up correctly before running the payroll. For example, 401(K) plan deductions for an employee must not exceed the legal limits. To prevent that, you have to set up the contribution limits for the registered savings plans in contribution rules.

Enhancements

Each business is unique. In some cases, SAP standard systems cannot meet the special requirement of the logic for benefit administration. Enhancement then can be brought into the picture. Enhancement will not change existing SAP codes, but provides you an opportunity to create extra logic based on standard processes. The user exits can be accessed by transaction code SMOD.

For example, let us suppose that a company uses a formula to determine coverage amount of an employee's insurance plan. Usually this is done by standard SAP function HR_BEN_CALC_COVERAGE_AMOUNT based on the master data and plan settings. In this case, the company wants to take the employee's coverage during past years into account while calculating. This makes the formula too complex for the standard function to perform the required calculation; the user exit can be used to replace the function.

Another example is the replacement of a feature with user-exit to determine default-values. Features can make decisions based on a certain field's value only if the value is directly available in a field. A feature cannot make a complex calculation to a field value before judgment. In this case, a user exit can be used to take over the feature's work.

Table 10.4 shows a list of all available enhancements in Benefits Administration, as well as the corresponding standard features and functions they will replace once they are implemented.

User exit	Replaces
PBEN0001	Feature BAREA
PBEN0002	Feature BENGR
PBEN0003	Feature BSTAT
PBEN0004	Feature CSTV1
PBEN0005	Feature CRDV1

Table 10.4 User Exits and Replacing Elements

User exit	Replaces
PBEN0006	Feature ELIGR
PBEN0007	Feature TRMTY
PBEN0008	Function HR_BEN_CALC_BENEFIT_COST
PBEN0009	Function HR_BEN_CALC_BENEFIT_CREDIT
PBEN0010	Function HR_BEN_CALC_BENEFIT_SALARY
PBEN0011	Function HR_BEN_CALC_COVERAGE_AMOUNT
PBEN0012	Form CALC_ELIG_DATE
PBEN0013	Form CALC_TERM_DATE
PBEN0014	Function HR_BEN_CALC_SAVE_ER_CONTRIB
PBEN0015	Form CHECK_ELIG_SERVICE
PBEN0016	Function HR_BEN_CALC_PARTICIPATION_DATE
PBEN0017	Feature EVTGR
PBEN0018	Feature COVGR
PBEN0019	Feature EECGR
PBEN0020	Feature ERCGR
PBEN0021	Function HR_BEN_CALC_SPEN_ER_CONRIB
PBEN0022	Function HR_BEN_GET_PROCESS_DATES
PBEN0023	Function HR_BEN_CALC_CUTOFF_AGE
PBEN0024	Function HR_BEN_CALC_CUTOFF_LOS
PBEN0025	Function HR_BEN_CALC_CUTOFF_SAL
PCOB0001	COBRA Letter
PCOB0004	Form HR_BEN_COB_GET_TOTAL_COSTS

Table 10.4 User Exits and Replacing Elements (cont.)

10.2.6 U.S. Specific Benefits

The Benefits Administration sub-module is designed to fit global needs; however, SAP also provides functionalities to administrate U.S. specific benefit requirements such as COBRA plans, Flexible Spending Accounts and Tax-Sheltered Annuity.

COBRA

The Consolidated Omnibus Budget Reconciliation Act (COBRA) requires most employers to provide employees the choice to continue the group health plan under certain circumstances so that they will not lose the group health plan coverage. The COBRA related plans are defined in IMG under **COBRA · Choose COBRA Plans** (see Figure 10.18).

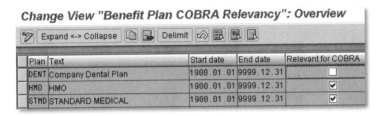

Change View "Benefit Plan COBRA Relevancy": Overview

Plan	Text	Start date	End date	Relevant for COBRA
DENT	Company Dental Plan	1900.01.01	9999.12.31	☐
HMO	HMO	1900.01.01	9999.12.31	☑
STMD	STANDARD MEDICAL	1900.01.01	9999.12.31	☑

Figure 10.18 COBRA Plan Selection

There are eight legally defined event types (circumstances) for COBRA plans:

▶ Termination of employment

▶ Reduction in working hours

▶ Death of employee

▶ Entitlement to Medicare

▶ Divorce

▶ Legal separation

▶ Loss of dependent status

▶ Bankruptcy of employer

For each event type, the permitted coverage periods have to be defined. SAP standard settings fulfil the minimal legal requirements. The IMG path is **COBRA · Define Qualifying Event Coverage Period**.

Personnel actions in Personnel Administration can be linked with event type termination, death of employee and reduction in hours. By establishing such a link, the event collection program can identify qualifying events by checking personnel actions. The IMG path for setting up the links is **COBRA · Assign COBRA Events to Personnel Actions** (see Figure 10.19).

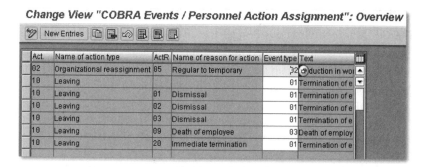

Figure 10.19 COBRA Event Settings

Event collection The event-collection program also checks the employee's master data to identify other qualifying events. Table 10.5 shows the information that the event collection program checks:

COBRA event	Personnel action	Other Infotype record
Termination	As defined, mandatory	-
Death of employee	As defined, mandatory	-
Reduction in hours	As defined, optional	New 0007
Medicare entitlement	-	New 0077, MEDIC = 'X'
Divorce	-	New 0021, SUBTY = 10
Separation	-	On 0021, SEPDT filled
Loss of dependent status	-	On 0021, over age limit
Bankruptcy	-	On 0000, status = retd.

Table 10.5 Master Data Checked During COBRA Event Collection

> **Note** COBRA event collection depends on how well work is done within the Personnel Administration module. It is very important to perform the right activity in the system to ensure that the master data accurately reflect the facts of the employee. For example, suppose that an employee gets divorced. The HR operator simply deletes the employee's 0021 Infotype for the spouse rather than using a family-status change action to make sure a new 0021 Infotype for ex-spouse is created. The event-collection program will not pick up this information as an event; therefore, the COBRA process will not start for this employee.

Once the event-collection program identifies events for employees, an Infotype 0211 is automatically created.

COBRA letter

Transaction RBENUSCOB02 is used to generate COBRA letters. For the settings of a COBRA letter template, please refer to the form setting in section 10.2.5.

After an employee accepts the offer within the permitted period, you can enroll the employee into COBRA plans using SAP Easy Access menu **COBRA · Participation**. Infotype 0212 and 0617 are created for each enrolled COBRA health plan and COBRA FSA plan. Infotype 0270 stores the COBRA plan participant's payment data.

If the employee declines the offer or his or her COBRA payment is overdue, termination will be carried out based on the settings.

Flexible Spending Accounts (FSA)

Flexible spending accounts enable employees to fund their own benefit plans. Employees choose to set aside a certain amount of their pay in FSA accounts. Then, their FSA account reimburses them for qualifying expenses, such as childcare or eldercare and medical deductibles after they submit a valid claim.

The setup of a FSA plan is simple compared with other plans. Only employer-contribution variants and rules are defined when needed. Employee contribution is freely entered during enrollment as long as the total falls into the contribution range. An Infotype 0170 record stores details of each FSA in which the employee is enrolled.

FSA Claim

An employee submits the claim with a receipt. The claim is entered into the system using transaction HRBENUS02. After entering the claim with all detailed information against the proper plan, the user assigns a status to the claim. There are four possible statuses for a claim:

▶ Not yet approved

▶ Approved

▶ Rejected

▶ Agreement given to rejection

For each claim the employee makes, a separate record of 0172 is created by the system. Only the claims with "approved" status are to be taken into account by payroll. Payments are made accordingly.

Tax-Sheltered Annuity (Infotype 0510)

Infotype 0510 is used to store amounts contributed to employees' 403(b) savings plans, including contributions made by the employee, current employer, and the employee's previous employers. This infotype should be maintained before the employee has his or her first payroll run. The cumulation numbers will be updated by the system automatically.

10.3 Critical Success Factors

▶ We strongly recommend that you make a copy of the benefit area and make changes only in the copy. This ensures that a copy of the original reference model is always clean and unchanged so that if later other requirements come out, no previous changes are brought in as defaults. This practice is advisable even when all the pre-defined plans and rules can be directly used without any modification. Thus if there is a need of change in the future, the benefit area does not need to be switched.

▶ Try to avoid using very complex features. If too many value fields are to be checked in a feature, the complexity of the feature will become a challenge during testing.

▶ The eligibility and cost rules must be strictly defined, especially when ESS is used. The presence of incomplete or incorrect rules may allow unwanted plans to be created. It is difficult to fix such defective plans, and they may also bring the company legal problems.

▶ The jobs of checking and updating the latest master data of employees should be scheduled to run automatically. It saves time if benefit administers are not running the jobs manually. It also helps protect the accuracy of the benefit information.

11 Personnel Controlling

Personnel controlling is often an important reason for implementing an integrated HR information system. However, its full potential is rarely realized. With the time constraints of implementation projects, personnel controlling is usually not given sufficient consideration during the design phase.

11.1 Business Principles

HR reporting, also known as personnel controlling, is a cross-application process that provides information from all processes. Reports can be restricted to information on individual processes, or they can combine the data from several processes.

The various chapters of this book will always mostly deal with the process-specific reports. It is in personnel administration (as well as in organizational management) that you design organizational structures and master data to lay the foundations for most other reports. In this way, you can also set up reports on personnel costs or working hours based on the structures from personnel administration, while also integrating some master data in most cases. For this reason, we will pay particular attention to reports in the area of master data.

This chapter uses extremely technical terms throughout. Readers who only have little knowledge of reporting in R/3 or similar standard software systems should only skim the technical passages at first. They are bound to read the same passages more carefully if the issues described occur while they are performing their everyday tasks.

11.1.1 Categorization of Personnel Reports

Personnel reports can be categorized according to different perspectives. When setting up reporting, you should also perform such a categorization and use it as a starting point when designing new reports:

▶ **Aggregated reports/Reports that are or can be specific to individual persons**
Whether a report contains any data of individual persons is a very important consideration for data privacy, and it often determines whether the report can be made available outside the HR department. The question of specificity to individual persons can be difficult to

decide. On the one hand, prepared lists can contain aggregations on too detailed a level (e.g., total salaries per cost center, if there are cost centers with only one salaried employee). On the other hand, you should consider this question very carefully when you not only provide prepared lists but also the option to create reports in a decentralized manner. In this case, it is very difficult to avoid the creation of person-specific lists. It is more a question of restricting access for users outside the HR department, such as departmental managers, to information on their own employees (see also Section 13.3) and of training them in the responsible use of report generators.

▶ **Ad-hoc reports/Recurring reports**
Ad-hoc reports are usually created for a specific purpose, and their concrete requirements cannot be predicted. It is a question of providing a defined information pool upon which the reports can be based. To ensure that reports can be compared, and to limit the workload, it is important in each case to assess the need for ad-hoc reports and the habit of constantly making slight alterations to standard reports.

▶ **Personnel inventory reports/Personnel change reports**
Personnel inventory reports generally refer to specific key dates and provide a snapshot (e.g., number of employees on 1st January, 2005). Personnel-change reports, on the other hand, reflect changes (e.g., new employees or employees leaving in 2005). Personnel-change reports have higher requirements, both for creation and interpretation.

▶ **Creation frequency**
Recurring reports can be classified by their frequency, for instance daily, weekly, and monthly.

▶ **Data sensitivity**
Some HR data can be available across the company (name, location, internal phone number), while other data should only be available for the manager responsible or the relevant HR representative. This is particularly relevant for person-specific reports.

▶ **Recipient group**
These can be public institutions, the executive board, employee representatives, managers, the HR department, all employees, etc.

▶ **Online reports/Paper lists**
Online reports are preferable as they are more up-to-date, with better distribution processes and availability. Paper lists are, however, always useful if you require frozen information for reasons of data security or in order to compare data.

11.1.2 Requirements for Setting Up Reporting

The objective is to set up a comprehensive reporting system that meets external requirements (especially from public institutions), supplies employees with sufficient information, and provides a good foundation for qualified decisions for controlling the company. The following requirements must be met in order to achieve this goal:

▶ Inclusion of the recipient group when defining content, usability, and processes

▶ Inclusion of employee representatives

▶ Definition of authorizations

▶ Structured definition of requirements and identification of redundancies, especially between different processes inside and outside of personnel management (e.g., controlling)

▶ Ensure standardized interpretation of report results

▶ Question the need for traditional lists and layout requirements

▶ Decentralization and use of online reports, wherever possible within the restraints of data security and complexity

▶ Definition of a core of standard reports that all users know how to use and interpret, enabling comparisons over longer periods of time

▶ Provision of a central instance (e.g., personnel controlling department) that deals with creation of complex and sensitive reports, as well as ongoing quality assurance, ensuring standardized interpretation, disposal of obsolete reports, as well as training and ongoing support for decentralized recipient groups

▶ Consolidation of information gained in a report hierarchy that provides the reports to more (for example to all managers) or fewer (for example to only three specialists within the HR department) people, based on data frequency, complexity and sensitivity. Figure 11.1 illustrates the structure of a reporting hierarchy.

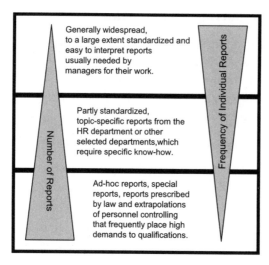

Figure 11.1 Reporting Hierarchy

11.1.3 Timeline for Reporting Data

Data quality   The report quality depends on the quality and timeliness of the data, as well as a clear structure. This is ensured by clear data retrieval and maintenance processes, as well as by structuring reporting as described above. Even where these requirements are fully met, however, data stocks are still subject to changes in terms of quality and completeness. This means they become outdated over time, just as paper lists do from the moment they are printed.

An important aspect here is an awareness of the timeline along which the report is moving. Both personnel inventory and personnel-change reports are always characterized by the following three time specifications:

▶ Report creation time

▶ Reference point or period of time for which data is to be evaluated

▶ One (or usually several) point(s) in time at which the recipient views the report

As a rule, these are three different points in time. The three times only converge for online reports that have the current day as the key date.

Even if this fact appears to be obvious and trivial, failure to take it into account can often lead to communication problems. For example, users often make the incorrect assumption that sets of figures that have already been evaluated and presented no longer change. In HR, however, it is standard practice (ideally) to enter information into the data-processing system as it becomes known. Basically, this means data is entered before the fact (i.e., on May 15, the system already reflects the fact that a specific employee will leave the company on May 31). In many cases, however, data is entered retroactively. Retroactive transfers or changes to payments are everyday occurrences in the personnel departments of many companies.

Payroll systems are enabled for retroactive accounting to take this situation into account, thereby improving the quality of the results. In reporting (and this generally applies to processes that go beyond personnel management as well), users often try to ignore these retroactive data changes. The reason is often frighteningly simple: Nobody wants to explain to the management why the last quarterly report was inaccurate.

The real explanation is quite clear. If you want to evaluate data for April 1, 2002, it is clear that the data will not be complete on March 7, 2002. The data used as the basis for the key date of April 1, 2002 is improved constantly as information is retrieved and maintained. New information can still become available on April 10, 2002, for example, even though the presentation to the board was made on April 5, 2002. Figure 11.2 represents an exemplary data-maintenance flow and the resulting ongoing improvement in data quality. Personnel controlling has the task of sensitizing the group that receives the report to this business reality. If you use "frozen data stocks" to avoid this problem, then you will be making decisions on the basis of reports that are of worse quality than those that could be based on the data actually available.

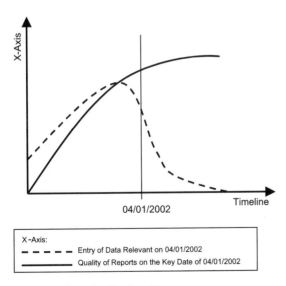

Figure 11.2 Data Quality Over Time

Regardless of this, the objective must still be to provide data as early as possible and at as high a level of quality as possible. This can be achieved with process changes to information distribution and authorization procedures, for example. The maintenance procedure in Figure 11.2, in particular, depends on other fixed dates. This means that users often work on a period-specific basis, in order to guarantee the best possible data quality at the date of payroll settlement. Personnel controlling, however, requires continuously updated data maintenance.

Future values Even with optimum processes, reporting still has its limits when it is restricted to the data stored as facts in the system. Future forecasts are often required to aid decision-making. Reporting uses two methods to facilitate this:

▶ Extrapolation or estimation of future values based on past data

▶ Collection of planning data, requirements, or objectives from managers and employees

For the extrapolation method, personnel costs are calculated based on current costs for known new appointments, departures, and payment changes. An adjustment factor based on empirical values can also be used.

In data-collection, managers specify the planned personnel changes, payment changes, and bonus payments. Here, too, prior experience shows that the value derived in this way also needs to be adjusted by a specific percentage.

Both methods have advantages and disadvantages. Data retrieval solely for report creation is extremely work-intensive. It is also important to find out whether those specifying the information may have an interest in deliberately specifying false data (e.g., because they would rather fall below a high budget than exceed a low budget). The more dynamic the environment, including internal company structures and objectives, the less precise the values determined purely from extrapolation based on past data.

11.1.4 Counting Method

In HR statistics, two basic types of counting methods are possible: headcount, or, or actual capacity. The latter can be counted in hours per week or as a percentage of the normal time worked per week. In both cases, it is also important to take unpaid absences into account.

If you want to define which tasks can be taken over by a given depart- **Fulltime**
ment, you should always consider the capacity as the full-time equiva- **equivalent**
lent, i.e., 0.5 for a part-time worker working half the standard weekly
hours. However in an employee-turnover statistic, for example, the headcount might also be the appropriate method.

11.1.5 Special Case for Turnover Statistics

Turnover statistics are an important tool for HR-related work. They are
often used to solve the following problems, for example:

▶ Recognition of problems with high turnover and the reasons for such
  problems

▶ Defining which channels are mainly used for recruitment

▶ Identifying channels via which personnel can be reduced

First, however, it is important to define the term "turnover." In this context, the following questions need to be answered:

▶ Which employees are taken into account in the statistics?

▶ Will the system only consider external turnover, or also internal turnover?

▶ What counts as an employee departure? (for example, change within
  the corporation, change to inactive employment such as parental leave)

▶ What grouping should the statistics use? (e.g., employer termination,
  employee termination, retirement, early retirement, inactivity period,
  death)

The final objective should be to identify the movements between the
areas relevant to the problem, as well as movements into and out of the
area considered. The company itself is generally the area considered. You
must also decide whether to include temporary staff in the evaluation.
Figure 11.3 displays a typical turnover overview, although it has been
simplified by omitting some of the arrows. The lesson behind the graphic
is clear: The company hardly ever recruits long-term employees directly,
but it first takes on apprentices and leased staff. Employees returning
from an inactive employment are very important.

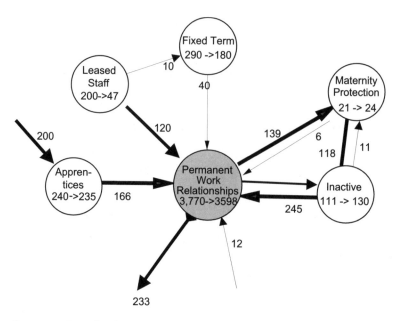

Figure 11.3 Example of a Turnover Overview (Simplified)

11.2 Implementation in mySAP HR

11.2.1 Structures in Personnel Controlling

For clear and meaningful personnel controlling, a clearly defined structure is indispensable for the individual reports. Only in this way can the reports be compared with each other, making it possible to combine the information provided by the different reports.

HR provides different structures that are introduced in Section 4.2.5. When structuring the company, you generally use the company code, personnel area, personnel sub-area, and cost center. These structure levels can also be used as the basis for personnel controlling. It is often the case, however, that the criteria for forming these structures do not correspond to the requirements of controlling. The personnel area and personnel sub-area, in particular, are meant to satisfy the requirements of payroll and time management.

For this reason, the use of organizational management is indispensable for efficient reporting in companies with more than 1,000 employees. For companies of this size, it might also be sufficient to use the fields **Organizational unit**, **Position**, and **Job** in Infotype 0001 without integration with Organizational Management.

Only the full implementation of Organizational Management, however, makes it possible to map an actual organizational structure for the company across any number of hierarchy levels. Also, different views of the organization (matrix organization) can be mapped and evaluated.

The fact that Organizational Management uses the general term "organizational unit" can often be problematic, however. While this guarantees maximum flexibility, it makes it more difficult to define an evaluation that needs to create subtotals at "division" level, for example. You may therefore need to find a way of indicating the neutral objects.

One possible solution is to indicate the individual organizational levels, e.g., using a customer-specific infotype. For a more detailed description of Organizational Management, see the book *HR Personnel Planning and Development Using SAP* by the same team of authors as this book, and also available from SAP PRESS.

Organizational levels

The employee structure presents a problem similar to that of the enterprise structure. The definition of employee groups and employee subgroups is also geared towards the requirements of payroll and time management. This is why there are employee subgroups such as "Employees with 13-month salary," "Industrial workers at old standard pay," etc. These criteria may be relevant for very specific evaluations, but they are generally not an appropriate basis for reporting.

On the other hand, in personnel controlling you want to be able to make selections using criteria such as: "inactive," "sick outside period of continued pay," "part time under 50%," "fixed term." Some of these could also be represented as employee subgroups, but this is not recommended. First, these details are already entered in the master data and entering the data again in another way would be redundant. Second, this would quickly lead to an "explosion" in the number of employee subgroups (mainly because this would have a multiplying effect: for every employee subgroup, a "part-time under 50%" version would have to be added, for example).

Because all the data is already stored in the master data, it can also be evaluated. The data is often not available as selection criteria, however. For this reason, users often perform different evaluations and then consolidate the results in a Microsoft Office product. Alternatively, using the Ad-hoc query's set operations or programming your own evaluations is an acceptable solution. At the same time, it is important that the underlying reporting structures are clearly defined on the basis of the system data. Only then is it possible to create reports that can be compared at a later date.

Another option is to use SAP BW (see Section 11.2.10). This includes various options for combining different selection and aggregation criteria. A very flexible example for defining a clean reporting basis is the definition of a company-specific logical database (LDB).

11.2.2 Tools for Personnel Controlling

Tools for Creating Evaluations

SAP R/3 and mySAP ERP provide various tools for creating evaluations. The main ones include:

► Standard reports

► Ad-hoc Query

► SAP Query

► Programming individual customer-specific reports

► Programming a customer-specific reporting basis using your own LDB

► SAP Business Information Warehouse (SAP BW)

The options above are listed in increasing order of flexibility and workload involved. For this reason, you should first clarify which requirements can be covered using standard reports and query. It is, however, the norm to program additional reports to supplement the standard functionality. If the requirements of personnel controlling are not fully reflected in the standard, and a large number of new developments are required, then you should also consider the last two alternatives: customer-specific reporting with a custom LDB, and using SAP BW.

Company-specific logical database An LBD (see the following section) can encapsulate a large portion of the company-specific logic, so that it does not need to be reprogrammed for every single report. This makes the programming more efficient and also ensures consistency.

There are, however, reasons that this method is rarely used:

► This option is not well known.

► The workload of developing a company's own LDB is overestimated.

► Customers develop the additional evaluations individually as required, but do not realize the potential of consolidating them.

- It is easier to have a small budget assigned for specific requirements than make a one-time investment for the future.
- The investment is wasted, if—from a business perspective—no clear structure is defined on which to base the various reports.
- Customers do not want to take on the workload involved in defining a full personnel-controlling concept and a clean structure.
- "Consulting companies" earn money for every report programmed, and they therefore generate more revenue from individual reports than from a one-time development of an LDB that significantly reduces future development effort.

Even if these obstacles are often difficult to overcome, it can be worth the effort in our experience. You must have previously clarified that the standard solution is not sufficient in some places and that several reports need to be programmed in any case.

The following criteria apply when a company intends to create its own LDB:

- Employee groups and subgroups are not suitable for reporting. In this case, special reporting groups can be encapsulated in the LDB.
- Complex personnel change statistics are required. In our experience, this logic can also be encapsulated very well in an LDB.
- Users constantly need aggregations at defined organizational levels that cannot be mapped using organizational criteria from Infotype 0001 and the neutral concept of the organizational unit in Organizational Management. Together with an "indicator" for the organizational units (e.g., as "team," "main department" or "sales branch") this type of logic can also be mapped very well in an LDB. For the evaluations based on the LDB, it then appears as though every employee has a team key, a main department key, and a sales branch key.

The Concept of the Logical Database (LDB)

R/3 works intensively with LDBs. They are used to make the programmers' jobs easier and to concentrate specific definitions and structures in a central location.

An LDB used by a program (or query) behaves in almost the same way as a "real" database, even though it does not physically store data (hence the name). A program or query requests certain data from the LDB, which then only really reads the individual tables. This means that the programmer has far fewer things to worry about. The most important logical databases in HR are the following:

- **PNP:** for HR master data
- **PNPCE:** for HR master data including concurrent employment (to remain future-oriented, you should work with PNPCE after changing to R/3 Enterprise)
- **PAP:** for applicant master data
- **PCH:** for objects in personnel planning and development (also includes HR master data)
- **PTRVP:** for travel planning and travel expenses

From this point onwards we will no longer use the term LDB PNP, but rather PNPCE. For Release 4.6C and earlier, continue to use PNP.

The logical database PNPCE provides the familiar standard selection screen and its variants, for example. It also relieves programmers of the tasks of authorization checks, personnel number selection, and period selection. If the criteria for the standard selection screen are insufficient, then the company-specific LDB can be used to provide other selection criteria without the programmer having to check them.

SAP BW and SAP SEM

Another tool that is increasingly important is *Business Information Warehouse* (*BW*). BW is a separate system that extracts data from SAP applications and other systems, if necessary. Using *InfoCubes*, BW provides the option of extremely flexible combination, selection, and aggregation of this data. For this reason, BW represents an extremely powerful tool and is mainly needed for very large data stocks. It does, however, require additional work to configure and maintain. From SAP ERP Central Component 5.0 onwards, a separate instance is no longer required for the installation of BW, which somewhat reduces the maintenance workload. SAP's current strategy is strongly BW-oriented (i.e., little investment in reporting outside BW).

Strategic Enterprise Management (*SEM*) is partly based on BW. A core component is the *Balanced Scorecard* (*BSC*), which can establish a relationship between aggregated key figures from different areas and trace those figures back to lower aggregation levels. The SEM principle is displayed in Figure 11.4.

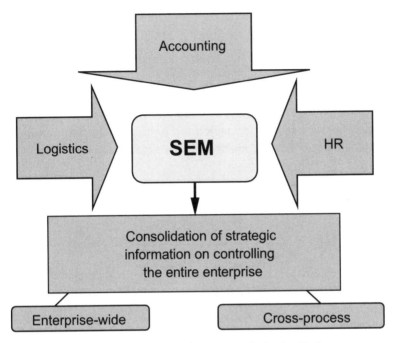

Figure 11.4 SEM as a Highly-Aggregated Cross-Area Evaluation Tool

Tools for Accessing Evaluations

Apart from the individual evaluations, easy access is also an important factor. The following options are provided for this in SAP R/3, as well as mySAP ERP and particularly in HR:

▶ Easy Access Menu

▶ Human Resources Information System HIS (see Section 11.2.8)

▶ Manager's Desktop (MDT, see Chapter 13, *Role-Based Portal Solution*)

▶ Manager Self Service (MSS, see Chapter 13, *Role-Based Portal Solution*)

The last two tools are specifically tailored to the requirements of managers who want to run reports on their employees. HIS makes it possible to start evaluations based on the organization chart, but is usually completely replaced by MDT.

The Easy Access Menu is not restricted to evaluations. This is the normal menu with which users work. Every evaluation and every query infoset can, however, be included in the menu based on users' roles. This means that every user can be provided with the required evaluation options in the most ergonomic position in the menu.

11.2.3 Standard Reports

Concept of
HR reports

HR reports generally must be assigned to the individual components. In the processes considered in this book (exception: Organizational Management), evaluations usually follow the basic pattern displayed in Figure 11.5. Here, we explain the principle in rather more detail, as it is extremely important for the correct usage of the broad range of reports on offer. The person-selection period and the data-selection period in particular are often used incorrectly even by experienced users.

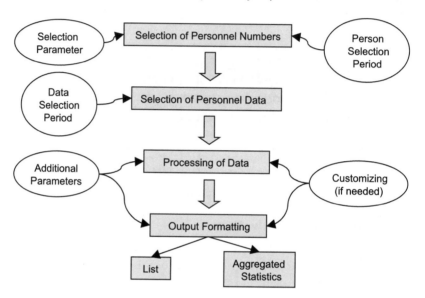

Figure 11.5 Basic Pattern for a Standard Report

First, you use the report's selection screen to determine which personnel numbers will be taken into account in the evaluation. This is done via selection parameters (e.g., employee subgroup, personnel area, etc.) and the person-selection period. The system considers the employees who meet the selection criteria at some point during the specified person-selection period.

You can use the data-selection period to define which data is to be output for the persons already selected. In this way, for example, you could select all employees that had been active in a specific personnel area at any time (leave the person selection period empty) and have the system issue the current (data selection period = current date) address for those employees.

Actual processing and output formatting for the data is report-specific and is partly controlled via other parameters in the selection screen or also in Customizing settings. See the online help regarding each specific report for more information (in the selection screen, follow the menu path **Help · Application Help**). The field help (**F1** help) may also provide information on any report-specific parameters of the selection screen.

The selection screens for the most commonly used standard reports are very similar. The standard selection screen from the PNPCE (PNP for older reports) logical database serves as the basis for these reports. It can and should also form the basis for individually programmed reports and SAP queries. Figure 11.5 displays a typical configuration for the standard selection screen. It generally provides the following functionality:

▶ Period selection

▶ Selection parameters (can be enhanced using the button **Other selections**)

▶ Selection via matchcodes

▶ Selection via the organizational structure of Organizational Management. Remember that—depending on the configuration of your system—selecting an organizational unit here may only include the people on the level directly below. In order to select the entire substructure, you must select it using the **Select sub-tree**.

Starting with the maximum configuration, it is very easy to adapt the selection screen for the use of specific individual reports. This is done in Customizing via the IMG path **Personnel Management · HR Information System · Reporting · Adjusting the Standard Selection Screen**. In the first step, you must create report categories (see Figure 11.6). These report categories define the following attributes:

▶ Selection options for period selection. Note that some evaluations only provide useful information when you use the key date selection.

▶ Immediately available and optional additional selection fields

▶ Availability of additional selection options (organizational structure, matchcode). The permissibility of the organizational structure as a selection criterion can significantly increase the value of many standard reports.

Report categories

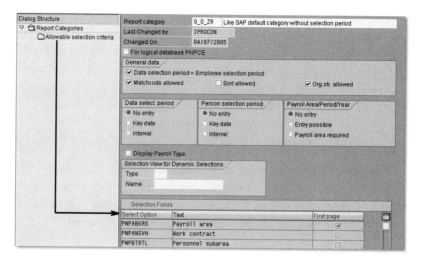

Figure 11.6 Defining a Report Class

When creating report classes, we recommend that you use an existing class as a copy template.

In the second step, these report classes are assigned to individual reports. When assigning report classes to standard reports, remember that enhanced options to the selection screen do not necessarily make sense. For example, a specific report only provides useful results on a key date.

The selection screens for most reports therefore provide many options. To avoid having to repeat the same entries each time you use the report, you should save frequently used selections as a variant. This also ensures quality and ease of comparison for recurring evaluations.

Note   When the structure is changed, you must also check and adapt variants. If, for example, a variant called "Employee list, East Coast" contains the personnel sub-areas "Boston, MA" "New York, NY" and "Washington, D.C." the new location "Charleston, S.C." can easily be overlooked. Variants that contain a selection across the entire organizational structure are particularly prone to errors. Note that the **Select sub-tree** functionality selects all organizational units below the organizational unit "East Coast" for the current period. A new "Team W4" set up in Washington must be maintained, as must a new personnel sub-area in "Charleston."

Examples

There is a very large supply of standard reports. Most of them are available via the menu. It is hardly possible to describe them all, and it is not necessary, as the online documentation is generally sufficient. We have, however, provided the following examples to give you an idea of the standard options.

The employee list is a very simple evaluation that you can access via the menu path: **Human Resources · Personnel Management · Administration · Info System · Reports · Employee · Employee list**.

Employee list

The system outputs a simple list of employees from the selected area (see Figure 11.7). In addition, the output screen provides the following possible options, for example:

▶ Sorting

▶ Filtering

▶ Print preview

▶ Transfer to a spreadsheet or word processor

▶ Save as local file

▶ Send as e-mail in SAP Office

▶ Display as SAP business graphic (with no numeric values in this report, there is no point in using this option)

▶ Column selection in the layout

Employee List

Key date: 04/07/2005
Number of selected employees: 221
Number of selected cost centers: 86
Parameter KOSTLTXT only allowed in connection with KOSTL

CoCd	PA	Cost Center	Text	Pers.no.	PersIDNo.	Name	Name at birth	Job Title	Entry Date	Leaving
3000	3000	2130	Accounts Payable	00100206	589492934	Mr. Tom Hays		Manager (US)	01/01/1996	
3000	3000	9301	Production 1	00100208	222111111	Mrs Monette Collins		Technician (US)	12/31/1998	
3000	3000	2250	Payroll Admin.	00100209	376898766	Mr. Timmy Tabasco		Manager (US)	01/06/1997	
3000	3000	4130	Warehouse	00100227	198871123	Mr. George Metzger		QM Personnel (US)	01/01/1997	
3000	3000	2220	Labor Relations	00100230	174871124	Mrs Jennifer Esposito		Administration (US)	02/01/1997	
3000	3000	4120	IT Service	00100235	674012887	Mr. Peter Laursen		PC Service Technician (US)	09/24/1999	
3000	3000	2100	Finance & Admin.	00100245	321455030	Mrs Amy Sombat		Assistant (US)	08/01/1997	
3000	3000	4120	IT Service	00100246	990999993	Mrs Elizabeth Davis		Director	10/19/2000	

Figure 11.7 Example of a Standard Employee List

It makes sense to try out all of these options (see Figure 11.8). Using them is far easier than providing a written description. Note, however, that problems that occur when transferring data to other applications (such as Microsoft Excel) could also be due to authorization problems.

Figure 11.8 Options for Further Processing a Report Output

The employee list contains all the options of the standard selection screen (sorting, matchcode selection ("search help"), selection via the organizational structure, and further selection fields) as well as report-specific selection fields. As a result it is also possible to select by various characteristics such as nationality or gender (see Figure 11.9). These are not contained in the standard selection screen and are therefore not available with most of the other reports. Furthermore, as the report has the capability to display the cost-center text, it also provides an example of how the form of the output is controlled via the selection screen.

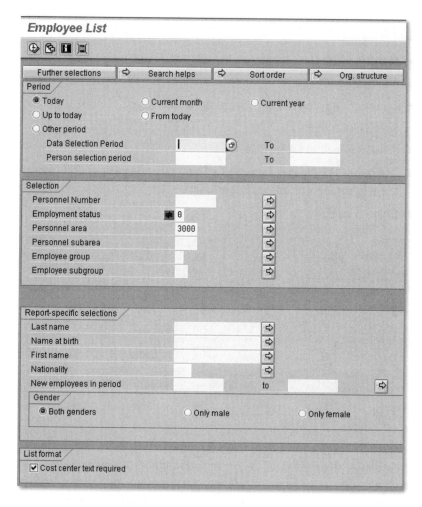

Figure 11.9 Selection Screen for the Standard Employee List

Apart from this, the employee list is simply provided as an example here.

You can access the report on flexible employee data via the menu path
**Human Resources · Personnel Management · Administration · Info
System · Reports · Employee · Flexible Employee Data**. Its extreme flexibility provides an extremely useful tool that can make it unnecessary to
create a query or program a separate report.

Flexible employee
data

A total of 105 fields from different infotypes are available for output.
These include some fields that are not saved in the database, but which
are calculated dynamically (e.g., the age of an employee). Figure 11.10
displays the selection of output fields.

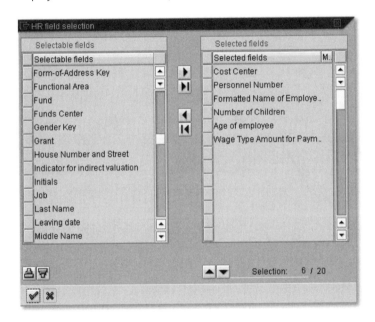

Figure 11.10 Selection of Output fields for the "Flexible Employee Data" Report

Because many of these fields are unequivocal only to given points in time,
they can only be selected for key dates, not for periods. Using the filter
function in the screen output, these 105 data fields can also be used to
select employees.

Important note for developers It is worth taking a closer look at this
report (RPLICO10) and possibly using it as a template for your own
development. Due to generic programming, it is very easy to add further fields if you know the structure of the program.

You can access the salary by seniority list via the menu path **Human
Resources · Personnel Management · Administration · Info System ·
Reports · Organizational Entity · Salary according to Seniority**. This
function calculates the payment for the selected employees (from the
master data, not from the payroll results) and lists the annual payments
aggregated by years of employment and cost centers (see Figure 11.11).
The report output can also be displayed as a graphic or broken down to
employee level (see Figure 11.12).

```
Salary Information

Cost center   2000 0000002100 Finance & Administration

Seniority     Number of employees              Average salary

01              1                               USD          14.736,00
03              4                               USD          28.440,00
08              5                               USD          19.200,00

Total salary                                    USD         224.496,00
Average salary per employee                     USD          22.449,60
Employee(s)                                                          10

Salary Information

Cost center   2000 0000002130 Accounts Payable

Seniority     Number of employees              Average salary

09              8                               USD          18.761,00
10              1                               USD          20.000,04

Total salary                                    USD         170.088,00
Average salary per employee                     USD          18.898,67
Employee(s)                                                           9
```

Figure 11.11 Annual Payments by Seniority and Cost Centers

```
04/07/2005   Salary list for key date  12/31/2005

Per.no.  Name                          Seniority   Annual salary


Cost center  2000 2130      Accounts Payable


00100126 Mr. Lawrence Carlton              9   USD        24.999,96
00100123 Mr. Harold Carson                 9   USD        15.000,00
00100128 Mr. Pamela Floyd                  9   USD        15.000,00
00100206 Mr. Tom Hays                      9   USD        18.000,00
00100124 Mr. Hubert Laws                   9   USD        17.088,00
00100001 Mr. Samuel Rainer                 9   USD        15.000,00
00100125 Mrs Kathy Trocolli               9   USD        30.000,00
00100127 Mr. Michael Watthers              9   USD        15.000,00
00100022 Mrs Noelle Manelli              10   USD        20.000,04
```

Figure 11.12 Annual Payments per Employee with Years of Employment

As well as the basic pay from Infotype 0008, it is also possible to include recurring payments and deductions (Infotype 0014), additional payments (Infotype 0015). For Infotypes 0014 and 0015, it makes sense to restrict the data used to specific wage types. The calculation is based purely on master data, and so it is also possible to perform evaluations for periods in the future. However, time-based variables can't be included (night-shift premium, etc.). This may often be correct for evaluations of this type, but the person interpreting the evaluation must be aware of this.

Integration in the Easy Access Menu

Standard reports, customer-specifically programmed reports, and even generated queries can easily be integrated in the Easy Access Menu using the role concept. You can maintain roles and collective roles via the menu path **Tools · Administration · User Maintenance ·** Role administration— **Roles**. This way Reports also can be included in the roles, making them available via the Easy Access Menu. Role definition should, however, only be performed by suitably experienced administrators responsible for authorizations. For data-security reasons, other users should not be allowed to define roles!

11.2.4 SAP Query

SAP Query is originally a cross-application component. For this reason, we will not go into greater detail on this here; we will just present the basic options and special characteristics within HR.

SAP Query is based on the same infosets and user groups as Ad-hoc Query (see the following section). Figure 11.13 illustrates the relationship between infosets, user groups, and queries. In the example, User A has access to all queries, while User B only has access to the queries in infosets 2 and 3.

In HR, it is easy to define and generate an infoset based on the PNPCE logical database. Of course, an infoset can also be created directly using the corresponding database tables if you are not using an LDB. We only recommend this, however, if you have a thorough knowledge of the underlying data structures and requirements cannot be met by the existing LDB (e.g., connection to data from the personnel master, time management and material master for evaluations in the area of incentive wages).

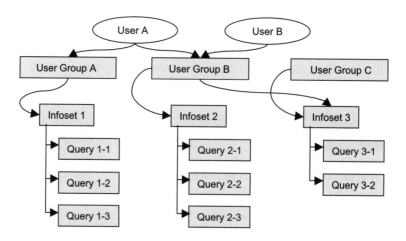

Figure 11.13 Infosets and User Groups

Based on the defined infosets, the use of SAP Query can be organized in
three different ways:

1. Queries are defined at a central location and are then simply executed
   by transactional users or executives.

2. Transactional users or executives create their own queries. In this case,
   clear conventions are needed.

3. Transactional users or executives use centrally provided queries and
   create their own ad-hoc queries (see the following section). Conventions are also needed here, although it is much easier to learn to use
   ad-hoc queries. This variant is probably the most practical, as the number of available fields for ad-hoc queries can significantly reduced in
   accordance with the wishes of the employee representatives.

SAP Query also provides Quick Viewer as an additional evaluation tool.
We do not, however, recommend that you use it in HR, as its functionality is restricted in this area.

The following section provides a brief description of creating an infoset
(e.g., based on the PNPCE logical database). You can define an infoset via
the following menu: **Human Resources · Information System · Reporting Tools · SAP Query · Environment · Infosets**. First, however, you
must select the correct query area (menu path: **Human Resources · Information System · Reporting Tools · SAP Query · Environment · Query
Areas**). In general, you work in the client-specific area (standard area).
You must also define the user group to which you are going to assign the

infoset (menu path: **Human Resources · Information System · Reporting Tools · SAP Query · Environment · User Groups**).

When creating the infoset, you must follow the steps displayed in Figure 11.14. In our example, PNPCE (or PNP for Release 4.6C and earlier) is selected as the database. Selection of the required infotypes and subsequent selection of the fields actually required in the individual field groups are intuitive. The system already proposes the most frequently used fields and assigns them to the field groups by infotype.

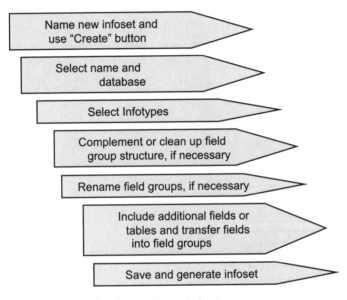

Figure 11.14 Procedure for Creating an Infoset

When maintaining infosets, you must always bear in mind that they will be used in the future as the basis for many queries and ad-hoc queries. For this reason, it is worth investing a little extra time when creating an infoset. The field names, in particular, should be self-explanatory. If they just have names like "Amount" or "Wage Type," then it will be very difficult to understand what the fields mean when they are used for a query. Changing an infoset for which queries already exist is restricted (in particular, you cannot remove fields used in queries). It is always possible to add new fields, however.

When the infoset has been created, it must be assigned to the user groups that will be allowed to access it.

It is then possible to create a query based on the infoset. The basic procedure is illustrated in Figure 11.15. You can access the initial screen via the following menu path: **Human Resources · Information System · Reporting Tools · SAP Query**. After you enter a name for the query and click on the **Create** button, the system opens a wizard that guides you through the query creation. Because this aspect is also not HR-specific, we are limiting our description to a few comments:

▶ If the infoset is based on LDB PNPCE, then its standard selection screen can be used. For this reason, fields already contained in the standard selection screen should not be defined as selection fields again. Otherwise, they will appear in the selection screen as duplicates.

▶ The control level concept is extremely important. Every field via which subtotals or similar are to be created must be indicated as a control level.

▶ If the result of the query is to be further processed in a spreadsheet, then you should select a single-line list.

▶ The field help (use the **F1** key) within the query creation is very helpful for most of the fields, and you should make full use of it from the beginning.

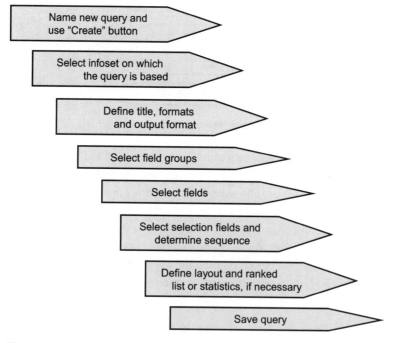

Figure 11.15 Procedure for Creating a Query

11.2.5 Ad-Hoc Query

Ad-hoc Query (outside of HR, this tool is also referred to as the "Infoset Query") is based on SAP Query. It is, however, significantly easier to use and can therefore be more widely used within departments and by managers and administrative staff. Just as with SAP Query, the Ad-hoc Query is based on the definition of the Infosets and user groups, as described in the previous section.

The Ad-hoc Query allows easy (single-line) lists, based on an LDB. Using PNPCE as an example, the following data is available (this also applies to SAP Query):

▶ All infotypes in Personnel Administration and Time Management

▶ The Payroll results, provided they are stored in a "Payroll results" infotype

▶ The results from Time Management (although only daily balances and no monthly ones), provided they are included in Customizing for simulated infotypes

▶ Long texts for the most relevant keys stored in the infotypes that have already been named

▶ A comprehensive set of additional fields, e.g., of PD infotypes, where a reference can be created to an individual personnel number (e.g., manager)

You can access the Ad-hoc Query via the following menu path: **Human Resources · Personnel Management · Administration · Info System · Reporting Tools · Ad-hoc Query**. The menu item **Reporting Tools** is also contained in other component infosystems and in cross-application infosystems. The Ad-hoc Query can also be accessed via the normal SAP Query transaction using the **Infoset Query** button.

If the user is assigned to a suitable user group, then the system will display the initial screen displayed in Figure 11.16 (after selecting the required infoset, if there are several for the user).

The screen section at the top left displays the available field groups representing infotypes. The top right of the screen displays the evaluation period, the additional restriction of the reporting set, and the selection screen. You can also use the hit list to display the number of data records selected by the query. The bottom section of the initial screen displays an output preview.

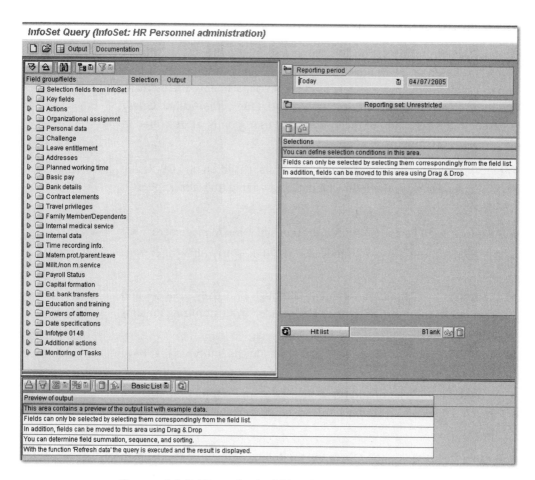

Figure 11.16 Initial Screen for the Ad-hoc Query

You actually define a query in the top left section of the screen. The infotypes and fields available here depend on the selected functional area (infoset). Every field can be used for output and/or selection. For each field, it is also possible to define whether the key or the long text is to be used (if you were using the field **Personnel Subarea**, for example, you could decide whether to use "0001" or "Seattle"). In some cases, it is quite surprising to find what the long text reveals. The text issued for the personnel number, for example, is the name of the employee. To choose between the key and the text, you click the right mouse button.

You can now select the required fields from the infotypes. The primary key should always be the personnel number. When you choose the **Selection** option, the corresponding field is added to the table on the right-hand side of the screen. You can use options and values to enter selection criteria. Check your selection first by using the hit list.

The output preview in the lower section of the screen displays the layout of the list. After selecting a column, you can move it using Drag&Drop. Figure 11.17 displays the individual screen areas for the Ad-hoc Query.

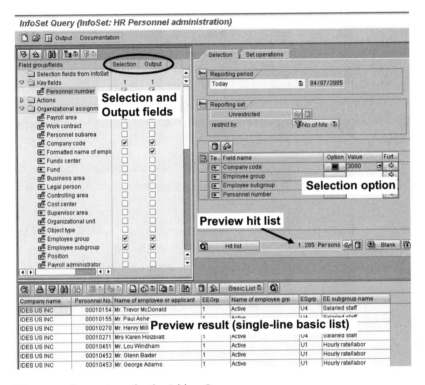

Figure 11.17 Screen Areas for the Ad-hoc Query

If you now click on the **Output** button, the system displays the result of your Ad-hoc Query (see example in Figure 11.18).

Personnel ...	Postal Co...	Location	Name of employee or applicant	CoCd	Company name	Subar...	P.subarea text
00010155	60609	Chicago	Mr. Paul Ashe	3000	IDES US INC	0001	Chicago
00010270	19111	Warminster	Mr. Henry Miller	3000	IDES US INC	0001	Philadelphia
00010271	19111	Burlington	Mrs Karen Holzblatt	3000	IDES US INC	0001	Philadelphia
00010451	30123	Atlanta	Mr. Lou Windham	3000	IDES US INC	0001	Atlanta
00010452	30112	Atlanta	Mr. Glenn Baxter	3000	IDES US INC	0001	Atlanta
00010453	30123	Atlanta	Mr. George Adams	3000	IDES US INC	0001	Atlanta
00010454	30112	Atlant	Mr. Jo Sallis	3000	IDES US INC	0001	Atlanta
00010455	30112	Atlanta	Mr. Alex Picket	3000	IDES US INC	0001	Atlanta
00010866	30112	Atlanta	Mrs Lou Bennett	3000	IDES US INC	0001	Atlanta
00010867	30111	Atlanta	Mr. Danny Smith	3000	IDES US INC	0001	Atlanta
00010868	30011	Atlanta	Mrs Chris Newton	3000	IDES US INC	0001	Atlanta

Figure 11.18 Output Example of an Ad-hoc Query

Return to the selection screen. If necessary, correct your selection and/or save the query if it provides the required output. Saving not only saves the definition of selection and output fields, but also the selection that has actually been made (as when saving a variant for standard reports).

Restricting the reporting set is particularly useful. For example, you can define an additional restriction using the organizational structure.

Set operations The ability to link selection sets from several queries provides extreme flexibility. This makes it possible to map intersections, set unions, and exclude one set from another. The result of these set operations is then transferred for subsequent use to the resulting set, as shown in Figure 11.19. This means that in two steps it is possible, for example, to select all the employees from a specific personnel area that do not have Infotype 0050.

It is often also useful to use the query as an aid for pre-selection, and to forward the reporting set to another report via the *report-report interface* (see Figure 11.20).

The Ad-hoc Query reaches its limits where more comprehensive calculation logic, control levels, special layouts, or multi-line lists are required. These requirements are at least partially covered by SAP Query.

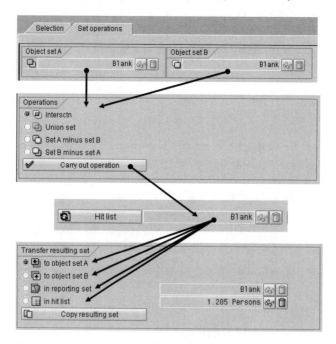

Figure 11.19 Set Operations in the Ad-hoc Query

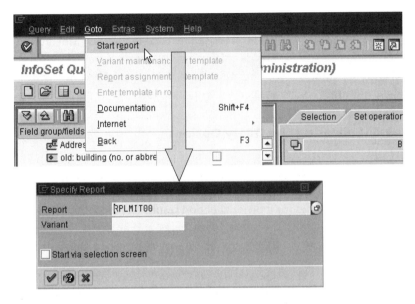

Figure 11.20 Calling a Report with the Resulting Quantity of a Query

Ad-hoc Query can be used by a broad range of users only if the infosets and user groups are clearly defined according to requirements. Even if it seems easy to use at first glance, users should be trained or at least have access to good, company-specific documentation. Otherwise, in our experience, errors made when selecting data and interpreting the results will often lead to confusion and contradictory lists.

> **Note** You should pay special attention to the following points:
>
> ▶ Clarification of the terms used when naming fields (especially for terms such as *basic salary*, *variable salary*, *basic pay*, and *hourly rate*, which are often understood differently by employees in the payroll department than by managers. It is important to clearly define the composition of these aggregations).
>
> ▶ Importance of the selection period (especially awareness that many reports only provide useful information when performed for a specific key date)
>
> ▶ Evaluation of actions (difference between Infotypes 0000 and 0302)
>
> ▶ Importance of object selection (HR-specific)

We strongly recommend the broad use of Ad-hoc Query within the framework of the restrictions imposed by data-security considerations and training costs. To ensure this, you must create a central concept (Personnel Controlling). You must have extensive knowledge of HR data and functionality to succeed with this work.

11.2.6 Enhancing the Query Options

Integration of Payroll Results

Payroll results cannot yet be accessed via the query. It is only possible to read the header lines for individual period results (Table WPBP). These do not, however, contain the actual wage types and amounts. In order to evaluate these using the query, they must first be provided in an infotype.

This is what the "Payroll results" infotype is used for. After you make the corresponding settings in Customizing, the system can automatically create person-specific infotypes containing the values for specific wage types. These infotypes can then be viewed in the normal infotype display and evaluated in queries and reports. You can carry out customizing via the IMG path **Personnel Management · HR Information System · Payroll Results** in the following steps:

▶ **Define Evaluation Wage Types**
These are the "wage types" that you will see later in the newly defined infotypes.

▶ **Assign "Real" Wage Types**
This assignment is made from the payroll results for the evaluation wage types. This can be a 1:1 assignment. It is also possible to accumulate or subtract several real wage types in an evaluation wage type. The principle is similar to that for customizing of cumulation wage types in the remuneration statement (see Chapter 9, *Payroll*).

▶ **Set Up One Or More Payroll Infotypes**
This is done by assigning the evaluation wage types.

▶ **Generate Payroll Infotypes**

▶ **Define Update Process**
The payroll infotypes can either be filled directly from payroll or via Report RPABRI00. In order not to restrict performance for payroll, we generally recommend that you update the infotypes separately using the report. Using the HR process workbench, you can add this update at the end of the process.

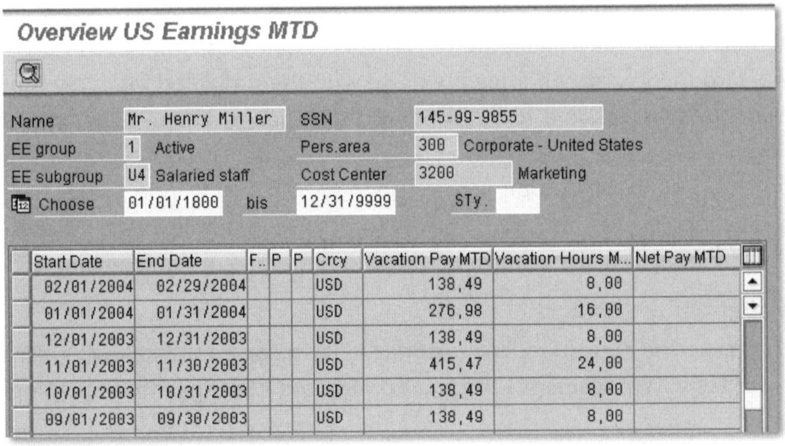

Overview US Earnings MTD

Name	Mr. Henry Miller	SSN	145-99-9855
EE group	1 Active	Pers.area	300 Corporate - United States
EE subgroup	U4 Salaried staff	Cost Center	3200 Marketing
Choose	01/01/1800 bis	12/31/9999	STy.

Start Date	End Date	F..	P	P	Crcy	Vacation Pay MTD	Vacation Hours M...	Net Pay MTD	
02/01/2004	02/29/2004				USD	138,49	8,00		
01/01/2004	01/31/2004				USD	276,98	16,00		
12/01/2003	12/31/2003				USD	138,49	8,00		
11/01/2003	11/30/2003				USD	415,47	24,00		
10/01/2003	10/31/2003				USD	138,49	8,00		
09/01/2003	09/30/2003				USD	138,49	8,00		

Figure 11.21 Payroll Infotype: List Screen

Figure 11.21 displays the list screen for a payroll infotype. This is a typical example, storing different gross and net salaries that are often required in evaluations. Just as often, hourly or daily rates are also stored, as is the value (in money) of a lifetime working account.

Integration of Time Evaluation Results

The result clusters for the time evaluation also are not directly available for evaluation via the query. In this case, SAP has decided to pursue a different method than the one it uses with payroll results. Instead of actually storing the results in an infotype, it uses simulated infotypes. These are defined in Customizing, and their "content" is calculated when a query is run without it ever actually being stored in a database table.

Simulated infotypes can contain different results for time evaluation. These are then summarized again, if necessary, as follows:

▶ Time types (values from the day table—but not the monthly cumulation) are summarized in reporting time types.

▶ Time wage types are summarized in reporting time types.

▶ Attendance and absence values are summarized in reporting time types.

▶ Attendance and absence quotas are summarized in reporting quota types.

▶ Leave quotas are summarized in reporting quota types.

For most applications, daily values in time types are unusable. As a rule, cumulated monthly values are relevant to evaluations. You have to use a workaround in order to integrate these with the simulated infotypes. For example, it is possible to store the monthly values in specially defined time types or time wage types as daily values at the end of the month. To do this, you must include a corresponding calculation rule in the time evaluation schema. An alternative is to provide monthly values in additional infoset fields. This technique is also described in the following section.

You make the corresponding customizing settings via the following IMG path: **Time Management · Information System · Settings for Reporting**.

Additional Fields

If the available fields are not sufficient, you can include additional fields. You do this via the corresponding menu points when defining the infoset. This requires programming experience and knowledge of the corresponding data structures and the underlying logical database. It is then possible, for example, to include additional details in the output, such as the SWIFT code for a bank code from Infotype 0009.

Special Query "Switches"

An improved Query Generator is provided with R/3 Enterprise, although it is also available via support packages for earlier releases. SAP Note 305118 applies to Release 4.6C, for example.

In this new generator, you can set switches that influence the processing logic. Some examples include the following:

▶ BL_ALLOW_DUP_LINES

Choose whether identical output lines are summarized or not

▶ PROCESS_LOCKED_RECORDS

Choose whether locked data records are considered or not

▶ NO_INDIRECT_EVALUATION

Choose whether the system performs indirect evaluation for outputting wage type amounts

You can view the full list in the documentation via the IMG path **Personnel Management · HR information System · HR settings for SAP query · Create infosets for HR**. First, it is important to understand the switching concept. Switches can only be included using additional "coding" in the infoset. If, for example, identical lines are to be printed, then switch BL_ ALLOW_DUP_LINES must be set using the following coding lines:

```
*$HR$ [COMMON]
*$HR$ BL_ALLOW_DUP_LINES = 'X'
```

Figure 11.22 illustrates how coding for switches is included.

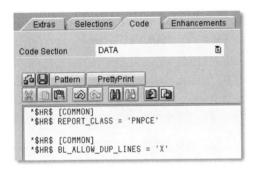

Figure 11.22 Including Two Switches

11.2.7 Programming Customer-Specific Reports

If the standard reports provided by SAP do not meet the requirements of your organization, and the query options are not sufficient, you can program customer-specific reports. You should first check, however, whether the additional workload (both for creating and maintaining reports) is really justified:

▶ Can you get by with compromises to the layout of standard reports?

▶ Can you avoid the need for programming by switching from paper reports to completely online reports? Standard reports are often simply not suitable for central printing (e.g., insufficient options for controlling page breaks).

▶ Are the reports you usually use really better? The options in the standard reports reflect best-practice experience, which can also be applied in your company.

When creating your own reports, they should be based on the PNPCE (or other) logical database where possible, for the following reasons:

▶ Authorization checks have already been implemented, they would need to be programmed again in your own reports.

▶ It provides a comprehensive standard selection screen.

▶ It is easier to read personnel data.

► You can log the start of PNPCE reports via the IMG menu path **Personnel Management · Personnel Administration · Tools · Revision · Log Report Starts** and evaluate them via Report RPUPROTD.

In some cases however, there can be good reasons to develop customer Advanced Business Application Programming (ABAP) applications without using an LDB. These reasons include:

► As a rule of thumb, performance of a reasonably designed report that doesn't use a LDB is much better that that of a LDB-based report.

► LDBs are focused on a specific part of the whole data in the system. If you want to combine, e.g., HR master data with data from the CO module and from travel management, you won't find it all in one LDB. As one report can only use one LDB, there is no possibility to combine several LDBs within one report.

11.2.8 HIS

The *Human Resource Information System* (*HIS*) is based on the structural graphic from Organizational Management. It makes it possible to start a structured range of evaluations easily via a section of the organizational structure that can be selected graphically.

You can access HIS via the menu path **Human Resources · Information System · Reporting Tools · HIS**. You select the required root organizational unit in the initial screen (see Figure 11.23). This is not quite the organizational unit for which you want to start an actual evaluation, but the upper-level area—often the entire company—from which you can select individual units of substructures. You can use the **Defaults** button to control selection and formatting for the structure graphic.

After confirming your entries, the system displays the selected structure and the two HIS selection screens. In the structural graphic, you select the organizational unit. In the **Reporting** pane, you select the subcomponents and the required evaluation (see Figure 11.24).

You make the settings for data selection, retrieval, and authorization in Customizing. You do this via the following menu path: **Personnel Management · HR Information System · HIS**.

In the standard version, HIS already contains comprehensive settings that facilitate company-specific enhancements.

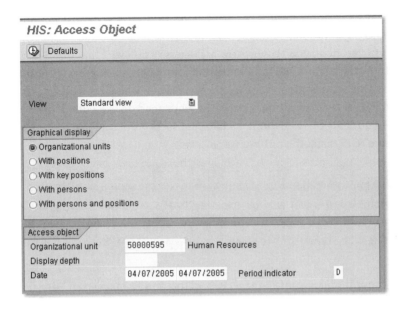

Figure 11.23 Starting to Use HIS

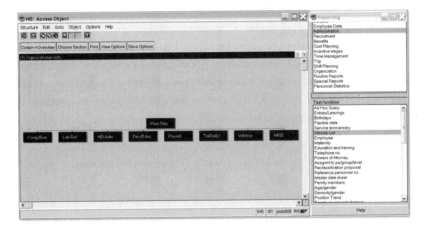

Figure 11.24 Example in HIS

The views and sub-areas are the results of the company-specific requirements that you make, especially the groups of HIS users. The **data
retrieval** point requires knowledge in the area of evaluation paths for
organizational management, which are not dealt with in this book. In
general, however, you should be able to get by with the existing examples
for data retrieval.

HIS makes it possible for less practiced users to make the right selections using the organizational structure, and it provides role-specific evaluation options. For decentralized use by managers, however, the Manager's Desktop (see Section 13.3) is more suitable. User-specific provision of reports, in the meantime, is feasible in other ways, using the role concept and the Easy Access Menu. For users who need to execute a clearly defined quantity of evaluations via different sections of the organizational structure, HIS is still the optimum solution.

> **Note** Because a query is also an (automatically generated) ABAP/4 program, queries can also be included in HIS. You can find out the report name for a query, for example, by calling the system status in the selection screen for the query.

With the introduction of Manager's Desktop and Manager Self Services (see Chapter 13, *Role-Based Portal Solution*), HIS has lost some of its importance. For decentralized use by managers who only evaluate their own section of the organization chart, MDT is better suited.

Customizing for HIS can, however, still be used. Entire sections of HIS can be linked to MDT. The standard version of the MDT function code HIS includes all HIS sub-areas to which the MDT view is assigned. This is programmed in this way in the function module HR_HIS_READ. A customer-specific copy of this module with simple adjustments, therefore makes it easy to include other HIS views in MDT.

You should, however, make a critical appraisal of whether it really makes sense to include HIS sub-areas in MDT. The elements derived from HIS Customizing form a fixed block in MDT, so MDT Customizing cannot insert any other reports in between. If you continue to expand MDT, this can easily lead to a loss of a clear, thematically organized reporting structure in MDT.

11.2.9 Limits of HR Reporting

All solutions for HR Reporting, no matter how technically perfect, reach their limits if the data quality and environment are not right. However, implementation in mySAP HR also reveals shortcomings.

Shortcomings of the PNPCE Logical Database

The LDB PNPCE and its underlying data structures are an important basis for all the forms of report creation described. Its shortcomings occur in nearly all reports. These are the following:

▶ Selection and aggregation via organizational structures is difficult. The structure concepts in Infotype 0001 are generally not sufficient to map lower-level structures. While Organizational Management can be layered as deep as required in a hierarchy, the individual organizational levels are not sufficiently described. As well as the department ID, HR controllers usually also like IDs for divisions, business areas, sub-departments, branch offices, teams, etc. A solution for this is to describe the organizational units using a company-specific infotype and possibly connect it to the selection of a company-specific logical database.

▶ Organizational structures with several dimensions (matrix organization, project structure) are not considered in the selection. A solution for this is the selection via PD structures and the transfer of the personnel numbers selected in this way to a PA report. In the standard version, this can be done by Report RHPNPSUB. A more flexible solution, which also creates an enormous workload, is to program a company-specific LDB that reflects these structures more closely.

▶ Selection and aggregation via the personnel structure are not always sufficient. As well as the employee subgroups and positions, personnel controlling also often requires a grouping of employees by more or less dynamic criteria. These can be criteria such as "outside continued pay period," "maternity leave," "national service" or "on night shift on this key date." It would be extremely time-consuming and also redundant to change employee subgroups for every change to these characteristics in order to be able to make clear selections in reports. Possible solutions are: individual programming of selection and aggregation in every evaluation, pre-selection using more work-intensive ad-hoc queries, and transfer of the selection set to the actual evaluation. This last approach only works partly and not for aggregation. Another way out is the extremely work-intensive creation of a company-specific LDB.

Limits to the Inclusion of Other Processes

Cross-process evaluations also often create problems. The inclusion of several of the processes described in this book is very well covered in the current release level. It is more difficult to include non-PA processes in PA evaluations:

▶ Processes for personnel planning and development are integrated very well up to this point. As described in Sections 11.2.4 and 11.2.5, SAP Query and Ad-hoc-Query already provide a significant amount of data, especially from Organizational Management. Furthermore, the PD LDB (PCH) fully includes PA infotypes. The standard reports still represented a weak point, as they are seldom set up as cross-process reports. A possible solution is the use of PCH as the basis for queries or company-specific programming.

▶ At the current release level, travel management provides a good range of standard evaluations, and it can also be evaluated via SAP Query, now that travel cost infosets are provided. The inclusion of travel data in PA evaluations could be better, however. A solution to this could be to define your own infosets based on the database tables, avoiding the LDBs. SAP queries can then also be created on this basis. To do this, however, you should be very familiar with the data structures and SAP Query.

▶ Evaluation of HR data that is linked to data from Financial Accounting, Logistics or industry solutions is not generally covered in the standard version. Very few standard reports are exceptions to this. This is only to be expected, as the requirements of individual companies differ greatly in this area and there are many possible combinations. While certain special cases can only be covered using company-specific programming without LDB support (provided that you have good knowledge of the data structures for several processes), BW does provide a comprehensive solution. It provides the opportunity to combine data from all SAP modules as well as external systems. Based on the large data quantities, however, the system does not work with real-time data, but with extracted data stocks, in order to safeguard system performance. BW is the most flexible and comprehensive evaluation tool, but it generates a heavy workload for implementation and maintenance.

11.2.10 Business Information Warehouse

BW is a self-contained system that enables a flexible evaluation of data from all R/3 modules and also of external data.

In addition to the wide range of possibilities offered by the definition of company-specific extractors (that transfer data from HR into BW) and company-specific InfoCubes (multi-dimensional data clusters that allow different selection and aggregation levels), SAP also provides comprehensive standard content for HR. This standard content represents a good basis for defining your own evaluations.

BW can be used via a WEB-interface or via the Business Explorer Analyzer (BEx Analyzer), a frontend based on Microsoft Excel (see Figure 11.25).

Leaving Rate

Employee
Employment Status
Gender
Nationality
Age in Years
Personnel area
Personnel subarea
Employee group
Employee subgroup
Master cost center
Leaving Rate
Organizational unit

Organizational unit	Average Headcount 2004	Number of Leavings 200	Leaving Rate
Overall Result	2.908,50	6	0,21 %
▽ Organizational plan	2.475,50	5	0,20 %
▷ OrgU PSales	253,00		
▷ IDES Japan	30,00		
▷ Test JT	7,50		
▷ Retail Organ	11,00		
▷ 50000675	6,00		
▷ OrgU Int.	44,00		
▷ OrgU Portal	41,00	2	4,88 %
▷ OrgU IS	63,00		
▷ OrgU Tec HR	239,00		
▷ CABB Group	574,00		
▷ IDES AG	1.207,00	3	0,25 %
▷ Not Assigned Organizational Unit (s)	433,00	1	0,23 %

Figure 11.25 BW Query Showing Various Criteria for Drill-Down

The queries in BW allow the user to sum up key figures according to various criteria on multiple levels. It is possible to start with a list on the highest level and then drill down to individual employees, wage types, and other levels.

Figure 11.26 shows such a query evaluating the number of employees as a key figure and organizational units (columns) and qualifications (lines) as the criteria. As the contextual menu in the upper right corner shows, other criteria such as age or gender can easily be chosen for drill down. This shows that BW is a very powerful tool when it comes to examining a problem online from various angles.

Qualifications per Employee by Organizationa

Menu:
- Back to Start
- Keep Filter Value
- Filter and drilldown according to ▸
- Add Drilldown According to ▸
- Swap Calendar Year/Month with ▸
- Sort ▸
- Goto ▸
- Calendar Year/Month ▸
- All Characteristics ▸
- Properties ...

Submenu:
- Age in Years
- Alternative Qualif.
- Employee
- Employee Group
- Employee Subgroup
- Employment Status
- Gender
- Nationality
- Personnel Area
- Personnel Subarea
- Proficiency Q/R
- Qualification Group
- Scale

Left panel:
Employee
Employment Status
Gender
Nationality
Age in Years
Personnel Area
Personnel Subarea
Employee Group
Employee Subgroup
Scale
Proficiency Q/R
Alternative Qualif.
Qualification Group
Calendar Year/Month   01.2005
Structure
Organizational Unit
Qualification

Calendar Year/Month	01.2005	01.2005	01.2005	01.2005	
	Number of employees	Number of employees	Number of employees	Number of employees	Number of en
Organizational Unit	300	3300	30015847	30019894	30019896
Qualification	US Exec.	Los Angeles	HR250	00 Ttl Rewds	01 Ttl Rewds
▽ Quali. catalog	1	3	31	1	
▽ Leadership C					
ProbSolv					
Interview					
▽ Educ					
▷ UnivEd					
▷ Trades					
▷ SCEd					
▽ Competencies			31	1	
▷ CoreComp			31		
▷ CoreMgmt			31	1	
▷ Leadership D					
▽ Empl Cmptncy			31		
▷ Soc. comp.			31		
▷ Cognitive					
▷ Core Rqmnts					
▷ Physical					
▽ Business KSA				1	

Figure 11.26 BW Query (Release 3.5) Using BEx Analyzer

The SAP PRESS publication *HR Personnel Planning and Development Using SAP* provides a quick overview of BW used in conjunction with HR. For more detailed information on BW, we recommend Norbert Egger's book: *SAP BW Professional*, also published by SAP PRESS in 2004.

11.3 Process Example: Company-Specific Reporting Concept

The process of personnel controlling often lacks a clear strategy. The following sections provide an example of how personnel controlling is set up with mySAP HR. This reporting concept consists of the following components:

▶ Role distribution between the personnel controlling department and managers

▶ Inclusion of other report recipients

▶ Definition of standard reports available decentrally

▶ Definition of standard reports available centrally

- ▶ Procedure for implementing new standard reports
- ▶ Tools for ad-hoc reports (centrally and decentrally)
- ▶ Tools for providing reports
- ▶ Authorization concept

Figure 11.27 displays the general structure of the reporting concept. At the same time, personnel controlling supports various internal customers:

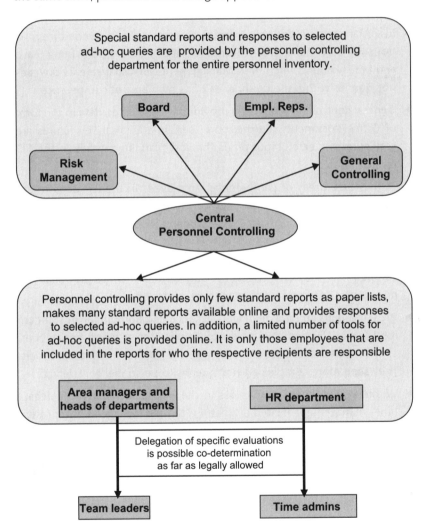

Figure 11.27 Reporting Concept: Recipients and Roles in Personnel Controlling

▶ The management board is provided with a few special standard reports and receives answers to ad-hoc queries. These reports are provided in the form of Office documents or paper lists.

▶ In R/3, the employee representatives can access many standard reports online. Some of these reports are legally required and some have been agreed upon within the framework of the reporting concept. They are also informed on all ad-hoc queries and included in the definition of new standard reports, as well as new tools for ad-hoc evaluations.

▶ Risk Management has online access to a few defined standard reports from HR Risk Management (turnover, age structure, remaining leave and time accounts, etc.). Risk Management can also create its own ad-hoc queries within the boundaries of its own area of competence.

▶ General controlling is regularly provided with selected data in the form of Office documents. Furthermore, certain statistical key figures are configured via batch input or via the cost-planning module in the CO module of R/3.

▶ Within their areas of competence, employees in the HR department can access data on the employees for whom they are responsible. They can access this data in R/3 via standard reports, company-specific reports, and queries. In addition, they can also perform ad-hoc queries based on infosets that provide very good coverage of their area of competence. They can process the data further in Office products. Ad-hoc queries are also sent to personnel controlling.

▶ Area and departmental managers access a certain number of standard reports via MDT and have access to simple infosets for ad-hoc queries. They cannot process the evaluation results further in Office products. They send more complex ad-hoc queries to personnel controlling.

▶ Within certain limits, employees in the HR department can delegate time- management-related evaluations to time management representatives. The time- management representatives access these reports via the Easy Access Menu.

▶ Managers can delegate non payment-related evaluations to team leaders. The team leaders access these evaluations via MDT, but only for their team members. It is expressly forbidden to delegate evaluations to secretarial staff.

This concept provides a rough framework. It is now necessary to fill it with actual reports and infosets, and to determine authorizations. This requires a certain amount of detailed work, but the process is not as work-intensive as you may think. In our experience, this kind of solution creates a usable and fairly stable personnel controlling environment far more quickly than the habit of just skipping from one requirement to the next.

11.4 Critical Success Factors

▶ When defining the HR Controlling strategy and the corresponding structures, internal customers must be included.

▶ The system must support the role of the HR department as a central framework, providing tools and advice for the interpretation of reports and creating more complex and wide-ranging evaluations.

▶ The system must support the role of managers who, with the support of the HR department, can create the reports they need online.

▶ The basis for high-quality personnel controlling is high-quality and up-to-date data entry.

▶ The requirements of personnel controlling should be included in the system design from the very start. They must definitely be regarded in a holistic way. Considering every single evaluation requirement in isolation rarely results in an ideal overall solution.

▶ Specific aspects of the authorization concept are relevant in personnel controlling. A well-configured authorization check, in particular, can have an extremely positive effect on performance.

▶ Employee representatives should be included in the process.

▶ You must define evaluation requirements very precisely. A general, verbal description of the contents is not usually sufficient. You should clarify the following in particular: Selection criteria, aggregation levels, numerical and non-numerical content, calculation formulae, layout, configurability, authorization check, and reusability of the results. Definitions must always clearly follow SAP terminology.

12 Quality Assurance

Quality has its price, especially if it is neglected. With forward planning and discipline, a pragmatic and thorough quality-assurance strategy usually pays off very quickly, because it improves usability and efficiency, thereby reducing process costs.

12.1 Quality in Software Projects

Implementation projects for IT systems are often subject to extreme time and budget pressure. Even if the initial project planning is realistic, this pressure often arises from the following factors:

Time and budget pressure

▶ Late or drawn-out project start

▶ Use of capacity elsewhere (especially if the workload for ongoing everyday tasks has been underestimated)

▶ Changes in membership of the project team during the project

▶ Changes in requirements

When projects are under pressure, quality assurance is often neglected in order to save resources. This is a short-term approach, however. It may help you to keep deadlines when running projects with short runtimes, but at the price of poorer quality. Targeted quality assurance—provided it is not implemented for its own sake—generally reduces total costs.

Typical quality problems can be divided into four categories:

▶ **Incorrect definition of requirements**
The first project phases are used to generate system requirements. Due to communication problems or the inclusion of the wrong group of people, the planned processes are often misunderstood. Just as frequently, individual processes or process variants are completely overlooked. In both cases, these mistakes may only come to light during end-user training or even during production operations.

▶ **Incorrect mapping of requirements**
This is the classic "quality problem" that users often describe as a "program error," leading to incorrect system behavior. Along with a clear concept and a well-qualified project team, structured tests are indispensable.

► **Incorrect use of the system**

System providers and consultants (even internal project teams) are often all to eager to call these problems "user errors," thereby removing them from their area of responsibility. Of course, users are not completely without responsibility in this situation. Change management in its broadest sense (including user-specific training) and optimal system support (e.g., via plausibility checks) can, however, significantly reduce these user errors during implementation.

► **The maintenance trap**

Quality problems that occur only some time after production starts can also often be traced back to implementation. Missing documentation or badly structured customizing or program coding can make maintenance significantly more difficult.

These categories apply to IT projects of all kinds. Project owners should therefore remember that both internal and external project teams almost always try to save money at these areas when "price" is the main factor considered at the beginning of a project.

For the rest of this chapter, we'll bear these four categories in mind when describing the use of quality assurance in HR projects. We will first consider some cross-process approaches and then individual HR sub-processes. Very general topics without any special reference to HR are mostly omitted. Figure 12.1 displays the listed quality- assurance fields and assigns the most important points to them.

Maintenance trap	• Bear in mind strong dynamics and complex customizing
Incorrect use of the system	• User guidance • Decentral use
Incorrect mapping of requirements	• Test helps, esp. for time evaluation and payroll
Insufficient definition of requirements	• Include decentral institutions • Service catalog • Process definition

Figure 12.1 Quality Assurance Fields

12.2 Cross-Process Quality Aspects in HR

12.2.1 Structured Procedure

There are many process models for implementing standard software products. Quality problems arise for the following three reasons:

▶ The selected process model is not used because it entails too great a workload.

▶ The selected process model is not used because it cannot be applied to the actual situation.

▶ The process model focuses on implementation and requires clear and sensible definition of the requirements.

An "off-the-rack" process model can only serve as a rough guide. One of the first tasks of a project team is to create a project-specific model from a general process model. The team must not only consider company-specific factors, but also the special characteristics of mySAP HR. It is not enough for a technically oriented process to stipulate the "definition of the most important structures." For an HR project, the team must define the company and employee structure (see Chapter 4, *Personnel Administration*), as well as the use of Organizational Management.

It is even more important to find a structured procedure for defining requirements. It is not very helpful to start describing or modeling processes with no clear structure. In the HR environment, in particular, the following dangers can arise:

▶ You concentrate too much on the HR department itself, and forget other users or potential users.

▶ You concentrate too heavily on mySAP HR terms. This means that processes that do not have their own modules in R/3 (e.g., personnel controlling, requirements planning, release, etc.) are often displaced.

A clear definition of requirements that clearly describes the planned processes is indispensable for quality assurance. The planned processes are, after all, the means for measuring the success and therefore the quality of the project.

There are varying opinions on the necessary formats for the requirements documentation or process documentation. The following points should, however, be clearly documented in some form:

- What services should the HR system support?
- How are the individual processes reflected in the most important variants?
- Which exceptions should you be aware of?
- What technical and organizational interfaces are provided?

These points should be supplemented with a detailed description of the data and interfaces that can be refined over the course of the project.

The service specifications, in particular, represent a useful guideline for quality assurance. It is important to ensure that the processes listed in the service specifications are supported and that additional functionalities aren't included merely because the system provides them.

12.2.2 Documentation and Customizing

HR is constantly changing. Constant changes in Customizing and also in programming are not only driven by real process improvements, but also by works agreements, wage agreements, and regulatory changes. Another measure of the HR dynamic is the number of support packages delivered by SAP. Between the appearance of Release 4.6C in the middle of 2000 until the middle of February 2003, 66 HR packages were delivered, as opposed to a total of 40 for all other R/3 modules. We strongly recommend a clean structure and ongoing cleanup of Customizing entries and report variants.

Also, easy-to-use documentation is very important for an ongoing maintenance. It is important to document the frequent small changes as quickly as possible. The IMG (Implementation Guide, see Appendix A) is a useful documentation tool in this area. There are other documentation tools, but IMG documentation is unbeatable, as it can be called directly from the Customizing screens of the IMG. The ease of simply clicking on the documentation button increases the likelihood that smaller changes will be documented immediately. However, you shouldn't succumb to the temptation of simply repeating the contents of the Customizing table in the documentation. Instead, you should concentrate on the following points:

- Reasons for certain settings
- Reference to laws, works agreements, process descriptions, or other documentation

- ▶ Naming conventions

- ▶ Modifiers or groupings (especially in HR)

The IMG can rarely replace the comprehensive documentation of cross-application processes and concepts. It is, however, very helpful for documenting individual settings.

12.2.3 Clear Customizing

Clear Customizing in both the implementation and maintenance phases represents a significant contribution to quality assurance.

During implementation, clear conventions are very important, especially when structuring tables that contain many entries. In HR, this applies when defining wage types or time types, for example. Also, the relationships between the different Customizing tables are often extremely complicated and multi-layered (e.g., absence valuation, TMW, MDT, etc.). It is precisely these relationships that are rarely clearly described in the standard documentation. Before you start making your settings in Customizing, you should first graphically display the dependencies for the area you work in, and create a configuration design with easy-to-use naming conventions. Every time a subsequent change is made to the settings, you will be rewarded for the initial time invested.

Many of the settings in HR are subject to extreme changes. You should therefore make sure that Customizing entries that are no longer required are time-restricted. It usually makes little sense to delete obsolete entries, as this then restricts the system's ability to do retroactive accounting as well as the option for displaying past data. The practice of time-restriction also gives you a better overview of the current entries. During system checks, we (the authors) often work with tools that search for entries that are no longer required (e.g., time types, time models). These tools are very easy to create for yourself.

Unfortunately, some table entries cannot be time restricted, as they are not stored with start and end dates. These include personnel areas and sub-areas, as well as employee groups and subgroups, for example. While most users do not seem to view this as a problem, it can often become one after several years of production-system operation. In Customizing, there is a way to improve input help for end users and to indicate obsolete entries. If you add "ZZ" to the beginning of the text description (not the key), then the corresponding settings can be recognized immediately. As most input help programs sort the entries by text, rather than by the key, these obsolete entries will appear at the end of the list (in other input help programs, there is still the option to sort by text after calling the help). Figure 12.2 displays an example of this solution as applied to a personnel sub-area. Although the offices in Houston and Jackson would appear in the middle of the list according to their keys, when the input help sorts the entries by long text, they appear at the end of the list. This makes it easier for the user when working with very long selection lists.

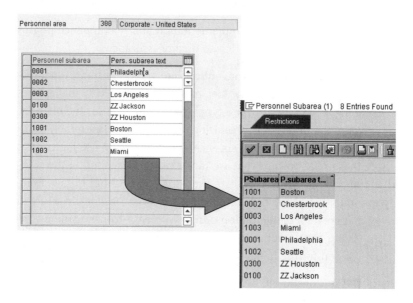

Figure 12.2 Placing Customizing Entries at the End

12.2.4 Test Concept

Tests in HR often focus on the correct calculation in the areas of Time Management, Remuneration Payroll, and the company pension plan. While there is no doubt that these areas require the heaviest testing, it is important not to forget the tests for more dialog-oriented processes and evaluations. To test dialog applications, CATT processes can be used, just as they can be outside of HR.

HR is characterized by strong relationships between individual components and changes to planned results over time. For this reason, it is particularly important to document the test cases in a structured way and to set up a lasting test dataset.

Setting up test data

Setting up test data can be time-consuming and labor-intensive. You have to take into account very different configurations and many exceptions. It is, however, possible to reduce the workload involved in setting up test data:

- Personnel data (HR master, including payroll results, travel expenses, etc.) can be copied if you use the right programs. This can be done within a system and across systems. Cross-system copying can be used to copy new configurations from the production system to test systems on a regular basis, in order to keep the test dataset up-to-date. You either can create a company-specific copy program, or purchase a ready-made tool or template from one of many providers.

- Objects in personnel planning and development can also be copied using a similar process. This means that you can use the production system to create a realistic environment in the test system. Some providers of copy tools also provide this functionality.

- Because test data in personnel planning and development is generally copied on a 1:1 basis from the production system (or for a section of the production system), it is also possible to copy the data without a special tool. Instead, you can use the standard ALE (Application Link Enabling) functionality to copy Organizational Management, for example, from the production system to the test system. This is not usually possible for HR master data, because the standard ALE functionality does not include all personnel data and does not render data anonymous during distribution.

Anonymity is probably the most critical factor when copying test data from a production system. For data-security reasons, it is not usually possible to use original data in the test system. Some companies deal with this problem by setting up the test environment within a quality assurance system, in which the use of original data is not critical. This means, however, that the QA system would have to be subject to the same access authorization restrictions that apply to the production system.

Usually, the test environment is created using anonymous data (i.e., with data that cannot be traced back to a real person). This applies both to the permanent test dataset, as well as to individual cases that are copied due to specific errors or Customizing changes.

The copy tools available on the market generally allow this kind of anonymity. However, the option to configure these on a company-specific basis is often extremely restricted. The scope depends heavily on specific requirements.

Anonymity of test data

For example:

▶ When testing age-dependant remuneration components, it makes no sense to assign a standard birth date to all test cases. At best—depending on the rule used—it can be set to 01.01 of the respective year.

▶ A company might enter the number of a company cell phone in a customer-specific subtype of Infotype 0040 ("Objects on Loan"). In this case, this field must also be made anonymous.

▶ If data that can identify an individual person has been entered in a customer-specific infotype, then this infotype must also be linked with an anonymization process.

For these reasons, a ready-made tool must also provide corresponding options that allow it to be adjusted to meet company-specific requirements. One alternative is to program the tool yourself, or to have one created based on a template. In the latter case, your own programming personnel should be included in the process so that they can make future changes themselves.

The following points list criteria that may be relevant when choosing a copy tool:

▶ Is cross-system copying also possible?

▶ Is data security guaranteed during cross-system copying?

▶ Is there an anonymization option?

▶ Is it possible to adapt the range of data to be copied and the anonymization process to your company-specific requirements?

▶ Apart from the HR master data, which data can also be copied (payroll results, business trips, applicant data, etc.)?

▶ How is the pricing, including maintenance (can it be adapted to new releases)?

▶ Can several people be copied in one run? What is the selection process and how long is the runtime?

▶ Is there a log that allows tracking of copy actions?

12.2.5 Authorization Concept

In HR, the authorization check is often seen as particularly critical. This is due to the sensitivity of HR data and the importance that employee representatives (rightly) place on this topic. Furthermore, the HR authorization concept is extremely complicated. In a strongly decentralized implementation of the system, creating, implementing, and testing of authorizations are often extremely labor-intensive tasks.

The following points list some aspects of HR authorizations that constantly lead to quality problems in practical project experience:

▶ HR contains many different authorization objects, some of which refer to the same data (HR master). Interaction between the different objects is often not taken into account. There are checks that are connected with "AND" as well as checks connected with "OR" operations.

▶ The default values of the profile generator (Transaction PFCG) are often very bad in the standard version. Authorization object P_ABAP in particular, is often proposed although we cannot be sure why. Also, users often misunderstand the way that this object works: It is not necessary for running a report; rather it fully or partially deactivates the master data authorization check for a report.

▶ The authorization check display behaves in a similar manner (Transaction SU53). When authorization problems arise, this check is intended to display the authorizations that are missing for a user. This check also often displays the object P_ABAP unnecessarily. Also, up to and including Release 4.6C, this check cannot be used in the area of structured authorizations. Where problems arise in this area, it often incorrectly indicates authorization object P_PERNR.

▶ Structural authorization, especially context-dependent variants from Release 4.7 onwards, is particularly time-consuming to test. In this case, we recommend that you use report RHAUTH00, which displays the authorized objects per profile and/or per user.

Because the authorization concept as such is not dealt with in this book,[1] we will finish the topic with these warnings. Above all, it is important to be aware that this area can easily become a minefield, and you cannot put off dealing with it until just before the production start. It is much more important to include the authorization concept from the very beginning of an HR project. In many cases, you can reduce the workload simply through early planning. Even if your budget for external consultants is tight, this sub-project is the one area in which you should try to avoid making savings your top priority. Consultants should, however, have a

---

1 See the following titles on this subject: Krämer, Lübke, Ringling: *HR Personnel Planning and Development Using SAP*, SAP PRESS 2004; Brochhausen, Kielisch, Schnerring, Staeck: *mySAP HR—Technical Principles and Programming*, SAP PRESS 2005; IBM Business Consulting Services: SAP Authorization System, SAP PRESS 2003

broad range of experience both in HR authorizations and the HR application, rather than just authorizations in general.

12.2.6 Decentralized Use of the System

HR is increasingly decentralized, i.e. implemented outside of the HR department. This is the best way to support HR processes while not being limited only to HR department processes.

This decentralized development can, however, create some quality problems. As well as the special requirements for the authorization concept, it is important to bear the following points in mind:

▶ For medium-sized companies, in particular, definition of processes is often implicit, as long as less than 30 people work on the system within the HR department. With decentralized implementation, user numbers quickly rise to more than 100 or more than 1,000 people. This means that process changes can no longer be made at will. Processes must be clearly defined and understood.

▶ Decentralized users only spend a small part of their working time in the HR system. Furthermore, it is generally not possible to give these users time-intensive training for this "part-time job." For this reason, the complexity of the application must be kept at a much lower level than for users in the HR department. This is done by efficiently using specific interfaces such as MDT, MSS, ESS, and TMW. You shouldn't forget, however, that it is not only the interface that can complicate the process. Long-winded rules, overloaded evaluations, and personnel-specific technical terminology can also make life difficult for users.

▶ The interfaces provided to decentralized users may be easier to use, but the users within the HR department are often unaware of them. This can lead to misunderstandings when users in the HR department have to answer questions from decentralized users. For this reason, it is important for employees in the HR department who are constantly in contact with decentralized users to also be familiar with the relevant interfaces, such as TMW, MDT, etc.

▶ While it is important for all users, it is crucial for users outside the HR department to adapt the user interface to the particular requirements as thoroughly as possible. It is a bad habit to have screens with various fields or buttons that users do not need. In most cases this can be avoided by Customizing (e.g., Table T555m for infotypes), GUIXT

screen variants. These techniques also allow you to make fields obligatory or to determine default values.

▶ When many users outside the HR department are involved, process
automation is especially useful in making processes more efficient and
secure. Section 4.4.2 shows how to use dynamic actions for this purpose. Other options are workflows or the generation of e-mails by custom ABAP development. The latter is not as difficult as it may seem at
first sight. The automatic generation of straightforward e-mails (going
to MS Outlook or Lotus Notes) can easily be implemented within one
or two days; such as, for example:

  ▶ Missing clock-in or clock-out stamps

  ▶ Missing travel expense records

  ▶ Birthday or anniversary mails

  ▶ Records in infotype 0019 when the due date is reached

12.2.7 Setting Up Your Quality-Management Project

Whether you have just completed the implementation of SAP HR and
you want to start a quality initiative as part of the continuous improvement process or your system is running for several years and you feel you
urgently need to improve usability and data quality: before going into the
details you should build a framework, set up an action plan and decide
about the priorities of each issue. The good news is: This project can be
spread over a longer period of time with low intensity. Once the framework and action plan are established, the project can be decomposed
into many small pieces of work, with each of them delivering some value
of its own.

The authors recommend a methodology they call "HR-Process-Check"
(see Figure 12.3). This is based on four steps and can be used in a similar
way for all projects that require an efficient analysis of the HR processes
of your organization. When reading through this four-step method, it
may look like an unbearable workload. As a matter of fact, the structured
procedure allows you to get through it quite swiftly. If you get the right
persons involved, it will probably take between four and 10 one-day
workshops to get the whole framework and action plan set up. Focusing
on a single process will make it even faster.

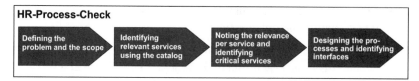

HR-Process-Check

Defining the problem and the scope → Identifying relevant services using the catalog → Noting the relevance per service and identifying critical services → Designing the processes and identifying interfaces

Figure 12.3 Four Steps of the HR-Process-Check

The four steps for setting up your quality management project are:

1. Decide on a high level which parts of the HR function are to be analyzed. For example, if there are parts that are not supported by SAP HR, you don't have to invest any effort there.

2. Now you must go into detail. You need a catalogue of each service or function within the scope of your project on a very detailed level. The authors use a reference model containing more than 600 typical functions within HR, because many organizations find it very difficult to tell right away which functions are performed within their HR.[2] This is something you have to build, no matter whether the work is based on your process documentation or on some reference model. At the end of this step, you'll have a catalogue with all the relevant functions that are supported by SAP HR. To give you a benchmark: When you are focusing on personnel administration, payroll and time management, you'll probably end up with about 150 to 400 functions.

3. Now, each function in your framework has to be assessed according to the criteria that tell you whether there is a need for action. These are the key performance indicators (KPIs) for your QM-project. To decide whether any effort has to be invested into a specific function, you may want to know:

   ▶ How often is the function performed per year?

   ▶ How much time is spent on it?

   ▶ Is it seen as critical?

   ▶ How do users assess usability and the potential for improving quality?

   ▶ Where is it supported within SAP HR (e.g., transaction, report, infotype)?

   ▶ Who is responsible?

---

2 For more information about using a template see *www.iprocon.de/int/leistungen/pprozesse.htm*

4. For some functions, you might need a detailed process description because they are very complex or contain an important interface between departments or IT-systems. However, this will be the case only for a minority of the functions involved. So, although the methodology is process-oriented, it avoids creation of a huge workload in process modeling.

Now, that your framework is built up, the fun-part of the project can start. With the information gathered, you can check out all the possibilities to improve quality that are outlined in this book and in other sources.[3] This provides you with your action plan, and you can implement it step-by-step. Some steps will only take an hour. Each step will improve your HR processes by some degree.

However, you must not think that the mission is over once your action plan is completed. Processes and system change with time, and new technical options may allow you to tackle a problem that seemed unsolvable two years ago. So, make sure that your framework is kept up-to-date by adding new functions or removing old ones. Regular meetings between users and SAP HR administrators have proved to be a key element of continuous improvement. It is a good idea to establish a monthly meeting schedule with those who rely on the system for their daily work and those who do the customizing and programming. When there are too many users to take part all at one time, let a group of five or 10 users join each meeting. It is astonishing, how easily some problems can be solved, once the persons involved are discussing them directly without any managers standing between them.

12.2.8 Auditing Tools

If your HR system is subject to an audit, the advice given in this chapter will definitely help you to get good rates. After all, the whole chapter is aiming at avoiding wrong procedures, wrong data, and miscalculations based on wrong configuration.

However, our approach is not so much that of an auditor as that of a business-process engineer. We want to avoid mistakes in the first place, while from the auditor's point of view, mistakes (often equaled with fraud) must be detected, and the responsible person must be found. If you can prove to the auditor that it is not possible to enter wrong data into the

---

3   For example, in the free newsletter all readers of this book are invited to subscribe to. See Section D.2.

system (a probably impossible task), he will be happy, of course. Other-wise, he may request a system that can trace any mistake or fraud. This approach, which focuses more on the end of the process, is what auditing tools are doing.

Basically, the auditing tool allows you

1. To define rules about what situations are considered to be exceptions, which lead to a warning message or an error.
2. To identify all exceptions with a reporting tool that allows you to deal with each exception (e.g., by approving it or by correcting the data). The tool will keep a track record of each exception and the way it was dealt with, so that the auditor will be able to assess the whole process.

A very sophisticated tool is "TheAuditor" from Pecaso. Besides audits focused on master data and payroll, it supports some other areas such as authorizations and system parameters with other areas to follow soon. Figure 12.4 shows the Customizing for a simple exception rule, which will create an error when wage type M120 in infotype 0015 is above 10,000. Besides checks based on master data, it is also possible to refer to payroll results.

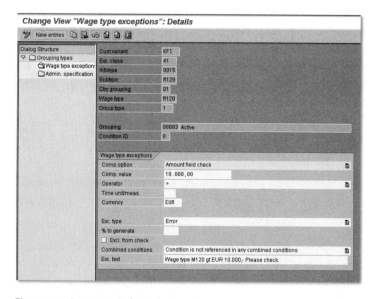

Figure 12.4 Exception Rule in TheAuditor

Figure 12.5 shows the payroll workbench. The exceptions are selected, categorized (left-hand side of the screen), and can be analyzed in detail and dealt with on the right-hand side of the screen.

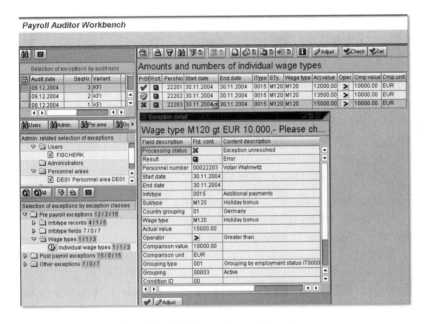

Payroll Auditor Workbench

Figure 12.5 The Payroll Workbench Showing Several Exceptions

12.3 Process-Specific Quality Aspects in HR

12.3.1 Quality Assurance in Organizational Management

Organizational Management represents the basis for many different processes. You must be aware of the fact that incorrect or obsolete data here leads to errors in the following areas:

▶ The wrong access rights are assigned via the structural authorization check.

▶ The wrong roles are assigned to users.

▶ MDT or TMW assign the wrong employees to managers or time management representatives.

▶ Cost centers are assigned incorrectly in the HR master, causing personnel costs to be posted incorrectly.

▶ Workflows flow to the wrong people.

▶ The wrong compensation components are assigned via compensation management.

▶ Too many or too few vacancies are specified in recruitment. In the worst case, job advertisements are started even though there are no open positions.

- Many of the evaluations provide incorrect results.
- Personnel cost planning provides incorrect results.

These examples should be motivation enough to make sure that you keep Organizational Management carefully maintained and up-to-date. The availability of information is often a big problem. Those responsible for entering data often receive information too late or only unofficially. In the latter case, they usually cannot make any data changes (e.g., because the employee representatives have not yet given authorization), although the new situation is effectively already in place.

This is essentially an organizational problem. There are different methods for improving information flow. In practice, sticking to official information and up-to-date maintenance often improves discipline if Organizational Management is broadly implemented and applied decentrally. If managers themselves receive incorrect evaluations online, if the organizational chart is incorrect on the Internet, or if cost centers are debited with personnel costs that are too high, then the communication process between the affected parties often changes quickly. It is important that these "educational measures" have the backing of top management. This should not be a problem if you can calculate the very high process costs due to insufficient communication.

12.3.2 Quality Assurance in Recruitment

In recruitment, you often have to deal with very poor data quality. This is because the only data that is entered carefully is the data required for processing day-to-day activities. To process an immediate rejection, for example, you do not necessarily require data such as "date of birth," "nationality," or assignment to a publication. This only becomes a problem if you need to evaluate this data later on.

For this reason you must be clear about the evaluation requirements from the very beginning and make sure that users are aware of the importance of the additional data. Recruitment is often implemented as part of R/3 due to its evaluation options, and it replaces the sort of application management that merely consisted of processing correspondence with applicants within Microsoft Office applications. The changeover often therefore means that significantly more data needs to be maintained. You should factor in the fact that this also impacts processing time. In no other process are such simple rules as the following so often misunderstood:

- "You can only evaluate data that you have entered into the system."

- "You cannot wait until the end of the year to retroactively define the data that you want to enter."

- "Standard software only has a limited stock of standard evaluations (in R/3 recruitment, this stock is unfortunately very restricted indeed). Evaluations that you will need regularly should be defined early. More complex ad-hoc evaluations create a high one-time workload."

- "The system is not aware of processes that take place outside the system (handing over a paper file or sending a letter) unless you enter these processes in a previously defined manner."

If you feel it is not necessary to formulate these statements, you should count yourself lucky. Otherwise, you should prepare to treat them as company policy.

The following are some of our tips on quality in recruitment:

- There are often communication problems between representatives in application management and personnel administration. This leads to the creation of new HR masters based on the file without reference to the applicant. On an organizational level, you should ensure that the file always contains the applicant number and that HR masters are only created in exceptional circumstances without transferring the applicant.

- The list of incomplete planned processes needs to be checked regularly. By correctly configuring process controls in Customizing, you also can use this list to prevent applicant documents from being mislaid.

- The PACTV feature, with its subfeatures and the action types, activity types, and text documents that it refers to, control the core of the application-management process. These relationships should be clearly documented.

12.3.3 Quality Assurance in Personnel Administration

Personnel administration suffers from similar problems to those of Organizational Management. Because HR master data forms the basis for many other processes, quality problems here often have wide-ranging consequences.

Along with documentation and training, plausibility checks and sensible default values lead to an improvement in data quality. The following sections describe various options.

Plausibility Check via Customizing

For a great many infotypes, plausibility checks can be defined in Customizing. For example, consider the permissibility of wage types for employee groups and subgroups, as well as for personnel areas and sub-areas. This is controlled via View V_511_B. Figure 12.6 displays an example in which wage type 8102 is only permitted for employees in employee Subgrouping 6 and personnel sub-areas in Groupings 1 to 4. It is also permitted with a warning message for employee subgroups in Grouping 5. The groupings used are those for primary wage types. For employee subgroups, for example, this is maintained in view V_503_ALL. For personnel sub-areas, it is maintained in View V_001P_ALL.

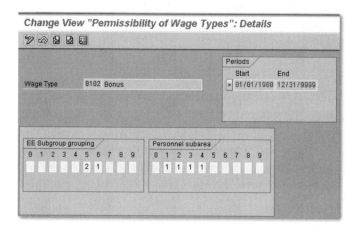

Figure 12.6 V_511_B: Permissibility of Wage Types

Similar checks that are often also controlled via groupings are also provided for the following:

▶ Wage types per infotype

▶ Work schedule rules

▶ Attendance types and absence types

Other checks also can be based purely on the permissibility of keys, such as

▶ Minimum and maximum amount of a wage type (e.g., in Infotype 0015 "Additional Payments and Deductions") via View V_511

▶ Minimum and maximum duration of attendances via View V_554S_B

These options are often used only to a very limited extent, either because not enough time is spent during the planning stage, or because users do not want to "break" anything. When a change is made, these settings are very easy to adjust.

Plausibility Checks via Programming

Customizing options are not always sufficient. Companies often need company-specific checks. This can be done with very little additional labor. You can use the function module exits for SAP enhancement PBAS0001 to store almost any number of checks (see Section 4.2.4). From Release 4.7, BAdi (Business Add-In) HRPAD00INFTY is also available (see Section 4.2.4).

"Emergency Brake" in Remuneration Payroll

In some cases, we recommend the use of the "emergency brake" concept. This means that certain configurations can be intercepted in remuneration payroll to trigger a termination. In many cases (e.g., missing tax data), this is already part of standard functionality. In other cases, these checks still have some gaps in the standard version. Also, software publishers cannot always plan for company-specific configurations. Users may then be unaware that they are making incorrect entries, a situation that leads to unwanted results in remuneration payroll or in evaluations. These errors may take a long time to uncover.

This concept mainly offers a way of finding missing infotypes. Because the checks listed above only work on the basis of the data in an infotype, they cannot be applied if the corresponding infotype has not even been created.

To avoid missing infotypes from the very beginning, you should configure Customizing for the optimum use of personnel actions and dynamic actions.

12.3.4 Quality Assurance in Time Management

Most of the information on plausibility checks in personnel administration also applies to time management. As well as the individual infotypes, you should also configure TMW (see Chapter 8, *Time Management*) for optimum performance with plausibility checks.

Test Procedures

A specific problem when maintaining data for time management is caused by intended or unintended changes that reach too far back into the past. This can be restricted by limiting retroactive accounting relevance. There are often situations where it should be possible to make corrections that extend one or two years into the past, but not every time-management representative should have the authorization to make such corrections.

This can be reflected using Infotype "Test Procedures" (0130). You can also use it outside of time management, but this is an area where it is frequently used. To configure this in Customizing, go to: **Personnel Management · Personnel Administration · Tools · Authorization Management · Test Procedures**. You can define one or more test procedures here. You then assign a number of infotypes and subtypes to each test procedure (see Figure 12.7).

For each test procedure defined in this way (= number of infotypes or subtypes), you can now define the point in the past to which data can be changed retroactively. In this way, every test procedure represents a subtype of Infotype 0130. Figure 12.8 shows that data in test procedure "T1" for personnel number 10270 can only be changed retroactively up to February 1, 2005.

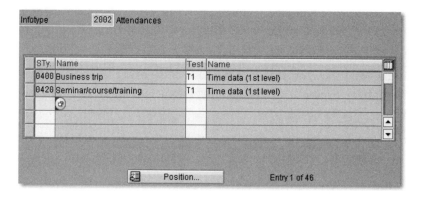

Figure 12.7 Assigning Subtypes to a Test Procedure

In this context, the term "released by" often causes confusion. It means that the data is checked up to this point in time and is released as correct, and therefore no more changes are allowed. Because no individual data-checking and maintenance are required for Infotype 0130, it is generally maintained automatically via a program. The following exception applies: Users who have maintenance authorization for the corresponding subtype of Infotype 0130 can also maintain the corresponding data in the past.

Pers. No.	10270		Pers.Assgn	00010270 Manager of Marketing A... ▤
Name	Mr. Henry Miller	SSN	145-99-9855	
EE group	1 Active	Pers.area	300 Corporate - United States	
EE subgroup	U4 Salaried staff	Cost Center	3200 Marketing	
Start	01/01/1800 To	12/31/9999		

Test Procedures

Test for	T1 Time data (1st level)		
Released by	01/31/2005		
Tested by	IPROCON	Tested on	04/12/2005
Tested using	MP013000	Tested at	14:42:28

Figure 12.8 Infotype 0130: Test Procedure

Automating Tests

Depending on the company, very complicated rules can underlie the time evaluation process. It is also very difficult to configure Customizing via schemas and rules. This makes testing very important and particularly difficult. A serious problem is created by the fact that when a particular rule is changed (or a specific error is corrected)—although the directly affected areas are tested—there are often unexpected consequences in completely different areas. It is not possible, however, to test the entire test database on every occasion.

This problem can be solved by partially automating the test. Tools are available on the market that compare the results of copied personnel numbers with those of the original in the production system. In many projects, it has proved worthwhile to set up successive, comprehensive test datasets (see Section 12.2.4) that are tested automatically at every change.

To do this, you need a program that stores reference results for all test cases. These reference results only need to be checked and declared correct once. Then, every time a change is made, the program can determine where the new results differ from the reference results. This kind of program is called a test workbench. Figure 12.9 illustrates the quality-assurance process when using a test workbench and a copy tool.

Automatic test workbench

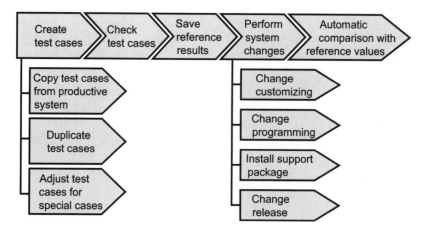

Figure 12.9 QA Process with Test Workbench and Copy Tool

We will use a specific example to demonstrate how this works. Figure 12.10 displays the selection screen for a simple test workbench that we (the authors) use in time management. It is possible to select the personnel numbers and the periods to be tested. It is also possible to restrict the test to specific time types and time-wage types. The tool in the example does not compare quota types. If these are not reflected in time types, then they must also be included. The most important selection option is the indicator **Update with new results**. This saves the current results as the new reference results. This is necessary, for example, if you want to include new test cases (new personnel numbers or new periods), or if a new rule means that a changed result is actually the correct version (e.g., a change to the flextime upper limit).

The result returned by the test workbench consists of the personnel numbers for which a difference compared to the reference result has been identified. Figure 12.11 displays a difference of three hours in several time types and three time-wage types for a personnel number. You must now check whether there is really an error in Customizing, or whether the change was deliberate. It is also possible that the test case data was changed. This should be avoided wherever possible, however.

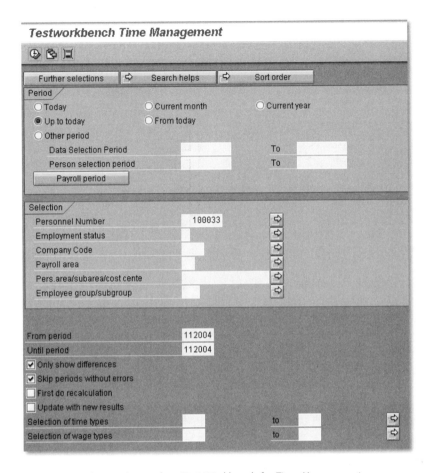

Testworkbench Time Management

| Further selections | ⇨ | Search helps | ⇨ | Sort order |

Period

- ◯ Today ◯ Current month ◯ Current year
- ◉ Up to today ◯ From today
- ◯ Other period
    - Data Selection Period [   ] To [   ]
    - Person selection period [   ] To [   ]
    - [Payroll period]

Selection

Personnel Number	100033	⇨
Employment status		⇨
Company Code		⇨
Payroll area		⇨
Pers.area/subarea/cost cente		⇨
Employee group/subgroup		⇨

| From period | 112004 |
| Until period | 112004 |

- ☑ Only show differences
- ☑ Skip periods without errors
- ☐ First do recalculation
- ☐ Update with new results

| Selection of time types | | to | | ⇨ |
| Selection of wage types | | to | | ⇨ |

Figure 12.10 Selection Screen for a Test Workbench for Time Management

It is still possible to make the automated test help even more comprehensive and easy-to-use, depending on the individual company requirements. The "basic model" presented here significantly improves quality and can be used in the following activities:

▶ Error-correction

▶ Customizing change due to new regulations

▶ Importing support packages

▶ Release change

```
Testworkbench Time Management

Recalculation done.


Personnel number: 00100033 Period: 11  / 2004

Time types
    0002                         178,00     178,00      0,00
    0003                          89,00      86,00      3,00-
    0005                          15,00-     15,00-      0,00
    0006                          89,00-     92,00-      3,00-
    0008                          15,00-     15,00-      0,00
    0020                          18,00      18,00       0,00
    0050                         249,00     252,00       3,00
    0051                       1.746,00   1.749,00       3,00
    0095                           0,00       0,00       0,00
    0097                           0,00       0,00       0,00
    0098                           0,00       0,00       0,00
    0099                           0,00       0,00       0,00
    0120                          18,00      18,00       0,00
    0130                          71,00      68,00       3,00-
    0600                          18,00      18,00       0,00
    1200                           0,00       0,00       0,00
    1301                           0,00       0,00       0,00
    1500                           0,00       0,00       0,00
    1501                           0,00       0,00       0,00
    ZD00                           0,00       0,00       0,00
    ZD12                           0,00       0,00       0,00
    ZD50                           0,00       0,00       0,00


Wage types
    1200                          71,00      68,00       3,00-
    1205                          89,00      92,00       3,00
    1206                          89,00      92,00       3,00
    1212                          54,00      54,00       0,00
    1250                          18,00      18,00       0,00
    /801 Partial period factor 1  18,00      18,00       0,00

Personnel number: 00100033 Period: 11  / 2004 Differences exist
```

Figure 12.11 List of Differences from the Test Workbench

12.3.5 Quality Assurance in Remuneration Payroll

The testing problems for remuneration payroll are the same as those for time management. They just seem more serious, due to the greater complexity of Customizing in this area.

For this reason, a Test Workbench would also be the ideal solution here. The methodology is the same as for time management, except that you do not need to worry about where you store the reference results. Because the results of remuneration payroll use version management, you can use this during implementation. Figure 12.12 provides an overview.

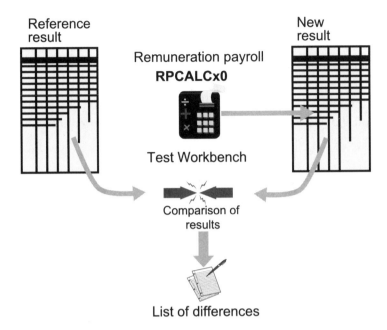

Figure 12.12 Using a Test Workbench

12.3.6 Quality Assurance in Personnel Controlling

The quality of personnel controlling mainly depends on the quality of the upstream processes. The evaluation is only useful if these processes can guarantee data that is up-to-date and of good quality.[4]

Here are a few tips on improving quality within personnel controlling:

▶ If reports (paper or online) are provided decentrally, then it is important to ensure that recipients can also interpret the data. Too much HR background knowledge is often required.

▶ If reports are being compared, it is important to know how those reports were generated. This often is not the case when decentralized users are using flexible evaluation options. Users will often, for example, try to compare a staffing report that has been developed based on headcount with one based on fulltime capacity. In this case, it is helpful if you add a selection log to printed reports. This displays exactly what has been included in the report and which parameters were set.

---

4 Frustrated controlling professionals responsible for reporting based on poor data quality coined the expression: "Shit in, shit out."

- ▶ Using the simplest possible report call with the fewest possible influencing factors will also make it easier to compare with other reports. You can achieve this using the MDT, for example, which includes reports with fixed variants.

- ▶ When creating SAP Queries or Ad-hoc Queries, it is very important to make the infosets user-friendly and easy to understand. This means that you should remove unnecessary fields and possibly replace standard texts with more meaningful terms.

12.4 Critical Success Factors

Quality assurance in itself is a critical success factor for an HR project. It should, however, be based on a clear concept and not simply be implemented for its own sake. Projects can also be needlessly stifled in the name of quality assurance.

13 Role-Based Portal Solution

With its Enterprise release of R/3, SAP delivered a completely new system for the underlying technical framework of what is known as the "Basis." When it was introduced, SAP's Web Application Server brought to the market a cross-system technology with open interfaces. Now, with the help of SAP NetWeaver, this concept has been continued and intensively extended in mySAP ERP. The interface that makes it possible to integrate heterogeneous systems in a mySAP ERP enterprise landscape is the mySAP Enterprise Portal.

The first part of this chapter deals with classic self-service scenarios such as *Employee Self Services* (ESS) and the *Manager's Desktop* (MDT), whose technology is based on the *Internet Transaction Server (ITS)* and on pure R/3 or ECC, and which are still quite relevant in the practical sense. The second part deals with the new developments in R/3 Enterprise, especially the *mySAP Enterprise Portal* and the self-services within the portal.

Because the role concept is an essential, cross-process element of the portal solution and the *R/3 Enterprise Core System*, the first part of this chapter focuses on the relevant roles.

13.1 Roles in mySAP HR

With its role concept, SAP is distancing itself from its previous focus on technical entities and structures. Instead, everything is now oriented towards the user and his or her daily tasks. Roles can be tailored to one specific user group and enable users to work efficiently, particularly inexperienced users, who usually use only a small set of functionalities.

13.1.1 General Remarks

The sheer scope of the functions provided by SAP's HR processes is considerable, and the inexperienced user is sure to feel overwhelmed. Added to this is the fact that, from the user's viewpoint, it often takes too many mouse-clicks to get to the required functionalities. Re-focusing the concept of the system on user roles represents a clear improvement in terms of efficiency and user acceptance.

There are two kinds of roles:

▶ In R/3 or the ECC, roles are simple collections of transactions and the associated authorizations for a user group.

▶ In the portal, SAP is increasingly providing "portal roles." Besides the functions mentioned above, these come with an interface specially tailored to the user group in question.

In this section, we shall concentrate on the first kind.

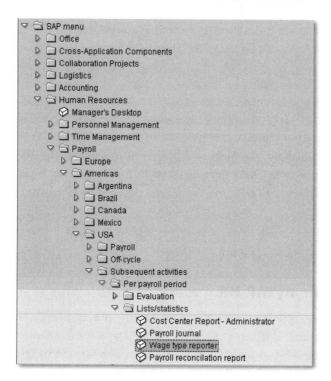

Figure 13.1 Access Without a Role Menu is Awkward

The fact that roles combine the Easy Access menu and authorizations provides the user with wonderfully useful options that he or she should not neglect to use. The Payroll menu and its benefits deserve particular mention. Imagine that staff in the payroll department of an American enterprise, for example, need only the payroll simulation, the remuneration statement, and some reports. Figure 13.1 shows the menu path to the report **"Wage type reporter"** (that is, how the function is accessed without the use of the role concept). A suitably designed role, on the other hand, makes accessing this function much easier, as shown in Figure 13.2.

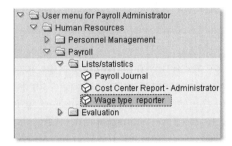

Figure 13.2 Access via a User-Specific Role is Efficient and Straightforward

The orientation of R/3 around user roles does not stop at role-specific menus. More and more applications within the system can be tailored to the individual user. In fact, this was already the case in older releases for the examples of actions and infotype menus given in Chapter 4, *Personnel Administration*. User-specific elements were further extended in release 4.6C and beyond. Also, various scenarios bundle together the typical functionalities of specific roles in one interface. A time administrator, for example, has an interface that is specially tailored to his requirements and enables him to perform exactly the activities he needs to perform in his daily work. The MDT provides similar functions for managers who require information about their team members.

The mySAP Workplace went even further than this by not restricting roles to the functionalities of an R/3 system. It is a role-specific portal that provides the user with access to multiple systems and applications. These can be different R/3 systems, or other applications or websites. Since then, the Enterprise Portal has replaced the Workplace.

SAP's original strategy of providing ESS only in conjunction with the mySAP Workplace in Release 4.6C was not successful, and so an interim solution was decided upon: ESS would be made available in Release 4.6C as an ITS-based solution and did not necessarily require the Workplace. The technical aspects of this solution are described in SAPNet and OSS in Note 321439. Project experience shows that this solution works in reality.

Because of the high levels of investment that implementing the Enterprise Portal requires, the ESS applications of most customers were still based on the "old" technology, even after the Portal became available. SAP will continue to support the older technology; but the new ESS scenarios it provides as standard are designed to work in the Enterprise Portal and may have only limited functionality without it.

13.1.2 Selected Roles in mySAP HR

Time Administrator

Time Manager's Workplace

The Time Manager's Workplace provides Time Administrators or persons who are responsible for central time management with functions similar to those that the employee area of the MDT provides to managers. It is accessed via the path **Human Resources · Time Management · Adminis-tration · Time Manager's Workplace** For detailed information on the Time Manager's Workplace, see Chapter 8, *Time Management*.

Employees in ESS

Employee Self Service

ESS provides very useful functions that improve the efficiency and quality of HR management. Simply put, it allows employees to display and maintain their own personal data. It can also generate reports that go beyond the data of the individual employee (for example, the "Who's Who" employee directory described in Chapter 4, *Personnel Administration*). ESS is described in detail below.

Managers

Manager's Desktop

In many enterprises, when managers need information about their employees, this is often still provided to them in paper form. Electronic lists created using any of the Office products are not much better, because—like paper lists—they are up-to-date only to the time of creation and do not allow for any interactivity (for example, a manager may have an overview list but may want to see detailed information for one particular item in the list).

However, many managers find it too time-consuming to access the information directly in the human resources information system that is used in their enterprise. This may be because the various pieces of information are stored in any number of different locations, and besides HR data, the manager may also require access to workflow data or cost center data.

The MDT in mySAP HR is designed to address exactly these needs. Using Organizational Management data, the system "knows" which employees are assigned to which manager. The tasks that each manager can perform in the system are set in Customizing.

13.2 mySAP Employee Self Service

The requirements of today's enterprises and employees are the best arguments for using ESS. What employees today require of a modern human resources management department is that their own data is guaranteed to be transparent to themselves, that their data is always up-to-date (for example, a change of address or new bank account number is immediately reflected in the system), that the human resources department is structured as a services department, and that they get more overall control and responsibility.

Enterprises have similar requirements, and also want HR departments to work in a more service-oriented manner, to align their work to the enterprise strategies, and to concentrate on these goals. Enterprises also require that the costs of operating HR processes be reduced.

ESS puts employees in the position where they have responsibility for keeping their own data up-to-date. The human resources department gets involved only if the employee needs assistance. This approach relieves the HR department of the associated administrative tasks, leaving staff there free to concentrate on their consulting tasks and core processes.

Sole responsibility for data maintenance

Besides fulfilling employees' and enterprises' requirements, Employee Self Services also have the following advantages.

▶ Data is up-to-date

▶ Long wait times are a thing of the past

▶ The HR department is relieved of routine administrative work

▶ There is more scope for qualitative HR work

▶ Administrative costs are reduced

▶ HR work is decentralized

What each employee has access to in ESS—that is, the range of data for which an employee can maintain or display—is specified by means of the ESS menu. This menu contains various categories that can contain multiple services.

By default, ESS functions from the following areas are available:

▶ Benefits

▶ Appraisals

▶ SAP Office (for example, e-mail inbox)

▶ Display/maintenance of employee's own master data

- ► Payroll (for example, remuneration statement)

- ► Time management (for example, time Statement, time posting)

- ► Seminars (for example, display catalog, booking)

- ► Recruitment (for example, internal applications)

- ► Travel management (for example, recording business trips or travel requests)

- ► Skills management (for example, maintaining employee's own qualifications)

The ESS is structured into two main parts: the ITS installation and its incorporation into the existing system structure; and the Customizing settings in R/3, which control the services provided via the ITS.

As a rule, because of the many dependencies, especially in the existing IT structure (network, Web browsers, Web servers, operating system, R/3 system), and the continuing high rate of change in this area, the ITS should be installed and maintained only with the support of an expert.

> **Note** The new self-service scenarios in the Enterprise Portal for mySAP ERP 2005 are not based on the ITS. Instead, they use Web Dynpro technology for Java and are optimized for use in the portal. It is also possible to use them using the architecture described above, but some functions, such as the navigation bar, are not available in this case.

13.2.1 The Internet Transaction Server (ITS)

Prerequisites   The ITS performs the necessary "translation" services between the R/3 systems and Web access. For a company to use the classic ESS, it needs a separate server (typically with Windows NT installed), on which the ITS software can be installed. The ITS then provides the Web interface for the Self Services and manages communication with R/3 (see Figure 13.3).

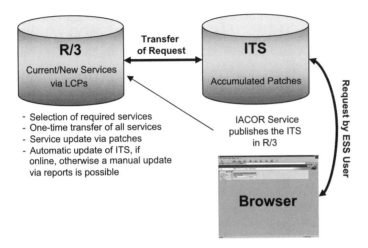

Figure 13.3 The ITS Concept

IACOR

Before the ITS is put into use, you should download the latest patches (*/general/its/patches/46DC3/NT/I386/setupits_7.exe* from sapserv3). SAP provides updates for the self-services on an ongoing basis in the form of Support Packages. Because the changes from support packages are always stored exclusively in R/3, there is a constant process of exchange between R/3 and the ITS. The IACOR service on the ITS side makes the ITS known to R/3, and the ITS can thus be automatically updated by publishing the services. So the R/3's Change and Transport System can be used too (see Figure 13.3). This is advantageous when, for example, new patches that contain updates of ITS services have to be imported into R/3. Note that the ITS should be online when the patches are imported, as otherwise the update process cannot work. However, if necessary, you can also manually update the ITS using report W3_PUBLISH_ALL_SERVICES.

With a normal system structure—one that contains at least one development or test system as well as the live system, possibly a quality assurance system, and an extra test ITS—it does not always make sense to copy the services to all ITS servers or instances at the same time. The R/3 test system should be connected to the test ITS, and the latter should be equipped with the latest new services. Just as the service settings are transported from the test system to the live R/3 system, the updated settings are transported from there to the live ITS system (this happens automatically via the IACOR service). It is thus sufficient to make the service settings in the test system and then to transport them.

Before you put the ITS into operation, you need to select the self-services you require in R/3 and transfer them to the ITS. For this to be possible, the ITS first has to be made known to the R/3 system. To do this, use the SAP menu to choose **Tools · ABAP Workbench · Overview · Object Navigator**. Then, on the **ITS · Publish** tab page under **Utilities · Settings**, select the server or **On all defined sites** (see Figure 13.4).

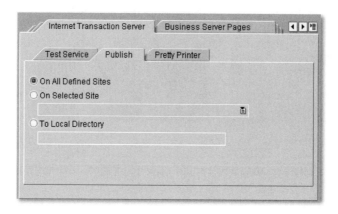

Figure 13.4 Connecting the ITS

Because the Web interface is administrated and maintained solely in R/3, you have to transfer the customized services to the ITS (you only need to do this once). If the server is known to the R/3 system, you can start the program W3_PUBLISH_ALL_SERVICES, which ensures that all services are transferred to the ITS.

Also, in R/3, you need to deactivate all service categories that are no longer required (see Figure 13.5). You do this using the view V_T77WWW_CDE (transaction SM31) under PZM3, and by selecting the **Deactivate** field.

ESS menu	Text	ServCat	Text	M...	Deact
PZM3	ESS	APPR	Appraisals	20	☑
PZM3	ESS	BENE	Benefits	9	☑
PZM3	ESS	OFFI	Office	1	☐
PZM3	ESS	PAY	Payment	13	☐
PZM3	ESS	PERS	Personal Information	15	☑
PZM3	ESS	QUAL	Skills	19	☐
PZM3	ESS	RECM	Jobs	11	☑
PZM3	ESS	TIME	Working Time	3	☐
PZM3	ESS	TRAV	Business Trips	5	☐
PZM3	ESS	VMAN	Training	17	☐

Change View "ESS Deactivate Catalog and Change Menu Item

Figure 13.5 Deactivating the Service Categories

Service categories are groups of self-services that are displayed when a user first opens the ESS. Figure 13.6 shows the ESS initial screen that opens when you select the service categories TIME (Working Time), TRAV (Business Trips), PAY (Payment), VMAN (Training), QUAL (Skills) and OFFI (Office).

Service categories

In addition to the service categories, you also have to select services for each category. You do this using the view V_T77WWW_SDE (see Figure 13.7).

Services

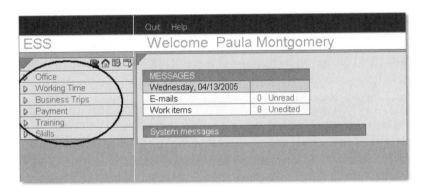

Figure 13.6 Service Categories in ESS

ServCat	Text	Service	Name of service	C...	Deact
TIME	Working Time	4	Display Time Statement	70	☐
TIME	Working Time	8	Display Work Schedule	60	☐
TIME	Working Time	9	Display Leave Information	50	☐
TIME	Working Time	21	Create Leave Request	20	☐
TIME	Working Time	23	Leave Request	30	☐
TIME	Working Time	33	Leave Requests - Overvi...	40	☐
TIME	Working Time	40	Record Working Time	10	☐
TRAV	Business Trips	68	Travel Management	10	☐
TRAV	Business Trips	114	Travel Manager	20	☐
TRAV	Business Trips	995	Exchange Rates	12	☐
TRAV	Business Trips	996	Travel Weather	11	☐
TRAV	Business Trips	998	Route Planning	5	☐
VMAN	Training	62	Training Center	10	☐
VMAN	Training	63	My Bookings	20	☐

Change View "ESS Deactivate Service and Change Catalog Item

Figure 13.7 Deactivating the Services

Services are actions that can be carried out in the ESS; for example, in the TIME service category (Time Management) of service number 4 (Time Statement). Figure 13.8 shows that the services are located under the service category.

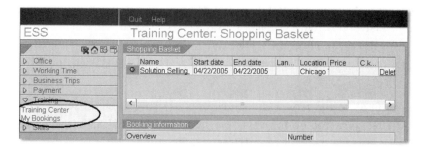

Figure 13.8 Services in ESS

Now, with these settings, you can already use the services in their standard form. However, in practice, requirements can very well arise that make it necessary to adapt the services, to extend the services, or even to create new services, as we shall explain below.

Customer-specific services can be created on the basis of different technologies. The simplest of these is the Web GUI functionality of the ITS, which makes it possible to display normal transactions in the Web browser. In this functionality, the ITS translates the R/3 data on the fly.

Note that the look and feel of these interfaces are not quite what the user of Web applications is used to. Therefore, it makes sense to invest a little more in designing the interface and to use the flow-logic technology. With this technology, an interface is created mainly in HTML and communicates with the backend system via a specially programmed function module.

13.2.2 ESS Time Management

Navigation in the ESS
This section presents some self-services, requirements, and points to note from the real-world experience of working with solutions in this area. However, let us first make an observation about navigating in ESS. The user navigates back and forth between the individual ESS areas using the service categories and services in the left-hand part of the browser (see Figure 13.8). Above the services are buttons that enable the user to cancel actions and return to the initial screen of the ESS. Users should navigate in the ESS using these buttons, rather than use the browser functions. This is because if a user uses the **Back** button in his browser, for example, synchronization may sometimes be lost. This has the result that incorrect data may be displayed, such as data from the last time the user used this screen. You can solve this problem by using additional JavaScript code to hide the **Back** button when the ESS is called.

Self-Service Time Management: Error List

Again, it may be necessary in some parts of the ESS to extend the services or to define new services. The process of defining new services, in particular, provides many options, two examples being design of new user-interfaces or inclusion of specially generated reports.

The process illustrated in Figure 13.9 shows a customer-specific example. **Process example** We have purposely not selected a standard example here, as SAP already provides many standard examples on the Internet in the form of live demos. Here, we want to show that enterprise-specific solutions that go beyond the standard can be created without an excessive amount of development work. However, we do still recommend that you use the comprehensive standard scenarios as much as possible.

We selected the Web GUI as the technology for this example, which allowed us to minimize the effort required for the implementation. It is easy to tell that we used the Web GUI, as the interfaces look almost the same as the normal R/3 interface that is called via the GUI for Windows.

The time management process shown above has to do with checking and correcting time management errors, a task that makes up a large part of the daily work of Time Administrators. Chapter 8, *Time Management*, describes how to do this without ESS. As a rule, the biggest part of this job is identifying the causes of the errors (such as a forgotten clock-out entry) and finding out the correct data (telephoning or e-mailing the employee in question to find out the correct clock-out time). The ESS scenario we have described allows the employee to do the following:

▶ Display and print his time statement via the Web browser (using a standard service)

▶ Get a detailed view of the errors that are relevant to him (see Figures 13.10 and 13.11 to see how standard error handling is adapted to and integrated into ESS)

▶ Send a correction message to the responsible Time Administrator (see Figure 13.12 to see how a customer-specific report is integrated into ESS)

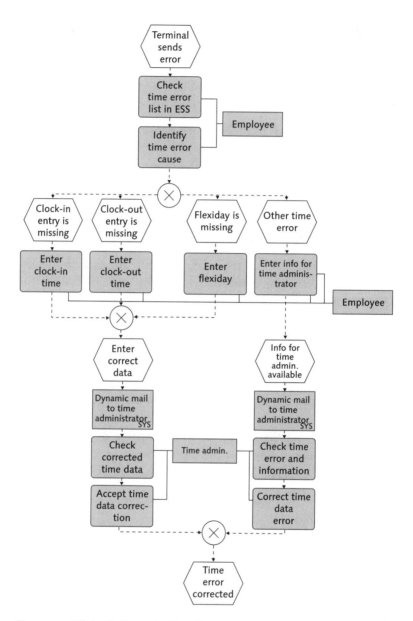

Figure 13.9 Efficiently Correcting Time Data in ESS

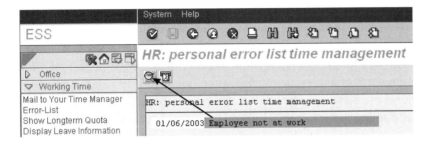

Figure 13.10 Employee's Time Errors in ESS

Because the employee is also notified of the existence of error messages at the time clock at which he enters his time data, he can also be instructed via this channel to make the corrections in ESS. Alternatively, a system for sending automatically generated e-mails (in MS Outlook or Lotus Notes, for example) can be set up to notify employees of time-management errors. This also involves customer-specific programming, but the amount of work required to implement a simple solution is reasonable (one to two days, for example).

The employee obtains the required information from the error-handling screen and maybe from the time statement, and he can then create the correction message. The interface should be programmed in an enterprise-specific way, so that the most common causes of error are already displayed and need only be checked when they occur (see Figure 13.12).

The employee selects the details for the error message to see more information about the day in question. In the example in Figure 13.10, the employee was obviously absent on a work day.

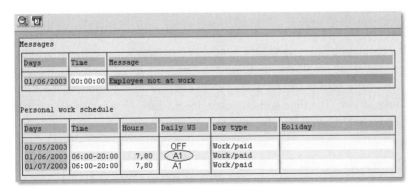

Figure 13.11 Details on a Time Management Error

The detailed view provides more detail on the case in question (see Figure 13.11). The lower part of the screen contains the **Personal Work Schedule**, which shows that the day in question is marked as a "Work" day. The employee can now use a special entry screen to contact the Time Administrator and explain the situation (see Figure 13.12). This screen is not contained in the standard; it was specially programmed in accordance with project-specific requirements.

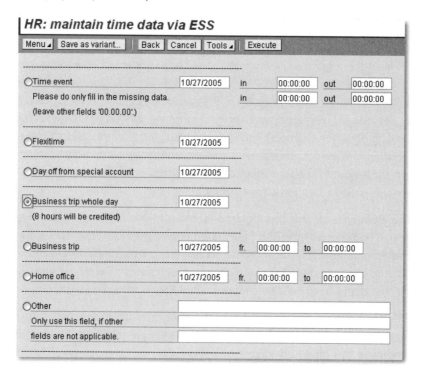

Figure 13.12 Contacting the Time Administrator

The employee can now tell the time administrator why he was absent on this day. If the employee has forgotten a posting, he can enter the missing time in the screen shown above and send this information to the time administrator. The time administrator, for his part, receives an executable mail in R/3, from which he can open a newly created transaction. This transaction provides the time administrator with an interface that he can use to check the correction in the mail (it allows him to go to the error list, the time statement, and the master data). Once checking is complete, the time administrator simply presses a button to activate the master data changes as specified in the mail. As soon as the time administrator corrects the error, the error message disappears from the employee's error list.

The error list (see Figure 13.10) is not a standard service; it was created along with a new service. The new service was defined in the relevant Customizing table (View T77WWW_SRV). The service number, the service type "S" (ITS server), and the associated transaction are also specified here. The transaction for the error list was newly created and linked with an ABAP/4 program, which was specially programmed for this purpose. The Web GUI was also activated for this transaction.

Note that in Web GUI transactions the input field for the transactions (OK code field) is shown by default. If you do not want this, you can hide it by entering *~noheaderokcode 1* in the *global.srvc* file on the ITS.

The error list functionalities thus enable employees to identify any time management errors they make (such as forgotten postings or missing leave requests) directly in the system and to send correction messages to the HR department via a straightforward procedure. This process is thus standardized and speeded up.

Self Service Time Management: time statement

The time statement is the second aspect of time management that we want to present here. The time statement as described here is a standard service, but with some customized aspects. To ensure that the time statement can be displayed correctly, the error list for the time period to be analyzed must be free of errors.

Customized standard service

Normally, the time evaluations, which create the time statements, are started in R/3 at regular intervals. Any additional events, such as the entering of absences, can be seen on the time statement only *after* the time evaluation has been processed. The standard time statement service reads the results of the most recently created time evaluation and forwards them to the ITS, whether or not any changes were made in the system since the last time evaluation.

However, to ensure that the most up-to-date data is always displayed to the employee when the time statement is started from the ESS, we need to make a small adjustment to the SAPMESSREP program. This adjustment has the effect that when the time statement is called up from the ESS, the system checks whether any relevant changes have been made in the system. If such changes have been made, a new time evaluation is started before the time statement is displayed.

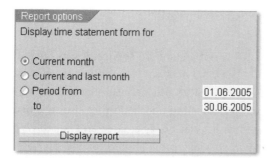

Figure 13.13 Selecting the Time Period for "Time Statement"

When the time statement service is called, the user enters the required evaluation period (see Figure 13.13). Once the user does this, the time statement is displayed in the browser and can be printed. If there is an error in the time data, the time statement is displayed only up to the day on which the error occurred.

13.2.3 ESS Remuneration Statement

Call time evaluation results

There is a standard service for displaying remuneration statements. This service allows employees to view their previous remuneration statements in the ESS. The employee can thus select the payroll results he requires from the list and view the relevant statement(s) (see Figure 13.14).

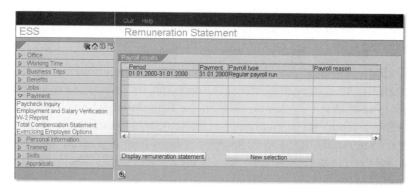

Figure 13.14 Calling Payroll Results

The remuneration statement can be displayed in HTML format or as a PDF document. We recommend that you use the PDF format, as this will be used more and more widely in SAP in the future (onward from mySAP ERP 2005).

In enterprises where not all employees have access to the ESS, and thus some employees cannot print out their remuneration statements themselves, it will still be necessary to print, send, or otherwise distribute these statements. There is a new HR infotype that prevents remuneration statements from being printed and sent for employees who have access to their remuneration statements via ESS. This is infotype 0655 (see Figure 13.15).

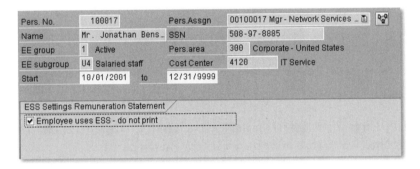

Figure 13.15 Infotype 0655, ESS Settings Remuneration Statement

13.2.4 ESS Personnel Administration

Personnel Administration (management of HR master data) is typical usage area for ESS. Providing employees with the facility to change their own address or bank details in the system relieves HR staff of these tasks, which can be very time-consuming, depending on the size of the enterprise.

Classic usage areas

The HR Employee Self-Services are as follows:

▶ Personal data (name, religion, family status, and so on)

▶ Address

▶ Bank details

▶ Next of kin/contact person (data of spouse or children)

▶ Previous employers

Figure 13.16 shows a customer-specific service developed on the basis of flow logic. It enables the ESS user to check and, if necessary, to change his own personal data. For example, the data entered in the system for birth name, place of birth, and country of birth is often inconsistent or incomplete. Allowing the employee himself to modify this data, if necessary, reduces the administrative work involved, should this data ever be required.

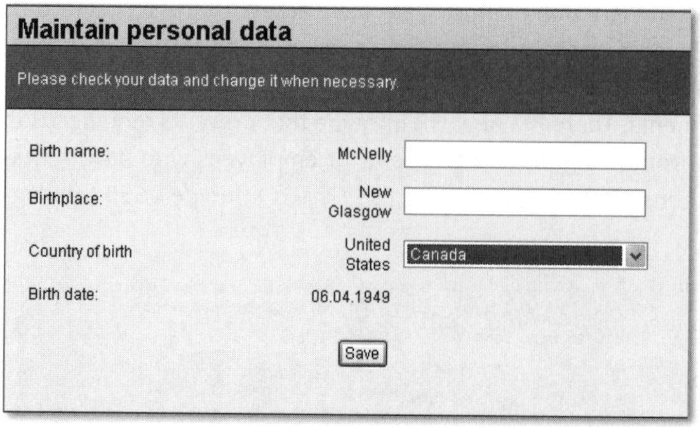

Figure 13.16 Customer-Specific Service on the Basis of Flow Logic

These kinds of services can be implemented with so little extra effort that it is often worthwhile using them even for one-off purposes.

As is clear from what we have already discussed, Employee Self-Services are also a good way to decentralize administrative work. At the same time, employees get more control over their own data.

For managers in an enterprise who also use self-services, there is another interface that provides all the data that a manager may need for his daily tasks and for employee management, monitoring budgets, and making decisions: the Manager's Desktop.

13.3 mySAP Manager's Desktop

Administrative and strategic tasks

MDT was inspired by managers' need for an easy-to-use tool that supports them in their daily administrative and strategic tasks. These tasks can be divided into the following areas:

▶ **Own employees**
Evaluations, approvals, employee appraisals, employee development

▶ **Organization**
Reports, organizational changes, and related items

▶ **Costs and budget**
Cost center information, headcount planning, budget management

▶ **Recruitment**
Evaluations, decisions, and related actions

▶ **Customer-specific functions**
Incorporating additional information and services

13.3.1 The User Interface

The MDT is divided into two main areas (see Figure 13.18). The left-hand Two main areas side contains the functions or theme categories that the manager can execute. The right-hand side contains the "objects" used to execute functions. For example, the HR administration area on the left contains the function for calling a list of all employees with anniversaries of years of service. An object is selected to perform the call; for example, an organizational unit or a person is selected on the right-hand side, and than assigned to the required function by Drag&Drop.

The main points in the initial screen and in the MDT—such as employee, organization, costs, and budget—are called theme categories. These categories are themselves divided into individual sub-categories, such as reports, education and training, employee appraisals, and personnel development (see Figure 13.17).

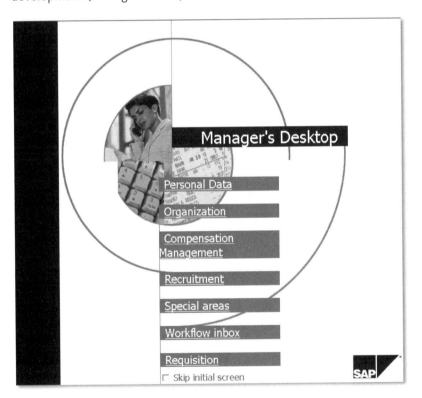

Figure 13.17 MDT Initial Screen

Figure 13.18 shows an example of very comprehensive functionalities for each of a manager's employees. The names of the employees are displayed in the right-hand side of the screen in accordance with the organizational structure. The left-hand side of the screen contains an Explorer bar with the functionalities that can be executed for each employee.

13.3.2 Adjustment Options

Besides adapting the design by selecting your own background image for the MDT initial screen, you can also make other adjustments in the Customizing settings by selecting the IMG path **Personnel Management · Manager's Desktop · Customer Adjustment · Define Scenario-Specific Settings**.

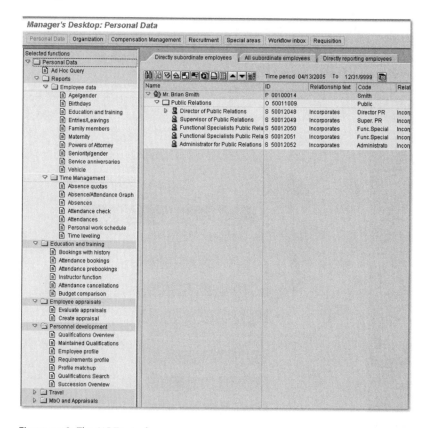

Figure 13.18 The MDT Interface

Scenarios

Making modifications "Scenario" is the term used to refer to all the applications that are available to the user within the Manager's Desktop. If you want to make modifications to standard scenarios, you should do so using the action "Define standard scenario," as modifications made in any other way may be

deleted when the system is updated (support package imports). However, we recommend that you copy a standard scenario rather than modify it, as this allows you to define all settings specifically for the scenario in
question.

Besides naming your scenario, one of the first things you have to do is
define its evaluation path. In the evaluation path, you specify how the
system will identify the employees that are subordinate to a particular
manager. By default, these are all the employees who belong either
directly or indirectly to the organizational unit that the manager is in
charge of (chief position). However, special relationships and evaluation
paths can easily be used to create a scenario that also gives an administrative assistant, for example, access to the MDT.

Define evaluation path

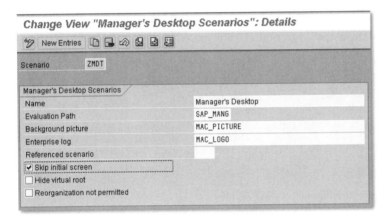

Figure 13.19 Define MDT Scenario

The initial screen of the MDT provides an overview of all the available categories. If, when you call up the MDT, you want to skip the initial screen
and go straight to the theme category and tab page that first appears in
Customizing (see Figure 13.19), check the **Skip initial screen** box.

The **Hide virtual root** option prevents the manager, as the root of the
organizational structure, from being displayed. This option is not activated in Figure 13.18, which is why the manager "Brian Smith" is shown
as the root of the "Personal Data" organizational units.

The **Reorganization not permitted** option (see Figure 13.19) enables the
user to specify that the manager who uses the MDT may not execute any
organizational changes by means of drag and drop inside his area of
responsibility. This also means that the "Reorganization" sub-category in
the function tree of the "Organization" topic category is no longer dis-

played. Last, the **Referenced scenario** field allows you to document which scenario was used as a template for the newly-created scenario. This also means that the new scenario automatically inherits all the entries of the referenced scenario from the tables T77MWBFCH (Scenario-specific settings), T77MWBD (views of organizational structure) and T77MWBK (views per category).

The scenario is now defined completely. The name of the scenario (ZMDT in the example) has to be entered in the user's user parameters (SAP menu: **System · User Profile · Own Data**). The user parameter is MWB_SCEN. Make absolutely sure that the scenario is entered in upper-case letters (see Figure 13.20).

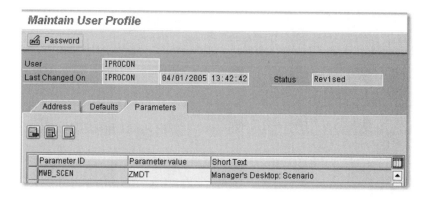

Figure 13.20 User Parameter MWB_SCEN

Views

Define views using the evaluation path

Once you have defined the scenario(s), you then have to specify the *Views*. You use an evaluation path (IMG: **Personnel Management · Manager's Desktop · Customer Adjustments · Determine Views of Organizational Structure**) to define which views will be used to determine the employee structure displayed in the MDT. Figure 13.21 shows, among other things, that the employee structure will contain the views "Directly subordinate employees," "All subordinate employees," and "Directly reporting employees." There is thus one tab page per defined view in the MDT. An evaluation path has to be specified for each of these views. Besides information about the evaluation path, the corresponding Customizing table (see Figure 13.21) also specifies the order of the tab pages. Alternatively, instead of specifying the start object in the evaluation path, you can specify a function module for identifying the start object in the **Start object function** field.

Scenario	Eval.path	Nu...	Evaluation path text	Seq...	Icon name	Column g...	Start object functi...	Start object ...
ZMDT	MDTDIREC	0	Directly reporting employees	3	ICON_EMPLOYEE	MDT_ORGS		
ZMDT	MDTSBES	0	Directly subordinate employees	1	ICON_EMPLOYEE	MDT_ORGS		
ZMDT	MDTSBESX	0	All subordinate employees	2	ICON_EMPLOYEE	MDT_ORGS		

Figure 13.21 Defining the Views of the Organizational Structure

You can use the IMG path **Personnel Management · Manager's Desktop · Customer Adjustments · Determine Views per Category** to make the views defined in the previous step available for each category (such as employee, organization, costs and budgets, and so on) in the organizational structure. You do this using the action "Composite Definition of views (evaluation paths)" (see Figure 13.22) and not the action "Determine views (evaluation paths) per category," as the latter entry is SAP specific and so will be overwritten when the next patch is imported.

Change View "Evaluation Paths for Each Category in Manager's Desktop

New Entries

Scenario	Function code	Eval.path	Num...
ZMDT	STANDARDFUNCTION	MDTDIREC	0
ZMDT	STANDARDFUNCTION	MDTSBES	0

Figure 13.22 Defining Views per Category

Note that only entries of categories in the **Function code** field with the function code type HOME have an effect in this table. Before you make any entries, use table T77MWBFCD (see Figure 13.23) to find out which function code has the type HOME. In our example, the function code STANDARDFUNCTION is used for employees. The definition of this function code specifies that only the views MDTDIREC (directly reporting employees) and MDTSBES (directly subordinate employees) are to be made available. Now that we have made these Customizing changes, if someone selects the theme category "Employees" in the MDT, he will see only two tab pages for the view of the organizational structure.

Display View "Function Codes for Manager's Desktop": Overview

Function code	Type	Org. ...	Obje...	Text	Function Module	
STANDARDFUNCTION	HOME	☐	☐	Personal Data		
STELLBESETZ	REPO	✓	☐	Staffing schedule		
STF_ASSIGN	REPO	✓	✓	Staff Assignments		

Figure 13.23 View of Table T77MWBFCD

Figure 13.24 summarizes the connection between the views of the organizational structure and the allocation of these views to theme categories.

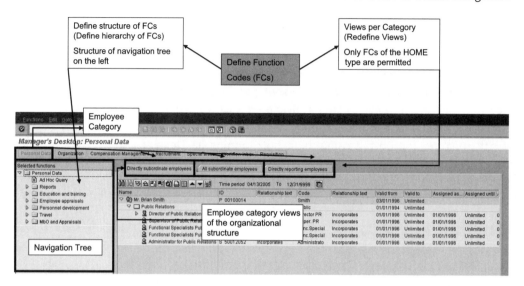

Figure 13.24 Connection Between Function Codes, Views, and Navigation Tree

Function codes

Type HOME   Function codes are objects that come in different types. Examples can be function codes of the type HOME representing root nodes or categories and function codes of the type REPO representing reports.

Let us concentrate initially on function codes of the type HOME, to which we have already assigned various views. If you want to define new function codes of this type, in order to be able to use them as categories, you have to do this before allocating them to the views. To open the Customizing for function codes (see figure 13.25), choose the following IMG path: **Personnel Management · Manager's Desktop · Enhancement of Function Codes**. Function codes of the type HOME are called categories.

An important consideration in creating function codes is the type, as this determines whether you are dealing with a node, a sub-node, report, or another executable object. The types HOME and NODE indicate nodes that are used to create the hierarchy. HOME is superordinate to the type NODE. Besides specifying the type of a function code, you can also specify whether the function is based on the organizational structure (as is usually the case) or whether it is executed in an object-specific manner, or both.

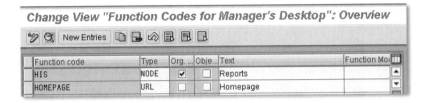

Function code	Type	Org. ...	Obje...	Text	Function Mo
HIS	NODE	☑	☐	Reports	
HOMEPAGE	URL	☐	☐	Homepage	

Figure 13.25 Table for Defining Function Codes

Set the "Organizational structure-based" flag for all function codes that are used with organization objects (including persons). If this flag is set for at least one executable node in a category, selecting the relevant button causes parts of the organizational structure to be displayed directly in the right-hand area of the screen. If, on the other hand, this flag is not set for any executable node, selecting the relevant theme category causes the first function to be started immediately. For example, this flag is set for the function code HIS, because the reports under this node are used for employee data and thus for organizational objects. If a theme category contains only URLs (that is, links to Internet or intranet sites); for example, calling this category causes the HTML page that is connected to the first URL to be displayed directly.

If, on the other hand, "object type specific" is set for a function code—something that is possible only for reports and function modules—then this report can be executed only on one level, for example the organizational unit level. If a function code is object-specific, you have to specify the object type for which the function can be executed. The path you use to do this is **Personnel Management · Manager's Desktop · Extend Function Codes · Define Object Type-Specific Function Codes**.

Extend function code structure

One more customizing option that we would like to show you at this point is the enhancement of the function-code structure. This option allows you, among other things, to integrate your own reports into the MDT. You can extend the hierarchy of the theme categories using the Customizing path **Personnel Management · Manager's Desktop · Extend Function Codes · Define Structure of Function Codes**. The Customizing settings shown in Figure 13.26 assign its own hierarchy of function codes in the user's own MDT scenario to the structure of the 'Employee' category. Figure 13.26 juxtaposes the settings with their associated functions, in order to further clarify how the hierarchy of function codes works.

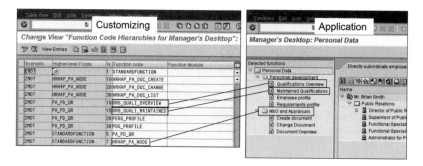

Figure 13.26 Connections Between Customizing Settings and Their Associated Functions in the MDT Interface

The function-code structure is thus the last step in defining the navigation tree in the left-hand part of the MDT screen. Both the scope and the sequence of the function codes are specified in this step. If you leave the **Higher-level Fcode** field empty, specify the sequence number in the **Sequence** field, and enter a function code of the type HOME, a new node representing a category is created in the navigation tree. The relevant entry is then made the **Higher-level Fcode** for any sub-nodes of this node.

Reports that are called inside the MDT never start with a selection screen. Instead, a variant of a report is always called. The variant name is stored in the function-code table. If you do still want to display selection screens for certain reports, you have to modify the system accordingly. One option is to create a customer-specific Customizing table for the function codes that are to be called by means of a selection screen, in order to define the number of reports that will be called by this method. A prerequisite for this is that the function module RH_MWB_FCODE_EXECUTE has been adjusted accordingly.

Other Customizing settings

Any other settings that need to be made via the MDT Customizing should be listed as follows, for the sake of completeness:

▶ Special settings for headcount planning (quota planning)

▶ Definitions of special workflows for using the SAP Business Workflow

Call reports from other systems

The MDT also enables you to call reports from other systems. For example, managers are very likely to want to start HR reports as well as FI and CO reports, and to be able to do so from one central point (that is, from the MDT), even though HR and FI/CO systems are often separate systems. We shall now briefly describe how to incorporate reports from distributed systems into the MDT.

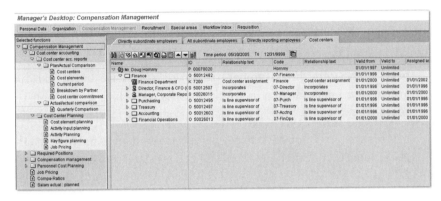

Figure 13.27 Cost-Center View of the Organizational Structure

When calling Accounting reports, you do so using function codes of the type RWRP from a view that also displays the cost centers of the structure (see Figure 13.27). However, when customizing the function codes (see Figure 13.28), you enter the abbreviation of the report group name from table T803VP, and not the ABAP name, in the program name field. This ensures that the correct report is selected, given that the ABAP name that is used in Report Writer reports in the development system is not the same as the name in the production system. The system standard contains an RFC (Remote Function Call) scenario for calling programs in other systems. The ALE Customizing is automatically checked in this scenario. If, for example, you have set up the cost centers that are assigned in HR to be checked with those in the CO system, the system also calls up the reports via the RFC destination stored in the respective ALE-scenario.

Function code	Type	Org. ...	Obje...	Text	Function M...	Progra...	Transaction
RWPLANACT	NODE	☑	☐	Plan/Actual Comparison			
RWREP1AIP	RWRP	☑	☐	Cost elements		1AIP	
RWREP1OAB	RWRP	☑	☐	Cost center commitment		1OAB	
RWREP1SHK	RWRP	☑	☐	Breakdown by Partner		1SHK	
RWREP1SIP	RWRP	☑	☐	Cost centers		1SIP	
RWREP1SLK	RWRP	☑	☐	Current period		1SLK	
RWREP1SQU	RWRP	☑	☐	Quarterly Comparison		1SQU	

Figure 13.28 Defining Function Codes

The authors' experience shows that the existing standard functionality for calling reports in other systems is often too inflexible in practice, in terms of the following points:

Real-world experiences

▶ Insufficient time frame available for selection

▶ No way of setting restrictions by cost type (except in fixed variants)

▶ No way of calling all kinds of reports (restricted to Report Painter/ Report Writer)

However, these problems are not insurmountable; some extra development in the form of a customer-specific RFC can solve them. You can include the required code in a function module, which can in turn be specified in the definition of the function codes (see Figure 13.25).

In these scenarios, you need to pay particular attention to the issue of target system authorizations, especially since only static cost-center authorizations can be assigned, and thus a considerable number of roles may be the result. However, as before, additional customer-specific development may be the answer to this problem.

Both the Manager Self Service and ESS have been incorporated into the mySAP Enterprise Portal in the Enterprise release of R/3. The next section deals with this subject in detail.

Figure 13.29 provides a final overview of the basic concepts of the MDT.

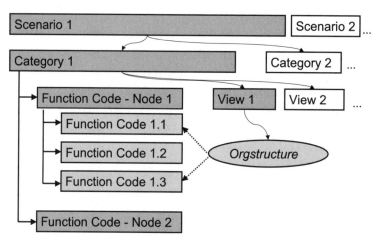

Figure 13.29 Overview of the Structure of the MDT

13.4 ESS and MSS in the Portal

13.4.1 Overview

New options in Personnel Management

The mySAP Enterprise Portal provides a whole range of new Personnel Management options. All the information, applications, and services that employees and managers need for their daily tasks are now available at the click of a mouse. This section presents an overview of the Employee Self Services (ESS) and the new Manager Self Services (MSS).

The mySAP Enterprise Portal is the successor to the mySAP Workplace. The portal provides employees with a consistent, browser-based interface to their personal work environments that gives them access to applications in different systems, information from external and internal sources, services, documents, forms, websites, and so on. There is no need to enter usernames and passwords multiple times, because with Single Sign-On (SSO), the user can log on to all systems at once.

In terms of HR work, the portal opens new horizons. Whereas administrating personnel data may have been the main task of HR departments, the portal adds new customer services to the HR spectrum, and allows HR staff to focus on the professional development of the individual employee.

mySAP HR is the basis of the portal. It is there that the administration of employee data takes place and where this data is prepared for use by other applications, so that employees can then access it via the portal.

mySAP HR as a basis

Employees get personally-tailored, HR-related services delivered quickly and directly to their desktops. Employee Self Services, which are accessed via the portal, enable employees to independently process their own routine HR tasks, such as holiday requests, changing personal data, and travel-cost reimbursements.

Benefits for employees

For managers, the portal is the medium that enables them to complete the HR-related tasks in their areas of responsibility more simply and, most important, more proactively than before. The portal provides managers with the functions and services they need to process a project request or transfer an employee, for example. Should managers require additional reports and statistics for their planning activities, the portal can provide this information from the SAP Business Information Warehouse or other sources.

Benefits for managers

As well as the ESS and MSS, other HR content is also available for the mySAP Enterprise Portal, in the form of the SAP Expert Finder and the SAP Learning Solution. However, the remaining chapters here deal only with the ESS and MSS business packages.

13.4.2 The mySAP Enterprise Portal

The mySAP Enterprise Portal uses open standards as the basis for integrating heterogeneous system landscapes in a unified platform. The portal also integrates enterprise information, including data from SAP and non-

Structure of the portal

SAP applications, data warehouses, desktop documents, and internal and external Web content and Web services (see Figure 13.30).

At the most basic level, the portal consists of a Web server, which is responsible for presenting the required data in the form of HTML by means of the HTTP protocol. A Java application server, preferably the J2EE Engine from SAP, is then connected to this Web server. The application server serves as the basis for the Page Builder, which is responsible for integrating the individual pages in the portal, and the iView server, which provides a runtime environment for the iViews that are currently running.

The portal uses a database for storing data. This database contains, among other things, information on the personalization settings for each user. The data regarding which user is assigned to which role, and the connections between portal users and back-end users, is stored in an LDAP directory. In summary, the simplest installation of a mySAP Enterprise Portal consists of a Web server, a Java application server, a database and an LDAP directory.

Content Management If you want to use the Content Management component, a search engine will be added to the above installation. The search engine is responsible for indexing and searching documents within Content Management. SAP provides a content-management system with the portal, but content-management systems from third-party vendors such as Documentum and Interwoven can also be used.

Drag&Relate If you want to use the oft-mentioned Drag&Relate function in the portal, you will also need to install the Unification Server. This server can analyze complex relationships between business entities and thus makes it possible to relate one entity to another. After it creates a relationship, the Unification Server then starts the appropriate business application from within the relationship.

Portal-based solutions can be looked upon as the holy grail of self services. Despite the substantial investment necessary to set up the SAP Enterprise Portal with ESS and MSS, many organizations achieved a good return on their investments by streamlining administrative processes, improving data quality, and providing the right information online to employees and managers.

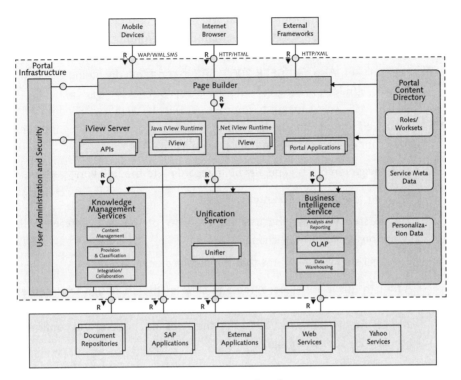

Figure 13.30 Components of the mySAP Enterprise Portal

In this book, we will not deal in detail with the technology of the SAP Enterprise Portal as this would easily double the book's size. Instead we will focus on the business benefits from the HR perspective. To adapt portal based HCM-applications, you need two skill sets:

▶ Skills specifically concerning mySAP ERP HCM, which are dealt with in this book and the other HR-books published by SAP PRESS

▶ Skills concerning the SAP Enterprise Portal, where we can recommend the SAP PRESS book *SAP Enterprise Portal: Technology and Programming* by Arnd Goebel and Dirk Ritthaler

ESS and MSS go perfectly together in many processes, given that managers have to approve or at least be informed about processes that are initiated by their staffs. While Web-based ESS can be used without a portal (though with some restrictions), MSS must be based on the SAP Enterprise Portal. MDT, a low-cost alternative, is not Web-based.

With mySAP ERP 2005, SAP migrates the standard ESS services from "old" technologies to WebDynpro for Java, which as a rule will be used for most Web-based applications within HCM. Many people regret that it's not WebDynpro for ABAP that will be used, as they believe this technology will provide a better development environment. Whatever your preference may be, with WebDynpro for Java it is necessary to acquire a new skill set. Also, with ERP 2005, SAP is constantly including the step-by-step "guided procedures" with the navigation bar for services in ESS as well as MSS. This is meant to improve usability by significantly complying with well-known standards used in Internet shops and other Internet sites your employees use in their private lives.

This navigation bar is generally built according to the following pattern:

1. One or more steps to enter the data
2. One step to show the user an overview of the data entered with options to confirm or change
3. A final step that confirms that the data has been saved/sent

Although this is a well accepted and state-of-the-art design for Internet applications, it may seem excessive for some applications. SAP takes this into account by allowing you to skip the steps for checking and confirmation in your custom design.

The navigation bar is a feature of the SAP Enterprise Portal. Therefore, when using ESS without portal, the navigation bar is not available.

13.4.3 Portal-Based ESS

ESS is but one among many applications in the Enterprise Portal as shown in Figure 13.31. Which applications will be available does not only depend on the custom configuration but also on the role of the user. A manager, for example, would have the MSS as an additional tabstrip.

Figure 13.31 shows a typical initial screen of ESS including some of the services delivered by SAP. These come from the following areas:

▶ General information such as search for other employees
▶ Payroll and benefits
▶ Job and career (skills profile, job opportunities)
▶ Working time
▶ Personal information
▶ Business trips
▶ Purchasing
▶ Work environment

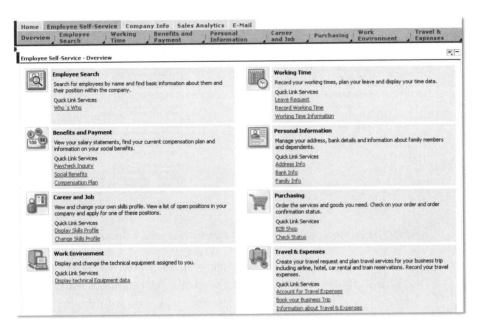

Figure 13.31 Starting Page of ESS Included in the Enterprise Portal

The two last areas deal with non-HR processes. They are included in ESS anyway, because they help the employees to minimize the time used for administrative tasks that are necessary for their daily work but beyond their core tasks.

Working Time in ESS

Working time is probably the area that comes first to most people's minds when talking about streamlining administrative processes via Web-based technology. This is because of the very high frequency of processes concerning working time (such as leave requests, clock-in/clock-out times, requests for paid overtime ...) and their rather low complexity (e.g., compared to business trips where much more data has to be entered).

Figure 13.32 shows the initial screen for working-time services. To make the solution as user-friendly as possible, it is always a good idea to include a short description of the services offered, as is done in this example. Employees are usually reluctant to refer to documentation stored at a different place each time they want to use a specific ESS Service.

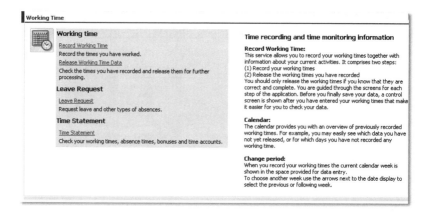

Working Time

Working time

Record Working Time
Record the times you have worked.

Release Working Time Data
Check the times you have recorded and release them for further processing.

Leave Request

Leave Request
Request leave and other types of absences.

Time Statement

Time Statement
Check your working times, absence times, bonuses and time accounts.

Time recording and time monitoring information

Record Working Time:
This service allows you to record your working times together with information about your current activities. It comprises two steps:
(1) Record your working times
(2) Release the working times you have recorded
You should only release the working times if you know that they are correct and complete. You are guided through the screens for each step of the application. Before you finally save your data, a control screen is shown after you have entered your working times that make it easier for you to check your data.

Calendar:
The calendar provides you with an overview of previously recorded working times. For example, you may easily see which data you have not yet released, or for which days you have not recorded any working time.

Change period:
When you record your working times the current calendar week is shown in the space provided for data entry.
To choose another week use the arrows next to the date display to select the previous or following week.

Figure 13.32 Working Time Services: Documentation for the User on the Right Side

The leave request as shown in Figure 13.33, Figure 13.34, and Figure 13.35 illustrates very clearly the use of the navigation bar. As there are only a few fields to maintain, this service makes do with the basic three steps described above. Note that the screens in this example always show the manager who is supposed to approve the request. Only after the approval through the responsible manager, the leave will be saved in HR.

This is a good opportunity to discuss approvals. The standard approval process in ESS and MSS is very much the digital equivalent of the classical paper-based process. However, it is a truism, that mapping inefficient traditional processes step by step with an IT system in most cases leads to digitalized inefficiency. It does not really streamline the process as a whole but only accelerates some of its steps. You should always check whether the new technology allows for a redesign of the whole process, maybe getting rid of some steps.

As to leave requests and similar processes, many organizations are happy without an approval step. Instead they provide the manager with the information necessary to intervene in critical cases. As a rule, leave planning is done before the formal request either in a conversation with the manager or within a whole team. As long as the formal leave requests remain within the limits agreed upon earlier, the approval is only a formal step causing unnecessary extra work. In normal circumstances, you can expect employees to observe the agreements made within the team. In practice, many managers at first worry because they feel they may lose control without the approval step. However, after some time, they see that in 999 in 1,000 cases the user will just confirm, and they think: "Well, we already talked about that one. Why bother me again?" So, in many cases it is only after a redesign of the solution that the approval step is dropped and managers content themselves with an appropriate information (either via e-mail or via a list they can check occasionally). From a purely process-focused perspective, it seems reasonable to do without the approval step from the very beginning. From a change-management perspective, it may be necessary in a transitional phase to convince managers that approval really is an unnecessary step.

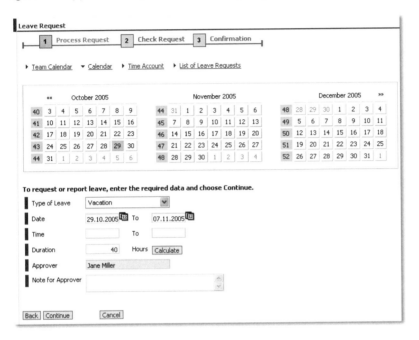

Figure 13.33 Starting a Leave Request: Step One

Figure 13.34 shows the overview of the data entered in step one. So, the employee has the opportunity to check whether everything is correct before submitting the request.

The last step (Figure 13.35) is confirmation, telling the employee, that the process was completed successfully and offering further options to work within ESS. This step proves very useful. Many users are not sure whether everything went all right and tend to enter the data a second time or call the HR department for a confirmation, thus causing extra work.

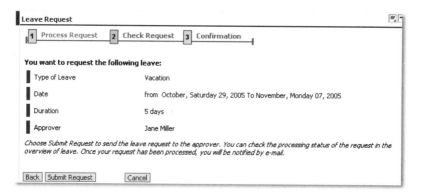

Figure 13.34 Check Leave Request: Step Two

Figure 13.35 Confirmation of Data Sent: Step Three

Business Trips in ESS

The business-trip scenarios are on the other end of the scale as far as complexity is concerned. Booking a trip requires a lot of data to be entered and information provided for the user, such as:

▶ Date and time of the trip

▶ Destinations

▶ Reason for the trip

▶ Flight data

▶ Hotel data

▶ Rental-car data

▶ Other

To deal with this complex process, the booking of tickets is included via different sub-processes. Figure 13.36 shows that the main process of booking a trip has just four steps, but the first step shown in the picture allows to branch into sub-processes via the buttons "Search for Flight," "Search for Hotel," "Search Rental Car," and "Search for Rail Connection."

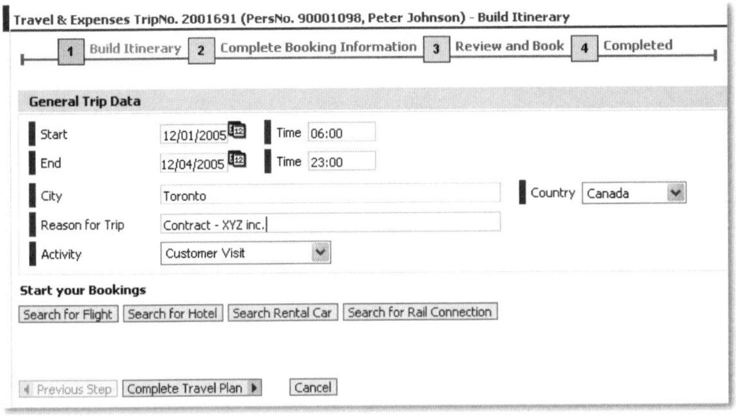

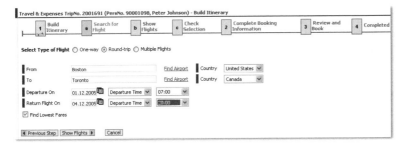

Figure 13.36 Booking a Business Trip with Sub-Processes

Each of these sub-processes can be very complex in itself. Booking a flight (the second step is shown in Figure 13.37 involves various data such as airports, stopovers, category (economy, business, etc.), airline, bonus program, and personal preferences. Doing this online in a well-designed portal proves very convenient for most people who are used to travelling. However, many employees who need a business trip every other year only, will have a hard time finding their way through the process. For these cases, it proved to be a good idea to have assistance available—e.g., through a secretary.

Figure 13.37 Booking a Flight

As mentioned above, ESS services need not to be restricted to typical HR processes. Based on the SAP procurement module, a service to purchase typical items needed for the everyday work can reduce costs significantly. You can define approval processes supported by SAP Workflow. These processes will observe rules for which person can buy items costing up to a certain price and who—if anyone—has to approve this. Figure 13.38 shows the purchasing of business cards as a typical example.

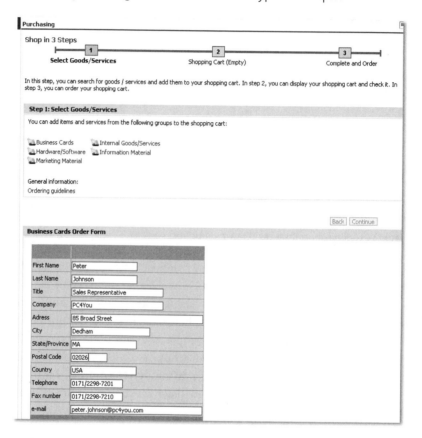

Figure 13.38 Purchasing Business Cards: An Example of Non-HR Processes in ESS

13.4.4 Portal-Based MSS

MSS is a more important tool for managers than ESS is for other employees. ESS mostly covers administrative processes that are not a part of the respective employees' core business, which is why most users spend very little time with ESS. MSS, however, deals with a core task of the managers: that is, managing people and other resources. This is a fact that managers on all levels have to understand before the organization is ready to implement MSS. Depending on the culture of your organization, this might be a greater issue than the technology. While in the early 1980s, having a computer in one's office was considered to be a symbol of high status, today many managers think that working with a mouse and keyboard is beneath their dignity. They expect to get their reports on paper, preferably served on a silver tray! It can be quite a challenge to convince those people that the user interfaces of a modern IT system provide information in a form far superior to a printed statistic. They have to understand that by relying on paper they deprive themselves of ways to view a problem from different angles: going into detail where it seems necessary but staying on the surface level when everything is proceeding smoothly. By leaving this to their assistants, they are not delegating a dull, administrative task but, rather, ceding actual power, because the assistants then will decide from which angles and on which levels they will present the data.

Furthermore, it is obvious that using a modern system it is more efficient to enter simple data directly than to instruct someone verbally or in writing to enter it. By entering important planning data directly into the system, a manager is able to see the effects immediately and can change the plan accordingly. This kind of interactive planning is far superior to paper-based planning, with respect to efficiency as well as to quality.

Besides their own ESS, managers have two major areas in the portal:

▶ Managing people (represented by the tabstrip "my staff" and

▶ Managing financials or resources in general (represented by the tabstrip "my budget")

HR processes are mostly intended to operate within the "my staff" area, and this is the area for which we want to show the most examples. Figure 13.39 shows a screen called "quick view" where you can include several applications considered to be the most important to be seen at one glance. In this example, these are an attendance overview for the current point of time, a list of important events such as birthdays and anniversaries, and a telephone list. The attendance overview shows an important option that you find in many MSS-services: The user can decide whether he or she wants to see the data for the people directly reporting to him or her, or the data for all subordinates. Such a quick view is certainly a good idea and can be filled with different applications for your organization.

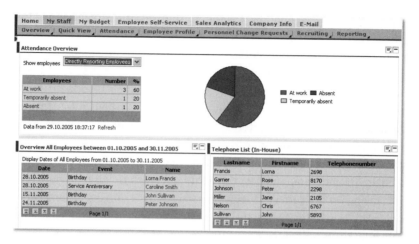

Figure 13.39 Custom Quick View with Three Applications

Employee profile

Another screen that is composed of many different components is the employee profile (Figure 13.40). Here, you can choose one subordinate and get a variety of data about him, such as:

▶ Contract data

▶ Address data

▶ Communication data

▶ Oranizational data

▶ Absences

▶ Employment history

▶ Skills profile

▶ Trainings

▶ Appraisals

▶ Objectives

▶ Company property held by the employee

▶ Other

Such an overview is very handy on various occasions, for example when preparing for a performance-review meeting with the employee.

Figure 13.40 Custom Employee Profile

Personnel Change Request

The personnel change request framework allows a manager to initiate the change of data for one of her employees. A variety of different changes can be included, all of which follow the same basic structure:

1. Select the employee the change has to be initiated for.

2. Select what process has to be initiated (as the process is represented by the form the data is entered in, this step is labeled "select a form").

3. Fill in the form with the data necessary to perform the intended change.

4. Review the data maintained and submit if OK.

5. The system confirms the successful completion of the process.

The fourth and fifth steps constitute the well-known final steps of most guided procedures. Depending on how each type of requests is configured, the changes can come into effect immediately or require an approval or other involvement of the HR department.

Figure 13.41 shows the first step, where one person from the list of directly reporting employees is selected. Note that this service also offers the above-mentioned option to show all subordinates or only direct reports.

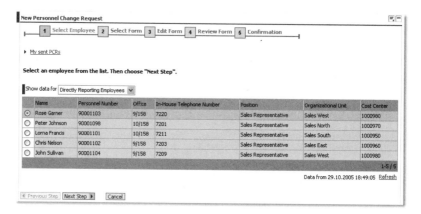

Figure 13.41 Personnel Change Request: Select an Employee

Figure 13.42 shows how the form for the change of working time is selected, thus initiating the corresponding process. In this screen as well as in the other screens of the whole process, the user can get a list of all personnel change requests (PCRs) initiated by him or her.

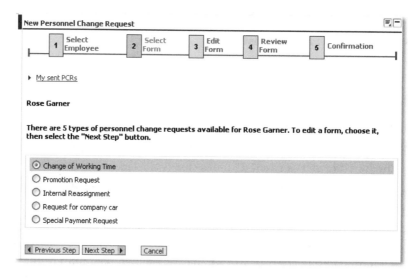

Figure 13.42 Personnel Change Request: Select an Activity

The third step represents the core part of the process, namely the form, in which the data has to be maintained. This is one example of new technology used in mySAP ERP 2005. Data is maintained here in an Adobe interactive form. Besides some other advantages such as good usability, Adobe forms are well suited for accessibility. As Figure 13.43 shows, the form can be adopted to your corporate design.

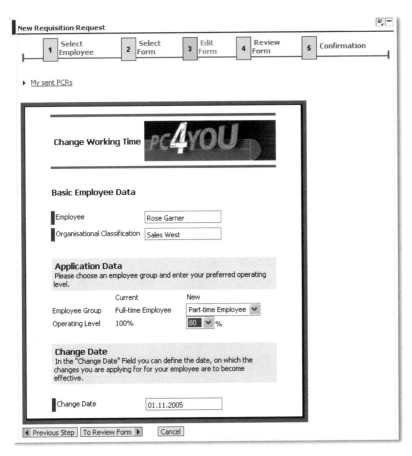

Figure 13.43 Personnel Change Request: Maintain Data Via Adobe Interactive Forms

My Budget

As can be seen in Figure 13.44, the "my budget" area does not only include financial data (especially cost-center reporting) but also planning functionalities from HR. It is not too important how different functions are divided between the "my Staff" and the "my Budget" tabstrips. The important point is that once logged in into the Enterprise Portal, the manager can access both his main responsibilities easily: his employees and his cost centers and other financial objects.

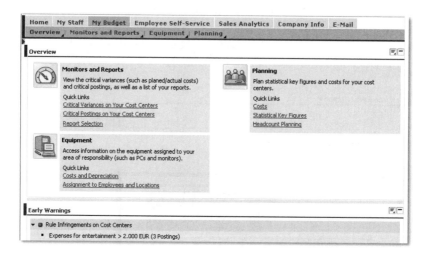

Figure 13.44 "My budget" Contains Not Only HR-Related Services but Foremost Financial Data

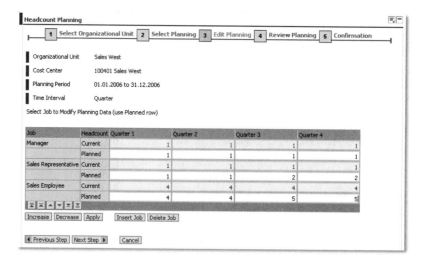

Figure 13.45 Headcount Planning

Besides cost planning, headcount planning is one of the major planning tasks for any manager. Figure 13.45 shows the core screen of the guided procedure for headcount planning. The user sees the current headcount of his department by quarter and job and can change these values in the "planned" lines. In this example, increases by one sales representative and one sales employee are planned for the third and fourth quarters of the year. The headcount-planning scenario is based on the quota planning functionality in R/3 respectively the ECC[1].

This is a very important point that does not only apply for this MSS application: The actual processing of the data is done in the backend system, which is the ECC (or the R/3 in earlier versions). The portal provides a sophisticated user interface, but to configure the process you first must understand how the core HR/HCM is working.

13.4.5 Process Example

In a portal-based solution, the look and feel of the user interface always matter greatly. Most companies work hard to ensure that the portal complies to their corporate design guidelines. Moreover, a portal is expected to deliver an application that not only can be used intuitively but that shows in one step all the information needed to deal with a specific process. Employees and managers, who use the portal or other SAP-based solutions only occasionally, don't want to master complex user guidelines. These professionals most often perceive the processes supported by ESS and MSS not as core components of their work but rather as administrative burdens.

So, to justify the significant investment in software licenses and implementation work, a portal-based solution with ESS and MSS must do the following.

▶ Fit into the corporate intranet environment smoothly and comply with corporate design and security guidelines. You often hear the requirement that users mustn't be aware that they are actually working with SAP software

▶ Reduce the overall time spent on adminsitrative processes while improving their quality at the same time

▶ Deliver an added value that the managers and employees who work with the system can clearly see

---

1 To learn more about headcount planning, see Chapter 14 (*Quota and Position Planning*) in *HR Personnel Planning and Development Using SAP* by Christian Krämer, Christian Lübke, and Sven Ringling, SAP PRESS 2004

These requirements can only be met by a solution that is tailored very closely to the actual processes of the specific organization. Design issues are the most obvious here but are hardly the only area where individual solitions are implemented. That's why we chose a process example that shows the portal of a real company. In B. Braun Melsungen AG, we found a company that built a solution that not only made HR more efficient but also more effective by improving service to its employees.

B. Braun—Sharing Expertise

In dialogue with the people who use the company's products, B. Braun is continually gaining new knowledge and incorporating it into product development.The company contributes innovative products and services that optimize working procedures in hospitals and medical practices all over the world and improve safety for patients, doctors, and nursing staff. With almost 30,000 employees in 50 countries, B. Braun achieved a turnover in 2004 of approximately 2.79 billion.

B. Braun is known to have innovative HR management. Its family-friendliness and modern office concept—among other points—have earned the company the "Top Employer Germany 2005" award. It ranked first in a research done by independent institute Corporate Research Foundation (CRF). The strategy of trusting employees with the responsibility for various processes, especially concerning their own working times, thus fits into the big picture. The first step was to implement a solution for all issues around time recording: This is often the first choice for ESS and MSS because there is a big potential for streamlining processes. B. Braun had five major objectives for this project:

▶ A tailored solution to support decentralized time management
▶ Consequent involvement of the employees into the processes of personnel administration and elimination of time administrators
▶ Getting rid of paper-based processes
▶ Instant and always up-to-date information for all users
▶ An easy-to-use system that does not require training

The start page (Figure 13.46) already shows how the solution is integrated into the so-called BKC (B. Braun Knowledge Center), the company's intranet portal. Corporate design is observed consequently. Besides the links to the individual functions on the right side of the screen, the user gets the most important information in one view. This includes lists with the status of his own requests and of requests waiting for his approval. He can work off these lists without having to navigate to any other screens.

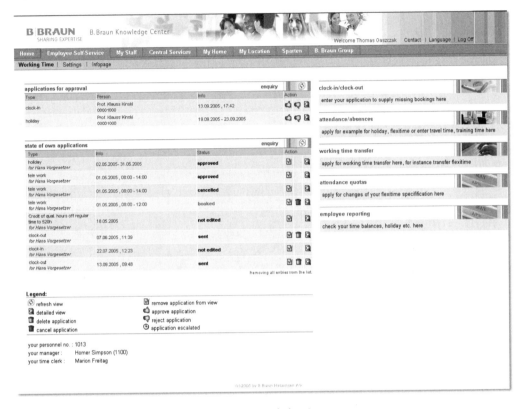

Figure 13.46 Start Page of ESS within the B. Braun Knowledge Center

The main functions for employees are:

▶ Supply missing clock-in/clock-out times

▶ Leave request

▶ Request for off-site work

▶ Request for overtime

▶ Transfer between different time accounts

▶ Various reports (such as the overview of one's leave entitlement as shown in Figure 13.47)

Managers can see corresponding information and a team calendar for their staff.

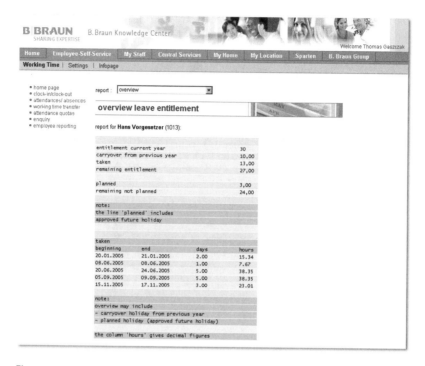

Figure 13.47 Overview Leave Entitlement

To achieve efficient processes, the workflow must be very sophisticated. It is clear that self-services for employees and for managers are supplementary to each other. Requests from the employee can be approved or denied by the manager. To ensure that this process runs smoothly, it has to be integrated into the corporate world not only technically but also from an organizational point of view. Because B. Braun uses Lotus Notes as an e-mail system, notifications are sent there and can be processed via a link directly from the e-mail. To meet the organizational requirements, the system observes substitutions and can forward requests to higher levels or substitutes automatically when they are not dealt with within a reasonable period of time. The system even notifies the employees when any error in time recording occurs, so that they can correct their data as fast as possible. Only such a high level of automation can ensure that no parallel processes are started via phone or paper to deal with delays.

Another important point is that errors

▶ Are reduced by extensive plausibility checks at the beginning of each process

▶ Can be corrected by the employees themselves through contra-entries

In order to guarantee efficiency and acceptance, it is critical that the user always has the necessary additional information for each particular process to hand without changing to another screen. This is a guideline closely observed by the B. Braun solution. Figure 13.48 shows but one example for this. When requesting a time transfer, the employee can see all the different time accounts and decide which transfer would be the best solution for him or her. All transfers from the last 12 month are displayed at the bottom of the screen. This is a good example of providing additional information for this particular process that is very important to this particular organization. Companies with fewer time accounts might choose to display other data for this process.

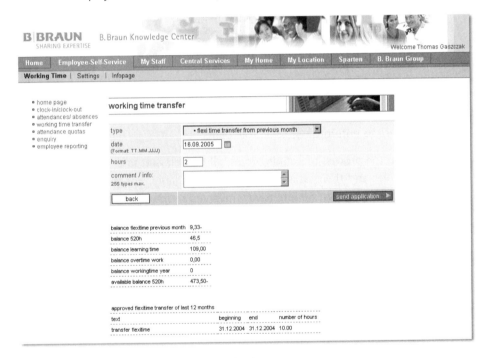

Figure 13.48 Working Time Transfer: Additional Information

There are lessons to be learned from the B. Braun process example. Probably the most important is that solutions within the portal—although based on a standardized framework—in most cases are very specific to the one organization. B. Braun made use of the SAP Enterprise Portal and some basic functionality, but also invested considerably in custom development. It is up to you to evaluate what amount of customization is necessary for your company to benefit from a portal-based solution.

Knowing this, you can decide whether the SAP Enterprise Portal will pay off for your organization or whether simpler solutions as described in the first sections of this chapter will suit you better. In the long run, you can expect that the ROI of the SAP Enterprise Portal will improve, because more and more functions will be included and because further job enrichment demands a single point of entry for various processes of everyone's day-to-day work.

13.5 Critical Success Factors

Because this chapter deals with a variety of topics, it is not possible to name critical success factors that apply to them all. Information specific to each individual area is provided below.

13.5.1 Success Factors: mySAP HR Roles

Recommendations A description of how to create roles and composite roles, including the relevant authorizations, is beyond the scope of this book. Below, we simply provide some recommendations that you should keep in mind in regard to enterprise-specific role concepts,

▶ In the process of defining roles, all the relevant information about the roles and their tasks must be made available. For this to be possible, the users must be intensively involved in the process, especially if the system in question is a decentralized one.

▶ Role-specific menus are strongly recommended, in order to really support the end users in their daily work.

▶ Use the options available to you for structuring the role concept in a modular way using composite roles.

▶ If you are upgrading from a lower release level to 4.6C, do not simply copy the old profiles into your role concept without first critically evaluating your role concept. If you do decide to copy old roles, SAP provides tools for this purpose.

▶ It is worthwhile displaying the structure of work centers, tasks, and task blocks in your department and those of dispersed users in overview form first, and only then dealing with the details of assigning authorizations.

▶ If multiple systems are in use, centralized user administration is the best option.

▶ First, compile a suitable menu for each role. Then, based on this, the profile generator creates a proposal for the access authorizations. This proposal is usually very good, but critically evaluate it anyway after filling in the empty fields. An intensive test is essential, due to the complexity of this topic.

13.5.2 Success Factors: ESS and MDT

The ESS provides a whole host of options for reducing paperwork. Here are some initial basic recommendations:

Recommendations

▶ Do not underestimate the technical requirements of integrating ITS into your enterprise-specific environment. Pay particular attention to users' PC installations, as interoperability with old Web browsers and graphics cards is restricted.

▶ It is very difficult to estimate the expected system load and to provide adequate hardware based on this estimate. The actual load depends very much on the usage behavior of the users. There is usually a usage peak in the initial phase, when the novelty value of a new system motivates users to use it frequently. However, if this high usage has too much of an adverse effect on system response times, the acceptance of the system will be jeopardized. Usage peaks also depend heavily on the type of services offered. The remuneration statement function, for example, always experiences heavy usage around payday.

▶ Ensure that the data displayed is self-explanatory. Otherwise, you will see exactly the opposite of the desired effect, when the staff of the HR department becomes overloaded with questions about the data presented in the ESS.

▶ If ESS access is functioning in a stable manner and the users have access to adequate documentation, it is certainly possible to reduce the amount of information exchanged in paper form and on the telephone. Otherwise, in the long term, the same processes will operate in two forms, and efficiency will decrease rather than increase. Providing remuneration statements, for example, both in paper and electronic form is not an indication of better service, but rather is a sign of serious inefficiency.

▶ A prerequisite for stopping the flow of certain information on paper is that everyone involved has access to the ESS. Thus, employees who do not have a PC will have to be provided with PC-based service terminals. In such cases, it is very important to avoid a situation where data relating to a user who has not logged himself out is accessible to anyone else who uses that terminal (auto-logout, for example, would solve this problem).

Here are some additional recommendations for implementing the Manager's Desktop:

▶ Management tasks must be clearly defined. This can be difficult in departments with temporary managers or with more than one manager. The more information is made available about the associated employees, the more complicated the situation becomes. For example, in departments with more than one manager, the question of who may view whose remuneration details is a problematic one.

▶ The process of updating the organizational and management structures in terms of Organizational Management must be clearly defined and should ensure that the structures are always up-to-date. Otherwise, functionalities will not be available to the employees who need them or will be only partially available, and the system will quickly lose acceptance amongst the employees.

▶ It is particularly important to involve the workers' council in the implementation process. Such bodies often have objections, as they are wary of unrestricted reporting functions and their potential for uncontrolled use by management.

▶ Therefore, start off with a small range of functions that are restricted to pure reporting.

▶ Ensure that competent contact persons are available for technical and content-related questions in the rollout phase. A step-by-step rollout may be required.

▶ Ensure also that the management supports the total replacement of paper-based procedures with reports in the Manager's Desktop. You must avoid a situation where, at the request of some managers, paper-based procedures run in parallel to electronic procedures (except for a short transitory phase).

▶ Take into account the realities in each department. In some cases, some tasks may be delegated to assistants. In this case, special roles will have to be created that do not contain any critical data or functions.

▶ Authorizations for MDT users should be largely similar to those of an employee with access to the personnel master data transaction PA30, in order to avoid from the very beginning potential errors in calling reports.

13.5.3 Success Factors: mySAP Enterprise Portal, ESS and MSS in the Portal

In the rollout phase of Employee Self Services and Manager Self Services, although the technical factors are of course very important, it is mainly the organizational and process-oriented success factors that make or break the success of the implementation in the enterprise.

▶ Including the various user departments in the project from the beginning is essential for accurately reflecting the processes in the scenarios. While ESS scenarios mainly involve just the HR department, MSS scenarios also involve the financial-accounting and controlling departments. Moreover, as mentioned above, the role of the workers' council must not be forgotten. Once the projects starts, the workers' council should be kept informed about what is involved in the project, and there should also be regular meeting with the council to discuss and achieve consensus on the outcome of the project.

▶ Before the implementation of the scenarios begins, a process input procedure should be conducted with all the parties involved in the project. Only this kind of process analysis allows certain important decisions to be made; for example, which iViews are important to managers and which views need to be provided. Also, it is always necessary in these kinds of projects to take into account the effects of the implementation on existing processes.

▶ Marketing is another aspect that should not be overlooked. At every stage of the project, it is worthwhile keeping the employees informed about its progress. This arouses the interest of individual employees and promotes their willingness to use the scenarios to maintain their own data or their employee data.

▶ It is likewise important to set up a pilot project with the aim of introducing a specific target group to the ESS or MSS scenarios. The project team can then use the experiences gained in this small user group for the benefit of the enterprisewide rollout. In a step-by-step implementation, it makes sense to employ a feedback system that users can use to notify the project team of problems and to tell them about any ideas they may have. This can be implemented in a special ESS scenario, for example. The feedback messages are not just important during the project; they can also be useful later on when the scenarios are live.

▶ After the rollout—and thus, after the maintenance of certain data has been decentralized—it must be made clear to the user departments that the relevant contact person will manually intervene in emergencies only. This is essential because certain employees will always take the easy option of avoiding the maintenance work and contacting the HR department instead, which would defeat the original purpose of reducing the administrative load of the HR department.

▶ Once the organizational and process-related aspects have been clarified, the technical aspects are the next to be analyzed. In other words, the customer's system and network landscape should be analyzed, and this should be done before, or, at the latest, in parallel to the process input procedure. For example, you have to ensure that the workplace of every employee is adequately equipped, or, at the least, that every employee has access to a PC. If the enterprise in which the rollout will be carried out is an international one, the analysis should be started very early on, so that there is enough time to carry out any activities that may be necessary.

▶ A mySAP Enterprise Portal rollout must be carried out within the context of an enterprisewide portal strategy. Theoretically, the mySAP Enterprise Portal can be used in a smaller environment, but its overriding utility is in the overall architecture.

14 Integration with Personnel Planning

mySAP HR provides a high degree of integration. It is there-
fore important to completely understand the interrelation-
ships between individual processes in terms of both their con-
tent and technology. Even though the administrative
processes can be easily separated from planning processes,
there are many interdependencies between them.

14.1 General Remarks on Integration

In some areas, the integration can be technically switched off. This is, for instance, the case in the integration of personnel administration with organizational management or skills. Interdependencies in terms of content still remain, however. If the system doesn't permit a highly integrated work process, it is particularly important to make every employee fully aware of his or her responsibility in the overall process.

Once mySAP HR has been implemented, users often regard the high degree of integration as very disturbing. This is because the legacy system (frequently consisting of several island solutions for the different HR areas) allowed employees to work in ways that were isolated from the overall process. The problem of data inconsistency and high redundancy caused by this hardly disturbed the users. On the contrary, they considered it very convenient to be able to work without having to take upstream or downstream processes into account. It is only a comprehensive overview that demonstrates the advantage of a high degree of integration, which in turn also requires more attention from the users. Despite the initial effort, a highly integrated system promotes a holistic way of thinking and working in the minds of users. However, the system cannot solve this problem by itself. This process should be accompanied by appropriate change management.

The following sections briefly describe the integration aspects relevant for the processes described in this book with regard to the essential processes in personnel planning and development.

14.2 Organizational Management

Organizational management can serve as a basis for each sensible implementation, even for that of the administrative processes. This is described in more detail in Chapter 5, *Organizational Management in mySAP HR*.

14.3 Training and Event Management

▶ HR master data and applicant master data are required for the booking of participation. Additionally, the HR master data is also used for assigning internal instructors.

▶ The master cost centre from Infotype 0001 is the default for the activity allocation.

▶ Attendances from Infotype 2002 are integrated for training participations or for the instructor function.

▶ Numerous values from HR master data are used for the automatic correspondence.

All these items described above also apply to the SAP Learning Solution.

14.4 Personnel Development and Performance Management

▶ Employee master data and applicant master data serve as a basis for the allocation of qualifications profiles and appraisals.

▶ In addition to the qualifications profile, the selection of employees to fill vacant positions also requires data from administration, such as the age and the gender.

▶ The applicant selection is generally based on data from personnel development.

▶ The maintenance of profiles can be called via Infotype 0024 within administration.

14.5 Compensation Management/Cost Planning

▶ The basic pay in Infotype 0008 and numerous other master data infotypes represent the basis for personnel cost planning.

▶ The results from payroll and their projection into the future is the most important basis for personnel cost planning.

▶ The pay data from the administration infotypes directly affects compensation management.

- The defaults of compensation management can be included in administration or used as a validation basis.
- The pay-scale customizing can represent the basis for the projected pay.
- The results from payroll that have been transferred to cost accounting can be compared with the results from personnel cost planning transferred earlier in the form of a target-actual analysis.
- In the context of the new cost planning in R/3 Enterprise, additional payment-relevant infotypes (e.g., 0014, 0015) are important for the integration into cost planning.

14.6 Workforce Planning/Shift Planning

By its very nature, shift planning is closely related to time management because the times recorded and managed in time management are used in shift planning in terms of both quantity and quality. At this point, however, it won't be helpful to provide a list of all the individual integration aspects.

14.7 Cross-Component Aspects

- Infotype 0105 is the basis for all Employee Self-Service (ESS) applications, including those in personnel planning and development.
- The communication language maintained in Infotype 0002 can be used in all components.

A   Cross-Process Customizing Tools

This appendix briefly describes the most important customizing tools used in the various components of mySAP HR. This presentation cannot replace practical experience or training on the system. Since the Implementation Management Guide (IMG), in particular, has a considerable range of customer-defined functions, this would scarcely even be possible.

The Features Editor

Features are used in all processes by mySAP HR to control system behavior in various respects. Basically, a feature represents a decision tree that arrives at a result in several branches. This result is referred to as the return value.

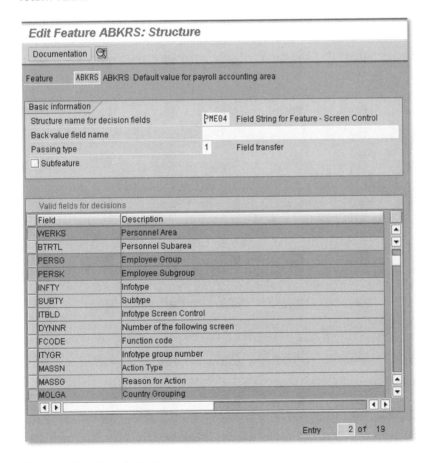

Figure A.1 Structure of a Feature

An example of this is the ABKRS feature that branches out to include the transaction class (personnel administration or recruitment), the country grouping (MOLGA), the employee group, and the employee subgroup. Finally, as a return value it provides the payroll area that is predefined as a default value in Infotype 0001.

Therefore the most important consideration in maintaining a feature is the structure of the decision tree. In this respect it is essential to know which decision criteria are available in order to create branches. The structure of the feature can give you a clue on this (see Figure A.1) as the available criteria are highlighted here. Highlighting additional criteria doesn't necessarily mean that these will also function. For this reason, you should restrict the selection to those criteria that are active by default.

There are two possible ways to maintain a feature. At first glance the table view may appear complex (see Figure A.2), with syntax that looks cryptic. However, an experienced user will quickly be able to handle it and will soon find out that this table actually provides a good overview of complex features.

Edit Feature ABKRS: Decision Tree

	Error text

Command	

Line	Variable key	F	C	Operations
000010			D	TCLAS
000020	B			&ABKRS=99,
000030	*		D	MOLGA
000040	* 26		D	PERSG
000050	* 26 E			&ABKRS=T1,
000060	* 26 8			&ABKRS=T2,
000070	* 26 4			&ABKRS=T2,
000080	* 26 3			&ABKRS=T1,
000090	* 26 2			&ABKRS=T1,
000100	* 26 1			&ABKRS=T1,
000110	* 26 *			&ABKRS=T1,
000120	* 01		D	PERSK
000130	* 01 DI			&ABKRS=D1,

Figure A.2 Feature Maintenance: Table View

The tree view (see Figure A.3) clearly displays the effectiveness of the decision tree. It is very useful to understand the structure of an unknown feature and also to check features you created by yourself.

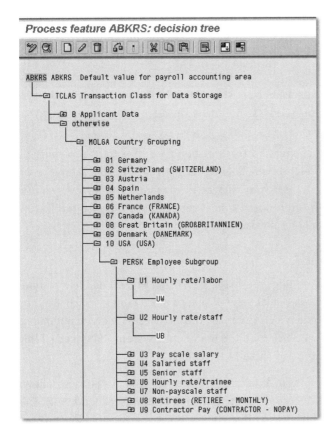

Figure A.3 Feature Maintenance: Tree View

You can navigate to the feature maintenance via Transaction PE03 or using the menu path **Human Resources · Time management · Administration · Tools · Maintain Features**.

We don't need to describe the exact syntax of features at this point, as the system itself provides sufficient guidance for this. It is more important to draw your attention to the following basic items:

▶ If the branching possibilities are insufficient due to the width of the variable argument, you can use the FLDID command to branch to a sub-feature.

▶ Checking and generating of features and their corresponding sub-features always happen simultaneously.

▶ Sub-features have to be identified as such in the attributes.

▶ Features are assigned to certain mySAP HR components and countries via their attributes.

▶ If you have modified an SAP feature in your client and want to reset it to the original status, you can simply delete it. In this case the system will automatically revert to Client 000, which contains the original status.

▶ Comprehensive decision trees should first be designed outside the system because you then can define a division into sub-features that makes sense.

▶ Not only must changes to features be saved, but they also must be generated before they can take effect. It is a popular pastime, even among experts, to search for alleged errors in a feature. However, the system behavior often doesn't meet expectations because the feature in question simply hasn't been generated.

View Maintenance

Most Customizing settings are made in what is known as *View maintenance*. This offers a particular view of one or more tables, which are then used to control system performance. You can access view maintenance using Transaction SM31 or with the menu path **System · Services · Table Maintenance · Extended Table Maintenance**.

In addition to directly maintaining the settings, the system also allows you to branch to IMG using the **Customizing** button (see Figure A.4). This is generally useful because it offers the possibility of using or adjusting the documentation of a project IMG.

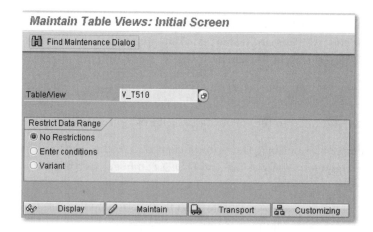

Figure A.4 Initial Screen of View Maintenance

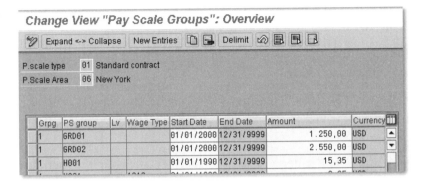

Figure A.5 Maintaining a Table View

In the actual maintenance (see Figure A.5), the following options are available:

▶ Change existing entries (Note: The grayed key fields cannot be changed. In order to do this, you would have to copy the entry.)

▶ Copy existing entries

▶ Create new entries

▶ Delete existing entries

▶ Admit entries in a transport request

If you have to process very extensive tables, the following functions are particularly helpful:

▶ You can use the menu path **Selection · By Contents...** to select specific table rows, for example, all those with an end date before December 31, 2003.

▶ You can use the menu path **Edit · Change Field Contents...** to make batch changes. You must previously have flagged all the entries to be changed prior to making these batch changes. Then you can change a certain field in all the marked entries in just one step. For example, you might use this option if you want to change working times. You could select all the work schedule rules with 38.5 hours per week and in one step change them all to 36 hours per week.

The Implementation Management Guide

The *IMG (Implementation Management Guide)* contains all customizing activities, organized according to component. In addition to the Reference IMG, which contains all activities, you can also create any number of project IMGs to support specific projects (for example, "Implementation of mySAP HR in France and Switzerland").

The use of the IMG in general, and the project IMGs in particular, offers the following advantages.

▶ It is easier to find the required activities because of clear structuring.

▶ You can use the documentation prepared by SAP for the individual steps.

▶ You can store enterprise-specific documentation for the individual steps.

▶ Project management is supported by status administration, time scheduling, and resource allocation.

Figure A.6 shows an example of a project IMG. In the left-hand side of the screen, you can see the component structure. The status, schedule, and resource allocation are maintained at the top right of the screen, and customer-specific documentation is stored below that in the form of notes.

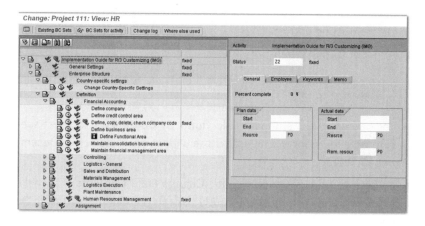

Figure A.6 Sample Project IMG

B   HR Infotypes

In Table B.1 below, you find nearly all the HR infotypes that are used to keep data for employees or applicants. The exceptions are those infotypes that have no description in English or that are not part of the SAP standard delivery (for example, infotypes for Central and Eastern Europe are only available via add-on solutions).

For each infotype, the table provides the following information.

▶ The third column ("RA PY") tells you whether this infotype triggers a retroactive calculation in payroll.

▶ The forth column ("RA TIM") does the same for time management.

▶ The fifth and sixth columns tell you whether the infotype is used for employees, applicants or both.

▶ The seventh column ("TC") contains the time constraint of the respective infotype.

▶ Finally, the column "Country" names the country the infotype is used for, providing it is only allowed for one country. If the infotype can be used for more than one country, the column is blank. In most cases, the content of this column depends on the standard customizing, which may sometimes be inaccurate.

All these settings can be changes via Customizing. Thus, this table does not necessarily reflect the usage of infotypes in your organization.

IT	Description	RA PY	RA TIM	Employee	Applicant	TC	Country
0000	Actions	X		X		1	
0001	Organizational Assignment		X	X	X	1	
0002	Personal Data			X	X	1	
0003	Payroll Status			X		A	
0004	Challenge			X		2	
0005	Leave Entitlement			X		2	
0006	Addresses		X	X	X	T	
0007	Planned Working Time		X	X		1	
0008	Basic Pay	X		X		T	

Table B.1 HR Infotypes

IT	Description	RA PY	RA TIM	Employee	Applicant	TC	Country
0009	Bank Details	X		X	X	T	
0010	Capital Formation		X	X		T	Germany
0011	External Transfers	X		X		T	
0012	Fiscal Data D		X	X		2	Germany
0013	Social Insurance D		X	X		2	Germany
0014	Recurring Payments/Deductions	X		X		T	
0015	Additional Payments and Deductions	X		X		T	
0016	Contract Elements		X	X		1	
0017	Travel Privileges			X		2	
0019	Monitoring of Tasks			X		2	
0020	DEUEV	X		X		1	Germany
0021	Family Member/Dependents		X	X		T	
0022	Education			X	X	3	
0023	Other/Previous Employers			X	X	3	
0024	Qualifications			X	X	3	
0025	Appraisals	X		X		2	
0026	Company Insurance		X	X		T	Germany
0027	Cost Distribution	X		X		T	
0028	Internal Medical Service			X		T	
0029	Workers' Compensation			X		2	Germany
0030	Powers of Attorney			X		3	
0031	Reference Personnel Numbers			X		B	
0032	Internal Data		X	X		2	
0033	Statistics			X		2	
0034	Corporate Function			X		T	
0035	Company Instructions			X		T	
0036	Social Insurance CH		X	X		1	Switzerland
0037	Insurance			X		3	
0038	Fiscal Data CH		X	X		1	Switzerland

Table B.1 HR Infotypes (cont.)

IT	Description	RA PY	RA TIM	Employee	Applicant	TC	Country
0039	Add. Org. Assignment CH		X	X		1	Switzerland
0040	Objects on Loan			X		3	
0041	Date Specifications			X		2	
0042	Fiscal Data A		X	X		1	Austria
0043	Family Allowance A		X	X		2	Austria
0044	Social Insurance A		X	X		1	Austria
0045	Loans	X		X		2	
0046	Company Pension Fund CH		X	X		2	Switzerland
0048	Residence Status			X		2	Switzerland
0049	Red. Hrs/Bad Weather	X		X		T	Germany
0050	Time Recording Info			X		2	
0051	ASB/SPI Data	X		X		1	Germany
0052	Wage Maintenance	X		X		2	
0053	Company Pension			X		3	Germany
0054	Works Councils	X		X		2	
0055	Previous Employer A			X		2	Austria
0056	Sickness Certificates A			X		T	Austria
0057	Membership Fees	X		X		T	
0058	Commuter Rate A		X	X		2	Austria
0059	Social Insurance NL	X		X		1	Netherlands
0060	Fiscal Data NL	X		X		1	Netherlands
0061	Social Insurance S	X		X		1	Spain
0062	Fiscal Data S	X		X		1	Spain
0063	Social Ins. Funds NL			X		T	Netherlands
0064	Social Insurance F	X		X		1	France
0065	Tax Data GB			X		1	U.K.
0066	Garnishment/Cession CA	X		X		2	Canada
0067	Garnishment: Claim CA	X		X		2	Canada
0068	Garnishment: Compensation CA	X		X		2	Canada

Table B.1 HR Infotypes (cont.)

IT	Description	RA PY	RA TIM	Employee	Applicant	TC	Country
0069	National Ins. GB		X	X		1	U.K.
0070	Court Orders GB		X	X		3	U.K.
0071	Pension Funds GB	X		X		T	U.K.
0072	Fiscal Data DK	X		X		1	Denmark
0073	Private Pension DK			X		3	Denmark
0074	Leave Processing DK			X		T	Denmark
0075	ATP Pension DK			X		1	Denmark
0076	Workers' Comp. NA	X		X		T	
0077	Additional Personal Data			X		1	
0078	Loan Payments	X		X		3	
0079	SI Additional Ins. D	X		X		T	Germany
0080	Maternity Protection/Parental Leave	X		X		3	
0081	Military Service			X		3	
0082	Additional Abs. Data			X		T	
0083	Leave Entitlement Compensation	X		X		3	
0084	SSP Control GB	X		X		1	U.K.
0085	SSP1(L) Form Data GB		X	X		2	U.K.
0086	SSP/SMP Exclusions GB	X		X		3	U.K.
0087	WFTC/DPTC GB	X				2	U.K.
0088	SMP/SAP/SPP GB	X		X		2	U.K.
0090	Additional Income E			X		3	Spain
0092	Seniority E			X		3	Spain
0093	Previous Employers D			X		2	Germany
0094	Residence Status			X		1	
0095	Tax data CAN			X		T	
0098	Profit Sharing F			X		2	France
0100	Social Insurance B	X		X		1	Belgium
0101	Fiscal Data B	X		X		1	Belgium
0102	Grievances NA			X		3	

Table B.1 HR Infotypes (cont.)

IT	Description	RA PY	RA TIM	Employee	Applicant	TC	Country
0103	Bond Purchases			X		2	
0104	Bond Denominations			X		3	
0105	Communication			X		T	
0106	Family/Related Person			X			
0107	Working Time B			X			Belgium
0108	Personal Data B			X			Belgium
0109	Contract Elements B			X			Belgium
0110	Pensions NL	X		X		2	Netherlands
0111	Garnishment/Cession D	X		X		2	Germany
0112	Garnishment Claim D	X		X		2	Germany
0113	Garnish. Interest D	X		X		2	Germany
0114	Garnishment Amount D	X		X		2	Germany
0115	Garnishment Wages D	X		X		2	Germany
0116	Garn. Transfer D	X		X		2	Germany
0117	Garn. Compensation D	X		X		2	Germany
0118	Child Allowance		X	X		2	Germany
0119	Definition of child allow. (pre1996)			X		2	Germany
0120	Company pension fund transaction CH			X		3	Switzerland
0121	RefPerNo Priority	X		X		1	
0124	Disruptive Factor D	X				3	Germany
0125	Garnishment B		X	X		T	Belgium
0126	Supplem. Pension D		X	X		T	Germany
0127	Commuter Traffic NL	X		X		2	Netherlands
0128	Notifications			X		T	
0130	Test Procedures			X		B	
0131	Garnishment/Cession	X		X		2	Austria
0132	Garnishment Claim A	X		X		2	Austria
0133	Garn. Interest A	X		X		2	Austria
0134	Garnishment Amount A	X		X		2	Austria

Table B.1 HR Infotypes (cont.)

IT	Description	RA PY	RA TIM	Employee	Applicant	TC	Country
0135	Spec. Garn. Cond. A	X		X		2	Austria
0136	Garn. Transfer A	X		X		2	Austria
0137	Garn. Compensation A	X		X		2	Austria
0138	Family/Rel. Person B			X			Belgium
0139	EE's Applicant No.			X		B	
0140	SI Basic Data JP			X		T	Japan
0141	SI Premium Data JP			X		T	Japan
0142	Residence Tax JP			X		2	Japan
0143	Life Ins. Ded. JP			X		T	Japan
0144	Property Accum. Sav. JP			X		T	Japan
0145	Personnel Tax Status JP		X	X		1	Japan
0146	Y.E.A. Data JP			X		2	Japan
0147	Pers. Appraisals JP			X		T	Japan
0148	Family JP			X			Japan
0149	Taxes SA		X	X		1	South Africa
0150	Social Insurance SA		X	X		1	South Africa
0151	External Insurance SA	X		X		T	South Africa
0154	Social Security data (IT)	X				1	Italy
0155	Additional administrative data (IT)			X		1	Italy
0156	Tax Deductions (IT)					1	Italy
0157	User Administration Data (IT)					1	Italy
0158	Amounts paid by Third Parties (IT)					2	Italy
0159	Seniority (IT)					1	Italy
0160	Family allowance (IT)	X				T	Italy
0161	IRS Limits USA			X		2	USA
0162	Ins. Y.E.T.A. Data JP			X		T	Japan
0165	Deduction Limits	X		X		3	
0167	Health Plans		X	X		2	
0168	Insurance Plans		X	X		2	

Table B.1 HR Infotypes (cont.)

IT	Description	RA PY	RA TIM	Employee	Applicant	TC	Country
0169	Savings Plans		X	X		2	
0170	Flexible Spending Accounts	X		X		2	
0171	General Benefits Information	X		X		1	
0172	Flexible Spending Account Claims	X		X		3	
0173	Tax card information (Norway)	X		X		1	Norway
0177	Registration of Country of Birth NL			X		2	Netherlands
0179	Tax SG		X	X		1	Singapore
0181	Additional Funds SG		X	X		1	Singapore
0182	Alternatative Names Asia			X		T	
0183	Awards			X		3	
0184	Resume Texts			X		2	Singapore
0185	Personal IDs		X	X		2	
0186	CPF		X	X		1	Singapore
0187	Family Add. (TH)			X			Thailand
0188	Tax Australia	X		X		1	Australia
0189	Construction Pay: Funds Procedure	X		X		2	Germany
0190	Construction Pay: Previous ER	X		X		2	Germany
0191	Construction Pay: Expenses	X		X		2	Germany
0192	Construction Pay: Assignment	X		X		2	Germany
0194	Garnishment Document	X		X		2	USA
0195	Garnishment Order	X		X		2	USA
0196	Employees Provident Fund			X		1	Malaysia
0197	Employees' Social Security			X		2	Malaysia
0198	Schedular Deduction Tax			X		T	Malaysia
0199	Addl. tax deduction			X		2	Malaysia
0200	Garnishments DK			X		3	Denmark
0201	Basic Pension Payments CPS	X				T	Germany
0202	Entitlements CPS		X			2	Germany
0203	Pension/Valuation Status BAV					A	Germany

Table B.1 HR Infotypes (cont.)

IT	Description	RA PY	RA TIM	Employee	Applicant	TC	Country
0204	DA/DS Statistics DK			X		T	Denmark
0205	Tax Card Information Finland	X				2	Finland
0206	Social Insurance InformationFinland	X				2	Finland
0207	Residence Tax Area	X		X		1	USA
0208	Work Tax Area	X		X		2	USA
0209	Unemployment State	X		X		2	USA
0210	Withholding Info W4/W5 US	X		X		2	USA
0211	COBRA-Qualified Beneficiary	X		X		T	USA
0212	COBRA Health Plans	X		X		2	USA
0213	additional family info			X			
0214	Loan Supplement, Denmark						
0215	CP: Transaction Data	X		X		T	Germany
0216	Garnish. Adjustment	X		X		2	USA
0217	Employment contract: addit. data			X		2	France
0218	Membership to insurance			X		3	France
0219	External Organizations		X	X		T	
0220	Superannuation Aust.	X		X		T	Australia
0221	Payroll Results Adjustment	X		X		3	
0222	Company Cars GB		X	X		2	U.K.
0225	Company Car Unavail. GB	X		X		2	U.K.
0227	TFN Australia		X	X		1	Australia
0228	Garnishments Finland	X				2	Finland
0229	Value Types BAV					2	Germany
0230	Supplement to P0008 PSG			X			Germany
0231	Supplement to P0001 PSG			X			Germany
0232	Child Allowance D		X	X		2	Germany
0233	Bilan social' (Social survey)			X		1	France
0234	Add. Withh. Info. US	X		X		2	USA
0235	Other Taxes US	X		X		2	USA

Table B.1 HR Infotypes (cont.)

IT	Description	RA PY	RA TIM	Employee	Applicant	TC	Country
0236	Credit Plans		X	X		2	
0237	Supplement to P0052 PSG			X			Germany
0241	Tax Data Indonesia		X	X		1	Indonesia
0242	Jamsostek Insurance Indonesia		X	X		2	Indonesia
0261	Loading Leave Aust.	X		X		3	Australia
0262	Retroactive accounting					T	
0263	Salary conversion	X				2	Germany
0264	Family NL						Netherlands
0265	Special Regulations	X		X		2	Germany
0266	Supplement to P0027 PSG			X			Germany
0267	Additional Off-Cycle Payments	X		X		T	
0268	Company Loans JP						Japan
0270	COBRA Payments	X		X		3	USA
0271	Statistics, Public Sector Germany						Germany
0272	Garnishment (F)			X		3	France
0273	Taxes SE	X		X		T	Sweden
0275	Garnishments SE	X		X		T	Sweden
0277	Exceptions SE	X		X		T	Sweden
0278	Basic Data Pension Fund			X		2	
0279	Individual Values Pension Fund	X		X		2	
0280	GB View for Contractual Elements						U.K.
0281	GB View for Beneficial Loans						U.K.
0283	Archived Objects			X		T	
0288	Family CH						Switzerland
0302	Additional Actions	X				3	
0303	Premium Reduction NL	X		X		2	Netherlands
0304	Additional Basic Pay Information	X		X		2	Germany
0305	Previous Employers (IT)					3	Italy
0306	Family add.						

Table B.1 HR Infotypes (cont.)

IT	Description	RA PY	RA TIM	Employee	Applicant	TC	Country
0309	IRD Nbr New Zealand		X	X		1	
0310	Superannuation NZ	X		X		T	
0311	Leave Balance Adj	X		X		3	
0312	Leave History Adj	X		X		3	
0313	Tax New Zealand	X		X		1	
0315	Time Sheet Defaults			X		2	
0317	Spec. Provisions NL	X		X		T	Netherlands
0318	Family view Indonesia			X			Indonesia
0319	Private Insurances Indonesia		X	X		T	Indonesia
0320	Official Housing	X		X		2	Germany
0321	Employee Accommodations	X		X		2	Germany
0322	Pension Payments	X				T	Germany
0323	Entitlement Group Type CPS					2	Germany
0326	Imputation of Pension		X			T	Germany
0329	Sideline Job					2	Germany
0330	Non-Monetary Remuneration	X				2	
0331	Tax PT	X				1	Portugal
0332	Social Security PT	X				1	Portugal
0333	Disability PT	X				2	Portugal
0334	Suppl. it0016 (PT)						Portugal
0335	Suppl. it0021 (PT)						Portugal
0336	Suppl. it0002 (PT)						Portugal
0337	Prof.Classificat. PT	X				2	Portugal
0338	Absence payment clearing PT	X				2	Portugal
0341	DEUEV Start			X		B	Germany
0342	Personal Data HK			X			Hong Kong
0343	Contract Elements HK			X			Hong Kong
0344	Additional Family HK			X			Hong Kong
0345	General Tax HK		X	X		1	Hong Kong

Table B.1 HR Infotypes (cont.)

IT	Description	RA PY	RA TIM	Employee	Applicant	TC	Country
0346	Contribution Plan HK	X		X		2	Hong Kong
0347	Entitlement Plan HK	X		X		2	Hong Kong
0348	Appraisal & Bonus HK			X		2	Hong Kong
0349	Cont/Ent Eligibility HK			X		2	Hong Kong
0351	Country Information			X		T	
0352	Additional Family Information (TW)			X			Taiwan
0353	Income Tax (TW)	X		X		1	Taiwan
0354	Labor Insurance (TW)		X	X		1	Taiwan
0355	National Health Insurance (TW)		X	X		1	Taiwan
0356	Empl. Stab. Fund (TW)	X		X		2	Taiwan
0357	Saving Plan (TW)	X		X		T	Taiwan
0358	EE Welfare Fund (TW)	X		X		2	Taiwan
0359	Tax Data Ireland	X				1	Ireland
0360	PRSI Ireland	X				1	Ireland
0361	Pensions Ireland	X				0	Ireland
0362	Membership view Indonesia			X			Indonesia
0363	Previous Employment Period			X		T	
0364	Tax TH	X		X		1	Thailand
0365	Social Security TH			X		T	Thailand
0366	Provident Fund TH			X		2	Thailand
0367	SI Notification Supplements A			X		T	Austria
0369	Social Security Data	X		X		1	Mexico
0370	INFONAVIT Loan	X		X		T	Mexico
0371	Retenciones en otros empleos	X		X		T	Mexico
0372	Integrated daily wage	X				3	Mexico
0373	Loan Repayment JP						Japan
0374	General Eligibility					T	
0375	HCE Information			X		2	USA
0376	Benefits Medical Information			X		2	

Table B.1 HR Infotypes (cont.)

IT	Description	RA PY	RA TIM	Employee	Applicant	TC	Country
0377	Miscellaneous Plans	X		X		2	
0378	Adjustment Reasons			X		2	
0379	Stock Purchase Plans		X			2	
0380	Compensation Adjustment			X			
0381	Compensation Eligibility			X			
0382	Award			X		3	
0383	Compensation Component					2	
0384	Compensation Package					1	
0386	Health Insurance Ireland	X				0	Ireland
0387	Starters Details Ireland	X				2	Ireland
0388	Union due Ded. JP			X		2	Japan
0389	Impuesto a las Ganancias AR			X		1	Argentina
0390	Impto.Ganancias: Deducciones AR			X		T	Argentina
0391	Impto.Ganancias: Otro empleador AR			X		3	Argentina
0392	Seguridad Social AR			X		1	Argentina
0393	Datos familia: Ayuda escolar AR			X		2	Argentina
0394	Datos familia: información adic. AR			X			Argentina
0395	External Organizational Assignment	X				3	
0396	Expatriation	X				3	
0397	Dependents BR						Brazil
0398	Contractual Elements BR						Brazil
0399	Income Tax	X		X		1	Venzuela
0400	Social Insurance	X		X		1	Venzuela
0401	Prestaciones/Antigüedad	X		X		1	Venzuela
0402	Payroll Results					3	
0403	Payroll Results 2					3	
0404	Military Service (TW)			X			Taiwan
0405	Absence Event	X		X		2	Germany
0406	Pension Information	X				T	Germany

Table B.1 HR Infotypes (cont.)

IT	Description	RA PY	RA TIM	Employee	Applicant	TC	Country
0407	Absences (Additional information)	X				Z	Italy
0408	CBS NL					2	Netherlands
0409	Execution of Employee Insurances					2	Netherlands
0411	Taxation Philippines	X				1	Philippines
0415	Export Status					B	
0416	Time Quota Compensation	X				3	
0419	Additional tax statement info (NO)					2	Norway
0421	Special remunerations (IT)	X				2	Italy
0422	Social Security Philippines	X				1	Philippines
0423	HDMF Philippines	X				1	Philippines
0424	Work Stopped (F)	X				2	France
0425	IJSS Summary (F)	X				2	France
0426	Orden jurídica México	X		X		2	Mexico
0427	Deudas por órden jurídica México	X		X		2	Mexico
0428	Additional data on beneficiary						
0429	Position in PS		X			T	
0430	Fam. Allowance for Processing		X			T	
0431	View Basic Pay	X				T	
0432	View: Type of Employment	X				2	
0433	GB View for Bank Details						U.K.
0434	GB view for External Transfers						U.K.
0435	ITF ADP 309 Free Format	X				3	France
0436	ITF ADP 409 Free Format	X				3	France
0438	Annual Tax additions SE					2	Sweden
0439	Data transfer information					B	
0440	Receipts & Misc. Information HK					T	Hong Kong
0442	Company Car	X				3	
0446	Payroll US Fed Taxes			X		3	USA
0447	Payroll US Fed Taxes MTD			X		3	USA

Table B.1 HR Infotypes (cont.)

IT	Description	RA PY	RA TIM	Employee	Applicant	TC	Country
0448	Payroll US Fed Taxes QTD			X		3	USA
0449	Payroll US Fed Taxes YTD			X		3	USA
0450	Payroll US State Taxes			X		3	USA
0451	Payroll US State Taxes MTD			X		3	USA
0452	Payroll US State Taxes QTD			X		3	USA
0453	Payroll US State Taxes YTD			X		3	USA
0454	Payroll US Local Taxes			X		3	USA
0455	Payroll US Local Taxes MTD			X		3	USA
0456	Payroll US Local Taxes QTD			X		3	USA
0457	Payroll US Local Taxes YTD			X		3	USA
0458	Monthly Cumulations					3	
0459	Quarterly Cumulations					3	
0460	Annual Cumulations					3	
0461	Tax Assignment CA	X				1	Canada
0462	Provincial Tax CA	X				1	Canada
0463	Federal Tax CA	X				1	Canada
0464	Additional Tax Data CA	X				2	Canada
0465	Documents					T	Brazil
0467	Add'l SI Notif.Data f.Comp.Agts A			X		T	Austria
0468	Travel Profile (not specified)					2	
0469	Travel Profile (not specified)					2	
0470	Travel Profile					2	
0471	Flight Preference					2	
0472	Hotel Preference					2	
0473	Rental Car Preference					2	
0474	Train Preference					2	
0475	Customer Program					3	
0476	Garnishments: Order	X				2	
0477	Garnishments: Debt	X				2	

Table B.1 HR Infotypes (cont.)

IT	Description	RA PY	RA TIM	Employee	Applicant	TC	Country
0478	Garnishments: Adjustment	X				2	
0480	Enhancement: Contracts Processing						
0482	Addit. data family/related person						
0483	CAAF data clearing (IT)					2	Italy
0484	Taxation (Enhancement)					T	
0485	Stage					2	
0486	Military Service (PS-SG)						Singapore
0487	Security/Medical Clearance					3	Singapore
0488	Leave Scheme					2	Singapore
0489	Voluntary Service/ ECA					3	Singapore
0490	Staff Suggestion					3	Singapore
0491	Payroll Outsourcing					2	
0493	Education (PS-SG)						Singapore
0494	Staff Suggestion Scheme—Evaluator					3	Singapore
0495	Retirement Benefits/Death Gratuity					1	
0496	Payroll US Benefits data			X		3	USA
0497	Payroll US Benefits data MTD			X		3	USA
0498	Payroll US Benefits data QTD			X		3	USA
0499	Payroll US Benefits data YTD			X		3	USA
0500	Statistical Data			X		3	USA
0501	Other Social Insurance Data			X		3	USA
0502	Letter of appointment					2	Singapore
0503	Pensioner Definition		X			2	
0504	Pension Advantage	X				3	
0505	Holiday certificate (B)		X			3	Belgium
0506	Tip Indicators	X		X		2	USA
0507	Superannuation						
0508	Prior Service					2	
0509	Activity with Higher Rate of Pay	X				2	

Table B.1 HR Infotypes (cont.)

IT	Description	RA PY	RA TIM	Employee	Applicant	TC	Country
0510	Tax-Sheltered Pension (US)	X		X		3	USA
0511	Cost-of-living allowance/amount		X			1	Switzerland
0521	Semiretirement D	X				2	Germany
0525	Child Care	X				2	Netherlands
0526	Work & Remuneration Confirmation A					3	Austria
0527	Payment Upon Leaving A	X				2	Austria
0528	Additional family information (CN)						China
0529	Additional Personal Data for (CN)					1	China
0530	Public Housing Fund (CN)	X				1	China
0531	Income Tax (CN)	X				1	China
0532	Social Insurance(CN)	X				T	China
0533	Personal File Management (CN)					1	China
0534	Party Information (CN)					1	China
0535	Project & Achievement (CN)					T	China
0536	Administration Information (CN)						China
0537	Going Abroad Information (CN)						China
0538	Separation payment					2	South Korea
0539	Personal Data						
0540	Family/Related Person						
0541	Personnel tax status	X				2	South Korea
0542	Year End Adjustment Data					2	South Korea
0543	Social insurance	X				T	South Korea
0544	Social insurance premium					T	South Korea
0545	Disciplinary measure					3	South Korea
0546	Termination Data		X			2	
0547	BIK(TAX) Infotype for Malaysia					3	Malaysia
0548	Supplementary pension funds (IT)					2	Italy
0551	Termination: General Data					2	Argentina
0552	Time Specification/Employ. Period					2	

Table B.1 HR Infotypes (cont.)

IT	Description	RA PY	RA TIM	Employee	Applicant	TC	Country
0553	Calculation of Service			X		2	USA
0554	Hourly Rate per Assignment	X				T	
0555	Military service					2	South Korea
0556	Tax Treaty	X		X		2	USA
0557	Additional personal data					2	South Korea
0559	Commuting allowance Info JP		X			3	Japan
0560	Overseas pay JP	X				2	Japan
0561	Tax Data	X				2	Mexico
0565	Retirement Plan Valuation Results					2	
0566	US Pension Plan QDRO Information			X		3	USA
0567	Data Container					B	
0568	Anniversary Date History		X			2	
0569	Additional Pension Payments	X				3	
0570	Offshore Tax GB					2	U.K.
0571	Offshore Social Security GB					2	U.K.
0572	Absence Scheme Override	X				2	
0573	Absence Infotype for Australia PS					2	Australia
0574	Contract Elements Austria PS						Austria
0576	Seniority for Promotion					3	
0578	PBS Accumulator Correction					3	Denmark
0579	External Wage Components						
0580	Previous Employment Tax Details					A	India
0581	Housing (HRA/CLA/COA)		X			1	India
0582	Exemptions		X			3	India
0583	Car & Conveyance	X				1	India
0584	Income From Other Sources					T	India
0585	Section 80 Deductions					2	India
0586	Investment Details (Sec88)					2	India
0587	Provident Fund Contribution		X			1	India

Table B.1 HR Infotypes (cont.)

IT	Description	RA PY	RA TIM	Employee	Applicant	TC	Country
0588	Other Statutory Deductions		X			T	India
0589	Individual Reimbursements					1	India
0590	Long term reimbursements					2	India
0591	Nominations					2	India
0592	Public Sector—Foreign Service		X			2	
0593	Rehabilitants		X			2	
0595	Family-Related Bonuses		X			2	Germany
0596	PhilHealth Philippines	X				1	Philippines
0597	Part-Time Work During ParentalLeave	X				Z	
0600	Employer Statement					2	Switzerland
0601	Absence History	X				2	
0602	Retirement Plan Cumulations					3	
0611	Garnishments: Management Data						
0612	Garnishments: Interest	X					
0613	Absence Donation/Withdraw (US)			X		3	USA
0614	HESA Master Data					2	
0615	HE Contract Data					2	
0616	HESA Submitted Data					2	
0617	Clinical Details					2	
0618	Academic Qualification					3	
0619	Equity and Diversity					2	
0622	Contract Elements (Public Sector BE)						Belgium
0623	Career History (Public Sector BE)					2	Belgium
0624	HE Professional Qualifications					3	
0626	Payment Summary					3	Australia
0632	Semiretirement A		X			2	Austria
0633	EEO/Grievance Case Management			X		3	USA
0634	Other/Previous Employers					3	Philippines
0646	FVP					2	Netherlands

Table B.1 HR Infotypes (cont.)

IT	Description	RA PY	RA TIM	Employee	Applicant	TC	Country
0647	GBA					T	Netherlands
0648	Bar Point Information					2	
0649	Social Insurance (Public Sector BE)						Belgium
0650	BA Statements					2	
0651	SI Carrier Certificates					2	
0652	Certificates of Training					2	
0653	Certificates to Local Authorities					2	
0655	ESS Settings Remuneration Statement					2	
0656	Nature of Actions			X		T	USA
0662	Semiretirement A—Notif. Supplmnts					2	Austria
0665	External Pension Rights					T	Netherlands
0666	Planning of Pers. Costs					3	
0671	COBRA Flexible Spending Accounts			X		2	USA
0672	FMLA Event			X		3	USA
0694	Previous Employment Details	X				2	
0696	Absence Pools					T	
0697	Drug Screening			X		T	USA
0698	Loan master to supplement for KR						
0699	Pension Provision Act	X				2	Germany
0701	End Point Australia					2	Australia
0702	Documents					3	
0703	Documents on Dependants					T	
0704	Information on Dependants					T	
0705	Information on Checklists					3	
0706	Compensation Package Offer					3	
0707	Activation Information					2	
0708	Details on Global Commuting					2	
0709	Person ID					A	
0710	Details on Global Assignment					2	

Table B.1 HR Infotypes (cont.)

IT	Description	RA PY	RA TIM	Employee	Applicant	TC	Country
0711	Employer number					1	Netherlands
0712	Main Personnel Assignment	X				2	
0713	Termination	X				2	
0715	Status of Global Assignment					T	
0717	Benefit point account					2	South Korea
0718	Benefit request		X			3	South Korea
0722	Payroll for Global Employees	X				2	
0723	Payroll for GE: Retro. Accounting					B	
0724	Financing Status					1	
0725	Taxes SA					3	South Africa
0734	View for IT Basic Pay Brasil						Brazil
0736	Alimony Brasil	X				2	Brazil
0737	Alimony Debt Brasil	X				2	Brazil
0738	Alimony Adjustment Brasil	X				2	Brazil
0739	Stock Option (Singapore)					3	Singapore
0742	HDB Concession					2	
0743	Discipline					3	
0744	Blacklist					2	
0745	HDB Messages in Public Sector					2	
0748	Command and Delegation					T	
0751	Company Pension Plan AT	X				T	Austria
0752	Declaration of Land/Houses/Property					3	
0753	Declaration of Shares					3	
0754	Declaration of Interest in Business					3	
0755	Declaration of Non-Indebtedness					3	
0758	Compensation Program					2	
0759	Compensation Process					3	
0760	Compensation Eligibility Override					3	
0761	LTI Granting					2	

Table B.1 HR Infotypes (cont.)

IT	Description	RA PY	RA TIM	Employee	Applicant	TC	Country
0762	LTI Exercising	X				3	
0763	LTI Participant Data					2	Netherlands
0764	Perm.Invalidity Ben.Act Netherlands					2	
0780	HR Pension Administration (PADM)					3	
0781	HR Pension Administration (PADM)					3	
0782	HR Pension Administration (PADM)					3	
0783	Job Title					2	
0784	HR Pension Administration (PADM)					3	
0785	HR Pension Administration (PADM)					3	
0786	HR Pension Administration (PADM)					3	
0787	HR Pension Administration (PADM)					3	
0788	HR Pension Administration (PADM)					3	
0789	HR Pension Administration (PADM)					3	
0790	HR Pension Administration (PADM)					3	
0793	Payment Made in Error GB	X				2	U.K.
0815	Multiple Check in One Cycle					3	
0900	Sales Data			X		2	
0901	Purchasing Data			X		2	
2001	Absences	X		X		Z	
2002	Attendances	X		X		Z	
2003	Substitutions	X		X		Z	
2004	Availability	X		X		Z	
2005	Overtime	X		X		Z	
2006	Absence Quotas			X		Z	
2007	Attendance Quotas			X		Z	
2010	Employee Remuneration Info	X		X		T	
2011	Time Events			X		Z	
2012	Time Transfer Specifications			X		Z	
2013	Quota Corrections			X		Z	

Table B.1 HR Infotypes (cont.)

IT	Description	RA PY	RA TIM	Employee	Applicant	TC	Country
3003	Materials Management			X		1	
4000	Applicant Actions				X	1	
4001	Applications				X	3	
4002	Vacancy Assignment				X	2	
4003	Applicant Activities				X	3	
4004	Applicant Activity Status				X	A	
4005	Applicant's Personnel Number				X	B	

Table B.1 HR Infotypes (cont.)

C   Explanations for Process Models

In order to read process examples, you should know the meaning of the following symbols.

Events

Events (see Figure C.1) are starting points for processes; in other words, a process is started because "something has happened." In Recruitment, for example, there is the event "applicant to be hired." For the hiring process, this means that a trigger event occurs and the process is started. Events can also be the results of decision-making processes. Example: After an interview, a decision must be made as to whether the candidate will be hired. Possible results of this decision-making process can be "applicant to be hired" or "applicant to be rejected."

Figure C.1 ARIS© Symbol: Event

Business Process Transactions/Functions

Functions (see Figure C.2) present activities. An example is "interview." In accordance with general ARIS convention, an event must be set after each function (see Figure C.3). Due to the lack of space in process models, the use of this "trivial event" is waived in this book. The relationships between functions, events, and the connectors are called *Connections*.

Figure C.2 ARIS© Symbol: Function

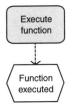

Figure C.3 ARIS© Symbol: Function • Event

System Functions

Actions carried out by the system—SAP in this case—are presented in *system functions* (see Figure C.4). These are actions that are run from the system without any user intervention.

Figure C.4 ARIS© Symbol: System Function

Process Interfaces

Process interfaces (see Figure C.5) create a connection between two processes. Example: The recruitment process ends with the event "candidate to be hired" then proceeding to the process "hiring."

Figure C.5 ARIS© Symbol: Process Interface

Jobs and Organizational Units

Jobs and *organizational units* (see Figure C.6) are linked to functions. They indicate who carries out the functions in question or in which organizational unit they are carried out.

Figure C.6 ARIS© Symbols: Job and Organizational Unit

Connectors

Connectors represent logical links between functions containing decisions and the results of these decisions. The relationship between an event and the functions resulting from it is also represented by connectors. The following connectors are used in the process examples shown.

The *AND connector* (see Figure C.7) means that after an event or a function, several functions are executed in parallel. It is used if *all* functions that emerge after an event or function *must* be carried out.

Figure C.7 ARIS© Symbol: AND Connector

If, on the other hand, not all functions that crop up after another function always need to be carried out, then the *AND/OR connector* (see Figure C.8) is used.

Figure C.8 ARIS© Symbol: AND/OR Connector

The *XOR connector* (see Figure C.9) is used to show that decisions must be made in a function. Figure C.10 shows an example of how the XOR connector is used.

Figure C.9 ARIS© Symbol: XOR Connector

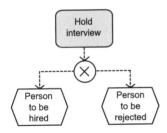

Figure C.10 Example XOR Connector

D Recommended Reading

D.1 Books

▶ Brochhausen, Ewald; Kielisch, Jürgen; Schnerring, Jürgen; Staeck, Jens: *mySAP HR—Technical Principles and Programming*. 2nd edition. SAP PRESS 2005.

▶ Buck-Emden, Rüdiger; Zencke, Peter: *mySAP CRM*. SAP PRESS 2004.

▶ Buckingham, Marcus; Coffman, Curt: *First, Break All the Rules: What the World's Greatest Managers Do Differently*. Simon & Schuster 1999.

▶ Davis, Rob: *Business Process Modelling with ARIS*. Springer Verlag 2001.

▶ Egger, Norbert: *SAP BW 3.1 Professional*. SAP PRESS 2004.

▶ Fitz-enz, Jac *The ROI of Human Capital: Measuring the Economic Value of Employee Performance*. AMACOM 2000.

▶ Hertleif, Werner; Wachter, Christoph: *SAP Smart Forms*. SAP PRESS 2003

▶ Huselid, Mark; Becker, Brian; Ulrich, Dave: *The HR Scorecard: Linking People, Strategy, and Performance*. Harvard Business School Press 2001.

▶ IBM Business Consulting Services: *SAP Authorization System. Design an Implementation of Authorization Concepts for SAP R/3 and SAP Enterprise Portal*. SAP PRESS 2003.

▶ Keller, Horst; Jacobitz, Joachim: *ABAP Objects: The Official Reference*. SAP PRESS 2003.

▶ Krämer, Christian; Lübke, Christian; Ringling, Sven: *HR Personnel Planning and Development Using SAP*. SAP PRESS 2004.

▶ McFarland Metzger, Sue; Röhrs, Susanne: *Change and Transport Management*. SAP PRESS 2005.

▶ Rickayzen, Alan; Dart, Jocelyn; Brennecke, Carsten; Schneider, Markus: *Practical Workflow for SAP. Effective Business Processes using SAP's Web-Flow Engine*. SAP PRESS 2002.

▶ SAP Labs: *System Administration Made Easy*, 4.6C/D. 2002.

▶ Scheer, August-Wilhelm et al.: *Business Process Change Management: ARIS in Practice*. Springer 2003.

D.2 Websites

▶ *help.sap.com* (note: the URL goes without "www"): Help portal of SAP AG. Free of charge.

- ▶ *www.admanus.de/english-newsletter*: SAP HR Newsletter. Free of charge.

- ▶ *www.asug.com*: Site of the American SAP User Group. Discussion boards, events, networking, etc. Most of the site is for members only. There is a charge for the membership.

- ▶ *www.hrexpertonline.com*: Online database of the HREXPERT newsletter, articles and how-to-guides in mySAP HR. There is a charge for the subscription. Among these, you will find contributions from the authors of this book.

- ▶ *www.sap.com/community*: Discussion boards and other information. Most of the site is for members only, but membership is free of charge.

- ▶ *www.sap.com*: Official site of SAP. A broad offer of documentation, white papers, life-demos, links, support sites, etc. While some parts of the site are accessible for everybody, others are for customers or partners only.

- ▶ *www.sapinfo.net*: Online version of the SAP INFO magazine. Interesting articles on all areas of SAP software.

- ▶ *www.thenewburyindex.com*: Not particularly focused on SAP HR but interesting for every HR professional who cares about the added value of HR (and HR software). This site gives a quick guide to a modern Human Capital Management System.

- ▶ *www.sapfans.com*: An online discussion board for SAP consultants and users. It's free and a great place to discuss SAP related topics.

E   About the Authors

This book is the result of a team effort. The authors are grateful to many contributors, without whom this project would never have attained its current standard of quality. These include, in particular:

▶ The staff of the healthcare company at B. Braun (*www.bbraun.com*), who provided interesting insights into their HR portal solution, described in the process example in Section 13.4.5. To contact the HR staff, e-mail to *info@bbraun.com*.

▶ Colleagues at iProCon GmbH—Anja Junold, Christian Lübke, and Jörg Edinger. They have made valuable contributions especially in the areas of payroll and technology. Over and above this, their assistance and suggestions were always helpful. Special thanks to Anja for producing more than 200 screenshots for the U.S. edition!

▶ The many helpful members of staff at SAP AG and SAP Deutschland GmbH, who have contributed much detailed information, particularly in the area of new developments. Special thanks to Stefan Ehrler, who made it possible for us to use the very latest version of the E-Recruiting solution.

▶ The technical support team at PIKON International Consulting Group (*www.pikon.com*), who ensured that we always had access to the IDES system, which was used as a source of numerous examples.

▶ Our Partners in the HR consulting network AdManus (*www.admanus. co.uk*), who always are prepared to share their wisdom.

▶ Last but not least, we want to thank the team at Galileo Press and SAP PRESS, and in particular, Eva Tripp and John Parker. They not only put up a brave fight against the dreaded typo monster; they also supported the authors in the conception of the book and have shown great confidence since the launch of the project.

▶ Hans-Jürgen Figaj from Projektkultur GmbH (*www.projektkultur.biz*) is among the most experienced consultants when it comes to time manager's workplace. He contributed the chapter on the TMW's calendar view.

We shall now briefly introduce the authors themselves (in the following order of appearance: "age before beauty"):

Sven Ringling

Sven Ringling is a co-founder and director of iPro-Con GmbH. He has worked on many projects aimed at optimizing the implementation of mySAP HR, with a focus on time management, reporting, and quality management, among other disciplines. He also has experience in managing personnel processes and selecting HR software and outsourcing service providers. Until early 2000, he was a manager at IDS Scheer AG, where he was second-in-command in the area of Human Resource Consulting.

Christian Krämer

Christian Krämer has been working as a senior consultant at iProCon GmbH since early 2001. He supports several customers in the area of mySAP HR with a focus that includes recruiting, pension plans, and TEM. He has developed extensive projects in process-oriented design for the implementation of mySAP HR and has experience in e-learning projects. Until early 2001, he was a senior consultant in the area of HR at IDS Scheer AG.

Song Yang

Song Yang has been providing SAP consulting services since 1998. He is experienced in personnel administration, payroll, benefits, and compensation. He has successfully supported many customers in Asia and North America. Song Yang is also recognized as an expert in Basis and ABAP. He joined Bearing Point Inc. as a senior consultant in early 2005. Before that, he served Atos Origin Inc. and Siemens Business Services as a senior consultant.

iProCon GmbH

Since early 2000, iProCon GmbH (www.iprocon.com) has set for itself the mission of optimizing personnel processes throughout their customer's enterprises. In so doing, it has achieved a sustainable improvement in competitiveness for its customers. In addition to process-oriented consulting, the implementation of modern HR systems and, in particular, mySAP HR, forms the core of its business. The idea of allowing requirements to flow directly from processes to the IT implementation is a foundation stone for this book. In addition to their high-quality project work (conducted in German as well as in English), the consultants of iProCon have written several publications on mySAP HR and on HR process management. They are in great demand as speakers in various conventions and workshops. To strengthen its leading position in the HR area, iProCon—together with other small companies—established the HR consulting network AdManus (*www.admanus.co.uk*).

Index

How to get most from your SAP HR systems

552 pp., 2004, 69,95 Euro / US$ 69,95
ISBN 978-1-59229-024-6

HR Personnel Planning and Development Using SAP

www.sap-press.com

Christian Krämer, Christian Lübke, Sven Ringling

HR Personnel Planning and Development Using SAP

How to get the most from your SAP HR systems

This compelling new reference book gives you a comprehensive view of the most important personnel planning and development functionality within SAP. Whether you need to implement, customize, or optimize your HR systems, the real-world insights this book provides will help you master the concepts essential for effective personnel planning and development. This book will help you leverage the many HR options and processes supported by SAP and gives you practical examples and key metrics to help you measure your success.

Integrate the Cross-Application
Time Sheet with SAP HR,
FI, PS, PM, CS and MM

Master employee time
management from various
decentralized locations

96 pp., 2006, 68,– Euro
ISBN 1-59229-063-9

Integrating CATS

www.sap-hefte.de

Martin Gillet

Integrating CATS

SAP PRESS Essentials 7

One of the most important aspects of the Cross
Application Time Sheet (CATS) is its integration with
other SAP modules. This unique new guide provides
readers with exclusive advice and best practices for
integrating CATS with other key SAP modules. First,
learn the fundamentals of CATS. Then, discover the
concepts, practical applications and possible
enhancements for CATS. You will quickly advance
your mastery of CATS as you uncover little known
tips, practical examples, and concise answers to your
most frequently asked questions. Full of practical
guidance and real-world scenarios, this book is for
anyone interested in CATS.

Efficient Reporting with BEx Query Designer, BEx Web, and SAP BW Information Broadcasting

Step-by-step instruction to optimize your daily work

Up-to-date for SAP BW 3.5

578 pp., 2006, 69,95 Euro / US$ 69,95
ISBN 978-1-59229-045-1

SAP BW Reporting and Analysis

www.sap-press.com

N. Egger, J.-M.R. Fiechter, J. Rohlf, J. Rose, O. Schrüffer

SAP BW Reporting and Analysis

Mastering reporting with BEx Query Designer, BEx Web, and SAP BW Information Broadcasting

In this book you'll find everything you need to configure and execute Web reporting and Web applications, as well as detailed instruction to take advantage of the resulting possibilities for analysis and reporting in SAP BW.
First, you'll be introduced to the basic topics of BEx Query Designer, BEx Web Application Designer, BEx Web Applications, BEx Analyzer, and SAP Business Content. Then, expert guidance shows you, step-by-step, how to master the process of creating custom reports and analysis. That's just for starters. You'll also learn best practices for creating your own SAP BW Web Cockpit and much more.

Expert advice to implement key
ETL processes

Complete coverage of master
data, transaction data and SAP
Business Content

Step-by-step instruction and
field tested solutions

552 pp., 2006, 69,95 Euro / US$ 69,95
ISBN 978-1-59229-044-4

SAP BW Data Retrieval

www.sap-press.com

N. Egger, J.-M.R. Fiechter, R. Salzmann, R.P. Sawicki,
T. Thielen

SAP BW Data Retrieval

Mastering the ETL process

This much anticipated reference makes an excellent
addition to your SAP BW Library. Read this book and
you'll discover a comprehensive guide to configuring,
executing, and optimizing data retrieval in SAP BW.

The authors take you, step-by-step, through all of the
essential data collection activities and help you hit the
ground running with master data, transaction data, and
SAP Business Content. Expert insights and practical
guidance help you to optimize these three factors and
build a successful, efficient ETL (extraction, transformation,
loading) process. This all-new edition is based on the
current SAP BW Release 3.5, but remains a highly valuable
resource for those still using previous versions.

How to succeed with InfoObjects, InfoProviders, and SAP Business Content

Step-by-step instruction to optimize your daily work

Up-to-date for SAP BW 3.5

437 pp., 2005, 69,95 Euro / US$ 69,95
ISBN 978-1-59229-043-7

SAP BW Data Modeling

www.sap-press.com

N. Egger, J.-M.R. Fiechter, J. Rohlf

SAP BW Data Modeling

This book delivers all the essential information needed for successful data modeling using SAP BW. In a practice-oriented approach, you'll learn how to prepare, store, and manage your data efficiently. Essential topics such as data warehousing concepts and the architecture of SAP BW are examined in detail. You'll learn, step-by-step, all there is to know about InfoObjects, InfoProviders, and SAP Business Content, all based on the newly released SAP BW 3.5.

Complete and targeted overview of all new BI features and functionalities

Comprehensive information on SAP NetWeaver Visual Composer and BI Accelerator

Up-to-date for SAP NetWeaver 2004s BI

656 pp., 2007, 69,95 Euro / US$ 69,95
ISBN 978-1-59229-082-6

SAP Business Intelligence

www.sap-press.com

N. Egger, J.-M.R. Fiechter, S. Kramer, R.P. Sawicki, P. Straub, S. Weber

SAP Business Intelligence

Up-to-date for SAP NetWeaver 2004s BI

This book provides information on all the important new BI features of the SAP NetWeaver 2004s Release. Essential subjects like data modeling, ETL, web reporting, and planning are covered along with all of the newest functions making this book an unparalleled companion for your daily work. Real-life examples and numerous illustrations help you hit the ground running with the new release. Plus, useful step-by-step instructions enable the instant use of new features like Visual Composer, and many more.

**SOA and the benefits
of the enterprise services
architecture approach**

**Architectural concepts, design
approach, and standards**

**Steps to successfully
deploy ESA**

144 pp., 2006, 49,95 Euro / US$ 49.95
ISBN 1-59229-095-7

Enterprise Services Architecture
for Financial Services

www.sap-press.com

Bruno Bonati, Joachim Regutzki, Martin Schroter

Enterprise Services Architecture for Financial Services

Taking SOA to the next level

Service-oriented architecture (SOA) has become an important topic for financial services organizations, offering new levels of flexibility, adaptability and cost savings. This book cuts through the confusion by clearly describing SAP's approach to SOA—the enterprise services architecture (ESA), shared with leading banks and insurance companies. By illustrating the principles and vision behind ESA, this invaluable guide shows you exactly how it can benefit your financial services firm. In a concise and easy-to-read format, the authors introduce you to ESA and explain exactly how it works. In addition, you'll get a detailed description of the key steps that financial services institutions need to take in order to successfully deploy ESA. This book is written primarily for CIOs, CTOs, IT managers, and consultants.

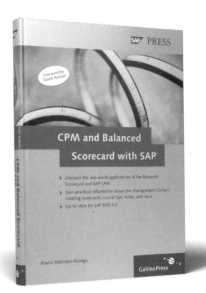

Uncover the real-world applications of the Balanced Scorecard and SAP CPM

Gain practical information about the Management Cockpit, creating scorecards, crucial tips, tricks, and more

Up to date for SEM 6.0

387 pp., 2006, 69,95 Euro / US $69.95
ISBN 978-1-59229-085-7

CPM and Balanced Scorecard with SAP

www.sap-press.com

Marco Sisfontes-Monge, Marco Sisfontes-Monge

CPM and Balanced Scorecard with SAP

Organizations planning to initiate the implementation of SAP CPM, using the Balanced Scorecard approach, need this practical guide. Get a clear understanding of the Balanced Scorecard and its relationship with SAP CPM, while gaining a thorough knowledge of the central concepts of both. With a foreword by Dr. David Norton, this book includes practical information about the management cockpit and teaches you how to create SAP CPM scorecards.

**The benchmark work
for release 4.0**

500 pp.,2006, 69,95 Euro / US$ 69,95
ISBN 978-1-59229-091-8

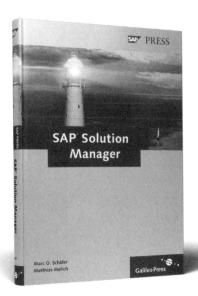

SAP Solution Manager

www.sap-press.com

M.O. Schäfer, M. Melich

SAP Solution Manager

This unique book helps administrators and IT managers to quickly understand the full functionality of SAP Solution Manager, release 4.0. Readers get a thorough introduction in the areas of Implementation and Operations, especially in the scenarios Project Management, Service Desk, Change Request Management, and the brand new function Diagnostics (root cause analysis).
The integration capabilities with third-party tools from the areas of Help Desk and Modelling, as well as the relation between the functionality and ITIL Application Management are also dealt with in detail.